Lecture Notes in Computer Science 8525

Commenced Publication in 1973
Founding and Former Series Editors:
Gerhard Goos, Juris Hartmanis, and Jan van Leeuwen

Randall Shumaker   Stephanie Lackey (Eds.)

Virtual, Augmented and Mixed Reality

Designing and Developing
Virtual and Augmented Environments

6th International Conference, VAMR 2014
Held as Part of HCI International 2014
Heraklion, Crete, Greece, June 22-27, 2014
Proceedings, Part I

 Springer

Volume Editors

Randall Shumaker
Stephanie Lackey
Institute for Simulation and Training
Orlando, FL, USA
E-mail: {shumaker; slackey}@ist.ucf.edu

ISSN 0302-9743   e-ISSN 1611-3349
ISBN 978-3-319-07457-3   e-ISBN 978-3-319-07458-0
DOI 10.1007/978-3-319-07458-0
Springer Cham Heidelberg New York Dordrecht London

Library of Congress Control Number: 2014939418

LNCS Sublibrary: SL 3 – Information Systems and Application,
incl. Internet/Web and HCI

Typesetting: Camera-ready by author, data conversion by Scientific Publishing Services, Chennai, India

Printed on acid-free paper

Springer is part of Springer Science+Business Media (www.springer.com)

Foreword

The 16th International Conference on Human–Computer Interaction, HCI International 2014, was held in Heraklion, Crete, Greece, during June 22–27, 2014, incorporating 14 conferences/thematic areas:

Thematic areas:

- Human–Computer Interaction
- Human Interface and the Management of Information

Affiliated conferences:

- 11th International Conference on Engineering Psychology and Cognitive Ergonomics
- 8th International Conference on Universal Access in Human–Computer Interaction
- 6th International Conference on Virtual, Augmented and Mixed Reality
- 6th International Conference on Cross-Cultural Design
- 6th International Conference on Social Computing and Social Media
- 8th International Conference on Augmented Cognition
- 5th International Conference on Digital Human Modeling and Applications in Health, Safety, Ergonomics and Risk Management
- Third International Conference on Design, User Experience and Usability
- Second International Conference on Distributed, Ambient and Pervasive Interactions
- Second International Conference on Human Aspects of Information Security, Privacy and Trust
- First International Conference on HCI in Business
- First International Conference on Learning and Collaboration Technologies

A total of 4,766 individuals from academia, research institutes, industry, and governmental agencies from 78 countries submitted contributions, and 1,476 papers and 225 posters were included in the proceedings. These papers address the latest research and development efforts and highlight the human aspects of design and use of computing systems. The papers thoroughly cover the entire field of human–computer interaction, addressing major advances in knowledge and effective use of computers in a variety of application areas.

This volume, edited by Randall Shumaker and Stephanie Lackey, contains papers focusing on the thematic area of virtual, augmented and mixed reality, addressing the following major topics:

- Interaction devices, displays and techniques in VAMR
- Designing virtual and augmented environments

- Avatars and virtual characters
- Developing virtual and augmented environments

The remaining volumes of the HCI International 2014 proceedings are:

- Volume 1, LNCS 8510, Human–Computer Interaction: HCI Theories, Methods and Tools (Part I), edited by Masaaki Kurosu
- Volume 2, LNCS 8511, Human–Computer Interaction: Advanced Interaction Modalities and Techniques (Part II), edited by Masaaki Kurosu
- Volume 3, LNCS 8512, Human–Computer Interaction: Applications and Services (Part III), edited by Masaaki Kurosu
- Volume 4, LNCS 8513, Universal Access in Human–Computer Interaction: Design and Development Methods for Universal Access (Part I), edited by Constantine Stephanidis and Margherita Antona
- Volume 5, LNCS 8514, Universal Access in Human–Computer Interaction: Universal Access to Information and Knowledge (Part II), edited by Constantine Stephanidis and Margherita Antona
- Volume 6, LNCS 8515, Universal Access in Human–Computer Interaction: Aging and Assistive Environments (Part III), edited by Constantine Stephanidis and Margherita Antona
- Volume 7, LNCS 8516, Universal Access in Human–Computer Interaction: Design for All and Accessibility Practice (Part IV), edited by Constantine Stephanidis and Margherita Antona
- Volume 8, LNCS 8517, Design, User Experience, and Usability: Theories, Methods and Tools for Designing the User Experience (Part I), edited by Aaron Marcus
- Volume 9, LNCS 8518, Design, User Experience, and Usability: User Experience Design for Diverse Interaction Platforms and Environments (Part II), edited by Aaron Marcus
- Volume 10, LNCS 8519, Design, User Experience, and Usability: User Experience Design for Everyday Life Applications and Services (Part III), edited by Aaron Marcus
- Volume 11, LNCS 8520, Design, User Experience, and Usability: User Experience Design Practice (Part IV), edited by Aaron Marcus
- Volume 12, LNCS 8521, Human Interface and the Management of Information: Information and Knowledge Design and Evaluation (Part I), edited by Sakae Yamamoto
- Volume 13, LNCS 8522, Human Interface and the Management of Information: Information and Knowledge in Applications and Services (Part II), edited by Sakae Yamamoto
- Volume 14, LNCS 8523, Learning and Collaboration Technologies: Designing and Developing Novel Learning Experiences (Part I), edited by Panayiotis Zaphiris and Andri Ioannou
- Volume 15, LNCS 8524, Learning and Collaboration Technologies: Technology-rich Environments for Learning and Collaboration (Part II), edited by Panayiotis Zaphiris and Andri Ioannou

- Volume 17, LNCS 8526, Virtual, Augmented and Mixed Reality: Applications of Virtual and Augmented Reality (Part II), edited by Randall Shumaker and Stephanie Lackey
- Volume 18, LNCS 8527, HCI in Business, edited by Fiona Fui-Hoon Nah
- Volume 19, LNCS 8528, Cross-Cultural Design, edited by P.L. Patrick Rau
- Volume 20, LNCS 8529, Digital Human Modeling and Applications in Health, Safety, Ergonomics and Risk Management, edited by Vincent G. Duffy
- Volume 21, LNCS 8530, Distributed, Ambient, and Pervasive Interactions, edited by Norbert Streitz and Panos Markopoulos
- Volume 22, LNCS 8531, Social Computing and Social Media, edited by Gabriele Meiselwitz
- Volume 23, LNAI 8532, Engineering Psychology and Cognitive Ergonomics, edited by Don Harris
- Volume 24, LNCS 8533, Human Aspects of Information Security, Privacy and Trust, edited by Theo Tryfonas and Ioannis Askoxylakis
- Volume 25, LNAI 8534, Foundations of Augmented Cognition, edited by Dylan D. Schmorrow and Cali M. Fidopiastis
- Volume 26, CCIS 434, HCI International 2014 Posters Proceedings (Part I), edited by Constantine Stephanidis
- Volume 27, CCIS 435, HCI International 2014 Posters Proceedings (Part II), edited by Constantine Stephanidis

I would like to thank the Program Chairs and the members of the Program Boards of all affiliated conferences and thematic areas, listed below, for their contribution to the highest scientific quality and the overall success of the HCI International 2014 Conference.

This conference could not have been possible without the continuous support and advice of the founding chair and conference scientific advisor, Prof. Gavriel Salvendy, as well as the dedicated work and outstanding efforts of the communications chair and editor of *HCI International News*, Dr. Abbas Moallem.

I would also like to thank for their contribution towards the smooth organization of the HCI International 2014 Conference the members of the Human–Computer Interaction Laboratory of ICS-FORTH, and in particular George Paparoulis, Maria Pitsoulaki, Maria Bouhli, and George Kapnas.

April 2014   Constantine Stephanidis
                                    General Chair, HCI International 2014

Organization

Human–Computer Interaction

Program Chair: Masaaki Kurosu, Japan

Jose Abdelnour-Nocera, UK
Sebastiano Bagnara, Italy
Simone Barbosa, Brazil
Adriana Betiol, Brazil
Simone Borsci, UK
Henry Duh, Australia
Xiaowen Fang, USA
Vicki Hanson, UK
Wonil Hwang, Korea
Minna Isomursu, Finland
Yong Gu Ji, Korea
Anirudha Joshi, India
Esther Jun, USA
Kyungdoh Kim, Korea

Heidi Krömker, Germany
Chen Ling, USA
Chang S. Nam, USA
Naoko Okuizumi, Japan
Philippe Palanque, France
Ling Rothrock, USA
Naoki Sakakibara, Japan
Dominique Scapin, France
Guangfeng Song, USA
Sanjay Tripathi, India
Chui Yin Wong, Malaysia
Toshiki Yamaoka, Japan
Kazuhiko Yamazaki, Japan
Ryoji Yoshitake, Japan

Human Interface and the Management of Information

Program Chair: Sakae Yamamoto, Japan

Alan Chan, Hong Kong
Denis A. Coelho, Portugal
Linda Elliott, USA
Shin'ichi Fukuzumi, Japan
Michitaka Hirose, Japan
Makoto Itoh, Japan
Yen-Yu Kang, Taiwan
Koji Kimita, Japan
Daiji Kobayashi, Japan

Hiroyuki Miki, Japan
Hirohiko Mori, Japan
Shogo Nishida, Japan
Robert Proctor, USA
Youngho Rhee, Korea
Ryosuke Saga, Japan
Katsunori Shimohara, Japan
Kim-Phuong Vu, USA
Tomio Watanabe, Japan

Engineering Psychology and Cognitive Ergonomics

Program Chair: Don Harris, UK

Guy Andre Boy, USA
Shan Fu, P.R. China
Hung-Sying Jing, Taiwan
Wen-Chin Li, Taiwan
Mark Neerincx, The Netherlands
Jan Noyes, UK
Paul Salmon, Australia

Axel Schulte, Germany
Siraj Shaikh, UK
Sarah Sharples, UK
Anthony Smoker, UK
Neville Stanton, UK
Alex Stedmon, UK
Andrew Thatcher, South Africa

Universal Access in Human–Computer Interaction

Program Chairs: Constantine Stephanidis, Greece, and Margherita Antona, Greece

Julio Abascal, Spain
Gisela Susanne Bahr, USA
João Barroso, Portugal
Margrit Betke, USA
Anthony Brooks, Denmark
Christian Bühler, Germany
Stefan Carmien, Spain
Hua Dong, P.R. China
Carlos Duarte, Portugal
Pier Luigi Emiliani, Italy
Qin Gao, P.R. China
Andrina Granić, Croatia
Andreas Holzinger, Austria
Josette Jones, USA
Simeon Keates, UK

Georgios Kouroupetroglou, Greece
Patrick Langdon, UK
Barbara Leporini, Italy
Eugene Loos, The Netherlands
Ana Isabel Paraguay, Brazil
Helen Petrie, UK
Michael Pieper, Germany
Enrico Pontelli, USA
Jaime Sanchez, Chile
Alberto Sanna, Italy
Anthony Savidis, Greece
Christian Stary, Austria
Hirotada Ueda, Japan
Gerhard Weber, Germany
Harald Weber, Germany

Virtual, Augmented and Mixed Reality

Program Chairs: Randall Shumaker, USA, and Stephanie Lackey, USA

Roland Blach, Germany
Sheryl Brahnam, USA
Juan Cendan, USA
Jessie Chen, USA
Panagiotis D. Kaklis, UK

Hirokazu Kato, Japan
Denis Laurendeau, Canada
Fotis Liarokapis, UK
Michael Macedonia, USA
Gordon Mair, UK

Jose San Martin, Spain
Tabitha Peck, USA
Christian Sandor, Australia

Christopher Stapleton, USA
Gregory Welch, USA

Cross-Cultural Design

Program Chair: P.L. Patrick Rau, P.R. China

Yee-Yin Choong, USA
Paul Fu, USA
Zhiyong Fu, P.R. China
Pin-Chao Liao, P.R. China
Dyi-Yih Michael Lin, Taiwan
Rungtai Lin, Taiwan
Ta-Ping (Robert) Lu, Taiwan
Liang Ma, P.R. China
Alexander Mädche, Germany

Sheau-Farn Max Liang, Taiwan
Katsuhiko Ogawa, Japan
Tom Plocher, USA
Huatong Sun, USA
Emil Tso, P.R. China
Hsiu-Ping Yueh, Taiwan
Liang (Leon) Zeng, USA
Jia Zhou, P.R. China

Online Communities and Social Media

Program Chair: Gabriele Meiselwitz, USA

Leonelo Almeida, Brazil
Chee Siang Ang, UK
Aneesha Bakharia, Australia
Ania Bobrowicz, UK
James Braman, USA
Farzin Deravi, UK
Carsten Kleiner, Germany
Niki Lambropoulos, Greece
Soo Ling Lim, UK

Anthony Norcio, USA
Portia Pusey, USA
Panote Siriaraya, UK
Stefan Stieglitz, Germany
Giovanni Vincenti, USA
Yuanqiong (Kathy) Wang, USA
June Wei, USA
Brian Wentz, USA

Augmented Cognition

**Program Chairs: Dylan D. Schmorrow, USA,
and Cali M. Fidopiastis, USA**

Ahmed Abdelkhalek, USA
Robert Atkinson, USA
Monique Beaudoin, USA
John Blitch, USA
Alenka Brown, USA

Rosario Cannavò, Italy
Joseph Cohn, USA
Andrew J. Cowell, USA
Martha Crosby, USA
Wai-Tat Fu, USA

Rodolphe Gentili, USA
Frederick Gregory, USA
Michael W. Hail, USA
Monte Hancock, USA
Fei Hu, USA
Ion Juvina, USA
Joe Keebler, USA
Philip Mangos, USA
Rao Mannepalli, USA
David Martinez, USA
Yvonne R. Masakowski, USA
Santosh Mathan, USA
Ranjeev Mittu, USA

Keith Niall, USA
Tatana Olson, USA
Debra Patton, USA
June Pilcher, USA
Robinson Pino, USA
Tiffany Poeppelman, USA
Victoria Romero, USA
Amela Sadagic, USA
Anna Skinner, USA
Ann Speed, USA
Robert Sottilare, USA
Peter Walker, USA

Digital Human Modeling and Applications in Health, Safety, Ergonomics and Risk Management

Program Chair: Vincent G. Duffy, USA

Giuseppe Andreoni, Italy
Daniel Carruth, USA
Elsbeth De Korte, The Netherlands
Afzal A. Godil, USA
Ravindra Goonetilleke, Hong Kong
Noriaki Kuwahara, Japan
Kang Li, USA
Zhizhong Li, P.R. China

Tim Marler, USA
Jianwei Niu, P.R. China
Michelle Robertson, USA
Matthias Rötting, Germany
Mao-Jiun Wang, Taiwan
Xuguang Wang, France
James Yang, USA

Design, User Experience, and Usability

Program Chair: Aaron Marcus, USA

Sisira Adikari, Australia
Claire Ancient, USA
Arne Berger, Germany
Jamie Blustein, Canada
Ana Boa-Ventura, USA
Jan Brejcha, Czech Republic
Lorenzo Cantoni, Switzerland
Marc Fabri, UK
Luciane Maria Fadel, Brazil
Tricia Flanagan, Hong Kong
Jorge Frascara, Mexico

Federico Gobbo, Italy
Emilie Gould, USA
Rüdiger Heimgärtner, Germany
Brigitte Herrmann, Germany
Steffen Hess, Germany
Nouf Khashman, Canada
Fabiola Guillermina Noël, Mexico
Francisco Rebelo, Portugal
Kerem Rızvanoğlu, Turkey
Marcelo Soares, Brazil
Carla Spinillo, Brazil

Distributed, Ambient and Pervasive Interactions

Program Chairs: Norbert Streitz, Germany, and Panos Markopoulos, The Netherlands

Juan Carlos Augusto, UK
Jose Bravo, Spain
Adrian Cheok, UK
Boris de Ruyter, The Netherlands
Anind Dey, USA
Dimitris Grammenos, Greece
Nuno Guimaraes, Portugal
Achilles Kameas, Greece
Javed Vassilis Khan, The Netherlands
Shin'ichi Konomi, Japan
Carsten Magerkurth, Switzerland

Ingrid Mulder, The Netherlands
Anton Nijholt, The Netherlands
Fabio Paternó, Italy
Carsten Röcker, Germany
Teresa Romao, Portugal
Albert Ali Salah, Turkey
Manfred Tscheligi, Austria
Reiner Wichert, Germany
Woontack Woo, Korea
Xenophon Zabulis, Greece

Human Aspects of Information Security, Privacy and Trust

Program Chairs: Theo Tryfonas, UK, and Ioannis Askoxylakis, Greece

Claudio Agostino Ardagna, Italy
Zinaida Benenson, Germany
Daniele Catteddu, Italy
Raoul Chiesa, Italy
Bryan Cline, USA
Sadie Creese, UK
Jorge Cuellar, Germany
Marc Dacier, USA
Dieter Gollmann, Germany
Kirstie Hawkey, Canada
Jaap-Henk Hoepman, The Netherlands
Cagatay Karabat, Turkey
Angelos Keromytis, USA
Ayako Komatsu, Japan
Ronald Leenes, The Netherlands
Javier Lopez, Spain
Steve Marsh, Canada

Gregorio Martinez, Spain
Emilio Mordini, Italy
Yuko Murayama, Japan
Masakatsu Nishigaki, Japan
Aljosa Pasic, Spain
Milan Petković, The Netherlands
Joachim Posegga, Germany
Jean-Jacques Quisquater, Belgium
Damien Sauveron, France
George Spanoudakis, UK
Kerry-Lynn Thomson, South Africa
Julien Touzeau, France
Theo Tryfonas, UK
João Vilela, Portugal
Claire Vishik, UK
Melanie Volkamer, Germany

HCI in Business

Program Chair: Fiona Fui-Hoon Nah, USA

Andreas Auinger, Austria
Michel Avital, Denmark
Traci Carte, USA
Hock Chuan Chan, Singapore
Constantinos Coursaris, USA
Soussan Djamasbi, USA
Brenda Eschenbrenner, USA
Nobuyuki Fukawa, USA
Khaled Hassanein, Canada
Milena Head, Canada
Susanna (Shuk Ying) Ho, Australia
Jack Zhenhui Jiang, Singapore
Jinwoo Kim, Korea
Zoonky Lee, Korea
Honglei Li, UK
Nicholas Lockwood, USA
Eleanor T. Loiacono, USA
Mei Lu, USA

Scott McCoy, USA
Brian Mennecke, USA
Robin Poston, USA
Lingyun Qiu, P.R. China
Rene Riedl, Austria
Matti Rossi, Finland
April Savoy, USA
Shu Schiller, USA
Hong Sheng, USA
Choon Ling Sia, Hong Kong
Chee-Wee Tan, Denmark
Chuan Hoo Tan, Hong Kong
Noam Tractinsky, Israel
Horst Treiblmaier, Austria
Virpi Tuunainen, Finland
Dezhi Wu, USA
I-Chin Wu, Taiwan

Learning and Collaboration Technologies

**Program Chairs: Panayiotis Zaphiris, Cyprus,
and Andri Ioannou, Cyprus**

Ruthi Aladjem, Israel
Abdulaziz Aldaej, UK
John M. Carroll, USA
Maka Eradze, Estonia
Mikhail Fominykh, Norway
Denis Gillet, Switzerland
Mustafa Murat Inceoglu, Turkey
Pernilla Josefsson, Sweden
Marie Joubert, UK
Sauli Kiviranta, Finland
Tomaž Klobučar, Slovenia
Elena Kyza, Cyprus
Maarten de Laat, The Netherlands
David Lamas, Estonia

Edmund Laugasson, Estonia
Ana Loureiro, Portugal
Katherine Maillet, France
Nadia Pantidi, UK
Antigoni Parmaxi, Cyprus
Borzoo Pourabdollahian, Italy
Janet C. Read, UK
Christophe Reffay, France
Nicos Souleles, Cyprus
Ana Luísa Torres, Portugal
Stefan Trausan-Matu, Romania
Aimilia Tzanavari, Cyprus
Johnny Yuen, Hong Kong
Carmen Zahn, Switzerland

External Reviewers

Ilia Adami, Greece
Iosif Klironomos, Greece
Maria Korozi, Greece
Vassilis Kouroumalis, Greece

Asterios Leonidis, Greece
George Margetis, Greece
Stavroula Ntoa, Greece
Nikolaos Partarakis, Greece

HCI International 2015

The 15th International Conference on Human–Computer Interaction, HCI International 2015, will be held jointly with the affiliated conferences in Los Angeles, CA, USA, in the Westin Bonaventure Hotel, August 2–7, 2015. It will cover a broad spectrum of themes related to HCI, including theoretical issues, methods, tools, processes, and case studies in HCI design, as well as novel interaction techniques, interfaces, and applications. The proceedings will be published by Springer. More information will be available on the conference website: http://www.hcii2015.org/

General Chair
Professor Constantine Stephanidis
University of Crete and ICS-FORTH
Heraklion, Crete, Greece
E-mail: cs@ics.forth.gr

Table of Contents – Part I

Interaction Devices, Displays and Techniques in VAMR

Designing Virtual and Augmented Environments

Avatars and Virtual Characters

Developing Virtual and Augmented Environments

Table of Contents – Part II

VAMR in Education and Cultural Heritage

Games and Entertainment

Medical, Health and Rehabilitation Applications

Industrial, Safety and Military Applications

Interaction Devices, Displays and Techniques in VAMR

Classification of Interaction Techniques
in the 3D Virtual Environment on Mobile Devices

Eliane Balaa[1], Mathieu Raynal[1], Youssef Bou Issa[2], and Emmanuel Dubois[1]

[1] IRIT, University of Toulouse, France
[2] Faculty of Engineering, Antonine University, Baabda, Lebanon
elianebalaa@yahoo.com

Abstract. 3D Virtual Environments (3DVE) are more and more used in different applications such as CAD, games, or teleoperation. Due to the improvement of smartphones hardware performance, 3D applications were also introduced to mobile devices. In addition, smartphones provide new computing capabilities far beyond the traditional voice communication. They are permitted by the variety of built-in sensors and the internet connectivity. In consequence, interesting 3D applications can be designed by enabling the device capabilities to interact in a 3DVE. Due to the fact that smartphones have small and flat screens and that a 3DVE is wide and dense, mobile devices present some constraints: the environment density, the depth of targets and the occlusion. The pointing task faces these three problems to select a target. We propose a new classification of the existing interaction techniques, according to three axis of classification: a) the three discussed problems (density, depth and occlusion); b) the first two subtasks of the pointing task (navigation, selection); and c) the number of targets selected by the pointing technique (1 or N). In this paper we will begin by presenting a state of the art of the different pointing techniques in existing 3DVE, structured around three selection techniques: a) Ray casting, b) Curve and c) Point cursor. Then we will present our classification, and we will illustrate the classification of the main pointing techniques for 3DVE. From this classification, we will discuss the type of interaction that seems the most appropriate to perform this subtask optimally.

Keywords: Interaction techniques, 3D Virtual environment, mobile devices, environment density, depth of targets, occlusion, Augmented Reality.

1 Introduction

Nowadays, with built-in mobile operating system, smartphones provide new computing capability and connectivity far beyond traditional voice communication [12]. Internet connectivity and applications, games, gyroscopic sensor [13], built-in camera, accelerometer, touchpad and touch screen are very common on such devices. In parallel, three-dimensional technologies have been recently introduced in different applications and areas such as desktop computing and CAD [8] (computer aided design systems), 3D games, VE (virtual environments), AR (augmented reality), ubiquitous computing and tele-operation [19]. Extending the use of 3D applications onto

R. Shumaker and S. Lackey (Eds.): VAMR 2014, Part I, LNCS 8525, pp. 3–13, 2014.
© Springer International Publishing Switzerland 2014

smartphone provides a greater value to both. Few applications to the concept are launched: 3D games and Head-tracking are some examples. Interesting 3D applications on mobile devices can be designed through the mapping of the device abilities to the interaction requirements in the 3D environment. Consequently, the smartphone will be promoted as the new generation of multi-use device. Researchers in 3D virtual environment have developed many new techniques and metaphors for 3D interaction to improve 3D application usability on mobile devices. But they are all facing the same kinds of problems or factors that are specific to the use of 3D on mobile devices. Indeed due to the fact that smartphones have small and flat screens and that a 3DVE is wide and dense with a large number of targets of various sizes, mobile devices present specific constraints:

1. The environment density [17]: to display a large number of targets with various sizes on the relatively small screen of mobile devices, the scene must be shrunk, and the virtual space size and its components must be minimized. Various objects are very close to each other. In this case, how to accurately select one of these objects?
2. The depth of targets [7]: the elements of the environment are displayed in 3D and are identified by three coordinates (X, Y, Z). They are arranged in several levels of depth while the display is a flat touch screen (x,y). But how to point at the appropriate depth to reach an object that is in depth and behind other, even transparent, layers? Depth causes two problems: On the one hand, to know where the pointer is in depth in relation to the target; on the other hand, to point target in depth quickly and with accuracy adds additional complexity to the pointing task.
3. The occlusion [18]: One or more elements of the scene can hide the target either partially or totally and thus reduce its visibility and ability to be selected. Furthermore, the user uses his finger to point a target using the touch screen which creates an additional occlusion while targeting a small object. How to reach an object if it is hidden by another or by the interaction process?

Designing an appropriate interaction technique for 3D on mobile devices must therefore consider these constraints in order to identify the most appropriate solution to the selected context.

In light of these three major concerns, and to contribute to the comparison and design of interaction techniques in 3D on mobile devices, we propose a new classification space. The originality of our approach is to particularly emphasize usage constraints (density, depth, and occlusion) in the context of the pointing task. It is no longer a technologically centered approach but a real user centered approach.

2   Classification

As a first step we chose to focus on the pointing task only, among the three well known tasks of Bowman [1]. Indeed, the pointing task, which is the most used, faces the three mentioned problems. Despite the large amount of different techniques proposed in the literature, these three problems are never solved at the same time. Typically, suggested interaction techniques are used to solve one or two of the three problems. To refine this analysis and better compare or design the pointing techniques in 3D, we propose to consider the pointing task as a set of three sequential subtasks:

1. Navigation refers to exploring the content of the 3DVE in different ways to search for the target and visualize it [4]. In this phase, the user may change his viewpoint through the environment or move the scene to visualize the target.
2. Selection refers to moving a pointer to reach the target position once the target is visible. [5]
3. Validation consists of validating or confirming the pointing task, when the pointer reaches accurately the target. When the technique selects multiple targets during the selection task, the validation task can also select the desired target from the N selected targets. [1]

In addition, the target environment can be either dense or sparse. In order to select a target in a dense environment, multiple objects close to the target may be hard to avoid while trying to select the target. As a result, the target will have to be selected from a first subset of objects. In a sparse environment, such kind of problem doesn't occur, and thus only one object is selected. Consequently we will consider two cases: a) the interaction techniques selecting multiple objects and: b) the interaction techniques selecting 1 object.

Finally problems that have been raised above can therefore be involved at different steps of the pointing task. This is why we propose a new classification of the existing interaction techniques, according to three axis of classification: a) the three subtasks of the pointing tasks (navigation, selection, validation); b) the three discussed problems (density, depth and occlusion) on the first two subtasks of the pointing task, and c) the number of targets selected by the pointing technique during the validation subtask (1 or N).

Table 1. Classification structure

1	2	3	4	5	6	7	8
PT	Navigation			Selection			Validation
	Dens.	Depth	Occl.	Dens.	Depth	Occl.	1 or N

Our classification space consists in a double-entry table. Each pointing technique (PT) is represented in a line. Columns depict the three sub-task of the pointing task. Subtasks are depicted by the columns and divided in sub columns with each encountered problems:

- The first column presents the name of the pointing technique and its reference.
- Columns 2 to 4 relate to the navigation subtask
  o In column 2, the target is in a high density environment but it is visible. Usually, navigation will not solve this problem of density because its goal is only to display the target. However, some interaction techniques can indirectly use navigation to bring target closer and therefore make easier the selection task.

> o   In column 3, the target is in depth, but visible. Like density, na-
>   vigation task is not necessarily required, but can be used to facili-
>   tate the selection task.
> o   In column 4, the target is occluded. To visualize it, the user has
>   to change the viewpoint searching for the target. This case covers
>   interaction techniques that benefit from the Navigation to solve
>   the occlusion problem.

- Columns 5 to 7 relate to the selection subtask
  > o   In column 5, the user must point a target that is close to several
  >   others (density problem). The technique must allow the selection
  >   with accuracy of the target among the N surrounding.
  > o   In column 6, the user must be able to point with the pointing
  >   technique the target that would be distant in depth. The technique
  >   must enable to quickly and accurately select this target.
  > o   In column 7, the position target is known but the target is oc-
  >   cluded or partially occluded. The technique must allow the selec-
  >   tion of the desired target despite obstacles.
- Column 8 treats the validation problem. We distinguish situations where
  one target is selected during the selection phase and the case where multiple targets are selected. In this last case, it requires a new selection from
  N preselected targets.

For each cell of the table, we note "-" if the sub-task is not covered by the pointing technique. If the subtask is covered, we note "**P**" if the problem is present but is not resolved by the pointing technique; "**PS**" if the problem is partially solved and "**S**" if the problem is solved by the pointing technique.

Thus this table allows to quickly see the advantages and disadvantages of a point-ing technique, and also allows comparing two techniques together. This representa-tion also allows us to study more precisely the resolution of a problem for a subtask by analyzing the various solutions proposed for this particular column.

In section 3 we use this classification space and its sub-categories to compare ex-isting interaction techniques. We highlight the differences of the various techniques to demonstrate that existing classifications do not sufficiently highlight the weaknesses and forces of each technique.

3   Existing Techniques

A well-established classification [4] proposes to classify the selection technique used in 3D Virtual Environment into 3 categories: point cursor, ray casting and curve. We will present the main techniques of these three categories and show the main prob-lems they face.

The simplest pointing technique consists of moving a pointer in the 3DVE. The pointer movement is controlled by a pointing device. For example, 3D Point cursor [5] is an interaction technique where a cursor is moved in the virtual environment to select a visible target. When the user press a button, the 3D position and orientation of an input device are linearly transformed into coordinates in the virtual environment where a cursor is displayed. To reach the target, the user moves his input device. Consequently, the coordinates of the cursor change. If the cursor points at the target, the target is highlighted. Then the selection is confirmed by clicking on the input device button. However, this task is complicated since it requires more accurate movements and multiple adjustments in depth.

In case of dense and crowded environment, the target can be occluded. Two problems may occur: the first is the occlusion of the target and the second is the density problem: due to the fact that the target is surrounded by multiple objects that makes the selection of this target a complicated task.

To point the target precisely, the user has to make fine displacement of the crosshair. To point the target accurately without making a big number of displacements, researchers introduce the volume selection with multiple occlusion levels. In the Silk cursor technique [20], the cursor is replaced by a semi-transparent rectangular volume cursor. The user hand is transformed into a silk cursor. When the target is inside the rectangular volume, the user close his hand and the selection is ended. The occlusion levels are used to solve the depth problem. Silk cursor provides information on where the object is placed relatively to another object with no measure of how much they are spatially separated. In the transparent sphere technique [4], the crosshair is replaced by a transparent sphere and the target is one of the objects inside the sphere. To select it, this technique uses list menu or circulation techniques. The menu technique solves the density problem but lose the information about the depth position.

In summary, pointing techniques, based on the point cursor, do not support the navigation phase. They require an additional accuracy effort from the user to point a target in depth. In the selection phase, Silk cursor and transparent sphere partially solve the depth problems. In transparent sphere, the density problem is partially resolved because it requires the search of the target from a set of items.

With the ray casting techniques, the depth problem is solved. In ray cursor [2,5] (see Fig.1-A), the user controls the origin position and the orientation of a virtual ray by adjusting the input device position. Then, a virtual ray is emitted from the user through the target direction. This ray intersects the targeted object. The first object intersected by the virtual ray is highlighted and the selection is confirmed by clicking the input device button. Therefore, this technique does not solve the occlusion problem because if a target is positioned in front of the desired target, it is the first target which is selected and not the desired target. In Go-Go technique [10] (see Fig.1-B), the virtual ray is replaced by a virtual hand. Go-Go is an arm-extension technique using a nonlinear transformation. The user real hand is transformed in a virtual hand in the virtual environment. The virtual hand is kept on the ray extending from the torso and going through the physical hand. Go-Go is limited by the real hand length and the difficulty of grabbing; these limitations are solved by the HOMER [3] interaction technique which combines a ray casting and an arm-extension techniques. HOMER can select objects at any position with no restrictions and perform easy selection and manipulation.

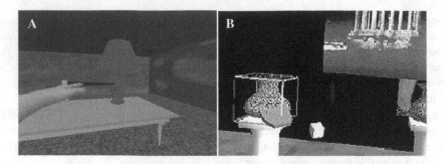

Fig. 1. A) Ray casting technique [3] B) Go-go technique [10]

In the selection phase, Ray cursor, Go-Go and HOMER solve the depth problem thanks to the virtual ray projected to infinity. These techniques are used in a sparse environment to point a visible target. However, they do not solve the occlusion problem because the pointer selects the first target encountered in the case of the ray cursor technique and a visible target in the case of the Go-Go and HOMER techniques. The density problem is not solved either: the Go-Go and HOMER techniques need multiple adjustments to point the target and the ray cursor requires a higher selection precision. Consequently, in case of a dense environment, these techniques are not accurate to select an object.

To solve the occlusion problem, when the ray passes through multiple targets, different techniques are proposed to identify and point the correct target from the group of the aligned objects. The "Ray With Variable Length" technique [4] aims to change the ray length by changing the position of the ray endpoint. The closest objet to the endpoint is highlighted and selected when the user pushes a tracked wand button. Another technique is the Depth ray [5], in addition to the ray, a depth marker travels between the objects following the input device displacements. Each time it comes close to an intersected object, the object becomes red. However, the Depth ray uses a continuous displacement of the input device that can cause modifications of the ray position. This limitation is solved by the Lock ray technique [5] which is a Depth ray version aiming of locking the ray then the depth marker appears to avoid confusion between selection and disambiguation phases. Another technique consists of using a menu to select a target from the N pointed objects of the ray casting. The menu technique consists of displaying the visible and the occluded objects intersected by the ray. Then the target is selected from the menu. Different techniques exist: a 2D flower menu in the Flower Ray technique [5] (which is a 3D extension of the splatter technique [11]) ; a virtual sphere menu in the Daisy menu technique [8] ; a circular menu in the Ring menu technique [8] or a list menu in the Floating menu technique [4, 11]. Using a ray cursor and adding a menu technique solves the occlusion and the depth problems in the selection phase. The limitation of these combined techniques is in the huge number of objects displayed in the menu. These techniques are efficient if the ray crosses exactly the target. Otherwise a density problem is detected.

To overcome the density problem, some techniques use a volume rather than a ray. A selection volume is defined by a ray and the volume around it. This volume can have different forms: a) a cone in the case of the spotlight technique [8] or a cylinder in the case of the transparent cylinder technique [4]. The transparent cylinder technique consists of displaying a cylinder around the ray (see Fig. 2 A.). All objects contained in the cylinder are selected. Then the target is selected using a circulation or Floating menu techniques. The huge number of objects inside the cylinder is solved using a dynamic selection volume (case of the spotlight). The spotlight technique consists of displaying a cone around the ray. The spread angle of the cone is adjusted to minimize the number of objects inside it. Then the target is selected using a special numeric algorithm. Once found, the area around the object is gradually shrunk to minimize the total number of the selected objects. Consequently, the transparent dynamic selection volume solves the density problem, in the selection phase.

Another way to solve the density problem consists of designing hybrid techniques. They combine techniques based on the point cursor metaphor to others based on the ray casting metaphor: for example, the hybrid technique formed by the combination of a ray cursor and a bubble cursor technique [5], or the one formed by the combination of a ray cursor and a transparent sphere technique [4] (see Fig. 2 B.). To do that, these techniques add a dynamic sphere volume at the ray endpoint to augment the selection area and minimize the pointing problem in a dense volume. The hybrid technique formed by the combination of the ray cursor and the bubble cursor provides a shape transformation and warp to select one target. And the hybrid technique formed by the combination of the ray cursor and the transparent sphere selects a group of objects. Based on the number of objects inside the dynamic selection area, researchers propose: a) circulation or menu techniques or b) a special numeric algorithm to select one target. In the selection phase, these techniques solve the depth and the density problems.

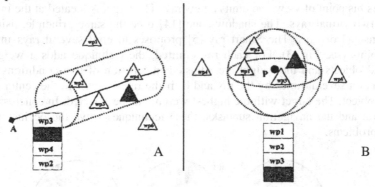

Fig. 2. A) Transparent cylinder and B) transparent sphere technique [4]

To resolve the occlusion problem during the selection phase, Curve technique presents a possible solution. Curve with fixed length [4] is an interaction technique where a fixed curve is moved in the virtual environment to select a visible target. Unlike the curve with fixed length where the user has to move many time in order to select a target, a Curve with variable length [4] technique move the destination endpoint along the three dimensions in order to select its target. In the selection phase, Curve with fixed length and Curve with variable length solve the depth and the occlusion problem because the curve help avoid targets which is in front of the desired target. In case of dense and crowded environment, the target can be occluded and the curve will select multiple objects. The curve techniques are based on the transparency of the environment. Thus, the user can detect the position of the target and make the adjustment to reach it. The Flexible pointer [9] technique is visualized by a flexible curve. The flexible pointer direction is determined by vector formed by the two hands. The amount of curvature is defined by the orientation of each the hand. It is used to point visible, partially or fully occluded objects and to point around objects. Using a curved ray has the advantage of selecting a deep target without passing through the environment objects. The problem of density is solved by the flexibility of the curve in the case of the flexible pointer technique or by using the Virtual pointer metaphor technique [16]. The Virtual pointer metaphor is a ray casting metaphor, using a dynamic area selection and a menu or selection algorithm, to point the target and then to draw a Bezier curve graph pointing the target. Curve also solves the depth problem. The transparency added to the curve metaphor solves the occlusion problem. Solving the density problem is achieved by two methods a) the form and the length of a flexible curve in a transparent environment or b) a ray based technique in a non-transparent environment. In the selection phase, the Flexible pointer length and the Virtual pointer metaphor solve the depth, the occlusion and the density problems.

Most of the presented techniques are only concerned with the selection phase. The navigation subtask is not supported by the proposed techniques and requires different approaches. This complicates the interaction task in the 3DVE. The following techniques cover the selection and the navigation phases. Using the two ray selection technique [4], a first virtual ray is emitted. Multiple targets could be intersected. To select the target from those that have been intersected by the first ray, the user changes his point of view and emits a new ray. The target is located at the intersection of the two virtual rays. The shadow cone [14] used the same principle, using virtual cone instead of rays. The Smart ray [5] proposes to emit several rays in different viewpoints (see Fig. 3). For each ray emitted, the technique adds a weight to the selected objects and the weight are adjusted in function of two conditions: a) if the target is hit several times by the ray and b) if the ray is closer to the center of the selected object. The target with the highest weight can be selected. In conclusion, in the selection and the navigation subtasks, these techniques solve the occlusion and the depth problems.

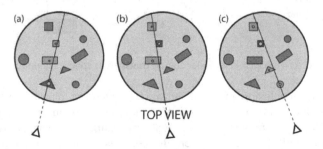

Fig. 3. Smart ray [5]

At last, the world-in-miniature (WIM) technique [15] uses a small representation of the environment to manipulate and interact with the environment objects. The user holds the small version. He uses a simple virtual hand for indirect manipulations of the full-scale object by interacting with their icon in the small version. The user manipulates the miniature objects then the full-scale objects are affected. The WIM is a point cursor technique and used for selection and navigation.

4   Discussion

Error! Reference source not found. summarizes the classification of the techniques we have presented in Section 3. We grouped the techniques in relation to the classification of [4].

Table 2.

	PT	Navigation			Selection			Validation
		Dens	Depth	Occl	Dens	Depth	Occl	
Point cursor	3D Point cursor [5]		-		P	P	S	1
	Silk cursor [20]		-		P	PS	S	1
	Transparent sphere [4]		-		S	PS	S	2
	WIM [15]		S		P	PS	S	1
Ray casting	Ray cursor [2,5]		-		P	S	P	1
	Go-Go [10]		-		P	PS	PS	1
	Homer [3]		-		P	S	S	1
	Variable Length [4]		-		P	S	S	N
	Depth ray [5]		-		P	S	PS	1
	Lock ray [5]		-		P	S	S	2
	spotlight [8]		-		S	S	S	2
	Transparent cylinder [5]		-		S	S	S	2
	Two ray selection [4]		S		S	S	S	2
	Shadow cone [14]		S		S	S	S	2
	Smart ray [5]		S		S	S	S	N
Hybrid	Ray cursor + Bubble cursor [5]		-		S	S	P	1
	Ray cursor + Transparent sphere[4]		-		PS	S	S	1
Curve	fixed or variable length [4]		-		P	PS	S	1
	Flexible pointer [9]		-		P	S	S	1
	Virtual pointer metaphor [16]		-		P	S	S	1

This table allows us to draw some information about the different techniques. At first, we can see that few of them can make both selection and navigation. The techniques we present are more specific to the selection.

We also note that point cursor techniques do not solve the problem of depth: it is difficult to locate the pointer position in depth relative to the target. In addition, the pointing task in depth is difficult with a pointer.

The depth problem is solved using ray casting techniques. However, this technique causes the occlusion problem. Indeed, the virtual ray emitted can cross another target before the desired. In this case, the validation should be done in several stages. On the one hand, point to the right target with the virtual ray, and then select the desired target among those crossed by the virtual ray. This generates two selection and/or validation steps. Therefore, it may increase the pointing time.

The occlusion problem can be solved by curves techniques. Curves techniques allow user to avoid targets located in front of the desired one. However, it poses afresh the depth problem because curves must be moved, and it can cause several movements to point precisely target.

5   Conclusion

In light of these considerations, this work proposes a categorization of interaction techniques. Our classification offers a different way of analyzing the existing interaction techniques which may help in the process of evaluating such techniques. The use of such categorization help users to choose the ones best suited for their needs, to improve existing techniques or to design new techniques. This new classification is based on two criteria: problems and factors affecting pointing performance and the interaction phases.

References

1. Bowman, D.A.: Principles for the Design of Performance-oriented Interaction Techniques, ch. 15
2. Bowman, D.A., Johnson, D.B., Hodges, L.F.: Testbed evaluation of virtual environment interaction techniques. In: Proceedings of the ACM Symposium on Virtual Reality Software and Technology (VRST 1999), pp. 26–33. ACM, New York (1999)
3. Bowman, D.A., Hodges, L.F.: An evaluation of techniques for grabbing and manipulating remote objects in immersive virtual environments. In: Proceedings of the 1997 Symposium on Interactive 3D Graphics (I3D 1997), pp. 35–38. ACM, New York (1997)
4. Dang, N., Le, H., Tavanti, M.: Visualization and interaction on flight trajectory in a 3D stereoscopic environment. In: IEEE 2003, pp. 9.A.5-1–9.A.5-10 (2003)
5. Grossman, T., Balakrishnan, R.: The Design and Evaluation of Selection Techniques for 3D Volumetric Displays. In: Proceedings of the 19th Annual ACM Symposium on User Interface Software and Technology (UIST 2006), pp. 3–12. ACM, New York (2006)
6. Grossman, T., Balakrishnan, R.: The bubble cursor: Enhancing target acquisition by dynamic resizing of the cursor's activation area. In: Proceedings of the SIGCHI Conference on Human Factors in Computing Systems (CHI 2005), pp. 281–290. ACM, New York (2005)
7. Hwang, M.S., Jeon, J.W.: Design of the 3D Input Method Based on Touch Device for Mobile. In: Fifth International Joint Conference on INC, IMS and IDC IEEE, NCM 2009, pp. 1607–1610 (2009)

8. Liang, J., Liang, O., Green, M.: Geometric Modeling Using Six Degrees of Freedom Input Devices. In: 3rd Int'l Conference on CAD and Computer Graphics (1993)
9. Olwal, A., Feiner, S.: The Flexible Pointer: An Interaction Technique for Augmented and Virtual Reality. In: UIST 2003, ACM Symposium on User Interface Software and Technology, pp. 81–82 (2003)
10. Poupyrev, I., Billinghurst, M., Weghorst, S., Ichikawa, T.: The Go-Go Interaction Technique: Non-linear Mapping for Direct Manipulation in VR. In: Proceedings of the 9th Annual ACM Symposium on User Interface Software and Technology (UIST 1996), pp. 79–80. ACM, New York (1996)
11. Ramos, G., Robertson, G., Czerwinski, M., Tan, D., Baudisch, P., Hinckley, K., Agrawala, M.: Tumble! Splat! Helping Users Access and Manipulate Occluded Content in 2D Drawings. In: Proceedings of the Working Conference on Advanced Visual Interfaces (AVI 2006), pp. 428–435. ACM, New York (2006)
12. Robbins, D.C., Cutrell, E., Sarin, R., Horvitz, E.: ZoneZoom: Map Navigation for Smartphones with Recursive View Segmentation. In: Proceedings of the Working Conference on Advanced Visual Interfaces (AVI 2004), pp. 231–234. ACM, New York (2004)
13. Schäfers, T., Rohs, M., Spors, S., Raake, A., Ahrens, J.: Designing Low-Dimensional Interaction for Mobile Navigation in 3D Audio Spaces. In: Proceedings of 34th International Conference of the Audio Engineering Society, AES (2008)
14. Steed, A., Parker, C.: 3D Selection Strategies for Head Tracked and Non-Head Tracked Operation of Spatially Immersive Displays. In: Proceedings of 8th International Immersive Projection Technology Workshop, pp. 13–14 (2004)
15. Stoakley, R., Conway, M., Pausch, R.: Virtual Reality on a WIM: Interactive Worlds in Miniature. In: Proceedings of the SIGCHI Conference on Human Factors in Computing Systems (CHI 1995), pp. 265–272. ACM Press/Addison-Wesley Publishing Co, New York, NY (1995)
16. Steinicke, F., Ropinski, T., Hinrichs, K.: Object selection in virtual environments using an improved virtual pointer metaphor. In: Proceedings of International Conference on Computer Vision and Graphics (ICCVG), pp. 320–326 (2006)
17. Vanacken, L., Grossman, T., Coninx, K.: Exploring the effects of environment density and target visibility on object selection in 3D virtual environments. In: IEEE Symposium on 3D User Interfaces, pp. 117–124 (2007)
18. Vanacken, L., Grossman, T., Coninx, K.: Multimodal selection techniques for dense and occluded 3D virtual environments. International Journal of Human-Computer Studies 67(3), 237–255 (2009)
19. Zhai, S., Milgram, P., Rastogi, A.: Anisotropic human performance in six degree-of-freedom tracking: An evaluation of three-dimensional display and control interfaces. IEEE Transactions on Systems, Man and Cybernetics, Part A: Systems and Humans 27(4), 518–528 (1997)
20. Zhai, S., Buxton, W., Milgram, P.: The "Silk Cursor": Investigating transparency for 3D target acquisition. In: Proceedings of the SIGCHI Conference on Human Factors in Computing Systems (CHI 1994), pp. 459–464. ACM, New York (1994)

Multimodal Interfaces and Sensory Fusion in VR for Social Interactions

Esubalew Bekele[1,*], Joshua W. Wade[1], Dayi Bian[1], Lian Zhang[1], Zhi Zheng[1],
Amy Swanson[3], Medha Sarkar[2], Zachary Warren[3,4], and Nilanjan Sarkar[5,1,*]

[1] Electrical Engineering and Computer Science Department
[2] Computer Science Department, Middle Tennessee State University, Murfreesboro, TN, USA
[3] Pediatrics and Psychiatry Department
[4] Treatment and Research in Autism Spectrum Disorder (TRIAD)
[5] Mechanical Engineering Department, Vanderbilt University, Nashville, TN, USA
{esubalew.bekele,nilanjan.sarkar}@vanderbilt.edu

Abstract. Difficulties in social interaction, verbal and non-verbal communications as well as repetitive and atypical patterns of behavior, are typical characteristics of Autism spectrum disorders (ASD). Advances in computer and robotic technology are enabling assistive technologies for intervention in psychiatric disorders such as autism spectrum disorders (ASD) and schizophrenia (SZ). A number of research studies indicate that many children with ASD prefer technology and this preference can be explored to develop systems that may alleviate several challenges of traditional treatment and intervention. The current work presents development of an adaptive virtual reality-based social interaction platform for children with ASD. It is hypothesized that endowing a technological system that can detect the feeling and mental state of the child and adapt its interaction accordingly is of great importance in assisting and individualizing traditional intervention approaches. The proposed system employs sensors such as eye trackers and physiological signal monitors and models the context relevant psychological state of the child from combination of these sensors. Preliminary affect recognition results indicate that psychological states could be determined from peripheral physiological signals and together with other modalities including gaze and performance of the participant, it is viable to adapt and individualize VR-based intervention paradigms.

Keywords: Social interaction, virtual reality, autism intervention, multimodal system, adaptive interaction, eye tracking, physiological processing, sensor fusion.

1 Introduction

Recent advances in human machine interaction enabled the use of computer technology [1], robot-mediated systems [2,3], and virtual reality (VR) based systems [4,5] for use in social interaction for autism spectrum disorders (ASD) intervention. ASD is characterized by a spectrum of developmental disorders that are associated with

---

* Corresponding authors.

R. Shumaker and S. Lackey (Eds.): VAMR 2014, Part I, LNCS 8525, pp. 14–24, 2014.
© Springer International Publishing Switzerland 2014

social, communicative and language deficits [6], generally poor social skills [7], deficits in facial and vocal affect recognition, social judgment, problem solving and social functioning skills [8] and deficits in the ability to use appropriate language in a social context [9]. Hence a deficit in social interaction is core deficit of ASD. Although, these common social and communicational deficits are observed in most children with ASD, the manifestation of these deficits is quite different from one individual to another [10]. These individual differences call for approaches to individualize the therapy as opposed to one-therapy-fits-all strategies.

Traditional intervention requiring intensive behavioral sessions results in excessive life time costs and inaccessibility of the therapy for the larger population [11]. Recent assistive technologies have shown the potential to at least lessen the burden of human therapists, increase effectiveness of the traditional intervention, and provide objective measures. Literature suggests that children with ASD are highly motivated by computer-based intervention tasks [12]. Predictability, objectivity, lack of judgmental behavior, consistency of clearly defined task and the ability to direct focus of attention due to reduced distractions from unnecessary sensor stimuli are among the benefits of technology-enabled therapy [9].

Virtual reality (VR) [13,5] have been proposed for ASD intervention. VR platforms are shown to have the capacity to improve social skills, cognition and overall social functioning in autism [14]. Explicit modalities such as audio visual for natural multimodal interaction [15] and peripheral physiological signals [16,5] and eye tracking [17] to identify the psychological states of the user and hence adapt the interaction accordingly is crucial in social interactions in general and VR in particular [18,19]. Despite this potential to automatically detect and adapt to the social interaction in VR systems, most existing VR systems as applied to ASD therapy focus on performance and explicit user feedback as primary means of interaction with the participant [20]. Therefore, adaptive interaction is limited in these systems. Adaptive social interaction using implicit cues from sensors such as peripheral physiological signals [14] and eye tracking [21] are of particular importance. For such a system to simulate some semblance of naturalistic social interaction, several components are required including conversational dialog management, body language (gesture), facial emotional expressions and eye contact in addition to the implicit user state understanding components. Conversational dialog is an important part of social interaction. Recently spoken conversational modules have been incorporated into VR systems to achieve more natural interaction instead of menu driven dialog management. Instead of large vocabulary, domain independent natural language understanding, limited vocabulary question-response dialog management, which is focused on the specific domain, has been shown to be effective [22,23]. Such multimodal interactions help in individualization of the therapy and in cases of inaccessibility of trained therapists, it may serve as a self-contained therapeutic system.

This paper describes details of an innovative adaptive VR-based multimodal social interaction platform. The platform integrates peripheral psychophysiological signal monitoring for affective state modeling, eye tracking and gaze metrics for engagement modeling and spoken question-answer-based dialog management for a more naturalistic interaction.

The remainder of the paper is organized as follows. Section 2 details individual components of the system. Section 3 presents preliminary physiology-based affective state modeling results. Finally, Section 4 concludes the discussion by highlighting future direction and extensions of the system.

1.1   VR System Details

The social task presentation VR system is composed of four major components: (1) an adaptive social task presentation VR module, (2) a spoken conversation management module (Q/A-based natural language processing, NLP module), (3) a synchronous physiological signal monitoring and physiological affect recognition module, and (4) a synchronous eye tracking and engagement detection module. Each component runs independently in parallel, while sharing data via light-weight network sockets message passing in a highly distributed architecture. The VR task presentation engine is built on top of the popular game engine Unity (www.unity3d.com) by Unity Technologies. The peripheral psychophysiological monitoring application was built using the software development kit (SDK) of the wireless BioNomadix physiological signals acquisition device by Biopac Inc. (www.biopac.com). The eye tracker application was built using the Tobii X120 remote desktop eye tracker SDK by Tobii Technologies (www.tobii.com).

1.2   The VR Social Task Engine

The VR environment is mainly built on and rendered in Unity game engine. However, various 3D software such as online animation and rigging service, Mixamo (www.mixamo.com), and Autodesk Maya were employed for character customization, rigging and animation. The venue for the social interaction task is a virtual school cafeteria (Fig. 1). The cafeteria was built using a combination of Google Sketchup and Autodesk Maya. A pack of 12 fully rigged virtual characters (10 teenagers and 2 adults) with 20 facial bones for emotional expressions and several body bones for various gestural animations were used as templates to instantiate most of the characters in the environment. Details of the VR development can be found in [24].

Fig. 1. The VR cafeteria environment for social task training. Dining area (top) and food dispensary area (bottom). The two areas are constructed in separate rooms.

Fig. 1. (*Continued.*)

1.3   Spoken Dialog Management

The verbal conversation component of the VR system creates context for social interaction and emotion recognition in a social setting and is managed by a spoken dialog management module. The dialog manager was developed using the Microsoft speech recognizer from the speech API (SAPI) with domain specific grammar and semantics. The conversation module is based on question-answer dialog and it contained conversational threads for easy (level 1, L1), medium (level 2, L2) and hard (level 3, L3) social tasks with each level having 4 conversational task blocks called missions that the participant is expected to accomplish. Each mission has further components called turns representing back and forth between the participant and the system. L1 missions have one turn, L2 missions have two turns and L3 missions have 3 turns (Fig 2). Each turn was represented by a tree of dialog with nodes representing each option and a particular branch in the tree representing the dialog alternative paths from the initial question to the final correct answer. Failure and success is measured in each conversational turn and there is a hierarchical scoring mechanism that keeps track of performance in conversation turn level as well as mission level. Options in each turn are presented to the participant using a list of items and the participant speaks out their choice through a microphone. Kinect is employed for this purpose as its microphones have superior sound directional localization and background noise cancellation features.

Overall performance, i.e., success/failure (S/F) is used to switch across missions (levels) as shown in Fig. 2 in the "performance only" version of the system. In the adaptive system, physiological affect recognition as well as eye tracking-based engagement detection are combined to adapt the level of difficulty of the interaction in addition to the overall performance of the participant.

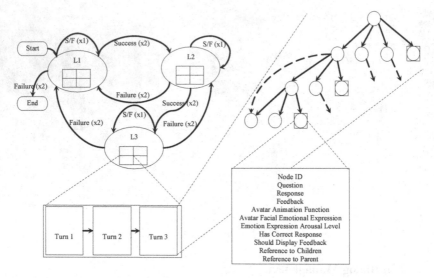

Fig. 2. Finite state diagram showing a level switching logic

1.4 Physiology-Based Affective State Modeling

The physiological monitoring application collects 8 channels of physiological data and was developed using the Biopac software development kit (SDK) and BioNomadix wireless physiological acquisition modules with a sampling rate of 1000 Hz. The physiological signals that were monitored were: electrocardiogram (ECG), pulse plethesymogram (PPG), skin temperature (SKT), galvanic skin response (GSR), 3 electromyograms (EMG), and respiration (RSP). Various features extracted out of these signals are used for supervised training of a machine learning algorithm for later affective state classification in the actual interaction. Training data was collected separately using a study designed to elicit target affective states such as liking, engagement, boredom, and stress. We developed and used computer-based pong and anagram solving cognitive games with trials carefully designed to elicit the states. Details of the cognitive tasks are presented in Table 1.

Table 1. Number of trials and trial durations for the games

Games	Sub-sessions	Number of Trials	Trial Duration
Anagram	sub-session 1	3	90 s
	sub-session 2	3	180 s
	sub-session 3	6	180 s
Pong	sub-session 1	3	120 s
	sub-session 2	3	120 s
	sub-session 3	9	120 s

The data were passed through various successive signal processing stages. First, the data was passed through very large signal uncorrelated outlier rejection block. Then, every channel was subsampled to lower frequency to keep most of the signal content while reducing computational burden. Signals such as EMG were subsampled at higher frequency whereas slow moving signals such as SKT, GSR, and RSP were down sampled at much lower frequency. The data were then filtered to remove high frequency uncorrelated noise, motion artifacts, very low frequency trending and DC bias, power line noise, and inter-channel interference (e.g.: ECG artifact on EMG). Finally, features were extracted from the channels for supervised training. For this preliminary comparative study, we choose four channels (which are prominent in capturing the autonomic system response), i.e., ECG, PPG, GSR, and SKT, and out of them 16 features were extracted.

Generally, people recognize emotions in speeches with an average 60% and from facial expressions with 70-98% [25]. Emotion recognition using peripheral physiological signals and machine learning techniques such as artificial neural networks (ANN) and support vector machines (SVM) under controlled experiments achieved a comparable recognition rates [26-29]. We comparatively studied the performance of SVM and ANN with three separate learning methods each. The most popular learning algorithm to solve the error minimization problem in ANN is the back propagation (BP) algorithm [30]. However due to its slow convergence and other issues such as convergence to local minima, a variety of methods have been proposed to improve time-space and error of performance BP. These methods range from adhoc methods with adaptive learning rate and momentum (GDX) [31] to using numerical approximations including Newton's secant method by Broyden, Fletcher, Goldfarb, and Shanno (BFGS) [32] and non-linear least squares called Levenberg-Marquardt (LM) [30]. To optimize the error margins of SVM, the performance of the quadratic programming (QP) [33], sequential minimal optimization (SMO) method that decomposes the larger QP problem in to a series of smaller QP problems [34], and the least square (LS) solver [33] were explored in this study.

1.5   Eye Gaze Based Engagement Modeling

The main eye tracker application computed eye physiological indices (PI) such as pupil diameter (PD) and blink rate (BR) and behavioral indices (BI) [21] such as fixation duration (FD) from raw gaze data. For each data point, gaze coordinates (X, Y), PD, BR, and FD were computed and logged together with the whole raw data, trial markers and timestamps in addition to being used as features for the rule-based engagement detection mechanism. The fixation duration computation was based on the velocity threshold identification (I-VT) algorithm [35].

A rule-based system for engagement detection is developed to infer engagement using the behavioral as well as physiological indices from the tracking data as features. The rules use adaptive thresholds and these thresholds are standardized using baseline data recorded before interaction.

1.6   Multimodal Decision Fusion

At this stage a decision tree based decision fusion for the multimodal interfaces is developed. The decision tree combines the outputs of the physiological affective state model, the engagement model, and performance of the participant as variables to come up with overall system difficulty level adjustment. This module will be used in the main pilot study of the overall system to illustrate its performance. In the results section, we present only the physiological-based affect modeling study that was briefly described in Section 2.3.

1.7   Experimental Procedures

With the designed distributed emotion modelling system based on computer games (Section 2.3), a total of 10 children with ASD participated in the study. Each participant went through all the Pong and Anagram sub-sessions as shown in Table 1. In each trial we monitored all the physiological signals described in section 2.3 and extracted 16 features out of each trial to obtain a total of 192 data points. These include 147 positive valence (liking and engagement/enjoyment) and 45 negative valence points (frustration/Boredom and anxiety). A trained therapist rated each trial on a Likert scale of 1-9 for each of the 4 perceived psychological states and the result was normalized and classified into positive and negative valence classes. All the data was trained to the three training methods of MLP and the three learning methods of SVM described in section 2.3.

2   Results

As described in Section 2, this system development is an ongoing effort which is tested for usability incrementally. The first phase was developing the virtual environment, the characters and endowing facial emotional expressions to the characters. This stage was evaluated with 10 children with ASD and 10 typically developing children in a separate study [19]. After that, this current study, develops more capabilities such as various animations, the cafeteria environment, the speech-based dialog management, affective modeling with supervised training methods and eye tracking based engagement modeling. The system development of the social task VR environment was presented in [24]. This paper presents the current status by adding results of the preliminary physiological-based affect modeling component.

2.1   Preliminary Physiological Modeling Results

We have conducted a separate study to collect training physiological data for affect modeling as described in Section 2.3.

Model Fitting. We performed model selection to get the best parameters for each learning algorithm. For multilayer perceptron (MLP) ANN, we fixed the number of epochs at 10,000, the error requirement at 0, minimum gradient at 1e-5, and the number of validation checks to 1,000 across all the model selection process. For SVM, we selected radial basis function (rbf) as the kernel and the variance of the rbf as 1.0.

We used minimum validation error as criteria to choose the best model (Fig. 3). However, whenever the testing error is not closer or at a local minimum when the validation is at global minima, we chose the next minimum validation error point. Table 2 shows the best model parameters.

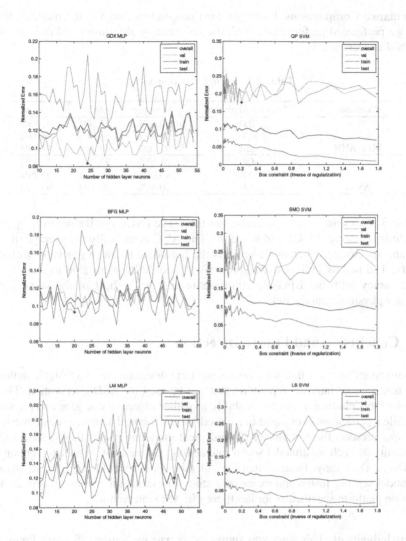

Fig. 3. Normalized Error vs. number of hidden layer neurons (MLP ANN) and vs. inverse of regularization parameter for SVM. Best validation parameters indicated by dark blue point on the green validation line.

Table 2. Selected Best Model Parameters

Classifier	Training Algorithm	Best Model Parameters
	GDX	29.00
	BFG	20.00
MLP ANN	LM	48.00
	QP	0.21
	SMO	0.55
SVM	LS	0.04

Performance Comparisons. Using the best parameters found in the model selection stage, we performed performance of all the six learning algorithms and two classifiers described in section 2.3.

Table 3. Performance Comparisons

Classifier	Training Algorithm	Accuracy	AUC	F_1-score
	GDX	89.09%	85.16%	92.85%
	BFG	94.80%	93.51%	96.58%
MLP ANN	LM	91.70%	89.24%	94.54%
	QP	91.67%	93.02%	94.33%
	SMO	90.62%	88.47%	93.79%
SVM	LS	90.63%	93.11%	93.53%

Table 3 shows the accuracy, area under the curve (AUC) of the receiver operating characteristics curve (ROC), and F1-score. The AUC is basically the average of sensitivity and specificity, whereas F1-score is the harmonic mean of precision with equal weights. The results indicated that both SVM and ANN were able to classify with high accuracy with the BFG algorithm achieving the highest performance for this particular physiological dataset.

3   Conclusion and Future Direction

The main contribution of this work is to present the development of a realistic multimodal VR-based social interaction platform that can be used for ASD intervention. The uniqueness of this platform relies on its ability to gather objective eye gaze and physiology data while a participant is engaged in a closed-loop VR-based adaptive social interaction. This paper presents the preliminary physiological modeling results that seem to indicate the viability of such multimodal social interaction environment as an intervention platform for ASD therapy. Future extensions of this system would add a more advanced multimodal sensory fusion and major pilot study to evaluate the whole system as an intervention platform specifically for its efficacy in ASD intervention.

Acknowledgement. This work was supported in part by National Science Foundation Grant 0967170 and National Institute of Health Grant 1R01MH091102-01A1.

References

1. Goodwin, M.S.: Enhancing and Accelerating the Pace of Autism Research and Treatment. Focus on Autism and Other Developmental Disabilities 23(2), 125–128 (2008)
2. Feil-Seifer, D., Matarić, M.: Toward socially assistive robotics for augmenting interventions for children with autism spectrum disorders. Paper presented at the Experimental Robotics 54 (2009)
3. Bekele, E., Lahiri, U., Davidson, J., Warren, Z., Sarkar, N.: Robot-Mediated Joint Attention Tasks for Children at Risk with ASD: A Step towards Robot-Assisted Intervention. In: International Meeting for Autism Research (IMFAR), San Deigo, CA (2011)

4. Andreasen, N.C.: Scale for the assessment of positive symptoms. University of Iowa, Iowa City (1984)
5. Welch, K., Lahiri, U., Liu, C., Weller, R., Sarkar, N., Warren, Z.: An Affect-Sensitive Social Interaction Paradigm Utilizing Virtual Reality Environments for Autism Intervention. Paper presented at the Human-Computer Interaction, Ambient, Ubiquitous and Intelligent Interaction (2009)
6. Lord, C., Volkmar, F., Lombroso, P.J.: Genetics of childhood disorders: XLII. Autism, part 1: Diagnosis and assessment in autistic spectrum disorders. Journal of the American Academy of Child and Adolescent Psychiatry 41(9), 1134 (2002)
7. Diagnostic and Statistical Manual of Mental Disorders: Quick reference to the diagnostic criteria from DSM-IV-TR. American Psychiatric Association, Amer Psychiatric Pub Incorporated, Washington, DC (2000)
8. Demopoulos, C., Hopkins, J., Davis, A.: A Comparison of Social Cognitive Profiles in children with Autism Spectrum Disorders and Attention-Deficit/Hyperactivity Disorder: A Matter of Quantitative but not Qualitative Difference? Journal of Autism and Developmental Disorders, 1–14 (2012)
9. Gal, E., Bauminger, N., Goren-Bar, D., Pianesi, F., Stock, O., Zancanaro, M., Weiss, P.L.: Enhancing social communication of children with high-functioning autism through a co-located interface. AI & Society 24(1), 75–84 (2009)
10. Ploog, B.O., Scharf, A., Nelson, D., Brooks, P.J.: Use of Computer-Assisted Technologies (CAT) to Enhance Social, Communicative, and Language Development in Children with Autism Spectrum Disorders. Journal of Autism and Developmental Disorders, 1–22 (2012)
11. Ganz, M.L.: The lifetime distribution of the incremental societal costs of autism. Archives of Pediatrics and Adolescent Medicine 161(4), 343–349 (2007)
12. Bernard-Opitz, V., Sriram, N., Nakhoda-Sapuan, S.: Enhancing social problem solving in children with autism and normal children through computer-assisted instruction. Journal of Autism and Developmental Disorders 31(4), 377–384 (2001)
13. Parsons, S., Mitchell, P., Leonard, A.: The use and understanding of virtual environments by adolescents with autistic spectrum disorders. Journal of Autism and Developmental Disorders 34(4), 449–466 (2004)
14. Kandalaft, M.R., Didehbani, N., Krawczyk, D.C., Allen, T.T., Chapman, S.B.: Virtual Reality Social Cognition Training for Young Adults with High-Functioning Autism. Journal of Autism and Developmental Disorders, 1–11 (2012)
15. Lang, P.J., Bradley, M.M., Cuthbert, B.N.: International affective picture system (IAPS): Technical manual and affective ratings. The Center for Research in Psychophysiology, University of Florida, Gainesville, FL (1999)
16. Herbener, E.S., Song, W., Khine, T.T., Sweeney, J.A.: What aspects of emotional functioning are impaired in schizophrenia? Schizophrenia Research 98(1), 239–246 (2008)
17. Lahiri, U., Bekele, E., Dohrmann, E., Warren, Z., Sarkar, N.: Design of a Virtual Reality based Adaptive Response Technology for Children with Autism. IEEE Transactions on Neural Systems and Rehabilitation Engineering: A Publication of the IEEE Engineering in Medicine and Biology Society PP (early access), (99), p. 1 (2012)
18. Zeng, Z., Pantic, M., Roisman, G.I., Huang, T.S.: A survey of affect recognition methods: Audio, visual, and spontaneous expressions. IEEE Transactions on Pattern Analysis and Machine Intelligence 31(1), 39–58 (2009)
19. Bekele, E., Zheng, Z., Swanson, A., Crittendon, J., Warren, Z., Sarkar, N.: Understanding How Adolescents with Autism Respond to Facial Expressions in Virtual Reality Environments. IEEE Transactions on Visualization and Computer Graphics 19(4), 711–720 (2013)

20. Parsons, T.D., Rizzo, A.A., Rogers, S., York, P.: Virtual reality in paediatric rehabilitation: A review. Developmental Neurorehabilitation 12(4), 224–238 (2009)
21. Lahiri, U., Warren, Z., Sarkar, N.: Design of a Gaze-Sensitive Virtual Social Interactive System for Children With Autism. IEEE Transactions on Neural Systems and Rehabilitation Engineering (99), 1–1 (2012)
22. Kenny, P., Parsons, T., Gratch, J., Leuski, A., Rizzo, A.: Virtual patients for clinical therapist skills training. Paper presented at the Intelligent Virtual Agents (2007)
23. Leuski, A., Patel, R., Traum, D., Kennedy, B.: Building effective question answering characters. In: Proceedings of the 7th SIGdial Workshop on Discourse and Dialogue, pp. 18–27. Association for Computational Linguistics (2009)
24. Bekele, E., et al.: A step towards adaptive multimodal virtual social interaction platform for children with autism. In: Stephanidis, C., Antona, M. (eds.) UAHCI/HCII 2013, Part II. LNCS, vol. 8010, pp. 464–473. Springer, Heidelberg (2013)
25. Picard, R.W.: Affective computing. MIT Press, Cambridge (1997)
26. Picard, R.W., Vyzas, E., Healey, J.: Toward machine emotional intelligence: Analysis of affective physiological state. IEEE Transactions on Pattern Analysis and Machine Intelligence 23(10), 1175–1191 (2001)
27. Liu, C., Conn, K., Sarkar, N., Stone, W.: Online affect detection and robot behavior adaptation for intervention of children with autism. IEEE Transactions on Robotics 24(4), 883–896 (2008)
28. Rani, P., Liu, C., Sarkar, N., Vanman, E.: An empirical study of machine learning techniques for affect recognition in human–robot interaction. Pattern Analysis & Applications 9(1), 58–69 (2006)
29. Kim, J., Ande, E.: Emotion recognition based on physiological changes in music listening. IEEE Transactions on Pattern Analysis and Machine Intelligence 30(12), 2067–2083 (2008)
30. Hagan, M.T., Menhaj, M.B.: Training feedforward networks with the Marquardt algorithm. IEEE Transactions on Neural Networks 5(6), 989–993 (1994)
31. Riedmiller, M., Braun, H.: A direct adaptive method for faster backpropagation learning: The RPROP algorithm. In: IEEE, vol. 581, pp. 586–591 (1993)
32. Battiti, R.: First-and second-order methods for learning: between steepest descent and Newton's method. Neural Computation 4(2), 141–166 (1992)
33. Suykens, J.A.K., Vandewalle, J.: Least squares support vector machine classifiers. Neural Processing Letters 9(3), 293–300 (1999)
34. Platt, J.C.: 12 Fast Training of Support Vector Machines using Sequential Minimal Optimization (1998)
35. Salvucci, D.D., Goldberg, J.H.: Identifying fixations and saccades in eye-tracking protocols. Paper presented at the Proceedings of the 2000 Symposium on Eye Tracking Research & Applications (2000)

Multi-modal Interaction System to Tactile Perception

Lorenzo Cavalieri, Michele Germani, and Maura Mengoni

Department of Industrial Engineering and Mathematical Sciences,
Polytechnic University of Marche, Italy
{lorenzo.cavalieri,m.germani,m.mengoni}@univpm.it

Abstract. Haptic simulation of materials is one of the most important challenges in human-computer interaction. A fundamental step to achieve it regards the definition of how human beings can encode the information acquired by different sensorial channels' stimulation. In this context, this paper presents the study, implementation and evaluation of a multi-modal cutaneous feedback device (CFD) for the simulation of material textures. In addition to tactile stimulation, two further sensory components (e.g. eyesight and hearing) are integrated to support the user to better recognize and discriminate different classes of materials and then, overcome previous identified drawbacks. An experimental protocol is tuned to assess the relevance of each stimulated channel in material texture recognition. Tests are carried out with real and virtual materials. Result comparison is used to validate the proposed approach and verify the realism of simulation.

Keywords: Elettrocutaneous feedback, haptic, multi-modal stimulation.

1 Introduction

Haptic interaction still represents one of the most important issues in human-computer studies due to the effects that touch has on product experience. Systems are classified in two main areas: kinesthetic and cutaneous [3]. Studies aim to develop solutions to recreate tactile stimulation in order to improve the user experience of virtual proto-types. However, most of them do not deepen the correlation among all involved senses (sight and hearing) that equally contribute to user sensations. The importance of multisensory interaction is demonstrated by the numerous researches about virtual reality environments where the integration of haptic, visual and auditory feedbacks are looked for to increase user perception of the outside world.

In this context, this paper presents the study, implementation and evaluation of a cutaneous feedback device (CFD) for the simulation of material textures. In addition to tactile stimulation, two further sensory components (e.g. eyesight and hearing) are integrated to support the user to better recognize and discriminate different classes of materials and then, overcome previous identified drawbacks.

The current research is a step forward a previous one, focusing on the development of an electrotactile device for texture simulation [1]. The main novelties, described in this paper, regard:

R. Shumaker and S. Lackey (Eds.): VAMR 2014, Part I, LNCS 8525, pp. 25–34, 2014.

- Improvement of tactile stimulation through the addition of mechanical vibration to stimulate deep skin mechanoreceptors;
- Addition of audio components through the reproduction of the sound emitted by a finger rubbing on the material and the subsequent application of an auralization algorithm;
- Extension of the 3D visualization by the implementation of a virtual prototyping-based system to represent human interaction with the material.

The experiments were organized in two phases. In the first one, system performance is tested by assessing responsiveness and synchronization. In the second phase, an experimental protocol is applied to verify if users recognizes the class of material. For each user, tests are replicated by changing the number of involved sensory channels.

2   Background

Haptic systems are classified in two categories: kinesthetic one provides to reproduce force feedback, while in the tactile one cutaneous feedback was applied.

In the field of cutaneous feedback, most researches focus on the development of devices producing stimuli of a single nature [20-24]. Three classes of tactile stimulations can be recognized:

- mechanical stimulation through vibration of physical elements or through the use of ultrasonic waves [20-22],
- electrical stimulation through application of a current flow or an electric potential on the contact surface [23-24];
- thermal stimulation through heating of the contact surfaces.

About the mechanical stimulation, Fukuyama [20] proposes a Shape Memory Alloy (SMA) that accepts a pulse-signal to generate a vibration in accordance with the pulse frequency of the signal. He developed a vibration actuator to create the tactile stimuli. Ikei [21] presents a tactile display, which has fifty vibrating pins to convey the surface texture sensation of object surfaces to the user's fingertip. Finally, Takasaki [22] proposed a tactile display using surface acoustic wave (SAW): a glass substrate, which is non-piezoelectric material, is combined with a piezoelectric material. These approaches allow the system to recreate a cutaneous feedback, but its granular density is so low that it is not able to reproduce the physical properties of a material surface.

On the other hand there are many contributions in the implementation of electrical stimulation. Yamamoto [23] developed a tactile display with a thin conductive film slider with stator electrodes that excite electrostatic forces. Olivier et al. [24] developed TeslaTouch, a tactile platform based on principle of electro vibration, which allows the creation of a broad range of tactile sensations by controlling electrostatic friction between an instrumented touch surface and the user's fingers. In both cases, the electrical stimulation is based on the properties of friction and does not implement the other key characteristics of surface texture.

Some studies focus on the correlation between the physical properties of materials and cutaneous stimuli for texture simulation via cutaneous feedback devices. Kyung [14] e Altinsoy [9] studied the possible correlation between the roughness of the materials and the amplitude and frequency of the vibrotactile stimulus; Hughes [11] investigated how the gradient density affects decoding of the texture by the tactile perception. Some researches recognize the key role of friction in the reconstruction of an actual perception of a given material. Developed devices can reproduce a variable friction of the user interface through mechanical vibrations [5, 15] or through the variation of an electric voltage applied on the contact surface [12].

Other important studies have been conducted to determine the properties and functions of the Low-Threshold MechanoReceptors (LTMRs), indicators of the sensitivity threshold of the human being [8]. In summary, many studies aim to investigate how the human being encoded information from the tactile channel coming from the real world.

In sensorial stimulation, an important issue regards the influence of different sensory channels on the perception of the outside world by the human being.

Calwell [10] proposes a glove providing both a mechanical and a thermal stimulus: in this case the multimodality is achieved by combining two types of stimuli with the aim to improve haptic interaction. Otherwise, none additional sensory channel is involved. Vitense [19] developed a system with multiple feedbacks (auditory, haptic and visual). The three considered stimuli have not a physical correlation between each other, but are implemented in order to provide enhanced user experience in performing tasks through a graphical interface. In addition, the system, designed to be a support for the visually impaired, is focused on the creation of a GUI that provides additional sensory channels as a force feedback (haptic) and earcon (auditory) to give or an enhanced use experience or an alternative user interaction mode.

A great contribution to multimodal sensory integration is provided by the works of Spence [17] that studied the importance of synchrony of stimuli of different sensory channels in a multimodal system and Turchet [18] that explored the relevance of semantic congruence of a bimodal system (haptic and auditory).

About the implementation of multisensory stimulation, a further key element seems to be how to make the developed technology wearable. For instance, Burch, D. et. al. [4] use an active display in combination with the wearable thimbles implementing a tactile stimulation varying according to current finger position. Calwell [10] uses a glove to implement a multimodal system described above. Although most systems appear effective, the use of a wearing device makes them intrusive and not barrier free. Their insufficient usability often influences user perception of materials.

Most analyzed devices stimulate one-by-one sensorial channel and do not investigate the cross-sensory connections of touch, sight and hearing in material discrimination. Taking into consideration current research drawbacks, the present work proposes a multi-modal system, called Ipertouch, able to differently stimulate all sensorial channels to achieve a proper texture simulation. The implementation of the system passes through a series of experiments on real material samples involving differently blind users to verify the mutual influences of senses on material perception, determination and discrimination. The lack of sight and hearing allowed users only to determine the material class the sample belongs to, but not to identify texture properties.

3 System Development

Ipertouch is the evolution of a previous developed platform for the single cutaneous stimulation [1]. The previous platform was formed by a tactile display that reproduces the spatial profile of the surface texture of real materials. This platform was driven by a PC and is used in passive touch mode (finger is placed on the touchpad and the electrical signal is done flowing below it). Previous researches focused on the elaboration and processing of roughness profiles. Tactile signals derived from scanning of real materials and their subsequent processing and mapping current [2]. Therefore, signals used to implemented tactile stimulation are connected with real properties of materials.

In this work, we have completed the simulation system adding a mechanical vibration through a shaker, a signal generator and a control software developed by LabView, adding an audio feedback with a record of rubbing finger on the material processed with a spatialization algorithm and developing a visual feedback software to show the finger movement on the chosen material.

This platform is created as a tool to reproduce tactile stimuli reconstructing texture properties of real materials: it is composed of a hardware component that can provide the stimulation of the three sensory channels and a software component able to manage the information of each class of material that is selected and the synchronism of information about every three sensory channels. The following describes in detail the different elements of the system.

The hardware platform is composed of three basic elements representing the user interface through which the three sensory channels are stimulated.

The conception of tactile component is based on the principle of selection stimulation [25]: touch is stimulated through two different types of signals, an electric and mechanical one, to excite all types of mechanoreceptors located at different skin layers.

In detail, the platform is composed of a pad with 256 pin electrodes arranged as a 32x8 grid to spatially distribute the current flow. The electrodes are 1-mm diameter and they are 2.5 mm away. The processing unit is a multiprocessor platform consisting of one master and four slaves. Two force sensors (Honeywell FSS-SMT) are located under the tactile pad layer to change signal amplitude based on the pressure of the finger. The pad is mounted on a shaker (PCB K2004E01) driven by a signal generator (Hantek 1025G) linked on PC. The shaker provides to give the high frequency (HF) stimulation to the users.

A Head Mounted Display (HMD) WRAP920AR by Vuzix connected to the Computing Hardware is used to supply auditory and visual stimuli. Figure 1 shows the system architecture and main modules.

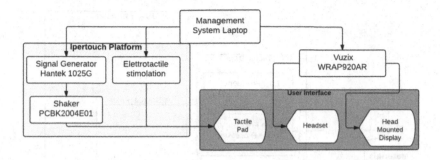

Fig. 1. Hardware Architecture of Ipertouch platform

The software components are shown in Figure 2. The human-machine software manages information and processes I/O data.

The system retrieves information to be processed from a database containing the initial roughness profiles, corresponding electrical and mechanical signals, pictures of material texture used as maps for graphic rendering and finally recorded sounds. Collected data are the outcomes of pre-processing operations carried out in Matlab R2013a to obtain proper signals for the different feedback devices. For instance, roughness profiles are split through low-pass and high-pass filtering operations to prepare the signals for both electrical and mechanical stimulation means. The cut-off frequency of filters is set to 250 Hz. An additional selective filter is applied on low frequency (LF) signals to eliminate the DC component. These actions were taken to ensure user safety in the electric signal.

The recording of sounds emitted by a finger rubbing on real material samples is carried out in semi-anechoic chamber with a 15dB background noise. The acoustic signal required a pre-processing due to the fact that the microphone was applied near the sample material during the registration. An auralization algorithm [7] is used first to process the audio records and then to add localization cues to the sound signal.

Finally, material visualization is achieved by representing a virtual hand sliding on a plane where the material texture is reproduced. The software has a computer graphic engine that renders the corresponding texture on the 3D object according to the class the configured material belongs to. The hand movement speed is the same of the sliding of the electro-mechanical signals and of the recorded audio. This setting guarantees the absolute semantic congruence between the different sensory channels.

The software is arranged into two parts. The first one ensures the synchronization of the signals reproducing the surface texture with the LF signals and HF signals. It is developed in CVI LabWindows to handle low-level commands and to assure the integration among the various hardware components (i.e. pad electrotactile, shaker and signal generator). The second one manages audio and video signals. It is implemented by adopting VB. NET programming language. The two software modules communicate with each other via a TCP-IP connection that is established automatically when the user starts with the application.

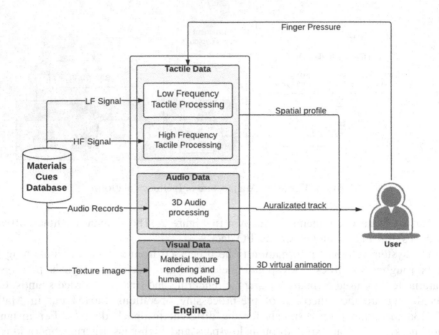

Fig. 2. Software architecture of Ipertouch Platform

4   Experiments and Results

In the experimental phase, two types of tests are conducted. The first regards the verification of system performance through the measurement of two parameters: responsiveness and synchronization. The second consists in evaluating the weight of three sensory channels through two experimental protocol.

In both experiments, testing sessions involved 20 participants (different persons for the two tests), 14 male (70%) and 6 female (30%). They were aged from 25 to 40 years old and the user sample has an average age of 32 years. Users were unaware of testing purposes and system functionalities. No user has finger sensibility problems.

System latency allows the analysis of responsiveness. It is achieved by measuring the time:

- from the moment when the user places his/her finger on the pad to the moment the system starts with the simulation and the user feels tactile sensations;
- from the moment the microcontroller varies the intensity of cutaneous stimulation according to finger pressure to the moment the user receives a feedback.

Times are measured from user input to completion of the system reconfiguration by a software routine in background. The management of the logic through the use of a microcontroller master and four slave controllers allows the system to perform operations in parallel, thus avoiding the congestion in the management of the operations. Average latency time results to be 5 ms in the start simulation, and 1 ms in the system reconfiguration.

Synchronization regards the simultaneous and coherent reproduction of three feedbacks. Software plug-in is developed to measure if the time of audio reproduction is coherent with the time of the texture visual representation and the signal speed. Tests shows an average time shift of 4.45 ms. Then a control routine is developed to realign the three signals in case of a time shift greater than 5 ms at the end of each cycle.

The efficiency of TCP-IP communication is critical to keep under control as tactile, visual and auditory components are not constantly synchronized, but with regular intervals. However, the TCP-IP connection results to be efficient because information is confined to a minimum of exchanged packages. The stability of connection is then ensured by an automatic routine that allows the reconnection and the automatic synchronism.

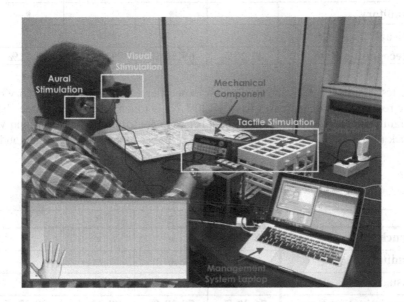

Fig. 3. View of setup test

In the second phase, user tests are carried out to verify material recognition. Experimentations are repeated on real and virtual materials in order to compare user sensations. The experimental protocol is the same adopted in [1].

First, a pre-testing procedure is necessary to set the system properly and calibrate the provided signals according to the user skin properties (electric impedance, humidity, saturation). Compared with the platform shown in [1], the calibration procedure has been automated, allowing the determination of the sensitivity threshold of the user through a simplified operation.

About material generation, ten sample materials were analysed for this study. Materials are classified in four classes: Paperboard, Wood, Textile Fabric and Rubber.

An experimental protocol is set to carry out first an absolute card-sorting experiment to assess material class discrimination in order to measure user ability to associate a tactile sensation to a given virtual material. The user receives virtual stimuli and makes judgments about which the correspondent real material class is.

Each user is submitted to 10 repetitions for each testing session and experts recorded and observed user's answers and behaviour. The test is carried out as follows: (1) the expert randomly chooses one material and communicates with the operator, (2) the stimulus is submitted to the user for 10 seconds at least (the user can ask for some more time if needed), (3) the user is asked to assign the material class. This procedure is repeated for the channel combination shown in Table 1.

Table 1. Results of Absolute Card–Sorting Test

	1	2	3	4
Touch	●	●	●	●
Auditory		●		●
Visual			●	●
Recognition Rate	47.20%	69.50 %	75.43 %	83.42%

The test results are relevant: in the first experiment, combining the sensory channel, the recognition rate increases from 47.20% (only touch) to 83.42% (three channel on). Significant results are the comparison between contributes of auditory and visual feedback (2-3): the visual stimulation reaches a higher recognition rate than auditory one.

Table 2. Results of Comparative Card–Sorting Test

	1	2	3	4
Touch	●	●	●	●
Auditory		●		●
Visual			●	●
Discrimination Rate	76.30 %	79.20 %	88.25 %	90.37 %

A subsequent experiment follows a comparative card-sorting procedure. The test is carried out as follows: (1) the expert randomly chooses one or two materials and communicates with the operator, (2) the first stimulus (real) is submitted to the user for 10 seconds at least (the user can ask for some more time if needed), (3) the second stimulus (virtual) is then submitted in the same way, (4) the user is asked to judge if it differs from the first or not.

In the second experiment, the users able to compare real and virtual material up to a maximum of 90% (76% only touch), as shown in Table 2. Trend of Experiment 1 is confirmed, but a reduced discrimination range is evident (40% against 14%). Therefore, This may mean that the virtual stimulation can reconstruct the sensation and interaction with a real object.

5   Conclusions

The study proposes a multisensory system for the simulation of texture surface materials. It allows the reproduction of visual, auditory and tactile sensations during the interaction with a given material. Absolute and comparative card-sorting experiments show that perception increases with the number of involved sensory channels. Moreover, the addition of a mechanical vibration to elicit deep skin mechanoreceptors significantly improves material recognition if compared with [1].

Contribution of each sensory channel on human sensations still remains an open issue. Despite a structured investigation has not been carried out, experiments highlight that visual contribution is more preponderance than the auditory one for tactile perception.

Future work will be focused on the integration of this system into an immersive Virtual Reality Environment and on a deep analysis of the contribution of each sensory channel in tactile stimulation in order to improve the developed technology.

References

1. Peruzzini, M., Germani, M., Mengoni, M.: Electro-tactile device for texture simulation. In: 2012 IEEE/ASME International Conference on Mechatronics and Embedded Systems and Applications (MESA), July 8-10, pp. 178–183 (2012)
2. Germani, M., Mengoni, M., Peruzzini, M.: Electro-tactile device for material texture simulation. International Journal of Advanced Manufacturing Technolog 68(9), 2185–2203 (2013) ISSN 0268-3768 (DOI 10.1007/s00170-013-4832-1)
3. Frisoli, A., Solazzi, M., Reiner, M., Bergamasco, M.: The contribution of cutaneous and kinesthetic sensory modalities in haptic perception of orientation. Brain Research Bulletin 85(5), 260–266 (2011) ISSN 0361-9230
4. Burch, D., Pawluk, D.: Using multiple contacts with texture-enhanced graphics. In: 2011 IEEE World Haptics Conference (WHC), June 21-24, pp. 287–292 (2011)
5. Marchuk, N.D., Colgate, J.E., Peshkin, M.A.: Friction measurements on a Large Area TPaD. In: 2010 IEEE Haptics Symposium, pp. 317–320 (2010)
6. Konyo, M., Tadokoro, S., Yoshida, A., Saiwaki, N.: A tactile synthesis method using multiple frequency vibrations for representing virtual touch. In: 2005 IEEE/RSJ International Conference on Intelligent Robots and Systems (IROS 2005), pp. 3965–3971 (2005)
7. Torres, J.C.B., Petraglia, M.R., Tenenbaum, R.A.: HRTF modeling for efficient auralization. In: 2003 IEEE International Symposium on Industrial Electronics ISIE 2003, June 9-11, vol. 2, pp. 919–923 (2003)
8. Abraira, V.E., Ginty, D.D.: The sensory neurons of touch. Neuron 79(4), 618–639 (2013), doi:10.1016/j.neuron.2013.07.051
9. Altinsoy, M.E., Merchel, S.: Electrotactile Feedback for Handheld Devices with Touch Screen and Simulation of Roughness. IEEE Transactions on Haptics 5(10), 1–8 (2012)
10. Caldwell, D.G., Lawther, S., Wardle, A.: Tactile Perception and its Application to the Design of Multi-modal Cutaneous Feedback Systems. In: International Conference on Robotics and Automation Minneapolis, Minnesota (April 1996)

11. Hughes, B., Wang, J., Rosic, D., Palmer, K.: Texture Gradients and Perceptual Constancy under Haptic Exploration. In: Second Joint EuroHaptics Conference and Symposium on Haptic Interfaces for Virtual Environment and Teleoperator Systems (WHC 2007), pp. 66–71 (2007), doi:10.1109/WHC.2007.109

12. Kim, S.-C., Israr, A., Poupyrev, I.: Tactile rendering of 3D features on touch surfaces. In: Proceedings of the 26th Annual ACM Symposium on User Interface Software and Technology - UIST 2013, pp. 531–538 (2013), doi:10.1145/2501988.2502020

13. Koritnik, T., Koenig, A., Bajd, T., Riener, R., Munih, M.: Comparison of visual and haptic feedback during training of lower extremities. Gait & Posture 32, 540–546 (2010), doi:10.1016/j.gaitpost.2010.07.017

14. Kyung, K., Kim, S., Kwon, D., Srinivasan, M.: Texture Display Mouse KAT: Vibrotactile Pattern and Roughness Display. In: 2006 IEEE/RSJ International Conference on Intelligent Robots and Systems, pp. 478–483 (2006), doi:10.1109/IROS.2006.282440

15. Lévesque, V., Oram, L., Maclean, K., Cockburn, A., Marchuk, N.D., Johnson, D., Peshkin, M.A.: Enhancing Physicality in Touch Interaction with Programmable Friction. In: CHI 2011, Vancouver, BC, Canada, May 7–12 (2011)

16. Marchuk, N.D., Colgate, J.E., Peshkin, M.A.: Friction measurements on a Large Area TPaD. In: 2010 IEEE Haptics Symposium, pp. 317–320 (2010), doi:10.1109/HAPTIC.2010.5444636

17. Spence, C.: Audiovisual multisensory integration. Acoustical Science and Technology 28(2), 61–70 (2007), doi:10.1250/ast.28.61

18. Turchet, L., Serafin, S.: Semantic congruence in audio–haptic simulation of footsteps. Applied Acoustics 75, 59–66 (2013), doi:10.1016/j.apacoust.2013.06.016

19. Vitense, H.S., Jacko, J.A., Emery, V.K.: Foundation for improved interaction by individuals with visual impairments through multimodal feedback. Univ. Access. Inf. Soc., 76–87 (2002)

20. Fukuyama, K., Takahashi, N., Zhao, F., Sawada, H.: Tactile display using the vibration of SMA wires and the evaluation of perceived sensations. In: 2009 2nd Conference on Human System Interactions, pp. 685–690 (2009)

21. Ikei, Y., Tsu, K.W.: Texture Presentation by Vibratory Tactile Display, pp. 199–205 (1997)

22. Takasaki, M., Kotani, H., Nara, T.: SAW Excitation On Glass Plates For A Tactile Display Application 00(c), pp. 819–822 (2005)

23. Yamamoto, A., Nagasawa, S., Yamamoto, H., Higuchi, T.: Electrostatic tactile display with thin film slider and its application to tactile telepresentation systems. IEEE Transactions on Visualization and Computer Graphics 12(2), 168–177 (2006)

24. Olivier Bau, Poupyrev, I., Israr, A., & Harrison, C, TeslaTouch: Electrovibration for Touch Surfaces. In: Disney Research (internal), Pittsburgh (2010)

25. Weiss, T., Straube, T., Boettcher, J., Hecht, H., Spohn, D., Miltner, W.H.R.: Brain activation upon selective stimulation of cutaneous C- and Aδ-fibers. NeuroImage 41(4), 1372–1381 (2008)

Principles of Dynamic Display Aiding Presence in Mixed Reality Space Design

Inkyung Choi and Jihyun Lee

Descart Lab., Graduate School of Culture Technology, KAIST, Republic of Korea
{ikstyle,jihyunlee}@kaist.ac.kr

Abstract. In this study, presence principles were developed for dynamic display design and evaluation of dynamic display for designing mixed reality space. This is a research to classify the indicators collected through the researches about the existing measurement and evaluation of the existence felling and information suggestion methods in mixed reality as the evaluation principles of the displays and multimodal's interfaces that construct the mixed reality. Additionally, by constructing QFD evaluation frame based on this presence principles and evaluating the interface that composes the mixed reality, research results were tried to be reflected in the future works.

Keywords: Spatial Presence, Dynamic Display, Mixed Reality, Presence Principles.

1 Introduction

According to Milgram(1999), MR space is where Real Components and Virtual Components are mixed together. Spatial characteristics are assigned within the range of Reality-Virtuality Continuum according to the occupation percentage of real component and virtual component environment, as well as whether the environment displaying the component is virtual or real [1]. This MR is an AR that creates overlap in virtual information with reality, or a form of VR that substitutes reality in altering the real space [8]. Accordingly, our Real World, in other words, elements that form the space with the existing static characteristics(wall, furniture, lighting and etc.) are absorbed into the components of the digitalized space and possess variable characteristic, and physical characteristics change to non-physical characteristics as well as others and thus mixed realitization can be expected [11]. There are various applications under research, which introduces MR space. In particular, early AR-related technologies were developed and studied for use with industry, military readiness, surgery training, computer games, and computer-supported collaboration. Research on AR-related technology is ongoing as the spread of small handheld devices and smartphones increases [8].

However, the current state of the matter is that if a task is performed in these MR spaces, the sense of presence and the sense of immersion from the virtual components projected in a manner of image, which the user feels, is lower than that of the physical feedback received from real components. In many research, it is stated that in order to

R. Shumaker and S. Lackey (Eds.): VAMR 2014, Part I, LNCS 8525, pp. 35–43, 2014.
© Springer International Publishing Switzerland 2014

overcome the lack of sense of presence, the MR environment must be similar to that of the actual physical environment[2]. Therefore, acquiring sense of presence and sense of immersion is a core objective in MR environment construction that supports effective interaction.

Heeter(1992) classifies the sense of presence into three different types, including Personal, Social, and Environmental[10]. Looking closely at research that increases sense of presence, centering around Environmental Presence which is closely related to MR space, we can classify the research field into two broad categories including data processing and interface field. In non-preprocess fields, 3d information modeling, dynamic information visualization methods among other solutions are used to increase visual reality, or research which allows for user context, usability among others in applying methodology in visualization of information that does not interfere with immersion in acquiring sense of presence, and there has also been research carried out using the method of supplementing the lack of sensory elements by providing other senses along with TUI, OUI, NUI, tactile interface and etc, as a way of expanding and supplementing sensory factor concentrated on the visualization of current GUI for the research in the interface field for MR presentation.

In order to design dynamic interface for MR presentation, a GUI and complementary, integrated interface concept model is necessary as opposed to the method of complete substitution of GUI. Furthermore, from the system aspect, it must not limit the systematic, cognitive, intelligent transform to only the types or forms of information, but rather expand out to interface search, assignment issues that can best support the modified form.

The contributions of this paper can be summarized as follows:

— *Develop dynamic display principles for MR space design based on criteria of presence.* All of the researches up to this point, have suggested principles based on factors covering the sense of presence in general. However, in this research, we have classified factors related to space and interface among the factors related to sense of presence, in order for new concept dynamic display model design, added and expanded a factor for sense of presence from the information stance, thus striving to advance it as the principle for the dynamic display for MR space.
— **Evaluation using QFD diagram of dynamic display principles we developed.** It has been put through the process of interface characteristic evaluation which made up the existing MR space by applying the principles developed for the purposes of dynamic display model design to QFD diagram. Via this process, weak points in the existing models were realized and the next step should be applied in order to achieve the applicable principle.

2   Literature Review

2.1   Presence in MR Space

The sense of presence in the virtual reality environment is defined as the level of certainty that one's self is actually in another environment different from that of the actual place of their presence [11], and the existence of medium environment as opposed to the physical environment. [12], In Schubert(2001) research, 8 factors were presented including Spatial presence(SP) Quallity of immersion(QI) [13]. Heeter(1992) also classified the sense of presence into 3 types; personal, social, and environmental presence [10]. And in case of environmental presence, there is a close relationship with the spatial presence within the MR environment. Looking closely at the comments related to conditions which satisfy spatial presence as an identifiable factor which assign spatial presence within these spatial characteristics, 'quick response regarding user input(Held & Durlach,1992)', 'level of comfort of the equipment and ease of transfer(Barfield & Weghorst, 1993)', 'the number of suggested and intervened level of senses and course (Steuer, 1992; Kim & Biocca, 1997; Lombard & Ditton, 1997)', 'the level of consistency in sensory information provided by the medium(Held & Durlach, 1992)' among others are mentioned.

Each of the factors in spatial presence have suggested requirements for maintaining the same, in particular spatial presence, 'the number of suggested and intervened level of senses and courses' was mentioned numerous times as an important requirement. Via this requirement, as a research which supports spatial presence, from (footnote) studies, multi-functional, multi-sensory system has been set as the goal. In other worlds, it is a method of approach which adds other sensory elements to the absence of physical, visual, sensory elements in MR space. As another requirement for spatial presence, 'the level of uniformity provided by the medium' can be mentioned. In many studies, it is stated that In order to overcome the lack of spatial presence, MR environment must be similar to that of the actual physical environment. Therefore, breaking away from the interface focused on visualization and conducting research related to interface which can provide sense of space consistent to that of the actual environment is also important. Increased effect of spatial presence can be expected only when the diversification of sensory Information and uniformity can be satisfied.

2.2   Information Presentation in MR Space

AR is a particularly useful visualization technique to overlay computer graphics on the real world. AR can combine visualization method to apply to many applications. However, even after having relocated the interface to MR and augmented reality, virtual components from the visualization methodology aspect still remains as a virtual component. A common problem that can occur in this situation with mixed reality visualization is the perception that the virtual component lies above the real component rather than below its surface. This ultimately serves as evidence that it was not able to provide uniform visual information with that of actual space. Information delivery in mixed real space could be considered as the method to strengthen and complement the information visualization to increase the existence felling and the trial to increase the existence felling along with other senses.

Research related to information presentation in MR has been focused mostly on studies related to decreasing occlusion between object and information, applying spatial context on color and transparency, transforming information, real component overlay method, and others which are related to the possibility of including visualized virtual components to the real space without a sense of foreign substance.

The trial to increase the existence felling by providing other senses has been executed through the realization of modalities research in intermodal, TUI, OUI and NUI. However, it is quite often that visual involvement requirements provided by

GUI are lost in the interfaces that try to provide these multi-sensing. For example in the study about Shape Display by Follmer(2013), limitations were raised like speed problem in information and image conversion, readability which is caused by the deceasing resolution [9].

3   Development of Presence Principles for MRs

In this study, principles of dynamic display supporting the presence, which is suitable for construction of MR space, are to be reorganized and to be developed as the quantitative evaluation indicator. For this, research of this chapter is conducted according to the order of Fig. 1.

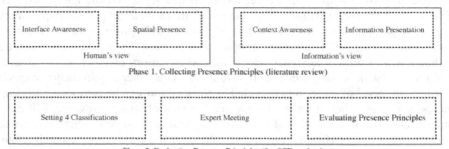

Fig. 1. Research framework

Through this, the evaluation frame focusing more on the interface and space construction elements are to be made ultimately by focusing the wide range presence indicator as the indicator for MR space design, and this frame is to be utilized for the alternative evaluation of next step research.

3.1   Collecting Presence Principles

Before suggesting and reviewing the dynamic display supporting the pesence which is suitable for construction of MR space, the indicator should be prepared which could measure and evaluate the 'Presence which is suitable for construction of MR space'. Therefore, indicators were collected which were officially approved by the existing collected presence principles studies like Table 1 and additionally, indicators about the Presence of the information which is suggested by this display were collected as well as by the people who are experiencing dynamic display.

When the information is suggested in the place which is mixed with real world, the presence about the space is required, which is different from the case when the information exist in complete virtual space. For example, based on the interpretation capability about information space and modality utilization capability in multimodal, it could mean how much this information has the autonomy in mixed reality. Like this, as the Presence indicator was added from the information perspective and duplicated contents in Presence indicator earlier suggested in Table 1 were arranged, the results could be summarized as 20 major categories like Table 2.

Table 1. Collected presence principles[2][4][7][9]

References	Presence Principles
Witmer et al.(1998)	Degree of control, Immediacy of control, Anticipation of events, Mode of control, Physical environment modifiability, Sensory modality, Environmental richness, Multimodal presentation, Consistency of multimodal information, Degree of movement perception, Active search, Isolation, Selective attention, Interface awareness, Scene realism, Consistency of information with the objective world, Meaningfulness of experience, Separation anxiety/disorientation
Schubert et al.(2001)	Spatial presence, Quality of immersion, Involvement, Drama, Interface awareness, Exploration of virtual environment, Predictability & interaction, Realness
+	
Information's Presence Principles	Context accepted state changes, Perception Location, Interaction tools (Kersten-Oertel et al, 2013), Affordance, Constraints (Follmer et al, 2013)

Table 2. Deleted and extended presence principles

Extended Presence Principles of MR space design
Interface awareness, Meaningfulness of experience, Perception Location, Affordance, Scene realism, Separation anxiety/disorientation, Spatial presence, Quality of immersion, Physical environment modifiability, Environmental richness, Consistency of information with the objective world, Information presentation accuracy, Diverse multimodal presentation, Consistency of modalities, Context accepted state changes

3.2 Classifying Presence Principles

In order to classify the determined presence principles and to make importance rating, 4 major categories were classified and meeting was conducted with 14 experts. For the presence of users and information, 4 categories of Interface awareness, Spatial Presence, Spatial Context Awareness, Degree of freedom in decision of Information Presentation method were classified as follows. The definitions of these groups are as follows.

- Factor 1. **Interface awareness:** The interface awareness group consists of principles related to the degree of understanding about the user MR space and level of communication.
- Factor 2. **Spatial Presence:** The spatial presence group consists of principles related to the immersion about the space and sense of existence that is equivalent to real world or better.
- Factor 3. **Spatial Context Awareness for Information Presentation:** The spatial context awareness group consists of principles related to the correspondence of the context information with MR space.
- Factor 4. **Degree of Freedom in Decision of Information Presentation Method:** The degree of freedom in decision of Information Presentation method group consists of principles related to the restriction in suggesting methods and ratios of degree of freedom.

Table 3. Results obtained from a principal component analysis

Principles	Factors			
	1	2	3	4
Interface awareness	.605			
Meaningfulness of experience	.614			
Perception Location	.782			
Affordance	.824			
Scene realism		.712		
Separation anxiety/disorientation		.891		
Spatial presence		.906		
Quality of immersion		.984		
Physical environment modifiability			.744	
Environmental richness			.612	
Consistency of information with the objective world			.673	
Information presentation accuracy				.745
Diverse multimodal presentation				.885
Consistency of modalities				.714
Context accepted state changes				.912

In this study, each factor included principles with factor loading of at least 0.6. The result of this process is shown in Table 3. As a result of the analysis of the main factors, extended presence principles were classified into four different groups (see Table 4).

Table 4. Classified presence principles

Interface Awareness	Spatial Immersion
-Interface awareness -Meaningfulness of experience -Perception Location -Affordance	-Scene realism -Separation anxiety/disorientation -Spatial presence -Quality of immersion

Information-Interface Communication	Information Presentation Method
-Physical environment modifiability -Environmental richness -Consistency of information with the objective world	-Information presentation accuracy -Diverse multimodal presentation -Consistency of modalities -Context accepted state changes

4   QFD Evaluation Followed Presence Principles for MRs

Quantitative analysis frame was prepared by substituting the expanded presence indicator, which was earlier deducted in QFD diagram. In order to increase the presence here, 1) application that has the method to strengthen the visualized information and 2) application providing diverse sensory information (e.g. Tangible User Interface) was QFD evaluated and analyzed. This has an objective to draw the necessary guidelines in designing the concept model of dynamic display in the future.

Based on the measurement of the degree of relation in each factor, 1 to 10 points were graded according to the importance of QFD diagram weight. After the evaluation of two applications, points were totaled and compared for each category by multiplying the scores and related weights in each principle.

Table 5. QFD Evaluation followed Presence Principles for MRs

Row	Weight / Importance	Demanded Quality (Extended Presence Principles)	Quality Characteristics	Column 1	Column 2
1	3.0	Interface Awareness	Interface awareness	0.561	0.653
2	3.0		Meaningfulness of experience	0.753	0.755
3	6.0		Perception Location	0.646	0.423
4	7.0		Affordance	0.417	0.879
5	3.0	Spatial Immersion	Scene realism	0.672	0.761
6	7.0		Separation anxiety/disorientation	0.659	0.756
7	8.0		Spatial presence	0.768	0.863
8	9.0		Quality of immersion	0.621	0.836
9	5.0	Information-Interface Communication	Physical environment modifiability	0.432	0.869
10	3.0		Environmental richness	0.534	0.521
11	4.0		Consistency of information with the objective world	0.722	0.475
12	6.0		Information presentation accuracy	0.892	0.753
13	8.0	Information Presentation Method	Diverse multimodal presentation	0.457	0.685
14	5.0		Consistency of modalities	0.856	0.673
15	9.0		Context accepted state changes	0.512	0.974
Total	88.0		Total Value	52.789	67.591
		Min Relationship Value in Column		Affordance =0.417	Perception location =0.423
		Max Relationship Value in Column		Information presentation accuracy =0.892	Context accepted state changes =0.974

In Application 1, relatively high scores were obtained in the categories of 'perception location', 'Consistency of information with the objective world' and 'Information presentation accuracy'. This gives a conclusion that existence felling is increasing from the direction not to restrict the involvement of users by 'providing correct information' or 'continuity and consistency of information providing methods'. In case of Application 2, positive scores were obtained in active information providing methods by the display, which are 'Affordance', 'Quality of immersion', 'Physical environment modifiability', 'Diverse multimodal presentation' and 'Context accepted state changes'. Reason why the scores in application 2 are high in spite of similar total score when weight values are totaled is that delivery power was increased by actively using the real world objects that were passive and static in information delivery methods. This proves that the information providing which interprets or utilizes the changing spaces positively in MR environments affects the increase in existence feeling as much as the continuous and consistent information providing does due to the dynamic characteristics of the space.

5   Conclusion

In this study, 15 presence principles were developed for dynamic display design and evaluation of dynamic display in mixed reality space. This is a research to subdivide and classify the indicators collected through the researches about the existing measurement and evaluation of the existence felling and information suggestion methods in mixed reality as the evaluation principles of the displays and multimodal's interfaces that construct the mixed reality. Additionally, by constructing QFD evaluation frame based on this presence principles and evaluating the interface, which composes the mixed reality, research results were tried to be reflected in the future researches. While the measurement of existence felling in the zone was a research that covers the entire range of mixed reality in Significant improvement, it was considered that output modality was rechecked by focusing through the space for information providing and information providing methods and the criteria could be extracted which could be used in dynamic display design.

It could be identified that the existence felling in the interface which supports the change of the space that becomes the interface is relatively high than the standardization and continuity of delivery method through QFD and the existence felling which is utilized in the interface is relatively high than the existence felling which is attached in the interface. However, if this interface is not supported by the correct information delivery, the capability that the existing visualization oriented interface maintains the existence felling is measured to be high. This study has some limitations. First, this evaluation frame should analyze and evaluate the characteristics of more diverse applications, but only two representative applications were evaluated. The procedures to draw the problems through this also remain as future assignments.

Therefore, future work should be expanded and subdivided as the indicators, which evaluate the mixed reality display method, UI composition and information delivery methods etc and subsequently, the criteria should be deducted by analyzing the problems. As the next step, complementing alternatives can be suggested and prototypes can be realized. It is considered that dynamic display optimization model based on mixed reality could be constructed through this and based on that, It could be possible that the development of applications providing the improved existence feeling to the users.

References

1. Milgram, P., Herman, C.: A taxonomy of real and virtual world display integration. In: Mixed reality: Merging real and virtual worlds, pp. 5–30 (1999)
2. Witmer, B.G., Singer, M.J.: Measuring presence in virtual environments: A presence questionnaire. Presence: Teleoperators and Virtual Environments 7(3), 225–240 (1998)
3. Slater, M., Steed, A.: A virtual presence counter. Presence: Teleoperators and Virtual Environments 9(5), 413–434 (2000)

4. Schubert, T., Friedmann, F., Regenbrecht, H.: The experience of presence: Factor analytic insights. Presence: Teleoperators and Virtual Environments 10(3), 266–281 (2001)
5. Schaik, P.V., Turnbull, T., Wersch, A.V., Drummond, S.: Presence within a mixed reality environment. CyberPsychology & Behavior 7(5), 540–552 (2004)
6. Tönnis, M., Plecher, D.A., Klinker, G.: Representing information–Classifying the Augmented Reality presentation space. Computers & Graphics 37(8), 997–1011 (2013)
7. Kersten-Oertel, M., Jannin, P., Collins, D.L.: The state of the art of visualization in mixed reality image guided surgery. Computerized Medical Imaging and Graphics 37(2), 98–112 (2013)
8. Ko, S.M., Chang, W.S., Ji, Y.G.: Usability principles for augmented reality applications in a smartphone environment. International Journal of Human-Computer Interaction 29(8), 501–515 (2013)
9. Follmer, S., Leithinger, D., Ishii, A.O.A.H.H.: inFORM: Dynamic physical affordances and constraints through shape and object actuation. In: Proceedings of the 26th Annual ACM Symposium on User Interface Software and Technology, pp. 417–426 (2013)
10. Heeter, C.: Being there: The subjective experience of presence. Presence: Teleoperators and Virtual Environments 1(2), 262–271 (1992)
11. Slater, M., Usoh, M., Steed, A.: Depth of presence in virtual environments. Presence 3(2), 130–144 (1994)
12. Steuer, J.: Defining virtual reality: Dimensions determining telepresence. Journal of Communication 42(4), 73–93 (1992)
13. Schubert, T., Friedmann, F., Regenbrecht, H.: The experience of presence: Factor analytic insights. Presence: Teleoperators and Virtual Environments 10(3), 266–281 (2001)

Combining Multi-Sensory Stimuli
in Virtual Worlds – A Progress Report

Julia Fröhlich and Ipke Wachsmuth

AI & VR Lab., Faculty of Technology, Bielefeld University
Universitätsstraße 25, 33615 Bielefeld, Germany
{jfroehli,ipke}@techfak.uni-bielefeld.de

Abstract. In order to make a significant step towards more realistic virtual experiences, we created a multi-sensory stimuli display for a CAVE-like environment. It comprises graphics, sound, tactile feedback, wind and warmth. In the present report we discuss the possibilities and constraints tied to such an enhancement. To use a multi-modal display in a proper way, many considerations have to be taken into account. This includes safety requirements, hardware devices and software integration. For each stimulus different possibilities are reviewed with regard to their assets and drawbacks. Eventually the resulting setup realized in our lab is described – to our knowledge one of the most comprehensive systems. Technical evaluations as well as user studies accompanied the development and gave hints with respect to necessities and chances.

Keywords: Multi-Sensory Stimuli, Wind, Warmth, Presence, Virtual Reality.

1 Introduction

Surprisingly today's virtual reality setups fall short on combining multi-sensory stimuli, even though virtual reality visionaries already included such. For instance Morton Heilig's Sensorama Simulator in 1962 [12] presented multi-sensory feedback like sound, wind, force feedback and smell. In 1992 David Zeltzer presented the AIP cube – aiming to provide dimensions for the comparison of virtual realities [26]. As seen in Figure 1 it consists of the three components: presence, interaction and autonomy. Zelzer introduced the presence axis as *"a rough lumped measure of the number and fidelity of available sensory input and output channels"* ([26] p.128).

In [11] we presented a user study on combining modalities in virtual worlds. Results suggested that there might be an uncanny valley effect, when only one additional cue is presented. We concluded that it is worthwhile to add as many modalities as possible which is supported by other evaluations (e.g. [6]). This has two effects: (1) the virtual world gets more believable the more out-put is generated and (2) the user is distracted from the real world if more senses are stimulated virtually.

R. Shumaker and S. Lackey (Eds.): VAMR 2014, Part I, LNCS 8525, pp. 44–54, 2014.
© Springer International Publishing Switzerland 2014

This paper will introduce a modern approach that includes a set of multi-modal stimuli as well as the integration of autonomy. It consists of a three-sided CAVE-like environment and is enhanced with 3D-sound, tactile feedback, wind and warmth.

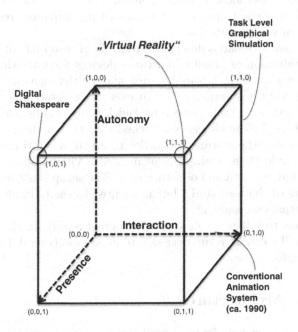

Fig. 1. The AIP-cube redrawn from [26]

2   Related Work

Many systems have been developed which add one modality to a visual virtual environment. This has mostly been **auditive** (e.g. [16], [19]) or **haptic** enrichment (e.g. [3], [23]). Some efforts including **olfactory** stimuli can be found, either presenting the scents via a wearable device (e.g. [24], [13]) or using global displays, which fill a whole room with odor. The main Problem with global approaches is fast neutralization. One System minimizing this problem is introduced by Yanagida et al. [25].

The integration of **wind** is realized either with a stationary system (constructed around the interaction space), or with a local system which is directly mounted onto the user. A real scooter is used for navigation inside the VR-Scooter-project [5] and generates wind in front of the user as well as tactile feedback with vibrotactile sensors. The authors state that perceived wind improved both, task performance and the subjective user experience. A disadvantage of this system is the inability to provide directional wind. Moon and Kim [22] introduced a setup which consists of 20 fans arranged in three levels around the user. Their evaluation showed that users cannot distinguish between winds which come from neighboring fans, if the angle between is less than 45 degrees. Another system was presented by Cadin et al. [4], consisting of eight CPU fans mounted circularly around the user's head. In order to evaluate the difference between stationary and local systems, Lehmann et al. conducted a user study [20]. The addition of wind significantly improved participants presence and the stationary system was preferred.

There is not much research describing the role of **warmth** in VR. Dionisio published an evaluation of possible hardware devices for warmth sensations in 1996, concluding that fans, infrared lamps and Peltier-elements are the best option for temperature sensations [7]. An exemplary setup was introduced as a "virtual hell" [8], with each three fans and infrared lamps arranged around the user as well as Peltier-elements attached directly on the skin. Only very few systems combine those stimuli in order to create a multi-modal sensation system. For example Dinh et al. [6] implemented a virtual office enriched with visual, audio, wind, warmth and olfactory cues. The setup was constructed to fit the requirements of the user study, but not suited to easily implement another multi-modal virtual environment.

In the sections to follow we describe a progress report on the development of a hardware and software setup designed to create multi-modal virtual worlds with minimum effort.

3   Software Architecture

The biggest problem with designing a multi-modal virtual world is that it is such a time consuming task. Often this effort does not seem to be worthwhile with regard to the benefits like improved immersion. One approach to simplify the creation of virtual worlds is to semantically enrich virtual objects. This concept has proven to be efficient in creating Intelligent Virtual Environments (IVEs) [21]. But until now this idea has mostly been used to store additional knowledge about the graphical representation only.

We have developed a framework in which objects, enriched with information about their multi-modal properties, are being processed to generate enriched virtual worlds. This is done with an automatic processing of the 3D-scene and therefore minimizes the effort needed to develop such multi-modal virtual worlds. The semantic annotation of objects works as a type declaration, and all further information like possible sound and haptic information are drawn from a database. This is employed in a 3-step process: parsing the file, comparing semantic annotation with a database, generating a new file which includes multi-modal properties. Our framework is based on InstantReality, a consistent, platform independent framework for fast and efficient application development for Virtual and Augmented Reality [9]. It employs the X3D standard for the description of 3D-models which uses the XML format. Therefore files have to be stored in the

X3D-format, in which objects can be annotated through the `<metadata>` tag. This knowledge is not held in a separate knowledge base, but anchored at the object itself. Figure 2 shows the process on the example of sound integration. An existing X3D file, with semantic annotation inside the `<metadata>`-tag is parsed. Database entries to the corresponding semantic annotation are searched and added to the scenegraph. Consequently the additional time to create such multi-modal worlds is minimized.

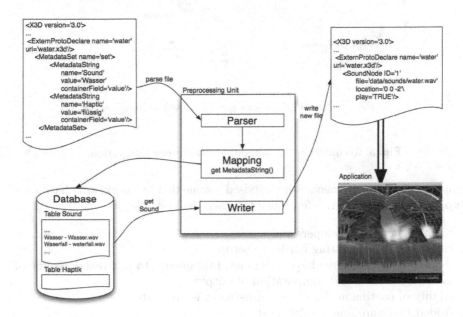

Fig. 2. Concept of enriched virtual objects to create automated multi-modal feedback

4   Hardware Setup

The original hardware setup installed 2003 consists of a three sided CAVE-like environment and an optical tracking-system (ART) with 11 infrared cameras. A collection of different interaction and navigation techniques is available. Eight speakers are installed in the corners of the interaction area, and subsonic sound devices underneath the floor, but not yet enabled with spatial sound. Figure 3 gives an overview.

During the last four years a system was constructed, enriching the original setup with improved auditory output, natural hand interaction now including tactile feedback and physical reaction, a wind setup and a warmth installation. Each step is subsequently described, giving advice on how to integrate such output modalities in CAVE-like environments. Technical and empirical evaluations accompanied the development process, to ensure a satisfactory system. In the

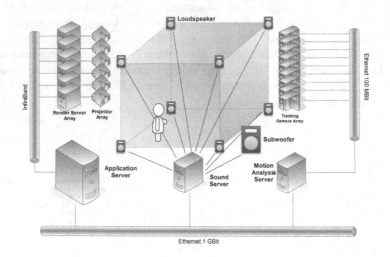

Fig. 3. Technical Setup without multi-sensory integration

beginning, some requirements were imposed – some tied to the existing hardware setup, others to enable transferability to other VR-systems:

1. Ensure safety of developers and users
2. Ensure safety of existing hardware setup
3. Real-time requirements have to be met, tantamount to fast reaction-time of hardware devices and computation of output
4. Ability of continuous hardware adjustment is preferable
5. Added hardware must be low-cost
6. Existing computational capabilities should be kept, therefore computational cost for additions should be minimized

4.1 Sound

Spatial sound is realized with the existing eight speakers (one in each corner) and two subwoofers underneath the floor. Because the integration of a realistic auditory rendering system (e.g. wave-field synthesis) did not meet *requirements 3, 5 and 6*, a vector based amplitude pannig (VBAP) approach was included. Even though two drawbacks exist (sweet-spots and the inability to simulate realistic output for sound sources close to the user's position), it is a good method with regard to computational and hardware costs and creates quite believable sound fields. For each sound the three speakers closest to the source are chosen, and the volume is regulated with regard to the distance, where doubling the distance results in a decrease of 6 dB [2]. A list with all sounds and activation levels of all speakers is passed on to the FMOD sound library which handles digital mastering [1]. The FMOD-library, which is free to use for non-commercial purposes, ensures real-time adjustments.

Our concept divides auditory output into three different types [10]. *Ambient sounds* represent a base level of output which is more or less constant over a larger region of a scene. As long as the user is within the defined area, ambient sound will be played without direction and steady volume. Only one ambient sound can be played at a time, thus all not applying ambient sounds are faded out if the user is in a subarea of the world . In addition, this concept allows for the definition of environmental properties which influence the audio rendering (e.g. adding reverberation), to fit the environment, such as an outside scenario, a dripstone cave or a concert hall. *Static sounds* are directly coupled to an object. They are adjusted in volume and direction with regard to their position relative to the user. *Event sounds* are only triggered when the related event occurs (e.g. a ball hitting the floor).

4.2 Tactile Feedback

Tactile feedback is accomplished by ART fingertracking devices which track the thumb, the index finger and the middle finger. At the tip of each finger three wires made of memory metal are attached which create a vibration, serving as tactile feedback when heated in short intervals.

To enable natural interaction the ODE physic engine in conjunction with a gesture-interaction are embedded. Collision detection allows for an appropriate visual reaction as well as generation of event sounds as mentioned above.

Technical evaluation showed a satisfactory result regarding the natural interaction, as long as a solid gesture training is performed in the beginning. The tactile feedback however was not perceived well enough in all cases – the vibration seems to be not strong enough to be noted by every participant. Further investigation of appropriate thresholds and feasible alternative hardware devices will be performed in future work. In general physical interaction is regarded essential to employ realistic feedback to user actions, but since physical calculation is costly the number of possible collisions is limited to approximately 40.

4.3 Wind

Wind effects are accomplished by eight low-cost controllable fans by ADDA Corp., which are located at the upper bound of the projection area. Since the user can rotate freely while being in the virtual world it was necessary to place them around the interaction space. In consideration of available space, costs, as well as fine-grained adaptation of wind direction we chose a setup in which the fans are mounted evenly distributed on a nearly circular arrangement [22]. The fans were chosen with a special focus on being as silent as possible and for this reason are driven with 115 Volt instead of 230 Volt. They have a diameter of 25.4 cm and a wind performance of roughly 13 m^3/min. To control all fans continuously, they are connected to a MultiDim MKIII Dimmerpack by ShowTec and driven via the DMX-Protocol.

Similar to the sound generation, wind sources are divided into three types [15]. *Directional wind* simulates the overall wind effect from one far away direction. *Spot wind* is coupled with a virtual object (e.g. a virtual fan) and therefore has a position and only influences a small region in front of it. Further, *event wind* was added in order to simulate sudden wind events. Due to reaction time, very short events, as the drift of a closing door, cannot be simulated, while the perception of a passing train enriched with wind worked quite well. The first system did not perform occlusion detection which was considered a major drawback during a pilot study and therefore was included later on.

To determine important thresholds, an exploratory study with N = 9 test subjects was conducted to measure accuracy of wind direction estimation, reaction times to recognize the effect and needed activation thresholds. Results show that the wind direction is detected with an accuracy of M = 24.13 degrees (SD = 30.25). It took participants about 3 seconds (M=3.1s SD=0.29s) to notice the wind stimulus, whereas the disappearance of wind was noticed much faster (M=1.3s, SD=0.85s). Activation levels needed to be about 50% in order to be sufficient. Detailed results are given in [14].

4.4   Warmth

To enable thermal stimuli as well, a heat display was added, consisting of six 250 Watt infrared lamps, which are mounted above the interaction area. Infrared lamps met all necessary requirements – a detailed discussion about the hardware considerations can be found in [15]. The height can be regulated to ensure users' safety and enable equivalent experience among different sized people. Maximum heat in front of the lamp is $100°C$, while temperature sensors are used to monitor the whole system and ensure safety requirements. Again, a differentiation between different heat sources is implemented. *Directional warmth* can be used to model effects like the heat of the sun, whereas *point warmth* is used to model smaller heat sources (e.g. a fireplace).

Since our tracking system uses infrared light, a major concern was whether the infrared lamps could disturb the performance of the user-tracking. Tracking coverage in the interaction space was tested and no influence was measurable. Although it must be suspected that in a different setting (e.g. with fewer cameras or more infrared lamps), the lamps may affect the tracking. The same test procedure as for wind suggests an activation threshold of 57% (SD = 21%). Mean time for perceiving the appearance of warmth was 2.5 seconds, whereas the disappearance was noticed faster (M = 2.0s).

5   Further Modalities

The enrichment with odor was not yet approached, because hardware availability is limited and therefore costly. Additionally our global setup should be preferably extended with a global scent system (e.g. [25]) which are not that common.

Referring back to the AIP-cube (cf. Figure 1), this system accomplished a great step towards point $(0, 1, 1)$, but in order to create an even better virtual experience, the autonomy axis has to be considered as well. It is defined as *"a qualitative measure of the ability of a computational model to act and react to simulated events and stimuli"* ([26] p.127). A lot of research is done in the field of virtual agents, which strives for this level of autonomy, but integration into virtual worlds where the virtual human interacts with the user and acts autonomously, is even less common in VR applications than multi-sensory stimuli. Therefore the integration of a virtual human introduces yet another level of possible presence enhancement. To make a step toward point $(1, 1, 1)$ the embodied conversational agent MAX was included in our virtual setup. MAX is an autonomous agent developed in the AI & VR Lab at Bielefeld University and for example is employed as a museum guide in Germanys biggest computer museum, the Heinz Nixdorf MuseumsForum in Paderborn [17]. The agent has the ability to generate speech and gestures naturally and in some scenarios acts as a virtual interaction partner [18]. A virtual lab setup was designed, where MAX acts as a virtual guide, including some interaction possibilities like bowling as well as some chit chatting. He shows people around, acts autonomously, and reacts to user input. The environment is enriched with sound, wind, warmth and tactile feedback as well. Figure 4 gives a glance at the setup.

Fig. 4. MAX (added as autonomy factor to a multi-modal virtual environment) in the virtual lab on a hoover disc, to take visitors along

6   Conclusion

The resulting system combines visual with auditory, tactile, wind and warmth stimuli (cf. Figure 5). Due to the earlier described software-architecture is it easy to include in existing or new virtual reality projects. To our knowledge this is a

VR-setup with one of the most extensive multi-sensory displays. Since low cost (hardware and computational wise) was one main criteria, the system may be added to another CAVE-based VR-system with little effort. In addition a major user study to examine the impact on perceived presence were performed, with promising results [11]. The addition of as many output modalities as possible seems to be worthwhile, especially if hardware costs are kept to a minimum as well as the effort needed to integrate the output modalities. In future work, the effects of multi-sensory stimuli will be investigated further, with an emphasis on cross-modal dependencies that might occur.

An evaluation of the integration of an autonomy factor as proposed by Zeltzer is desirable. Within the proposed lab setup, test subjects are guided either by a real or virtual human. Further investigation of the impact on perceived presence with regard to the absence or presence of an autonomous agent, is assumed to help with the design of more comprehensive virtual reality systems.

Fig. 5. Hardware devices used with exemplary position in the overall setup

Acknowledgements. The authors are indebted to Felix Hülsmann, Nico Lüdike, Patrick Renner and Timo Dankert who assisted in this research.

References

1. Fmod - interactive audio middleware (2010), http://www.fmod.org
2. Begault, D.R.: 3D Sound for Virtual Reality and Multimedia. Academic Press (1994)
3. Burdea, G., Burdea, G.C., Burdea, C.: Force and touch feedback for virtual reality. Wiley, New York (1996)
4. Cardin, S., Thalmann, D., Vexo, F.: Head Mounted Wind. In: Computer Animation and Social Agents, pp. 101–108 (2007)
5. Deligiannidis, L., Jacob, R.J.K.: The VR Scooter: Wind and Tactile Feedback Improve User Performance. In: 3DUI 2006, pp. 143–150 (2006)
6. Dinh, H.Q., Walker, N., Song, C., Kobayashi, A., Hodges, L.F.: Evaluating the Importance of Multi-sensory Input on Memory and the Sense of Presence in Virtual Environments. In: Proceedings of the IEEE Virtual Reality, VR 1999, pp. 222–228. IEEE Computer Society, Washington, DC (1999)
7. Dionisio, J.: Temperature feedback in Virtual Environments. In: Imaging Sciences and Display Technologies, pp. 233–243 (1996)
8. Dionisio, J.: Virtual Hell: A Trip Through the Flames. IEEE Comput. Graph. Appl. 17(3), 11–14 (1997)
9. Fellner, D., Behr, J., Bockholt, U.: Instantreality - a framework for industrial augmented and virtual reality applications. In: The 2nd Sino-German Workshop Virtual Reality & Augmented Reality in Industry
10. Fröhlich, J., Wachsmuth, I.: A phong-based concept for 3D-audio generation. In: Dickmann, L., Volkmann, G., Malaka, R., Boll, S., Krüger, A., Olivier, P. (eds.) SG 2011. LNCS, vol. 6815, pp. 184–187. Springer, Heidelberg (2011)
11. Fröhlich, J., Wachsmuth, I.: The Visual, the Auditory and the Haptic – A User Study on Combining Modalities in Virtual Worlds. In: Shumaker, R. (ed.) VAMR/HCII 2013, Part I. LNCS, vol. 8021, pp. 159–168. Springer, Heidelberg (2013)
12. Heilig, M.L.: Sensorama simulator, u.s.patent no.3050870 (August 1962)
13. Hirota, K., Ito, Y., Amemiya, T., Ikei, Y.: Presentation of Odor in Multi-Sensory Theater, pp. 372–379 (2013)
14. Hülsmann, F., Fröhlich, J., Mattar, N., Wachsmuth, I.: Wind and Warmth in Virtual Reality: Implementation and Evaluation. In: VRIC 2014: Proceedings of the Virtual Reality International Conference: Laval Virtual. ACM (in press, 2014)
15. Hülsmann, F., Mattar, N., Fröhlich, J., Wachsmuth, I.: Wind and Warmth in Virtual Reality – Requirements and Chances. In: Virtuelle und Erweiterte Realität: 10. Workshop der GI-Fachgruppe VR/AR, pp. 133–144 (2013)
16. Husung, S., Mikalauskas, R., Weber, C., Kästner, T.: Modelling of sound propagation of technical systems for real-time VR-applications. MECHANIKA (4), 33–37 (2010)
17. Kopp, S., Gesellensetter, L., Krämer, N.C., Wachsmuth, I.: A conversational agent as museum guide - Design and evaluation of a real-world application. In: Panayiotopoulos, T., Gratch, J., Aylett, R., Ballin, D., Olivier, P., Rist, T. (eds.) IVA 2005. LNCS (LNAI), vol. 3661, pp. 329–343. Springer, Heidelberg (2005)
18. Kopp, S., Jung, B., Leßmann, N., Wachsmuth, I.: Max - A multimodal assistant in virtual reality construction. KI - Künstliche Intelligenz 4(03), 11–17 (2003)
19. Larsson, P., Västfjäll, D., Kleiner, M.: Ecological acoustics and the multi-modal perception of rooms: Real and unreal experiences of auditory-visual virtual environments. In: Proc. of the Conf. on Auditory Display, pp. 245–249 (2001)

20. Lehmann, A., Geiger, C., Wöldecke, B., S.J.: Poster: Design and Evaluation of 3D Content with Wind Output. In: IEEE Symposium on 3D User Interfaces, pp. 152–152 (2009)
21. Luck, M., Aylett, R.: Applying Artificial Intelligence to Virtual Reality: Intelligent Virtual Environments. Applied Artificial Intelligence 14(1), 3–32 (2000)
22. Moon, T., Kim, G.J.: Design and Evaluation of a Wind Display for Virtual Reality. In: VRST 2004 Proceedings of the ACM Symposium on Virtual Reality Software and Technology, pp. 122–128 (2004)
23. Weber, B., Sagardia, M., Hulin, T., Preusche, C.: Visual, Vibrotactile, and Force Feedback of Collisions in Virtual Environments: Effects on Performance, Mental Workload and Spatial Orientation. In: Shumaker, R. (ed.) VAMR/HCII 2013, Part I. LNCS, vol. 8021, pp. 241–250. Springer, Heidelberg (2013)
24. Yamada, T., Yokoyama, S., Tanikawa, T., Hirota, K., Hirose, M.: Wearable Olfactory Display: Using Odor in Outdoor Environment. In: VR, pp. 199–206 (2006)
25. Yanagida, Y., Kawato, S., Noma, H., Tomono, A., Tetsutani, N.: Projection-Based Olfactory Display with Nose Tracking. In: VR, pp. 43–50 (2004)
26. Zeltzer, D.: Autonomy, interaction, and presence. Presence: Teleoper. Virtual Environ. 1(1), 127–132 (1992)

R-V Dynamics Illusion:
Psychophysical Influence on Sense of Weight
by Mixed-Reality Visual Stimulation of Moving Objects

Satoshi Hashiguchi, Yohei Sano, Fumihisa Shibata, and Asako Kimura

Graduate School of Information Science and Engineering, Ritsumeikan University
1-1-1 Noji-Higashi, Kusatsu, Shiga, 525-8577, Japan
hasiguti@rm.is.ritsumei.ac.jp

Abstract. When humans sense the weight of real objects, their perception is known to be influenced by not only tactile information but also visual information. In a Mixed-Reality (MR) environment, the appearance of touchable objects can be changed by superimposing a computer-generated image (CGI) onto them (MR visual stimulation). In this paper, we studied the psychophysical influence on the sense of weight by using a real object that has a CGI superimposed on it. In the experiments, we show CGI representing the inertial force caused by the movable objects inside, while the subject swings the real object. The results of the experiments show that the subjects sensed weight differently when being shown the CGI animation.

Keywords: Mixed Reality, Sense of Weight, Visual Stimulation, Psychophysical Influence.

1   Introduction

Using mixed reality (MR) technology, real and virtual worlds can be merged [1][2]. In an MR environment, the visual information of the virtual object can be superimposed on a real object with no change in tactual sense. In other words, users have the tactile feeling of the real object while viewing the superimposed digital data [3]. This implies that material and/or shape of the object can differ between visual and tactual sense. In such a situation, what kind of psychophysical phenomenon could be occurring? Based on this question, we have systematically performed various experiments to investigate this influence of "MR visual stimulation" on tactile sense and have found various illusions. For example, we had indicated that when objects with different degrees of virtual roughness are presented to both visual and tactile senses and the tactile stimulus are over a certain threshold of roughness, the subjects perceive the objects to be tactually different although the objects have no physical difference [4][5]. This implies that the tactile impression can be intentionally changed by providing the appropriate visual stimulation. We also confirmed that when a subject pushes the real object on which the virtual object that deforms differently from the real object is superimposed, he/she perceived the object as being harder or softer than the real

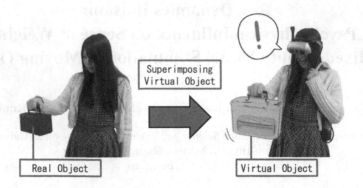

Fig. 1. R-V Dynamics Illusion

object. We found that, in some cases, visual stimulation had a significantly larger effect than the actual hardness of the real object [6][7].

Additionally, we focused on the center of gravity (COG) and examined the influence of superimposing virtual objects having different COG positions onto real objects. As a result, we confirmed that COG perception can be influenced by superimposing virtual objects, and we named this illusion the "Shape-COG Illusion [8]." In the experiments of "Shape-COG Illusion," we only focused on the rigid object for both real and virtual stimulation whose COG position is clear for the subjects. However, through the experiments, new question has raised. That is, if real and/or virtual objects are non-rigid (deformable or having movable portion in it), how are they perceived?

In this study, we firstly focus on a situation in which a virtual object that has movable portion in it is superimposed on a real rigid object (Fig. 1). This paper describes the experiments we conducted to analyze the influence.

2   Related Work

"Dynamic Touch" is a haptic perception with motion [9][10]. With this perception, a person can sense and recognize the information, such as the size, shape, and weight, of a holding object without looking at it by swinging it. Even if the object is deformable or has movable portion in it, he/she can recognize its movement roughly. In this paper, we focus the case that this deformation or internal movement differs between visual and tactual sense.

"Pseudo-Haptics [11-14]" and "Size-Weight Illusion [15]" is known as illusions occurred by interaction between visual and tactual sense. "Pseudo-Haptics" is an illusion in which a person can perceive tactual sense, such as softness, texture, and viscosity of an object, only by controlling visual stimulation. This phenomenon could be closely-related to our study on the point that both changes tactual sense only by changing visual sense (with no use of haptic display).

"Size-Weight Illusion" is a well-known and typical illusion of weight [15][16]. When grasping objects of the same weight but different sizes, a person perceives the bigger object to be lighter than the smaller one. Moreover, Roch et al. confirmed that when a cube in a subject's hand appears larger through a magnifying glass, he/she perceives it as being lighter than actual [17]. In these studies show that perception of mass can be influenced by visual stimulation. However, internal movement of an object is not considered in these studies.

There are some studies about the influence of MR visual stimulation on haptic perception, including our previous studies [4-8]. Kitahara et al. confirmed that visual stimulation in an MR environment affects the haptic perception of texture and sharpness of an edge [18]; this idea is similar to [4]. Nakahara et al. described the result of experiments on the curvature factor of edges [19]. However, these studies examined only the haptic sense of the material and/or haptic exploration of the object's shape [20]. Ban et al. report that the color of superimposing objects affects weight perception [21]. However, a study which addresses the case having different internal movement between visual and tactual sense has yet been conducted.

3   Purpose and Preparation of Our Study

3.1   Purpose of Our Study

We conducted experiments to verify the influence of dynamic change of MR visual stimulation on the tactile sensation. There could be many kind of combinations of experiments, for example, a case that a real object is rigid and a virtual object is dynamically changeable, a case that both of them are dynamically changeable, a case that movable objects are solids, a case that movable object is liquid, and so on. Therefore, in this paper, we start from a condition in which a real object is rigid case with handle and as MR visual stimulation it is superimposed by the same size virtual case filled with liquid.

In the experiment 1, we superimpose MR visual stimulation on real rigid object, which is reminded of moving liquid in an object to confirm whether tactual perception is different between a case that liquid in the object moves according to the user's hand movement and a case that liquid dose not move. In experiment 2, we verify the influence of virtual liquid level in the virtual object.

3.2   Experimental Environment

In the following experiments, we adopted an MR system with a video see-through mechanism that visually merges the real and virtual worlds (Fig. 2). Wearing a head-mounted display (HMD) (VH-2002, Canon Inc.) with a pair of built-in video cameras, the subject viewed the stereoscopic images that are computer-generated images (CGIs) in the scene in front of his/her eyes. In other words, the subject saw the CGIs that were texture-mapped onto the objects with high geometric precision. Head position and position of real object was constantly tracked with six degrees of freedom (6-DOF) by a magnetic sensor (3SPACE FASTRAK, Polhemus Inc.), which allows the subject to move his/her head freely.

3.3   Preparation of Experiments

The real rigid object used in the experiments was a plastic case (165 mm width × 90 mm height × 80 mm depth) with the handle (Fig. 3). The weight of the plastic case was adjusted to 750 g, which was the weight of a case filled with water up to the level of 45 mm (50 % of the case height).The size of virtual object used as MR visual stimulation was the same as the real object. In the virtual object, water colored virtual liquid was filled. We prepared five liquid levels, CG1 27mm (30% of the virtual object's height), CG2 36mm (40%), CG3 45mm (50%), CG4 54mm (60%), and CG5 63mm (70%) for the experiments (Fig. 4). Table 1 shows patterns of MR visual stimulation used in the experiments. There were ten patterns of CGI which is the combination of liquid level and liquid motion (moving/not moving).

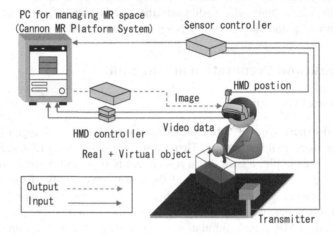

Fig. 2. System Configuration

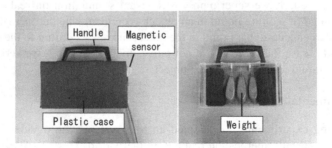

Fig. 3. Real Object Used in Experiments

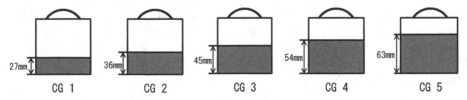

Fig. 4. Virtual Stimulation Used in Experiments

3.4   Evaluation Methods

In the experiments, we used Thurstone's paired comparison method for the subjective evaluation. This method is a simple psychological measure and can prevent confusion due to the large number of choices. The objective response was measured by electromyography (EMG). To measure electromyographic signals during the experiment, we attached disposable electrodes to the subjects' forearm (Fig. 5). The measurement of EMG uses surface electromyography meter (ATR-Promotions, TS-EMG01). If the force is affected by the MR visual stimulation, then the difference should be observed in the EMG. Therefore, we measured the objective response to this illusion by the EMG. In the experiments, a subject swings the plastic case to the right and left. Since this motion is a pronation-supination movement, we put a electrodes on a supinator muscle. The distance between electrodes was set at 25 mm. We put a ground electrode on the olecranon. The analog signal was derived from the surface EMG meter and the sampling frequency was 500 Hz.

Table 1. Variety of MR Visual Stimulation Used in Experiments

Pattern	Motion	Levels
1		27 mm (CG1)
2		36 mm (CG2)
3	Moving	45 mm (CG3)
4		54 mm (CG4)
5		63 mm (CG5)
6		27 mm (CG1)
7		36 mm (CG2)
8	Not moving	45 mm (CG3)
9		54 mm (CG4)
10		63 mm (CG5)

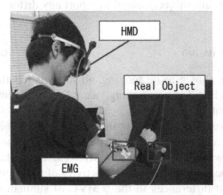

Fig. 5. Experimental Scene

In order to evaluate the muscle activity in the supinator in the swinging operation, we used the %MVC (Maximal Voluntary Contraction) index of the degree of activity of the muscle, which is calculated from the amplitude information [22]. After the full-wave rectified waveform was obtained from EMG and the normal MVC was measured for each subject, the %MVC was calculated.

4 Experiment 1

4.1 Purpose

In experiment 1, we superimpose MR visual stimulation on real rigid object, which is reminded of moving liquid in an object to confirm whether tactual perception is different or not between two patterns; pattern 3 and 8 in Table 1. In pattern 3, a CGI of liquid was shown moving inside the cases according to the swinging of the case. In pattern 8, the liquid CGI was not moving.

4.2 Experimental Procedure

The liquid level of superimposed CGI was 45 mm (pattern 3 and 8 in Table 1). The subjects were five men. The experimental procedure is described below:

1. The subjects wear the HMD and electrodes are attached on their forearms.
2. Either pattern 3 (liquid is moving) or 8 (not moving) was superimposed onto the same real rigid object presented to subjects' HMD. Patterns are selected randomly with each subject.
3. The subjects asked to bend their elbows about 90 degrees and hold the real object and swing them right and left according to a metronome (100 strokes/min).
4. The subject rests for 3 sec and repeat steps (3) to (4) three times.
5. Sufficient breaks are provided to eliminate the effect of muscle fatigue.
6. For the other pattern (a pattern not selected at step (2)), steps (3) to (5) are repeated.
7. After the experiment, the subjects asked to report any difference in the tactual sensation in each trial.

4.3 Results and Discussion

When the liquid CGI is shown to be moving, all subjects felt the object to be lighter than the case where the liquid is not moving, according to the interviews conducted at the end of the experiment.

Fig. 6 shows the results of calculating the average of the %MVC supinator in the interval. The period of analysis was 3 sec from the start to the end of the swinging motion. The figure shows that, by presenting MR visual stimulation in which a CGI of liquid is shown to be moving, the muscle activity of the supinator was reduced. A t-test showed significant differences in the %MVC of supinator motion between the patterns ($p < 0.01$).

From these results, it appeared that the MR visual stimulation having movable portion could affect the sense of weight.

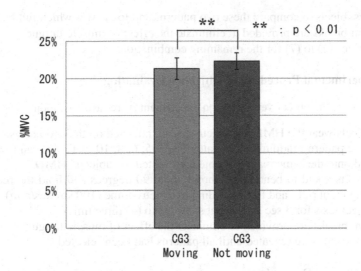

Fig. 6. Results of Experiment 1 (Average %MVC)

We named this psychophysical influence caused by the difference between dynamics of the real object (R) and the virtual object (V) movement, the "R-V Dynamics Illusion."

5   Experiment 2

5.1   Purposes

The aim of experiment 2 was to detect any change in the sense of weight caused by changing the volume of the movable portion of the MR visual stimulation.

The objective evaluation and subjective evaluation were conducted separately in this experiment.

5.2   Experimental Procedure of Subjective Evaluation

The experimental procedure was based on the Thurston's paired comparison method. If the sense of weight was affected by the MR visual stimulation, bias should be seen in the psychological measure. There were 10 subjects in this experiment (nine males and one female). The experimental procedure is described below:

1. The subjects wear the HMD.
2. Two patterns are randomly selected from the 10 patterns shown in Table 1
3. One of the two patterns selected step (2) was superimposed onto the same real rigid object presented to subjects' HMD.
4. The subjects asked to bend their elbows about 90 degrees and hold the real object and swing them right and left according to a metronome (100 strokes/min).
5. Repeat (3) to (4) with the remaining pattern in step (3).

6. Ask the subjects to compare these two patterns and to answer which felt heavier.
7. Sufficient breaks are provided to eliminate the effect of muscle fatigue.
8. Repeat steps (2) to (7) for the remaining combinations.

5.3   Experimental Procedure of Objective Evaluation

The subjects for the objective evaluation experiment were also five men.

1. The subjects wear the HMD and electrodes are attached on their forearms.
2. Select one pattern randomly from pattern 1, 3, 5, 6, 8, 10 in Table 1 and was superimposed onto the same real rigid object presented to subjects' HMD.
3. The subjects asked to bend their elbows about 90 degrees and hold the real object and swing them right and left according to a metronome (100 strokes/min).
4. The subject rests for 3 sec and repeat steps (3) to (4) three times.
5. Sufficient breaks are provided to eliminate the effect of muscle fatigue.
6. Steps (2) to (5) were repeated until all patterns had been selected.

5.4   Results and Discussion

Fig. 7 shows the results of subjective evaluation and it can be seen that;

1. Regardless of the height of liquid level, when the liquid CGI is shown to be moving, the object is perceived lighter than the case where the liquid is not moving.
2. Though the weight of the case is not changed, the subject feels the object is heavier when the liquid measure is increased.

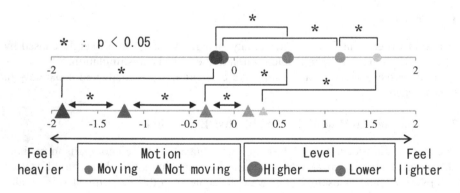

Fig. 7. Results of Experiment 2 (Thurstone's paired comparison method)

3. Fig. 8 shows the r average of the %MVC supinator in the interval. The period of analysis was 3 sec from the start to the end of the swinging motion. The figure shows that;
4. (iii) When the CGI liquid was shown to be moving, the amount of muscle activity in the supinator decreased.

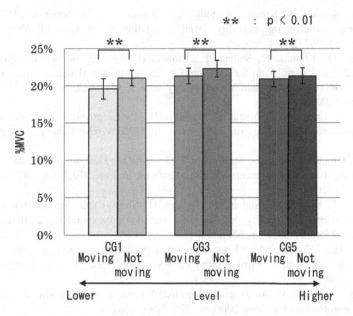

Fig. 8. Results of Experiment 2 (Average %MVC)

6   Conclusion

In this paper, we conducted experiments to examine the influence of superimposing virtual objects having movable portion in it onto real rigid objects. As a result, we confirmed that weight perception can be influenced by superimposing virtual objects though the weight of real object is not changed (experiment1), and we named this illusion the "R-V Dynamics Illusion." In Experiment 2, we examined the volume of the movable portion of the MR visual stimulation. As a result, regardless of the liquid measure, when the liquid CGI is shown to be moving, the object to be perceived lighter than the case where the liquid is not moving. We also found that the lower the liquid level become, the lighter real object is perceived.

"R-V Dynamics Illusion" may still present many unanswered questions, and hence we must conduct additional experiments to address them. For the future, we will continue to study the occurrence of this illusion in other situations.

References

1. Ohta, Y., Tamura, H. (eds.): Mixed Reality—Merging real and virtual worlds. Springer, Heidelberg (1999)
2. MacIntyre, B., Livingston, M.A.: (Special Session) Moving mixed reality into the real worlds. IEEE Computer Graphics and Applications 25(6), 22–56 (2005)
3. Ohshima, T., Kuroki, T., Yamamoto, H., Tamura, H.: A mixed reality system with visual and tangible interaction capability: Application to evaluating automobile interior design. In: Proc. 2nd IEEE and ACM Int. Symp. on Mixed and Augmented Reality, pp. 284–285 (2003)

4. Iesaki, A., Somada, A., Kimura, A., Shibata, F., Tamura, H.: Psychophysical influence on tactual impression by mixed-reality visual stimulation. In: Proc. IEEE Virtual Reality 2008, pp. 265–267 (2008)
5. Kagimoto, M., Kimura, A., Shibata, F., Tamura, H.: Analysis of tactual impression by audio and visual stimulation for user interface design in mixed reality environment. In: Shumaker, R. (ed.) Virtual and Mixed Reality. LNCS, vol. 5622, pp. 326–335. Springer, Heidelberg (2009)
6. Hirano, Y., Kimura, A., Shibata, F., Tamura, H.: Psychophysical influence of mixed-reality visual stimulation on sense of hardness. In: IEEE Virtual Reality 2011, pp. 51–54 (2011)
7. Sano, Y., Hirano, Y., Kimura, A., Shibata, F., Tamura, H.: Dent-softness illusion in mixed reality space: Further experiments and considerations. In: Proc. IEEE Virtual Reality 2013, pp. 153–154 (2013)
8. Omosako, H., Kimura, A., Shibata, F., Tamura, H.: Shape-COG Illusion: Psychophysical influence on center-of-gravity perception by mixed-reality visual stimulation. In: Proc. IEEE Virtual Reality 2012, pp. 65–66 (2012)
9. Solomon, H.Y., Turvey, M.T.: Haptically perceiving the distances reachable with hand-held objects. Journal of Experimental Psychology: Human Perception and Performance 14, 404–427 (1988)
10. Yao, H.Y., Hayward, V.: An experiment on length perception with a virtual rolling stone. In: Proc. EuroHaptics Int. Conf. 2006, pp. 275–278 (2006)
11. Lecuyer, A., Coquillart, S., Kheddar, A., Richard, P., Coiffet, P.: Pseudo-haptic feedback: can isometric input devices simulate force feedback? In: Proc. IEEE Virtual Reality, pp. 83–90 (2000)
12. Biocca, F., Kim, J., Choi, Y.: Visual touch in virtual environments: An exploratory study of presence, multimodal interfaces, and cross-modal sensory illusions. Presence: Teleoperators and Virtual Environments 10(3), 247–265 (2001)
13. Lecuyer, A.: Simulating haptic feedback using vision: A survey of research and applications of pseudo-haptic feedback. Presence: Teleoperators and Virtual Environments 18(1), 39–53 (2009)
14. Lecuyer, A., Burkhardt, J.M., Etienne, L.: Feeling bumps and holes without a haptic interface: the perception of pseudo-haptic textures. In: Proc. SIGCHI Conference on Human Factors in Computing Systems, pp. 239–246 (2004)
15. Charpentier, A.: Experimental study of some aspects of weight perception. Archives de Physiologie Normales et Pathologiques 3, 122–135 (1891)
16. Ellis, R.R., Lederman, S.J.: The role of haptic versus visual volume cues in the size-weight illusion. Attention, Perception & Psychophysics 53(3), 315–324 (1993)
17. Rock, I., Harris, C.S.: Vision and touch. Scientific American 216, 96–104 (1967)
18. Kitahara, I., Nakahara, M., Ohta, Y.: Sensory property in fusion of visual/haptic stimuli using mixed reality. Advances in Haptics. Intech (2010)
19. Nakahara, M., Kitahara, I., Ohta, Y.: Sensory property in fusion of visual/haptic cues by using mixed reality. In: Proc. World Haptics Conference 2007, pp. 565–566 (2007)
20. Lederman, S.J., Klatzky, R.L.: Extracting object properties through haptic exploration. Acta Psychologica 84, 29–40 (1993)
21. Ban, Y., Narumi, T., Fujii, T., Sakurai, S., Imura, J., Tanikawa, T., Hirose, M.: Augmented Endurance: Controlling fatigue while handling objects by affecting weight perception using augmented reality. In: Proc. CHI 2013, pp. 69–78 (2013)
22. Ernst, M.O., Bulthoff, H.H.: Merging the senses into a robust percept. Trends in Cognitive Science 8, 162–169 (2004)

Expansion of the Free Form Projection Display Using a Hand-Held Projector

Kaoru Kenjo[1] and Ryugo Kijima[2]

[1] Gifu University Graduate School of Engineering,
1-1 Yanagido, Gifu 501-1193, Japan
[2] Gifu University Faculty of Engineering, 1-1 Yanagido, Gifu 501-1193, Japan

Abstract. We developed the multi projection system that supplement the free form projection display (FFPD) that virtual object image projected onto the real object with the projection of hand-held projector. This system enabled the users to expansion of projection area and look see the interesting area by covert to high-definition display. Furthermore, we investigated the effects of user's stereoscopy by visual gap of images projected each projector.

1 Introduction

One example of mixed reality technology is projection mapping, which displays a computer-generated (CG) image on a real object by projection. Moreover, the hand-held projector that the user can handle with one hand has been developed, and expected to be applied to various type of mixed reality application. We have developed a so called free form projection display (FFPD) technology[1] that merges virtual and real objects. The CG image is projected on the curved surface of a semitransparent real object. The virtual object is observed as if embedded inside this real object. The user's viewpoint is measured and reflected in the CG image to provide a sense of motion parallax. The position and orientation of the real object is also measured and used to fix the virtual object with respect to the real one and to cancel the distortion in the observed image caused by a projection on the curved surface. The virtual anatomical model (VAM)[2] is one of the applications of FFPD and is used for medical education. For this purpose, a movable white torso is used as the screen (real object). The internal organs, blood vessels, and bones are then embedded virtually in this torso.

There are three unresolved problems with the VAM system. The first is the resolution problem. Using the existing projector, the size of the pixel projected on the life-size human body is a couple of millimeters, which is not enough to represent the detailed texture of an organ's surface, for example. The second is the shadow problem. One projector cannot cover the whole surface of the torso; at least half of the torso cannot be used as screen. Further, the pixels are stretched in the boundary area between the projected and shadow area. The image becomes darker and the resolution, lower, in this area. For example, when the user looked into the side of the body, the lower half of the side is in the shadow area without image and the dissolving of organs is observed. The third

R. Shumaker and S. Lackey (Eds.): VAMR 2014, Part I, LNCS 8525, pp. 65–74, 2014.
© Springer International Publishing Switzerland 2014

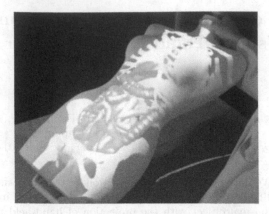

Fig. 1. Vitual Anatomical Model (VAM)

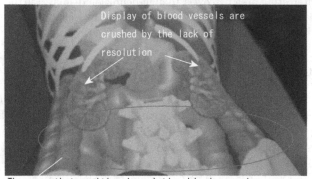

Fig. 2. Lack of resolution and the area that positional relationship is complex

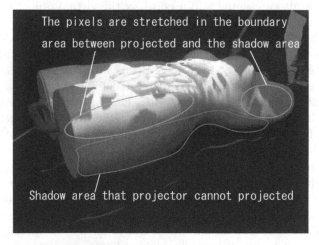

Fig. 3. Shadow area that projector cannot projected

problem is concerning the interface to control the content of the display. One important aim is to use the anatomical model in medical education to present the positional relationship of organs. However, since the internal organs hide each other, it is impossible to show all organs at once. There is hence a strong need to control which organ or which part of an organ is to be visible.

These problems could be reduced by adding a hand-held projector to the original VAM system. When the hand-held projector comes closer to the torso, the size of the pixel projected by it becomes smaller. The user can then achieve the necessary resolution by aiming the hand-held at the area of his/her interest. The hand-held projector can be used to cover the shadow area, simply by turning the line of projection to the shadow area where the user wants to observe the organs. In short, the primary projector covers the whole torso in relatively low resolution, and the hand-held projector is used to observe the area of interest. Further, it would be useful to feed the hand-held an image that is different from that for the primary projector. A simple example is to use the detailed model of organs for the image to the hand-held to produce the high density pixel area. Another aim is to use the different image to control the content of the image. When part of the image from the primary projector is erased to avoid overlap in the area of projection by the hand-held, the user feel as if the hand-held projector cuts a hole in the image from the primary projector and embeds the image from the hand-held inside this hole. By showing the whole organs with the primary projector and providing images of the organs deep inside the body to the hand-held, the user can cut a hole in a set of organs and unearth the hidden organs to be visible in this hole. The aim of this study was to solve the three problems in the VAM system and to validate a method of efficient stereoscopy.

2   Materials and Method

The original VAM system consists of a PC, a projector above the torso screen, a magnetic sensor on the torso to measure the position and orientation, and a sensor on the user's head to measure the viewpoint. The shape of the torso, and the relative position and orientation of the torso to the projector are considered both for embedding the virtual organ in the screen and for eliminating the distortion in the image caused by the projection onto the curved surface. The position of the user's eye is used for creating motion parallax by generating the organ's image as viewed from this viewpoint. Before starting the system, the projector's internal and external parameters are estimated by using a calibration tool[3]. A hand-held laser projector was added to this VAM system. Since the projection distance of the hand-held projector varies considerably with the user's manipulation, the laser projector has to forms a clear image at any distance. The internal parameters of the laser projector were measured in advance. A magnetic position/orientation sensor was attached to this projector. The data it produces are used to cancel the distortion in the image in the same manner as in the case of the primary projector. The projection frustum was also dynamically calculated for each frame based on the position and orientation data from the sensor and used to cut a hole in the content of the image from the primary projector.

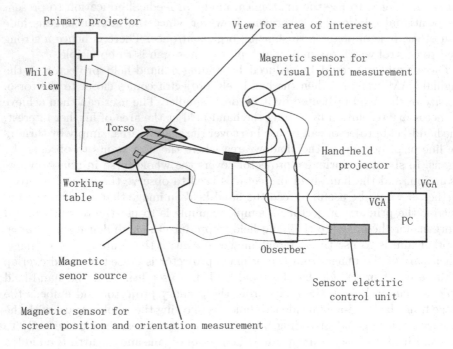

Fig. 4. Diagram of proposed system

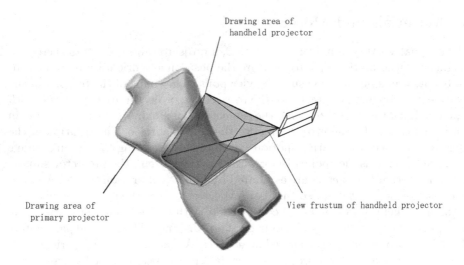

Fig. 5. Part of projection area is masked to avoid overlap

3   Result

In this section, the reduction of the three problems described in the first section is confirmed.

3.1   Improving the Resolution of the Display

The projection from the introduced hand-held projector helped achieve the necessary resolution to observe the detail of organs. It was easy and natural to choose the high-resolution area by facing the hand-held projector to the area of the user's interest. It was also possible to control the pixel density by changing the distance between the projector and the screen's surface. However, it seemed like there was more improvement in the size of the projection area than in the resolution. On the other hand, the image became brighter as the hand-held projector came close to the screen's surface, and the large difference in brightness between the two projection areas broke the constancy of the content's appearance. This defect was eliminated by adding a brightness control to the hand-held projector based on the projection distance. The table below shows the relation between the projection distance and pixel density. In our current system, the resolution of the primary projector was 1920 by 1080 pixels and the projection distance was set to 180 centimeters. This configuration provided 323 pixels per square centimeter. In contrast, although the resolution of the hand-held projector was only 848 by 480 pixels, the density of pixels was 1146 pixels per square centimeter when the projection distance was 30 centimeters.

Table 1. Pixel number per unit area of primary projector

Projection distance(cm)	Area(cm^2)	Resolution(px)	Pixel number per unit area(px/cm^2)
180	6420	848 × 480	63.40
180	6420	1024 × 768	122.5
180	6420	1920 × 1080	323.0

Table 2. Pixel number per unit area of hand-held projector

Projection distance(cm)	Area(cm^2)	Pixel number per unit area(px/cm^2)
10	50	8141
15	112	3634
20	185	2200
25	268.75	1515
30	355.25	1146
35	470.25	865.6
40	612	665.1

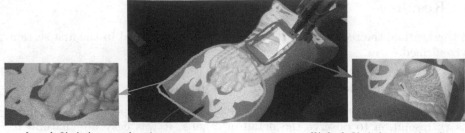

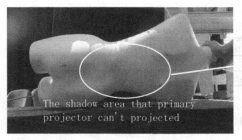

Low-definition projection
of primary projector

High-definition projection
of handheld projector

Fig. 6. Projected images by primary and hand-held projector

3.2 Extending the Field of View

As shown in Fig.7, the hand-held projector could fill part of the shadow area
where the primary projector was not able to create an image. The operation of
facing the projector to the area of the user's interest was easy and natural, and
this ability of adding a new visible part was felt to be effective. When the hand-
held was turned to the boundary area between clear projection and shadow,
the accuracy of stitching the images from the two projectors together was not
enough. Sometimes this improper connection made a bad impression on the user.
When a gap between the images from the hand-held and primary projector was
introduced, this error in image alignment was not disturbing, though the unity
of two images was lost.

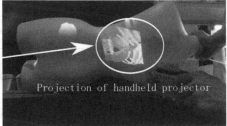

The shadow area that primary
projector can't projected

Projection of handheld projector

Fig. 7. Expansion of projection area

3.3 Switching Image Content by Hand-Held Projector

It is not easy to understand the positional relationship between organs in com-
pacted shape in three dimensions. A typical example is the digestive organs that
are layered in the stomach, such as the gastric organ, duodenum, pancreas, liver,
and the blood vessels around them. As described above, our approach is to provide the image of the organs in upper layer to the primary projector and the

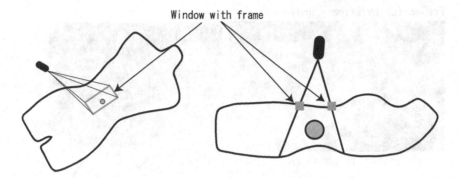

Fig. 8. The method that window with frame on surface to show boundary between projection areas

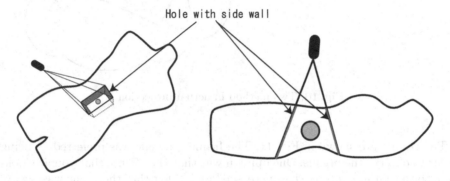

Fig. 9. The method that hole with side wall in torso to show boundary between projection areas

image of the lower layer to the hand-held projector. The image from the hand-held projector had priority over that from the primary projector, avoiding an overwrap between them. As a result, by using the hand-held projector user cuts a hole in the surrounding organs projected by the primary projector, and could watch the organs inside this hole displayed by the hand-held projector. Since this situation was still visually complicated, we added a cue to show the boundary between organs from different projectors. Two different cues were used and compared in experiments with the subjects: (1) a window frame on the surface of the torso and (2) side walls of the hole in the torso. The subjects were asked to try the system with the two types of cues and evaluate the result by choosing one among five answers about the easiness to understand the positional relationship between organs inside and outside the hole. The subjects were also asked to write freely about their impressions of the two types of cues. The subjects were 13 men and women, 20 - 24 years old. The duration of experiment was about 5 minutes for each case.

Projection by primary projector

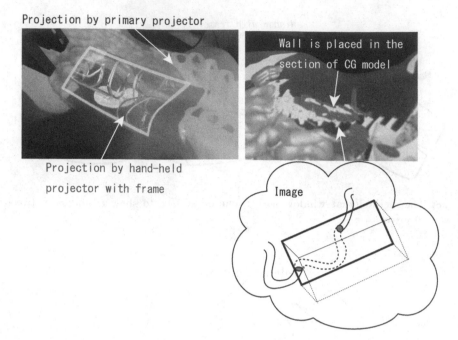

Wall is placed in the section of CG model

Projection by hand-held projector with frame

Image

Fig. 10. Two method in actual projection

The results are shown in Fig. 11. The frame type cue was preferred as being easier to observe the organs. One opinion was that the "Sense that you are looking into the cut in the frame has increased" and "I felt that the frame was always closest to viewpoint and on the torso's surface, and the organs are present in it". The result score and the opinions suggested that the frame worked to help the users distinguish organs inside the hole from outside the hole, avoiding visual confusion. This could be considered as an indirect help to understand the positional relationship between the organs. However, there were subjects who complained that the presence of frame confused some part of the three dimensional visual perception. A typical opinion was "When the frame exists, the organs in the frame is no longer appeared to be buried inside". The wall type cue generates a relatively complicated image on the screen's surface as compared to the frame type cue, since the former is three-dimensional inside the torso and the latter is two-dimensional on the torso's surface. The wall sometimes overlaps other organs displayed by the hand-held projector and this overwrap varies in each frame. Opinions from the subjects such as "the wall was visually disturbing" would be caused by this phenomenon. On the other hand, opinions such as "I felt like I was looking into the hole by recognize the cutting surface" suggested that the presence of the property placed walls improved the three dimensional perception. Our interpretations of this user test are; (1) the frame on the torso's surface was visually simpler and easier to understand, and worked to clearly

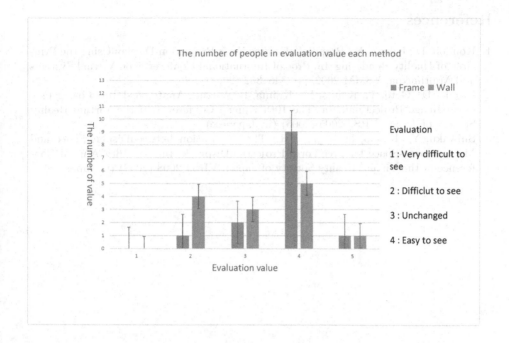

Fig. 11. The number of people in evaluation value each method

divide the organs displayed by the primary projector from that by the hand-held projector. (2) The sidewalls worked to connect the contents displayed by different projectors when the walls were perceived at the proper location in 3D space, but this was visually complicated and difficult to understand.

4   Conclusions

The improved image resolution and expanded visible projection area were successfully achieved by adding a hand-held projector to the existing VAM system. The hand-held projector was a natural tool to indicate the region of interest for the user. Furthermore, two types of cues were introduced to show the boundary between the contents from different projectors, i.e., a frame and sidewalls. These cues are expected to help reduce the difficulty in understanding the relationship between organs in different layers. The result of a user test suggested that the frame type cue promotes the division between layers and was preferred by the users. It was suggested that the wall type rather connects the layers and promotes an understanding of positional relation between organs in different layers, while the complexity in the projected image was magnified. Though the experiment with subjects described in this paper was preliminary, we suspect that the potential merit of the wall type cue would be to connect different layers by different projectors. The precise implementation to provide three-dimensional localization and improved visual appearance of the wall could draw on this potential merit.

References

1. Kondoh, D., Kijima, R.: Proposal of a Free Form Projection Display Using the Principle of Duality Rendering. In: Proc.of International Conference on Virtual Systems and Multimedia, VSMM 2002, pp. 346–352 (2002)
2. Kondo, D., Goto, T., Kouno, M., Kijima, R.: Virtual Anatomical Torso using Free Form Image Projectionh. In: The 10th Annual Conference of the Virtual Reality Society of Japan, VRSJ 2005 (2005) (in Japanese)
3. Shiwaku, Y., Kondo, D., Kijima, R.: The Calibration betweenDisplay-Space and Measurement-Space for Free-Form ProjectionDisplayh. In: The 13th Annual Conference of the Virtual Reality Society of Japan, VRSJ 2008 (2008) (in Japanese)

Study of an Interactive and Total Immersive Device with a Personal 3D Viewer and Its Effects on the Explicit Long-Term Memories of the Subjects

Evelyne Lombardo

Kedge Business School, LSIS,
Laboratory of Science of Information and Systems, CNRS, France
evelyne.lombardo@hotmail.com

Abstract. We studied an interactive (functional and intentional interactivity) and immersive (technical and psychological immersion) device with a personal 3D viewer (360° vision and environmentally ego-centered) and its effects on the explicit long-term memories of the subjects (4 groups of 30 students for a total of 120 subjects) (2007 and 2012).We have tested memory, communication and feeling of presence in our virtual environment with a canonic test of presence (Witmer and Singer, 1998). This article is a reflection on these 3D devices and their impact on the long term memory of the students, and on their presence sensation.

1   Introduction

Observing the virtual world is a stage that allows us to prepare ourselves for other actions and that is necessary for understanding the virtual world.   Navigating, acting and communicating presume an action on the user's part. The structure of our experiment can thus be considered as interactive in the sense that it allows the user to perform these four actions. We can therefore describe the structure of our experiment as an immersive, interactive structure, giving the sensation of presence. We must too describe the type of memory that we have tested in our experiment and, for that purpose, call on the theories inherent in the memorization processes within the learning programs, notably in the domain of cognitive sciences. Our experiment entails a 3D device in the setting of media-based, educational communication. Our initial hypothesis was calling upon an increasing number of sensory modes simultaneously makes it possible to increase performance of the long-term explicit memory of the information delivered by the didactic content (Paivio, 1986 and 1991), double coding theory (Paivio and Caspo 1969). As far as our experiment is concerned, we have tested long term / explicit memory. In fact, that is the form of memory at work when memorizing a course, even if learning brings several forms of memory into play.   We begin by defining our framework by distinguishing immersion, interaction and feeling of presence. In a second part, we define the different types of memory to explain what sort of memory we have tested in our experiment. In the third section, we describe our protocols of experiment. In the fourth part, we give the results of our experiment.

R. Shumaker and S. Lackey (Eds.): VAMR 2014, Part I, LNCS 8525, pp. 75–84, 2014.
© Springer International Publishing Switzerland 2014

2   Framework

2.1   Virtual Reality

The notion of Virtual Reality (VR) has given rise to many definitions in the literature. In 1986 Jaron Lanier used the term « virtual reality » (VR) for the first time. He defined it as being a reality:

— that we can apprehend through our senses,
— with which we can interact,
— that can be synthesized and shared with other persons,
— which does not affect our individuality but only our senses.

There are two types of approaches to VR: a psychological approach and a technical approach.

1. The psychological approach to VR emphasizes its sensory and cognitive aspect:
   «*VR is above all a mental construct formed by the observer when confronting sensory stimuli that have been supplied to him by technological devices.* » (Schneider, 2001).
2. The computer science specialists, in turn, choose a technical definition of VR and are interested in it as an interface:
   «*VR is an immersive experience in which the users wear screen headsets provided with position sensors, see stereoscopic images, hear 3D sounds, and can explore an interactive world in three dimensions*» (Pimentel and Texeira, 1993).

The last definition suggests that VR in a 3D context necessarily presumes advanced technology. In fact, the equipment used is made up of a work station (PC unit or Silicon Graphics station and a monitor), plus components for data retrieval and capture:

— Stereoscopic vision headset or vision helmet.
— Spatial position tracker or detector necessary for the computer to integrate and analyze the representation of the human body and its numerical model, its position, and its movements.
— A stereophonic sound retrieval system for reproducing 3D sound effects.
— An array of interface variables: joystick and other secondary accessories, vibration suit, dynamic chair…

Therefore, these definitions presume that Virtual Reality is inherent in the 3D image. Now, certain researchers oppose this understanding. For example, Daniel Schneider, psychology and education sciences professor at the University of Geneva, thinks that a 2D or text environment is enough to immerse the user in VR.

We can reach a consensus on the definition of Virtual Reality: a system which gives its users the sensation of presence in virtual spaces and allows them to interact with the system's components. The notion of Virtual Reality is therefore inherent in that of immersion which we must now elaborate.

Immersion. Many authors have likened this term to a technical notion which might act on the user's senses.

Cadoz (1994) asserts that immersion is *«a technology, an interface technique between man and machine and does not involve the psychological state of the subject»*. The physical immersion of a subject in a virtual environment is performed by sensory information (sight, hearing, etc.) alone.

For Pimentel and Texeiria (1993), immersion is *«the state of a participant when one or more of his senses... is isolated from the exterior world and he no longer registers any information that does not come from the computer»*.

According to Seipel (2003), a virtual environment is considered :

1. *Immersive* when the totality of the user's senses is called upon on the one hand, while on the other hand there is total immersion of each sense (even if this total immersion is seldom attained in practice).

   According to Slater and Usoh (1993) and Slater and al., (2001), in an immersive environment, the users have an:

   • **egocentric** view of the virtual world, that is, a view from the inside of the environment or of the phenomenon, as opposed to an:
   • **exocentric** view from the outside of the environment, where the user does not directly take part in the virtual world. For systems of these types, immersive technologies are used: data gloves, CAVE or HMD headsets, etc. Technologies of this kind allow visual immersion of the user in a virtual environment.

2. *Semi-immersive* when users can interact with both real and virtual worlds at the same time. Semi-immersive technologies utilize fixed visualization systems covering a large part of the visual field or going beyond it, these systems generally originate in simulation systems (Kalwaski, 1993). They cover a field of vision of 130 degrees. With semi-immersive technologies several persons can interact on the objects. An example of this kind of environment would be the systems used in artificial reality, such as «responsive workbenches» or projection rooms.

3. *Non-immersive* is when one uses a «desktop» display (Psotka and al., 1993). These are generally computer screens. This kind of VR reduces the user's contact with the virtual world to a window. This does not give the sensation of being present but simply of being in contact with a virtual environment. These worlds are made up of three-dimensional images. They are interactive in real time; they are navigable; and they can be accessed via the Internet. They do not use vision headsets.

The Feeling of Presence. The feeling of being present in a virtual environment is sometimes combined with that of immersion, but it forms the psychological aspect, while the notion of immersion refers rather to the technological aspect. The notion of *«presence is the psychological feeling of being there in the environment, of which immersion is the technological basis»* (Slater and Usoh, 1993). The presence sensation in a virtual environment is sometimes mixed with that of immersion, but actually refers to the psychological side, whereas the notion of immersion refers more to the technological side. The notion of *"presence... is the psychological sensation of being in an environment whose technological base is the immersion"* (Slater and al., 2001). Moreover, the immersive solution system does not necessarily include the presence sensation for the user (Slater and Usoh, 1993, Slater and al., 2001). Indeed, the presence sensation is not characteristic of Virtual Reality and could also be associated with other media such as cinema, literature, or theater. The presence sensation can therefore appear in a non-immersive environment. In an experimental study, Shubber (1998) demonstrated the existence of a presence sensation during the playing of video games, considered as non-immersive virtual environments. The interactive aspect, user action on the environment and the action of images on their perceptions appear to be sufficient to provoke a presence sensation in the user and *"the perceived image coupled with the action (is) sufficiently strong to make the player react and experience a presence sensation"*. The presence sensation therefore seems to be independent of the degree of immersion in the environment. In order to perceive the sensation of being present in an environment of virtual reality rather than in other media, Barfield and Hendrix (1995) distinguished "virtual" presence from presence in the physical environment: *"virtual presence is generally conceived as being a subjective and hypothetical state of consciousness and implication in a non-present environment"* (Barfield and Hendrix, 1995). The term telepresence is sometimes designated by some researchers as being synonymous with the presence sensation: *"telepresence is defined as the experience of presence in a virtual environment..."* (Steuer (1992). For Steuer, the term presence refers to the natural perceptions of an environment whereas telepresence refers to the mediatized perception of an environment. *"This environment can be a non-existent animated virtual environment that is synthesized by a computer (for example, an animated world created in a video game)"* (Steuer, 1992).

Functional Interaction. In virtual environments, the user's interactions are said to be subordinated to four tasks, according to Fuchs et al. (2001), as regards functional interaction.

The user's four tasks are:

— Observe the virtual world
— Navigate in the virtual world
— Act upon the virtual world
— Communicate

We can therefore describe the structure of our experiment as an immersive (technical and psychological immersion with a structure giving the feeling of presence) and interactive structure.

— **Immersive:** our experiment entails a 3D device in the setting of media-based, educational communication. The students were equipped with a HMD and had a 360 degrees vision in the virtual world (with egocentric view of the virtual world). The immersion was technical (with the HMD) and psychological, giving the feeling of presence in the virtual environment (this kind of immersion was tested by a questionnaire of presence of Witmer & Singer 1998).
— **Interactive:** (functional interactivition) because the students could act upon the virtual environment, observe the virtual world, navigate in the virtual world.

Our initial hypothesis was calling upon an increasing number of sensory modes simultaneously makes it possible to increase performance of the long-term explicit memory of the information delivered by the didactic content (Paivio, double coding theory (Paivio and Caspo 1969).

We must now describe the type of memory that we have tested in our experiment and, for that purpose, call on the theories inherent in the memorization processes within the learning programs, notably in the domain of cognitive sciences.

2.2   Cognitive Theories of Memory

Memory Systems. According to Lieury and Clavez (1986), we distinguish:

— **short term** memory from
— **long term memory.** In long term memory, the cognitivist researchers distinguish visual and verbal memory, semantic and episodic memory, implicit and explicit memory, declarative and procedural memory.

Long Term Memory

Visual Memory and Verbal Memory. According to Paivio (1991) and his theory of double coding: the images can give rise at one and the same time to verbal coding and to imaged coding.

1. Hence, information can be recovered via either one of these two codes or via both.
2. The imaged code is always more effective than the verbal code (Paivio and Caspo, 1969).

Semantic Memory and Episodic Memory: Tulving (1972). According to Tulving (1972), we may distinguish:

1. Semantic memory which has to do with the comprehension of speech and the memory of general knowledge that the subject possesses about the world.
2. Episodic memory that refers to the storage of information corresponding to a particular event experienced by the subject. It contains temporal and spatial information that specifies where and when this piece of information was acquired.

Implicit Memory and Explicit Memory

1. Implicit memory shows up in the tasks that do not require conscious or intentional retrieval of information on the subject's part (indirect measurement method).
2. Explicit memory covers the tasks of direct memory (recall and recognition) in which the retrieval of information previously presented is conscious and even prescribed by the task (direct measurement method).

Declarative Memory and Procedural Memory

1. The information stored in declarative memory corresponds to the knowledge of something
2. Procedural information corresponds to knowing how to do something.

As far as our experiment is concerned, we have tested long term / explicit memory. In fact, that is the form of memory at work when memorizing a course, even if learning brings several forms of memory into play.

3   Protocols of the Experiment

Initial Hypothesis. Calling upon an increasing number of sensory modes simultaneously would make it possible to increase the level of the processes implicated in memorizing information delivered by the didactic content (Paivio, 1991).

Experiment. We formed 5 homogeneous groups of students (18 students per group in the 2nd year of initial training, DUT of TC at the IUT of Toulon, in the setting of our courses in the Psycho-sociology of Communications).

The Equipment Used for the Course in 3D. For our experiment, the students were equipped with:

— A HMD (Head Mounted Display, that is, a Sony Glasstron LDI-D100B ruggedized vision headset (LCD screen, Resolution 800x600, non-stereoscopic, visual field 26° Horizontal, 19.6° vertical, headphones with stereophonic sound).
— A Tracker (movement detector) Intersense intertrax² (3 degrees of freedom, angular resolution: 0.02°, latency time 4 ms : internal refresh rate of 256Hz), mouse buttons as navigation tools.
— Software used: Unreal 2004, 3D Studio max, Actor X, PowerPoint.

The Personnel Involved in the Project. Close collaboration with:

— A physician and neuro-psychologist doctor, who has elaborated a system conceived within a virtual environment in order to treat patients suffering from phobias by successive habituation. He conceived the story-board of the course in virtual imagery, the animations and the course in virtual imagery.
— A media engineering student from the University of Toulon and the South, a specialist in synthetic images, has created, in the framework of a proficiency grant, the 3D images for the course in virtual imagery.

Experiment: Report, the Courses

1. An oral, media-based course: the course was dictated, the students did not take notes.
2. A media-based course in PowerPoint alone but without taking notes. The images and the diagrams were the same as those that were used in the course in synthetic images.
3. A media-based course in PowerPoint, with note taking. The images and the diagrams were the same as those that were used in the course in synthetic images.
4. A media-based course in virtual imagery (3D, vision headset, total immersion).
5. A control group course, the pre-test and the post-test only.

Hypotheses

— H1: a course by means of virtual images makes it possible to memorize better compared with other types of media-based presentations (auditory, PowerPoint without notes, PowerPoint with notes);
— H2: the type of media-based presentation acts on the communication of course content and the students experienced the four types of media-based presentation differently.

Approach. Our approach combined:

• a quantitative analysis based on hypothetical-deductive reasoning in order to ana-lyze whether an immersive 3D structure in the framework of our courses on the Psycho-sociology of Organizations can have effects on memorization (with a pre-test and a post-test 3 months later with Anova to compare the results).
• a qualitative analysis a) in order to understand how the students experienced the different communications situations across the four types of med ia-based presenta-tion; and b) to test the sensation of presence in the course presented by means of virtual images (with qualitative interviews).

Methodology H1. A way of verifying hypothesis H1 was to construct a quasi-experimental system that allowed us to vary the different dimensions of the Indepen-dent Variable (IV) and to create teaching structures each one of which corresponded to a mode of the IV that we wanted to test, that is, the structure of the media-based presentation.

Data Processing H1

• The IV has several modes: course A auditory, course B PowerPoint without note taking, course C PowerPoint with note taking, course D by means of virtual images in immersive 3D.
• The differences in results obtained by the courses were calculated by variance analysis (Anova), and by a test T. of the Student.

4   Results

Anova Results H1

• Group 3 (PowerPoint with note taking) is the one that had the clearest significant improvement in performance.
• By decreasing order of performance, group 2 came next (PowerPoint without note taking), then group 4 (virtual images with HMD, immersive and interactive course), then group 1 (auditory) and last came group 5 (the control group).

Results of the Qualitative Treatment H2. The recurrent themes in the group 4 (virtual images with HMD, immersive and interactive course) were the following;

- **theme 1: positive aspects of the structure**, examples of sub-themes: playful, interactive, animated, convivial;
- **theme 2: constraining aspects of the structure**, examples of sub-themes: difficulties: technical, physical, pedagogical, communications;
- **theme 3: immersive aspects of the structure**, examples of sub-themes: immersion: physical, real, feeling of presence, feeling of involvement;
- **theme 4: proposals for improvement**, examples of sub-themes: technical improvements, pedagogical improvements, communications improvements ;
- **theme 5: cognition and learning**, examples of sub-themes: memory, attention, learning, comprehension;
- **theme 6: perception of the general course of the Psycho-sociology of organizations**, examples of sub-themes: pleasant memories;
- **theme 7: perception of the experimental course in virtual images**, examples of sub-themes: fantasy, motivating, disappointment.

Results of the Test of Presence H2. The results show that the students had a feeling of presence within the virtual environment of the course in immersive 3D.

5   Discussion and Conclusion

1. Our study showed that in the course in virtual imagery (total immersive device with HMD) the performance of long-term memory is no better than in the other courses. Group 3 (PowerPoint with note taking) is the one that had the clearest significant improvement in performance. And by decreasing order of performance, group 2 came next (PowerPoint without note taking), then group 4 (virtual images), then group 1 (auditory) and last came group 5 (the control group).
2. The results show that the students had a feeling of presence within the virtual environment of the course in immersive 3D. This feeling of presence is physical and psychological.

We assume that the average score of students in the group virtual images could be explained:

1. The cognitive load theory: in fact, students were sometimes embarrassed by the HMD, they experienced headaches or heart, the hardware could cause mental or cognitive overload. Mayer and Anderson (1991), Mayer (1998), Sweller (1994, 1999) take into account in their models the notion of mental activity associated with multimedia learning, Sweller, Ayres, Kalyuga (2011) defined the concept of cognitive load by placing it in the problems of multimedia learning. Cognitive load is defined by these authors as the mental workload that the execution of a task imposes on the cognitive system. Varies depending on the quantity and quality of information presented in a multimedia educational product, the cognitive load is assumed to depend on storage capacity and processing information in working memory learners. The theory of cognitive load may partly explain the poor performance of students in memory if the current 3D immersive virtual images;

2. the effect of habituation may be too long (we had planned to let students get used to the device for a quarter of an hour, but this time perhaps has not been sufficient, also another experiment might be to lead by allowing students to have time to get used the device much longer).

References

1. Barfield, W., Hendrix, C.: The effect of update rate on the sense of presence within virtual environments. Virtual Reality: The Journal of Virtual Reality Society 1(1), 3–16 (1995)
2. Cadoz, C.: Les réalités virtuelles, p. 125. Dominos-Flammarion, Paris (1994)
3. Kalawsky, R.S.: The Science of Virtual Reality and Virtual Environments. Addison-Wesley, Reading (1993)
4. Lieury, A., Calvez, F.: Code imagé et traitement séquentiel. Inl'année Psychologique 86(3), 329–347 (1986)
5. Fuchs, P., Moreau, G., Papin, J.-P.: Le traité de la réalité virtuelle, p. 517. Techniques Ingénieur, Paris (2001)
6. Mayer, R.E., Anderson, R.B.: «Animations need narrations: An experimental test of dual-coding hypothesis. Journal of Educational Psychology 83, 484–490 (1991)
7. Mayer, R.E.: Cognitive, metacognitive and motivational aspects of problem solving. Instructional Science 26(1-2), 49–63 (1998)
8. Paivio, A.: Dual coding theory: Retrospect and current status. Canadian Journal of Psychology 45, 255–287 (1991)
9. Paivio, A.: Mental representations: A dual coding approach, p. 323. Ox-ford University Press, Oxford (1986)
10. Paivio, A., Csaspo, K.: Concrete images and verbal memory codes. Journal of Experimental Psychology 80(2), 279–285 (1969)
11. Pimentel, K., Teixeira, K.: La réalité virtuelle: De l'autre côté du miroir, p. 338. Addison Wesley, Paris (1993)
12. Plass, J.L., Moreno, R.: Cognitive Load Theory. Cambridge University Press, New York (2010) (ISBN 9780521677585)
13. Psotka, J., Davison, S., Lewis, S.: Exploring Immersion in Virtual Space (1993)
14. Schneider, D.K.: Le rôle de l'Internet dans la formation supérieure: Scénarii et technologies. Colloque International: Enseignement des Langues et Multimédia, Alger.ual Reality Systems 1(2), 70–92 (2001)
15. Seipel, S. (2003). Visualizations technologies. Uppsala Universitet,
    http://www.it.uu.se/edu/course/homepage/igs/ht03/lectures/ igs_07_visualization_techniques.pdf (retrieved March 23, 2013)
16. Shubber, Y.: Les réalités virtuelles et la présencede la conceptualisation à l'opérationnalisation. Recherches en Communication 10, 161–185 (1998)
17. Slater, M., Linakis, V., Usoh, M., Kooper, R., Street, G.: Immersion, presence, and performance in virtual environments: An experiment with Tri-Dimensional Chess. In: ACM Virtual Reality Software and Technology (VRST), pp. 163–172 (2001)
18. Slater, M., Usoh, M.: Presence in immersive virtual environments. In: Virtual Reality Annual International Symposium, pp. 90–96 (1993)
19. Steuer, J.: Defining virtual reality: Dimensions determining telepresence. Journal of Communication 42(4), 73–93 (1992)

20. Sweller, J., Ayres, P., Kalyuga, S.: Cognitive Load Theory (2011)
21. Sweller, J.: Cognitive Load Theory, learning difficulty, and instructional design. Learning and Instruction 4 (1994), doi:10.1016/0959-4752(94)90003-5
22. Sweller, J.: Instructional design in technical areas, Camberwell, Australie. Australian Council for Educational Research (1999) (ISBN 0-86431-312-8)
23. Tulving, E.L.: Organization of memory: Quo vadis? In: Gazzaniga, M. (ed.) The Cognitive Neurosciences. MIT Press (1975)
24. Witmer, B., Singer, M.: Measuring presence in virtual environments: A presence questionnaire. Presence 7(3), 225–240 (1998)

Research and Simulation on Virtual Movement Based on Kinect

Qi Luo[1] and Guohui Yang[2]

[1] College of Sports Engineering and Information Technology,
Wuhan Sports University, 430079, China
[2] School of Computer Science, Wuhan Univesity, 430079, China
emeinstitute@126.com

Abstract. Kinect is a line of motion sensing input devices by Microsoft for Xbox 360 and Xbox One video game consoles and Windows PCs. Based around a webcam-style add-on peripheral, it enables users to control and interact with their console/computer without the need for a game controller, through a natural user interface using gestures and spoken commands. The virtual simulation system is designed in the paper. Key Technologies of the Simulation System based on Virtual movement such us Characters in skinned binding technology, Kinect data capture, Movement data extraction and processing model, Depth of the image to bone, Sports redirection module and Skeleton model with motion data node bound are introduced in the paper.

1 Introduction

There are mainly three methods in traditional virtual movement simulation: manual driven, model driven and data driven. With an increasing demand for simulation authenticity, image quality, action complexity, low cost in virtual movement simulation and so forth, the three methods has revealed their deficiencies. To be specific: Manual drive need professional animators to set a key frame by hand first, and then finish simulating the movement with difference method, which relies solely on the animators' experiences and is inefficient. Model driven need mathematical model to abstractly present human movement process, which is more convenient. However large amount of calculation usually cannot put real human motion data into virtual model. Data driven uses mechanical, electromagnetic, acoustic or optical methods to realize motion data capture, but people must carry some external sensor equipment during the process. It can guarantee high quality movement data, but the external sensor equipment will bring inconvenience to the motion of the body. Most importantly, motion capture equipment has a high price, which is difficult to prompt and put in use [1].

Therefore, it has an important practical meaning to study on virtual movement simulation based on Kinect. Kinect is a body feeling peripherals designed by Microsoft for Xbox360 main engine. It is different from traditional camera, which not only has color image acquisition function as ordinary camera, but also can realize depth data acquisition by two infrared transceiver in front of the camera. This function can help

R. Shumaker and S. Lackey (Eds.): VAMR 2014, Part I, LNCS 8525, pp. 85–92, 2014.

Kinect to get depth data of 3D scene with a low cost. And by the use of machine learning and pattern recognition methods, it can extract three dimensional space and direction of human skeleton model and articulation point from the depth data. Finally, the data will be applied to the virtual character model after real-time processing based on the single frame to complete the human movement simulation.

Movement simulation based on Kinect is still at the research stage home and abroad. It is mostly used in game development, action recognition and so forth, such as dancing, racing game, etc, which at the most time lacks of interaction between virtual characters and virtual scene.

The virtual simulation system is designed in the paper. Key Technologies of the Simulation System based on Virtual movement such us Characters in skinned binding technology, Kinect data capture, Movement data extraction and processing model, Depth of the image to bone, Sports redirection module and Skeleton model with motion data node bound are introduced in the paper.

2   Kinect

Kinect is a line of motion sensing input devices by Microsoft for Xbox 360 and Xbox One video game consoles and Windows PCs. Based around a webcam-style add-on peripheral, it enables users to control and interact with their console/computer without the need for a game controller, through a natural user interface using gestures and spoken commands [2]. The first-generation Kinect was first introduced in November 2010 in an attempt to broaden Xbox 360's audience beyond its typical gamer base. A version for Windows was released on February 1, 2012. Kinect competes with several motion controllers on other home consoles, such as Wii Remote Plus for Wii, PlayStation Move/PlayStation Eye for PlayStation 3, and PlayStation Camera for PlayStation 4. Kinect for Xbox 360 see Figure 1.

Fig. 1. Kinect for Xbox 360

Kinect builds on software technology developed internally by Rare, a subsidiary of Microsoft Game Studios owned by Microsoft, and on range camera technology by Israeli developer PrimeSense, which developed a system that can interpret specific gestures, making completely hands-free control of electronic devices possible by using an infrared projector and camera and a special microchip to track the movement of objects and individuals in three dimensions. This 3D scanner system called Light Coding employs a variant of image-based 3D reconstruction.

Kinect sensor is a horizontal bar connected to a small base with a motorized pivot and is designed to be positioned lengthwise above or below the video display. The device features an "RGB camera, depth sensor and multi-array microphone running proprietary software", which provide full-body 3D motion capture, facial recognition and voice recognition capabilities. At launch, voice recognition was only made available in Japan, United Kingdom, Canada and United States. Mainland Europe received the feature later in spring 2011. Currently voice recognition is supported in Australia, Canada, France, Germany, Ireland, Italy, Japan, Mexico, New Zealand, United Kingdom and United States. Kinect sensor's microphone array enables Xbox 360 to conduct acoustic source localization and ambient noise suppression, allowing for things such as headset-free party chat over Xbox Live.

The depth sensor consists of an infrared laser projector combined with a monochrome CMOS sensor, which captures video data in 3D under any ambient light conditions. The sensing range of the depth sensor is adjustable, and Kinect software is capable of automatically calibrating the sensor based on game play and the player's physical environment, accommodating for the presence of furniture or other obstacles.

Described by Microsoft personnel as the primary innovation of Kinect, the software technology enables advanced gesture recognition, facial recognition and voice recognition. According to information supplied to retailers, Kinect is capable of simultaneously tracking up to six people, including two active players for motion analysis with a feature extraction of 20 joints per player. However, Prime Sense has stated that the number of people the device can "see" (but not process as players) is only limited by how many will fit in the field-of-view of the camera.

This infrared image shows the laser grid Kinect uses to calculate depth .The depth map is visualized here using color gradients from white (near) to blue (far)Reverse engineering has determined that the Kinect's various sensors output video at a frame rate of ~9 Hz to 30 Hz depending on resolution. The default RGB video stream uses 8-bit VGA resolution (640 × 480 pixels) with a Bayer color filter, but the hardware is capable of resolutions up to 1280x1024 (at a lower frame rate) and other colour formats such as UYVY. The monochrome depth sensing video stream is in VGA resolution (640 × 480 pixels) with 11-bit depth, which provides 2,048 levels of sensitivity. The Kinect can also stream the view from its IR camera directly (i.e.: before it has been converting into a depth map) as 640x480 video, or 1280x1024 at a lower frame rate. The Kinect sensor has a practical ranging limit of 1.2–3.5 m (3.9–11.5 ft) distance when used with the Xbox software. The area required to play Kinect is roughly 6 m2, although the sensor can maintain tracking through an extended range of approximately 0.7–6 m (2.3–19.7 ft). The sensor has an angular field of view of 57° horizontally and 43° vertically, while the motorized pivot is capable of tilting the sensor up to 27° either up or down. The horizontal field of the Kinect sensor at the minimum viewing distance of ~0.8 m (2.6 ft) is therefore ~87 cm (34 in), and the vertical field is ~63 cm (25 in), resulting in a resolution of just over 1.3 mm (0.051 in) per pixel. The microphone array features four microphone capsules and operates with each channel processing 16-bit audio at a sampling rate of 16 kHz.

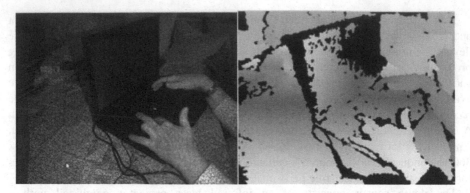

Fig. 2. The laser grid Kinect uses to calculate depth and The depth map is visualized here using color gradients from white (near) to blue (far)

Because the Kinect sensor's motorized tilt mechanism requires more power than the Xbox 360's USB ports can supply, the device makes use of a proprietary connector combining USB communication with additional power. Redesigned Xbox 360 S models include a special AUX port for accommodating the connector, while older models require a special power supply cable (included with the sensor) that splits the connection into separate USB and power connections; power is supplied from the mains by way of an AC adapter.

3   Key Technologies of the Simulation System Based on Virtual Movement

The paper proposes a simulation system based on the virtual movement, and conduct detailed description about the integrated design of this project. It is included data capture, data analysis and processing, redirection for the movement data, skeletal model binding and action instruction design module and so on.

This system combines Kinect and Unity3D, for use human body directly as a controller input to achieve the control for real-time movement of the role model in the virtual scene. At the same time, to design simulation movement instruction for the completion interaction between virtual role and scene object.

At last, the system can achieve real-time movement simulation and also can recognize interaction instruction to realize the interaction between virtual role model and scene. It mainly consists of four modules: (1) 3D point cloud acquisition module; (2) human bone skeleton extraction and movement data capture module; (3) movement data processing and redirection module; (4) action figures simulation module.

3.1   Characters in Skinned Binding Technology

The first step of virtual action figures simulation is to set up the role virtual model. 3D virtual role model consists of skeleton model and skin. Skeleton is a tree structure, which is generally formed by the connected relation between the nodes, just shown in

Figure 3. Skin is a skin mesh, including the top point coordinate information, texture coordinate information and texture information of skin grid. In generally, skeleton model can reflect the action figures information accuracy. Therefore, after conduct with the motion data captured by motion capture device, apply the data to skeleton model, through each frame skeleton movement data to realize model driven, as usual as the reuse of the movement data. Skin is bound to one or more special bone joints, through the skeleton movement to drive the skin movement. The skin binding technology is a technique method, which is to complete this correspondence relation between skin and bone joints, reappear complex movement information through simple skeleton movement and drive the movement of skin model [3].

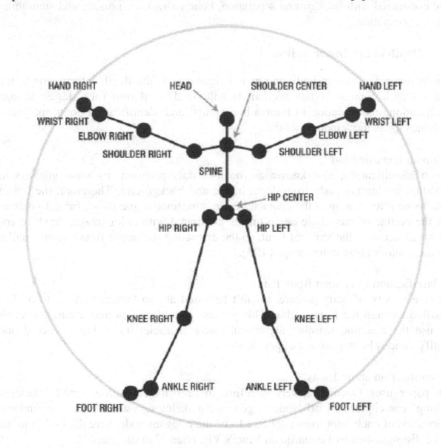

Fig. 3. Illustrated skeleton joints

3.2 Kinect Data Capture

The image data stream maybe can be understood as a contiguous of a collection still picture group. At initialization, you can set related option, including image resolution ratio, image type and video streaming buffer size. Next, open the image and set the video streaming buffer size, usually the application should acquit data before the relief area filled. Otherwise, with the coming of the data frame, the old data frame will be lost. Users can interview two kinds of data from Kinect, first is color flow image data, and the other is depth image data.

3.3   Movement Data Extraction and Processing Model

By Kinect somatosensory camera, 3D world can be seen, but it is important content during research about how to extract the human body and its movement information from the 3D information. The 3D color information and depth information got by Kinect can't be served as movement data directly to drive any 3D model, so it needs to be conducted with background separation, bone extract, de-noising and smoothing treatment operation.

3.4   Depth of the Image to Bone

How to recognize human body and action figures with the depth information is the main research content in this section. It will be divided into four stages: human identification, classification of human body parts, and identification about the joints and bones joints movement smooth.

1) Human Identification
Human identification, also known as the user data partition, its main goals is to individual the human body from depth image and background. Therefore, the object needs to be filtered around the character operation, remove the noise. First, to extract with the outline of the whole depth image, compared with color image, depth image will not affect with the ambient light, so the extracting the target figure to be smaller than the contour noise color image [4][5].

2) Classification of Human Body Parts
Due to a variety of body posture, it can't be listed all, so human body is to be fast classified through the Eigen value. This process should go fast and accurate enough will use the machine learning algorithm, using characteristic value to record and identify various body postures of people [6].

3) Identification about Joints
This paper uses OpenNI driver, therefore in accordance with OpenNI "skeleton tracking" can capture 14 off Node to generate a skeleton system. This is to find out the location of each joint from the body 14 of the relevant node, here the body's joints can be distinguished by Leonardo da Vinci's Vitruvian Man diagram[7].

4) Skeletal Joints Smooth Movement
In skeletal tracking process, due to noise, hardware performance and other factors can lead to incoherent action figures, bone joints. The relative position between the large changes from frame to frame jitter or jumping generated, resulting in false operation of the virtual. To solve this problem is to smooth the data by the coordinate standardization to reduce bone joints of the frame and the frame of difference between the joint positions [8].

3.5   Sports Redirection Module

Sports redirection is a technology, which is referred to when apply the original motion data to the virtual scene role through 3D movement of the device, the virtual character size ratio and the ratio may not be captured exactly the same entity, even different skeleton results under circumstances such action may lose the original features, then you can redirect the movement of data through the movement through a series of operational re-directed to the virtual character models leaving the action to maintain the original characteristics[9].

3.6   Skeleton Model with Motion Data Node Bound

In this paper, to take the Unity3D game development platform for virtual human motion simulation, Unity3D is a more powerful integrated game engine and editor that allows you to quickly and efficiently create objects, import external resources, and use the code to connect them together . Unity3D provides a visual editor, in principle it is that you can use to build a simple drag and drop actions to complete any task, or even a script to connect, create complex variable assignment or resource contains multiple parts. Meanwhile Unity3D also includes an integrated scripting environment, command-driven and action control model simulation process is mainly controlled by writing a script to implement virtual models and simulation-driven action command module.

At beginning, Kinect was designed for game console of Xbox360, which conduct the body as a controller to control the virtual role movement. In order to Kinect can be widely application to other fields, such as telemedicine, animation production, game character control, virtual assembly and other fields. The interaction between virtual role and scene is essential. By studying the previous section, now we can use the movement data with Kinect through redirecting way to drive the virtual scene role model. So how to achieve a deeper level of interaction, such as the interactions between objects in virtual characters and scenes, including virtual characters can grab objects in the scene, assembly, mobile and other operations are the main research in this paper.

4   Conclusions

The virtual simulation system is designed in the paper. Key Technologies of the Simulation System based on Virtual movement such us Characters in skinned binding technology, Kinect data capture, Movement data extraction and processing model, Depth of the image to bone, Sports redirection module and Skeleton model with motion data node bound are introduced in the paper.

References

1. Shang, H.: Dissertation, p. 1–2. Submittted to Hangzhou Dianzi University for the Degree of Master (2012)
2. http://blog.seattlepi.com/digitaljoystick/2009/06/01/e3-2009-microsoft-at-e3-several-metric-tons-of-press-releaseapalloza/

3. James, D.L., Twigg, C.D.: Skinning mesh animations. In: Association for Computing Machinery, pp. 399–407 (2005)
4. Shotton, J.: Real-time human pose recognition in parts from single depth images, pp. 1298–1299. IEEE Computer Society, Colorado Springs (2011)
5. Knoop, S., Vacek, S., Dillmann, R.: Sensor fusion for 3D human body tracking with an articulated 3D body model, pp. 1686–1691. Institute of Electrical and Electronics Engineers Inc. (2006)
6. Bindiganavale, R., Badler, N.I.: Motion abstraction and mapping with spatial constraints. In: Magnenat-Thalmann, N., Thalmann, D. (eds.) CAPTECH 1998. LNCS (LNAI), vol. 1537, pp. 70–75. Springer, Heidelberg (1998)
7. Sidenbladh, H., Black, M.J., Sigal, L.: Implicit probabilistic models of human motion for synthesis and tracking. In: Heyden, A., Sparr, G., Nielsen, M., Johansen, P. (eds.) ECCV 2002, Part I. LNCS, vol. 2350, pp. 784–800. Springer, Heidelberg (2002)
8. Pronost, N., Dumon, G.: Dynamics-based analysis and synthesis of human locomotion. Visual Compute 23(7), 513–522 (2007)
9. Hsieh, M.K., Chen, B.-Y., Ouhyoung, M.: Motion Retargetting and Transition in Different Articulated Figures. In: CAD/Graphics, pp. 457–462 (2005)

A Natural User Interface for Navigating in Organized 3D Virtual Contents

Guido Maria Re and Monica Bordegoni

Politecnico di Milano, Dipartimento di Meccanica,
Via La Masa, 1, 20156 Milano, Italy
{guidomaria.re,monica.bordegoni}@polimi.it

Abstract. The research activity presented in this paper aim at extending the traditional planar navigation, which is adopted by many desktop applications for searching information, to an experience in a Virtual Reality (VR) environment. In particular, the work proposes a system that allows the user to navigate in virtual environments, in which the objects are spatially organized and sorted. The visualization of virtual object has been designed and an interaction method, based on gestures, has been proposed to trigger the navigation in the environment. The article describes the design and the development of the system, by starting from some considerations about the intuitiveness and naturalness required for a three-dimensional navigation. In addition, an initial case study has been carried out and consists in using the system in a virtual 3D catalogue of furniture.

Keywords: Virtual Reality, Natural User Interfaces, Navigation, Gestures, Virtual Catalogue.

1   Introduction

A considerable amount of time that users spend interacting with a computer is usually devoted to information search. These pieces of information are virtual contents, such as pictures, news, music and videos or, in other more articulated cases, also 3D models, and they are usually represented by means of thumbnails spatially organized. The reason behind their disposition is to make them clearly visible and easy to recognize. The disposition side by side of these elements is often carried out according to logical reasons or a classification. Typical examples are the e-commerce websites, in which goods on sale are ordered by relevance or price, or the slideshow visualization mode to select a tune to play, where the music albums are arranged in alphabetical order or by genre.

Traditional interaction devices, such as keyboard and mouse, provide the browsing experience to the user. The navigation is performed by a scrollbar or other dragging interaction metaphors that limit the user's experience in one direction. Hence, the navigation through these pieces of information is limited along a single direction, which could be the vertical or the horizontal one.

From these considerations, it turns out that searching information is a common aspect for many traditional computer applications and websites. However, the visualization

R. Shumaker and S. Lackey (Eds.): VAMR 2014, Part I, LNCS 8525, pp. 93–104, 2014.
© Springer International Publishing Switzerland 2014

and interaction methods for these purposes limit the user navigation experience. They are actually oriented to desktop-like user interfaces. The effectiveness of these navigation methods dramatically decreases if used in particular HCI systems, such as in Virtual Reality (VR) environments. Therefore, new solutions for browsing in virtual spaces become necessary.

The objective of this research work is to overcome the limitations of the current navigation interfaces across organized objects in a tri-dimensional VR environment and to extend the user's navigation possibilities by means of Natural User Interfaces (NUI) [1]. In this way the user is not in a flat virtual space and he can experience a free 3D navigation.

The proposed navigation system is oriented to use spatial gestures to enable a 3D navigation experience in an organized Virtual Reality (VR) environment. The items in the VR environment are sorted according to common features. Moreover, in order to promote and expand new contexts of use for VR, the gestures must be as natural as possible and the technologies involved must be cheap. Actually, the need of interactive methods, which are easy to learn and remember, and the use of mass-market devices, which are highly available and for a low price, are the two requirements for a large-scale deployment of NUIs.

The paper is organized as follows. Section 2 gives an overview of the state of the art of the NUIs and virtual navigation systems. Section 3 describes the system while Section 4 the design of the gestures used for the interaction. Section 5 presents an initial case study. The paper closes with a discussion and conclusions.

2   Background

NUI's are computer-interaction modalities that have been growing up in the last years. The term "natural" is due to the possibility of managing a computer through usual gesture and minimally invasive devices. NUI enables the user to provide inputs to a machine by means of his whole body and movements in the space, differently to the traditional mouse and keyboard [2]. This modality is particularly convenient in wide interactive environments, such as the ones provided by a CAVE [3]. In these cases, in fact, the user is free to move and he does not have to hold any bulky device. Finally, the possibility of interacting with natural gestures makes the NUIs intuitive, easy to learn and increases the user's engagement during the use. According to these considerations, NUIs are more usable than traditional interaction devices [4].

The great progress in the miniaturization, the development of powerful technologies and efficient software brought to new NUI device available for a cheap price in the last decade. In particular, several new devices came out in the video-game mass market. These devices have been nicely integrated into research projects in the field of virtual navigation and interaction. One of the first examples was the use of the Balance Board from Nintendo[1] as input device for moving in a virtual space [5]. However, these game devices require a physical interaction between them and the user in order to provide an input to the machine.

---

[1] Nintendo Balance Board - http://wiifit.com/

Advances in Computer Vision (CV) and HCI brought also the whole human body to become an interface without wearing any device. Smart systems are currently able to recognize a user by means of cameras [6], and interpret his/her movements as computer inputs avoiding the touch interaction. [7] evaluated a simple system, based on a single camera, to detect the hands and the head of a user in a CAVE for navigation purposes. More recently, the release of Microsoft Kinect for Xbox 360[2] pushed further the boundaries of NUI devices by providing a cheap motion capture system. Kinect couples the video stream of a normal RGB camera with depth information and it is also able to detect a user and the position of 21 joints of his/her body in real time. [8] proposed to use this device for map navigation purposes by detecting hand direction and motion by means of the depth data. An important contribution on the spread of Kinect has been given by the middleware called FAAST [9], which is able to recognize body gestures and consequently trigger keyboard events. A gesture-driven navigation system for VR environments by using Kinect and FAAST is described in [10].

Differently to the previous researches, this work deals with a virtual environment where objects are precisely organized in the space according to a three-dimensional grid. The objects are sorted and arranged in the space according to classification features. For this reason, free navigation in the space is not requested because the browsing is from a precise coordinate point to another one. These two points correspond to the spatial position of two different objects. [11] proposed a similar approach to navigate through the media contents on a television by means of gestures and a camera sensor. [12] developed a system addressed to browsing a database of medical images in a hospital, with the advantage for the doctor to avoid touch interactions in a sterile environment. [13], finally, developed a similar system to browse items by using Kinect. The research described in this paper takes into account these previous works and it contributes to extend the navigation user's experience to three dimensions.

3   System Description

The system proposed provides a 3D navigation through a large display and a NUI. As depicted in Fig. 1, the system is made up of hardware and software components that work all together to allow the user to experience the navigation. The components are organized in two main modules according to their task; an event driven approach triggers the communication between the modules. The first module regards the user interaction experience and its task is to detect the user's gesture and to provide the related event. The second module provides the navigation experience to the user, according to the triggered event, by rendering the camera motion in the VR space. The components and the two modules are described in depth in the following.

---

[2] Microsoft Kinect - http://www.xbox.com/en-US/kinect

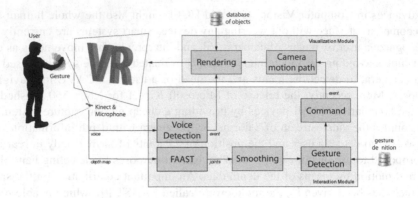

Fig. 1. Schematic representation of the system

3.1   System Components

The main hardware components of the system are the Microsoft Kinect and a Pow-erWall. Kinect is a motion capture controller that integrates a RGB camera, a depth sensor and an array of microphones. The color camera has 8-bit VGA resolution (640 x 480 pixels) working at 30 Hz. The depth sensor consists of a monochrome VGA camera working in the infrared spectrum (IR) and an IR laser projector. The sensor is able to detect the 3D scene in a distance range from 0.8 to 3.5 meters. The PowerWall is a retro-reflective display, whose size is 3x2.25 meters. The image stream is pro-vided by a color projector with a resolution of 1400 x 1050 at 80 Hz. All the devices are connected to a laptop, which manages all the data in order to elaborate the naviga-tion experience. The laptop is equipped with a 2.66 GHz processor, 4 GB RAM and a NVIDIA GeForce GT 330M GPU.

3.2   Interaction Module

The purpose of the interaction module is to trigger the navigation through the recogni-tion of user's gestures. In order to do this, the depth map generated by Kinect is elaborated in real time by FAAST. As in Fig. 2, FAAST extracts the user shape in the scene and calculates a 3D skeleton model of the user. This skeleton is a simple repre-sentation of the biomechanical structure of the whole user body in the space and it is made up of 24 joints. Then, FAAST makes the position of each joint available to other applications through a VRPN communication network [14].

The command recognition software collects the VRPN data of the joints and works to define in real-time what the user wants to command through gestures. This soft-ware has been developed by means of Virtools 5.0[3], which is a game engine by Das-sault Systèmes. As a first step, the command recognition software filters the received data along time, in order to remove high frequency noise. This step is carried out by means of a low-pass filter. In this way, the system makes smooth the raw user's

---

[3] 3DVIA Virtools - http://www.3ds.com/products-services/3dvia/
3dvia-virtools/

movements captured by Kinect. Subsequently, the command recognition software uses the data and detects precise gestures according to information stored in a database. Since the navigation is in a 3D organized space, the system requires six different gestures to move in all of the main directions. The system compares the user movements with the gestures described in the database and an event is generated in order to trigger the navigation in case of matching. The definitions of the gestures and the detection algorithm are reported in Section 4 in detail.

Lastly, additional events are generated by voice commands. A microphone placed in the environment captures the user voice and detects precise words. In particular, the two words are "select" and "release". The system recognizes these two words and allows the user to pick or leave a virtual object in the 3D environment.

Fig. 2. The visualization of the depth map from Kinect by means of FAAST. The light blue area corresponds to the user, while the red lines indicate his simplified skeleton.

3.3   Visualization Module

The Visualization Module enables the user to see the virtual space and to browse across the objects, which are arranged in a particular way. The objects are placed on fixed positions in the space so that they are at the same distance to each other. In addition, these objects are located in the virtual space according to three classifications. Actually, each object can be described according to some qualitative and quantitative features. The three common features among the objects are associated to the three dimensions of the environment. Consequently, they can be arranged in a sort of visual 3D array, where each place corresponds to a value or a quality of a feature. Figure 3 represents an example of such arrangement by means of coloured primitive solids. Different kinds of objects are arranged in the space according three features:

- Shape, (cone, pyramid, cube, cylinder, sphere)
- Size, (extra small, small, medium, large, extra large)
- Colour (red, orange, yellow, green, light blue, blue, purple)

Thus, each feature is associated with a dimension and the navigation along one direction allows the user to browse through the objects with different values associated with one of the features. In this particular example, the user switches to a different colour by moving horizontally, changes the object dimension going forward and backward, selects another shape going up and down.

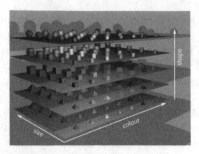

Fig. 3. Several 3D objects are arranged in the space according to the shape, size and colour

The navigation through these objects is performed by means of the motion of the point of view of the virtual camera on a precise path. The path is a straight line along one direction and it connects one object with the neighbouring one. The total motion time to switch from two objects has been set to 0.8 seconds.

In particular cases, navigation in a direction is impossible, since the user is watching an object at the border of the environment. Thus, the system provides a visual feedback to the user, in order to alert him/her that he cannot move towards the selected direction. The feedback is a horizontal shaking motion of the camera.

4   Gesture Interface

This section describes the definition of the gestures and the implementation of the interface in detail. In particular, it focuses on the design according to the human-based approach proposed in [15]. The objective is to provide a NUI with gestures that are easy to make from an ergonomic point of view, easy to remember and logically coupled to the functions they have to perform. Therefore, six different gestures have been designed and an algorithm to detect them has been developed. Finally, useful parameters for the algorithm have been evaluated by measuring some human movements.

4.1   Design of Gestures

The function of the six gestures is to indicate the moving direction of the virtual camera to the system. All of the gestures start from the position called *neutral* in Fig. 4a. No commands are executed while the arm is in this position. The position consists of placing the right hand in front of the shoulder, by keeping the elbow relaxed and bended.

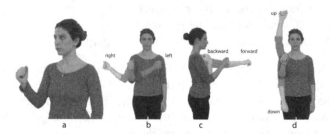

Fig. 4. The neutral position (a) and the six gestures defined for the navigation in the virtual environment (b, c and d)

The gestures involve the motion of the hand and the arm to six different positions. Abduction of the arm from the neutral position means a camera motion to the right, while an adduction on the horizontal plane means a motion to the left (Fig. 4b). Extension and contraction of the arm indicate respectively forward and backward movement (Fig. 4c). Finally, an extension of the forearm to the hip specifies a downward movement of the camera, while an upward flexion of the arm entails the camera to move above (Fig. 4d).

4.2   Gesture Detection Algorithm

The developed detection algorithm receives the position of all the user's joints and recognizes if the user is performing one of the gestures previously defined. The data coming from FAAST are elaborated in order to estimate the position of the right hand, relative to the right shoulder, and the two angles, as shown in Fig. 5. The coordinates of the hand are expressed by the following vector,

$$\overrightarrow{V_{hand}} = \begin{bmatrix} x_{hand} \\ y_{hand} \\ z_{hand} \end{bmatrix} \tag{1}$$

where x_{hand}, y_{hand} and z_{hand} correspond to the values of the coordinates in the three principal direction. Figure 5 represents also the thresholds that define the spatial limits of the neutral position. The designed gestures lie outside of these thresholds.

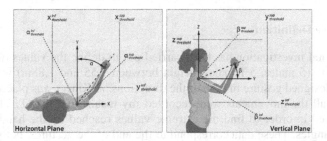

Fig. 5. Representation of the reference system used to detect the gestures. The yellow line indicates the user's skeleton while the dashed lines are the thresholds used for the detection.

Since the gestures involve the motion of the hand all the time, its position in the space according to the defined coordinate system is used for the recognition. However, these data are not completely reliable due to different arm dimension and joints mobility among the users. The two angles α and β have been taken into account in order to overcome the issue related to the dimension. The angle α is defined as the rotation of the hand around the shoulder on the horizontal plane and it is possible to calculate it by the following equation:

$$\alpha = {}^{\pi}/_{2} - atan2(x_{hand}, y_{hand}). \tag{2}$$

On the other hand, β is the rotation of the hand around the shoulder on the vertical plane. Its equation is :

$$\beta = atan2(z_{hand}, y_{hand}).$$ (3)

Once all of these measures are calculated, the algorithm detects if a user's movement corresponds to one of the gestures according to the comparison represented in the scheme in Fig 6.

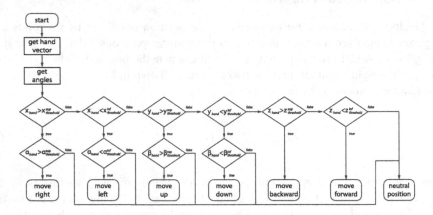

Fig. 6. The schematic representation of the detection algorithm

4.3   Gesture Definition

An experimental investigation has been carried out to define the values of the thresholds. Ten users (5 males, 5 females, height between 1.55 and 1.88m) were asked to perform the designed gesture in both of the directions. A Kinect was placed in front of the user and all the movements were recorded my means of FAAST. The measures were elaborated in order to find the extreme values reached by the hand and by the width of the angles. These data correspond to the end of the gestures, before returning to the neutral position. Each threshold corresponding to a gesture in a direction is related with these data. In particular, it is equal to the 85% of the minimum value between the peaks. Table 1 reports the values of the thresholds.

Table 1. The values of threshold

	Superior	Inferior
X	26.5 cm	-12.6 cm
Y	39.1 cm	11.0 cm
Z	28.5 cm	-32.4 cm
α	38.3 deg	-22.9 deg
β	83.6 deg	-45.5 deg

5   Case Study

This section reports a case study where the system is used in the field of furnishing. Nowadays, many e-commerce stores allow the customers to browse in large catalogues of objects, but they are limited on a planar navigation on a web-like application. Therefore, the searching activity does not differ much to the ones on a paper catalogue. The system developed makes the searching activity different to the traditional one because it is in a 3D space.

Figure 7 shows the forty-eight different objects that have been used to populate the environment. They are pieces of furniture addressed to housing and they are arranged in a virtual space according to three features. Tab. 2 gives a map of the objects. The first feature corresponds to the recommended location in the house where the object should be placed. In particular, the objects are addressed to three different places: kitchen, living room and bedroom. A vertical move of the camera in the virtual environment enables the user to switch between these three kinds of locations.

The second feature is the function of the objects. The environment is populated by furniture addressed to support the person, such as chairs and beds, to support other objects, like in case of tables, and to keep objects like a wardrobe. The user can navigate across the three functions by moving back and forward.

The last feature is the style used for designing the objects. The user can switch to different kinds of styles by moving left and right.

Fig. 7. The virtual catalogue

Table 2. The objects in the virtual space. For each object, models with different style have been arranged in the space.

		Function		
		Support people	Support objects	Keep objects
	Livingroom	Sofas	Coffe tables	Book cases
Location	Bedroom	Beds	Night tables	Wardrobe
	Kitchen	Chairs	Tables	Cupboard

As it is possible to see in Fig. 8, the user stands in front of the PowerWall and navigates the virtual catalogue by means of gestures. Once he finds the piece of furniture he wants, the user can select it by means of voice commands. In this case, a HUD appears in order to show to the screen auxiliary information, such as a brief description and also a list of further available colours (Fig. 8).

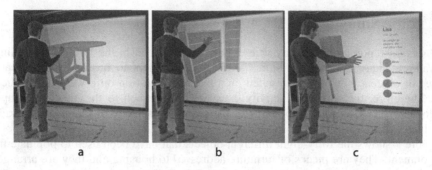

a   b   c

Fig. 8. The user during the case study

6   Discussion

The case study shows how the system can be used to navigate in a virtual environment with sorted objects by means of gestures. In particular, it reveals an approach to move across different pieces of furniture. The big advantages of this system are due to the integration of the 3D visualization and the natural interaction. The objects are organized in the space so that the user is able to search easily several of them. In a traditional desktop application for browsing information, the user sees a planar space and he can switch only from a selected object to the previous or the next one. In this case, instead, each virtual object is surrounded in all of the directions by other six. Therefore, the compact organization of the virtual items in the environment allows the user to move quickly his research towards what he is looking for. The gestures are simple to learn and it turns out the system is able to detects them precisely. The ease of gestures is given by the strict association between the user movement and the function. For these reasons, the developed system provides some benefits regards traditional approaches for browsing.

However, during the use of the system in the case study, a problem regarding the user orientation in the virtual space came out. The traditional interfaces give a clue to the user about his position between the items by means of visual feedbacks. The scrollbar usually provides this clue. The proposed system misses a graphic way to represent the user location in the 3D space and it informs the user only when he is at the last objects along a direction by means of a trembling movement.

7   Conclusion

The work in this paper describes the feasibility of a visualization and interaction system to navigate in a VR environment. The system is specifically addressed to environment in which the virtual objects are spatially organized on a three dimensional grid. The objects are arranged along the three spatial directions according to three different classifications.

The Authors believe this system can have a large use in many activities that involve searching information or items. Actually, the NUI technologies available today are spreading in many fields and can be integrated in several useful applications. In particular, the system can be easily integrated in commercial activities, in order to show products, as also demonstrated by the reported case study. The use of VR visualization and natural interactive gestures can increase the user involvement and consequently improve the user experience while seeking information.

Further studies can be carried out in this field. The Authors intend to continue investigating this kind of navigation. In particular, they want to develop new natural interaction techniques, by increasing and improving gestures. They want also to demonstrate the effectiveness of the system in other navigation contexts. Finally, comparative tests will be carried out in order to evaluate the user performances and satisfaction during the use of the system.

References

1. Jaimes, A., Sebe, N.: Multimodal human–computer interaction: A survey. Comput. Vis. Image Underst. 108, 116–134 (2007)
2. Wachs, J.P., Kölsch, M., Stern, H., Edan, Y.: Vision-based hand-gesture applications. Commun. ACM 54, 60–71 (2011)
3. Cruz-neira, C., Sandin, D.J., Defanti, T.A.: Surround-Screen Projection-Based Virtual Reality The Design and Implementation of the CAVE. In: Proceedings of the 20th Annual Conference on Computer Graphics and Interactive Techniques, pp. 135–142 (1993)
4. Bowman, D.A., McMahan, R.P., Ragan, E.D.: Questioning naturalism in 3D user interfaces. Commun. ACM 55, 78–88 (2012)
5. de Haan, G., Griffith, E.J., Post, F.H.: Using the Wii Balance Board™ as a Low-Cost VR Interaction Device. In: Proceedings of the 2008 ACM Symposium on Virtual Reality Software and Technology, pp. 289–290 (2008)
6. Moeslund, T.B., Hilton, A., Krüger, V.: A survey of advances in vision-based human motion capture and analysis. Comput. Vis. Image Underst. 104, 90–126 (2006)
7. Cabral, M.C., Morimoto, C.H., Zuffo, M.K.: On the usability of gesture interfaces in virtual reality environments. In: Proceedings of the 2005 Latin American Conference on Human-Computer Interaction, pp. 100–108 (2005)
8. Fang, Y., Chai, X., Xu, L., Wang, K.: Hand Tracking and Application in Map Navigation. In: Proceedings of the First International Conference on Internet Multimedia Computing and Service, pp. 196–200 (2009)
9. Suma, E.A., Lange, B., Rizzo, A.S., Krum, D.M., Bolas, M.: FAAST: The Flexible Action and Articulated Skeleton Toolkit. In: IEEE Virtual Reality Conference, pp. 247–248. IEEE (2011)
10. Roupé, M., Bosch-Sijtsema, P., Johansson, M.: Interactive navigation interface for Virtual Reality using the human body. Comput. Environ. Urban Syst. 43, 42–50 (2014)
11. Jeong, S., Song, T., Kwon, K., Jeon, J.W.: TV Remote Control Using Human Hand Motion Based on Optical Flow System. In: Murgante, B., Gervasi, O., Misra, S., Nedjah, N., Rocha, A.M.A.C., Taniar, D., Apduhan, B.O. (eds.) ICCSA 2012, Part III. LNCS, vol. 7335, pp. 311–323. Springer, Heidelberg (2012)

12. Wachs, J.P., Stern, H.I., Edan, Y., Gillam, M., Handler, J., Feied, C., Smith, M.: A Gesture-based Tool for Sterile Browsing of Radiology Images. J. Am. Med. Informatics Assoc. 15, 321–323 (2008)
13. Chai, X., Fang, Y., Wang, K.: Robust hand gesture analysis and application in gallery browsing. In: IEEE International Conference on Multimedia and Expo, pp. 938–941 (2009)
14. Ii, R.M.T., Hudson, T.C., Seeger, A., Weber, H., Juliano, J., Helser, A.T.: VRPNA Device-Independent, Network-Transparent VR Peripheral System. In: Proceedings of the ACM Symposium on Virtual Reality Software and Technology, pp. 55–61 (2001)
15. Nielsen, M., Störring, M., Moeslund, T.B., Granum, E.: A procedure for developing intuitive and ergonomic gesture interfaces for HCI. In: Camurri, A., Volpe, G. (eds.) GW 2003. LNCS (LNAI), vol. 2915, pp. 409–420. Springer, Heidelberg (2004)

Requirements for Virtualization of AR Displays within VR Environments

Erik Steindecker, Ralph Stelzer, and Bernhard Saske

Technische Universität Dresden, Faculty of Mechanical Engineering, Chair of Engineering
Design and CAD, Dresden, Germany
{ralph.stelzer,erik.steindecker,bernhard.saske}@tu-dresden.de

Abstract. Everybody has been talking about new emerging products in augmented reality (AR) and their potential to enhance our daily life and work. The AR technology has been around for quite a while and various use cases have been thought and tested. Clearly, the new AR Systems (e.g. Vuzix m100, Google Glasses) will bring its use to a new level. For planning, designing and reviewing of innovative AR systems and their application, virtual reality (VR) technology can be supportive. Virtual prototypes of AR Systems can be expired and evaluated within a VR environment (e.g. CAVE).

This paper proposes the virtualization of AR displays within VR environments and discusses requirements. A user study investigates the necessary pixel density for the legibility of a virtual display in order to verify the significance of guidelines given by ISO 9241-300. Furthermore, equations examine the suitability of various VR systems for display virtualization within VR environments. This will enable reviews of various display systems in a virtual manner.

Keywords: Virtual Reality, Augmented Reality, Virtualization, Display, User Study.

1 Introduction

Augmented reality (AR) is a technology, which can be apply to support technicians in their work of operating and maintaining technical products by the depiction of instructions, status and warnings through mobile devices (e.g. handhelds, tablets, head-mounted displays) [1, 2]. The necessary documents and dialogs should be planned, designed and reviewed within the product development phase in order to provide high-quality manuals at the time of product release. The use of AR technology in virtual reality (VR) [3] is a promising approach, which ensures the quality of AR instructions and enables service training in advance.

The goal of the project "Virtualization of AR systems for maintenance planning in immersive environments", founded by the German Research Foundation (DFG), is to integrate AR technology into the product development process seamlessly. Previous research has investigated the possible combination of AR technology and VR technology (AVR) for the review of AR instruction by developing the prototypes displayed by Fig 1. Fig 1-1 shows AR information being depicted by an AR Display

R. Shumaker and S. Lackey (Eds.): VAMR 2014, Part I, LNCS 8525, pp. 105–116, 2014.

in a VR environment (VRE) [4]. This allows the evaluation of an actual AR System and its dialogs. Another multi-display approach is the use of a tracked mobile device (e.g. tablet, see Fig 1-2) within a VR system [5, 6] enable a high fidelity view into a VRE.

This paper focuses on the possible virtualization of an AR display within a VRE. This virtualization would enable the enhancement of the virtual prototypes by depicting documents and dialogs for maintenance directly within the VRE (see Fig 1-3). The design and review can be achieved without the use of physical AR systems. Within a narrow time frame, issues can be identified and solved in early development stages. Furthermore, a huge variety of AR systems can be tested and even not yet existing/available systems can be evaluated.

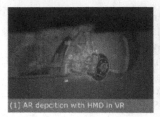

(1) AR depiction with HMD in VR   (2) AR depiction with tablet in VR   (3) AR depiction by VR

Fig. 1. Tree different approaches to bring AR into VREs

2   Investigation of Virtual Displays in VR Environments

According to Azuma [7], an AR system consists of the following functional units: controller, computer and presenter. Since the design of documents and dialogs is primarily visual, the AR display plays an unique role as a presenter. In principle displays are called virtual when the image plane is shifted by optical or holographical system. This technique is used for near-to-eye micro displays (e.g. HMDs) to generate a virtual image, where the perceived distance is larger than the real distance of the micro display. In addition, the representation of an AR display within a VE can be termed a virtual display as well. For this representation the content legibility is fundamentally. The depiction of legible signs, symbols, texts and illustrations essentially depends on the applied VR system. Influencing attributes such as contrast, brightness, viewing distance, pixel density and character properties are described and standardized in ISO 9241-300 [8]. Since the applied rules are based on requirements for electrical visual displays, it is unclear whether the calculated values are applicable for a virtual display within VRE or not.

Essentially, the achievable fidelity of a display depends on its specifications (e.g. contrast, brightness and pixel density). For virtual displays, contrast and brightness are attributes directly determined by the VR system. However, the pixel density of a virtual display depends on the pixel density of the VR system and also on the operator's position in the VR system. Consequently, the AR content is depicted with a altering pixel density, resulting in various virtual display qualities (see Fig 2).

The viewing distance is the distance (d) between the point of sight and a display. In case of virtual displays there are two viewing distances to be considered:

- d_{RD} defines the distance to the physical screen of the VR system.
- d_{VD} is the distance between point of sight and virtual display.

If d_{RD} and d_{VD} are equal, the pixel densities are corresponding (d_{RD1} in Fig. 2). Since the viewing distance (d_{VD}) remains constant (e.g. virtualization of HMDs), a larger screen area is used for depicting the virtual display by increasing the distance to the VR screen (d_{RD}). Therefore the achieved pixel density of the virtual display increases (d_{RD2} and d_{RD3} in Fig. 2).

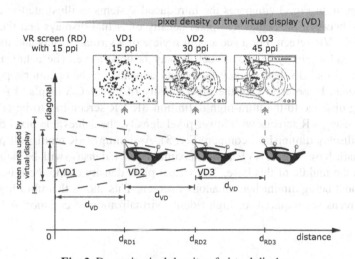

Fig. 2. Dynamic pixel density of virtual displays

In principle the pixel density of a display (ppi_{RD}) is calculated by the quotient of the display height/width and its resolution. However as presented in the graph above, the dynamic pixel density of a virtual display (ppi_{VD}) is defined by the ratio of the current viewing distance to VR screen (d_{RD}) and the specific viewing distance of the virtual display (d_{VD}) is multiplied by the actual pixel density of the VR system (ppi_{RD}):

$$ppi_{VD} := ppi_{RD} * \frac{d_{RD}}{d_{VD}} \tag{1}$$

To support the upcoming investigations, introduces examples of AR and VR systems with their specifications. The four VR systems distinguish in their resolution, but not in their dimension, resulting in different pixel densities. The dimension of the VR projection corresponds to the CAVE available at our facility. The SVGA AR display is based on the specification of the Nomad ND2000 [9], also available at our facility. A system with an higher SXGA resolution is assumed to the second AR display.

Table 1. Illustrative AR systems and VR systems

VR screen	Screen diagonal	Pixel density	Viewing distance
1.6K	4500 mm	11,29 ppi	< 3600 mm
2K	4500 mm	14,45 ppi	< 3600 mm
4K	4500 mm	28,90 ppi	< 3600 mm
8K	4500 mm	57,80 ppi	< 3600 mm
AR Display	Screen diagonal	Pixel density	Viewing distance
SVGA	200 mm	127,00 ppi	400 mm
SXGA	200 mm	203,20 ppi	400 mm

The diagram in Fig. 3 compares the introduced systems to illustrate the described dependence between the achievable pixel density of virtual displays and the viewing distance to the VR screen. For a successful review of a virtual display and its content, the quality and legibility of the virtual display is imperative. The achievable pixel density of a virtual display is a key factor and depends on the operator's position in the VR system. In order to gain the pixel density of the SVGA display of ND2000, the viewing distance to the ultra-high definition 8K VR screen has to be at least 0,9 meters. By using VR screens with lower pixel density, the achievable pixel density of the virtual display diminishes (compare Fig. 3). Assuming a 4K multi wall projection with a square base (e.g. CAVE), the maximum pixel density will be achieved by standing in the middle of this base. The virtual pixel density cannot be raised on one screen without being diminished on another screen. This shows that ultra-high definition VR screens are required for high fidelity virtualization of common AR displays in a VRE.

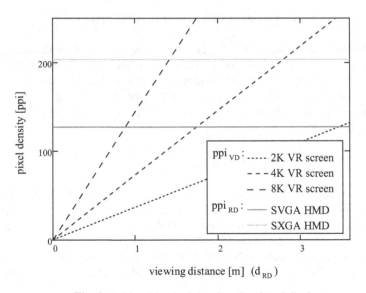

Fig. 3. Achievable pixel density of a virtual display

Illustrations consist of graphics, symbols and text and are presented within VRE by the virtual display. A low pixel density reduces the fidelity of the display. For legibility of single characters a guidance is provided by ISO 9241-300. Considering this the width to height ratio of the character matrix has to be at least 7 by 9 pixels to ensure the legibility. Another requirement for legibility is a character subtense of at least 11 minutes of arc (rms). The chosen character size in the illustration determines the necessary pixel density of the virtual display to guarantee the legibility of the depiction. Taking into account the character matrix requirement, an equation can be introduced to calculate the necessary pixel density of the virtual display (ppiVD), ensuring the legibility of a certain character size within a virtualized AR display:

$$ppi_{VD} := \frac{px_h * d_{VD}}{\frac{inch}{72} * pt * ppi_{RD}} \tag{2}$$

This ensures the legibility of a certain character size within a virtualized AR display. For the calculation of $ppi_{VD,}$ the constant viewing distance of the virtual display (d_{VD}), the pixel density of the VR system (ppi_{RD}) and the character height (pt) must be given. The character height in pica point can be converted into the metric system by the multiplication with 1/72 inch [10]. In correlation with ISO 9241-300, the height of the character matrix (px_h) is set to 9 pixels.

Considering the CAVE in our facility with 1600 by 1200 pixels per screen and the virtualization of a Nomad ND2000 (), the following results appear for various character subtenses. The viewing distance (d_{RD}) is calculated by using equation (1):

Table 2. Calculated minimum viewing distance to the VR screen for various character subtense

Parameters				Results		
min. character matrix	pixel density (ppi$_{RD}$)	viewing distance (d$_{VD}$)	character height (pt)	character subtense	pixel density (ppi$_{VD}$)	viewing distance (d$_{RD}$)
9 px	11,29 ppi	400 mm	22 pt 7,46 mm	47,3'	29,46 ppi	1,04 m
			16 pt 5,64 mm	34,4'	40,50 ppi	1,44 m
			11 pt 3,88 mm	23,6'	58,91 ppi	2,09 m

Larger character subtenses allow a shorter viewing distance to the VR screen. By virtualizing the Nomad ND2000 in our CAVE and by depicting a character height of 16 pt, the viewing distance to the VR screen as to be at least 1,44 meter ensures legibility. This distance allows a movement range of 0,36 meter relative to the CAVE center, considering the width of the CAVE, which is 3,6 meter. Within this area the legibility is guaranteed. Provided that all parameter stay the same, the movement area escalates as the VR screen resolution increases.

3   User Study

Since the calculation is based on ISO 9241 for electrical optical displays, it will be investigated whether equation (2) can be applied to the virtualization of displays. A user study aims to clarify this question using the setup described in Table 2.

As former studies [11–13] have shown, the stereoscopic view is the most unfavorable for legible depiction of content. So the eye charts used for the study are depicted in stereoscopic manner. Eye charts containing different sized single characters, word groups or illustrations, are used to determine the necessary viewing distance for legibility. The eye charts are depicted through a virtual display into the participant's field of vision. The parameters of the virtual display correspond to the Nomad ND2000, which is virtualized within our CAVE. Fig. 4 shows a participant during the experiment observing a chart in our CAVE.

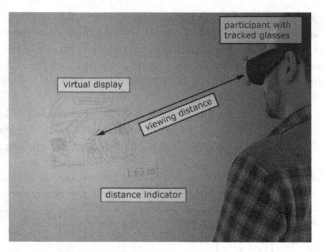

Fig. 4. Setup of the experiment

The chart is a texture mapped on a plane rendered in an independent viewport. Since this viewport does not swap the color buffer but only the depth buffer of the graphic renderer, all mapped textures will overlay the VRE depicted by the screen viewport. This effect of virtual information overlaying other objects emulates the behavior of information depicted through an AR display. While the tracked participant is moving through the CAVE, the relative position and orientation to the virtual display and its information does not change. The chart's content always appear to be fixed 400 mm in front of her/him. Considering that the screen area facilitated by the virtual display fluctuates depending on the participant's position in the CAVE, one may conclude that the   pixel density (for depicting the chart information) will also vary . The label below the virtual display indicates the current viewing distance to the VR screen. The distance is calculated by the tracked position of the participant and the known dimensions of the CAVE. A larger viewing distance to the screen results in a higher pixel density. For the experiment different combinations of charts and viewing distances are investigated. The used charts are static slides without animations.

The experiment in the CAVE can be divided in 4 parts:

- PRT0: Participant moves freely to get an idea of virtual display and its behavior,
- PRT1: Validate the calculated viewing distance for legibility with an eye chart,
- PRT2: Determine the individual viewing distance for legibility with an eye chart,
- PRT3: Validate and estimate the legibility of an illustration for the calculated viewing distance.

A total of 20 people aged between 20 and 34 years (avg. 23 years old) participated in the experiment and just 20 % of them were females. Most of the participants are fifth semester students of mechanical engineering and had not yet experienced a CAVE. During the 30 minutes of experiment, participants observe a virtual display and its content depicted into their vision. In order to guarantee sufficient eyesight for legibility under normal conditions, all participants had to perform a standard vision test which has shown the following outcomes:

35% had a weak but corrected vision; all participants passed the test with 100 % or more sight (normal or better vision); just one participant had an impair stereo vision (50') and however it remains unclear if or how this condition has an impact on his ability to read in VREs, his results were considered and not separated from the other participant´s results.

3.1   Experiment PRT0

At the beginning (**PRT0**) of the experiment the participant can move freely in the CAVE to get a feeling for how the virtual display is depicted and behaves. In order to demonstrate the dependency between viewing distance and legibility, participants are asked to look normal to screen and to step close (~0.5 meters) to the VR screen of the CAVE. The virtual display depicts some characters with a height of 22 pt. Closely to the screen the participant is not able to read the characters. Then he steps further away slowly until the distance is about 1 meter. At a determined distance she/he is able to recognize and to read the characters and understand the basic issue, which was addressed.

3.2   Experiment PRT1

After completing the introduction, the main experiment starts. In the first part, (**PRT1**) the calculated viewing distance for legibility is validated (compare Table 2). To start, the participant looks straight and keeps a viewing distance of 1,44 meters to the VR screen. The first sequence of charts shows lines with single characters or word groups of 16 pt height. All charts in this experiment used the font Verdana, optimized for digital depiction and natively supported by various OS. The participant tries to read each sequence. Fig. 5 shows two complete sequences. The second sequence of charts also shows single characters and word groups with a height of 11 pt. As represented by Table 2, the viewing distance is 2,09 meters.

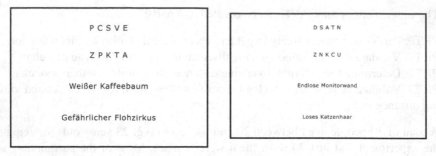

Fig. 5. Chart examples for 16 pt (left) and 11 pt (right)

Considering that all participants were able to read each sequence, we can generally assume that the guidance of ISO 9241-300 may be applied to virtual displays. The diversity of the individual viewing distance for legibility remains unclear up to this point.

3.3   Experiment PRT2

The next part (**PRT2**) addresses the individual viewing distance for legibility. In this second phase, the participant stands 1 meter away from the VR screen and looks straight to it. Once again, sequences of single characters or word groups are depicted. Three different types are distinguished:

1. Single upper characters (*ABC* type)
2. Single lower characters (*abc* type)
3. Word groups (*txt* type)

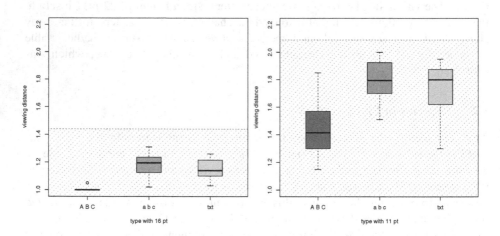

Fig. 6. Results for individual viewing distance (PRT2)

For each of these types, the participant increases the viewing distance step by step until he/she can read the first line of the sequence. In order to ensure the legibility at this point, additional lines of the same type are depicted. If the participant is unable to read the additional line, the viewing distance is increased. The described procedure is made for both character sizes 16 and 11 pt of each of the types separately. The determined viewing distances (for 16 and 11 pt) are shown in Fig. 6.

Over all, the determined viewing distances are below their expected value of 1,44 meters for 16 pt and 2,09 meters for 11 pt (compare Table 2). The *abc* type was the most difficult to read, since less pixels were available for depiction in comparison to *ABC* type. This fact has lead the median of the viewing distance for *abc* type to be higher in comparison to the other tested types.

Despite the presence of lower characters the legibility of the *txt* type is better than the legibility of *abc* type. This is caused by the contextual support of the words and word groups.

The upper characters (*ABC* type) are legible within a smaller distance than the other types, which is not surprising. Regarding the ISO 9241, the character matrix must be at least 5 by 7 pixels in order to ensure the legibility of alphanumeric and upper characters. Based on this assumption the calculated viewing distance for this type is 1,12 meters (16 pt) and 1,62 meters (11 pt). Most of the participants can identify the *ABC* type with 16 pt already at the initial distance of 1,0 meter. Only one participant exceeds the calculated viewing distance.

For a stereoscopic setup the legibility depends also on the personal ability to focus the virtual display plane properly. This plane appears distant form the real display (VR screen) and can cause an ambiguous reception. Therefore the charts were provided with a frame to support proper focus. Furthermore the proper focus can be supported by placing a hand near the virtual display plane. With further distance it is harder to focus properly. If the participant's focus is not proper, the chart appears blurry and it is illegible. For this reason the distance variation for the chart with 11 pt is larger.

3.4   Experiment PRT3

At this point there is still no statement on the quality of the depiction and how well the participants can read the content following the guidance of ISO 9241. At the last part (**PRT3**) of the experiment the participants rate the legibility of an illustration including text and symbols. The viewing distance is once again 1,44 meters. The different elements are displayed in the following order: text field, edge image, highlighted image elements, symbols and arrows. When a new element is displayed, the participant is expected to describe the change, its content and rate its legibility. The illustration in Fig. 7 shows the complete chart with all elements.

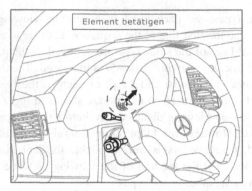

Fig. 7. Chart with illustration and additional elements

All elements were correctly identified by the participants. For the assessment of the legibility, a scale of 1 to 6 was applied (scale see Fig. 8). Most participants have perceived the text field with a character size of 16 pt as "*well legible*" (2). Only one of the participants has rated the text field with a grade of "*legible*" (3). The assessment of the graphic shows similar results. Just one participant has rated the legibility as "*very well*" (1). The rest of them has perceived the graphic as "*well legible*" (2). A larger variation of the assessments has occurred in the case of the symbol and the arrow. Some of the participants described the symbol and the arrow as legible, where others described the legibility as well or even very well. Fact is that with the available pixel density of 40,50 ppi, the hand symbol (as illustrated in Fig. 7) can be perceived but not all of its features. Some participants were not able to detect the arrow head. The average grade for the symbol was 2,3 and for the arrow 2,6. In a situation where the operator is acquainted with the symbol library, the perception and identification of symbols are possible even if they are not depicted in every detail.

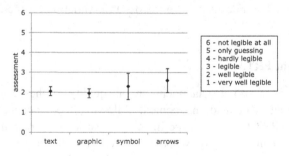

Fig. 8. Results for legibility of the illustration (PRT3)

4   Conclusion

Essentially, the user study has shown that the legible depiction of AR displays in VREs is possible. In order to guaranty legibility, the guidance of ISO 9241 has to be considered. This paper has investigated the relationship between pixel density and legibility for virtualization of displays and its dynamic behavior. Besides the pixel density, the motion blur and display parameters (e.g. contrast, brightness and response time) also influence the legibility but have not been further discussed in this paper.

The introduced equations may be used to estimate the pixel density for the virtualization of a display by a VR system. For the virtualization of state-of-the-art AR displays with full pixel density, ultra-high definition VR screens with at least 8K are required. VR screens with 4K and less resolution can still provide the legibility of virtualized displays, although with less details. Besides the evaluated CAVE System, other systems such as video glass and powerwall can be applied. The requirements described by this paper apply to these systems as well. Another alternative to enable virtualization of displays with low definition screens is to adopt a multi-display approach by employing tracked high definition mobile devices to depict high fidelity content in low definition VR systems.

The paper has mainly described the virtualization of head mounted displays, however the equations may also be used to estimate the achievable pixel density of a virtualized stationary display (e.g. dashboard, control panel). In contrast to head mounted displays, the viewing distance between this display and the operator may change. The achievable pixel density depends on the current position of the operator and also on the fixed position of the display in the VRE. For a valuable estimation, the achievable pixel density has to be calculated for each crucial position of the design review.

For full comprehension of the visual effects for virtualization, further influential display parameters for legibility shall be investigated (e.g. contrast, brightness, response time). For most immersive planning, designing and reviewing processes, the complete AR system must be modeled in VREs. Therefore all components and their relations to each other must be mapped. It is not necessary that all components are virtualized but connected. These tasks were not discussed in this paper, but investigated as part of the project "Virtualization of AR systems for maintenance planning in immersive environments".

Acknowledgments. The authors gratefully acknowledge the German Research Foundation (DFG) for funding this research (grand STE1451/12-1). Furthermore, the authors acknowledge the Mercedes-Benz Commercial Vehicles Division of the Daimler AG for providing product data and prototypes for the creation of the test scenario. The support of the Daimler colleagues Gregor Tauscher and Tea-Soo Kim (Virtual Reality Support Center) was particularly greatly appreciated.

References

1. Henderson, S., Feiner, S.: Exploring the benefits of augmented reality documentation for maintenance and repair. IEEE Trans. on Vis. Comput. Graph. 17, 1355–1368 (2011)
2. Saske, B.: Augmented Reality in der Instandhaltung: Konzept zur effizienten Nutzung und Integration in das Product Lifecycle Management

3. Stelzer, R., Steindecker, E., Saske, B., Lässig, S.: Augmented Reality Based Maintenance within Virtual Environments. Presented at the Proceedings of the 11th Biennial Conference on Engineering Systems Design and Analysis, Nantes (July 2012)
4. Stelzer, R., Steindecker, E., Saske, B.: AR-Systeme für die Wartungsplanung in immersiven Umgebungen. In: 11. Paderborner Workshop: Augmented & Virtual Reality in der Produktentstehung, pp. 237–250. HNI-Verlagsschriftenreihe, Parderborn (2013)
5. Bader, T.: Multimodale Interaktion in Multi-Display-Umgebungen. KIT Scientific Publishing (2011)
6. Sakurai, S., Itoh, Y., Kitamura, Y., Nacenta, M.A., Yamaguchi, T., Subramanian, S., Kishino, F.: A middleware for seamless use of multiple displays. In: Graham, T.C.N. (ed.) DSV-IS 2008. LNCS, vol. 5136, pp. 252–266. Springer, Heidelberg (2008)
7. Azuma, R.: A Survey of Augmented Reality. Presence 6, 355–385 (1997)
8. ISO 9241-300, Ergonomics of human-system interaction – Part 300: Introduction to electronic visual display requirements (2008)
9. NOMAD Expert Technician System: Configuration & Specification. Microvision Inc., Bothell (2004)
10. DIN 16507-2, Printing technology - Type sizes - Part 2: Digital typesetting and related techniques (2008)
11. Dittrich, E., Brandenburg, S., Beckmann-Dobrev, B.: Legibility of Letters in Reality, 2D and 3D Projection. In: Shumaker, R. (ed.) VAMR 2013, Part I. LNCS, vol. 8021, pp. 149–158. Springer, Heidelberg (2013)
12. Gaggioli, A., Breinlng, R.: Perception and cognition in immersive Virtual Reality. Commun. Virtual Technol. Identity Community Technol. Commun. Age. 1, 71 (2001)
13. Wann, J.P., Rushton, S., Mon-Williams, M.: Natural problems for stereoscopic depth perception in virtual environments. Vision Res. 35, 2731–2736 (1995)

Robot Behavior for Enhanced Human Performance and Workload

Grace Teo and Lauren Reinerman-Jones

Institute for Simulation and Training, University of Central Florida,
3100, Technology Parkway, Orlando, FL 32826
{gteo,lreinerm}@ist.ucf.edu

Abstract. Advancements in technology in the field of robotics have made it necessary to determine integration and use for these in civilian tasks and military missions. Currently, literature is limited on robot employment in tasks and missions, and few taxonomies exist that guide understanding of robot functionality. As robots acquire more capabilities and functions, they will likely be working more closely with humans in human-robot teams. In order to better utilize and design robots that enhance performance in such teams, a better understanding of what robots can do and the impact of these behaviors on the human operator/teammate is needed.

Keywords: Human-robot teaming, Robot behavior, Performance, Workload.

1 Introduction

In recent years, robots have been deployed in more areas than before. Although robots are used for a variety of reasons ranging from being able to perform tasks that are impossible for humans to accomplish, undertaking tasks that endanger human lives, and being more cost effective to deploy, one of the most often-cited reason for their use is that they can enhance human performance and relieve workload.

2 Robots in Context

2.1 Military

The military uses robots to carry out tasks that are too difficult or dangerous for soldiers. For instance, *Daksh* is a teleoperated military robot that clears improvised explosive devices. It can maneuver in various environments, including climbing stairs, and has an X-ray device on board to scan objects. The *MARCbot* is a military robot that inspects suspicious objects. It has a camera that is elevated in a post that enables it to look behind doors. It can operate for 6 hours on a full battery charge and soldiers have used it in the Iraq to detect hazardous objects. On the other hand, the *Goalkeeper* from the Netherlands helps defend military assets by tracking incoming missiles with its autocannon and advanced radar in its close-in weapons system. Another robot with

R. Shumaker and S. Lackey (Eds.): VAMR 2014, Part I, LNCS 8525, pp. 117–128, 2014.

a similar defence function is the *Guardium*, an Israeli unmanned security robot that guards and attacks any trespassers with its lethal and less-lethal weaponry. The *Pack-Bot* series is a set of robots that can be fitted with particular kits that allow them to perform various tasks ranging from identifying, disarming and disposing IEDs, to detecting snipers through localizing gunshots from azimuth, elevation and range, to collecting air samples in order to detect chemical and radiological agents. *PackBots* were the first robots deployed to the Fukushima nuclear disaster site. Likewise, the *TALON* robots are used for a variety of tasks depending on the sensor or weapon modules that they are fitted with. They were used in Bosnia to safely remove and dispose of live grenades, and deployed in search and recovery missions, such as that in Ground Zero after the September 11 attack on the World Trade Center ("Current Use of Military Robots," 2014).

2.2   Healthcare

Robots have also been used in the medical field. With the *da Vinci* surgical assistant robot, surgeons have performed minimally invasive delicate surgeries with the help of its high-definition 3D vision system and robot arms with "wrists" that are able to make smaller, more precise movements because they bend and rotate far more than the human wrist. To date, the *da Vinci* has helped with approximately 1.5 million various surgical procedures worldwide (da Vinci Surgery, 2013). On the other hand, other robots make surgeries unnecessary. The *Magnetic Microbots*, developed in Switzerland, are each about the width of a strand of human hair. They are maneuvered and controlled with great precision by a series of electromagnetic coils, and have been used to treat a type of blindness that traditionally requires surgery (Liszewski, 2013). *Magnetic Microbots* have also been used to remove plaque from patients' arteries, as well as in disease screening, and in the treatment of cancer (Martel, 2012). Another robot that is used directly in therapy is the *Walk Training Assist* robot developed by *Toyota*. Attached to the patient's paralyzed leg, it helps patients walk and balance through a number of motion detectors and supports the patient as he moves to walk. On the contrary, other robots in healthcare are "service robots" that perform tasks of caregivers. For example, the *Bestic Arm* robot is fitted with a spoon on the end and helps patients who are unable to move their arms or hands to eat without requiring help, and the *Aethon TUG* and *RobotCourier* are both robots that move through hospital corridors, elevators and wards to deliver medication on schedule, or lab results and bed linen. There are claims that they are able to do the work of three full-time hospital staff, and yet cost less than one. Other robots like the *Vasteras Giraff* are equipped with a camera, a monitor, and a two-way video call system that enable doctors in hospitals to monitor and communicate with their elderly patients at home. In contrast, the *CosmoBot*, is used in therapy for developmentally disabled children. *CosmoBot's* cartoon-like appearance helps the child patient to warm up to it so that it is able to collect data on the child's performance, allowing the therapist to evaluate progress. (McNickle, 2013).

2.3 Manufacturing/Domestic Applications

In the manufacturing industry, robots boost productivity, as they are able to manipulate materials and objects in assembly lines with great precision and speed. Australia's *Drake Trailers* saw a 60% increase in productivity due to the inclusion of a welding robot (ABB Australia, 2010), and the *Unimate* robot, that is used to pour liquid metal into die casts and weld auto bodies, has improved processes in the manufacture of automobiles at General Motors (Lamb, 2010). Another robot that performs mechanical tasks with high precision and speed is the *Selective Compliance Assembly Robot Arm or Selective Compliance Articulated Robot Arm (SCARA)*, which has "arm" joints that enable it to move deftly in and out of confined spaces to install delicate and tiny components (Kuka, 2013). More recently, in addition to performing different repetitive tasks, industrial robots have developed to work more closely with humans. For instance, *Baxter* the robot is a human sized, two-armed robot with an animated face. Unlike its predecessors, it does not come pre-loaded with programs that direct it to operate. Instead, through a series of prompts, the robot can be "taught" to perform certain tasks by moving its arms in the desired motion and having it "memorize" the movements. Equipped with a range of cameras and sensors, *Baxter* also has a degree of "behavior-based common sense" and is capable of sensing and adapting to its task and environment (Guizzo & Ackerman, 2012).

Robots are also used as domestic help both indoors and outdoors. The *Roomba*, vacuums the carpet, while the *iRobot Scooba 230* washes the floor. Both are able to navigate around the house and are relatively small in size, allowing them to clean in tight spaces and under furniture. Outdoor robots like the *LawnBott LB3510* and *Husqvarna Automower 230 ACX* are able to mow uneven lawns and at an incline, and the latter is also equipped with an antitheft alarm (Swan Robotics, 2014). Others, like *Jazz Security*, are security robots that are outfitted with night-vision capable wide-angle cameras that shoot videos and sensors that detect motion on the grounds. The robots would also alert the house owner of activities on the suspicious activity on the property. This concept of patrolling has been extended to telepresence. The *Jazz Connect* is a robot that can be stationed at home while its operator is away. It allows the operator to move around the house and communicate with the people present as though he/she were at home. This application permits caregivers to check on their stay-in patients or parents to check on their children while at work (Aki, 2012).

2.4 Entertainment

Robots have also been developed for recreational purposes. They may take the form of a pet, like a dog (e.g. *Poo-Chi* or *Aibo*), or guinea pig (e.g. *Gupi*). Some are interactive and can perform various tasks and tricks on command like *Teksta*, the robot dog that does backflips and wags its tail when its name is called, expresses emotions through its eyes, and responds to touch. Other robots serve as art pieces and installations (Bubblews, 2013). For instance, *Paparazzi Bots* were developed as a statement against modern culture's obsession with images of ourselves and celebrities. The robots, which are about the height of a human and move at human speed, are outfitted with a range of cameras, actuators and sensors, and behave like paparazzi, moving among people capturing photographs of people and making them accessible to the world (Rinaldo, n.d.). Furthermore, there is *ARTI,* an interactive robot driven by artificial intelligence that functions like a museum curator as well as exhibit. It is capable of recognizing faces and understanding speech, and teaches museum guests about the history and exhibits of the Intel Museum (West, 2008).

In all these applications, robots display a variety of behaviors, befitting of their intended function. However, it is important to understand how these behaviors affect the human, particularly in enhancing performance and reducing workload and stress. This calls for an understanding of the stages involved in information processing and performing tasks.

3   Relating Robot Behaviors to Human Information Processing

In the attempt to understand how automation may help enhance performance and reduce workload, Parasuraman, Sheridan and Wickens (2000), proposed that automation can support the human in four primary areas: (i) information acquisition, (ii) information analysis, (iii) decision selection, and (iv) action implementation. This classification of tasks was based on a simple four-stage model of human information processing (Parasuraman et al., 2000).

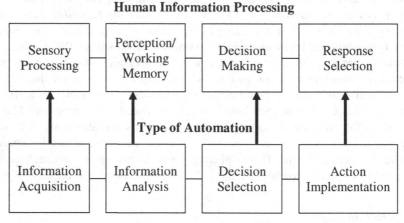

Fig. 1. Simple four-stage model of human information processing and types of automation. Adapted from Parasuraman, Sheridan, and Wickens (2000).

The framework provides a way to classify factors and dimensions that impact performance and workload in both human-computer and human-robot systems For example, researchers have identified taxonomic elements that contribute to usability and user satisfaction in human-computer systems that include interface design, input/output devices, learnability, perceptual factors, memory load required, and perceived usefulness (e.g. Çalişir & Çalişir, 2004). Likewise, from reviewing multiple studies, Prewett et al. (2010) proposed several guiding principles and propositions for reducing operator workload in human-robot interaction. These include the type of visual display, number of multimodal displays/cues, amount of system delay, and environmental complexity, and can be traced to the cognitive processes they affect, attesting to the value of such a framework. In addition, a taxonomy of human-robot interaction proposed by Yanco and Drury (2002; 2004) included factors that relate more to the task at hand, as well as factors that drive the human-robot interaction. Their list comprised task type, task criticality, robot form/morphology, ratio of humans to robot, composition of robot teams, level of shared interaction among teams, interaction roles, type of physical interaction between human and robot, decision support for operators, time/space relationship between human and robot, and level of autonomy of robot.

These factors and taxonomic dimensions can be mapped onto the information processing stages that they impact. For instance, number of displays, camera type, lags in system visual image processing mostly affects information acquisition, while the number of robots controlled and ratio of humans to robots impact more information processing stages, and potentially have more influence on workload, performance and stress. Such an approach to understanding robot behaviors would enable developers of automation to understand the human cognitive processes that their automation supports, and how the automation affects performance and workload. This would facilitate development of robots that work and collaborate better with humans, thereby increasing the possibility that robots would be able to team effectively with humans in the near future.

4   Next Generation Robots: Robots That Team with Humans

In 2013, the Defense Advances Research Projects Agency (DARPA) acknowledged that presently, robots operate mostly in controlled and well-defined environments, doing simple, repetitive tasks as they require too many step-by-step commands. To be effective in the unpredictable real world, the robots of the future should operate in novel situations without requiring extensive reprogramming and should still be able to operate even when communications with the human are delayed or interrupted. This entails robots having "task-level" autonomy, as opposed to being teleoperated (DRC, 2013). Such capabilities would also render robots more able to work more closely and team with humans. This vision of robots was also echoed in a recent announcement that the National Science Foundation (NSF), in partnership with the National Institutes of Health (NIH), U.S. Department of Agriculture (USDA) and the National Aeronautics and Space Administration (NASA), has made new investments totaling approximately \$38 million for the development and use of robots that are able to work collaboratively with humans to enhance human capabilities, performance, and safety (R&D, 2013).

If human-robot teaming is to be the goal in the coming decades, then understanding the influence of robots on humans is imperative. In developing a framework for robot behaviors in human-robot teams, we draw upon theories from team research, including theories of team roles and social support.

5   Review of Related Team Research

5.1   Team Roles and Functions/Behavior

A team differs from a social group in that all teams are formed to achieve certain goals or to perform a task. Belbin (2013) proposed that teams can be more productive, high-performing, and team members can be more self-aware and personally effective when there is an understanding of the strengths and weaknesses of each member. He proposed that there are nine team roles, and each fall into one of three categories; (i) action-oriented roles, (ii) people-oriented roles, and (iii) thought-oriented roles. Under the action-oriented roles, there is the *Shaper*, who challenges the team to improve and move forward, the *Implementer*, who puts ideas into action and is well-organized, and the *Completer/Finisher*, who works to ensure that the team completes the task in a thorough, timely manner. The people-oriented roles include the *Coordinator*, who acts as a chairperson, delegating and clarifying goals, and promoting decision-making, the *Team Worker,* who, being a good listener, works to resolve social problems and encourages cooperation, and the *Resource Investigator*, who explores outside opportunities and develops contacts that can help the project. Under the thought-oriented roles, there is the *Plant*, who presents new ideas and approaches, the *Monitor-Evaluator*, who analyzes the options, and the *Specialist*, who provides specialized skills (Belbin, 1981; 2013).

Some team roles (i.e. action-oriented roles) serve to move the team towards achieving its goals, while other roles are more focused on fostering relationships and communication that facilitates goal-attainment (i.e. people-oriented roles). On the other hand, some team roles that encourage the team to generate new ideas, self-evaluate, and examine its strategy and approach in reaching the goals (i.e. thought-oriented roles).

The main concept behind the various team roles is that there are different sets of behaviors found in an effective team (Belbin, 1981; 2013). Behaviors may pertain directly to the task/goal (e.g. clarifying goals or generating new ideas) or indirectly to the task/goal (e.g. communicative and self-evaluate behaviors).

5.2   Types of Support

Apart from team roles, there are theories that address various types of help or support behaviors. House (1981) postulates that there are four basic types of support that members of a social network may offer each other: (i) informational support, (ii) instrumental support, (iii) emotional support, and (iv) appraisal support. Informational support refers to the provision of suggestions and information that the individual in need can use to address the problem faced, while instrumental support involves the giving of tangible aid and services that directly help the individual in need. On the other hand, emotional support refers to the sharing of emotions and provision of empathy, love and caring, while appraisal support refers to the provision of constructive feedback and affirmation for the individual's self-evaluation. These four types of support may broadly be classified as (i) direct, and (ii) indirect support. Informational and instrumental support pertain directly to need or problem encountered, while emotional and appraisal support may help the individual cope of the problem better, but do not address the problem directly.

Applying this notion to a human-robot team, it is then possible to conceptualize potential robot behaviors as being directly or indirectly aiding the human.

5.3   Structure in Teams

Drawing on the language of management and industrial psychology, automation and HCI researchers have proposed theories that incorporate the relationships and roles of supervisor, peer and subordinate. In his work on automation, Sheridan (1992) describes five generic supervisory functions that comprise planning the task, programming the computer, monitoring the automation's actions to detect failure, intervening with a new goal or taking over control in the event of failure, and learning from experience. Furthermore, a theory of human-robot interaction proposed by Scholtz (2003) outlines several relationship and roles that may be found in human-robot teams. These roles, based on Norman's stages of HCI interaction (Norman, 1986), include the (i) supervisor, (ii) operator, (iii) mechanic, (iv) peer, and (v) bystander, and differ in terms of the level of involvement of the human and the autonomy of the robot. The theory acknowledges that the different roles are associated with various levels of autonomy, for instance, the supervisor has more autonomy and operates at a higher goal level than the peer role. This is similar to that in human teams, where the supervisor typically has more autonomy than the peer, who has more autonomy than a subordinate does.

5.4   Gradations of Autonomy

Despite their benefits, there are some detrimental effects of automation on human performance. These include problems such as complacency, decreased vigilance and loss of situation awareness (Endsley, 1987; Carmody & Gluckman 1993; Parasuraman et al., 1993; Endsley & Kiris, 1995; Parasuraman & Riley, 1997). Researchers describe the underlying problem as having the human out-of-the-loop (OOTL) (Young 1969; Kessel & Wickens, 1982). To address this, strategies to manage the use of automation have been suggested. These broadly fall under the levels of automation approach and the adaptive automation approach. Billings (1997) proposed two approaches to automation, while Sheridan and Verplank (1978) described more explicit levels of automation. Adaptive automation, on the other hand, has been studied by researchers such as Rouse (1977; 1988), Parasuraman, Mouloua and Molloy (e.g. 1996), among others.

Management-by-Exception and Management-By-Consent. Billings (1997) proposed two approaches to use automation in aviation: management-by-consent and management-by-exception. Management-by-consent occurs when automation only takes action when explicit consent has been obtained by the operator to do so, whereas when the management-by-exception strategy is adopted, automation is able to initiate and execute actions without explicit consent from the operator, who retains the option to override or reverse the actions taken or initiated.

Levels of Automation. Another theory incorporating the similar idea of gradations of automation is Sheridan and Verplank's (1978) levels of automation (LOA). The theory involves a scale with ten degrees or levels at which automation can aid with decision and action. Higher LOA represent increased machine autonomy while lower LOA denote greater human involvement and diminished automation (Parasuraman et al., 2000). For instance, operating at high LOA in the information acquisition stage may provide the operator "decluttered" and filtered information already categorized according to certain criteria such that the "raw" data is unavailable to the operator (Yeh & Wickens, 2001). On the other hand, medium LOA in the same stage only tentatively classifies incoming data, allowing the operator to see the "raw" data (Parasuraman et al., 2000). In the information analysis stage, lower LOA merely provide a simple trend lines, providing only minimal support with regard to the evaluation of the information. The main concept of LOA is to automate the system only to a moderate degree to minimize the problems associated with excessive automation.

Incorporating this concept of levels of automation, Save & Feuerberg (2012) further developed the four-stage model of information processing to include gradations within each stage that reflect the degree to which automation was involved. For instance within the decision selection stage, the level of automation can range from being fully human-driven ("human decision making") to fully automated ("automatic decision-making"), with intermediate levels such as "artifact-supported decision making", "automated decision support", "rigid automated decision support", "low-level automatic decision-making", and "high-level automatic decision making".

Adaptive Automation. In addition to having multiple levels of automation, or, in the case of a human-robot teams, multiple levels of robot autonomy, there can also be a customization of the robot's level of autonomy to the changing needs of the human teammate. In automation research, this is the concept of adaptive automation (AA) (Rouse, 1988). While LOA identifies the degree to which automation is implemented, AA pertains to when the different levels of automation are invoked (Taylor, Reinerman-Jones, Szalma, Mouloua, & Hancock, 2013).

The effectiveness of the AA strategy has been observed empirically (Rouse, 1977). For instance the adaptive automation scheme where the automated tool was only used during high traffic conditions, resulted in the smallest increase in mental workload among Air Traffic Controllers compared to the constant automation and constant manual schemes (Hilburn, Jorna, Byrne & Parasuraman, 1997). Parasuraman et al. (1996; 1993) found that adaptive automation improved detection of system failures in a multitask flight simulation. In addition, adaptive automation was found to improve performance especially when the type of automation was matched to the type of task demand (Taylor et al., 2013).

Incorporating these theories and ideas in a human-robot team, it is proposed that the level of autonomy of the robot can be managed in terms of the roles that it assumes. In most situations, the robot would be a subordinate, having limited autonomy, as reflected by the set of behaviors that it can exhibit. These behaviors are likely to be "passive" and are responses to explicit commands. However, applying the AA idea, under certain circumstances, it may assume a role with greater autonomy, such as that of a peer, which entails a set of more "active" behaviors that are associated with greater autonomy and initiative.

6   Dimensions of Robot Behaviors

Drawing from the various related theories and literature, robot behaviors can then be (i) active or passive, corresponding to different levels of autonomy, as well as (ii) impacting performance, workload and stress directly or indirectly. Table 1 shows some examples of behaviors in each category:

Table 1. Taxonomy of robot behaviors

	DIRECT	INDIRECT
ACTIVE	Robot shows affirmative behaviors that aid with operator's main task. Example behaviors: • Takes over operator's task entirely. • Aids operator with his task by taking over parts of the main task. • Aids by preventing others' inputs from hindering operator from main task.	Robot shows affirmative behaviors that aid with operator's secondary tasks or indirectly helps with the main task. Example behaviors: • Aids operator with his main task by reminding him (indirect help) of certain aspects of the task. • Aids operator by relieving him of secondary tasks. • Aids by preventing others' inputs from hindering operator from secondary tasks.
PASSIVE	Robot helps by withdrawing its own inputs from hindering the operator from his main task. Example behaviors: • Stops feeding inputs that may disrupt operator from main task.	Robot helps by withdrawing its own inputs from hindering the operator from his secondary tasks. Example behaviors: • Stops feeding inputs that may disrupt operator from secondary tasks.

Hence, with a human-robot team, in line with the levels of automation/autonomy notion, there should be different roles and correspondingly, different sets of behavior that the robot can exhibit. This will help minimize issues associated with having the human out-of-the-loop. Additionally, applying the idea of adaptive automation/autonomy, the robot should be able to assume different roles and the associated behavior sets depending on the workload and stress experienced by its human teammate.

7   Conclusion

The field of human-robot teaming is a relative new but a promising one. Although development of robots and programming of their behaviors are usually first driven by functional specifications, the resultant product may or may not meet intended functions because in human-robot teams, it is the interface and interactions that are key. Hence, much research and a multi-disciplinary approach is required to develop robots that can be shown to enhance human performance while mitigating workload and stress.

References

1. ABB Australia. ABB robot keeps trailer make competitive with 60% productivity increase (2010), http://www.abbaustralia.com.au/cawp/seitp202/88d442f2225b9957c1257766003896be.aspx (retrieved January 21, 2014)
2. Aki, L.: 7 Must-have domestic robots – R2D2 & C3PO eat your hearts out (2012), http://www.amog.com/tech/153161-domestic-robots/ (retrieved January 21, 2014)
3. Belbin, M.: Management Teams. Heinemann, London (1981)
4. Belbin, M.: Method, reliability & validity, statistics and research: A comprehensive review of Belbin's team roles (2013), http://www.belbin.com/content/page/5596/BELBINuk-2013-A%20Comprehensive%20Review.pdf (retrieved January 21, 2013)
5. Billings, C.E.: Aviation automation: The search for a human centered approach. Erlbaum, Mahwah (1997)
6. Bubblews, Entertainment Robots (2013), http://www.bubblews.com/news/552216-entertainment-robots (retrieved January 21, 2014)
7. Carmody, M.A., Gluckman, J.P.: Task specific effects of automation and automation failure on performance, workload and situational awareness. In: Jensen, R.S., Neumeister, D. (eds.) Proceedings of the 7th International Symposium on Aviation Psychology, pp. 167–171. Department of Aviation, The Ohio State University, Columbus (1993)
8. Current use of military robots (2014), http://www.armyofrobots.com/current-use-military.html (retrieved January 21, 2014)
9. Çalişir, F., Çalişir, F.: The relation of interface usability characteristics, perceived usefulness, and perceived ease of use to end-user satisfaction with enterprise resource planning (ERP) systems. Computers in Human Behavior 20(4), 505–515 (2004)
10. da Vinci Surgery, Changing the experience of surgery (2013), http://www.davincisurgery.com/ (retrieved January 21, 2014)
11. DRC, DARPA Robotics Challenge 2013 (2013), http://www.theroboticschallenge.org/about (retrieved January 10, 2013)
12. Endsley, M.R.: The application of human factors to the development of expert systems for advanced cockpits. In: Proceedings of the Human Factors Society 31st Annual Meeting, pp. 1388–1392. Human Factors and Ergonomics Society, Santa Monica (1987)
13. Endsley, M.R., Kiris, E.O.: The out-of-the-loop performance problem and level of control in automation. Human Factors 37, 381–394 (1995)

14. Guizzo, E., Ackerman, E.: How Rethink Robotics built its new Baxter robot worker. IEEE Spectrum, http://spectrum.ieee.org/robotics/ industrial-robots/rethink-robotics-baxter-robot-factory-worker (retrieved January 21, 2014)
15. Hilburn, B., Jorna, P.G., Byrne, E.A., Parasuraman, R.: The effect of adaptive air traffic control (ATC) decision aiding on controller mental workload. In: Mouloua, M., Koonce, J. (eds.) Human-automation interaction: Research and practice, pp. 84–91. Erlbaum Associates, Mahwah (1997)
16. House, J.S.: Work Stress and Social Support. Addison-Wesley, Reading (1981)
17. Kessel, C.J., Wickens, C.D.: The transfer of failure-detection skills between monitoring and controlling dynamic systems. Human Factors 24, 49–60 (1982)
18. Kuka, Scara robots (2013), http://www.kuka-robotics.com/usa/ en/products/industrial_robots/special/scara_robots/ (retrieved January 21, 2014)
19. Lamb, R.: How have robots changed manufacturing? (2010), http://science.howstuffworks.com/ robots-changed-manufacturing.htm (retrieved January 21, 2014)
20. Liszewski, A.: Magnetic microbots perform eye surgery without a single incision (2013), http://gizmodo.com/magnetic-microbots-perform-eye-surgery- without-a-single-598784256 (retrieved January, 2014)
21. Martel, S.: Magnetic microbots to fight cancer. IEEE Spectrum (2012), http://spectrum.ieee.org/robotics/medical-robots/ magnetic-microbots-to-fight-cancer (retrieved January 21, 2014)
22. McNickle, M.: 10 medical robots that could change healthcare. Information Week (2012), http://www.informationweek.com/mobile/10-medical-robots- that-could-change-healthcare/d/d-id/1107696 (retrieved)
23. Norman, D.: Cognitive Engineering. In: Norman, D., Draper, S. (eds.) User-Centered Design: New Perspectives on Human-Computer Interaction, pp. 31–62. Erlbaum Associates, Hillsdale (1986)
24. Parasuraman, R., Riley, V.: Humans and automation: use, misuse, disuse and abuse. Human Factors 39, 230–253 (1997)
25. Parasuraman, R., Mouloua, M., Molloy, R.: Effects of adaptive task allocation on monitoring of automated systems. Human Factors 38, 665–679 (1996)
26. Parasuraman, R., Mouloua, M., Molloy, R., Hilburn, B.: Adaptive function allocation reduces performance costs of static automation. In: Jensen, R.S., Neumeister, D. (eds.) Proceedings of the 7th International Symposium on Aviation Psychology, pp. 178–185. Department of Aviation, The Ohio State University, Columbus (1993)
27. Parasuraman, R., Sheridan, T., Wickens, C.: Model for types and levels of human interaction with automation (English). IEEE Transactions on Systems, Man, and Cybernetics. Part A. Systems and Humans 30(3), 286–297 (2000)
28. Prewett, M.S., Johnson, R.C., Saboe, K.N., Elliott, L.R., Coovert, M.D.: Managing workload in human–robot interaction: A review of empirical studies. Computers in Human Behavior (2010), doi:10.1016/j.chb.2010.03.010
29. R & D, National Robotics Initiative invests $38 million in next-generation robotics (2013), http://www.rdmag.com/news/2013/10/national-robotics- initiative-invests-38-million-next-generation-robotics (retrieved 10 January 2013)
30. Rinaldo, K.: Paparazzi Bot, http://www.paparazzibot.com/ (retrieved January 21, 2014)

31. Rouse, W.B.: Human–computer interaction in multi-task situations. IEEE Transactions on Systems, Man and Cybernetics 7, 384–392 (1977)
32. Rouse, W.B.: Adaptive aiding for human/computer control. Human Factors 30, 431–438 (1988)
33. Save, L., Feuerberg, B.: Designing human-automation interaction: a new level of automation taxonomy. In: de Waard, D., Brookhuis, K., Dehais, F., Weikert, C., Rottger, S., Manzey, D., Biede, S., Reuzeau, F., Terrier, P. (eds.) Human Factors: a view from an integrative perspective. Proceedings HFES Europe Chapter Conference Toulouse, France (2012)
34. Scholtz, J.J.: Theory and evaluation of human robot interactions. In: Proceedings of the 36th Hawaii International Conference on System Science (2003), doi:10.1109/HICSS.2003.1174284
35. Sheridan, T.B.: Telerobotics, Automation, and Human Supervisory Control. MIT Press, Cambridge (1992)
36. Sheridan, T.B., Verplanck, W.L.: Human and computer control of undersea teleoperators. Cambridge University Press, Cambridge (1978)
37. Swan Robotics, Domestic robots (2014), http://www.swanrobotics.com/Domestic%20robots (retrieved January 21, 2014)
38. Taylor, G.S., Reinerman-Jones, L.E., Szalma, J.L., Mouloua, M., Hancock, P.A.: What to automate: Addressing the multidimensionality of cognitive resources through system design. Journal of Cognitive Engineering and Decision Making 7(4), 311–329 (2013)
39. West, D.: Intel Museum tourist attraction (2008), https://suite101.com/a/intel-museum-sightseeing-attraction-a85734 (retrieved January 21, 2014)
40. Yanco, H.A., Drury, J.J.: A Taxonomy for Human-Robot Interaction. AAAI Technical report FS-02-03 (2002)
41. Yanco, H.A., Drury, J.J.: Classifying Human-Robot Interaction: An Updated Taxonomy. In: Proceedings of The 2004 IEEE International Conference on Systems, Man & Cybernetics, The Hague, The Netherlands, pp. 2841–2846 (2004)
42. Yeh, M., Wickens, C.D.: Attentional filtering in the design of electronic map displays: A comparison of color-coding, intensity coding, and decluttering techniques. Human Factors 43, 543–562 (2001)
43. Young, L.R.A.: On adaptive manual control. Ergonomics 12, 635–657 (1969)

Designing Virtual and Augmented Environments

Subjective-Situational Study of Presence

Nataly Averbukh

Ural Federal University, Ekaterinburg, Russia
NataAV@olympus.ru

Abstract. The paper is devoted to the description of the interview approach to reveal presence state and its types such as environmental, social and personal presence. The questions of the interview is described and analyzed in detail. The questions were formulated in view of the subject's behavior and the reactions during tests. Also the answers of the test subjects are analyzed from a perspective of sense of presence revealing. The interview method proved its efficiency. This method allowed to identify in practice types of presence being under researching. In addition, it has enabled a better understanding of the dynamics of the perception changes in the case of presence. The flexibility of this method allows to adjust it under specific virtual environment, and to clarify all key aspects to understand presence.

Keywords: sense of presence, interview approach, types of presence.

1   Introduction

Virtual reality is widely used in educational, medical and scientific applications in the last two decades. Also the phenomenon of virtual reality is the object of scientific research. This paper is devoted to the research of the sense of presence.

The sense of presence (feeling of "being there") is a factor which defines virtual reality. The sense of presence distinguishes virtual reality from "traditional" 3D Computer Graphics. [2]—[4], [7]. There is a number of publications devoted to the problems of specific states occurring in connection with virtual reality. The important conceptions of virtual reality such as presence, absorption, immersion, involvement, and cybersickness are described and discussed. Also the methods and techniques of the measurement and the study of sense of presence are described. Its contributing factors are analyzed. But the finding of effective methods for the presence measurement remains a challenging open problem.

Behavioral, *physiological*, and *subjective* approaches to the measurement and to the study of sense of presence are offered traditionally.

Presence in any case reduces to definition "sense of being there". In our opinion this is the only true criterion of the presence condition. Therefore it seems correct to use in the first instance the subjective method since no one but the person cannot say where she/he felt her/him self. Thus objective methods are subsidiary, confirming introspections of subjects.

R. Shumaker and S. Lackey (Eds.): VAMR 2014, Part I, LNCS 8525, pp. 131–138, 2014.

Thus, our approach is based on the subjective opinion of an user. It's about her/his sensing that she/he was "there", was in the virtual reality. An user can say "no, I was not able to control events, I was uncomfortable, I was not able to survey or search the virtual environment, I had not lost track of time, but I was there." And we may make a conclusion, that an user experienced the state of presence.

Presence is defined as a sensing of immediate interaction with the environment or the object of the environment. International Society for Presence Research said presence is the state arising in interaction with the special technology in which part or all of the individual's perception fails to accurately acknowledge function the role of the technology in the experience.

The question of how to determine whether the presence of? "Being there" is too broad term. Presence can be of different types, can exist in varying degrees, can be experienced at any one instant of interaction with the technology and the lost to the next instant.

We propose to expand presence and include in criteria not only user actions or her/his feelings about the event happened already, but the user's expectations and expectancy. The technology may not always make the sense of touch or other interaction; the imagination does not help relive a nonexistent touch. But an user believes that a touch is possible.

When the user says "I was afraid of being hit by clashes", "I wanted to touch", "I waited for sensation of wind on my face" experimenter says "there is a sense of spatial (environmental) presence."

When the conditions of the experiment or technology does not allow another person to be in the environment, but the subject says "you were near to me", the experimenter said "there was a Social presence or Co-presence".

In this paper some results of our previous researches are used [1]. In those researches we have considered the problem of influence the presence effects on the performance of the intellectual task. As such Kohs Block design test was selected. The study involved two groups. The subjects in one of them decided the task in stereo glasses. The members of the second (control) group performed exactly the same task, but on the desktop. To motivate the subjects of both groups they after experiment may see demos with nature views. A sense of presence after the Kohs Block design test was measured using the Presence Questionnaire of Witmer and Singer [8]. That is mentioned most often in literature. Questions in that questionnaire are constructed taking into account factors which cause the sense of presence. We received the results coinciding with described in literature. Despite of it we were not completely satisfied with the results of research. The main defect of a questionnaire as the method is preset strictly fixed questions. Questions in any way concern neither the concrete virtual environment, nor concrete activity of the subject of the experiment in frameworks of this environment. Therefore the elaboration more flexible technique is seemed to be useful.

In this regard, we propose our version of a technique for the presence research. It's not a questionnaire, which would have to be modified "toties quoties" (each time). It is an interview where in advance the only the general direction of questions is specified. The questions of our interview depend on many factors. Among them the type of the virtual environment, the behavior of the test subject, a task that she/he performed in the environment. Besides, the questions depend on the subject's messages during operating in the virtual environment, as well as during the interview.

We analyzed the different data, such as the records of the subjects after the test run in stereo-glasses, the reports about the virtual reality demos viewing by both main and control groups, as well as the subject's stories about viewing of 3D movies. The analysis was supplemented by our own impressions of the CAVE-system and 3D movies.

As a result we drew a conclusion that it is appropriate to conduct not quantitative but qualitative studies of presence state. Such approach relieves of the need to connect this low-studied phenomenon with others often too low-studied states. Similarly it isn't necessary to look for quantitative indices of actually unknown objects and concepts.

Types (levels) of presence were described in detail in [6]. We think that it is suitable to base a survey-interview on these types. However, the preliminary results of our analysis induced us to redefine the descriptions of these types.

For example, **environmental** (or spatial) presence within frameworks of our study assumes the interaction with the environment, the reaction environment on the subject, and the expectation of interaction. The determining factor is the expectations of the subject. As we said above, when the user says "I was afraid of being hit by clashes, I wanted to touch", "I waited for sensation of wind on my face", the experimenter may say "there is a sense of spatial (environmental) presence".

Social presence is considered if the subject believes that she/he interacts with others human beings within virtual reality. Moreover technologies may allow being present into an environment really and may not allow. But if the subject says during the interview "you were near to me", then the experimenter may say "there is a Social presence or Co-presence".

Personal presence is the most profound presence. Subject remembers how she/he appears in the initial state of virtual reality. She/he knows the background and previous experience into this environment.

Below we consider a set of interview questions which correspond to the selected types of presence.

The first, **environmental,** set of questions in turn may be divided onto following subtypes:

- questions about *impressions,* formed into virtual environment;
- questions about *expectations* (for example *did you want to touch objects, did you afraid of crash with wall, or tree, or another object of environment,* etc.),
- questions about *self-sentiments* (for example *where have you been - in the virtual environment or in the real world?*).

The second set of questions is the **social** set. In this part of the interview it should be asked about other subjects of the virtual environment, about the experimenters and the technical staff if they were in the room. The aim of the social set of questions is to find out whether other people intensify the sense of fidelity of a virtual environment or they hinder sense of "being there". Possible such co-presence is ignored as unnecessary for the interaction with the environment.

The third set consists of questions about **personal** presence. The task of these questions to reveal exactly whom the subject feels in virtual reality. Presumably she/he can identify with the character, proposed a specific system or come up with something else, or may be her/himself. In the latter case it is necessary to ask if she/he remembers how and why was in this virtual environment.

In addition, at the beginning of the interview the general questions about impressions have to offer.

2   Methods

The virtual environment containing various objects and allowing to move inside, helps to reveal the factors influencing experience of presence. We have chosen the environment to involve the maximum number factors which may influence the experience of presence. We paid special attention to ease of the interface, the reality of the imagery, the user control of the events occurring in the environment and realistic feeling of movement through the environment. The popular computer game *Grand Theft Auto: San-Andreas* was chosen. The game world in this case is rather rich. There is the possibility to navigate a helicopter demonstrating the reasonably realistic "behavior". *Multi Theft Auto* is the modification of *Grand Theft Auto*. It makes possible to create various scenarios basing on the game.

The eighteen subjects were selected. They were acquainted earlier with virtual reality based on the stereo glasses. They had the opportunity to fly over a town, a forest, and a lake. The flight took place in the low cloud. The timescale was 1 hour = 1 minute. Flights began with since midday and finished ten o'clock P.M. The total time spent in the virtual reality should not exceed ten minutes. There was the "first-person" flight, that is subjects obtained an overview from a helicopter cockpit. The helicopter itself and its cockpit panel weren't shown to the subjects. USB-joystick ThrustMaster Top Gun Fox 2 Pro was used as the controller. Two series with a small break were offered to the subjects. The subjects independently controlled flight in one series. The operator controlled helicopter in another series. In some cases subjects initiate voice commands according to which the operator directed the helicopter.

The questions of interview were formulated taking into account the virtual environment. These questions are:

1. Describe your feelings and impressions.
2. What is your mood after the "flight"?
3. Did you feel the flight? As far as this feeling was realistic?
4. Did you wait for the crash?
5. Are you afraid of the crash?
6. Did you wish to examine the environment?
7. Had you another wishes and expectations connected with the virtual environment?
8. Where did you feel you self: a) airborne; b) in the helicopter, c) in the room (where test was carried out), d) at the same time in the room and in the helicopter?

9. Who, in your opinion, did control the helicopter (in cases when the test operator have controlled the helicopter)?
Options: a) a test operator, b) a character from the virtual environment, c) the helicopter was controlled by itself.
10. How did you perceive the flight operator?
Options: a) as a character from the virtual environment, b) a person from other world (i.e. from real world), controlling the helicopter, c) some tool, d) without a thought.
11. Where, in your opinion, have the experimenter (or the experimenter together with the operator) been in the case of the independent flight? a) Near you in the helicopter? b) Near you in the room? c)You didn't think of them? d) They were absent at all.
12. Whom did you feel yourself? a) a game character, b) other person (describe), c) your old self?
13. Do you remember how you have became airborne?
14. Had you sense of presence? In what series this sense was more – in passive where you watched the flight, or in active where you controlled flight?

Note, that in each case the questions were formulated in view of the subject's behavior and the reactions during "flight".

The purpose of the first two questions is to bring the opportunity for the subjects to share impressions, to state what is most excited them at present and only then to return to the topic, that is interesting the experimenter.

The third question related to the realism and fidelity of virtual environment. This question allowed to correlate the impressions emerged from virtual environment, to the impressions emerged usually from the real world.

Points concerning presence directly begin with the fourth question. The questions from the fourth to the eighth were the environmental questions. The questions from the fourth to the seventh were about the impressions received from the virtual environment and the interaction with the environment. The eighth question was about the subjective localization. These questions were made more exact on the basis of direct observation over subjects: "What emotions the expected collision did trigger?", "When you almost collided with the wall what did you feel: fear of trauma, misgiving of penalties for failure, etc."

The questions from the ninth to the eleventh were about social presence. As we said above in our investigation other participants of virtual environment did not present visual, but they presented in environment functionally (for example the operator who controlled the helicopter in half of series).

Twelfth and thirteenth questions were about personal presence.

The last question was proposed as the final, and its main goal is to summarize the interview. Also, we tried to verify how important for presence experience is an own subject activity in the virtual environment.

3   Results

Usually answers to the first two questions had rather emotional nature. They were reduced to exclamations such as "Cool", "Fablonic", "I like it", "I also want a helicopter!", etc. Less enthusiastic answers also took place. Subjects complained of the fatigue, the difficulty with control, inability to look around the corner, the discrepancy between the visual and vestibular sensitivity. However generally one may say that flying in a virtual environment has attracted interest.

3.1   Answers to the Third Question

The part of the subjects had no real flight experience. They could compare their virtual experience to flights in a dream. One subject considered the virtual flight as more similar to swimming. However the majority (10 of 18) specified that the flight was seemed to them like a flight in the real world. There were also such subjects who reported that flight in the virtual environment is even more realistic than in the real plane since a view from a window of the passenger plane doesn't provide such visibility.

3.2   Answers to Environmental Questions

The answers to the questions from the fourth to the eighth are ranged from the belief that there is a "picture" or "Game World" to the confidence that one can be knocked on the trees and swim in the lake. The subjects were exposed to the dangers of the virtual collision with buildings, trees or the ground. It is interesting that they responded differently to these dangers. For example, one of the subjects described its presence in virtual reality as an extremely high. Her description largely corresponds to an altered state of consciousness. For her the collision was a way to explore the world, "to touch the world by helicopter if you can not feel it by own hands". Others said that they felt themselves rather in a room where the test was conducted, than in the air over the city or inside the helicopter. But at the sight of the approaching wall they shuddered and tried to dodge.

3.3   Answers to the Social Questions

Despite the fact that our subjects were well aware of the operator being in the room and some of them even gave him commands, part of the subjects claimed that in a passive series the helicopter flied by itself, operated by "the roundabout mechanism". Others considered her/his own voice giving commands as the instrument of control and ignored the person to whom they were addressed. There were subjects who included the operator in the virtual environment, identifying him with the pilot. In some cases we received the answer "you were beside me, but you were in the room, but I was in a helicopter over the city".

3.4   Answers to the Personal Questions

In our study we observed some situations. In some cases the subjects felt "as themselves, together with whole their memory" (i.e. they didn't experience personal presence). In others they felt "as themselves, but without the burden of habitual experiences". In third they felt themselves even as the character of the virtual environment with the biography that is different from the biography of the subject. In only two cases we observed personal presence. The subjects were built in themselves on virtual environment on the level of reminiscences, imagining the background to their appearance in the virtual world, and even a "virtual biography". Once the identification of her and the virtual character was full. The subject could tell us "her" (virtual) biography, the flight purpose, the duty station, and even a grade title of character. The second case was rather intermediate. The subject thought up a character backstory, but did not convince herself in the authenticity up to the end. In our opinion, there were elements of the game to another person here.

Only two subjects answered negatively on the generalizing question, and three subjects pointed that the experience of presence was higher during passive rather than active series.

4   Conclusion

The main advantage of the interview approach is a lack of prearranged constraints on the set of questions. Thus this method is applicable for the different environments and the experimental conditions. Certainly, under other conditions questions will be formulated differently. The environment set of questions may be strengthened, the social or personal set may be weakened. Other expectations and fears may appear in other experiments.

Besides, the free form of the interview allows subjects to describe intermediate forms of presence which they tested. It allows to reveal nuances of the phenomenon.

We have to remind, the term presence, especially spatial presence dubbed as the sense of "being there." Spatial presence is a product of an unconscious effort to correctly register oneself into the virtual environment in a consistent manner. this process is perceptual, and bottomup in nature, and rooted in the reflexive and adaptive behavior to react and resolve the mismatch in the spatial cues between the physical space where the user is and the virtual space where the user looks at, hears from and interacts with [5].

Our method helps to notice when this mismatch is resolved not completely. In our research subjects in most cases ignored a contradiction. For example, the subjects claimed that they were in the helicopter, and spoke about experimenters "you was near me, in the room". They noticed a paradoxicality of the words only after speaking. Thus, one may consider that our method revealed partial spatial presence.

Then the interview method proved its efficiency. This method allowed to identify in practice types of presence being under researching. In addition, it has enabled a better understanding of the dynamics of the perception changes in the case of presence. Finally, the flexibility of this method allows to adjust it under specific virtual environment, and to clarify all key aspects to understand presence.

References

1. Averbukh, N.V., Shcherbinin, A.A.: The Presence Phenomenon and Its Influence upon Intellectual Task Performance within Virtual Reality Settings. Psychology. Journal of the Higher School of Economics 8, 102–119 (2011)
2. Fencott, C.: Content and creativity in virtual environment design. In: Proceedings of Virtual Systems and Multimedia 1999, pp. 308–317. University of Abertay Dundee, Dundee (1999)
3. Insko, B.E.: Measuring Presence: Subjective, Behavioral and Physiological Methods. In: Riva, G., Davide, F., Jsselstein, W.A.I. (eds.) Being There: Concepts, Effects and Measurement of User Presence in Synthetic Environments. IOS Press, Amsterdam (2003)
4. Huang, M.P., Himle, J., Beier, K., Alessi, N.E.: Comparing Virtual and Real Worlds for Acrophobia Treatment. In: Westwood, J.D., Hoffman, H.M., Stredney, D., Weghorst, S.J. (eds.) Medicine Meets Virtual Reality: Art Science, Technology: Healthcare (R)evolution, pp. 175–179. IOS Press, Amsterdam (1998)
5. Lee, S., Kim, G.J., Rizzo, A., Park, H.: Formation of Spatial Presence: By Form or Content? In: Raya, M.A., Solaz, B.R. (eds.) Proceedings of 7th Annual International Workshop on Presence, pp. 20–27. Universidad Politècnica de Valencia, Valencia (2004)
6. Sadowski, W., Stanney, K.M.: Measuring and managing presence in virtual environments. In: Stanney, K.M. (ed.) Handbook of virtual environments: Design, Implementation, and Applications, pp. 791–806. Lawrence Erlbaum Associates, Mahwah (2002)
7. Stanney, K.M., Salvendy, G.: Aftereffects and Sense of Presence in Virtual Environments: Formulation of a Research and Development Agenda. International Journal of Human-Computer Interaction 10, 135–187 (1998)
8. Witmer, B.G., Singer, M.J.: Measuring Presence in Virtual Environments: A Presence Questionnaire. Presence 7, 225–240 (1998)

Development of a Squad Level Vocabulary
for Human-Robot Interaction

Daniel Barber[1], Ryan W. Wohleber[1], Avonie Parchment[1], Florian Jentsch[1],
and Linda Elliott[2]

[1] Institute for Simulation and Training, University of Central Florida, Orlando, FL, USA
{dbarber,rwohlebe,aparchme}@ist.ucf.edu, florian.jentsch@ucf.edu
[2] Army Research Laboratory, Fort Benning, GA, USA
linda.r.elliott.civ@mail.mil

Abstract. Interaction with robots in military applications is trending away from
teleoperation and towards collaboration. Enabling this transition requires technologies for natural and intuitive communication between Soldiers and robots.
Automated Speech Recognition (ASR) systems designed using a well-defined
lexicon are likely to be more robust to the challenges of dynamic and noisy
environments inherent to military operations. To successfully apply this approach to ASR development, lexicons should involve an early focus on the target audience. To facilitate development a vocabulary focused at the squad level
for Human Robot Interaction (HRI), 31 Soldiers from Officer Candidate School
at Ft. Benning, GA provided hypothetical commands for directing an autonomous robot to perform a variety of spatial navigation and reconnaissance tasks.
These commands were analyzed, using word frequency counts and heuristics, to
determine the structure and word choice of commands. Results presented
provide a baseline Squad Level Vocabulary (SLV) and a foundation for development of HRI technologies enabling multi-modal communications within
mixed-initiative teams.

Keywords: Human-robot interaction, human-robot teaming, mixed-initiative
teams, speech recognition.

1   Introduction

The U.S. military is increasingly looking to robots to perform complex and hazardous
tasks such as reconnaissance and Explosive Ordinance Disposal (EOD). According to
General Robert Cone of the U.S. Army Training and Doctrine Command (TRADOC),
robots could replace one-fourth of combat Soldiers by 2030[1]. Today's robots bring
advanced technology to the field, helping to keep Soldiers out of harm's way. As of
2011, the U.S. deployed over 2,000 ground robots to Afghanistan supporting EOD
teams and entry control points [2]. However, state-of-the-art robotic ground systems
currently serve as tools for Soldiers, not teammates. To enable unmanned systems
operating in teams with Soldiers and manned vehicles as described by Department of

R. Shumaker and S. Lackey (Eds.): VAMR 2014, Part I, LNCS 8525, pp. 139–148, 2014.

Defense (DoD) Unmanned Systems Roadmap [3], advanced Human-Robot Interaction (HRI) capabilities are needed.

Current HRI paradigms utilize teleoperation, with control through physical input devices such as joysticks, track balls, and touch screens. These input devices constrain the robot operator in that they often require operation from stationary positions, hand eye coordination to map controls to output, dexterity to operate controls, and additional training and practice time [4]. Teleoperated robots also inherently add an additional step in the chain of communication, where a commander must direct a robot through a specially trained operator [5]. Advancements in robot perception, intelligence, and mobility will soon enable Soldiers to work with robots as collaborators rather than tools [6]. A key aspect of these advancements is communication using modalities Soldiers are already familiar with, facilitating Soldier-Robot (SR) collaborations without the addition of workload or training.

Speech provides a natural method of communication to robots. Research into speech for commanding robots clearly demonstrates it to be quicker, more intuitive, and superior to manual control for discrete tasks and Soldier multitasking and situation awareness [7], [4]. Ideally, continuous speech recognition systems would allow Soldiers to speak naturally to a robot collaborator as one might speak to another person. Unfortunately, full Natural Language Processing (NLP) and Automatic Speech Recognition (ASR) technology is limited [8]. Current systems have trouble with word classification accuracy and limited semantic understanding of continuous speech [9], [10]. Manual control is still more effective for continuous tasks than speech control [4]. A further challenge for true continuous speech NLP is working within the environment of military operations which includes noise from background sounds such as gunfire, echoes, and reverberations. Additional factors characteristic of this atmosphere including stress, fear, sickness, and pain may induce voice variability [11]. Moreover, special circumstances may change the way words are spoken [4], [11], [12]. Finally, common use of discrete words (e.g. commands) instead of normal speech in military environments may also inhibit speech understanding [7].

Due to current limitations in ASR technology and the use of discrete word commands typical of a military setting, programming systems to understand discrete commands using a limited lexicon is likely to show better overall performance and robustness in challenging environments. Such was the approach taken by Tellex et al. [8] who developed a body of natural language commands for operating a robotic forklift for the purposes of training and evaluating a robust robot speech recognition system.   Applying a lexicon scoped to the application domain limited the NLP search space, resulting in the robotic forklift demonstrating an ability to competently handle discrete commands [8]. To successfully apply this same approach to develop ASR systems for SR teaming, development of lexicons should involve an early focus on the target audience, such as U.S. Soldiers [13], [4].

Until new methods and algorithms, along with the hardware necessary for quickly handling large search spaces are developed to enable robots to fully interpret natural speech, a Squad Level Vocabulary (SLV) facilitating natural and intuitive communication within mixed-initiative teams is needed. A SLV scoped to commands Soldiers already use supports improved reliability of ASR technologies by reducing the input search space [14]. Further, by tailoring the speech commands to the preferences and conventions of the user, the language used for commands can be better retained and would allow for more efficient operation. Finally, this approach eliminates the need for additional training for robot specific communications. The goal for the present study was to inform the development of a SLV within   spatial navigation and reconnaissance tasks.

2   Method

2.1   Participants

A total of thirty-one (N = 31; 25 male, 6 female, mean age = 24.9) Soldiers assigned to   11B (Infantry) or similar (e.g., Combat arms, Officer Candidate School) Military Occupational Specialty (MOS), located at Ft. Benning, GA participated in the study. Researchers informed participation in the study was voluntary and that they may withdraw at any time.

2.2   Spatial Navigation and Reconnaissance Survey

A Spatial Navigation and Reconnaissance (SNR) survey was created to begin development of an initial SLV within SNR tasks. In this survey, Soldiers were instructed to issue commands to a robot based on their level of experience and training. The survey consisted of four parts comprised of open ended and multiple choice questions regarding commands to give an autonomous robot. Commands for Parts 1 through 3 involved either (Check) reporting obstructions in lines of movement, (Move) moving to a location, or (Survey) performing surveillance at a location. Each command prompt included an image of a landscape with two buildings, the participant's avatar within the scene, and the robot. Participants were instructed to pretend they were in the scene and use the spatial information provided to issue one of the three commands. Language used within the survey training materials and questions was chosen to avoid words that may influence the responses from participants.

In Part 1, the images presented with each item included the location of the robot and the area of interest for commands. Participants were informed that the robot only has information about its current location, where buildings are, and where their avatar is, but not command marker in the image. The command markers in all images included a circle or arrow highlighting where the robot was in the scene and an 'X' representing the point of interest to command the robot to move to or observe. Command markers in the images complemented the questions and aided participants in understanding what the intent of each command they must give was while limiting use of words that may bias their responses (e.g. near building, right side). Fig. 1 illustrates an example Move command question with command markers from Part 1 of the survey.

Using the image below, please describe what command you would give to the robot, to direct it to the marked side of the target location.

Fig. 1. Example question and image from Part 1 of the SNR Survey. In the image command markers include the 'X' that represents the location to command the robot (circle marker) to move to.

Part 2 of the survey augmented the images from Part 1 to include an aerial strip map with cardinal directions and building labels that could be used to help guide the robot. Similar to Part 1, participants were instructed that the robot had the same information as them (including the map), except for command markers in the scene and on the aerial strip map. Fig. 2 represents an example question from Part 2 of the survey.

Part 3 included multiple choice questions for Move commands using images from Parts 1 and 2. For each question, participants answered three multiple choice questions comprising a complete Move command sequence comprised of: a move command, position designation, and stop criteria. An example answer choice could result in the command, "Move to the South side of the left building." Part 3 was comprised of four images from Part 1 and four from Part 2 (with aerial strip map). Answer choices for the images from Part 1 used spatial phrases relative to the user (e.g. left, right, near, far), where images from Part 2 also included cardinal directions and building labels from the map (e.g. North, South, Building Alpha). Multiple choice answer options for Part 3 were derived from U.S. Army Field Manuals and the DoD Dictionary of Military Terms and were reviewed by a Non-Commissioned Officer (NCO) at Ft. Benning, GA. Fig. 2 represents an example question from Part 3 of the survey.

Using the image and strip map provided below, please describe what command you would give to the robot, to direct it to the marked side of the target location.

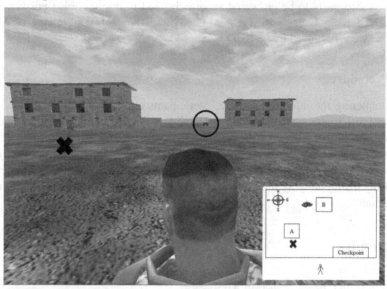

Fig. 2. Example question and image from Part 2 of the SNR Survey. In the image the 'X' represents the location to command the robot (circled) to move to

Using the provided figure, please build a speech command by circling the selections that you believe are the most intuitive, based on your experience and training, when commanding the robot to the marked side of the target location. Mark a choice for Column A, Column B, and Column C.

Column A	Column B	Column C
a) Travel to	a) the front side of	a) of the near building
b) Go to	b) the 6 o'clock side of	b) of my 11 o'clock
c) Drive to	c) the South side of	c) of the front building
d) Maneuver to	d) The near side of	d) of the left building
e) Move to		e) of the West building

Fig. 3. Example question and image from Part 3 of the SNR Survey. In the image the 'X' represents the location to command the robot (circled) to move to. Each column (A, B, and C) represents an answer choice to construct a command.

Part 4 presented no visual aids, and questions were different from the previous sections. At least one open-ended and one multiple-choice question addressed each of five new command types. Similar to Part 3, some multiple choice questions split the commands into parts to be answered separately, and multiple choice answer options were derived from U.S. Army Field Manuals and the DoD Dictionary of Military Terms and were reviewed by an NCO.

2.3   Procedure

After completing the informed consent, participants completed a demographics questionnaire. Participants were asked if they have any type of color blindness, and if so, or didn't know, the Ishihara Color Test, [15], was administered. Participants then completed the SNR Survey on paper. Participants completed one section of the survey at a time, returning each section upon completion to the experimenter. This prevented participants from changing their answers when presented with new information from later sections.

3   Results

3.1   Multiple Choice Question Analysis

Multiple-choice questions from Part 3 and Part 4 of the survey were analyzed using Chi-squared tests and word choice frequency counts. For Part 3, there are two categories (map, no map) of commands, each with three sub phrases: move command, position designation, and stop criteria. Table 1 lists overall recommended phrases comprising a full command based on word frequency counts, with significant values noted.

Table 1. Recommended phrases for commanding a robot to a location from Part 3 of the survey

Map	Phrase 1	Phrase 2	Phrase 3
No	Move to*	the {North,South,East,West} side of*	the {near, far} building
Yes	Move to*	the {North,South,East,West} side of*	building {Alpha, Bravo}*

Note: Words within braces represent options within the phrase part.
*Significant for $p < .05$

For multiple choice questions in Part 4, each section was self-contained and a single recommendation is made for each question. Recommended commands are based on mean frequency across questions in each set analyzed, Table 2.

Table 2. Recommended phrases for commanding a robot from Part 4 of the survey

Command Question	Recommended Command
Follow a person of interest	Follow* | The target*
Retreat	(No clear recommendation)
Skip location	Avoid* | Location
Skip location	Skip landmark
Identify your location	Give | (No clear recommendation)
Identify your location	Identity your location

Note. Questions with two choices to build a full command are arranged with a divider between parts when necessary.
*Significant for $p < .05$

3.2   Free Response Question Analysis

Handwritten answers to open-ended questions were transcribed onto a spreadsheet. After standardizing words (variations of "building" included "bldng," "Building," and "bldg") and correcting typographical errors to reduce redundancies, a frequency count of each word for each Part of the SNR survey was generated. These words were then categorized by the parts of speech (noun, verb, adjective, etc.) to determine which words were used for each command response. These frequency counts ascertained the preferred word choice once the structure of each archetypal command was determined.

To determine the archetypal structure, it was first established heuristically whether the participant was verbally teleoperating the robot or assumed the robot had autonomous capabilities. Generally, it was assumed that the participants were trying to teleoperate if commands reached a certain level of detail where the responses indicated micromanaging the execution of the higher level task. If the Soldier gave direction or distance information in addition to the destination command, or if the Soldier walked the robot through the steps to get to the destination (e.g. "move North 75 meters. Move East 25 meters") the Soldier was assumed to be teleoperating the robot. Commands for teleoperating the robot were not consistent with automated robot capabilities and were therefore not included in final recommendations.

Commands given by participants who had assumed autonomous capabilities were broken down into phrases. These phrases were grouped into broad command categories such as move commands, position designation, and stop commands. Command categories were then divided into specific phrase types such as *zone-relative-object*, *zone-relative-self*, or *zone-relative-direction* for position designation category, or *stop-at-destination* or *stop-on-command* for the stop commands category, see Fig. 4.

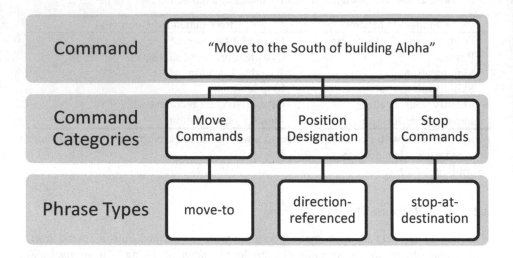

Fig. 4. Example of Move command mapped to command categories and then phrase types

The most frequently used phrase type was then chosen from each category to build an archetypal command phrase for each command type (Check, Move, and Survey). An example archetype command phrase consistent with "Move to the left of the building" would be *move-to / zone-relative-direction / stop-at-destination*. Word frequency counts from the data within chosen phrase types determined the words used for the command ultimately recommended. Final command recommendations for each command type are contained in Tables 3, 4, and 5.

Table 3. Recommendations for each command type (Check, Move, and Survey) for Part 1

Command Type	Recommended Command
Check	Report obstacles in your path to {left, right, front, back} side of building at my X o'clock
Move	Move to {left, right, front, rear, back} of building
Survey	Report recon Y meters to your {left, right, front, back}

Note: Words within braces represent options within the command. The variable X represents a unit of time on a clock [1-12] and variable Y a distance in meters.

Table 4. Recommendations for each command type (Check, Move, and Survey) for Part 2

Command Type	Recommended Command
Check	Report obstacles from your location to {North, South, East West} side of building {Alpha, Bravo}
Move	Move {North, South, East West} to building {Alpha, Bravo}
Survey	Report recon {North, South, East, West} of current location

Note: Words within braces represent options within the command. Alpha and Bravo building names were within provided maps and may be substituted for other labels.

Table 5. Recommendations for each command type from Part 4

Command Objective	Recommended Command
Follow Person	Follow target
Retreat	Retreat back to point
Skip specific building	Move past building
Return to starting point	Return back to start point
Identify current location	Report location

4   Conclusion

The phrases produced by this heuristic-driven process are useful for future research and design of robotic command languages and interfaces, but they should not be mistaken for conclusive or exact recommendations, with the possible exception of some of the multiple-choice based recommendations. However, consistent with the exploratory goal for this effort, these phrases serve as a necessary first step for a better understanding of preferred word choice and ordering for Soldiers commanding a robot within a reconnaissance and surveillance task. Moreover, this baseline SLV provides a foundation for the development of HRI technologies enabling true multi-modal communication within mixed-initiative teams using a well-known lexicon that is intuitive to Soldiers.

Acknowledgements. This research was sponsored by the Army Research Laboratory and was accomplished under Cooperative Agreement Number W911NF-10-2-0016. The views and conclusions contained in this document are those of the author's and should not be interpreted as representing the official policies, either expressed or implied, of the Army Research Laboratory or the U.S. Government. The U.S. Government is authorized to reproduce and distribute reprints for Government purposes notwithstanding any copyright notation herein.

References

1. CBS News: U.S. Army general says robots could replace one-fourth of combat soldiers by 2030. In: CBS News, http://www.cbsnews.com/news/robotic-soldiers-by-2030-us-army-general-says-robots-may-replace-combat-soldiers/ (accessed January 23, 2014)
2. Magnuson, S.: "Robot Army" in Afghanistan surgest past 2,000 units. In: National Defense Magazine, http://www.nationaldefensemagazine.org/blog/Lists/Posts/Post.aspx?ID=300 (accessed February 2, 2011)
3. Office of the Secretary of Defense: Unmanned Systems Integrated Roadmap: FY2013-2038., Washington D.C (2013)
4. Redden, E., Carstens, C., Pettit, R.: Intuitive speech-based robotic control. Aberdeen Proving Ground, MD (2010)
5. Cosenzo, K., Capstick, E., Pomranky, R., Dungrani, S., Johnson, T.: Soldier Machine Interface for Vehicle Formations: Interface Design and an Approach Evaluation and Experimentation. Technical Report ATRL-TR-4678, Aberdeen Proving Ground (2009)
6. Ososky, S., Schuster, D., Jentsch, F., Fiore, S., Shumaker, R., Lebiere, C., Kurup, U., Oh, J., Stentz, A.: The importance of shared mental models and shared situation awareness for transforming robots from tools to teammates. In: Proceedings of the 2012 SPIE Defense Security & Sensing Symposium (Unmanned Systems Technology XIV Conference DS114), Baltimore, MD (2012)
7. Pettitt, R.A., Redden, E., Carsten, C.B.: Scalablity of Robotic Controllers: Speech-based Robotic Controller Evaluation (ARL-TR-4858). Aberdeen Proving Ground, MD: US Army Research Laboratory, 1-46 (2009)
8. Tellex, S., Kollar, T., Dickerson, S., Walter, M., Banerjee, A., Teller, S., Roy, N.: Understanding natural language commands for robotic navigation and mobile manipulation. In: Proceedings of the National Conference on Artificial Intelligence (2011)
9. Anusuya, M., Katti, S.: Speech recognition by machine: A review. International Journal of Speech Technology 6(3), 181–205 (2009)
10. Yucong, D., Cruz, C.: Formalizing semantic of natural language through conceptualization from existence. International Journal of Innovation, Management and Technology 2(1), 37–42 (2011)
11. Pigeon, S., Swail, C., Geoffrois, E., Bruckner, G., Van Leeuwen, D., Teixeira, C., Orman, O., Collins, P., Anderson, T., Grieco, J., Zissman, M.: Use of Speech and Language Technology in Military Environments, North Atlantic Treaty Organization, Montreal, Canada (2005)
12. Williamson, D., Barry, T., Liggett, K.: Flight Test Results of ITT VRS-1290 in NASA OV-10, Wright-Patterson AFB, OH (1996)
13. Karis, D., Dobroth, K.: Psychological and Human Factors Issues in the Design of Speech Recognition Systems. In: Syrdal, A., Bennett, R., Greenspan, S. (eds.) Applied Speech Technology, pp. 359–388. CRC Press, Ann Arbor (1995)
14. Phillips, E., Rivera, J., Jentsch, F.: Developing a tactical language for future robotic teammates. In: Proceedings of the Human Factors and Ergonomics Society Annual Meeting, Santa Monica, CA (2013)
15. Ishihara, S.: Tests for color-blindness. Hongo Harukicho, Handaya (1917)

Towards an Interaction Concept for Efficient Control of Cyber-Physical Systems

Ingo Keller, Anke Lehmann, Martin Franke, and Thomas Schlegel

Technische Universität Dresden, Junior Professorship in Software Engineering of
Ubiquitous Systems, 01062 Dresden, Germany
{firstname.lastname}@tu-dresden.de
http://seus.inf.tu-dresden.de

Abstract. In this work, we introduce our interaction concept for efficient control of cyber-physical systems (CPS). The proposed concept addresses the challenges of the increased amount of smart/electronic devices along with increasingly complex user interfaces. With a dual reality approach, the user is able to perform the same action in the physical world as well in the virtual world by synchronizing both. We solve thereby the most important compelling issue of ease of use, flexibility, and bridging the gap between both worlds. Our approach is substantiated by two test scenarios by means of a characteristically CPS setting.

Keywords: cyber-physical system, smart home, dual reality interaction, synchronized environments.

1 Introduction

Nowadays, smart electronic devices enable us to build intelligent home automation systems for everybody, so called *smart homes*. These systems aim for assisting users assuring their independence as long as possible and improving overall quality of life [1]. The current state shows that these systems are usually constructed by integrating a wide range of standalone, network-compatible embedded systems with the aim to construct an all-in-one solution. These embedded systems range from simple sensors and actuators to small computational units, like smart phones, up to workstations.

Besides, every physical component comes with a corresponding virtual data representation. Those embedded systems form so called cyber-physical systems (CPS) [2]. CPS monitors and controls physical and virtual processes by so called *feedback loops* that affect the real and the virtual world simultaneously. Sensors or sensor compounds measure the current state of the environment (e.g., temperature, CO_2) and push these information to a particular software component. This component forwards the information to a subscribed software component over a networked connection. As this component holds an actuator, it manipulates the physical world, which causes an effect on all sensors.

The development, composition and optimization of this networked CPS is a complex process. However, ordinary people should be able to configure and interact with their smart environment with respect to their personal needs. Current

R. Shumaker and S. Lackey (Eds.): VAMR 2014, Part I, LNCS 8525, pp. 149–158, 2014.

approaches in smart home control, such as smart phones, tablets or workstations, provide inefficient user interfaces (UI) and a high configuration overhead.
For instance, graphical user interfaces based on list views are used to handle devices and tasks but are unsuitable for growing amounts of devices or performing
complex tasks. Moreover, the user has to become familiar with the UI but new
devices and tasks may introduce new concepts and views which lead to further
training periods.

To overcome these limitations we propose a dual reality interaction approach
for cyber-physical systems by combining a three-dimensional smart home simulator (virtual world) with our smart home infrastructure (real world). Supporting
interaction in both worlds we require for every real sensor and actuator a virtual counterpart with an identical visual representation. To provide the dual
reality interaction we have to, semi-automatically, synchronize objects, actions
and effects initiated by user inputs and environmental changes from the real and
virtual world.

2   Related Work

Due to the inexorable growth of data in all areas of life, people face more and
more the problem to understand the datasets they are confronted with. Thus, information visualization tools are required to assist end users who are not familiar
in creating effective graphical representations [3].

Green et al. [4] explored in a study the user's expectations and demands for
smart homes. They identified the following requirements from a user's point of
view: *cost, reliability, security/privacy/safety.* To justify the cost of a smart home
system the reliability, security, safety, and privacy are key issues and as such are
intensively addressed by current CPS research [2]. In addition they identified
flexibility, ease of use, keeping active, and *controlling* the smart home which
are aspects of interaction. Controlling a smart home system demands an user
interface which provides an easy and flexible way to interact with.

In the study of smart home usability and living experience conducted by
Koskela et al. [5], it was found that two main user activity pattern can be distinguished on controlling smart home environments. The *pattern control* which
is utilized to handle familiar and recurrent activity patterns whereas the *instant
control* is used for impulsive and unexpected tasks. They suggest that these
control patterns should be supported differently by provided user interfaces for
smart home environments. Based on these findings they conclude to use desktop-
based graphical user interfaces for *pattern control* tasks whereas usage of mobile
devices is more suitable for *instant control* in real-use context. They argue that
the diverse input methods available to desktop systems will support the work of
planning and predetermination while in the *instant control* case the key aspects
are the immediate availability, fast response and a centralized control device.

Introducing the concept of *dual reality,* Lifton et al. [8] bridges the gap between the real and the virtual world by using networked sensors and actuators,
thus creating an implicit bi-directional communication channel. This approach

facilitates to visualize the gathered data within the sensor network and hence it is perceptible by the user.

Kahl and Bürckert [10] have developed and used an event-based infrastructure and a dashboard-like visualization to combine the dual reality approach with an intelligent environment. The virtual environment is used to monitore and to visualize changes or problems in realtime. In their smart shopping environment the smart physical objects are recognized in the real world (e.g., product position and stock of products) and the items state are synchronized with their virtual representation.

Franke et al. [9] shows a model-based CPS middelware to handle this bi-directional communication and which is suitable for domestic environments. This type communication helps to create and maintain the so called "synchronized realities", a concept introduced by Stahl et al. [11] creating an assistance system to increase social connectedness. It is motivated to synchronize a virtual environment with a remote intelligent environment, which means the system knows the status of devices and appliances in the real environment and their digital representation in the virtual world. Furthermore, the 3D environment model can be used for designing and evaluating smart homes. By the mean of context menu that is attached to the virtual object, the user is able to control real devices or he can switch on a real light by manipulating the virtual light cone. In contrast, a state change in the real world, like switching on the light is updated in the virtual world with a visualization, like drawing a light cone.

Current approaches to customize and control smart home environments are based on graphical user interfaces [6], [7]. While this is sufficient for pattern control activities we will show a different approach for instant control according to the requirements found by Koskela et al. [5].

3   A Concept of Synchronized Interaction

According to [8] the virtual world can be described as being an immersive 3D environment that allows for fluid interaction among inhabitants and enables them to shape their environment to a certain extent.

A typical interaction in the physical or the virtual environment can be decomposed into smaller actions. These actions form a workflow which starts with navigating to an object, followed by selecting, and finally performing a manipulation task on or with the object.

While moving towards an object (e.g., walking towards it) can be easily distinguished from other kinds of actions in the real world the interaction decomposition might not be obvious at any time. For instance, selecting an item (e.g., grabbing an physical object) becomes a manipulation (e.g., moving it) naturally without the user noticing. As a consequence of the physical interaction, the user is fully aware which object he is currently manipulating since he usually has physical contact to it. However, the manipulation tasks can range from a simple action (e.g. turning a lamp on and off) to rather complex ones (e.g., controlling a robot to get an item from a room).

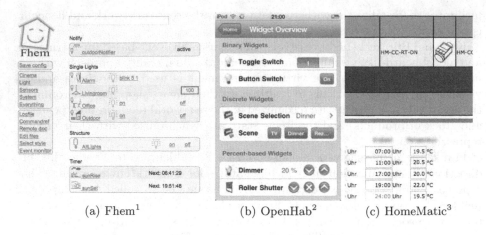

(a) Fhem[1]   (b) OpenHab[2]   (c) HomeMatic[3]

Fig. 1. Example of user interface based on list views

In smart home environments the situation is different. To start an interaction, the user needs to navigate to a desired item by using a hierarchical or list view provided through browser-based control centers, apps (see Fig. 1) or by means of even more complex programs. After selecting the item in the graphical user interface the user gets listed the available manipulation operations and chooses one. These user interfaces often vary with the complexity of the tasks that can be performed. While a light switch can easily be represented by a toggle button, complex user interfaces are required in more sophisticated scenarios such as controlling a smart home robot. However, in contrast to real world interaction the user is not necessarily aware which item he is currently handling. Usually the selected item is a text label or icon on the screen without a visible relation to the corresponding physical object. Since the user does not get a natural feedback, either of its location by means of navigation towards it, or its appearance by means of having physical contact to it, the users awareness is not efficiently supported. On the other hand, the performed actions are not distinguishable from each other, because starting a manipulation task is usually done by the same user action, e.g. a button click gives no natural feedback about the task performance.

In 3D virtual environment (VE), the interaction shares properties with real world and smart home interaction. While navigating can be seen as similar to the real world, selection and manipulation actions feature similar properties to the smart home environment. Additionally, VE provides the opportunity to enhance the user experience by incorporating information which is not visible in the real world but helps the user to understand his environment better. It is also possible to give the user more flexibility by providing interaction short cuts.

---

[1] http://fhem.de

[2] https://code.google.com/p/openhab/wiki/WebAppUI

[3] http://www.homematic.com

Fig. 2. Correlation detection between the physical and virtual environment

According to the cyber-physical system definition, we use a unique one-to-one correspondence between physical and virtual objects with the focus on mapping the real environment into the virtual world. This means, e.g., that every light switch in our physical environment get its virtual counterpart in the VE. To be efficient, this is done semi-automatically using a combination of sensing devices and actuators. For instance, we could detect correlations between a switch of a stationary ceiling light by means of an ambient light sensor in the same room (Fig. 2) This approach reflects the feedback loops and synchronizes the physical and virtual world permanently. However, it must be adjusted by requesting the user from time to time. Furthermore, we can visualize these - physically - relations between the elements in our virtual world.

Using mobile devices such as tablets or smart phones to interact with the virtual environment, the instant control activities can be supported by a single centralized device. These devices can either be carried around or are available in each room. Since the smart home is an all-in-one system the described virtual environment represents a viewport into the same shared world regardless of the used device.

Another benefit of our concept is the user's flexibility to achieve a goal. The smart home environment is adjusting to the user's performed actions. Normally, the user wants to perform a task himself whereas occasionally he wants support from the smart home for the same task, e.g., while being injured or disinclined. Whatever he decides to perform the smart home environment will be kept in synchronicity and therefore models the real world.

In the real world existing informal or invisible information about physical objects or environmental states can not be seen. Incorporating additional information into the virtual world can enhance the user experience and provides additional cues about smart home system states. Thus, the awareness of otherwise hidden information can be raised, e.g., visualization of CO_2 measurements in a sleeping room or showing the temperature state of a boiler or stove. Also, linking between physical and virtual objects can be visualized, e.g., the virtual representation of a physical light switch can be visually connected to the corresponding lamp within the VE by highlighting both in the same manner or by providing visual connection elements.

Overall, the user benefits from our comprehensible interaction concept, as we provide an abstracted and unified view on simple and complex control operations, as well as assisted configuration for smart home environments.

4   Proposed Setup

After explaining our interaction concept we present our proposed system realization. It is constructed by using three state of the art frameworks. Hence, we introduce the used components and show afterwards how the interplay between them leads to synchronized environments. We clarify the workflow and the interaction approach using two different scenarios.

4.1   Components

As shown in Fig. 3, we use the Modular OpenRobots Simulation Engine (MORSE) [12] to visualize the virtual world providing human and robot models. Information gathering from real world sensors and for communicating with actuators of our environment we use the Semantic MiddleWare (SeMiWa) [9]. To combine the virtual world of MORSE with the physical world of SeMiWa we utilize the Robot Operating System (ROS) [13] mapping the virtual and physical items and to localize them within a global shared coordinate system. Fig. 3 illustrates our entire system and the communication between the individual parts.

SeMiWa: All sensors and actuators are abstracted by our model-based, semantic middleware (SeMiWa) [9]. For instance, this middleware abstracts sensor stations of the Tinkerforge[4] toolkit. Each station consists of a temperature, a humidity and an ambient light sensor. In smart home all stations are assigned to a specific location, which is described by spatial coordinates. Beside the sensors SeMiWa controls the actuators in the real world transmitting control instructions to these components.

ROS: Firstly, we use ROS to synchronize the sensor's and actuators physical coordinates with the simulated world. We apply the *Simultanous Localization and*

---

[4] http://www.tinkerforge.com

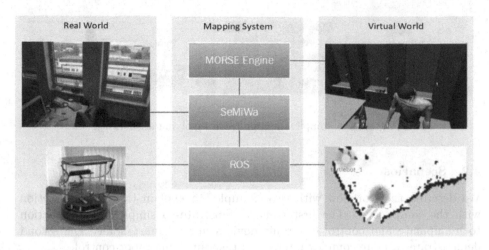

Real World   Mapping System   Virtual World

Fig. 3. The dual reality component architecture bridging the gap from the physical to synchronized reality

Mapping (SLAM) method integrated in ROS, a technique where a robot builds a map of the environment and estimates simultanously its pose within the environment. The measured SLAM map is the reference of our coordinate system, as this format can be used efficiently for mapping and localization. Additionally, this format was integrated in forehand in the MORSE simulator. In our scenario, we will use Turtlebots[5] for mapping purposes. Secondly, we reuse the modules of ROS to get an abstraction of robot abilities, e.g., object identification, picking and carrying with the Turtlebot.

MORSE: To interact in this dual reality, we use the human-robot interaction (HRI) module of MORSE [12]. In contrast to the classical intention, we permanently update the simulated virtual world with the real one. This means, each physical sensor updates the state of its virtual representation and vice versa. To achieve this behavior, we had to extend the MORSE simulator using the middleware infrastructure SeMiWa. The HRI module provides an *avatar* to pick and release objects, and investigate object states. As illustrated in Fig. 3 the human can walk with the avatar through the VE in order to manipulate it. Regarding to our ceiling light example, a person can switch on a particular lamp in a specific room without the demand to search for this lamp in a classical user interface. The MORSE simulator also gives us the capability to teleport the avatar to a specific room supporting interaction short cuts. Thus, the step-by-step navigation through the environment is not necessary but is nevertheless possible.

---

[5] http://www.turtlebot.com/

Fig. 4. A complex manipulation involving a robot

4.2 Scenarios

We describe the workflow with two examples to explain the user interaction with the components. The first scenario illustrates a simple user interaction to manipulate and control electronic devices in the smart home. The second demonstrates a more complex interaction task involving robot control.

Scenario 1: Simple user interaction controlling electronic devices.

As a common task we choose the control of a physical lamp. In the real world the user turn on the light by using a physical switch. Since the switch is connected to the smart home the system recognizes the action and in consequence it turns on the corresponding light. Additionally, the virtual worlds gets updated with the new state of the lamp. Whereas in the virtual world the user can turn on the light by clicking on the corresponding virtual switch. The user input is recognized by MORSE and creates an light switch event within SeMiWa which relays the event to the real world actuator to switch on the physical lamp.

As a failure detection mechanism the Tinkerforge sensor station controls the execution of the task by measuring the ambient light and checks for possible mismatching world states. If the measurement is within an expected range the system recognized the successful execution and updates the world model accordingly, thus keeping the real and the virtual environment synchronous. Otherwise the system informs the user about the failed action.

Scenario 2: A complex manipulation involving a robot.

As CPS consists also of complex devices like robots, we abstracted our concept from direct robot interaction to a more sophisticated object interaction. For instance, the user moves to a room, marks an object of interest and gets an overview of available manipulation tasks.

This more complex scenario involves mainly two objects, a carried object and a carrier robot (Fig. 4). As these worlds are synchronized, the user is able to decide an appropriate interaction path for itself, e.g., to order a robot to get the pill organizer from the kitchen or to go to the kitchen and get it themselves. If the user is currently within the kitchen its more efficient to grab it by hand. In contrast if the user stays in another room it might be easier to task an assisting robot. For example, the room is out of reach for the current user situation due to distance or other circumstances. In the virtual world, he is able to select the room or teleport to it, look around to find the pill organizer and define it as a goal for the robot by clicking on the virtual representation. Afterwards, the user have to call for the simulated robot and in the same way, the real robot gets for its journey. After both robots reach their goal, the avatar put the object on the simulated robot. In the real world, a gripper, which is installed in the kitchen, puts the real object onto the physical robot. The avatar instructs the robot to go for the human, which finally gets its object physically.

5 Conclusion and Outlook

Our interaction concept supports the instant control activities according to the study by Koskela et al. [5]. The favored mobile devices are supported by our approach by means of using tablets and smart phones as interaction devices. With our approach we created an interaction concept and virtual environment that can be utilized by such devices. This setup also supports dynamic changes by e.g., using robots or other actuators. The utilized dual reality approach from [8] which we extended by an semi-automated, synchronized reality concept allowed us to support the ease of use of such systems, according to Green et al. [4], by using real world user actions in a 3D virtual world to control smart home environments. As a result we get a smart home environment based on the previous mentioned components which is able to recognize some failure states and is able to inform the user. Besides the convenience requirement we also fulfill the requirement of flexibility mentioned by Green et al. The user can decide which actions to take without the system demanding a certain interaction style thus seamlessly incorporating people's lifestyle.

With the usage of robots to map the environment before or even while using it, we are able to localize sensor and actuator positions and synchronize those in the virtual world. In future work this could be extended to automatically create the 3D representation of the smart home utilizing indoor 3D reconstruction based on vision or other cues.

Due to the focus on the domestic environment this concept is directed to handle single user and small user groups such as families. We do not envision a utilization of the proposed interaction concept for larger groups. While the usage in such a scenario is possible to some extend adjustments would be necessary to coupe for issues that large user groups raise such as permission and access control. Also in contrast to [11] in which the authors motivate to bring different locations into a shared virtual environment to support communication between inhabitants, we used the "synchronized realities" approach to combine the real and virtual world of a single smart home environment at one location to support our interaction concept.

Currently, we are planning to conduct an exhaustive evaluation on identifying more classes of objects that are neccessary to synchronize. In addition, we are working on preparing a long-term user study in an elderly care environment to measure the suitability of our interaction concept. Furthermore, we intend to enhance our system to work not only on direct manipulation of objects, but also on a cooperative manner between the smart environment and the user.

Acknowledgment. This work was partly funded by the European Social Fund and the Federal State of Saxony in Germany within the projects VICCI (ESF-100098171) and SESAM (ESF-100098186).

References

1. Bayer, A.H., Harper, L., Greenwald, M.: Fixing to stay: A national survey of housing and home modification issues. American Association of Retired Persons 00102 (2000)
2. Lee, E.A., Seshia, S.A.: Introduction to embedded systems: a cyber-physical systems approach. Lee & Seshia (2011)
3. Voigt, M., Franke, M., Meißner, K.: Using expert and empirical knowledge for context-aware recommendation of visualization components (2013)
4. Green, W., Gyi, D., Kalawsky, R., Atkins, D.: Capturing user requirements for an integrated home environment. In: Proceedings of the Third Nordic Conference on Human-computer Interaction, NordiCHI 2004, pp. 255–258. ACM, New York (2004)
5. Koskela, T., Väänänen-Vainio-Mattila, K.: Evolution towards smart home environments: empirical evaluation of three user interfaces. Personal and Ubiquitous Computing 8(3-4), 234–240 (2004)
6. Piyare, R., Lee, S.R.: Smart home-control and monitoring system using smart phone, 00000 (2013)
7. Humble, J., Crabtree, A., Hemmings, T., Åkesson, K.-P., Koleva, B., Rodden, T., Hansson, P.: "Playing with the Bits" User-Configuration of Ubiquitous Domestic Environments. In: Dey, A.K., Schmidt, A., McCarthy, J.F. (eds.) UbiComp 2003. LNCS, vol. 2864, pp. 256–263. Springer, Heidelberg (2003)
8. Lifton, J., Paradiso, J.A.: Dual reality: Merging the real and virtual. In: Lehmann-Grube, F., Sablatnig, J. (eds.) FaVE 2009. LNICST, vol. 33, pp. 12–28. Springer, Heidelberg (2010)
9. Franke, M., Seidl, C., Schlegel, T.: A Seamless Integration, Semantic Middleware for Cyber-Physical Systems. In: 2013 10th IEEE International Conference on Networking, Sensing and Control (ICNSC), Evry, France, pp. 627–632. IEEE (2013)
10. Kahl, G., Burckert, C.: Architecture to enable dual reality for smart environments. In: Proceedings of the 2012 Eighth International Conference on Intelligent Environments, IE 2012, pp. 42–49. IEEE Computer Society, Washington, DC (2012)
11. Stahl, C., Frey, J., Alexandersson, J., Brandherm, B.: Synchronized realities. Journal of Ambient Intelligence and Smart Environments 3(1), 13–25 (2011)
12. Lemaignan, S., Echeverria, G., Karg, M., Mainprice, J., Kirsch, A., Alami, R.: Human-robot interaction in the morse simulator. In: Proceedings of the Seventh Annual ACM/IEEE International Conference on Human-Robot Interaction, HRI 2012, pp. 181–182. ACM, New York (2012)
13. Quigley, M., Conley, K., Gerkey, B., Faust, J., Foote, T., Leibs, J., Wheeler, R., Ng, A.Y.: Ros: an open-source robot operating system. In: ICRA Workshop on Open Source Software, vol. 3 (2009)

3D Design for Augmented Reality

Ivar Kjellmo

NITH (The Norwegian School of IT), Schweigaardsgate 14, 0185 Oslo
kjeiva@nith.no

Abstract. How do you define a good concept when designing augmented reality apps for mobiles? This paper focuses on design processes technically, graphically and conceptually in the development of 3D content for Augmented Reality on mobile devices. Based on experiences in the development and implementation of a course in 3D design for Augmented Reality at NITH (The Norwegian School of IT), challenges and methods in creating concepts, optimized graphics and visually coherent content for AR will be discussed.

Keywords: Augmented Reality, Virtual Reality, Mixed reality, Education, 3D design, Concepts, Presence in augmented and virtual reality.

1   Introduction

With the increased use of smart phones and tablets, development of Augmented Reality apps for a wide range of use has increased. Numerous games with AR content are available on Google Play and the App Store. There is a significant yearly increase in the amount of research being conducted on AR technology. According to numbers from Google Scholar [1], articles on augmented reality have risen from 4,020 in 2008 to 5,920 in 2010, 9,200 in 2012 and finally 11,500 in 2013. The numbers from Google Scholar may vary depending on search criteria. A similar search was done by Geroimenko in 2012 [2] with a different result, but the trend is similar. It seems that it is a technology that, to mention a few, is embraced by disciplines ranging from research, art and entertainment to marketing, architecture, engineering, military and medicine. A common impression is that most research on the topic still tries to enhance the technology, but the industry has also, to some degree, started to use AR concepts. As an example when Volkswagen launched their concept car, XL1 2014, an AR app by the German company Metaio [17] was developed [3]. By pointing the camera of a cell phone against the open engine room, the user can trigger animations displaying maintenance instructions superimposed on the camera image of the engine.

Augmented Reality as concept triggers the normal question about what AR is. The focus of this paper will not go into a long discussion about definitions. Wikipedia has one definition [4] that covers a wide range of different technical solutions and concepts. Stating the following: "*Augmented reality (AR) is a live, copy, view of a physical, real-world environment whose elements are augmented (or supplemented) by computer-generated sensory input such as sound, video, graphics or GPS data.*". The key issue is the merging of the "real reality" with the "virtual reality", speaking in

R. Shumaker and S. Lackey (Eds.): VAMR 2014, Part I, LNCS 8525, pp. 159–169, 2014.

the same language as Geroimenko [1]. In this paper,"real reality" as camera images from a mobile device merged with "virtual reality" as 3D graphical scenes. So to refine this paper, it will focus on augmented reality for mobile with the merging of 3D graphics and real time camera images of the mobile device.

As an example the new Google Glasses would be covered under the definition as they have a potential to merge text information with real-world environment through the glasses will not be covered.

2   Background

The first Augmented Reality interface dates back to the 1960's with a head mounted display called "sword of Damocles" by Ivan Sutherland [5].

In the beginning, creating AR applications required a massive setup of hardware and custom work. A pioneer project in Norway was the research of AHO (The Oslo School of Architecture and Design) regarding the visualization of the Margaretha Church in Maridalen, Oslo in 2005[6]. The project was a recreation of an old church in 3D. The ruins of the church were covered by markers in order to project the 3D model in the right place [Ill.1]. The project was viewed from a custom made portable screen that the viewer could carry around the area.

Fig. 1. Ill. 1. Margaretha Church ruins covered with AR markers

With today's tools for developing AR apps and the spread of smart phones and tablets, it is no longer a big technical challenge to make AR apps if only thinking in terms of making graphics superimposed with a camera image on a mobile device. Tools for making AR such as Unity 3D with the Vuforia packages makes it easier, but there are still technical challenges. More or less, the same technical research topics are outlined in the 2008 paper, "Trends in augmented reality tracking, interaction and display: A review of ten years of ISMAR" [7] are still relevant, such as tracking and how to represent realistic virtual graphics. There are also still limitations when developing AR when it comes to hardware and graphical possibilities. Another challenge lies in designing the content of AR apps visually and conceptually. Which choices do designers make on how to make good quality graphics? Developing AR concepts leads to a question of how and when to use augmented reality. With the rapid development of apps it is easy to see AR often used as a marketing gimmick or simple entertainment where the fascination of superimposing graphics with camera images can be seen as the main driving force. As the "magic of AR" becomes more advanced, storytelling and content that utilize AR as media becomes increasingly important.

The 3D graphics students of NITH (The Norwegian School of Information Technology) have designed augmented reality apps where they learn about these challenges in their course, "3D Design for Mobile Augmented Reality."

3   3D Graphics in Education

The AR course at NITH is an elective course for third year 3D graphic students at the school. It was run for the first time in the autumn of 2012 and developed by NITH, the visual effect company Placebo Effects and Labrat - a company specializing in games for mobile devices. The companies have firsthand experience in developing AR apps for the industry and brought important experiences into the course.

The goal of the course was that the students should learn all steps from start to end in developing a simple Augmented Reality app for either iOS or Android. The main assignment in the course was to develop a concept for an artist or band which would include sound, 3D graphic scenery and figure animation. The 3D content should pop up from a CD cover of the artist/band. This made it ideal to use the CD cover as an image tracker for the augmented reality app. An image tracker for AR is a picture or symbol which the camera on the mobile device would recognize and then be able to place and merge the 3D content into the camera image.

The chosen AR technology for the course was Qualcomm Vuforia packages for the Unity game engine. The choice of using the Vuforia libraries was motivated both because it is free to use and the easy integration with Unity 3D. By using this technology it is possible to upload images to the Vuforia developer website [8] to create image targets.

The course is organized in iterations with three assignments. The first assignment would be the design of an image tracker for the 3D content. The image tracker should both be technically stable and visually coherent with the graphical style of the chosen artist. When designing the marker for the AR app, the students had to make their own design of a CD cover for the artist/band. The importance of making the cover instead of just using an already existing CD cover was mainly a pedagogical issue in order to get the students to understand how an image marker works. It was also important to introduce the students to the concept of adapting to an existing graphical style in the assignment.

The second assignment was to design the 3D scene for the artist/band together with the working image tracker and the complete AR setup in the game engine. The students had 1 year of experience with 3D graphics, and this assignment was focused on the technical setup in Unity 3D with the Vuforia packages for the AR. On the artistic side, the students were encouraged to follow the graphical style from the image marker and to study the visual concepts of the chosen artist/band. This in order to make a scene that was visually coherent with the marker and applying typical elements as coloring, symbols and design of scenery elements that the given artist/band would use.

The third assignment was the full setup with an animated figure as a cartoony version of the artist/band. The students would typically make the figure both look and move like the original artist.

4   Design and Artistic Challenges

4.1   Tracking the Scene

In order to place the virtual scene correctly in place relative to the camera image, there are different techniques available. This will very dependent on the software used. In the course, Qualcomm's Vuforia was chosen as the technology to use. There could be different challenges with other software than those described here.

The Vuforia developer website contains a tool for making image trackers. By uploading an image to be used as a tracker, the tool will show with a rating of stars how good the tracking capabilities are. It will also show the overall distribution of track marks in the image. The technology works by finding contrast and non-repeating patterns in the image. As an example of a very good image tracker is the sample images that follows the Vuforia packages. It is only an image of small stones. However, the image has no repeating pattern and the contrast in and between the stones will distribute tracking marks uniformly over the whole image [Ill.2.]. The tool on the website will then embed the image into a downloadable Unity package which works directly on an AR camera in the virtual scene.

The challenges lay both in designing a good marker with an even distribution of tracking marks all over the image and to visually represent the artist/band. Another issue to consider is the size of the image marker compared to the virtual scene. For example if the image marker is very small and the virtual scene is very big with an extent far out on the sides of the marker, stability problems could occur, which is described as the pendulum effect, making it difficult to keep the virtual scene steady when watching it together with the "real reality".

Fig. 2. Image tracker with rating and evenly distributed tracking marks all over the image

4.2   Illuminating the Scene

A key issue in AR is the lighting of the 3D graphics that is supposed to be merged with camera images on the mobile device. In order to have a believable blending between the 3D graphics and the camera images, the first crucial element is how shadows appear in the virtual scene. The problem with realistic lighting in an augmented reality scene is obvious since the camera images in which the virtual scene will be rendered in are not predictable. This means that the coloring, direction and brightness of the lights would be different all the time depending on where the app is used.

There is no doubt of the importance of shadows in a 3D scene. Already in an early paper "The Effect of Shadow Representation in Virtual Objects in Augmented Reality" from 2003 [9], the authors discuss the strong effect of shadows in an augmented reality scene. This is useful, not only for a stronger connection between the real and virtual world but also as an element for creating depth. The paper shows examples with shadows in the virtual scene pre-rendered from one angle. The authors provide tests that show the importance of shadows despite the fact that they would come from an incorrect light direction when rendered together with real time camera images. This leads to the conclusion that it is probably better to have incorrect shadows than none at all.

Newer research has tried to solve the problems with shadow direction. A promising paper titled "Estimation of Environmental Lighting from Known Geometries for Mobile Augmented Reality" [10] discusses how to extract shadow direction based on facial geometry from the camera of the mobile. Still there are problems since the proposed system is only tuned for one light source and is only functional outdoors. In addition, the example seems to only produce sharp shadows.

In computer graphics, a well-known method to obtain photorealistic images is by using HDRI (High dynamic range image) based lighting of the 3D scene. This affects the coloring, direction of shadows and reflections in the scene. This is no longer a big problem to do when it comes to the rendering of 3D graphics for still images or video. Even most commercial game engines have support for using HDRI solutions, which, in computer games, is referred to as HDRR(High dynamic range rendering) [11]. With Augmented Reality, it is different since optimally all light information should be calculated in real time. This is discussed in the paper "Mobile AR Rendering Method using Environmental Light Source Information" [12]. The authors describe a system for capturing light sources and images from the cameras of a cell phone. The system also uses the gyro in the phone for direction of lights related to the image tracker of the virtual scene. Finally, the captured images would be used as an environmental light for the virtual scene. The method seems promising with multiple soft shadows generated in the scene.

5   Industrial Implications

5.1   AR Concepts

Developing good concepts for AR where the content, story and technical aspects of AR fully utilize the media can be a challenge. The mentioned car maintenance AR app by Volkswagen combines the actual car with important information on the user's own car and can be used in any place the car would be. Another good example is how the Norwegian dairy producer Tine utilizes the medium with their AR milk marketing campaign. The TineMelk AR app was created by Placebo Effects and Labrat in collaboration with the Try advertising agency.

In an interview, Kim Baumann Larsen shared his thoughts on developing engaging AR concepts and storytelling for the TineMelk AR app. His insight was also presented at Siggraph Asia 2013 [13] and ACM Siggraph 2012 [14]. Tine had, in several TV commercials, established a story world wherein computer-animated, highly photorealistic cows talked to each other with different Norwegian dialects in the cultural landscapes of Norway.

The most common arena for consuming milk would be the breakfast table. For the second AR app for Tine, a more interactive AR app was designed by Baumann Larsen. By having the milk carton as AR marker children can start a 3D coloring game where they colorize a farm scene with a stylized barn that drops down onto their milk carton. Animated cows will walk around in the scene, telling jokes and encourage the user to color the barn. Every now and then, they tell the children to drink their milk and eat their food. The app combines the important start of the day in a family setting with a healthy product with a fun and a potential social game. In addition to developing a concept that builds on an existing brand story world, Baumann Larsen believes there are three distinct features that should be included when developing a story based AR app. Each of these features will make the most out of the media and make for a more immersive and engaging augmented experience for the user:

1. Include the marker and the physical room into the story. In the first Tine app, the animated cows interact with the milk carton (the marker) by reading from it and by talking in the same local dialect in Norway as the area in which the milk carton was produced.

2. The location of the user (device) is inherent to AR, so one should create a visual connection between the virtual world and the user. In the case of the Tine Kuer AR app, the cows would look around and talk to the user to ask for help in the coloring of the scene, including the user into the story.

3. Enable user interaction with the scene. In the first TineMelk AR app, the user could only poke the cows, and they would react to it by replying with one-liners. In the last app, the interaction was a complete 3D coloring game.

5.2   Cartoony vs Photorealistic 3D Graphics

When designing 3D content for AR, the designers must choose a visual style for the virtual scene. Should the virtual scene be graphically stylized/cartoony or as photorealistic as possible? The examples in the research papers on lighting have a clear goal of developing techniques for a direction towards a photorealistic illumination of the virtual scene, something which is a difficult task, if even possible, at the current state of mobile graphics.

In the process of transferring the concept from TV to AR, the developers of the Tine app ended up with a style they call stylized realism. This means basically that the scene have a bit of both where it ends up somewhere in the middle but not photorealistic. Baumann Larsen argues that going away from the photorealistic towards a cartoony style, actually makes it more believable. The illusion breaks since it is more apparently "wrong" when something pretending to be photorealistic doesn't succeed 100%. When some elements in a scene are photorealistic, users would, to a larger degree, have higher expectations because one knows the notion of reality so well. An overly cartoony style would break too much with reality for the users to be able to accept it for what it is since one of the goals of AR is to seamlessly blend the digital scene with the physical world.

Baumann Larsen explains further that in the case of the apps made for Tine, instead of going for a complete realism, the developers lit the scene primarily with a dome light. This means that the main light is coming from a hemispherical dome illuminating the scene from all directions. A soft key light was added to give the 3d scene more form. This produces subtle contact shadows between the objects in the scene and there is no apparent direction in light/shadows. This makes the scene functional from all directions in an AR app. Materials and textures were baked in to single unlit materials where all the light information is stored in the textures. This is to keep the shaders simple and effective when it comes to hardware demands. From an industrial point of view, this was meant to work on as many smartphones and tablets as possible. This is a huge challenge, especially on the Android platform, since there are a large number of different types of devices. To further integrate the AR scene with the physical reality, an organically formed alpha map was used for the edge of the scene.

Based on the industry best practice experiences from Placebo Effects and Labrat, both the method of lighting with dome lights, simple materials (bake all information into one unlit map) and the choice to encourage the students to go for a more cartoony graphical style was included into the course.

6   Results and Discussion

The first time the course was conducted, the last assignment contained figure animation. Since the course in 3D animation went parallel to the AR course, they had to
learn animation simultaneously. Figure animation is complicated and potentially quite
time consuming. Extra lessons on animation were provided in order to help out. The
result was that the students used a significant amount of time on animating and learning to animate. The produced apps would typically have nice graphics, based on the
lighting methods described, but the apps would only contain the scene, sound and an
animated figure placed on the image tracker. There would be no interaction or other
elements to strengthen the experience. In the evaluation of the course, the students
also had, only to some degree, tried to have a coherency between all the parts of the
assignments. For example, in some cases they would have one style in the design of
the marker that didn't necessarily connect to the scene visually.

Based on those experiences, the next time the course was conducted there was a
more theoretical focus on coherency and on adaption of existing style. A lucky issue
that had an impact on the structure of the course was that the 3D animation course was
moved to earlier in the education, so the students who elected to take the 3D design for
AR course already had learned animation. This freed time to use on other elements.

The animation in the AR course would instead have a focus on making animated
behavior loops that could be reused, which was more time efficient. Another element
that was taken into the course was a bit of scripting for interaction. 3D graphic students are by nature not the most adept programmers, so this was just a very basic C#
intro, with some simple trigger scripts. The students where then encouraged to make
intros for their scenes. This, combined with trigger scripts, would make a way of manifesting the Virtual Reality in the Real Reality by some simple interaction. This
could be as simple as using a start button to start the animation of the 3D content to
more advanced scripting features. The teaching of lights and shadows was also developed to include a technique to make a connection between the virtual and the real by
making alpha maps with subtle contact shadows.

Finally it was also focused on designing splash screens and icons for the app in
order to have complete product from start to end.

The results of the assignments after the second time the course was completed was
overall significantly better in terms of graphics, coherency and overall total experience. The interaction - even in the cases when it was very simple makes the viewer
engage in the app. Some of the students used the scripting more than other depending
on their skills with programming. In one case a student made it possible to trigger
fireworks on the stage by touching it. Another student made a Stevie Wonder concept,
scripted with a graphical equalizer as a scene element, which moved according to the
music [Ill.4]. It also included loudspeakers in the scene that where controlled by a
script to trigger the bass elements in time with the music.

One good example on scene adaptation is one of the student works featuring the
artist Pink where the scenery from the artists "Funhouse" show was used as inspira-
tion [Ill.3]. The design process of the tour was already well documented on the artist's
webpage, with photographs from the actual show and 3D renderings from the

planning of the stage design. The student adopted the design of the scene with clear elements from the original, with the circuslike forms, the panels back on the stage and in the use colors, concept and design from the real show. An animated Pink figure would appear by poking a little hatch on the scene floor.

Fig. 3. On the left: The original designs of the funhouse show [16]. Right: AR funhouse designed by Kine Marie Sæternes 2013.

The illustrations [3 and 4] also show the effect with the dome lighting that produces soft contact shadows and space in the virtual scenes. This makes uniform lighting that can be viewed with the same quality from all directions of the scene. With static,

Fig. 4. Stevie Wonder AR app by Philip Stevju Løken 2013. Scene with subtle contact shadows with alpha channel and scene with scripted equalizer and bass elements.

sharp shadows as described by Sugano, Kato and Tachibana [9], it may enhance the scene compared to not having shadows at all, but it might also be perceived as disturbing if it breaks too much with the physical lighting of the camera image. As seen in the Stevie Wonder concept [Ill.4], soft and subtle shadows rendered to alpha maps make the virtual scene connect to the surface it is projected to.

So far a cartoony/stylized representation seems to visually work for AR in many cases. However the intensive research on AR, computer graphics in general and hardware enhancements makes a future hope of photorealistic virtual content for AR likely.

7   Conclusion and Further Development

The overall technical goal of making AR apps is to have a believable blending between the real and the virtual, but the human factor is about content and what to present. The course was designed with experiences from the industry, which makes a high demands from their customers. Bringing in the industrial side of the production makes a focus on completeness and coherency. Although the apps produced by the students have a simple and limited narrative focus, it seems that focusing on coherency in the design and completeness seemed to enhance the quality of the products the students made.

The introduction of scripting had significant value where it brought interaction as an element into the work.

The fact that the students had a year with experience with 3D graphics and especially that they could do some figure animation before the course started made them more capable of doing a fun and interesting story.

Further development of the course would enhance the conceptual side in the planning in order to have more consistent stories. More scripting could also be considered, enabling even more interaction from the user into the virtual scene.

References

1. Augmented reality, search criteria "anywhere in the article",
   http://scholar.google.co.uk
2. Geroimenko, V.: Augmented Reality Technology and Art: The Analysis and Visualization of Evolving Conceptual Models. In: 16th International Conference on Information Visualisation, p. 1 (2012)
3. http://gigaom.com/2013/09/30/this-bit-goes-there-vw-and-metaio-show-off-what-ar-can-do-for-car-service-technicians/
4. http://en.wikipedia.org/wiki/Augmented_reality
5. http://en.wikipedia.org/wiki/The_Sword_of_Damocles_%28virtual_reality%29
6. Lecture notes of Professor Søren Sørensens at AHO covering different early AR projects, http://www.ife.no/en/ife/departments/software-engineering/files/ar/ar-in-architectural-and-urban-planning.pdf

7. Zhou, F., Been-Lim Duh, H., Billinghurst, M.: Trends in augmented reality tracking, interaction and display: A review of ten years of ISMAR. In: ISMAR 2008, pp. 1–2 (2008)
8. https://developer.vuforia.com/
9. Sugano, N., Kato, H., Tachibana, K.: The Effect of Shadow Representation in Virtual Objects in Augmented Reality. In: ISMAR 2003 Proceedings of the 2nd IEEE/ACM International Symposium on Mixed and Augmented Reality (2003)
10. Koc, E., Balcisoy, S.: Estimation of Environmental Lighting from Known Geometries for Mobile Augmented Reality. In: International Conference on Cyberworlds (2013)
11. http://en.wikipedia.org/wiki/High-dynamic-range_rendering
12. Jung, Y., Kim, T., Oh, J., Hong, H.: Mobile AR Rendering Method using Environmental Light Source Information. In: International Conference on Information Science and Applications, ICISA (2013)
13. Baumann Larsen, K.: Interactive 3D coloring with mobile AR. In: SIGGRAPH Asia 2013 Symposium on Mobile Graphics and Interactive Applications (2013)
14. Baumann Larsen, K., Siver, T., Jones, D.: Mobile augmented reality in advertising: the TineMelk AR app - a case study. In: SIGGRAPH 2012 (2012)
15. http://rockartdesign.com/gallery/rock-shows/pink/pink-2009-design-process/
16. http://www.tpimagazine.com/production-profiles/274964/pink_the_funhouse_tour.html
17. http://www.metaio.com

Don't Walk into Walls: Creating and Visualizing Consensus Realities for Next Generation Videoconferencing

Nicolas H. Lehment, Philipp Tiefenbacher, and Gerhard Rigoll

Institute for Human-Machine Communication
Technische Universität München
{Lehment,Philipp.Tiefenbach,Rigoll}@tum.de

Abstract. This contribution examines the problem of linking two remote rooms into one shared teleconference space using augmented reality (AR). Previous work in remote collaboration focusses either on the display of data and participants or on the interactions required to complete a given task. The surroundings are usually either disregarded entirely or one room is chosen as the "hosting" room which serves as the reference space. In this paper, we aim to integrate the two surrounding physical spaces of the users into the virtual conference space. We approach this problem using techniques borrowed from computational geometric analysis, from computer graphics and from 2D image processing. Our goal is to provide a thorough discussion of the problem and to describe an approach to creating consensus realities for use in AR videoconferencing.

1 Introduction

To date, videoconferencing is a mode of communication constrained to displays or specialized projective equipment. With current innovations like Google Glass and advanced Head Mounted Displays (HMDs), we can however envision a future where our remote conversation partner is no longer banished to flat displays. Instead our Avatars will appear to walk in far-away offices and labs, rendered as three-dimensional personalities by displays integrated into our glasses. This leads to the question of how we are to define the consensus reality in which we engage. Since we cannot guarantee that all participants are located in infinite, uncluttered spaces, there are bound to be discrepancies between our surroundings. If our opposite were to inhabit a large corner office, while we were to reside in a smaller cubicle, such conflicts would inevitably arise. As our conversation partner strolls over to his desk, his Avatar on our side of the connection might happen to walk right through our cubicle wall. In order to deal with such discrepancies in our environments, we aim to define a consensus reality which uses 3D scans of both rooms in order to identify common layout features. A simplified illustration of our target system is shown in Fig. 1. Note that in this paper we focus on the details of computing the consensus reality, leaving the details of user streaming and rendering to other parties (e.g. [1,2]).

In the following, we start by clarifying the context and present an overview over previous related research. We then present our method for computing the consensus reality,

R. Shumaker and S. Lackey (Eds.): VAMR 2014, Part I, LNCS 8525, pp. 170–180, 2014.

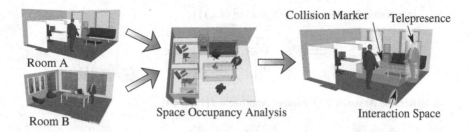

Fig. 1. Example of an augmented reality videoconference with two participants and heterogeneous environments. In a first processing step, the rooms are aligned and obstacles are identified. A map of common uncluttered floorspace is generated and used as the basis for the consensus reality. In the right image, the scene as perceived by participant A is shown: The conversation partner is added to the scene as an Avatar, the uncluttered floorspace is shown in green and a single obstacle, the desk, is represented as a red box. Participant A can thus avoid stepping into the desk and knows the basic layout of the consensus reality.

followed by a description of a simple visualization scheme. Subsequently we summarize our experiences in the conclusion and give a brief outlook on open questions.

2   Related Work and Context

Videoconferencing is a wide field of research. For our scenario, we focus on concepts which place the conversation partner directly into our environment, e.g. using augmented reality (AR) or at least mobile displays. Our previous work explored the inclusion of AR-elements into classic videoconferencing [3]. Sodhi *et al.* [4] realize a similar concept for hand-held devices in limited tabletop workspaces. Other groups have attempted to integrate conversation partners into remote locations using cylindrical displays [5], mobile social proxies [6,7] or stationary social proxies [8,9]. When we categorize previous work on virtual telepresence by the handling of the physical surroundings, we arrive at three different approaches which are illustrated in Fig. 2.

Firstly, there is the total immersion of both participants in a virtual space. This VR approach disregards the actual environment of the participants and instead provides a virtual meeting space in which interactions and discussions take place. Typical examples would be [10,11]. Another approach uses window metaphors in order to connect two real, physical spaces. In its simplest implementation, this leads to video-conferencing as familiar to users of Skype or Google Hangouts. In recent years, more elaborate versions have evolved such as the perspective sensitive display by Maimone *et al.* [12] or our AR-enhanced videochat [3]. Using the window approach, the participant's spaces are clearly separated as "things on my side of the window" and "things on the other side of the window", effectively avoiding conflicts by suspending immersion. Finally, there is the wide field of remote assistance systems. For these approaches, one user space is selected as the "hosting" space into which the remote supporter is immersed. The space on the side of the remote participant is usually disregarded, since the focus lies on solving a problem in the primary space. Typical examples are found in [13,14,4,15].

Immersive Telepresence Conferencing [10, 11]

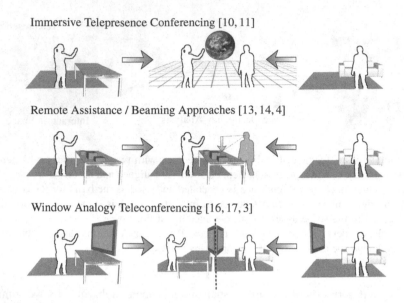

Remote Assistance / Beaming Approaches [13, 14, 4]

Window Analogy Teleconferencing [16, 17, 3]

Fig. 2. Current approaches to treating surrounding physical space in remote collaboration research

None of these approaches considers the scenario of mutually integrating conversation partners into each other's physical environment. Therefore we ask: How can we treat scenarios where both participants want to meet on equal footing, talking between themselves in their offices? We propose a distributed augmented-reality approach: We create a consensus reality by combining both participants' offices into one shared virtual space which encompasses both locations.

Thus, we touch upon issues of scanning the room [18,19], computational geometric operations on the resulting scans [20], tracking the conversation partners [21,22] and visualizing the consensus reality [4,23,24].

3   Defining a Consensus Reality

Our approach relies on existing scans of the participating spaces. Such scans can be obtained easily and cheaply using commodity depth sensing cameras and subsequent analysis programs (e.g. using Kinect Fusion [25]). The resulting 3D meshes are then analysed by applying computational geometry techniques such as boolean operations [20]. We thus distinguish between 3 types of spaces: Those unobstructed on both sides of the conversation, those occupied by objects at one conversation partner and finally those occupied on both sides. Unobstructed spaces are then defined as free floor space, while both other types are marked as non-enterable spaces. Optionally, we can identify similar surfaces and mark these as consensus surfaces. Such surfaces can be used to place virtual content objects or 3D models. Since we know for these consensus planes that there is a similar, physical surface in both participants' environment, we can avoid having virtual objects floating mid-air. In a further refinement, we could even create a

Fig. 3. Visualization of a conference in a consensus reality with static mock-up avatars. The table marked in red is not present in the local environment, but marks a table standing in the conversation partner's office. For the sake of illustration, HMDs and their fields of view are ignored.

shared physical space, i.e. using the consensus surfaces as entities in a shared simulation of physical properties of virtual objects.

For our work, we assume the two participating rooms to have an even and uninterrupted floor plane. We do not consider multi-level rooms, stairs or sloped surface planes. We also require the scans to cover the entire floor of the intended interaction space and all obstacles within. Fig. 4 shows an exemplary scenario where a consensus reality spanning two rooms is constructed. A triangular mesh of counter-clockwise connected vertices is assumed, but does not need to be complete or closed. However, the mesh describing the floor plane of the intended workspace must be complete and free of holes. In the following, we shall consider the meshes $\mathcal{M}_A$ for room A and $\mathcal{M}_B$ for room B. The meshes are made up of individual polygons P_k which in turn consist of three vertices $\mathbf{V} = (V_x, V_y, V_z)$:

$$\mathcal{M}_i = \{P_1, P_2, \ldots, P_n\} \tag{1}$$

$$P_k = \left\{ \begin{pmatrix} V_{1,x} \\ V_{1,y} \\ V_{1,z} \end{pmatrix}, \begin{pmatrix} V_{2,x} \\ V_{2,y} \\ V_{2,z} \end{pmatrix}, \begin{pmatrix} V_{3,x} \\ V_{3,y} \\ V_{3,z} \end{pmatrix} \right\} \tag{2}$$

In a first step, we consider the submeshes $\mathcal{M}_{i,\,\text{Furniture}}$ containing only Polygons P lying at least partially above the floor plane (i.e. $V_{j,z} > 10\,\text{cm}$ $\exists j \in \{1, 2, 3\}$) and entirely below the ceiling (i.e. $V_{j,z} < 2\,\text{m}$ $\forall j \in \{1, 2, 3\}$). We use an orthographic projection to render the Vertices V_j contained in $\mathcal{M}_{i,\,\text{Furniture}}$ to the 2D floor plane. In order to facilitate subsequent processing, we define the floor plane $\mathbf{I}_{i,\,\text{Furniture}}$ as an 2D array of fixed size $S_f = s_r \times s_y = 10\,m \times 10\,m$ and discretize coordinates in that plane with a sampling factor of $d_{\text{floor}} = 1/50m$. Note that $\tilde{\mathbf{T}}_{\text{floor}}^{\text{world}}$ denotes the absolute world transformation of the floor plane, while $\triangle_{ABC}^{\text{filled}}$ signifies a filled triangle drawn by the half-space function or a similar suitable rendering function.

$$\forall P_k \in \mathcal{M}_i$$
$$\forall V_{kj} \in P_k$$
$$\hat{V}_{kj} = \tilde{\mathbf{T}}_{\text{floor}}^{\text{world}} V_{kj} \tag{3}$$
$$\hat{v}_{kj,\text{x}} = \lfloor d_{\text{floor}} \cdot \hat{V}_{kj,x} + 0.5 \cdot s_x \rfloor \tag{4}$$
$$\hat{v}_{kj,\text{y}} = \lfloor d_{\text{floor}} \cdot \hat{V}_{kj,y} + 0.5 \cdot s_y \rfloor \tag{5}$$
$$\forall P_k \in \mathcal{M}_i$$
$$t_k = \frac{\hat{V}_{k1,z} + \hat{V}_{k2,z} + \hat{V}_{k3,z}}{3} \tag{6}$$
$$\triangle_{ABC}^{\text{filled}}(A : \hat{v}_{k1} \rightarrow B : \hat{v}_{k2} \rightarrow C : \hat{v}_{k3}, \text{value} : t_k) \Rightarrow \mathbf{I}_{i,\,\text{Furniture}} \tag{7}$$

In order to account for walls, we repeat this procedure for all polygons P contained in a single rooms mesh and arrive at a second 2D array $\mathbf{I}_{i,\,\text{InvWalls}}$ where only the areas without data are set to zero. We perform a bitwise thresholding operation on each pixel $\mathbf{p}(x, y)$ of this array in order to arrive at a map where the volumes behind walls or columns are set to 2.0 m:

$$\forall \mathbf{p}(x, y) \in \mathbf{I}_{i,\,\text{Walls}} : \quad \mathbf{I}_{i,\,\text{Walls}}(x, y) = \begin{cases} 2.0\,m & \text{if } \mathbf{I}_{i,\,\text{invWalls}}(x, y) = 0 \\ 0.0\,m & \text{else} \end{cases} \tag{8}$$

We then construct the final map of a single room by combining both maps into the room map $\mathbf{I}_i$:

$$\forall \mathbf{p}(x, y) \in \mathbf{I}_i : \quad \mathbf{I}_i(x, y) = \begin{cases} \mathbf{I}_{i,\text{Walls}}(x, y) & \text{if } \mathbf{I}_{i,\text{Walls}}(x, y) > \mathbf{I}_{i,\text{Furniture}}(x, y) \\ \mathbf{I}_{i,\text{Furniture}}(x, y) & \text{else} \end{cases} \tag{9}$$

As we compute the equally sized maps $\mathbf{I}_A$ and $\mathbf{I}_B$ for both rooms A and B, we can then use these to find a map $\mathbf{I}_{\text{Floor}}$ of open floor space common to both rooms:

$$\forall \mathbf{p}(x, y) \in \mathbf{I}_A \wedge \mathbf{I}_B :$$

$$\mathbf{I}_{\text{OR}}(x, y) = \begin{cases} \mathbf{I}_A(x, y) & \text{if } \mathbf{I}_A(x, y) > \mathbf{I}_B(x, y) \\ \mathbf{I}_B(x, y) & \text{else} \end{cases} \tag{10}$$

$$\mathbf{I}_{\text{Floor}}(x, y) = \begin{cases} 1 & \text{if } \mathbf{I}_{\text{OR}}(x, y) > 0.1\,m \\ 0 & \text{else} \end{cases} \tag{11}$$

Thus we have a first 2D map of shared free space for both participants. Similary, we can use our room maps in order to identify obstacles unique to one room. We can compute $I_{Obst. A}$ and $I_{Obst. B}$ with boolean operators as follows:

$$\forall \mathbf{p}(x, y) \in \mathbf{I}_A :$$
$$\mathbf{I}_{AND}(x, y) = \mathbf{I}_A(x, y) \wedge \mathbf{I}_B(x, y) \tag{12}$$
$$\mathbf{I}_{Obst. A}(x, y) = \neg (\mathbf{I}_{AND}(x, y)) \wedge \mathbf{I}_A(x, y) \tag{13}$$
$$\mathbf{I}_{Obst. B}(x, y) = \neg (\mathbf{I}_{AND}(x, y)) \wedge \mathbf{I}_B(x, y) \tag{14}$$

Finally and maybe most importantly, we can identify not only obstacles common to both rooms in a map $\mathbf{I}_{Common}$, but also find consensus surfaces $\mathbf{I}_{Surfaces}$:

$$\forall \mathbf{p}(x, y) \in \mathbf{I}_A :$$
$$\mathbf{I}_{HeightDiff}(x, y) = \|\mathbf{I}_A(x, y) - \mathbf{I}_B(x, y)\| \tag{15}$$
$$\mathbf{I}_{Common}(x, y) = \begin{cases} \mathbf{I}_{AND}(x, y) & \text{if } \mathbf{I}_{AND}(x, y) \leq 1.6\,m \\ 0 & \text{else} \end{cases} \tag{16}$$
$$\mathbf{I}_{Surfaces}(x, y) = \begin{cases} \mathbf{I}_{AND}(x, y) & \text{if } \mathbf{I}_{HeightDiff}(x, y) \leq 0.05\,m \\ 0 & \text{else} \end{cases} \tag{17}$$
$$\tag{18}$$

We thus arrive at 2D maps of the 5 different types of spaces. These are also illustrated in Fig. 4.

- $\mathbf{I}_{Floor}$ shows the consensus free space available to both conversation partners.
- $\mathbf{I}_{Obst. A}$ shows obstacles present only in room A, but not in room B.
- $\mathbf{I}_{Obst. B}$ shows obstacles present only in room B, but not in room A.
- $\mathbf{I}_{Common}$ shows obstacles present in both rooms, but not of equal height.
- $\mathbf{I}_{Surfaces}$ shows obstacles present in both rooms and of equal height, e.g. table tops present in both rooms.

For initializing the consensus reality, we need to determine a reference point prior to map computation. In simple implementations, this might be done using a simple planar marker which serves as a reference point. More interesting however is the dynamic optimization of the map alignment transform $\mathbf{T}_{align}$. This can be formulated as an optimization problem with the goal of maximizing consensus free space and consensus surfaces. Using a suitable energy function E_{align}, we can solve the following equation for an optimal alignment:

$$\mathbf{T}_{align} = \text{argmin}_{\mathbf{T}} \, E_{align}(\mathbf{I}_A, \mathbf{I}_B, \mathbf{T}) \tag{19}$$

In the next step, we can use the resulting maps to communicate the similarities and discrepancies of their surroundings to the conversation partners.

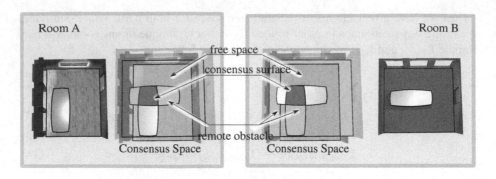

Fig. 4. Consensus Reality as seen from two different rooms. Note especially the different layout of remote obstacles (in red) for the two rooms.

4   Visualizing the Consensus Reality

The procedures described so far are based on geometrical analysis of meshed 3D models. The next challenge lies in communicating the extend and limits of the consensus reality to the conversation participants. In order to study this problem, we use a test-bench approach. The entire AR communication scenario is replicated in the virtual environment of a 4-wall CAVE VR system, an approach suggested in [26,27].

Hence we are free to quickly define and evaluate different modes of display, minutely control scenario parameters and reduce possible experimental noise. Furthermore, we are able to evaluate a wide range of different display technologies simply by simulation. We can evaluate not only existing devices, but also technologies still under development. This enables an effortless and cheap review of different approaches for future systems, ranging from simple Google Glass-style visors up to HMDs covering nearly the entire field of view.

After the mapping procedure described in the previous section, we are presented with the problem of visualizing these 2D maps in a 3D space on devices with a limited field of view (FOV). Here we have to consider different demands and constraints on the visualization. The goal is to provide a non-distracting, intuitive and clear rendering. We consider the different maps in turn, assuming the point of view of an participant in room A:

- I_{Floor}: Rendering the free floor space can help confidently navigating the consensus space. However, care must be taken to make this visualization as non-intrusive and uncluttered as possible.
- $I_{Obst. A}$: As we are already standing in room A and seeing the obstacles directly, no rendering of this map is necessary.
- $I_{Obst. B}$: Rendering this map is important. This map contains information crucial to remote obstacle avoidance, such as walls or furniture in the remote location. This visualization helps in avoiding walking through the conversations partners wall, desks etc.
- I_{Common}: As there is also a local obstacle present, rendering these common obstacles would only make sense if there is a marked difference in shape or height.

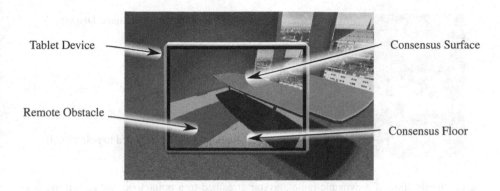

Fig. 5. Consensus Reality rendered as pointcloud on a simulated tablet device. Shown is the view from room A, as seen in Fig. 4. Different colors denote different maps, in this case $I_{Surfaces} \equiv$ blue, $I_{RemoteObstacle} \equiv$ red and $I_{Floor} \equiv$ green.

– $I_{Surfaces}$: Rendering this map enables the conversation partners to find flat surfaces common to both rooms. Thus, the local user in room A would be able to place a virtual object on the remote's user table in room B instead of having it hang mid-air.

We use a pointcloud rendering approach in order to visualize the different maps. Since the maps also contain height information, we can draw the point clouds such that they appear to hover over the real objects themselves.

The pointclouds $\mathcal{P}_i = \{\mathbf{A}_{i1}, \mathbf{A}_{i2}, \ldots, \mathbf{A}_{iN}\}$ are computed using the reverse mapping from the map array to the 3D space of the room:

$$\forall \mathbf{p}_j(x,y) \neq 0 \in \mathbf{I}_i :$$

$$\mathbf{A}_{j,x} = \frac{x - 0.5 \cdot s_x}{d_{floor}} \tag{20}$$

$$\mathbf{A}_{j,y} = \frac{y - 0.5 \cdot s_y}{d_{floor}} \tag{21}$$

$$\mathbf{A}_{j,z} = \mathbf{p}_j(x,y) \tag{22}$$

These pointclouds can then be rendered into the scene, as shown in Fig. 5, or used as the basis for more elaborate visualizations, e.g. using surface meshes or wireframe models.

5 Discussion and Conclusion

In this paper, we show a method for computing and visualizing consensus realities from existing 3D scans of rooms. These consensus realities are intended for use in 3D AR videoconferencing scenarios with non-homogeneous surroundings. The 2D mapping approach is a rather simplistic solution and easily implemented. The reduction to a 2D plane also reduces computational complexity especially for full room models: Whelan et al. [28] arrive at 1.2×10^6 vertices for a single room (LAB dataset). The simplification to the floor plane therefore significantly accelerates the consensus space computation,

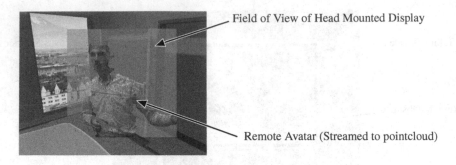

Field of View of Head Mounted Display

Remote Avatar (Streamed to pointcloud)

Fig. 6. Visualization of a dynamic remote avatar streamed to a pointcloud and seen through a simulated HMD device in our CAVE

however at the cost of losing height information during the projection. Our approach performs well for rooms of limited size with an even, continuous floor plane. In the implementation presented here, we assume a rigid mapping of participating conference rooms, i.e. no *redirected walking* [29,30].

The visualization with pointclouds in flat planes is a technically elegant solution, but suffers from the limited field of view of the users' devices. If mapped to the floor plane, the point cloud becomes barely visible at times and requires the user to look down in order to orient himself in the consensus reality. For remote obstacles, the rendering often results in pointclouds and artifacts floating in space without a visible connection to the physical surroundings. We therefore propose the introduction of more powerfull visualization techniques in future incarnations of our system. Nevertheless, pointclouds are a viable starting point for more elaborate displays and will remain attractive especially due to their flexibility in rendering and interaction. As we can see in Fig. 6, the pointcloud approach can also be used for rendering the users themselves. This is an active field of research in itself [1,2].

The use of a CAVE for fast evaluation of different rendering methods has proven to be very promising. We found that considering the same visualization techniques on different devices can lead to surprising insights which might have been missed otherwise. For instance, just varying the field of view for a see-through HMD can lead to a markedly different perception of the consensus space. In future works, we aim to extend the parallel testing and development of AR visualizations using the flexibility provided by the CAVE to a more formal and systematic development approach for AR experiences.

In the coming years, we are likely to see a convergence of three major technological developments: Affordable and lightweight consumer HMDs, as foreshadowed by the OculusRift and W. Steptoes current adaption to AR scenarios, cheap depth sensing cameras similar to the Kinect and the spread of high-bandwidth network connections. In consequence, we can expect AR videoconferencing to become a serious alternative to window-constrained videochats. As we move away from window analogies and virtual meeting spaces, the inclusion of our surroundings is bound to become an important factor in this development. We hope that the methods and insights outlined in this paper will help bringing videoconferencing away from limited flat screens into the rich and complex spaces of our everyday life.

References

1. Kammerl, J., Blodow, N., Rusu, R., Gedikli, S., Beetz, M., Steinbach, E.: Real-time compression of point cloud streams. In: ICRA, pp. 778–785 (2012)
2. Ruhnke, M., Bo, L., Fox, D., Burgard, W.: Compact rgbd surface models based on sparse coding. In: AAAI (2013)
3. Lehment, N.H., Erhardt, K., Rigoll, G.: Interface design for an inexpensive hands-free collaborative videoconferencing system. In: ISMAR, pp. 295–296 (2012)
4. Sodhi, R.S., Jones, B.R., Forsyth, D., Bailey, B.P., Maciocci, G.: Bethere: 3d mobile collaboration with spatial input. In: ACM SIGCHI, pp. 179–188 (2013)
5. Kim, K., Bolton, J., Girouard, A., Cooperstock, J., Vertegaal, R.: TeleHuman: Effects of 3D perspective on gaze and pose estimation with a life-size cylindrical telepresence pod. In: Human Factors in Computing Systems, pp. 2531–2540 (2012)
6. Adalgeirsson, S.O., Breazeal, C.: Mebot: a robotic platform for socially embodied presence. In: HRI, pp. 15–22 (2010)
7. Michaud, F., Boissy, P., Labonte, D., Corriveau, H., Grant, A., Lauria, M., Cloutier, R., Roux, M.A., Iannuzzi, D., Royer, M.P.: Telepresence robot for home care assistance. In: Multidisciplinary Collaboration for Socially Assistive Robotics, pp. 50–55 (2007)
8. Venolia, G., Tang, J., Cervantes, R., Bly, S., Robertson, G., Lee, B., Inkpen, K.: Embodied social proxy: mediating interpersonal connection in hub-and-satellite teams. In: SIGCHI, pp. 1049–1058 (2010)
9. Steptoe, W., Normand, J.M., Oyekoya, O., Pece, F., Giannopoulos, E., Tecchia, F., Steed, A., Weyrich, T., Kautz, J., Slater, M.: Acting rehearsal in collaborative multimodal mixed reality environments. Presence: Teleoperators and Virtual Environments 21(4), 406–422 (2012)
10. Gross, M., Würmlin, S., Naef, M., Lamboray, E., Spagno, C., Kunz, A., Koller-Meier, E., Svoboda, T., Van Gool, L., Lang, S., Strehlke, K., Moere, A.V., Staadt, O.: Blue-c: A spatially immersive display and 3D video portal for telepresence. In: SIGGRAPH, pp. 819–827. ACM (2003)
11. Kurillo, G., Bajcsy, R.: 3D teleimmersion for collaboration and interaction of geographically distributed users. Virtual Reality 17(1), 29–43 (2013)
12. Maimone, A., Fuchs, H.: Encumbrance-free telepresence system with real-time 3D capture and display using commodity depth cameras. In: ISMAR, pp. 137–146 (2011)
13. Adcock, M., Anderson, S., Thomas, B.: Remotefusion: Real time depth camera fusion for remote collaboration on physical tasks. In: VRCAI, pp. 235–242 (2013)
14. Gurevich, P., Lanir, J., Cohen, B., Stone, R.: Teleadvisor: A versatile augmented reality tool for remote assistance. In: SIGCHI, pp. 619–622 (2012)
15. Oyekoya, O., Stone, R., Steptoe, W., Alkurdi, L., Klare, S., Peer, A., Weyrich, T., Cohen, B., Tecchia, F., Steed, A.: Supporting interoperability and presence awareness in collaborative mixed reality environments. In: VRST, pp. 165–174 (2013)
16. Billinghurst, M., Cheok, A., Prince, S., Kato, H.: Real world teleconferencing. IEEE Computer Graphics and Applications 22, 11–13 (2002)
17. Maimone, A., Yang, X., Dierk, N., State, A., Dou, M., Fuchs, H.: General-purpose telepresence with head-worn optical see-through displays and projector-based lighting. In: IEEE VR, pp. 23–26 (2013)
18. Salas-Moreno, R.F., Newcombe, R.A., Strasdat, H., Kelly, P.H., Davison, A.J.: Slam++: Simultaneous localisation and mapping at the level of objects. In: CVPR, pp. 1352–1359 (2013)
19. Newcombe, R.A., Davison, A.J., Izadi, S., Kohli, P., Hilliges, O., Shotton, J., Molyneaux, D., Hodges, S., Kim, D., Fitzgibbon, A.: Kinectfusion: Real-time dense surface mapping and tracking. In: ISMAR, pp. 127–136 (2011)

20. Granados, M., Hachenberger, P., Hert, S., Kettner, L., Mehlhorn, K., Seel, M.: Boolean operations on 3D selective nef complexes: Data structure, algorithms, and implementation. In: Di Battista, G., Zwick, U. (eds.) ESA 2003. LNCS, vol. 2832, pp. 654–666. Springer, Heidelberg (2003)
21. Shotton, J., Fitzgibbon, A., Cook, M., Sharp, T., Finocchio, M., Moore, R., Kipman, A., Blake, A.: Real-time human pose recognition in parts from a single depth image. In: CVPR (2011)
22. Baak, A., Müller, M., Bharaj, G., Seidel, H.P., Theobalt, C.: A data-driven approach for real-time full body pose reconstruction from a depth camera. In: CVPR, pp. 1092–1099 (2011)
23. Livingston, M., Gabbard, J., Swan, J., Edward, I., Sibley, C., Barrow, J.: Basic perception in head-worn augmented reality displays. In: Human Factors in Augmented Reality Environments, pp. 35–65. Springer, New York (2013)
24. Kantonen, T., Woodward, C., Katz, N.: Mixed reality in virtual world teleconferencing. In: IEEE VR, pp. 179–182 (2010)
25. Izadi, S., Newcombe, R.A., Kim, D., Hilliges, O., Molyneaux, D., Hodges, S., Kohli, P., Shotton, J., Davison, A.J., Fitzgibbon, A.: Kinectfusion: real-time dynamic 3d surface reconstruction and interaction. In: SIGGRAPH, pp. 23:1–23:1 (2011)
26. Ragan, E., Wilkes, C., Bowman, D., Hollerer, T.: Simulation of augmented reality systems in purely virtual environments. In: IEEE VR, pp. 287–288 (2009)
27. Lee, C., Bonebrake, S., Hollerer, T., Bowman, D.: A replication study testing the validity of ar simulation in vr for controlled experiments. In: ISMAR, pp. 203–204 (2009)
28. Whelan, T., McDonald, J., Kaess, M., Fallon, M., Johannsson, H., Leonard, J.J.: Kintinuous: Spatially extended kinectfusion. In: Workshop on RGB-D: Advanced Reasoning with Depth Cameras (2012)
29. Steinicke, F., Bruder, G., Jerald, J., Frenz, H., Lappe, M.: Analyses of human sensitivity to redirected walking. In: VRST, pp. 149–156 (2008)
30. Kulik, A., Kunert, A., Beck, S., Reichel, R., Blach, R., Zink, A., Froehlich, B.: C1x6: A stereoscopic six-user display for co-located collaboration in shared virtual environments. In: SIGGRAPH Asia, pp. 188:1–188:12 (2011)

Transparency in a Human-Machine Context: Approaches for Fostering Shared Awareness/Intent

Joseph B. Lyons and Paul R. Havig

Air Force Research Laboratory, 711 Human Performance Wing/Human Effectivess Directorate, Wright-Patterson AFB, OH 45433
{Joseph.Lyons.6,Paul.Havig}@us.af.mil

Abstract. Advances in autonomy have the potential to reshape the landscape of the modern world. Yet, research on human-machine interaction is needed to better understand the dynamic exchanges required between humans and machines in order to optimize human reliance on novel technologies. A key aspect of that exchange involves the notion of transparency as humans and machines require shared awareness and shared intent for optimal team work. Questions remain however, regarding how to represent information in order to generate shared awareness and intent in a human-machine context. The current paper will review a recent model of human-robot transparency and will propose a number of methods to foster transparency between humans and machines.

Keywords: transparency, human-machine interaction, trust in automation, trust.

1 Introduction

Robotic platforms have been projected to revolutionize the landscape of modern life with applications ranging from support of the elderly, customer service, education, rehabilitation, and medicine [1]. These systems may offer advantages over human-based operators in situations where humans are not available, not capable, nor motivated to perform the necessary actions. Robotic platforms (also called autonomous systems within the Department of Defense, or DoD, vernacular) could be used in a military context to perform missions such as high-risk reconnaissance, search and rescue, logistics (e.g., transport), training, defensive security/crowd control, firefighting, and potentially kinetic operations. Full autonomy, where a system is permitted to execute complete decision and behavioral initiative, has yet to be realized for the vast majority of systems, though technology advances may enable greater autonomy in the future. Yet, despite technological advances in many areas related to robotics, humans maintain a critical role in executing supervisory control and serving as collaborators (some may suggest partners) with novel technology. The need for humans to be involved with robotic systems as controllers, supervisors, or teammates will not likely change in the near future, at least not for Department of Defense (DoD) -oriented technologies. Thus, it is critical that human-centric requirements be engineered into robotic platforms to encourage optimal use and reliance on newly developed systems.

R. Shumaker and S. Lackey (Eds.): VAMR 2014, Part I, LNCS 8525, pp. 181–190, 2014.
© Springer International Publishing Switzerland 2014

Much of the research in this area has focused on human-robot interaction (HRI) and has been driven in recent years by advances in commercial-off-the-shelf platforms, advances in the science of human-like robotic interfaces, and advances in the design of robotic platforms in terms of navigation and locomotion. A growing interest has emerged in understanding HRI using a more social orientation. There has been a movement toward considering robotic platforms as teammates rather than as tools [2]. Moving from tools to teammates requires that systems be designed with more naturalistic interaction styles which may attempt to leverage the nuances of human-human interactions. Regardless of the approach used, human resistance or acceptance of these systems will be a key factor in shaping the success or demise of robotic systems. "The human ability to accept robots into teams ultimately will determine the success or failure of robot teammates. Although the technical capabilities of robots to engage in coordinated activity is improving (as visible for robot-only teams at RoboCup), we believe humans' innate expectations for team-appropriate behavior pose challenges to the development of mixed teams that cannot be fixed with technology innovation." [3; p.486]. Research has consistently demonstrated that humans naturally anthropomorphize technology [4], and this phenomenon may be more prominent within an HRI domain as humans may seek to ascribe "intention" to robotic systems given their appearance and planned usage in socially-oriented contexts [2].

Human-human teams can be effective or not effective depending largely on a number of social elements including development of shared mental models [5], team processes (e.g., communication, conflict management, coordination [6]) and training [5]. Effective teamwork has a number of socio-emotional components including: shared goals, shared awareness, desire to be interdependent, motivation toward team goals, performance toward team activities, and trust among team members [3]. Many of these same principles will apply to a human-machine context, particularly when the system exhibits human characteristics, is used for social tasks, and is used in the context of uncertainty. One of the keys for optimizing the human-machine relationship will be to present the human partner with cues related to the team-orientation and mission-centric performance of the robotic system. Yet, this is easier said than done.

Autonomy for robots may include autonomous sensing, planning, or acting [7]. A robotic platform that is programmed to behave autonomously can face a number of "decision points" during dynamic environmental constraints. Complicating matters is the fact that many DoD missions could involve both high levels of uncertainty and threat, as well as time pressure. Robotic platforms in the commercial world could also include high-risk domains such as aviation or driving, both of which can involve life-threatening consequences when errors occur. Robotic platforms could be used in tandem with manned platforms and the number of platforms on the battlefield could be considerable, placing high demands on the human's ability to monitor the battlefield [8]. The demands of monitoring the performance of multiple robotic systems could foster sub-optimal decision strategies, suggesting that systems be designed to present the right information at the right time without overloading their respective operator/teammate [8]. In order to address the dynamics of environmental changes, the nuances of various tasks, and the need for team-oriented social cues robotic systems should be designed to foster transparency.

1.1   Transparency in a Human-Machine Context

Transparency in a human-robot context can be defined as a method to establish shared intent and shared awareness between a human and a machine [9]. The concept of transparency emerged from the trust in automation literature as way to reduce uncertainty regarding the performance and or behavior of an automated tool. Interestingly, providing information to human users of automation can also create greater uncertainty when done poorly (i.e., when overloading the users or when presenting users with irrelevant information). Therefore, the type and amount of information presented to users must be tailored to the unique situation in which the information is to be used. Prior research on trust in automation found that providing human operators with information related to the reliability of an automated tool promoted more optimal reliance strategies on the tool [10]. Further, information related to the limitations of an automated tool aids in trust recovery following errors of the automation [11]. This added information appears to be useful in deciphering the boundary conditions under which the tools are more or less capable. Thus, providing humans with information related to the performance of an automated tool appears to be beneficial. Kim and Hinds [12] applied a similar logic within a human-robot context and found that providing explanations of anomalous robotic behavior was related to more attributions of blame when the system made an error, though only when the system was described as having higher versus lower autonomy. The added information seems to add value for humans interacting with technology, perhaps because it offers clues regarding the performance of the system. Further, this information seems to be more important when the system has greater control over its actions (i.e., when it is more autonomous). This is logical given that performance is the strongest predictor of trust within a human-robot context [13]. The competence (i.e., ability) of a person is also a critical driver of interpersonal trust; however, so is the benevolence and integrity of a person [14]. Given the social-emotional engagement that is possible between humans and robotic platforms and the social nature in which robotic platforms may be used, it is plausible that both performance-oriented and socially-oriented transparency factors matter within a human-robot scenario.

In this spirit, Lyons [9] outlined a novel model of human-robot transparency involving an intentional model (including social intent and purpose), task model, analytical model, environment model, teamwork model, and human state model. The intentional model highlights the overall purpose of the system and provides cues to the human regarding the social intent of the system. The task model may include an understanding of the particular task (perhaps via a cognitive task analysis or a task analysis), information that communicates the robot's goals, information that characterizes the robot's progress in relation to the goals, information to communicate awareness of capabilities in relation to the goals, and finally communications that signify awareness of performance/errors in relation to the goals. The analytic model should communicate the decision logic used by the robot to initiate action. The environment model should communicate awareness of constraints present within the mission context (e.g., weather, relevant variations in terrain, threat information, etc.). The teamwork model should visualize the division of labor between the partners in real-time, adjusting to the dynamic nature of tasks as activities as traded off between partners. Finally, the human state model should display relevant metrics related to the human's performance (i.e., workload, stress, performance trends) in the human-robot context. The notions of shared intent and shared awareness are key objectives related to transparency. Thus, the methods for fostering transparency are clustered around each of these higher-level domains of shared intent and shared awareness. Below we outline some initial thoughts we have on how HRI should evolve for effective teaming. Note that an interesting research question is the amount of anthropomorphizing one may (or may not) want to incorporate in a human-machine team. These ideas are put forward as an attempt to get the community to discuss how this teaming should most effectively be instantiated and then eventually tested.

Shared Intent. From the perspective of functionality, appearance seems to matter quite a bit in a human-robot context. Appearance of a robot may confer functionality to the humans interacting with it based on expectations [1; 15]. Some of these expectations conform to gender roles. Research by Eyssel and Hegel [16] compared robots with typical male features such as short hair to robots with female features such as long hair and found that "male" robots were perceived as being more agentic than females and more suitable for masculine tasks such as security or repairs. In contrast, "female" robots were perceived as more warm, better suited for care giving, and service relative to "males". Further, research by Broadbent [17] found that robots with a human-like appearance were perceived as being more amicable, social, and having the most personality relative to robots that were less human-looking. The critical point from a transparency perspective is that the desired functionality of the system should map directly into its appearance as much as possible.

In addition to the function-orientation of the intention model, a robot also needs to confer social intent to its human teammate. Rich social information exchanges may enhance human-robot interactions as this added information could serve as a useful cue to the human representing the system's understanding, engagement, and intent [18]. The social style of the system will be an important factor in determining the "intent" of the system (as perceived by the human) which will likely have significant implications for one's trust of the system. Given the uncertainties inherent to human-robot interactions, understanding the social intent of a system will help humans to anticipate "why" a robot took a particular action, which is equally as important as understanding what the action was. Further, understanding robot intent will allow the human to anticipate a range of actions given particular environmental constraints. The latter would be useful for DoD operations since the DoD operates with a number of guidelines/rules for conflict (e.g., the Law of Armed Conflict) and understanding social intent, which may include adherence to a set of ethical – albeit – programmed principles of a robotic platform, will aid human operators and partners in making informed decisions regarding how much behavioral initiative to provide to the robotic system (see [19] for a review). Understanding the drivers of robotic behavior could also be important for autonomous systems used in the commercial domain. For instance, it will be important for humans to understand the driving etiquette of autonomous cars, particularly during congested traffic, inclement weather, or urban routes involving high pedestrian traffic. This information will help humans to anticipate the behavior of the robotic platforms. Social cues can also provide humans with rich information regarding how the robot "views" their human teammate [20]. Akin to human-human social exchanges, it is often not what is said but how it is said that shapes one's reactions to others. These social cues could represent concepts such as benevolence, social etiquette, and team-oriented communication.

Shared Awareness. Many human-robot interaction scenarios involve collocation between the human and the system. However, many DoD-relevant scenarios will involve distributed interactions, and having shared awareness in the latter context will be critical to ensuring optimal HRI. The transparency model by Lyons [9] outlines a number of awareness-based requirements between humans and robotic platforms. First, the robot should communicate knowledge about the task. The robot should communicate what task, or which step embedded within a series of tasks, it is currently working on. Inputs for this task model could originate from a task or cognitive analysis, which would specify the facets of each task to be accomplished. The robot should communicate progress within the task, and where possible identify when it has encountered obstacles that prevent task completion. The system should also communicate the decision logic used to initiate behaviors. This will be particularly useful when a behavior violates the expectations of the human. A key element of distributed teaming between humans and robotic platforms will be developing a shared awareness of the environmental constraints within a task domain. This has been shown to be important for deep space missions where humans cannot be collocated with robotic platforms [7]. Finally, the robotic platform should communicate awareness of the distribution of labor in team-based tasks, and an awareness of human state characteristics such as workload and stress. In the section below, the authors outline a few high-level ideas for creating these transparency facets within a HRI context.

2 Interface Techniques

2.1 Shared Intent

The importance of shared intent cannot be overlooked if trying to form an effective Human-Robotic team. It is clear from watching team failures in any environment (e.g., sports, work, familial, etc.) that the potential for miscommunication and misunderstanding easily arises when the intent of all players is ambiguous. The same will likely hold true for human-machine partnerships. In a DoD context, perhaps the most important sharing of intent would be when the robot has to update the human partner as to why it deviated from the original plays/programming (i.e., what was the intent of the change and what are the follow-on consequences). This is especially important if there is a reliance on the human to help form a new course of action. Shared intent can flow from the appearance, social cues, and prescribed behavioral repertoire of the system. From a non-DoD perspective, shared intent would be extremely helpful in Human-Robotic teams for disaster relief. Robotic systems have been used to survey damage associated with events such as the Tsunami that hit Japan in 2011 and the super typhoon that hit the Philippines in 2013. If the systems were given the mission of finding individuals in need following these natural disasters they would need to be flexible in their planned routes. When the systems had the decision initiative to deviate from flight plans, they humans interacting with them would need to understand the intent of the system or else the system would run the risk of being overridden by the human. Take the example of plan deviation; it would be important for the intent to be communicated quickly and accurately so the human partner could make a more effective decision.

From an appearance standpoint, researchers have demonstrated that the form of a robotic system tends to shape the human expectations associated with the system [1]. Thus, the key for establishing transparency in purpose is to align the appearance with the desired function. The more socially-oriented the desired function, the more anthropomorphic the system should be designed. Robots intended for mechanistic functions such as loading/unloading, transport, assembly may not need anthropomorphic features as much as those engaging in social-oriented activities. Robots designed for security purposes may want to incorporate features that are useful for deterrence such as size or the presence of a weapon to shape perceptions of relative formidability [21]. Spider legs, relative to regular legs or tracked capabilities, have also been shown to be associated with higher perceived aggressiveness in prior research [22]. More research is needed in this area to better understand how different robotic forms relate to human expectations.

Non-verbal cues from robotic systems can be used to decipher intent from the systems. Social cues like gaze can signal attention, facial expressions can be used to communicate emotion, and action can represent intention [20]. Gaze seems to foster greater recall of information when humans interact with robotic instructors [23]. Gaze may help to establish shared attention and it may help to foster social norms or social etiquette within a task context. Gaze may be particularly useful in situations where the human and the system must exchange a lot of information. For instance, service robots taking orders for merchandise or food may be equipped with gaze features to demonstrate engagement with a particular person. Exploring social etiquette within an automated scenario, Parasuraman and Miller [24] found that automated tools were more effective when they avoided interrupting humans during tasks and when they used a polite versus impatient style. Social etiquette between humans and robotic systems may benefit from having an established social etiquette that is appropriate for the particular task context in question. It may also be imperative for the social etiquette to evolve as the dynamics of a situation change. For instance, it is possible that when a robot encounters a time-sensitive constraint the humans will respond better to etiquette that reflects this temporal demand and urgency.

The communication exchanges between humans and robots will also serve as a key indicator of robot intention. Communications that exemplify the notion of benevolence, the belief that a trustor has the trustee's best interest in mind [14], may promote a human's perceived benevolence from the robot when the robot suggests a change of behavior is needed. Robots could use phrases such as, "My recommended course of action is in your best interests based on my assessment of your goals." That phrase communicates an awareness of the human's needs and that the suggested action would be the best course of action in relation to those needs. Robotic communications may also influence human perceptions of their competence. The use of specific versus more general nouns has been shown to be related to greater perceived persuasion [23]. Also, robots tend to be perceived as having greater expertise when they use a combination of vocal variability, gaze, and gestures [23]. Other research has found that robot-expressed emotions are more easily perceived by humans when multiple information channels are used at once (e.g., gestures coupled with expressions) [25]. Thus, the use of social cues and corresponding behavior may provide information to the human about the capabilities and intent of the robot.

Understanding the social intent of robotic systems will also involve the concept of robot ethics. Researchers discussed the idea of ethical governors for robotic systems [19]. Such systems may identify the thresholds for risk based on established conventions in warfare – this could incorporate a decision logic tree for behaviors. Presenting this logic to humans may provide useful information pertaining to the social intent of the robot. This could also be represented via robotic emotional displays where the robot interface could portray particular emotions in contexts where it might be expected to display emotions such as guilt [19]. Expressed guilt would signify that the system is aware that it has violated the desired state of the human. Emotion expressions, even digital emotional displays, signify an awareness of consequences and thus one can infer intent from them [26]. In fact, it is often the extrapolation of intent through an emotional appraisal process that drives human behavioral reactions to agent-based emotional displays [26]. Thus, the idea of robot "intent" will be fundamental in predicting how humans respond to robotic social cues. Designers need to be cognizant of such effects lest their systems fall victim to misaligned perceptions among user communities. The issue of alignment between perceived intent (i.e., appraisals of intent [26]) and robotic emotional displays will increase with importance as robots gain more behavioral and decision authority, and as robots are used in more team-based scenarios.

2.2   Shared Awareness

Prior research has outlined a number of recommendations for the design of automated tools: it should be aware of progress towards goals, suggest actions that support goals, be inquisitive when uncertainty is high, communicate intentions and limitations, and serve as a collaborator [27]. Many of these concepts are consistent with the idea of the task model of transparency. Robots could use a real-time indicator within a human-machine interface to signify which step in a particular task, or set of tasks, that a robot is currently working on. Simple process flow diagrams could be used to represent a set of tasks and as the robot completes one step and moves on to the next step a real-time indicator could be used to track progress within the process map. When the robot encounters an obstacle or is otherwise unable to complete a task it should communicate this limitation/constraint to the human, and where possible share the reason for the failure. Geo-registering could be used to track the location of distributed platforms. In the event of a disturbance in signal, which is possible in military domains characterized by Anti Access Area Denial (A2AD) domains, the interface could provide a range of possible locations based on historical waypoints. The showing of robotic moves/interactions on a geospatial world view would be a most logical step for the majority of current concepts for HRI. If the true concept of autonomous vehicles of the future is "autonomous action" then the human needs only be a passive viewer of the work (i.e., the human is on-the-loop as opposed to being in-the-loop) and would only need to intercede when there is an operationally relevant teaming decision to be made. However, simple route information may not be enough. In current military operations, it is up to the pilot to pay attention to things such as fuel, time-on-station, sensor capabilities, and then make the decision through the operations floor if a change in plans is required based on the mission goals. In this future scenario, an automated system may be capable of monitoring its fuel status for example, but may not have the ability to effectively hand-off operations to another autonomous vehicle. In this case, the human operator would have to intervene and re-route the appropriate asset. In such situations, it would be optimal for the human to have complete knowledge of the "health" of the system and so the aforementioned characteristics (e.g., fuel) would need to be depicted and/or reported in some way that is actionable by the human. An initial design concept could involve creating a display to represent the health status on any platform similar say to the status board one may have in a hospital setting. The hospital metaphor is important as the most important health information should be highlighted in some logical manner so the human can more quickly assess the situation and make a decision.

Understanding the analytical underpinning of a robot during a performance context is also very important. Human collaborators need to understand the logic tree for the system [7] particularly when the system evidences some anomalous behavior. For instance, when the human expects the platform to be in location A and it emerges in location C, it needs to immediately explain the anomalous behavior to the human partner. In this situation, it would be best for the robot to report changes in a clear and logical manner that allows the human to quickly re-assess the situation and prepare for new operations. One way this could be done is to have the robot report with a quick verbal protocol as to when the mission changed, why it changed, and what was accomplished due to the change (or what was not) accomplished due to the change. After this quick debrief then, depending upon the mission and thorough explanation, using the original planning interface would then help in the re-planning process. The idea of the quick debrief is to get the human on the same page as the robot much in the same way a human would do when reporting back to a commanding officer (i.e., quick debrief then details as needed). The importance of understanding the logic driving behavior increases as systems gain initiative to execute mission objectives. In other words, the greater autonomy afforded to a robotic system, the greater the need for the human to understand the robot's decision logic driving its behavior.

As robots are used in novel domains they are certain to encounter unexpected constraints within the environment. These constraints may come in the form of difficult weather, terrain obstructions, or even hostile threats within military operations. Robotic interfaces should be designed to foster shared awareness between the human and robot regarding any environmental changes that may influence mission effectiveness. This shared awareness could be enabled through the use of sensors on the platform to gauge weather patterns, as well as cameras to display physical constraints and threats in the area.

Finally, robots need to communicate an awareness of the division of labor when engaging in team-based tasks with human partners. Using the same notion of a process map or task analysis described above, the interface could represent which activities were under the robot's control and which were the responsibility of the human. Taxonomies for representing different levels of automation such as those outlined in [28] could be used to signify the degree of autonomy currently allocated to the robot for a particular task. This could be particularly useful when a human is collaborating with more than one robotic platform and is responsible for supervising and adjusting them within an operational context.

3   Conclusion

The future of HRI and design approaches to foster transparency within this domain is ripe for future research. Indeed, there is considerable human-human teaming research on-going that can be leveraged as the HRI moves forward, and this has been evidenced by the growth of social robotics. The key evolution in recent years is the consideration of the robot as a partner not a thing, tool, or vehicle. Once a true teaming concept is accepted and adopted, our supposition is that the interface will follow naturally though the HCI of implementing effective transparency methods aiming to engender shared intent and shared awareness between the human and his/her robotic teammate.

References

1. Veloso, M., Aisen, M., Howard, A., Jenkins, C., Mutlu, B., Scassellati, B.: WTEC Panel Report on Human-Robot Interaction Japan, South Korea, and China. World Technology Evaluation Center, Inc., Arlington (2012)
2. Ososky, S., Schuster, D., Phillips, E., Jentsch, F.: Building appropriate trust in human-robot teams. In: Proceedings of AAAI Spring Symposium on Trust in Autonomous Systems, pp. 60–65. AAAI, Palo Alto (2013)
3. Groom, V., Nass, C.: Can robots be teammates? Benchmarks in human-robot teams. Interaction Studies 8(3), 483–500 (2007)
4. Nass, C., Moon, Y.: Machines and mindlessness: Social responses to computers. J. of Social Issues 56, 81–103 (2000)
5. Salas, E., Cooke, N.J., Rosen, M.A.: On teams, teamwork, and team performance: Discoveries and developments. Human Factors 50(3), 540–547 (2008)
6. Cohen, S.G., Bailey, D.E.: What makes teams work: group effectiveness research from the shop floor to the executive suite. J. of Management 23, 239–290 (1997)
7. Stubbs, K., Wettergreen, D., Hinds, P.J.: Autonomy and common ground in human-robot interaction: A field study. IEEE Intelligent Systems, 42–50 (2007)
8. Chen, J.Y.C., Barnes, M.J., Harper-Sciarini, M.: Supervisory control of multiple robots: Human performance issues and user interface design. IEEE Transactions on Systems, Man, and Cybernetics – Part C: Applications and Reviews 41(4), 435–454 (2011)
9. Lyons, J.B.: Being transparent about transparency: A model for human-robot interaction. In: Proceedings of AAAI Spring Symposium on Trust in Autonomous Systems, pp. 48–53. AAAI, Palo Alto (2013)
10. Wang, L., Jamieson, G.A., Hollands, J.G.: Trust and reliance on an automated combat identification system. Human Factors 51, 281–291 (2009)

11. Dzindolet, M.T., Peterson, S.A., Pomranky, R.A., Pierce, L.G., Beck, H.P.: The role of trust in automation reliance. Int. J. of Human-Computer Studies 58, 697–718 (2003)
12. Kim, T., Hinds, P.: Who should I blame? Effects of autonomy and transparency on attributions in human-robot interactions. In: Proceedings of the 15th International Symposium on Robot and Human Interactive Communication (RO-MAN 2006), pp. 80–85. IEEE, Hatfield (2006)
13. Hancock, P.A., Billings, D.R., Schaefer, K.E., Chen, J.Y.C., Ewart, J., Parasuraman, R.: A meta-analysis of factors affecting trust in human-robot interaction. Human Factors 53(5), 517–527 (2011)
14. Mayer, R.C., Davis, J.H., Schoorman, F.D.: An integration model of organizational trust. Academy of Management Review 20, 709–734 (1995)
15. Fischer, K.: How people talk with robots: Designing dialogue to reduce user uncertainty. AI Magazine, 31–38 (2011)
16. Eyssel, F., Hegel, F.: (S)he's got the look: Gender stereotyping of robots. J. of App. Soc. Psych. 42(9), 2213–2230 (2012)
17. Broadbent, E., Kumar, V., Li, X., Sollers, J., Stafford, R.Q., MacDonald, B.A., Wegner, D.M.: Robots with displays screens: A robot with more humanlike face display is perceived to have more mind and a better personality. PLoS ONE 8(8), e72589 (2013)
18. Breazeal, C., Aryananda, L.: Recognition of affective communicative intent in robot directed speech. Autonomous Robots 12(1), 83–104 (2002)
19. Arkin, R.C., Ulam, P., Wagner, A.R.: Moral decision-making in autonomous systems: Enforcement, moral emotions, dignity, trust, and deception. Proceedings of the IEEE 100(3), 571–589 (2012)
20. Coradeschi, S., Ishiguro, H., Asada, M., Shapiro, S., Thielscher, M., Breazeal, C., Mataric, M., Ishida, H.: Human-inspired robots. IEEE Intelligent Systems 21(4), 74–85 (2006)
21. Fessler, D.M.T., Holbrook, C., Snyder, J.K.: Weapons make the man (larger): Formidability is represented as size and strength in humans. PLoS ONE 7(4), e32751 (2012)
22. Sims, V.K., Chin, M.G., Sushi, D.J., Barber, D.J., Ballion, J., Clark, B.R., Garfield, K.A., Dolezal, M.J., Shumaker, R., Finkelstein, N.: Anthropomorphism of robotic form: A response to affordances? Proceedings of the Human Factors and Ergonomics Society Annual Meeting 49, 602–605 (2005)
23. Mutlu, B.: Designing embodied cues for dialogue with robots. AI Magazine, 17–30 (2011)
24. Parasuraman, R., Miller, C.: Trust and etiquette in high criticality automated systems. Communications of the ACM 47, 51–55 (2004)
25. Zecca, M., Mizoguchi, Y., Endo, I.F., Kawabata, Y., Endo, N., Itoh, K., Takanishi, A.: Whole body emotion expressions for KOBIAN Humanoid Robot: Preliminary experiments with different emotional expression patterns. Paper presented at the 18th IEEE International Symposium on Robot and Human Interactive Communication. Toyama, Japan (2009)
26. de Melo, C., Carnevale, P., Read, S., Gratch, J.: Reverse appraisal: The importance of appraisals for the effect of emotion displays on people's decision-making in a social dilemma. In: Proceedings of the 34th Annual Meeting of the Cognitive Science Society, Sapporo, Japan (2012)
27. Geiselman, E.E., Johnson, C.M., Buck, D.R.: Flight deck automation: Invaluable collaborator or insidious enabler? Ergonomics in Design: The Quarterly of Human Factors Applications 21, 22–26 (2013)
28. Parasuraman, R., Sheridan, T.B., Wickens, C.D.: A model for types and levels of human interaction with automation. IEEE Transactions on Systems, Man, and Cybernetics—Part A: Systems and Humans 30, 286–297 (2000)

Delegation and Transparency: Coordinating Interactions So Information Exchange Is No Surprise

Christopher A. Miller

Smart Information Flow Technologies (SIFT), 211 First St. N. #300,
Minneapolis, MN USA 55401
cmiller@sift.net

Abstract. We argue that the concept and goal of "transparency" in human-automation interactions does not make sense as naively formulated; humans *cannot* be aware of everything automation is doing and why in most circumstances if there is to be any cognitive workload savings. Instead, we argue, a concept of transparency based on and shaped by delegation interactions provides a framework for what should be communicated in "transparent" interactions and facilitates that communication and comprehension. Some examples are provided from recent work in developing delegation systems.

Keywords: flexible automation, adaptive/adaptable automation, Playbook®, delegation, Uninhabited Aerial Systems, trust, transparency, supervisory control.

1 Introduction

"Transparency" has been held up as a goal for automated systems that assume or require a substantial human interaction ([1], though the term is not used in this paper), and on its surface this seems a laudable and reasonable goal. But what does transparency in human-automation interaction mean anyway? What can or should it mean?

Naively, it would seem that "transparency" is a straightforward property such that all a system's functions and behaviors, as well as the rationale behind them, are available and obvious to human users. The automated system is "like glass" in that its workings are apparent to all. Achieving such transparency might be a substantial challenge for user interface designers, and understanding all the behaviors and rationales transparently presented might require specialized knowledge (e.g., aeronautical mechanics and flight controls for an autopilot), but these do not seem to be impossible goals, at least in principle.

The problem is that this form of transparency is fundamentally at odds with the goals of most human-automation interaction in the first place. Automation is generally created and deployed to save the human operator effort and/or to achieve performance speed or accuracy beyond what a human alone could do. This means that if transparency demands that the human maintain awareness of every sensed observation, decision and executed behavior the automation performs, then there is no time or

R. Shumaker and S. Lackey (Eds.): VAMR 2014, Part I, LNCS 8525, pp. 191–202, 2014.

(cognitive) effort saved. Full transparency in automation (and the human responsibility to make full use of it) would eliminate most benefit from the automation[1].

2   The Problem of Transparency

In earlier work [2], we formulated a concept of the relationship and tradeoff between human cognitive load, unpredictability to the human in automation behaviors and the achieved competency of the overall human-automation system (that is, performing correct behaviors in context). See Figure 1. Very frequently, we implement automation with the objective of achieving greater competency (the ability to achieve more behaviors more accurately, precisely or rapidly, etc.)—this corresponds to expanding the length of the triangle base. The relationship to the other legs of the triangle, however, illustrates two additional principles. First, that an increase in competency can only be achieved via an expansion of one or the other (or both) of the other two dimensions. Second, that a given level of competency can be achieved in a variety of ways that will differ in impact on workload and unpredictability.

Competency is achieved by giving the responsibility for monitoring, assessing and making decisions and executing actions to some agent—either human or machine. If the added responsibility (and the corresponding added tasks) for performing these steps are all given to the human, then clearly, added workload will be

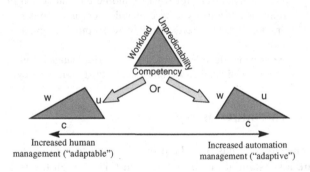

Fig. 1. The spectrum of tradeoffs between competency, workload and unpredictability (from [2], used with permission)

the result. If those added responsibilities are given to automation, the human cognitive load will not increase, but the knowledge, awareness and control which comes from performing those tasks will also not accrue to the human. If the human is required to maintain awareness of everything the automation is sensing, assessing and deciding, as in a fully "transparent" system, then awareness will not decrease, but the human will have performed at least all of the cognitive work that s/he would have had to perform to achieve the task in the first place. In short, for competency increases without cognitive workload increases, it is inevitable that some of the sensing, assessing

---

[1]   There are exceptions to this general formulation. Some automation enables performance at times or places where humans cannot. It might well be acceptable to use "transparent" automation in the sense described above in situations hostile to human presence, but where sufficient time and human resources are available to fully understand everything the automation is doing—such as in Martian rovers and nuclear reactor maintenance.

and deciding activities be taken out of the human's hands—that is, they must be "obscured, not "transparent" in the sense above if any cognitive work is to be saved.

We have not previously considered the meaning of the height of the triangle, but it seems reasonable that it represents an abstract measure of work complexity: the amount of cognitive work which *must be done by someone* (humans or automation), for the level of competency. Work complexity is probably not as independent of the competency dimension as implied by the triangle figure—a point at which the analogy breaks down. Work may be made less complex by better system design, reduction in the number of interacting components, etc.—and such reductions can reduce both human cognitive workload and system work producing unpredictability. For example, by most accounts, jet engines are less complex than traditional piston driven turbines because there are fewer moving parts. This implies that to be fully aware of the state and behaviors for operating a jet engine is "simpler" than for a piston-driven turbine, whether it is a human or automation doing it.

Transparency in a human-automation system is essentially the opposite of the unpredictability leg of the triangle in Figure 1 and, therefore, "transparent design" would imply striving to minimize that leg. As for competency though, for a given level of work complexity, this can be accomplished only by reducing either human cognitive workload or the competency of the overall human-automation system, or both. If the goal is to preserve overall system competency and if no reduction in the underlying work complexity is possible, then the only way to accomplish that while concurrently reducing unpredictability is by increasing human cognitive workload.

A pair of objections to this reasoning seems valid. First, this reasoning only applies to cognitive workload. Some automation performs mainly or solely physical tasks. Reducing unpredictability through increased transparency for such a system would still increase the human's cognitive load, but there could be substantial savings in physical workload. Second, one might object that "transparency" does not refer to the human's need to be aware of all operations of the automation concurrently, but only to the availability of that information. Automation should be transparent, but the human has to decide when and what to look at. I would agree that removing the need that the human maintain awareness of everything avoids the problems above, but relaxing that requirement begs the question of how to design, select and train the human-automation system to afford the right kind of awareness for good performance and safety. We will advance some thoughts on that in the next section below.

3   Practical Transparency—The Role of Delegation

So if "transparency" cannot, practically speaking, mean that the human knows everything about what the automation is doing, then what can or should it mean? Chen, et al., [3] define automation transparency as "… the descriptive quality of an interface pertaining to its abilities to afford an operator's comprehension about an intelligent agent's intent, performance, future plans, and reasoning process." If this cannot reasonably mean full awareness of all these elements, then the emphasis is on "operator's comprehension" and the key question becomes how much and what type of awareness is necessary to promote comprehension in a multi-agent system?

This question requires a decision about the roles and relationships of the system's actors. Most current and near-future visions of human-automation interactions leave the human in charge of automation in a *supervisory control* relationship [4]—that is, both responsible for directing the automation and for ensuring all functions are accomplished. This relationship demands more awareness of a greater range of functions than other possible ones, and it is subject to the fundamental limitation described above: the human cannot be aware of everything the system is doing if any cognitive workload is to be saved. Humans in supervisory positions exert control through *delegation*—the act of giving instructions or orders that the subordinate is expected to attempt to follow and perform, with some reporting throughout execution and discussion when compliance with the directives are difficult, impossible or sub-optimal.

In multiple efforts, we have explored enabling humans to express intent and delegate to subordinate automation with the same flexibility possible in human supervisory control [2,5]. We use the metaphor of a sports team's playbook. Our Playbook® systems allow humans and automation to share a conceptual, hierarchically-structured framework for the goals and methods of a pattern of activity (a "play") and to delegate instructions and discuss performance within that framework.

Flexible delegation achieves *adaptable*, rather than adaptive, automation [2]. To achieve a greater range of competency from automation than available in traditional, static automation, researchers turned to adaptive automation approaches [6], which exhibit a wider variety of behaviors but which leave decisions about when and how to shift behaviors to the automation itself. By contrast, in adaptable automation, the human initiates behaviors by "delegating" at flexible levels of specificity; automation is then responsible for planning and executing within the delegated instructions. Adaptive automation is targeted at saving the user workload and may result in superior performance in some contexts, but when the user and automation are at odds as to what should be done, the human has little opportunity to influence, override or even understand the automation and may end up "fighting" it for control.

We have argued for adaptable approaches [2] in most contexts due to this potential for mismatch. Adaptable, delegation approaches have been shown to result in improved overall system performance when examined across unpredictable and/or unexpected contexts [7] and reduced human workload relative to adaptive systems in some circumstances [8]. There is also reason to believe that the act of expressing intent is an important part of the naturalistic decision making process [9], serving to "crystalize" intent for both the declarer and the hearers. Moreover, the process of declaring intent to subordinates should facilitate situation awareness of what the subordinate is doing (alleviating the 'what is it doing now' problem [1]) and even, potentially, improving trust accuracy by providing the "truster" with an explicit, declared intent to evaluate the "trustee's" performance against. Many of these effects have been observed for adaptable automation approaches in recent studies [7,8,10,11].

The question considered below is whether intent declaration and intent-focused interactions inherent in delegation systems may have an impact on "transparency" and transparent design. Since the key is to convey information which will "afford operator comprehension" as appropriate to the operator's role as the supervisor in a supervisory control system, delegation informs the behavior expected of the subordinate.

3.1   What Is Delegation?

Collaborative interactions in work domains are primarily about intent—to perform an action, use a resource—and the need or desire to notify others, receive permission, elicit cooperation, report status, etc. against it. When the operator is a supervisor, these interactions become instructions (as Sheridan defines for supervisory control [4]) with an expectation of compliance. This is delegation.

Intent may be expressed in one of five ways (cf. Table 1). The supervisor may express a goal (a world state) to be achieved or a plan (a series of actions) to be performed. Constraints and stipulations on actions, methods or resources to be used may also be expressed. Finally, less specifically, the supervisor may also express values or priorities. These refer to the relative goodness or badness of states, actions, resource usages, etc. if they are achieved or used. These methods are rarely mutually exclusive and may be combined to achieve various methods of delegation as appropriate to the domain, and the capabilities of both the supervisor and subordinates.

Delegation is inherently hierarchical. Goals and tasks are composed hierarchically in a causal means-ends fashion—as expressed in traditional task analysis techniques [12]. Our Playbook implementations have used this structure to facilitate optional operator input in a fashion that enables AI planners to create plans adhering to both the shared play definition and to any additional stipulations the operator provides [2]. Even delegation interactions which center on re-

Table 1. Five methods of intent expression in delegation

Supervisor Method	Subordinate Responsibility
Goal	Achieve goal if possible; report if incapable
Plan	Follow plan if possible; report if incapable
Constraint	Avoid actions/states if possible; report if not
Stipulation	Achieve actions/states if possible; report if not
Value Statement	Work to optimize value

source usage also participate in hierarchical decompositions along part-whole dimensions—such that resources are usually parts of larger wholes, and may involve decompositions into smaller sub-parts.

Thus an act of delegation expresses the operator's intent for a constrained, but still under-specified, set of behaviors, expressed either implicitly or explicitly, to be accomplished by one or more subordinates. This expression of delegated intent, we argue, frames the interaction and helps to determine the kinds of information which will "afford operator comprehension" in a transparent system—in ways discussed below.

3.2   Delegation, Situation Awareness and Trust—The "Intent Frame" Effect

We argued, in [2], that any workload savings from efficient automation design could be devoted to maintaining or achieving better overall situation awareness about the context of use. While true, this phenomenon is partially countered by the unpredictability effect (described above) resulting from giving tasks to subordinates who, almost inevitably, must also be accorded some autonomy in their performance.

Situation Awareness (SA), as traditionally defined and measured [13], refers to all situational knowledge required to perform one's job. Knowledge specifically about what a subordinate is doing and why is surely part of that set, but it is more specific and subject to different influences. SA reduction specifically about delegated tasks is tolerated, even embraced, in exchange for competency improvements and/or work-load reductions as discussed earlier. That said, the reduction in automation-related SA can differ in different human-automation interactions. In adaptive or traditional auto-mation, behaviors are disconnected from human intent and therefore, an additional element of unpredictability enters into the human's experience. This is summed up in Sarter, Woods & Billings [1] work on "automation surprises"—instances in which non-transparent automation does unexpected, difficult-to-explain things. While trans-parency can alleviate automation surprises by giving humans insight into what the automation is doing, this comes at the expense of cognitive workload—since it requires the human to monitor and interpret those interfaces. This is akin to having a subordinate who one has to watch all the time to make sure what s/he is doing is appropriate.

Delegation provides another way. By tasking the subordinate, the act of delegation provides an *Intent Frame* that expresses and defines expectations about the subordi-nate's behavior for both parties. In communication, this frame explicitly details what the supervisor expects the subordinate to do, therefore that aspect of SA should im-prove for both parties. But delegation also helps awareness and interpretation of ob-served subordinate behaviors as well because it creates a cognitive expectation about what the subordinate is *supposed* to do. If a task (or "play") is delegated, then certain behaviors are expected and others are not. This framing narrows the set of behaviors that need be attended to by the superior: instead of checking to see what behaviors, from all possible ones, the subordinate is doing, s/he may simply check to see whether the subordinate is doing what was expected or not. Even unanticipated behaviors can be interpreted more directly for whether they are reasonable within the intent instead of for what they could possibly accomplish. In short, explicitly delegated intent shifts the operator's task in monitoring and interpretating automation from one of "what is it doing now?" to a cognitively simpler one of "is it doing what I told it to do?"

The same Intent Frame effect likely has an impact on trust formation. Lee and See [14] define trust as "...the attitude that an agent will help achieve an individual's goals in a situation characterized by uncertainty..." (p. 51). Thus, delegation impacts trust by making it clear(er) to both parties what those goals are. While this may or may not lead to increased trust depending on the subordinate's behaviors, it does "sharpen" the test for trust and should, therefore, speed trust tuning [cf. 15].

These hypothesized effects on trust and automation-specific SA have largely not been tested directly, but there is some indirect support for them. Several studies [8,11] report improved performance and/or faster response times on secondary tasks when using adaptable delegation—which might imply either improved SA or reduced work-load or both, though the former was not explicitly measured. In [8], experimenters conducted a direct comparison of adaptive vs. adaptable automation on tasks repre-sentative of multi-UAS operations, and reported higher subjective confidence ratings (a loose analog for trust) under adaptable vs. adaptive control. Finally, Layton, Smith and McCoy [16] had pilots interact with three kinds of automated route planning support in a commercial aviation context: a "low" automation level where operators sketched routes and automation computed route details such as fuel consumption and arrival times, a "high" level providing expert system-like support proposing a single complete route to the pilot, and an "intermediate" level where the pilot had to request a route with specific constraints (e.g., 'going to Kansas City and avoiding Level 3 turbulence') before automation developed it. Pilots with the intermediate and high automation levels explored more routes because manual sketching was too difficult to allow much exploration, but with full automation, users tended to accept the first route suggested without exploring it or alternatives deeply. Particularly in trials where automation performed suboptimally (e.g., failing to consider uncertainty in weather predictions), humans using the intermediate level produced better overall solutions. Although SA was not directly assessed, this suggests that pilots were most able to bring their own knowledge to bear, and most aware of the automation's plans when they explicitly instructed it as to what they needed.

3.3   Delegation and Dialog Framing—Improvements in Communication

While the prototypic delegation interaction is the supervisor conveying intent to the subordinate, other interactions flow from both parties. Delegation dialogs, and the hierarchical structures which underlie them, also serve to frame and facilitate communication from automation to the supervisor in a variety of ways and are therefore relevant to transparency, as will be discussed for a suite of different technologies below.

"Explanation" and Negotiation through Relaxed Constraint Planning. "Transparency" in human interactions is greatly facilitated by natural language explanations, but human-understandable explanation of the complex reasoning of a mathematical control or symbolic logic system has been a canonically difficult problem in Artificial Intelligence for decades [17]. Furthermore, explanation is a key to effective, multi-dimensional negotiation since it facilitates understanding of the parties' goals and identification of potential tradeoffs they may be willing to make.

In one Playbook® implementation, we provided a simple explanation and negotiation approach integrated with our automated planner [18]. Prior Playbook versions had simply tried to create an executable plan given the supervisor's instructions. If this failed, the system reported the failure but did not otherwise indicate *why* the user's instructions were impossible. This is akin to a subordinate who, responding to instructions, says simply "I can't"—a non-transparent (and unhelpful) behavior. To improve, we implemented a "Relaxed Constraint Planning" (RCP) approach. Under RCP, when the system receives instructions it cannot achieve, instead of responding "I can't" it seeks to progressively relax constraints until a valid plan can be provided. This now is akin to saying "I can't do that, but here's something close I can do. How's this?" This has many benefits, including a form of increasing transparency.

RCP not only provides a valid plan that can be executed immediately, it also gives insight into what the subordinate system had to change to achieve performability. If, say, the system had to arrive later than requested, the user can decide whether relaxing a different constraint (say fuel consumption) is preferable. Thus, RCP can serve as the first "move" in a negotiation process. Constraints in our initial RCP system were relaxed via an ordered list of static priorities, but this could be both more dynamic and knowledge-based. Communication of multiple alternatives and/or visualization of the effects of alternate constraint dimensions would speed the "negotiation" process by increasing transparency to the system's underlying reasoning system. Importantly, however, framing this negotiation in a task-based delegation process keeps the goals and methods grounded in a shared understanding of possible approaches.

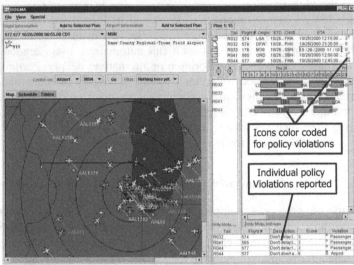

Fig. 2. Implemented policy visualization system

Policy Visualization. Particularly for policy and values (cf. Table 1), delegation offers another method to support explanation and negotiation. If a supervisor provides an explicit (and, ideally, quantified) set of policy statements about conditions or approaches with associated values, then plans and projected outcomes can be evaluated against them and the results shown in a variety of ways ranging. We used this approach in a prototype system developed for dispatchers in commercial airlines [19] who must make decisions about where to divert airplanes when they, unexpectedly, cannot make their destinations (e.g., due to weather events, etc.). These diversion decisions can affect many stakeholders in the organization, each with differing priorities. Worse, values change in different contexts—e.g., during holidays. Finally, dispatchers have ~5-15 minutes to make decisions that can affect many flights and it is exceedingly difficult to maintain awareness of the priorities of all stakeholders.

By capturing a numerically-weighted value for each state of concern and "bundling" these policies by stakeholder, we provided optimization functions that could serve to visualize the good or bad aspects of potential outcomes or, with a search algorithm, to generate criteria-optimized outcomes. Separating policy statements by context and by stakeholder allows the dispatcher to assert or weight different policy bundles. As plans are developed, they can be reviewed against values either separately (to determine effects on different stakeholders) or in aggregate. Policy bundles can be weighted differently to reflect permanent or temporary variations in the importance of different stakeholders. Figure 2 illustrates an implemented prototype, developed by Honeywell Laboratories, using this approach for visualizing alternate dispatch plans.

In short, policy value statements, especially if "bundled" by various concerns, enable rapid conveyance of how well alternate plans do against the values, how specific policy concerns are contributing to that value, which concerns are satisfied more or less, etc. Insofar as automation is creating or critiquing plans for a supervisor, such reports can go a long way toward transparently conveying the automation's reasoning.

Information Expectations from Delegation. Delegation and negotiation produce an agreed-upon plan that carries assumptions about what should be communicated back to the supervisor—under normal and abnormal circumstances. These expectations do not promote full transparency so much as *principled information reduction* to satisfy Chen, et al's goal of "operator comprehension" while maintaining reasonable workload. This principle manifests in various ways, many of which have been explored as part of the Flexible Levels of Execution—Interface Technologies (FLEX-IT) project [4]. FLEX-IT is developing an adaptable delegation approach to controlling multiple UASs via highly flexible automation interactions—from manual flight control to high level, multi-vehicle play calling, all via multiple interface modalities.

First and most obvious, as part of the act of delegation, the supervisor may explicitly include instructions about reporting. FLEX-IT uses versions of this approach via incorporating "decision" and "notification points" in plays. These are "points" tied to absolute or route-based geographic locations (or, potentially, to temporal- or event-

based "points") at which the subordinate is to report to the supervisor (for notifications) or ask for further instructions (decisions). In essence, they permit the supervisor to say "Do X, and when or if Y happens, let me know [ask me what to do next]." Figure 3 illustrates a notification point from FLEX-IT.

Beyond explicit instructions, FLEX-IT also uses delegated activities as a "vocabulary" to

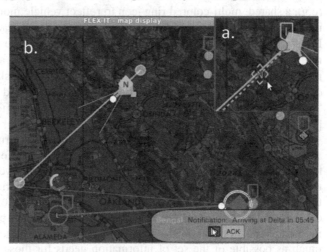

Fig. 3. Notification point behaviors showing (a) insertion of a point, and (b) activation of the point when reached by the UAS

Fig. 4. Activities Panel showing vehicles allotted to specific tasks and under "Short Term" control (available)

facilitate and organize information exchange. FLEX-IT initially organized information and status presentations around the individual vehicles being controlled—a typical format for Air Force displays—but it became clear with multiple vehicles involved in different tasks that organization around the task itself was at least as useful. Thus, in addition to the typical map display, we added an "Activity Panel" which organized vehicle icons by the activity they were engaged in, presented task-relevant status of those vehicles (e.g., whether they were currently in position to transmit imagery for a monitoring task), provided links to more detailed information about the task and, potentially, to temporal views of task performance, etc. (See Figure 4). The human or automation could move vehicles from task to task within the Activity Panel. The motion itself was salient, helping to mitigate change blindness, thereby maintaining SA about who was doing what. Vehicle tasks were also reflected by icons and glyphs (e.g., a shared, multi-colored ring icon to reflect vehicle monitoring ranges in a shared monitoring task) and could be extended to reflect task status (e.g., on time or not). Finally, the vocabulary of task labels also served multiple purposes in the design of multi-modal interactions—allowing operators to designate a group of UASs to halt or modify their stealth profile by referencing their shared task or by using the sub-task decomposition as an underlying structure for sketch and speech interactions (i.e., "Ingress like this [sketch route], then monitor here [touch] using this pattern [sketch]").

A final use of the delegation interaction to manage information flow is more subtle and largely untried to date. We have created dynamic information management systems in the past (e.g., [20]) which were essentially adaptive automation for an operator's displays. Our approach has been to represent information needs abstractly for the types of tasks an operator is likely to perform and then, either through inference or explicit declaration, assess the tasks that are actually being performed from moment to moment throughout the mission. Available displays are then configured to supply as much as possible of the set of information needs for those tasks. A similar approach could be formulated for adaptable automation by developing heuristics for how to interpret delegated instructions in terms of their information reporting requirements. For example, it seems reasonable that supervisors will want to be informed of task completion and of any circumstance that makes task completion impossible. Resource consumption (including time) is probably not important information to report if it is proceeding as expected in the agreed-upon plan. For example, a vehicle performing a steep dive is not overly noteworthy if the plan included that action, but is highly noteworthy if it did not. When deviations are expected to exceed a pre-defined threshold, however, then reporting becomes important. For specific resources (e.g., a vehicle that the supervisor is holding in reserve, entering a restricted airspace) or specific actions (e.g., firing a munition, decreasing stealth by descending below a specified altitude), notification might always be required. We have not worked out this method completely, but we believe a reasonable and general approach to information reporting could be built around delegated task heuristics such as these.

4   Conclusions

In the multiple examples provided above, we have illustrated how taking a "delegation perspective" on the concept of transparency may lead us out of the impossible and counterproductive attempt to achieve "full transparency" and toward a more productive goal of conveying specifically what is necessary to "afford operator comprehension" of the behavior of a subordinate. Furthermore, we have argued for how task-based delegation can frame the human-automation interaction both to improve communication to and comprehension of the automated subordinate, but also to improve and tune communication, expectations and interpretations for the supervisor. It does this by establishing an "Intent Frame" between the supervisor and subordinate (and, at least as important, within the mind of the supervisor) which serves to restrict the space of what must be communicated and shape and speed the interpretation of that which is communicated. While much of what is argued above remains to be proven, it seems to flow reasonably from the nature of delegation interactions in both human-human and human-automation interaction.

Acknowledgments. The thoughts expressed here are the work of the author, but related work has been supported and augmented over many years by many individuals. Particular thanks are due to Drs. Mark Draper and Gloria Calhoun of AFRL/RHCI, Heath Ruff and Tim Barry of Ball Aerospace & Technologies, Dr. Jay Shively and Ms. Lisa Fern of the U.S. Army AeroFlightDynamics Directorate, Drs. Raja Parasuraman and Tyler Shaw of George Mason University, Dr. Michael Dorneich of Honeywell and Mr. Josh Hamell of SIFT. The FLEX-IT project was funded by AF/A2Q ISR Innovations Division and managed by at Wright-Patterson Air Force Base under Air Force Contract FA8650-08-D-6801. The Policy Visualization system was supported by funding from Honeywell Laboratories.

References

1. Sarter, N.B., Woods, D.D., Billings, C.E.: Automation Surprises. Hndbk. of HFES 2, 1926–1943 (1997)
2. Miller, C., Parasuraman, R.: Designing for Flexible Interaction Between Humans & Automation: Delegation Interfaces for Supervisory Control. Human Factors 40(1), 57–75 (2007)

3. Chen, J.Y.C., Boyce, M., Wright, J., Procci, K., Barnes, M.: SA-based Agent Transparency. ARL Technical Report (in prep.)
4. Sheridan, T.: Humans and Automation. Human Factors and Ergonomics Society, Santa Monica (2002)
5. Miller, C.A., Draper, M., Hamell, J.D., Calhoun, G., Barry, T., Ruff, H.: Enabling Dynamic Delegation Interactions with Multiple Unmanned Vehicles; Flexibility from Top to Bottom. In: Harris, D. (ed.) EPCE 2013, Part II. LNCS, vol. 8020, pp. 282–291. Springer, Heidelberg (2013)
6. Kaber, D.B., Riley, J.M., Tan, K.W., Endsley, M.R.: On the Design of Adaptive Automation for Complex Systems. Int'l J. of Cog. Ergo. 5(1), 37–57 (2001)
7. Parasuraman, R., Galster, S., Squire, P., Furukawa, H., Miller, C.: A Flexible Delegation-Type Interface Enhances System Performance in Human Supervision of Multiple Robots: Empirical Studies with RoboFlag. IEEE Sys., Man & Cybernetics—Part A 35(4), 481–493 (2005)
8. Kidwell, B., Calhoun, G., Ruff, H., Parasuraman, R.: Adaptable and Adaptive Automation for Supervisory Control of Multiple Autonomous Vehicles. In: 56th Annual Human Factors and Ergonomics Society Meeting, pp. 428–432. HFES Press, Santa Monica (2012)
9. Klein, G.: Naturalistic Decision Making. Human Factors 50(3), 456–460 (2008)
10. Shaw, T., Emfield, A., Garcia, A., de Visser, E., Miller, C., Parasuraman, R., Fern, L.: Evaluating the Benefits and Potential Costs of Automation Delegation for Supervisory Control of Multiple UAVs. In: 54th Annual Human Factors and Ergonomics Society Meeting, pp. 1498–1502. HFES Press, Santa Monica (2010)
11. Miller, C.A., Shaw, T.H., Hamell, J.D., Emfield, A., Musliner, D.J., de Visser, E., Parasurman, R.: Delegation to Automation: Performance and Implications in Non-Optimal Situations. In: Harris, D. (ed.) Engin. Psychol. and Cog. Ergonomics, HCII 2011. LNCS, vol. 6781, pp. 322–331. Springer, Heidelberg (2011)
12. Diaper, D., Stanton, N. (eds.): The Handbook of Task Analysis for Human-Computer Interaction. Erlbaum, Mahweh (2004)
13. Endsley, M.R.: Measurement of Situation Awareness in Dynamic Systems. Human Factors 37(1), 65–84 (1995)
14. Lee, J.D., See, K.A.: Trust in Computer Technology: Designing for Appropriate Reliance. Human Factors 46(1), 50–80 (2004)
15. Miller, C.: Trust and Delegation: Achieving Robust Interactions with Subordinates. In: Burke, J., Wagner, A., Sofge, D., Lawless, W.F. (eds.) AAAI Spring Symposium on Robust Intelligence and Trust in Autonomous Systems. AAAI Press, Cambridge (in press)
16. Layton, C., Smith, P.J., McCoy, C.E.: Design of a Cooperative Problem-Solving System for En-Route Flight Planning: An Empirical Evaluation. Human Factors 36(1), 94–119 (1994)
17. Sørmo, F., Cassens, J., Aamodt, A.: Explanation in Case-Based Reasoning–Perspectives and Goals. Artificial Intelligence Review 24(2), 109–143 (2005)
18. Goldman, R., Miller, C., Wu, P., Funk, H., Meisner, J.: Optimizing to Satisfice: Using Optimization to Guide Users. In: American Helicopter Society International Specialists Meeting on Unmanned Rotorcraft. AHS Press, Alexandria (2005)
19. Dorneich, M.C., Whitlow, S.D., Miller, C.A., Allen, J.A.: A Superior Tool for Airline Operations. Ergonomics in Design 12(2), 18–23 (2004)
20. Miller, C.: Bridging the Information Transfer Gap: Measuring Goodness of Information "Fit". J. Visual Languages and Computing 10(5), 523–558 (1999)

Trust and Consequences: A Visual Perspective

Emrah Onal[1], John O'Donovan[2], Laura Marusich[3], Michael S. Yu[4], James Schaffer[2], Cleotilde Gonzalez[4], and Tobias Höllerer[2]

[1] SA Technologies, Inc., Marietta, GA, USA
emrah@satechnologies.com
[2] Department of Computer Science, University of California, Santa Barbara
{jod,james_schaffer,holl}@cs.ucsb.edu
[3] U.S. Army Research Laboratory, Aberdeen Proving Ground, MD, USA
laura.r.marusich.ctr@mail.mil
[4] Department of Social and Decision Sciences, Carnegie Mellon University
{msyu,coty}@cmu.edu

Abstract. User interface (UI) composition and information presentation can impact human trust behavior. Trust is a complex concept studied by disciplines like psychology, sociology, economics, and computer science. Definitions of trust vary depending on the context, but are typically based on the core concept of "reliance on another person or entity". Trust is a critical concept since the presence or absence of the right level of trust can affect user behavior, and ultimately, the overall system performance. In this paper, we look across four studies to explore the relationship between UI elements and human trust behavior. Results indicate that UI composition and information presentation can impact human trust behavior. While further research is required to corroborate and generalize these results, we hope that this paper will provide a reference point for future studies by identifying UI elements that are likely to influence human trust.

Keywords: Trust, cooperation, user interface, visualization, design, typology, model.

1 Introduction

The user interface (UI) is a key component of any system that involves user interaction – including desktop and mobile applications, Web, social media tools, Virtual Reality interfaces, and robot control systems. The UI can be defined as the space where humans interact with other entities, such as machines. What is included in a UI (composition) and how it is displayed (information presentation) can impact performance, workload, situation awareness (SA), and usability. As a consequence, UI composition and information presentation may influence human perceptions and behavior, including trust. Trust is important in many contexts, including commercial transactions, military command and control, social media, and teleoperation. This paper reviews four studies that examine the relationship between UI components and trust – spanning different UI designs as well as different trust contexts. First, we

R. Shumaker and S. Lackey (Eds.): VAMR 2014, Part I, LNCS 8525, pp. 203–214, 2014.

define trust and identify factors that affect trust. Next, we review the four studies individually, focusing on what each of the studies reveal about the relationship between UI design and trust. Finally, we integrate the results, discussing overall conclusions, open questions, and further avenues of investigation.

2   Background

Trust is a complex concept studied by diverse disciplines such as sociology [1], psychology [2], economics [3], and computer science [4]. While definitions of trust have varied across contexts, researchers attempting to reconcile these literatures have proposed a general definition of trust as "a psychological state comprising the intention to accept vulnerability based upon positive expectations of the intentions and behaviors of another [5]." As trust dictates how people interact with others, including other people or machines, trust can drive user behaviors and, ultimately, overall system performance. Indeed, research has shown trust to be important in improving performance ([6], [1]), aligning motivations [7], improving cooperation [8], and improving knowledge transfer [9].

2.1   Types of Trust and Affecting Factors

McKnight and Chervany [10] identify three major components in their typology of trust. Dispositional trust represents personal traits that promote trusting behavior. Institutional trust represents expectations regarding the current situation. Interpersonal trust represents beliefs about the trustworthiness of others. Some researchers use the terms interpersonal and institutional trust to distinguish between trust in people and organizations. In this paper, institutional trust refers only to the situation. This McKnight model is complemented by computer science research, which finds that experience can shape trust [11], as in Figure 1.

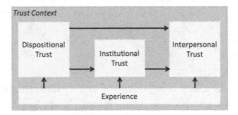

Fig. 1. This model, adapted from McKnight and Chervany [10], shows how experience affects dispositional, institutional, and interpersonal trust components

Through repeated interactions, feedback changes a person's general willingness to trust (dispositional), understanding of the environment (institutional), and belief in the reputation of others (interpersonal). Experience is relevant in social media, where iterative effects of incoming information affect trust behavior of the user, such as the

TasteWeights we will examine in this paper. In economic and psychology research, experience has been shown to directly affect dispositional and interpersonal trust [12].

Hancock et al. [13] proposed a similar model of trust, in the context of human-robot interactions. They identify three major categories: human-related factors (e.g., abilities and characteristics such as propensity to trust), robot-related factors (e.g., performance- and attribute-based), and the environment (e.g., task characteristics). Note that categories of human-related factors, robot-related factors, and the environment overlap significantly in their scope with dispositional, interpersonal, and institutional trust components of the McKnight model, respectively. Most of the robot-related factors (e.g., dependability, reliability, level of automation, and performance) are largely applicable to interactions with other systems or agents beyond human-robot interaction. Some of the key factors influencing trust in technology have been summarized as involving system reliability, validity, and understandability [14]. Understanding how the trust environment works (i.e., institutional trust or environment-related factors) can have an important effect on what trust-related behaviors are actually realized. Martin et al. [15] studied how different levels of information regarding the presence and performance of other "participants" influenced behavior in the repeated Prisoner's Dilemma – a game from economics in which both players are independently better off defecting, but are jointly better off cooperating. In this case, cooperation increased as participants better understood how their actions influenced the other's performance. Computational models that elaborated on the dynamics of the emergence of cooperation over time, suggest that the increased level of cooperation with more information is associated with an increased level of trust. Trust emerges as a gradual reduction of "surprising" actions occurring between the pairs with repeated interactions, where expected actions are increasingly in agreement with actual actions taken by an opponent over time. The UI is positioned between users and a broader system that may include other human (or non-human) actors. As the UI can influence the user's understanding of the environment either directly (e.g., information-provision, transparency) as well as through reducing demands on human cognition (e.g., reducing operator workload), UIs are likely to have an important influence on trust-related behaviors.

3   UI and Trust

The relationship between UI and human trust behavior has been studied in e-commerce and Web page design. There are UI principles and guidelines for promoting trust in users (e.g. [16]), and empirical studies of aspects of UI design, showing that page layout, navigation, style, graphics, and content elements can have significant effects on the perceived trustworthiness of e-commerce sites [17]. A strong relationship between UI quality and user reported trust can be observed in Web retailer page designs [18]. In addition, the user's trust increases with perceived system usability [19]. Still, empirical studies on the impact of specific aspects of UI on trust are limited. In this paper, we explore the relationship between UI elements and human trust behavior by looking at commonalities and patterns across four past studies we conducted in this domain. The types of trust studied include interpersonal trust (e.g., trusting a team member to convey accurate information, trust in information sources, and trusting an agent to behave in a certain way) and institutional trust (e.g., aspects of UI and source reliability). Two of these studies are in the context of an abstract game, the iterated Diner's Dilemma (DD) ([20], [21]). The High Value Target (HVT) study explores trust within the context of a command and control (C2) scenario. The last study, TasteWeights (TW), is on user behavior when using a recommender system, focusing on "inspectability" and "control" aspects [22]–[24].

3.1   First Diner's Dilemma Study (DD1)

The goal of this experiment was to study how UI and the behavior of others influenced situation awareness, cooperation, and self-reported trust in the Diner's Dilemma (DD) [20]. The scenario involves three individuals who agree to split the bill evenly before going out to dinner. At dinner, each individual chooses to order either the expensive, higher-quality dish (lobster), or the inexpensive lower-quality dish (hot dog). Each diner's goal was to maximize his or her 'Dining Points.' Dining Points were calculated based on the quality of the diner's own meal divided by the diner's share of the bill. The experiment involved one human participant playing repeatedly against the same two computer-based co-diners for 50 rounds. There were six co-diner strategies divided into "cooperation encouraging" and "cooperation discouraging" categories based on how the computer-based opponents played. Twenty-four undergraduates at the University of California volunteered for the study. Participant ages ranged from 18 to 25, and 63% were female.

UI Elements. Three different UIs were used in this study, identified as UI Levels 1 through 3 (Fig. 2). Each UI level added new UI elements.

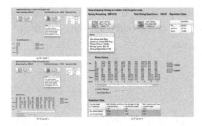

Fig. 2. The first Diner's Dilemma study with three UI levels

UI Level 1. This UI included a display to indicate the user's remaining money and total dining experience points gained, which was updated after each decision. Additionally, a panel labeled "Current Round Score" presented the user's and co-diners' decisions and scores from the previous round, presented as a bar that was color-coded to distinguish between menu items. Additionally, a panel labeled "Reputation Table" displayed the percentages of times the participant and co-diners decided to cooperate (i.e., chose hot dog).

UI Level 2. For this visualization, the "Current Round Score" was augmented with "Game History" that provided a segmented bar display that illustrated all past decisions of each player and the scores of those decisions. Information on past rounds were intended to help the user understand the impact of their decisions and to investigate trends in their co-diners' decisions.

UI Level 3. Here, a "Prediction Table" presented the expected probability of one, both, or neither of the co-diners to cooperate, assuming that their decisions to cooperate were independent. The table also includes the possible scores the participant would receive if they chose to cooperate or not, given each of those scenarios.

Results. An analysis of variance (ANOVA) revealed a significant effect of UI Level on cooperation, $F(2,105) = 5.45$, $p = 0.012$. A post-hoc Tukey-Kramer test found higher cooperation in UI Level 1 compared to UI Level 2, $p = 0.025$, and to UI Level 3, $p = 0.042$; but no significant differences between UI Levels 2 and 3. Overall, the simpler UI appeared to improve cooperation, and by implication, trust.

3.2   Second Diner's Dilemma Study (DD2)

The second study was designed as a follow up to the previous Diner's Dilemma study (DD1) [20]. Similar to DD1, the goal was to study how UI and the behavior of others affected SA, trust, and performance; however, the UI elements were updated as described below. In addition, objective SA was measured using the Situation Awareness Global Assessment Technique. Participants were matched with simulated co-diners, as before, which played one of five strategies. Ninety-five participants were recruited from Amazon Mechanical Turk. Participant ages ranged from 19 to 60, and 39% were female.

UI Elements. Three different UIs were used in this study, identified as UI Levels 1 through 3. Similar to the previous study, each UI level built on the previous level by adding new UI elements (Fig. 3).

UI Level 1. This UI level shows the user their current dining points, the food quality and cost of each menu item, the current round, and the results from the previous round in terms of dining points. Only the most current and recent game states are presented. The difference between DD1 [20] and this study is that this omits the reputation display along with general graphical and visual changes.

UI Level 2. This UI level includes all UI features from Level 1 UI, and adds a 'History' panel to provide historical game information to the participant. The difference between DD1 [20] and this study is that this omits the score display feature.

UI Level 3. This UI level adds a "Long Term" panel to help estimate the user's longer-term dining score under cooperation or defection scenarios. This is an interactive panel where the participant can enter his or her assumptions about opponent behavior and calculate the expected dining points. Compared to the previous study, this panel is interactive and emphasizes long-term outcomes.

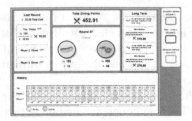

Fig. 3. The second Diner's Dilemma study with three UI levels

Results. A two-factor ANOVA on cooperation showed a significant main effect for the co-diner strategy, $F(4,80) = 4.87$, $p = 0.001$, a marginal effect of UI Level, $F(2, 80) = 2.56$, $p = 0.084$, and no interaction. Post-hoc Tukey HSD tests indicated significantly higher cooperation for UI Level 2 compared to UI Level 3. Overall, UI Levels 1 and 2 appeared to improve cooperation, and by implication, trust.

3.3   High-Value Target Study (HVT)

This study was designed to explore issues of trust in a human partner as well as trust in information sources in a simulated command and control (C2) task. Participants completed the task in pairs, and their goal was to find and capture a series of high value targets (HVTs) on a grid-based map as quickly as possible. Within each pair, one participant was assigned the role of the Intelligence (Intel) Officer, and the other was assigned the role of the Operations (OPS) Officer. The Intel player's responsibility was to process incoming messages that provided information about the possible location of HVTs. These messages came from two different sources, Source A and Source B. In each round of game play, one of these sources was randomly assigned to be 90% accurate, while the other was 10% accurate. The OPS player's responsibility was to assign 4 platoons under his/her command to various locations on the grid map in order to capture HVTs.

UI Elements. There were two manipulations in this study. The first was whether the information available to each player was shared or limited. In the Limited condition,

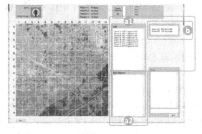

Fig. 4. The HVT study with varying UIs. The first manipulation is whether (1) a1 and a2 are shown to both players, or (2) a1 is shown to Intel and a2 is shown to OPS only. The second manipulation is whether (1) b is hidden, (2) b is visible presenting congruent information, or (3) b is visible presenting incongruent information.

players only had access to the information pertinent to their own role (e.g. only the Intel player could see the incoming messages from Source A and Source B). In the Shared condition, players were able to view the same information. Our interest was in determining if having access to all information, including the information the other player was using, was helpful or detrimental to performance, trust, and SA.

The second manipulation was what information was provided on each round to the participants about the reliability of each of the two sources. There were three conditions: None, Congruent, and Incongruent. In the None condition, no information was provided. In the other two conditions, an additional UI element was visible that displayed information about the accuracy of each source. In the Congruent condition, the information displayed matched the actual accuracies of the two sources. In the Incongruent condition, the opposite information was displayed (Fig. 4; so, for example, if Source B was assigned to be the 90% accurate Source in a given round, the displayed information would label Source A as 90% accurate and Source B as 10% accurate in the Incongruent condition).

Results. Results indicated that self-reported trust in one's partner was lower in the Shared condition than in the Limited condition (F(1,54) = 6.40, p = 0.014). There was a marginal effect upon self-reported trust in one's partner, with lower levels of trust in the Incongruent condition (F(2,108) = 2.49, p = 0.088). Supporting this finding, target capture times were slower in the Incongruent condition than in either the None or the Congruent conditions (F(2,52) = 7.96, p = 0.001). Participants only rated the two sources as much more similar in their reliability in the None condition than in the Congruent and Incongruent conditions (F(2,78) = 20.50, p<0.0001).

3.4   TasteWeights Study (TW)

It is important to consider how the UI impacts trust at the system [25] or institutional [10] levels. To exemplify this, we now describe the TasteWeights visual recommender system [23] and an associated user study [22] that was designed to explore the roles played by interface on the development of trust and general acceptance of the system's recommendations. In particular, the study focused on the UI properties of "inspectability" and "control".

Fig. 5. The TasteWeights visual recommender system showing musical artist recommendations for one user based on a preference profile. Profile items are shown on the left column and recommendations are shown on the right, generated by recommendation sources in the center.

TasteWeights is a visual representation of a collaborative filtering recommendation algorithm [26] that leverages multiple sources to generate recommendations for one target user. The system builds on previous research on interactive UIs for recommender systems [27][24]. Fig. 5 shows the three-column interface with the user profile on the leftmost column, recommendation sources in the center and a list of recommendations (output) on the right. Bostandjiev et al. [23] explain how the ranked lists of social, semantic and expert nodes in the center column and ranked, filtered and combined to produce the personalized recommendation list on the right. The column views and associated interactions support both inspection (leading to explanation), and control of the algorithm. A study n = 297 was performed to evaluate the effect of inspection and control on the overall user trust in the system's recommendations, as determined by various satisfaction and perception metrics. Details of the study are reported by Knijnenburg et al. in [22].

UI Elements. Participants were assigned one of two inspection conditions: right column only (the typical "list view" as a benchmark), or the full provenance graph shown above. Participants were allowed to manipulate weights on nodes through the horizontal sliders (Fig. 5). Three control conditions were tested: item-level, neighbor-level, and full control. Subjective experiences were assessed through pre and post questionnaires. Recommendation accuracy was evaluated by gathering post-hoc item ratings from participants.

Results. Knijnenburg et al. [22] discusses structural equation model of the key results from this study. To summarize with respect to UI influence on system level trust: the UI provides an explanation of what the algorithm is doing to produce recommendations. The authors call this feature "inspectability". In turn, the explanation generates a level of understanding that enables an end user to control the system via interactions with the UI. In particular, manipulations on profile items or connected neighbor weightings vs. the benchmark no-control condition impacted understanding of the system and algorithm, which in turn increased perceived satisfaction with and control over the output. This had a strong positive effect on perceived quality of the system's recommendations and overall satisfaction (seen as a proxy for trust) in the system. This relation was impacted by domain expertise and trust propensity.

Table 1. Trust components explored through experimental design

Study		Interpersonal	Institutional Trust
Diner's Dilemma	DD1	Co-diners (computer strategies)	- Current and previous scores - Score histories with opponent score - Prediction panel (short-term focus)
	DD2	Co-diners (computer strategies)	- Current and previous scores - Score histories without opponent score - Long-term panel (long-term focus)
High-value Targets	HVT	Human operator (partner)	- Shared/limited information
		Information sources	- Reliability of sources
TasteWeights	TW	Recommendation system	- Provenance graph - Control over UI (weights)

Table 2. This table summarizes the observed effect of UI elements from a trust perspective. Legend: "⇑"=increase; "⇓"=decrease; "--" no change in trust.

Study	UI Element	Impact on Trust	Trust Measurement
DD1	#1. Score histories with opponent score	⇓ (co-diners)	*User's cooperation proportion / rate was used as a proxy to trust*
DD1	#2. Prediction panel (short-term)	-- (co-diners)	
DD2	#3. Score histories without opponent score	⇑ (co-diners)	
DD2	#4. Long Term panel (interactive & long-term focused)	⇓ (co-diners)	
HVT	#5. All information presented to all users (Shared)	⇓ (partner)	*Self-reported trust in one's partner and subjective ratings of information source reliability (used as a proxy to trusting sources)*
HVT	#6. Only user-pertinent information presented (Limited)	⇑ (partner)	
HVT	#7. Incongruent information	⇓ (partner) ⇓ or ⇑ (info sources)	
HVT	#8. Congruent information	⇓ or ⇑ (info sources)	
TW	#10. Increased control over UI (item/neighbor vs. no control over weights)	⇑ (system)	*Overall satisfaction and perceived recommendation quality as a proxy to trust*

4   Conclusion

In this section we investigate how the four studies fit into a trust classification and where there may be gaps that future studies can fill. We also look at summary results across these studies for commonalities and differences. These four studies focus on different aspects of the model in Fig. 1. Table 1 organizes these studies by types of trust investigated. In this paper, institutional trust refers to the user's expectations regarding the situation, encompassing the UI that mediates trust formation by affecting the user's interaction with the situation. Dispositional trust is expected to have an effect on all types of trust, as shown in Fig. 1. In future efforts, analyzing dispositional trust as a covariant might allow us to observe stronger effects in studies like DD1, DD2, and HVT. Table 2 summarizes UI elements presented across these studies and their effect on the user from a trust perspective. The generalizability of the results presented in this table is limited for multiple reasons. First, the four studies are not directly comparable, since their context and experimental setups are different. While DD1 and DD2 are very similar studies, HVT and TW are very different. Second, it is difficult to isolate the effect of a UI element without the context that surrounds it. Third, there may be unidentified factors that cause the observed behavior other than the UI. Nevertheless, we hope this table will provide a starting point for researchers who study the relationship between UI and trust, and help focus efforts on UI elements that might impact human trust behavior.

An interesting finding is the effect of presenting historical transaction information (i.e., game history in the context of DD1&2) to the user (#1 and #3 in Table 2).

In DD1, interpersonal trust decreased with the inclusion of this visualization, whereas in DD2 trust actually increased. The two visualizations were not identical and DD1 included co-diner scores while DD2 did not. Taken at face value, these results suggest that at least under certain scenarios seeing the opponent's historical scores may reduce cooperation, hence trust in one's opponent. A follow-up study with a larger sample size is necessary to verify these results. This has implications for systems where both collaborative and competitive behaviors are possible. Another interesting finding is the effect of the projection panel (#2 and #4 in Table 2) added to help support higher levels of user SA. The two versions of this panel used in DD1 and DD2 did not provide the intended effect. Instead, it either had no effect or reduced trust. These results highlight the challenges involved in providing higher levels of SA support. For example, #2 was intended to be a prediction panel to provide projection SA support, but it focused on one (the next) round only, without factoring in long-term consequences of not cooperating. On the other hand, while #4 attempted to emphasize long-term consequences of user's actions, the added UI complexity or information might have made it hard to learn and use. This is consistent with #5 that sometimes more information can have a detrimental effect. In the HVT study, presentation of incongruent information (#7; mismatch between the actual and advertised quality of information streaming from sources) has the expected effect of affecting trust in information sources. However, this has a spillover effect of reducing trust in partner, even though ideally one would expect participants to make accurate trust attributions. This has implications for UI tool and visualization design to help users develop better trust attributions. For #7 and #8, the direction of change in trust was not recorded, though one might suspect trust in information sources was reduced in #7 and increased in #8 given the nature of the UI change.

5   Discussion and Future Work

This paper reviews four studies and organizes their results in a trust framework. There are many challenges associated with running studies that explore trust. Differentiating between different types of trust can be difficult because of overlap in definitions.

Future studies should make an attempt to isolate and analyze the effects of individual UI elements on trust. This will help design and build UIs that produce the right level of trust. Also, there are many aspects of trust. A systematic approach to methodically study all aspects of trust will help paint a more complete picture of our understanding of human trust behavior. Some of these goals may be as elusive as trust itself. There are many definitions and classifications of trust. Different domains look at it from different perspectives. Still, there are commonalities. Regardless of the domain, we hope that this paper will guide future research in terms of where to focus efforts and what UI elements may result in trust behavior changes.

Acknowledgments. This material is based in part upon work supported by the U.S. Army Research Laboratory (ARL) under cooperative agreements W911NF-09-2-0053 and W911NF-09-1-0553 and by NSF grant IIS-1058132. The views and conclusions contained in this document are those of the authors and should not be interpreted as representing the official policies, either expressed or implied, of the ARL, NSF, or the U.S. Government. The U.S. Government is authorized to reproduce and distribute reprints for Government purposes not-with-standing any copyright notation here on.

References

1. Helbing, D.: A mathematical model for the behavior of individuals in a social field. J. Math. Sociol. 19(3), 189–219 (1994)
2. Rotter, J.B.: A new scale for the measurement of interpersonal trust1. J. Pers. 35(4), 651–665 (1967)
3. Granovetter, M.: Economic action and social structure: the problem of embeddedness. Am. J. Sociol., 481–510 (1985)
4. Hughes, D., Coulson, G., Walkerdine, J.: Free riding on Gnutella revisited: the bell tolls? IEEE Distrib. Syst. 6(6) (2005)
5. Rousseau, D.M., Sitkin, S.B., Burt, R.S., Camerer, C.: Not So Different After All: A Cross-Discipline View of Trust. Acad. Manage. Rev. 23(3), 393–404 (1998)
6. Zaheer, A., McEvily, B., Perrone, V.: Does Trust Matter? Exploring the Effects of Interorganizational and Interpersonal Trust on Performance. Organ. Sci. 9(2), 141–159 (1998)
7. Dirks, K.T., Ferrin, D.L.: The Role of Trust in Organizational Settings. Organ. Sci. 12(4), 450–467 (2001)
8. McAllister, D.J.: Affect- and Cognition-Based Trust as Foundations for Interpersonal Cooperation in Organizations. Acad. Manage. J. 38(1), 24–59 (1995)
9. Levin, D.Z., Cross, R.: The Strength of Weak Ties You Can Trust: The Mediating Role of Trust in Effective Knowledge Transfer. Acad. Manage. J. 50(11), 1477–1490 (2002)
10. McKnight, D.H., Chervany, N.L.: What trust means in e-commerce customer relationships: an interdisciplinary conceptual typology. Int. J. Electron. Commer. 6, 35–60 (2002)
11. Artz, D., Gil, Y.: A Survey of Trust in Computer Science and the Semantic Web. Web Semant. 5(2), 58–71 (2007)
12. M. Yu, M. Saleem, and C. Gonzalez: Developing Trust: First Impressions and Experience (manuscript submitted for publication)
13. Hancock, P.A., Billings, D.R., Schaefer, K.E., Chen, J.Y.C., de Visser, E.J., Parasuraman, R.: A meta-analysis of factors affecting trust in human-robot interaction. Hum. Factors 53(5), 517–527 (2011)
14. Seong, Y., Bisantz, A.M., Bisantz, A.M.: Judgment and Trust in Conjunction with Automated Decision Aids: A Theoretical Model and Empirical Investigation. Proc. Hum. Factors Ergon. Soc. Annu. Meet. 46(3), 423–427 (2002)
15. Martin, J.M., Gonzalez, C., Juvina, I., Lebiere, C.: A Description–Experience Gap in Social Interactions: Information about Interdependence and Its Effects on Cooperation. J. Behav. Decis. Mak., n/a–n/a (2013)
16. Shneiderman, B.: Designing Trust into Online Experiences. Commun. ACM 43(12), 57–59 (2000)
17. Stephens, R.T.: A Framework for the Identification of Electronic Commerce Visual Design Elements that Enable Trust Within the Small Hotel Industry (2004)
18. Roy, M.C., Dewit, O., Aubert, B.A.: The impact of interface usability on trust in Web retailers. Internet Res. 11(5), 388–398 (2001)
19. Flavián, C., Guinalíu, M., Gurrea, R.: The role played by perceived usability, satisfaction and consumer trust on website loyalty. Inf. Manage. 43(1), 1–14 (2006)

20. Teng, Y., Jones, R., Marusich, L., O'Donovan, J., Gonzalez, C., Höllerer, T.: Trust and Situation Awareness in a 3-Player Diner's Dilemma Game. In: Proc. 3rd IEEE Conf. Cogn. Methods Situaiton Aware. Decis. Support CogSIMA 2013, pp. 26–28 (2013)
21. Onal, E., Schaffer, J., O'Donovan, J., Marusich, L., Yu, M.S., Gonzalez, C., Höllerer, T.: Decision-making in Abstract Trust Games: A User Interface Perspective. Manuscr. Rev.
22. Knijnenburg, B.P., Bostandjiev, S., O'Donovan, J., Kobsa, A.: Inspectability and control in social recommenders. In: Proceedings of the Sixth ACM Conference on Recommender Systems, pp. 43–50 (2012)
23. Bostandjiev, S., O'Donovan, J., Höllerer, T.: TasteWeights: A Visual Interactive Hybrid Recommender. In: Proceedings of ACM RecSys 2012 Conference on Recommender Systems, Dublin, Ireland (2012)
24. O'Donovan, J., Smyth, B., Gretarsson, B., Bostandjiev, S., Höllerer, T.: PeerChooser: visual interactive recommendation. In: Proceedings of the SIGCHI Conference on Human Factors in Computing Systems, pp. 1085–1088 (2008)
25. Marsh, S. P., U. of S. D. of C. Science, and Mathematics: Formalising trust as a computational concept. University of Stirling (1994)
26. Resnick, P., Iacovou, N., Sushak, M., Bergstrom, P., Riedl, J.: GroupLens: An Open Architecture for Collaborative Filtering of Netnews. In: ACM Conference on Computer Supported Cooperative Work, Chapel Hill, NC, pp. 175–186 (1994)
27. Gretarsson, B., O'Donovan, J., Bostandjiev, S., Hall, C., Höllerer, T.: SmallWorlds: Visualizing Social Recommendations. Comput. Graph Forum 29(3), 833–842 (2010)

Choosing a Selection Technique
for a Virtual Environment

Danilo Souza[1], Paulo Dias[1,2], and Beatriz Sousa Santos[1,2]

[1] DETI/UA- Department of Electronics, Telecommunications and Informatics
[2] IEETA- Institute of Electronics and Telematics Engineering of Aveiro
University of Aveiro
Campus Universitário de Santiago, 3810-193 Aveiro, Portugal
danilo@danilo-souza.net, {paulo.dias,bss}@ua.pt

Abstract. Bearing in mind the difficulty required to create virtual environments, a platform for Setting-up Interactive Virtual Environments (pSIVE) was created to help non-specialists benefit from virtual applications involving virtual tours where users may interact with elements of the environment to extract contextual information. The platform allows creating virtual environments and setting up their aspects, interaction methods and hardware to be used. The construction of the world is done by loading 3D models and associating multimedia information (videos, texts or PDF documents) to them.

A central interaction task in the envisioned applications of pSIVE is the selection of objects that have associated multimedia information. Thus, a comparative study between two variants of the ray-tracing selection technique was performed. The study also demonstrates the flexibility of the platform, since it was easily adapted to serve as a test environment.

Keywords: Virtual Reality, Virtual Environments, Selection.

1 Introduction

Setting up a virtual environment is a complex process that requires a large amount of time and resources, and also specific knowledge in programming languages and computer graphics. This is true even when it is created with the aid of specialized frameworks that abstract part of the complexity, therefore excluding part of the possible benefit to be obtained from a virtual environment. Aiming to alleviate these problems, a platform for Setting up Interactive Virtual Environments (pSIVE) was developed to allow non-specialists to setup interactive virtual environments that can be applied for virtual visits in the scope of different application areas such as training, education, marketing, etc. Besides setting up the virtual environment, the platform also allows to associate additional information to 3D models in the environment. This gives the possibility to select an object and view the available information about it, such as documentation, videos, etc.

A central interaction task in the envisioned applications of pSIVE is the selection of those objects that have associated multimedia information. Because of the relevance of

R. Shumaker and S. Lackey (Eds.): VAMR 2014, Part I, LNCS 8525, pp. 215–225, 2014.

selection in this context, the fact that object selection is one of the fundamental tasks in 3D user interfaces and thus poorly designed selection techniques often have a significant negative impact on the overall user performance [1], a comparative study to evaluate the selection techniques that should be available on the platform was conducted. In what follows a brief overview of pSIVE is given, the comparative study between two variants of the ray-tracing selection technique is described, and some conclusions are drawn.

2   pSIVE Platform

2.1   Architectural Decisions

From the frameworks analyzed, VR Juggler (VRJ)1 was chosen as the basis for our system since it had all the qualities needed to fulfill the project requirements and its community is active developing new features and supporting users to solve problems from its creation back in the late 90's. The project activity was the main point that made VRJ the chosen framework, as while it had a very active community other possible frameworks such as inVRs2 had reduced activity.

The graphics engine was tied to the base framework. For VRJ, even though it supports a number of graphics engines, some are more developed, accepted and therefore, easy to work with. The decision was between OpenSceneGraph and OpenSG. Both were complete solutions to meet pSIVE's requirements. However, the project activity was again decisive and OpenSceneGraph[3] was chosen since OpenSG[4] is outdated and lacks updates and improvements.

The alternative of using a well-known game engine such as Ogre[5] and Unity[6] was also considered, yet in general they are more specialized with focus on game applications, and more generic graphics engines, as scene graphs, more easily cover a wide variety of applications, and adapt to different application types.

2.2   Platform Development

Figure 1 shows an overview of pSIVE's structure. The Virtual Environment (VE) depends on a series of settings to be configured before running using the configuration tool. While the Virtual Environment is built on top of a group of frameworks, namely VR Juggler to handle input/output devices along with VRPN[7] (that adds an extra set of supported devices to VR Juggler through network). VR Juggler also handles the window system creation and the system calls (to the operating system).

---

[1] http://vrjuggler.org/
[2] http://www.invrs.org/
[3] http://www.openscenegraph.com/
[4] http://www.opensg.org/
[5] http://www.ogre3d.org/
[6] http://unity3d.com/
[7] http://www.cs.unc.edu/Research/vrpn/

OpenSceneGraph is the graphic rendering framework, however most of its features are encapsulated by VR Juggler. The top four elements in Fig. 1 are the modules built using elements of both frameworks to manage the whole Virtual Environment.

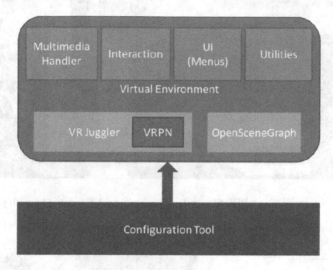

Fig. 1. Platform Overview

pSIVE must be flexible enough to allow a simple simulation (one could load a single model just to see and rotate it in a VE) or load a complex environment such as a whole factory with machinery in which the user could interact with a document describing the machines or watch a documentary on the maintenance of a part on its location. The platform must also cope with several possible devices, file formats to show as contextualized information, as well as the interactions that trigger and control all of it. A group of modules was developed to allow flexibility:

- Multimedia Module: handles the input and exhibition of multiple formats of 3D models and its multimedia contents, the multimedia module takes advantage of the plugin architecture from OpenSceneGraph which loads dynamically the plugin needed for different kinds of formats. Besides the 3D models, the currently supported formats for additional information are: PDF Files, Videos and text files. An example is shown in Fig. 2.
- Interaction module: takes care of the whole interaction allowing navigation, selection and manipulation. An example of selection is presented in Fig. 3, where the user is pointing at a dinner table. The name of the model is presented as visual feedback indicating the existence of additional information related to the model.

Fig. 2. User inspecting a PDF file while immersed in a VE created by with pSIVE

Fig. 3. User selecting an object (dinner table) by head orientation (HOS) while immersed in a VE created with pSIVE

- Menus module: provides a way for the user to access information inherent to virtual elements. The Virtual Environment presents 2D adapted menus created accordingly to the elements that are available for a certain model. In Fig. 4 a three item menu is presented indicating the existence of a video, a pdf file and text information associated to the fridge model.
- Utilities module: provides elements that aid the development and programming of pSIVE such as mathematical and text processing functions.

Fig. 4. A three item menu concerning information associated to a model in a VE created with pSIVE

2.3   pSIVE Configuration

The configuration tool is a simple JAVA application designed to generate the XML file that will control the whole application. It allows users to configure the layout and tell VR Juggler which hardware to use on the Virtual Environment. Its interface was designed to rely on tabs, each one controlling a specific aspect of the system. The hardware Tab allows the user to choose from a list (previously defined by the developer) of equipment supported by pSIVE, dividing them into three classes: Head Tracking, Hand Tracking/Controller and Output. Models tab loads the 3D files giving the possibility of adding information to each file and adjust its position/orientation.

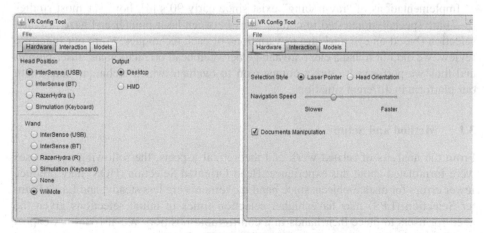

Fig. 5. pSIVE configuration tool

The last tab controls the interaction styles to be used on the environment: Navigation speed, Selection style and Manipulation (of the documents). Fig. 5. presents some views of the configuration tool created.

The list of devices to be used is sent to pSIVE transparently for the user. The configuration tool modifies the VR Juggler files that define each device so the correct ones can be loaded by the platform.

3   Comparison of Selection Techniques

As mentioned, object selection is a fundamental interaction task in Virtual Environments in general, and particularly in the envisioned applications of pSIVE to select those objects that have associated multimedia information. Thus, during the latest stages of development of pSIVE a study was proposed to assess the effectiveness and to find out which selection technique was better applied to different situations, given the characteristics of the platform, and the several possible selection methods, two variants of the "ray-tracing" technique, a well know and very popular selection technique [2], were compared. Both techniques are considered pointing techniques [3] which require the user to perform a set of movements to place a selection tool (on this case, a ray) inside the target (the object to be selected).

The first variation used the hand to control the selection tool with its orientation and position, and to become the selection tool start point. This recalls a laser pointer located in the user's hand. On the second variant the selection tool is controlled by the head, this also is its origin point, requiring the object to be on the center of the user's viewpoint. The two methods share common aspects, however by detaching the viewpoint to the control of the selection tool, the laser pointer technique suffers from the eye–hand visibility mismatch which, according to Argelaguet et al. [2] "bias how the user perceives the difficulty of the task; some objects might seem easy to select but in practice they are not".

Implementations of "ray-tracing" exist since early 90's [4], however most studies [5–7] are specially interested in comparisons between laser pointer and gaze oriented selection (based on eye tracking) or variations of each techniques. From our literature review, we did not found a clear advantage between head orientation and laser pointer and thus we performed a direct comparison to evaluate which technique suits more our platform in different situations.

3.1   Method and Setup

From the analysis of related work and theoretical aspects, the following hypotheses were formulated about this experience: Head Oriented Selection (HOS) may produce fewer errors for distant objects since hand movements are less steady, and Laser Pointer Selection (LPS) may have higher selection times in initial selections given the need for users to place their hands in a comfortable position. We also did not expect any influence of the initial method (HOS or LPS) on users' performance, if they had to use both methods in sequence.

The selection method was the input (or independent) variable, with two levels (HOS or LPS). The output variable (or dependent variable) considered was the user performance and satisfaction with both techniques, assessing basically the number of mistakes and the time elapsed as well as difficulty and preferences. The learning effect according to the initial selection method was considered a secondary variable.

During the evaluation participants had to perform a series of selection tasks that were considered representative of what users would typically do in the applications intended for pSIVE: select a green cube (55cm size) on a grid of 3x3 cubes (Fig. 6.). The position of the green cube to select is random, and after each selection the distance to the grid increases (starting at 5 meters and increasing 5 meters each step until the final position 70 meters away from the user) in order to assess how user performance varies with distance. After performing the tasks, all participants answered a questionnaire concerning their profile and impressions on different aspects of their experience (easy to orientate, pleasant, etc...), the satisfaction rate for each selection method, the preferred method and any comment about difficulties or any other experiment related subject.

The evaluation had the participation of 16 volunteers (14 male and 2 female) with ages between 19 and 26 years. All users performed the selection with both methods, however to compensate for possible learning effects, half of the participants started with Laser Pointer (LPS) and the other half with selection by Head Orientation (HOS) in a within-groups experimental design [8]. The participants were observed while performing these tasks.

This evaluation layout was based on a previous experiment performed by Bowman et al. [9], differing on the selection methods and without manipulation of the selected object.

This experiment also served to test the platform flexibility. The test environment was created using pSIVE, that was modified to record measures characterizing users' performance.

Any device supported by pSIVE could have been used, yet the Razer Hydra[8] (an electromagnetic tracker including two controls) was chosen as it is easy to operate and provides 6DOF allowing to easily emulate the natural act of pointing. Since the Hydra is composed of two controllers, one was placed on the back of each participant's head, to track its orientation, along with the VR2000[9] head mounted display since the built-in tracker is not yet supported neither by VR Juggler nor the VRPN. The other controller was held for inputting commands to start the simulation and to trigger the selection. The second controller was also used as a laser pointing, by tracking the position and orientation of the hand.

---

[8] http://www.razerzone.com/minicite/hydra
[9] http://www.vrealities.com/products/head-mounted-displays/vr2000-pro-dual

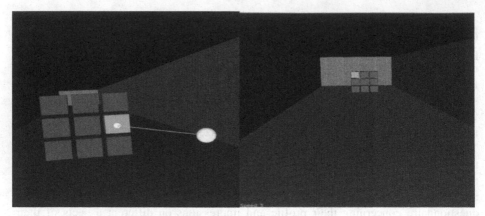

Fig. 6. Selection of a cube using the LPS method (left); next grid position with the object to be selected highlighted (right)

3.2   Results

As mentioned, several measures were automatically recorded by the platform, corresponding to the user's performance: number of errors (an error corresponded to a wrong object selection), time elapsed from the activation of the test and the selection, the distance of the grid and the position of the correct object on each step. The method that the participants began with was also recorded (HOS or LPS).

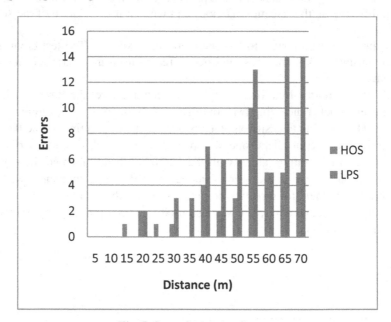

Fig. 7. Sum of errors by distance

Regarding errors, as shown on Fig. 7, users performed fewer errors (wrong selections) with HOS for almost all distances, and the number of errors obtained with both techniques increased with distance; both results were expected.

Regarding the average elapsed time needed to perform the selection at each distance, Fig. 8 shows that participants took longer times while using LPS, in most instances. However, the original difference tends to decrease in the range of 10 to 25 meters. As expected, users needed higher selection times with LPS in the first selections probably due to the fact that they took some time to find a comfortable position for the hand as reported by 8 of the 16 participants.

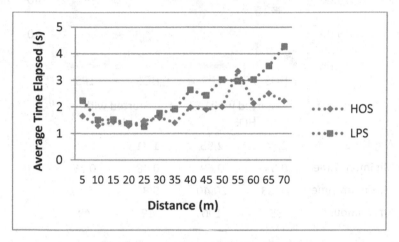

Fig. 8. Average time to select by distance

An interesting result was a noticeable increase in both selection time and number of errors for those who started using the LPS method. Fig. 9 shows clearly that the number of errors accounted for those who began with HOS and were currently using LPS was approximately two times higher than those who started with LPS and were currently using HOS. A possible explanation is the fact that both techniques require small, precise and especially steady movements, which are more easily obtained when controlling the beam with the head. The change from steady movement (with the head) for an unstable movement (with the hand) or vice versa was reflected in the learning rate of the user. It is probable that those who started with LPS were subjected to a method requiring more training to be used, as the users reported (see Table 1), and thus had to be more focused to understand how to interact with the system resulting in a performance improvement when using even HOS.

On the other hand, users generally obtained worse results while using LPS independently of the initial method. These results are reflected on the opinions provided by the participants. On a 5 level Likert-like scale, where 1 means strongly disagree and 5 strongly agree: it can be seen on Table 1 that despite the fact both techniques are pleasant, LPS presents irritant features and requires more training than HOS.

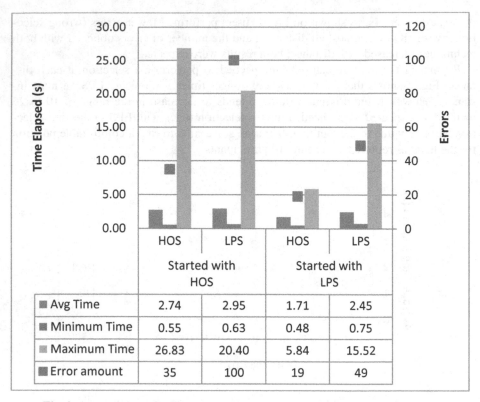

	Started with HOS		Started with LPS	
	HOS	LPS	HOS	LPS
■ Avg Time	2.74	2.95	1.71	2.45
■ Minimum Time	0.55	0.63	0.48	0.75
■ Maximum Time	26.83	20.40	5.84	15.52
■ Error amount	35	100	19	49

Fig. 9. Average elapsed time and errors according to the starting selection method

Table 1. Questionnaire results (median of each index in a scale of 1-disagree to 5- agree)

	HOS	LPS
Ease of Orientation	4	4
Is Pleasant	4	4
Has Annoying features	2	4
Is Intuitive	4	4
Requires Training	3	4
Is Useful for near Obj.	5	4
Is Useful for Distant Obj.	4	3
Satisfaction Rate	4	3

From the results, it is clear that that HOS was the technique preferred by most users (Table 1) and along with the results concerning performances, HOS was better for these tasks regardless of the position and distance of the object.

4 Conclusions and Future Work

This paper presents pSIVE, a platform that abstracts the usage of several frameworks to setup Virtual Environments, allowing even laymen to work with it. Albeit several frameworks already ease the creation of Virtual Environments none addressed in a satisfactory way the need to interact directly with code or configuration files, difficult to non-experts. Results suggest pSIVE is flexible enough to allow extending it for domain specific applications, as it was the case for the user study performed. The results of the tests indicate the selection performed with the head orientation allow users to have better overall performance, when directly compared to the results for the selections performed with the laser pointer. However the laser pointer analogy was more intuitive and delivered a better learning effect so that those who started with it could finish the tasks with lower times and fewer errors than those who started with the head orientation.

The current version of pSIVE is a prototype and still requires further refinement concerning its structure and modules. Furthermore, it is still limited and does not have the elements to provide a better and more natural usage of the Virtual Environment, for instance allowing new selection methods supported by the interactions with different types of equipment.

Acknowledgements. This work was partially funded by FEDER through the Operational Program Competitiveness Factors – COMPETE – by National Funds through Foundation for Science and Technology – FCT (references FCOMP-01-0124-FEDER-022682 and PEst-C/EEI/UI0127/2011) and by Produtech PTI - New Processes and Innovative Technologies for Manufacturing Technologies (reference QREN 13851).

References

1. Bowman, Kruijff, E., LaViola, J., Poupyrev, I.: 3D User Interfaces: Theory and Practice. Addison-Wesley Professional (2004)
2. Argelaguet, F., Andujar, C.: A survey of 3D object selection techniques for virtual environments. Comput Graph. 37, 121–136 (2013), doi:10.1016/j.cag.2012.12.003
3. Mine, M.: Virtual environment interaction techniques. UNC Chapel Hill Comput. Sci. Tech. Rep. (1995)
4. Liang, J., Green, M.: JDCAD: A highly interactive 3D modeling system. Comput Graph 18, 499–506 (1994)
5. Jimenez, J., Gutierrez, D., Latorre, P.: Gaze-based Interaction for Virtual Environments. J. Univers Comput. Sci. 14, 3085–3098 (2008)
6. Cournia, N., Smith, J.D., Duchowski, A.T.: Gaze- vs. hand-based pointing in virtual environments. In: CHI 2003 Ext. Abstr. Hum. factors Comput. Syst. - CHI 2003, p. 772. ACM Press, New York (2003)
7. Sanz, F.A.: Pointing facilitation techniques for 3d object selection on virtual environments (2011)
8. Dix, A., Finlay, J.E., Abowd, G.D., Beale, R.: Human-Computer Interaction, 3rd edn. Prentice-Hall (2003)
9. Bowman, D.A., Johnson, D.B., Hodges, L.F.: Testbed evaluation of virtual environment interaction techniques. In: Proc. ACM Symp. Virtual Real. Softw. Technol - VRST 1999, pp. 26–33. ACM Press, New York (1999)

Augmented Reality Evaluation: A Concept Utilizing Virtual Reality

Philipp Tiefenbacher, Nicolas H. Lehment, and Gerhard Rigoll

Institute for Human-Machine Communication,
Technische Universität München, Germany
{Philipp.Tiefenbacher,Lehment}@tum.de
http://www.mmk.ei.tum.de

Abstract. In recent years the field of augmented reality (AR) has seen great advances in interaction, tracking and rendering. New input devices and mobile hardware have enabled entirely new interaction concepts for AR content. The high complexity of AR applications results in lacking usability evaluation practices on part of the developer. In this paper, we present a thorough classification of factors influencing user experience, split into the broad categories of rendering, tracking and interaction. Based on these factors, we propose an architecture for evaluating AR experiences prior to deployment in an adapted virtual reality (VR) environment. Thus we enable rapid prototyping and evaluation of AR applications especially suited for applications in challenging industrial AR projects.

1 Introduction

The AR technology has advanced rapidly over the last years and the number of real world applications increases. Industrial AR applications have always been targeted, but until today only partly succeeded. The development of AR applications for industrial settings is challenging. The development process of industrial plants is complex and in general years pass until the plant is reality. AR applications, on the other side, need to be adapted to the exact use-cases to yield real value. Therefore, we present a mixed reality (MR) environment, which enables early development of AR applications through the visualization of the CAD data of the industrial line in the virtual reality (VR). Besides the benefits of an earlier development, the isolated and controlled environment of the VR allows advanced user evaluation for AR applications.

A survey by Dunser *et al.* showed that only 8 % of all considered publications in AR conducted user evaluations. Swan *et al.* conclude in [17] that there is still space to identify proper user interfaces and user interaction requirements to known usage domains, which is reflected by the rising importance of evaluation in AR publications [6,21]. We therefore see a high potential in frameworks, which enable thorough evaluation of AR systems under a wide range of conditions. In this paper we propose a general concept for evaluating AR applications, which takes advantage of the controlled conditions afforded by full VR systems.

R. Shumaker and S. Lackey (Eds.): VAMR 2014, Part I, LNCS 8525, pp. 226–236, 2014.
© Springer International Publishing Switzerland 2014

Hereby, the system is able to simulate Head-Mounted Displays (HMD) as well as to integrate mobile device like smart phones. We feel that the success of AR depends on the acceptance by the users and aim to improve said acceptance by providing a reliable and reproducible test bench for future AR applications. Section 2 discusses current work in the field of mixed reality evaluation concepts. Then, Section 3 presents the architecture of the evaluation bench with the corresponding parameters. Also the CAVE is described shortly. The following Section 4 presents a variety of different properties, which affect the AR experience and should be evaluated. Lastly, Section 5 summarizes the work and gives an outlook.

2   Related Work

Khan et al. describe in [11] a CAVE setting for evaluating the intrusiveness of virtual ads on a smart phone. Here, the CAVE solely supports the evaluation of the user experience. Furthermore, only the head of the subjects are tracked and based on the position of the user, virtual content is displayed on the smart phone. The mobile device itself is not tracked.

First approaches investigating the influence of tracking failures in AR scenes like jitter are presented in [15,19]. Vincent et al. test in [19] the influence of jitter based on artificial normal distributed noise. Ragan et al. provide in [15] a proof of concept for simulating an AR system in a virtual environment, the experiment results show a significant influence of jitter to the task completion time.

Besides the evaluation of the tracking accuracy also approaches for evaluating the impact of the latency in AR scenes exist [13]. VR systems have also been used for simulating outdoor AR systems. Gabbard et al. present in [7] an AR scene in a CAVE, the users wore an optical see-through display, which showed virtual objects registered within the VR environment. Here, different designed virtual texts overlay heavily textured outdoor scenes. In the controlled environment of the CAVE, the users chose the best recognizable text designs. Another work about the human perception of AR scenes was done by Knecht et al. in [12]. Knecht focused on the influence of rendering global illumination for augmented objects to allow for photo-realistic augmented reality scenes. The different types of rendering did not change the completion time for a positioning task of a virtual cube.

Furthermore, Lee et al. compare in [14] different levels of visual quality for searching tasks in a mixed reality (MR) environment. The results show that the completion time of most searching tasks are independent of the visual quality of the rendering part of the MR. Also the completion times of the same task in MR and AR are not significantly different, which further motivates our approach.

3   Evaluation Architecture

Our main contribution is an overview of experience criteria for AR applications, which are depicted in the evaluation concept called Augmented Reality Evaluation (ARE). Figure 1 shows this concept. ARE works as a link between the physical hardware to any AR application.

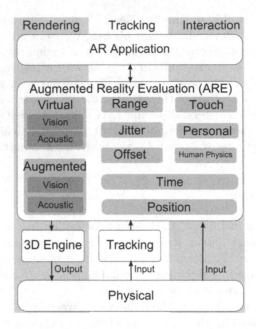

Fig. 1. The test bench separated into rendering, tracking and interaction. Each part is subdivided into possible evaluation criteria.

It is implemented as a CAVE virtual reality (VR) system, which in turn simulates the entire AR experience and partly real hardware. This constrained environment enables complete control of AR related parameters. We separate these parameters into the three different main parts of any AR system [3]: rendering, tracking and interaction. Azuma defined these parts in [3] as *scene generator*, *tracking and sensing* and *display device*. We extend the definition of the displaying part to the interaction part, as the display is generally more than just a visualization. Commonly the touch display is also used as interaction device for the AR scene. In the case of a HMD, the interaction part also may include gesture or speech recognition. The computational unit is neglected as it is included in every mentioned main part.

The physical layer includes all the necessary hardware for the MR environment like the canvas, projectors, tracking targets and PCs. The rendering encompasses both the stimulation of the real world and the augmented reality content, which is just visible in the field of view of a Head-Mounted Display or on the surface of a tablet PC, as demonstrated in Figure 3. Section 4.1 describes the quality metrics of the rendering part in more detail. A professional tracking system (DTrack), which works on the basis of infrared cameras and reflecting tracking targets, delivers precise tracking data with a rate of 60 Hz to our ARE concept. The tracking results of the DTrack system are altered according to the five depicted properties in Figure 1. Then ARE forwards this modified tracking data to an arbitrary AR application. The subject's view is tracked using glasses with

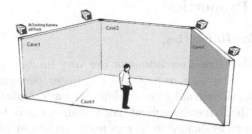

Fig. 2. Scheme of the four sided CAVE and the setup of the tracking cameras. Each of the four walls is projected through two *projectiondesign* projectors. The projectors are equipped with *Infitec* filters, which enable a 3D experience.

tracking targets mounted on it. The position of the head defines the rendered scene in the CAVE. When simulating a virtual HMD display, an additional camera with an arbitrarily defined field of view renders the contents of the AR scene. Besides the simulated HMD also physical mobile devices can be included. For this, tracking targets are also equipped at the mobile device. In this case, the tracking system registers both the head of the subject and the mobile device. The mobile device has to render the virtual scene in the CAVE, as well as the additional AR content. Thus, the mobile device has to fulfil high performance requirements. The smaller field of view of the mobile device, however, limits the virtual space which has to be rendered. Lastly, the interaction with the AR scene is also split into five different properties. The simulated HMD has currently no input options, consequently the only way for the subject to directly interact with the scene would be through gesture or/and speech recognition using a Wizard-of-Oz approach. Nevertheless, AR tasks like searching for 3D content can be performed and the user experience evaluated.

Fig. 3. A user with a tracked mobile device stands inside a virtual industrial line, which is also visible on the mobile device. The user interacts with additional AR content only accessible on the touch device. In this scenario the head of the subject, as well as the mobile device are tracked.

4   Evaluation Properties

4.1   Properties for Rendering

The side effects in the virtual environment are very limited, enabling to simulate real world conditions with respect to actual user perception. This can be achieved by rendering the virtual scene in different ways, imitating possible limitations and noise of the real environment. For instance, the influence of changing outdoor illumination as evaluated in [7] can easily be tested within a controlled environment. For a start, we propose four different environmental properties, which might influence the visual AR experience and are easily reproducible in our concept:

◆ available light
◆ background texture
◆ disruptive visual environment (dust, powder)
◆ acoustic noise

The first three items are part of the visual rendering property, the last belongs to the acoustic property of previous Figure 1. The available light includes the brightness of the virtual scene as well as the number and the spots of light sources. In a plant or an other indoor environment, it is very likely that more than one light source brightens the setting.

The background texture can be changed from very simple, flat ones to more rich ones, which is similar to the idea in [7]. It should be noted that, our main goal is not an easier reproducibility of outdoor scenes in the VR simulation. The influence of disruptive visual environment shares the same features as the background textures, however this time the distractions are of a more dynamic nature and overlays the background textures. Finally, the acoustic noise in the VR rendering part provides an additional disturbance factor to the task. Hereby, the noise can surround the subject or be perceived in a more directional fashion, where the source of the noise comes from a distinct direction. The Head-related transfer function for the audio output, however, is not implemented yet.

The type of noise should fit to the presented scene in the CAVE. In our case an industrial plant is visualized and typical sounds of heavy machinery are the best choice.

The camera of the portable device, which displays the augmented reality content is purely virtual. Hence, we can control the following camera parameters of the AR rendering part:

◆ rendering latency
◆ rendering quality
◆ focal length
◆ field of view
◆ aperture

A holding parameter defines the update rate of the AR content, which only affects the user experience in the case of animated 3D items. The quality of the

3D items has to be detailed offline. The basis of the 3D items is CAD data, thus through reducing the faces and vertices, the rendering quality of the 3D items can be decreased from very realistic to sketchy. A volumetric lens renders not the whole 3D data as we are culling specific parts of the 3D items [18] based on the view frustum. A view frustum is a geometric shape similar to a pyramid. The position of the pyramid's peak specifies the position of the lense. The shape of the volume defined through the view frustum is rigid, so moving the viewer's head has no affect on the volume of the frustum. The focal length is determined by setting the near and far plane for the view frustum, whereas the field of view can easily be changed through setting the left, right, top and bottom of the view frustum. The brightness of the light in the virtual scene defines the aperture of the virtual camera.

4.2   Properties for Tracking

Tracking is a crucial part in any AR scenario as bad content registration impairs user experience and task fulfilment. The precise tracking available in a virtual environment allows for measuring the influence of important performance metrics of a tracking system. In our test bench approach, we can alter four different tracking metrics and evaluate their impact on user experience. These metrics are:

- ◆ update rate
- ◆ precision
- ◆ jitter (spatial and temporal)
- ◆ necessary range of tracking (see Figure 4)

As stated above, the tracking system delivers new tracking data with a frequency of 60 Hz, which also defines the upper threshold of the update rate. Based on this maximum rate, slower update rates can be simulated by emitting the same tracking data for multiple new inputs. At this step, an additional temporal random noise can be added to the update rate. The random jitters of both the spatial and temporal jitter are Gaussian distributed. The temporal jitter is just added to the altered update rate.

The precision of the tracking data can be separated into the rotational precision and the translational precision. Therefore, two additional sources of noise may influence the tracking outcome respectively. First, the translational position is modified. For that, a fixed translational offset vector $\mathbf{T_o}$ is subtracted from the original position of the object $\mathbf{X}$

$$\mathbf{X_o} = \mathbf{X} - \mathbf{T_o}. \tag{1}$$

Hereby, $\mathbf{T_o}$ holds the offset for each axis. Then, the spatial jitter is added to each axis.

Huynh et al. analysed different metrics for 3D rotation in [5]. We choose an easy to calculate metric, which overcomes the problem of ambiguous representation and is also bi-variant, when calculating a metric for the distance between two rotations. Therefore, the proposed metrics in [5] cannot be used for determining a new rotation matrix based on such a distance metric.

Hence, the three Euler angles are separately defined based on the Equation

$$\alpha_o = \alpha - r_o. \tag{2}$$

The offset r_o to the current angle ranges between $-\pi \leq r_o \leq \pi$. Finally, the random rotational jitter is added to each angle. For evaluation purposes a rotational distance metric m_r between the final rotation matrix $\mathbf{R}_o$ and the original rotation $\mathbf{R}_x$ is computed with Equation (3).

$$m_r = ||\mathbf{I} - \mathbf{R}_o\mathbf{R}_x^T||_F \tag{3}$$

Here, $\mathbf{I}$ denotes the identity matrix. The *Frobeniusnorm* is defined as follows

$$||\mathbf{R}||_F = \sqrt{\sum_i \sum_j R_{i,j}^2}. \tag{4}$$

The distance of the altered rotation to the original rotation changes with every update of the tracking data. The reason therefore lay in the fact that for each update a fix offset r_o is added but also random noise (jitter). So the metric m_r records the changes in the rotational distance. Lastly, the tracking system follows the targets not in the whole area of the CAVE. An upper and lower threshold for each axis determine the valid area for delivering valid tracking data.

Marker based tracking is still widely used as it leads to quite accurate tracking and also to little performance requirements. A drawback of marker based tracking is the limited range of available tracking, as in each frame a fiducial marker must be recorded and detected. Furthermore, when working at an industrial plant, markers can only attached at certain spots on the machine. Either way the tracking is limited to specific regions. Thus, we also restrict the range of the tracking to examine the influence to certain AR applications in the mixed reality environment. In the best case, we are able to recommend a necessary tracking area to fulfil a certain AR task, like maintaining a part of the machine in a satisfactory manner.

Figure 4 shows the favoured positions of 18 different subjects in bird's-eye view of a study. Here, the subjects had to interact with three AR items in the CAVE.

4.3   Properties for Interaction

Now that we can control experimental conditions, the interaction metrics can be exercised. Widely used questionnaires are the System Usability Scale [4] and the NASA TLX [9] for more challenging tasks. Our system, however, can gather a host of additional data, such as:

◆ amount of touch points
◆ area and range of touch points (see Figure 5)

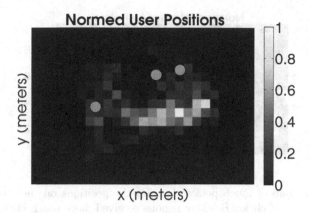

Fig. 4. The heat map of positions displays the favoured positions of the subjects during an AR task. Here, the green dots describe the location of AR models. Brighter rectangles indicate the favoured positions of the participants during the whole test.

◆ human physics
◆ time (task, interaction)

Human physiology need to be taken to account as in the one hand the interaction happens in real places, which sometimes might be hard to reach. On the other hand the human biometrics like the size of the hand may influence the usability of an AR application according to different sized touch devices.

In first studies, we concluded that in some cases it is beneficial to separate the completion time into the whole task time and the interaction time. The interaction time is just the time, in which the subjects are really touching and interacting with the scene. In the case of evaluating different interaction concepts for an AR scene, the whole completion time is additionally influenced by repositioning tasks of the subjects. The difficulty of a certain task also influences the completion time, as the participants have to find the right way to solve the task. This affects the study outcome, when performed as within-subject design as it is hard to counterbalance the training effects. The consideration of just the interaction time reduces such training effects. Figure 5 depicts an heat map of exemplary touch points on the touch-screen of the tablet. Here, a lot of touch points are indicated in the middle of the screen, thus the human hands need to be big enough to perform touch events in these area easily.

5   Detailed Properties vs. Evaluation Categories

The ARE architecture features the parts initially proposed by Azuma, however, there exists also a classification of different types of evaluation concepts of AR systems. In the following the rendering, tracking and interaction part are linked to these new types of classification. Dunser *et al.* classified in [6] four different types of evaluation concepts for AR systems. Three of them were initially introduced by Swan *et al.* in [17].

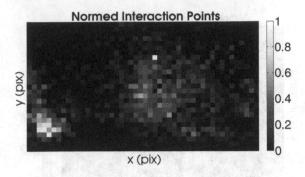

Fig. 5. The heat map of touch points classifies the positions on the screen in regard to the total number of clicks. Brighter regions received more touch clicks than darker regions.

Experiments determining how the subjects perceive and realize the AR context belong to the *Perception* type. The second type of evaluation is classified as *Performance*. These experiments mainly examine the users' task performance with the goal to improve the task execution through the help of AR. The *Collaboration* experiments detail the interactions in an AR scene between multiple users. The collaborative AR can be split into face-to-face [1,10] and to remote collaboration [8,20]. The new category introduced in [6] is called *Interface or system usability studies* abbreviated as *Usability*. This type does not need to involve the measurement of the task performance, instead the user experience is identified. Figure 6 combines the evaluation criteria with the three components

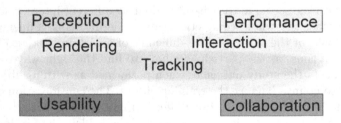

Fig. 6. Relation of the three parts every AR systems consists of to the evaluation criteria in [6]

every AR system consists of. The rendering part of an AR scene mainly belongs to the *Perception* category. Since the proposed properties in the rendering part affect primarily the cognition of the scene.

The interaction with the AR scene and the quality of the tracking are measured as the *Performance* of the task. The AR task mostly depends on the featured interaction idea, when a certain quality in tracking is guaranteed. Photo-realistic rendering, calculation of lightning effects [12] and the visualization of occlusion [2] improve the user experience (*Usability*). Therefore, the rendering part plays an important role. Shah *et al.* show in [16], however, that neglecting occlusions in AR scenes lead to incorrect display, which might be noticed by the user. So, the users' perception might be wrong in some cases, which lead to wrong task operations and might also influence the performance.

Lastly, when working with multiple user's in an AR scene, the interaction parts within the group are of main interest (*Collaboration*).

6 Conclusion and Outlook

Inspired by the definition of the main AR parts by Azuma, we envisaged individual evaluation metrics for each part on the basis of a mixed reality environment. The detailed description of evaluation criteria for AR applications gives other researchers a guideline for their AR evaluations. We use a CAVE setting for the evaluation architecture as AR applications can be evaluated more rapidly and easily in VR scenes than in real scenes.

The use of a mixed environment, however, also implies some shortcomings. The area for the AR scene is limited to a desktop scenario due to the size of the CAVE. Testing AR applications in wide area scenarios is not possible.

Furthermore, the use of projectors for the presentation of the virtual scene restricts the maximum intensity of ambient light. A brighter room reduces the quality of the virtual experience as the projectors have a limited luminance. So, the experiments can only be conducted in an almost dark room.

Beside this, the evaluation architecture can be advanced to include photo realistic rendering or occlusion aware rendering of the AR objects, which is currently not integrated. The forth evaluation category, *Collaboration*, is also not included, yet. Hence, face-to-face as well as remote scenarios for collaborative AR have still to be incorporated in the CAVE environment.

Acknowledgement. The research leading to these inventions has received funding from the European Union Seventh Framework Programm (FP7/2007-2013) under grant agreement n° 284573.

References

1. Morrison, A., Mulloni, A., Lemmelä, S., Oulasvirta, A., Jacucci, G., Peltonen, P., Schmalstieg, D., Regenbrecht, H.: Collaborative use of mobile augmented reality with paper maps. Computers & Graphics 35(4), 789–799 (2011)
2. Allen, M., Hoermann, S., Piumsomboon, T., Regenbrecht, H.: Visual occlusion in an augmented reality post-stroke therapy scenario. In: Proc. CHINZ. ACM (2013)
3. Azuma, R.: A survey of augmented reality. Presence 6(4), 355–385 (1997)
4. Brooke, J.: Sus-a quick and dirty usability scale. Usability Evaluation in Industry 189, 194 (1996)
5. Du Huynh, Q.: Metrics for 3d rotations: Comparison and analysis, Mathematical Imaging and Vision 35(2), 155–164 (2009)

6. Dünser, A., Grasset, R., Billinghurst, M.: A Survey of Evaluation Techniques Used in Augmented Reality Studies. Technical report (2008)
7. Gabbard, J.L., Swan, J.E., Hix, D., Lucas, J., Gupta, D.: An empirical user-based study of text drawing styles and outdoor background textures for augmented reality. In: Proc. VR, pp. 11–18, 317. IEEE (2005)
8. Gauglitz, S., Lee, C., Turk, M., Höllerer, T.: Integrating the physical environment into mobile remote collaboration. In: Proc. MobileHCI, pp. 241–250. ACM (2012)
9. Hart, S.G., Staveland, L.E.: Development of nasa-tlx (task load index): Results of empirical and theoretical research. Human Mental Workload 1(3), 139–183 (1988)
10. Kaufmann, H., Schmalstieg, D.: Mathematics and geometry education with collaborative augmented reality. Computers & Graphics 27(3), 339–345 (2003)
11. Khan, V., Nuijten, K., Deslé, N.: Pervasive application evaluation within virtual environments. In: Proc. PECCS, pp. 261–264. SciTePress (2011)
12. Knecht, M., Dünser, A., Traxler, C., Wimmer, M., Grasset, R.: A framework for perceptual studies in photorealistic augmented reality (2011)
13. Lee, C., Bonebrake, S., Hollerer, T., Bowman, D.A.: The role of latency in the validity of ar simulation. In: Proc. VR, pp. 11–18. IEEE (2010)
14. Lee, C., Rincon, G.A., Meyer, G., Hollerer, T., Bowman, D.A.: The effects of visual realism on search tasks in mixed reality simulation. Visualization and Computer Graphics 19(4), 547–556 (2013)
15. Ragan, E., Wilkes, C., Bowman, D.A., Hollerer, T.: Simulation of augmented reality systems in purely virtual environments. In: Proc. VR, pp. 287–288. IEEE (2009)
16. Shah, M.M., Arshad, H., Sulaiman, R.: Occlusion in augmented reality. In: Proc. ICIDT, vol. 2, pp. 372–378. IEEE (2012)
17. Swan, J.E., Gabbard, J.L.: Survey of user-based experimentation in augmented reality. In: Proc. VR, pp. 1–9. IEEE (2005)
18. Viega, J., Conway, M.J., Williams, G., Pausch, R.: 3d magic lenses. In: Proc. UIST, pp. 51–58. ACM (1996)
19. Vincent, T., Nigay, L., Kurata, T.: Handheld augmented reality: Effect of registration jitter on cursor-based pointing techniques. In: Proc. IHM, pp. 1–6. ACM (2013)
20. Shen, Y., Ong, S.K., Nee, A.Y.C.: Augmented reality for collaborative product design and development. Design Studies 31(2), 118–145 (2010)
21. Bai, Z., Blackwell, A.F.: Analytic review of usability evaluation in ISMAR. Interacting with Computers 24(6), 450–460 (2012)

Avatars and Virtual Characters

Good Enough Yet? A Preliminary Evaluation of Human-Surrogate Interaction

Julian Abich IV[1], Lauren E. Reinerman-Jones[1], Gerald Matthews[1],
Gregory F. Welch[2], Stephanie J. Lackey[1], Charles E. Hughes[2], and Arjun Nagendran[2]

[1] University of Central Florida (UCF), Institute for Simulation & Training (IST),
Applied Cognition in Virtual Immersive Training Environments Laboratory (ACTIVE Lab)
Orlando, FL, USA
{jabich,lreinerm,gmatthew,slackey}@ist.ucf.edu
[2] University of Central Florida (UCF), Institute for Simulation & Training (IST),
Synthetic Reality Lab (SREAL)
welch@ucf.edu, {ceh,arjun}@cs.ucf.edu

Abstract. Research exploring the implementation of surrogates has included areas such as training (Chuah et al., 2013), education (Yamashita, Kuzuoka, Fujimon, & Hirose, 2007), and entertainment (Boberg, Piippo, & Ollila, 2008). Determining the characteristics of the surrogate that could potentially influence the human's behavioral responses during human-surrogate interactions is of importance. The present work will draw on the literature about human-robot interaction (HRI), social psychology literature regarding the impact that the presence of a surrogate has on another human, and communications literature about human-human interpersonal interaction. The review will result in an experimental design to evaluate various dimensions of the space of human-surrogate characteristics influence on interaction.

Keywords: human-robot interaction, human-surrogate interaction, communications, social psychology, avatar, physical-virtual avatar.

1   Introduction

The past decades have seen a tremendous social role change for robots and virtual avatars, as many have forecasted (Dragone et al., 2006). One such manifestation is the inception of their use as non-traditional surrogates (Welch, 2012). Surrogates, although the term has other meanings (McFarland et al., 2002), are considered for the present purpose to be a substitute for another person in a context-specific role. These surrogates can range from being purely virtual characters to real human beings. In the broadest sense, the term 'surrogate' captures the interest in human representations, while not being encumbered by traditional distinctions between digital and physical form (of the virtual characters) or the nature of the agency (intelligence model of the virtual characters). Basically, the concentration here is on the 'vessel' that will house the surrogate and to describe how to conceptualize the future social roles of non-traditional surrogates.

R. Shumaker and S. Lackey (Eds.): VAMR 2014, Part I, LNCS 8525, pp. 239–250, 2014.
© Springer International Publishing Switzerland 2014

As the average person in many industrialized nations becomes more tech savvy, they are less likely to perceive interactions with robots as negative (Bartneck et al., 2005). The substantial increase in computer-mediated communication (CMC) is a factor in this acceptance (Halpern & Katz, 2013). Haraway (1985) even made arguments stating the social response humans have towards robots can be attributed to the societal trend of blending computers, machines, and organisms. This has created an environment in which people are more willing to at least entertain the idea of interacting with surrogates in the forms of robots and virtual avatars. Reeves and Nass (1996) also found that humans are likely to socially accept computer entities as equal peers as long as they consistently portray competent social behavior. Therefore, on a larger scale, research should seek the benefits of implementation of non-traditional surrogates for current social roles held by a human. Before this accomplishment, basic lines of research revealing the perception of the human user should lay foundational work and provide recommendations for non-traditional surrogate design and application. Despite the acceptance of these newly acquired avenues of interaction, little is known about the factors that influence the behavioral response from the human user. Specifically, it is unknown how the perceived interaction of the human user will be affected by the characteristics of these non-traditional surrogates and if the same forms of communication that apply to human-human interactions still hold true for human-surrogate interaction, in all its forms (Welch, 2012).

An initial review of the current state of human-surrogate interaction is presented. The work will then draw on the literature about human-robot interaction (HRI). However, it should be noted in relation to the developmental progress of physical-virtual avatars, that much of the work has centered on improving the functionality and capabilities of the robot to resemble a human, such as the motion and behavior, but fewer efforts have focused on the appearance (Lincoln et al., 2010) or the human's perception of the robotic entities. To that end, best practices for experimentation will also draw on the social psychology literature regarding the impact that the presence (actual, imagined, or implied) of a surrogate has on another human (Fiske, 2004) and the communications literature about human-human interpersonal interaction.

The first step in this line of research is understanding each of these disciplines separately and then integrating the concepts into a shared mental model from which surrogate research can flow. This process, in particular identifying specific constructs, will be highlighted in the present paper. The evaluation of various approaches to studying similar domain areas and their importance to driving novel surrogate research will be discussed in more detail. The result of this review is an initial experimental design constructed from a truly integrated, multi-disciplinary viewpoint. That experimental design will be outlined with the expected impact on a newly developed systematic approach to studying human-surrogate interactions.

1.1   Human-Surrogate Interaction

Traditionally, human surrogates have played a variety of roles within social settings, such as medical, military, educational, and entertainment. Waytz (2013) argues that meaningful connections with "social substitutes" are possible. Even in other species, surrogates have been shown to elicit a social response (Harlow, 1958). There is an apparent innate desire to develop social ties. Some might argue that from an evolutionary perspective, successful socialization increases the likelihood of survival and reproduction. Therefore, one must take advantage of this motivation to socialize when developing the role of a non-traditional surrogate.

Advances in computer science technology have led to the development of many forms of surrogates, including virtual and physical-virtual. The vision of future surrogate roles is one of a widespread generality. Imagine classrooms all over the world that are each equipped with a human-like surrogate that receives input from a single teacher and portrays her dynamic image from a remote location (Welch, 2012). This allows people to be in more than one place at a time, disseminating thoughts, ideas, and knowledge to a larger population. Now replace that teacher with a doctor, and now the doctor has the ability to visit with patients, nurses, or other colleagues without having to be physically present (Lincoln et al., 2010). Use the role of a search and rescue team instead, and now teams can access areas that are potentially dangerous or impenetrable for a human, but not for a surrogate (Goodrich & Schultz, 2007). As one can see, this opens up the door to new ways of interacting and communicating, expanding the physical and mental capabilities of both surrogates and users. Research has explored the successful implementation of non-traditional surrogates in areas such as training (Chuah et al., 2013), education (Yamashita, Kuzuoka, Fujimon, & Hirose, 2007), and entertainment (Boberg, Piippo, & Ollila, 2008), yet the field is still in its infancy.

One type of possible physical-virtual surrogate is a robotic replica of a person (Lincoln et al., 2010; Welch, 2012). Determining the characteristics of the surrogate that could potentially influence the human's behavioral responses during human-surrogate interactions is of importance for effective interactions. It would be advantageous for these robotic replicas to capitalize on the extensive research within the field of HRI to aid non-traditional surrogate development.

1.2 Human-Robot Interaction

HRI is the "field of study dedicated to understanding, designing, and evaluating robotic systems for use by or with humans" (Goodrich & Schultz, 2007). The interaction, therefore, necessitates some form of communication to occur between both the human and robot. Several forms of communications are possible, but are dependent upon proximity to each other (Mumm & Mutlu, 2011). Entities can either be distant or nearby. In reference to human-surrogate interaction, research should compare the effectiveness of interacting and communicating with surrogates that are remote or co-located in a variety of contexts to establish when it is appropriate to use one or the other.

Goodrich & Shultz (2007) described five attributes in which interaction between a human and robot is possible. Of the five, two are most relevant to the current review. One centers on the nature of information exchange and the other, of a lesser immediate relevance, refers to the adaptation, learning and training of humans and robots. Many of the characteristics of the former attribute indicates the way information is passed, such as the format, medium, or rules (Chan et al., 2005; Gunhee Kim et al., 2004; Sidner et al., 2004), and reaches out to the human factors and communication literature for support. HRI addresses, in this context, the parameters of the information need to be in order for the human perceptual system to effectively receive such input. The ability to satisfactorily understand, communicate, or interpret the behavior of a robot or avatar will factor into the perceived usability of interacting with the surrogate (Yanco, Drury, & Scholtz, 2004). The second attribute takes two approaches, maximizing or minimizing the amount of training required to effectively interact with the robot. For naturalistic interactions and increased likelihood of technological acceptance, minimization is preferable (Salvini, Laschi, & Dario, 2010).

From a once common teleoperated or supervisory control, these entities have acquired more autonomous capabilities to allow free roaming interaction in the social environment with other robots, computers, humans, or a combination thereof. If surrogates are going to be used for a myriad of social roles, then ideally, extensive training should not be required to learn how to communicate with each other. They should both hold a similar mental model as to how the interaction or communication should take place (Crandall & Goodrich, 2002). By leveraging the anthropomorphic tendency of humans to ascribe human characteristics to animals and objects, mental models of human-human interactions will transfer to a human-robot interaction, facilitating the transition of utilizing a robot or virtual avatar as a medium through which surrogates are portrayed (Halpern & Katz, 2013). A look at the role of human perception as a motivational factor for socializing with surrogates borrows explanations from the discipline of social psychology.

1.3   Social Psychology

Social Psychology refers to the "scientific attempt to understand and explain how the thoughts, feelings, and behaviors of individuals are influenced by the actual, imagined, or implied presence of other human beings" (Fiske, 2002, 2004; Stevens & Fiske, 1995). Presence is the key word here. Social psychology deals with how individuals think and behave when in the presence of others. Research showed that a physically present robot was associated with changes in participant engagement when compared to a video image of the same robot, suggesting that physical presence is an influential factor (Welch, 2012). What is unknown is the context or situation in which the physical or imagined presence of a surrogate is most effective for human-surrogate interaction.

Individuals can express themselves in ways that can influence a social group and vice versa. If certain criteria are met, such as perceived benefits or trust, individuals within the social group develop interpersonal relationships, increasing dependence on each other (Yuan, Fulk, Monge, & Contractor, 2010). This increase leads to interdependence of individuals working together to accomplish a shared goal because of the perceived benefits they will gain by a collective effort, rather than individual. Therefore, for successful instantiation of non-traditional surrogates, interdependence is crucial. To increase the success rate of interdependence, it is valuable to identify and understand the motivation for individuals to socialize.

The core social motives framework describe by Fiske (2004) attempts to describe the psychological processing that underlies human cognition, affect, and behavior within a social context. One core social motive, belonging, underlies the other four motives, which include controlling, understanding, self-enhancing, and trusting. For example, in applied settings, it may be useful to foster a sense that humans and robots 'belong to the same team.' Social thoughts, feelings, and behaviors are argued to be linked to satisfying these core social motives. In terms of human-surrogate interaction, the relationship built between the two should aim to meet these motives. By securing these motives, a shared goal can be met and the level (i.e. strength, frequency, diversity) of interdependence will increase (Fiske, 2004; Yuan, Fulk, Monge, & Contractor, 2010). There are also many individual factors that can affect the way in which humans socialize, such as culture (Bartneck et al., 2005), gender (Nomura & Takagi, 2011; Schermerhorn, Scheutz, & Crowell, 2008), and religion (Shaw-Garlock, 2009), and must be taken in account when defining the context in which human-surrogate interaction will occur. The context will suggest the way in which communication will ensue during human-surrogate interaction.

1.4   Communication

Communicating is an act of transmitting verbal and non-verbal information (Lackey et al., 2013). Transmission refers to a message being communicated from one entity to another (i.e. asking a question). Communication entails a bi-directional passage of information between two entities through a common system (i.e. symbols, signs, behavior). Human communication is comprised of more than just the information conveyed, but a composition of psychological, physiological, behavioral, and environmental factors (Floyd & Afifi, 2011), with goals to establish/maintain a relationship, persuade changes, understand others, and/or reach a common goal. When applying these concepts to the human-surrogate interaction domain, the content of the message is not conveyed alone, but a synthesis of explicit and implicit information in communication forms that fluctuate depending on the content and context of the message.

Of the forms of human communication, the most relevant to construct positive human-surrogate interactions are a mix of interpersonal, interviewing, and CMC. Interpersonal communication suggests a relationship exists or builds between the two interacting partners. Interviewing consists of more direct questions and answers, but still has interpersonal value. CMC is a general form in which communication is facilitated by a computer or computer-related device. By allowing the form of human-surrogate communication to vary, it will resemble the forms used during human-human communication, likely increasing the social presence of the surrogate from the perspective of the user.

Though communication seems to be expressed rather explicitly through these various forms of communication, there are a host of implicit cues that are expressed as well (Lackey et al., 2011; Reinerman-Jones, Sollins, & Hudson, 2013). Effective communication depends not just on the clarity and relevance of verbal utterances, but also on non-verbal cues that facilitate understanding of the speaker and regulation of the dialogue (Breazeal et al., 2005). These cues include gestures and displays of emotion. Indeed, in some accounts, facilitating communication is a primary function of emotion (Oatley & Johnson-Laird, 2014). To some degree, both emotional and gestural cues are processed unconsciously. Thus, an effective surrogate needs, at least to some degree, to elicit implicit processing of cues similar to human-human interaction. Ideally, the interaction feels natural to the human participant, even if he or she is unaware of the cues that facilitate communication. These concepts are theorized in a transactional model of communication.

According to the transaction model, communication is never a one-way street, but a simultaneous, mutual interaction (Barnlund, 1970; Watzlawick, Beavin, & Jackson, 1967; West & Turner, 2009), unlike the linear models that argue communication is more one-sided. The term transaction implies a supportive interaction to attain a collective meaning (West & Turner, 2009). That is the goal of human-surrogate interaction, to build a trusting relationship in order to work together to develop a shared meaning of the situation and progress towards a cooperative solution.

2   Interaction Investigation Recommendations

The purpose of these general logic statements is to suggest the areas of investigational importance and how they relate to achieve successful human-surrogate interaction. This logic, ideally to increase the successful implementation of non-traditional surrogates, is based on the disciplines described above.

- Perception: if humans perceive the surrogate as beneficial or coherent to their mental models, then they will trust it
- Trust: if humans trust the surrogate, then they will use it
- Usability: if humans are able to use the surrogate, then they will accept it
- Technological acceptance: if humans accept the surrogate, then interactions will be effective and performance will meet or exceed set standards
- Performance: if human performance meets or exceeds standards, then human-surrogate interaction is successful

Graaf and Allouch, (2013) suggested including both hedonic and utilitarian factors to assess the social role of these surrogates. The first two relate to the hedonic factors of the user's perspective and interpersonal relationships, while the following three evaluate the utilitarian aspects of interaction and experience. A salient interpretation of the human-surrogate interaction experience will begin to emerge by looking at both factors, informing the ultimate decision to either use non-traditional surrogates or not. This is intended not as an exhaustive effort to categorize all human-surrogate interaction research areas, but as a guiding framework to add or remove logical investigative statements or sub-statements to direct human-surrogate interaction research based on contextual purposes.

2.1   Experimental Approach

The novel experimental approach proposed here seeks to combine the guiding theories and principles as interdisciplinary solutions to the interdisciplinary investigation of manifesting a surrogate from the combination of human, virtual avatar, and robotic features to effectively communicate with a human to achieve a shared goal. The term human-surrogate interaction implies the cooperation of two or more individuals, meaning no single entity (i.e. human, robot, avatar) can provide all the solutions. This consideration implicitly directs the approach that must be taken in order to address the research issues. The manifestations of virtual and physical-virtual surrogates typically are represented with many anthropomorphic features, come in a variety of shapes and physical forms, and have varying levels of intelligence, but the degree to which these features influence the human's response, and therefore potentially impact the effectiveness of communication, is less understood (Dragone et al., 2006; Halpern & Katz, 2013; Welch, 2012). Thus, it is important to conduct controlled experimental studies of the impact of specific types of surrogate on the experience of the human who interacts with them.

3   Experimental Overview

Central to the methodology is the use of multiple metrics for evaluating participant experience. These metrics include both scales for explicit aspects of experience, and implicit behavioral measures. Scales for explicit response may be located within the research literatures already reviewed, i.e., those on HRI and the human factors of interfaces, on social perceptions, and on conscious perceptions of communication. Implicit behavioral measures may be derived primarily from communications research on objective measures of speech behavior and postural cues to speaker and listener engagement. Statistical analysis can then be used to determine whether and how surrogate type influences these various metrics.

3.1   Variables

Independent. The independent variable is surrogate type, manipulated within-subjects, includes a human, 2D virtual avatar, and a physical-virtual avatar (PVA). All three types of surrogates should be used because the participant's experience may be so profoundly influenced by interacting with a virtual figure as opposed to a human, that the experience becomes qualitatively different. One aim is then to compare the participant's responses to human and virtual surrogates along relevant metrics to determine whether it is feasible to use responses to the human as a reference point for evaluating a range of different surrogates.

The gender, age, voice, clothing, and form of interaction should be held constant across all surrogate types, the difference being solely the medium in which the surrogate is presented. The surrogates should express the seven universal primary emotions (Ekman, 1992) through tone of voice, gestural cues, and facial expression while interacting with participants. Gestural cues (head movements) and facial emotion expressions can be programmed or practiced (depending on the surrogate type) to represent the use of cues in human-surrogate interaction.

Dependent

Subjective Measures. Questionnaires should be based on the multidisciplinary approach described and used to gather subjective information from the participants about their experience with each surrogate. They should cover areas related to the user's perception, trust, usability, and technology acceptance. As described in section 1 above, the literature provides several relevant constructs. From a social psychological perspective, it is important also to assess the user's interpretation of their experience of the interaction with the surrogates in relation to constructs such as social presence. The assessment of trust should look at the perceptions of the reliability, functionality, and social attributes of the surrogates. As with any form of technology, the ability to effectively and efficiently use it should be addressed by a usability questionnaire. Technology acceptance refers to the interest and enjoyment of the interaction with the surrogates. Especially in the early stages of research, it is important also to obtain qualitative responses, which may illuminate data obtained from quantitative rating scales. Qualitative data may be obtained from free responses to questions probing key elements of the user experience. The free response format also allows assessment of the user's experience of communication with the surrogate, and any specific issues arising from the visual and auditory components of communication.

Objective Measures. Validated questionnaire scales may be more effective in evaluating explicit rather than implicit responses. As implicit measures, postural measures may pick up unconscious reactions that may not be evident in the questionnaires (Knapp, Hall, & Horgan, 2013).

Postural Measures. A head-tracking system can be used to objectively assess the participant's head position and a body-tracking system can be used for assessing the torso and arms/hands of the participants while engaged in transactional conversations with the surrogates.

Verbal Communication Measures. Objective measures of the participant's verbal responses can be assessed during communication with each surrogate of interest. Measures include frequency counts of utterances, average duration, and average response time to surrogate speech.

3.2   Procedure

It is important to maintain experimental control of participants' interactions with the three surrogates of interests (human, virtual, and physical-virtual) through verbal communication. Both the participant and the surrogate should remain at a constant distance from each other and never be in physical contact to first assess characteristics of the surrogate without taking into account other factors such as proximity. Communication can take the form of structured verbal exchanges between the participant and the surrogate, resembling casual conversation about both non-emotional (i.e., asking the participant's age) and emotional topics (i.e. asking about emotional reactions to being cut off while driving). The suggested post-exposure questionnaires can be administered following interaction with each surrogate. The order of experimental conditions (exposure to each surrogate) must also be counter-balanced across participants to minimize any order effects.

4   Conclusion

Our proposed methodology will potentially identify characteristics of surrogates that can affect human perceptions of transactions with surrogates, achieved through a multi-disciplinary method. The multi-disciplinary approach is encouraged to explore the area of human-surrogate interaction. Specifically, in our research, we aim to compare the participant's experience of three surrogate types across a range of quantitative metrics derived from the relevant disciplines. We can then evaluate differences between surrogates in terms of constructs derived from HRI (e.g., usability), social psychology (e.g., presence) and communication (e.g., postural engagement). We anticipate finding different patterns or profiles of response to the three surrogates, patterns that can be interpreted qualitatively on the basis of the relevant research literatures, aided by the participant's free-response accounts of their experience.

Two specific types of comparison are of most important. First, we can compare participants' reactions to human versus virtual surrogates. The cultural trend towards increased interaction with artificial systems (Bartneck et al., 2005) implies that people may have broadly similar experiences of interacting with the two types of entities, at least in highly structured settings, such as that developed for this study. On the other hand, the distinction between human and virtual presence may be so salient that the experiences cannot be considered comparable. Based on the outcome of the comparison, we can explore a defined single domain for human-surrogate interaction or pursue two separate lines of investigation. That is, if there are major qualitative differences in interacting with the two forms of surrogate, it may not be productive to compare interactions with virtual surrogates (whether human or artificial) with those with physically-present human beings.

Second, within the field of virtual systems, the research may begin to inform about optimal design, for example, the auditory and visual characteristics that optimize natural interaction. The current study should be informative about one specific design question, whether to use a 2-D or 3-D figure. Questionnaires also probe some specific design issues such as the acceptability of the visual and auditory aspects of the stimuli, and the realism of the emotional displays. Future studies might explore the impact of other design features, such as proximity between the human and surrogate (Halpern & Katz, 2013; Mumm & Mutlu, 2011).

The applied contribution of the research will be to guide practitioners, designers, and trainers in managing some of the tradeoffs faced when creating human surrogates (Welch, 2012). It will also make a methodological contribution towards developing protocols for evaluating the person's experience with surrogates, which might be directed towards a range of surrogate systems and contexts for interaction. The findings will advance the understanding and framework of human-surrogate interaction and its social role as investigated through the use of virtual and physical surrogates.

Acknowledgements. This work was in part supported by the Office of Naval Research (ONR) (N00014-12-1-0052). The views and conclusions contained in this document are those of the authors and should not be interpreted as representing the official policies, either expressed or implied, of ONR or the US Government. The US Government is authorized to reproduce and distribute reprints for Government purposes notwithstanding any copyright notation hereon.

References

1. Barnlund, D.C.: A transactional model of communication. Foundations of Communication Theory, 83–102 (1970)
2. Bartneck, C., Nomura, T., Kanda, T., Suzuki, T., Kato, K.: Cultural differences in attitudes toward robots. In: Proceedings of Symposium on Robot Companions: Hard Problems and Open Challenges in Robot-human Interaction (SSAISB 2005), pp. 1–4 (2005)
3. Boberg, M., Piippo, P., Ollila, E.: Designing avatars. In: Proceedings from the 3rd International Conference on Digital Interactive Media in Entertainment and Arts, pp. 232–239. ACM (2008)
4. Breazeal, C., Kidd, C.D., Thomaz, A.L., Hoffman, G., Berlin, M.: Effects of nonverbal communication on efficiency and robustness in human-robot teamwork. In: Proceedings of IEEE/RSJ International Conference on Intelligent Robots and Systems, pp. 708–713. IEEE (2005)
5. Chan, A., MacLean, K., McGrenere, J.: Learning and identifying haptic icons under workload. In: Eurohaptics Conference, 2005 and Symposium on Haptic Interfaces for Virtual Environment and Teleoperator Systems, 2005. World Haptics 2005. First Joint, pp. 432–439. IEEE (2005)
6. Chuah, J.H., Robb, A., White, C., Wendling, A., Lampotang, S., Kopper, R., Lok, B.: Exploring agent physicality and social presence for medical team training. Presence: Teleoperators and Virtual Environments 22, 141–170 (2013)
7. Crandall, J.W., Goodrich, M.A.: Characterizing efficiency of human robot interaction: A case study of shared-control teleoperation. In: Proceedings from International Conference on Intelligent Robots and Systems, vol. 2, pp. 1290–1295. IEEE (2002)
8. Dragone, M., Duffy, B.R., Holz, T., O' Hare, G.M.P.: Fusing realities in human-robot social interaction. VDI BERICHTE 1956, 23 (2006)
9. Ekman, P.: Are there basic emotions? Psychological Review 99(3), 550–553 (1992)
10. Floyd, K., Afifi, T.D.: Biological and physiological perspectives on interpersonal communication. The SAGE Handbook of Interpersonal Communication 87 (2011)
11. Fiske, S.T.: Five core social motives, plus or minus five. In: Spencer, S.J., Fein, S., Zanna, M.P., Olson, J. (eds.) Motivated Social Perception: The Ontario Symposium, pp. 233–246. Erlbaum, Mahwah (2002)
12. Fiske, S.T.: Social beings: A core motives approach to social psychology. John Wiley & Sons, Hoboken (2004)
13. Garau, M., Slater, M.: Pertaub & D, Razzaque, S, The responses of people to virtual humans in an immersive virtual environment. Presence 14(1), 104–116 (2005)
14. Goodrich, M.A., Schultz, A.C.: Human-robot interaction: a survey. Foundations and Trends in Human-Computer Interaction 1(3), 203–275 (2007)
15. De Graaf, M., Ben Allouch, S.: Exploring influencing variables for the acceptance of social robots. Robotics and Autonomous Systems 61(12), 1476–1486 (2013)

16. Gunhee Kim, W.C., Kim, K.-R., Kim, M., Han, S., Shinn, R.H.: The autonomous tour-guide robot Jinny. In: Proceedings from IEEE/Robotics Society of Japan International Conference on Intelligent Robots and Systems. IEEE (2004)
17. Halpern, D., Katz, J.E.: Close but not stuck: understanding social distance in human-robot interaction through a computer mediation approach. Intervalla 1 (2013)
18. Haraway, D.J.: A manifesto for cyborgs: Science, technology and socialist feminism in the. Socialist Review 80(15), 65–107 (1985)
19. Harlow, H.F.: The nature of love. American Psychologist 13(12), 673–685 (1958)
20. Knapp, M.L., Hall, J.A., Horgan, T.G.: Nonverbal communication in human interaction, 8th edn. (2013)
21. Lackey, S., Barber, D., Reinerman, L., Badler, N.I., Hudson, I.: Defining Next-Generation Multi-Modal Communication in Human Robot Interaction. In: Proceedings of the 55th Annual Meeting of the Human Factors and Ergonomics Society, HFES (2011)
22. Lackey, S., Barber, D., Reinerman-Jones, L.E., Ortiz, E., Fanfarelli, J.: Human Robot Communication. In: Hale, K., Staney, K. (eds.) Handbook of Virtual Environments, 2nd edn. (2013)
23. Lincoln, P., Welch, G., Nashel, A., State, A., Ilie, A., Fuchs, H.: Animatronic shader lamps avatars. Virtual Reality 15(2-3), 225–238 (2010)
24. McFarland, H.F., Barkhof, F., Antel, J., Miller, D.H.: The role of MRI as a surrogate outcome measure in multiple sclerosis. Multiple Sclerosis 8(40) (2002)
25. Mumm, J., Mutlu, B.: Human-robot proxemics: physical and psychological distancing in human-robot interaction. In: Proceedings of the 6th International Conference on Human-robot Interaction, pp. 331–338. ACM (2011)
26. Nomura, T., Takagi, S.: Exploring effects of educational backgrounds and gender in human-robot interaction. In: Proceedings of 2011 International Conference on User Science and Engineering (i-USEr), pp. 24–29. IEEE (2011)
27. Oatley, K., Johnson-Laird, P.N.: Cognitive approaches to emotions. Trends in Cognitive Sciences (2014), Advance online publication doi: 10.1016/j.tics.2013.12.004
28. Reeves, B., Nass, C.: The media equation. Cambridge University Press, Cambridge (1996)
29. Reinerman-Jones, L.E., Sollins, B., Hudson, I.: Evaluating Human-Robot Implicit Communication using Psychophysiology. In: Proceedings of the Annual Meeting of AUVSI Unmanned Systems North America (2013)
30. Salvini, P., Laschi, C., Dario, P.: Design for acceptability: improving robots' coexistence in human society. International Journal of Social Robotics 2(4), 451–460 (2010)
31. Schermerhorn, P., Scheutz, M., Crowell, C.: Robot social presence and gender: do females view robots differently than males. In: Proceedings of the 3rd ACM International Conference on Human-Robot Interaction, pp. 263–270 (2008)
32. Shaw-Garlock, G.: Looking forward to sociable robots. International Journal of Social Robotics 1(3), 249–260 (2009)
33. Sidner, C.L., Kidd, C.D., Lee, C., Lesh, N.: Where to look: a study of human-robot engagement. In: Proceedings of the 9th International Conference on Intelligent User Interfaces, pp. 78–84. ACM (2004)
34. Stevens, L.E., Fiske, S.T.: Motivation and cognition in social life: A social survival perspective. Social Cognition 13(3), 189–214 (1995)
35. Watzlawick, P., Beavin, J.H., Jackson, D.D.: Pragmatics of Human Communication. W.W. Norton, New York (1967)
36. Waytz, A.: Social connection and seeing human. In: Dewall, C.N. (ed.) The Oxford Handbook of Social Exclusion. Oxford University Press, New York (2013)

37. Welch, G.: Physical-virtual humans: challenges and opportunities. In: Proceedings from ISUVR 2012: International Symposium on Ubiquitous Virtual Reality (2012)
38. West, R., Turner, L.H.: Understanding interpersonal communication: Making choices in changing times, vol. 2. Wadsworth Cengage Learning, Boston (2009)
39. Witmer, B., Singer, M.: Measuring presence in virtual environments: A presence questionnaire. Presence 7(3), 225–240 (1998)
40. Yanco, H.A., Drury, J.L., Scholtz, J.: Beyond usability evaluation: Analysis of human-robot interaction at a major robotics competition. Human–Computer Interaction 19(1-2), 117–149 (2004)
41. Yamashita, J., Kuzuoka, H., Fujimon, C., Hirose, M.: Tangible avatar and tangible earth: a novel interface for astronomy education. Proceedings from CHI 2007, Extended Abstracts on Human Factors in Computing Systems. ACM (2007)
42. Yuan, Y.C., Fulk, J., Monge, P.R., Contractor, N.: Expertise directory development, shared task interdependence, and strength of communication network ties as multilevel predictors of expertise exchange in transactive memory work groups. Communication Research 37(1), 20–47 (2010)

A Design Methodology for Trust Cue Calibration in Cognitive Agents

Ewart J. de Visser[1,2] , Marvin Cohen[1], Amos Freedy[1], and Raja Parasuraman[2]

[1] Perceptronics Solutions, 3141 Fairview Park Drive, Suite 415
Falls Church, VA 22042, USA
`edevisser@percsolutions.com`
[2] George Mason University, Human Factors & Applied Cognition, MSN 3F5
4400 University Drive, Fairfax VA 22030, USA

Abstract. As decision support systems have developed more advanced algorithms to support the human user, it is increasingly difficult for operators to verify and understand how the automation comes to its decision. This paper describes a design methodology to enhance operators' decision making by providing trust cues so that their *perceived* trustworthiness of a system matches its actual trustworthiness, thus yielding *calibrated trust*. These trust cues consist of visualizations to diagnose the actual trustworthiness of the system by showing the risk and uncertainty of the associated information. We present a trust cue design taxonomy that lists all possible information that can influence a trust judgment. We apply this methodology to a scenario with advanced automation that manages missions for multiple unmanned vehicles and shows specific trust cues for 5 levels of trust evidence. By focusing on both individual operator trust and the transparency of the system, our design approach allows for calibrated trust for optimal decision-making to support operators during all phases of mission execution.

Keywords: Trust, Trust Calibration, Trust Cues, Cognitive Agents, Uncertainty Visualization, Bayesian Modeling, Computational Trust Modeling, Automation, Unmanned Systems, Cyber Operations, Trustworthiness.

1   Introduction

As decision support systems have developed more advanced algorithms to support the human user, it is increasingly difficult for operators to verify and understand how the automation comes to its decision. It is therefore harder for users to diagnose the true reliability of the system and to calibrate their trust appropriately in the recommendation made by a decision-aid based on both its reliability and the mission context [1]. If users trust automation too much, they risk becoming complacent and can miss critical mistakes made by recommendations, especially when advice is unreliable [2]. Conversely, users have been shown to have high self-reliance on their own decisions even if automation performance is superior to their own [3]. Additionally, if operators trust automation too little, they may spend too much time verifying the accuracy of

R. Shumaker and S. Lackey (Eds.): VAMR 2014, Part I, LNCS 8525, pp. 251–262, 2014.
© Springer International Publishing Switzerland 2014

the aid, which can be costly in time-critical situations [4], [5]. Consequently, the challenge is to ensure calibrated trust in the automated aid – that is, for users to tune their trust to the aid's true capability.

Figure 1 illustrates the key issue of trust calibration. If operators are calibrated, their trust as shown on the y-axis will match the trustworthiness of the automated aid as shown on the x-axis [6]. That is, calibrated operators have trust proportional to actual automation capability, as shown by the dotted line. When operators trust automation more than it deserves, they are over-trusting the system. Operators who trust automation less than it deserves, are classified as under-trusting the system. Over-trust and under-trust are associated with misuse and disuse of automation [7].

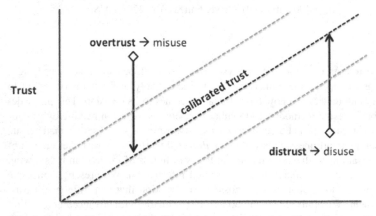

Fig. 1. Trust calibration with calibrated (green) and mis-calibrated zones (red)

We propose that providing more contextual information to the operator about the automation can lead to calibrated trust. Visual cues to diagnose the actual trustworthiness of the system by showing the risk and uncertainty of the associated information can support increased understanding of the automation. This strategy involves providing trustworthiness cues to the operator directly. By providing more information about the automation to the operator it is likely that calibration in the automation will increase [3], [6]. The effectiveness of this strategy has been shown empirically. For instance, one study showed that pilots were able to calibrate their trust in an automated aid that detected the possibility of icing conditions [8]. This automated aid showed its confidence level in its ability to estimate the likelihood of the icing condition. As a result, pilots relied on the aid more selectively and this led to improved landing performance.

The goal of this paper is to describe a trust cue design methodology to promote calibrated trust within operators. Specifically, we propose that the use of trust cues will cause over-trusting operators to reduce their trust and under-trusting operators to increase their trust into the automated system. Appropriate trust will lead to more appropriate reliance on automated systems, which will ultimately lead to better mission performance.

2   Trust Cue Design Methodology

A trust cue is any information element that can be used to make a trust assessment about an agent. In order to understand how an effective trust cue may be designed, we must first examine the trust process. We first outline five steps of a typical trust process, derive a trust cue design taxonomy based on this analysis, and describe how a trust cue may be effectively designed.

2.1   The Trust Process

The trust process can be likened to a person's attempt to construct an ad-hoc theoretical model about another human being, or generally, an agent. This process is not unlike the theory of mind abilities attributed uniquely to humans [9]. The process is updated continually over time in a loop, which can be likened to a Bayesian updating process. We have identified five steps that encompass the trust decision-making process.

Step 1: Who is to be trusted? The first step in the trust process is to consider who is to be trusted. An initial belief is formed about the object to be trusted, which has been termed dispositional-based trust [10]. During this step information is collected about the other object and is driven by both the characteristics of the trustor [10], [11], beliefs/biases about the source to be trusted. In this context, trust can be seen as a personality trait which can be measured as the propensity to trust [11], [12]. Traits of the trustor, or individual trust differences, can explain up to 52% of the variance [12]. Other biases may come from experiences, culture, etc. that have shaped general beliefs in the trustor. Knowing the source is a second great way to derive information which can, in part, explain the differences in judging machines [13], organizations [11], and interpersonal relationships [14]. Both pieces of information set the initial belief in the trustor.

Step 2: What information is available about the agent? The second consideration is what information needs to be considered to make a trust judgment. Much theorizing and classification has focused on the this step of the trust evolution, which has been labeled history-based trust [10]. The second step pertains to the evidence that is actively sampled from the trustee. As Lee and See [6] note, this can be done at various levels of abstraction using three general categories: 1) performance, which refers to the actions that are performed, 2) process, which is the consistency of those actions over time, and 3) purpose, which is the positive or negative disposition of the trustee towards the trustor. Most trust evidence can be broken down according to these dimensions. Barber [15] calls them competence, predictability, and responsibility. Mayer et al. [11] calls them ability, integrity, and benevolence. Rempel et al. [16] call them predictability, dependability, and faith. It is apparent that these different dimensions give different levels of information about the object and have different value. The order of sampling this information may occur randomly. People could start with determining the purpose, which is often the case when people are introduced to automation [6]. In such a case, one can set up their theoretical model and automatically make more assumptions then necessary which are then easily violated when observing real behavior. In addition, information can be sampled at different levels of detail. With regard to automation, an entire system can be observed or just a sub-system. This has also been referred to as the trust resolution of a system [1].

Step 3: How to judge the available information? The third step is to evaluate and judge the presented information. This step involves calculating the belief based on the prior information and the collected information to produce a final 'posterior" trust belief, as in a Bayesian updating process. This trust belief is then evaluated (weighted) based on the constraints of the situation (completeness of information, time constraints, etc.). Lee and See [6] propose three process dimensions, including analytical, analog, and affective processes. This process can be seen as analogous to how people assess risk in general. Analytical approaches mirror the rational economic based approach. Analog processes are also called category-based trust and follow rules, expectations and contracts that have been made according to which judgments can be made. Third, the trust belief can be evaluated affectively based on affective tagging of the belief as generally favorable or unfavorable according to the risk-as-feelings, and affect heuristic paradigms [17], [18].

Step 4: What is the situation like?. The fourth step is to determine the benefit/utility of trusting the trustor compared to other alternatives (self-reliance, another person, etc.). Factors that have been found to influence this decision are self-confidence, task load, amount of effort needed, perceived risk, and exploratory behavior. This value is combined with the belief value to arrive at the utility of relying on the person to be trusted. If this value is regarded as positive, the decision will be to rely on the trustee. If it is regarded as negative, no such reliance will be observed.

Step 5: What is my reliance decision? The final step is to decide whether to rely on the automation or to seek more information. Steps one through five describe the trust decision making process. Several authors have recognized that this process is a perpetual process and repeats itself over many cycles [6], [19], [20] This has also given rise to many other classification schemes. For example, Rousseau et al. [20] propose three phases of trust including the building phase, the stability phase, and the dissolution phase. Others have proposed a dichotomous classification of trust and distrust which has been useful in classifying different sampling behaviors of evidence [19], [21]–[23]. Finally, there is an observed time phenomenon known as the inertia of trust. Lee & Moray [24] found that it took time for people to adjust their trust after experienced faults, showed residual effects over time, and found slow trust repair. In contrast to this finding, some have proposed that swift trust can be established rather quickly with a team of experts who know to look for a certain level of expertise [25].

2.2   The Trust Cue Design Taxonomy

To date there have been limited efforts to classify all information that could lead to a possible cue for trust. Typical trust dimensions are ability, integrity, and benevolence in the human-human trust literature and performance, process and purpose in the human-automation literature [6]. These bases of trust classify what task an agent is performing and how well, how the task is being performed, and the purpose/disposition of the agent towards the trustor. These are course classifications and do not form a good basis to identify information that can lead to specific design of trust cues. There is a need to develop a rigorous taxonomy of trust cues.

Figure 2 shows our trust cue design taxonomy, with levels of trust evidence shown in the first column. With reference to the taxonomy: Intent is the overall current goal of the automation and why certain tasks are being executed. Performance is what and how well the automation is executing a particular task. Process is how an agent is executing a particular task. Expressiveness is the mode of interaction in which the automation communicates with the operator. Origin is the background information and reputation of the system. These levels of evidence include those identified in the literature as well as our own developed dimensions. In the columns are the classic information processing stages important for human performance in most tasks, including perception, comprehension, projection, decision, and execution [26]. Together these present a complete overview of the types of information that can serve as a trust cue.

Trust Cue Taxonomy		Information Processing Stages				
		perception	comprehension	projection	decision	execution
Trust Evidence Levels	Intent	perceptual intent & goals	comprehension intent & goals	projection intent & goals	decision intent & goals	execution intent & goals
	Performance	perceptual errors	classification errors	prediction errors	decision-making errors	execution errors
	Process	perceptual steps	comprehension steps	projection steps	decision steps	execution steps
	Expressiveness	perceptual indicators	comprehension indicators	projection indicators	decision indicators	execution indicators
	Origin	design of perceptual capability	design of comprehension capability	design of projection capability	design of decision capability	design of execution capability

Fig. 2. Trust cue design taxonomy

2.3   Trust Cue Design

Given a typical trust process and our trust design taxonomy, we can now provide a procedure for designing trust cues for a specific case. The procedure is as follows:

1. Select a scenario that involves trust in a cognitive agent
2. Conduct a task analysis to identify critical trust related tasks
3. Identify key pieces of information for operator decision making
4. Verify pieces of information against the trust cue taxonomy
5. Construct a visual display representing this information

In the next section we show the results of applying this procedure to a scenario in which an automated aid assists with the management of multiple unmanned vehicles.

3   Case Study: Trust Cue Library for Unmanned Vehicle Control

3.1   Case Study: UAV Scenario

Our use case involves an On Station Operator (OSO), as a representative multi-Remotely Piloted Aircraft (RPA) operator. The OSO exercises supervisory control over all unmanned air platforms. The three main tasks of the operator include planning missions for unmanned aerial vehicles, monitoring those missions as they are executed, and reviewing these missions upon completion. Automation assistance is provided for each of these tasks and can either be fully automated or manually executed based on the level of automation [26], [27].

Since each of these tasks can be automated in our paradigm, the operator can supervise the automation performing each of these tasks. Different types of cues can be provided indicating whether the automation is succeeding in each of these tasks. In our scenario, a Situation Awareness Mixed Initiative (SAMI) module is presented as an agent acting as a subordinate mission planner that guides mission planning, execution, monitoring, and re-planning functions [28], [29]. Previous research has shown that cognitive agents can foster relationships between humans and automation [30]. Operators are first presented with a library of missions from which they can select a mission of interest. When a mission is selected, a brief description of the mission is provided to explain the actions of each UAV and the goal they will execute.

Table 1 summarizes our designs for trustworthiness cues developed according to the trust dimensions of the trust cue taxonomy and applied to the automated agent example. We elaborate on the more complex cues of performance and process in the following sections.

Table 1. Trustworthiness cue designs for each trust evidence dimension

Trustworthiness Cue	Design
Intent	**Goal Indicator**
Intent is the overall current goal of the automation and why certain tasks are being executed. The goal indicator shows the overall current goals of the agent in question. Sharing the goals of automation with a user has been shown to be an effective way to increase the trustworthiness of an adaptive cruise control system [31]; in this study, merely showing the goals of the automated agent and the user goals had the desirable effect [31].	**S.A.M.I. Goal** Mission success ▲ Safety ▲ Fuel efficiency ▲ Speed ▲ Accuracy

Table 1. (*Continued.*)

Performance	DICON
Performance is what and how well the automation is executing a particular task. The *Decision Information Icon* (DICON), a dynamic configural display, shows decomposition of uncertainty about how well the agent is performing. Showing performance feedback has been shown to increase trust and performance [8].	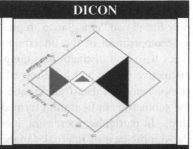
Process	**Mission Model**
Process is how an agent is executing a particular task. The mission model visualization module shows how SAMI executes a model step-by-step and provides valuable insight into the complex mission models created by the SAMI automation (see Table 1). Conveying the mode of automation has been shown to increase understanding of the automation and subsequent trust [32].	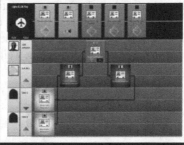
Expressiveness	**Etiquette Module**
Some have argued that one of the reasons for the trust mis-calibration with automation is that the behavior of an automated device does not conform to human-human etiquette [33], [34]. Increasing etiquette has also been shown to lead to better performance, reduced situation awareness, and improved trust [34]. Scripted avatars are a way of providing a rich user interface to communicate with operators through facial communication like gaze.	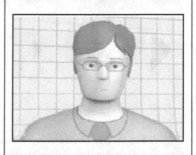
Origin	**Reputation Module**
Origin is the background information and reputation of the system. Certificates and background information are another method to establish credibility and foster trust. This is a heuristic people often use to determine whether an agent can be trusted. The reputation module is designed to provide more background information about the automated agent. Providing a rationale and background for automation system has been shown to increase trust [3].	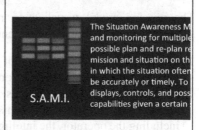

3.2   Performance: DICON

Figure 3 shows the Decision Information Icon (DICON), a dynamic configural display for: (1) an "at a glance" representation of uncertainty about a hypothesis, and (2) a decomposition of the uncertainty surrounding that hypothesis into three different types based on distinctions among task input-output relationships. The DICON uses distinctive colors and locations of triangles to differentiate the performance (green), completeness of data (black), and conflict (red) components of uncertainty and uses the geometric configuration formed by the triangles to represent their current relationships. In particular, increasing incompleteness of data or team participation reduces the significance of internal variability (e.g., conflict in evidence or disagreement on the team) as well as discrimination (the preponderance of evidence or opinion in one direction or the other). These relationships are reflected in dynamics that change the size of one triangle as a function of the size of the others. Figure 3 shows how the DICON display updates over time to confirm or disconfirm the hypothesis that an automated agent is performing well.

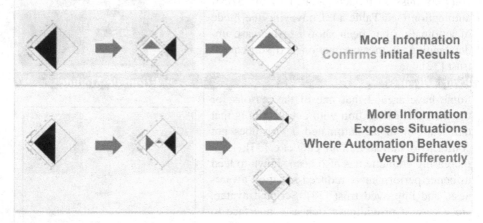

Fig. 3. The *Decision Information Icon* (DICON) dynamic changes over time

3.3   Process: Mission Model

The mission model visualization module is comprised of several components as shown in Figure 4. These components are:

1. **Mission Phases.** The top row of the mission model shows the phases or segments of each mission. Users can click on each phase to see the detailed task structure.
2. **Mission Role Timeline Tracks.** The mission role column shows the roles for the mission and which actor fills this role. In this particular mission, there are 4 roles including the operator, the intelligent automation SAMI, and two UAVs.
3. **Decision Nodes.** Operator decisions are displayed using a special operator decision node (purple) for the mission visualization. The node can be set to either accept the automation recommendation or reject the automation recommendation.

4. Task Status. Petri-net transitions and arcs are shown on the timeline tracks. These elements indicate which part of the plan is currently being executed (orange), which parts have been successfully completed (green), and which parts still need to be completed (blue).

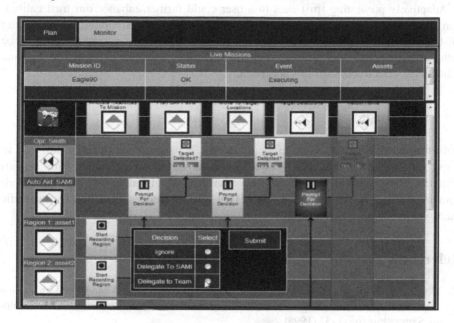

Fig. 4. The Mission Model Visualization

4 Discussion

The goal of this paper was to describe a trust cue design methodology for trust calibration in advanced automated systems. We provided background on the trust process, provided a guide for trust cue design, and gave example cases of trust cue designs.

Our focus in this paper was to describe a trust taxonomy that is domain and task independent. The trust process itself is a general process used by people on a daily basis. Most of the differences in trust is driven by the characteristics of the task and the variation in agents that assist in this task. By applying the general framework to a specific task, trust cues can be developed for any domain or task, which we believe is the strength of our approach.

The current paper described mainly visual trust cues. Our taxonomy can be applied to cover other modalities as well. Previous research has shown how best to cue humans using a cognitive-agent spectrum that varies primarily on human machine characteristics has yet to be defined [30]. These machine characteristics vary greatly in both the real world and in studies of trust. It may thus be more useful to classify machines on a cognitive agency spectrum in which some machines are more like humans and others are closer to the traditional machine. Various trust cueing dimensions of this spectrum are visual appearance, audition, motion, and personality.

Adaptively presenting trust cues to a user could further enhance our trust calibration approach. Trust varies significantly from individual to individual. By measuring trust in real-time and adaptively showing relevant trust cues, an individual may be better able to adjust and calibrate their trust. Further research is needed to test and validate the effectiveness of this approach.

5   Conclusion

With this general trust cue design methodology, novel trust cues can be designed to assist with understanding and transparency with advanced automation for various domains. These types of designs will become increasingly important with the development of advanced automated systems. This work presents a guideline with specific examples to develop such designs.

References

1. Cohen, M., Parasuraman, R., Freeman, J.: Trust in decision aids: A model and its training implications. In: Proceedings of the 1998 Command and Control Research and Technology Symposium, pp. 1–37 (1998)
2. de Visser, E.J., Parasuraman, R.: Adaptive aiding of human-robot teaming: Effects of imperfect automation on performance, trust, and workload. J. Cogn. Eng. Decis. Mak. 5(2), 209–231 (2011)
3. Dzindolet, M., Peterson, S., Pomranky, R.: The role of trust in automation reliance. Int. J. Hum. Comput. Stud. 58(6), 697–718 (2003)
4. Bahner, J., Huper, A., Manzey, D.: Misuse of automated decision aids: Complacency, automation bias and the impact of training experience. Int. J. Hum. Comput. Stud. 66(9), 688–699 (2008)
5. Parasuraman, R., Manzey, D.: Complacency and Bias in Human Use of Automation: An Attentional Integration. Hum. Factors 52(3), 381–410 (2010)
6. Lee, J., See, K.: Trust in automation: Designing for appropriate reliance. Hum. Factors 46(1), 50–80 (2004)
7. Parasuraman, R., Riley, V.: Humans and automation: Use, misuse, disuse, abuse. Hum. Factors 39(2), 230–253 (1997)
8. McGuirl, J., Sarter, N.: Supporting trust calibration and the effective use of decision aids by presenting dynamic system confidence information. Hum. Factors 48(4), 656–665 (2006)
9. Adolphs, R.: Cognitive neuroscience of human social behaviour. Nat. Rev. Neurosci. 4, 165–178 (2003)
10. Kramer, R.: Trust and distrust in organizations: Emerging perspectives, enduring questions. Annu. Rev. Psychol. 50, 569–698 (1999)

11. Mayer, R., Davis, J., Schoorman, F.: An integrative model of organizational trust. Acad. Manag. Rev. 20(3), 709–734 (1995)
12. Merritt, S.M., Ilgen, D.R.: Not All Trust Is Created Equal: Dispositional and History-Based Trust in Human-Automation Interactions. Hum. Factors J. Hum. Factors Ergon. Soc. 50(2), 194–210 (2008)
13. Madhavan, P., Wiegmann, D.A.: Similarities and differences between human-human and human-automation trust: An integrative review. Theor. Issues Ergon. Sci. 8(4), 277–301 (2007)
14. Rotter, J.: Generalized expectancies for interpersonal trust. Am. Psychol (1971)
15. Barber, B.: The logic and limits of trust, p. 190. Rutgers University Press, New Brunswick (1983)
16. Rempel, J., Holmes, J., Zanna, M.: Trust in close relationships. J. Pers. Soc. Psychol. 49(1), 95–112 (1985)
17. Loewenstein, G., Weber, E., Hsee, C., Welch, N.: Risk as feelings. Psychol. Bull. 127(2), 267–286 (2001)
18. Slovic, P., Finucane, M., Peters, E., MacGregor, D.: The affect heuristic. Eur. J. Oper. Res. 177(3), 1333–1352 (2007)
19. Lewicki, R.J., Tomlinson, E.C., Gillespie, N.: Models of Interpersonal Trust Development: Theoretical Approaches, Empirical Evidence, and Future Directions. J. Manage. 32(6), 991–1022 (2006)
20. Rousseau, D., Sitkin, S., Burt, R.: Not so different after all: A cross-discipline view of trust. Acad. Manag. Rev. 23(3), 393–404 (1998)
21. Muir, B., Moray, N.: Trust in automation: Part II. Experimental studies of trust and human intervention in a process control simulation. Ergonomics 39(3), 429–460 (1996)
22. Jian, J., Bisantz, A., Drury, C.: Foundations for an empirically determined scale of trust in automated systems. Int. J. (2000)
23. Parasuraman, R., Sheridan, T., Wickens, C.: Situation awareness, mental workload, and trust in automation: Viable, empirically supported cognitive engineering constructs. J. Cogn. Eng. Decis. Mak. 2(2), 140–160 (2008)
24. Lee, J., Moray, N.: Trust, control strategies and allocation of function in human-machine systems. Ergonomics 35(10), 1243–1270 (1992)
25. Meyerson, D., Weick, K., Kramer, R.: Swift trust and temporary systems. In: Kramer, R., Tyler, T.R. (eds.) Trust in Organizations, pp. 166–195. Sage Publications, Inc., Thousand Oaks (1996)
26. Parasuraman, R., Sheridan, T., Wickens, C.: A model for types and levels of human interaction with automation. IEEE Trans. Syst. Man Cybern. Part A Syst. Humans 30(3), 286–297 (2000)
27. de Visser, E.J., LeGoullon, M., Freedy, A., Freedy, E., Weltman, G., Parasuraman, R.: Designing an Adaptive Automation System for Human Supervision of Unmanned Vehicles: A Bridge from Theory to Practice. Proc. Hum. Factors Ergon. Soc. Annu. Meet. 52(4), 221–225 (2008)
28. Brooks, N., de Visser, E.J., Chabuk, T., Freedy, E., Scerri, P.: An Approach to Team Programming with Markup for Operator Interaction. In: 12th International Conference on Autonomous Agents and Multiagent Systems (2013)
29. de Visser, E.J., Kidwell, B., Payne, J., Parker, J., Chabuk, T., Scerri, P., Freedy, A.: Best of both worlds: Design and evaluation of an adaptive delegation interface. In: Human Factors and Ergonomics Society Annual Meeting (2013)

30. de Visser, E.J., Krueger, F., McKnight, P., Scheid, S., Smith, M., Chalk, S., Parasuraman, R.: The World is not Enough: Trust in Cognitive Agents. Proc. Hum. Factors Ergon. Soc. Annu. Meet. 56(1), 263–267 (2012)
31. Verberne, F.M.F., Ham, J., Midden, C.J.H.: Trust in Smart Systems: Sharing Driving Goals and Giving Information to Increase Trustworthiness and Acceptability of Smart Systems in Cars. Hum. Factors J. Hum. Factors Ergon. Soc. 54(5), 799–810 (2012)
32. Degani, A., Shafto, M., Kirlik, A.: Modes in human-machine systems: Constructs, representation, and classification. Int. J. Aviat. Psychol. 9(2), 125–138 (1999)
33. Parasuraman, R., Miller, C.A.: Trust and etiquette in high-criticality automated systems. Commun. ACM 47(4), 51–55 (2004)
34. Hayes, C., Miller, C.A.: Human-Computer Etiquette: Cultural Expectations and the Design Implications They Place on Computers and Technology, p. 406. Auerbach Publications (2011)

Effects of Gender Mapping on the Perception of Emotion from Upper Body Movement in Virtual Characters

Maurizio Mancini[1], Andrei Ermilov[2], Ginevra Castellano[3], Fotis Liarokapis[4], Giovanna Varni[1], and Christopher Peters[5]

[1] InfoMus Lab, University of Genoa, Italy
{maurizio.mancini,giovanna.varni}@unige.it
[2] Faculty of Engineering and Computing, University of Coventry, UK
ermilova@uni.coventry.ac.uk
[3] School of Electronic, Electrical and Computer Engineering,
University of Birmingham, UK
g.castellano@bham.ac.uk
[4] Interactive Worlds Applied Research Group & Serious Games Institute,
Coventry University, UK
aa3235@coventry.ac.uk
[5] School of Computer Science and Communication,
Royal Institute of Technology (KTH), Sweden
chpeters@kth.se

Abstract. Despite recent advancements in our understanding of the human perception of the emotional behaviour of embodied artificial entities in virtual reality environments, little remains known about various specifics relating to the effect of gender mapping on the perception of emotion from body movement. In this paper, a pilot experiment is presented investigating the effects of gender congruency on the perception of emotion from upper body movements. Male and female actors were enrolled to conduct a number of gestures within six general categories of emotion. These motions were mapped onto virtual characters with male and female embodiments. According to the gender congruency condition, the motions of male actors were mapped onto male characters (congruent) or onto female characters (incongruent) and vice-versa. A significant effect of gender mapping was found in the ratings of perception of three emotions (anger, fear and happiness), suggesting that gender may be an important aspect to be considered in the perception, and hence generation, of some emotional behaviours.

1 Introduction

Several studies explored the perception of behaviour in virtual characters [1,2]. Results from these studies are significant, as they can be used to contribute to the design and development of more efficient and plausible simulations of artificial entities, with applications in important and complex fields such as virtual and

R. Shumaker and S. Lackey (Eds.): VAMR 2014, Part I, LNCS 8525, pp. 263–273, 2014.
© Springer International Publishing Switzerland 2014

augmented reality. Perhaps of equal significance, these studies also have impact on deepening our understanding of how humans perceive other humans and biological versus artificially generated motions.

While studies have started to investigate the relationship between emotion and body movement by using virtual characters [3], little is known about the effect of gender on the perception of emotion from body movement. This issue is important for creating expressive social entities that are able to successfully communicate with humans. For example, if humans are more sensitive to motions of anger from male embodiments, this suggests that such behaviour needs to be moderated in order to create more desirable impressions.

In this paper, we present a pilot experiment investigating the perception of six basic emotions (anger, disgust, fear, happiness, sadness and surprise) from upper body movements that have been mapped onto virtual characters of the same and opposite gender from actors who originally conducted the movements. A corpus of emotional gestures was recorded from the performances of male and female actors using a Microsoft Kinect [4]. These movements were mapped onto virtual character as follows: movements generated by a Female Actor (FA) were mapped onto both Female and Male Characters (FC and MC) and movements generated by a Male Actor were mapped onto both Male and Female Characters (MC and FC).

We expected that when the gender of the virtual character was congruent with the gender of the original actor, the recognition rate of the expressed emotion would be higher. An online experiment was performed to test our hypothesis, in which videos of the virtual characters were shown to twenty-four subjects. The results indicated that when the virtual character's gender is congruent with the gender of the original actor, the recognition rate of the expressed emotion is higher for a subset of the six emotions considered here.

This paper is organised as follows. The next section (Section 2) provides a summary of relevant literature. Section 3 presents the corpus that was recorded with the Microsoft Kinect as part of this study, detailing the mapping process and the virtual stimuli used in the experiment. Section 4 describes a pre-experiment and Section 5 provides details of the mapping from actors to virtual characters. Section 6 describes the online perceptual experiment, summarising and discussing the main results. Finally, Section 7 summarised the contributions and limitations of the work in the context of future studies of impact in this domain.

2   Related Work

In the affective computing and computer animation communities, there has been growing interest in the study of perception of emotion from body movement using virtual characters. McDonnell and colleagues [1], for example, investigated the perception of emotion expressed by virtual characters with different embodiments and, more recently, the ability of humans to determine the gender of conversing characters based on facial and body cues [5]. Ennis and Eggs [6] explored the use of complex emotional body language for a virtual character and found that participants are better able to recognise complex emotions with negative connotations rather than positive. Castellano et al. presented an experiment investigating the perception of synthesized emotional gestures performed by an embodied virtual agent based on actor's movements with manual modulations [3].

In previous work on copying behaviour of real motion in virtual agents [7], it was shown that movement expressivity can convey the emotional content of people's behaviour, e.g., if a virtual agent's expressivity is not altered, then emotional content cannot be conveyed effectively. Investigations in [8] considered whether and how the type of gesture performed by a virtual agent affects the perception of emotion, concluding that a combination of type of movement performed and its quality are important for successfully communicating emotions.

In relation to gender perception from body movement, early studies by Kozlowski and Cutting [9] argued that the gender of walkers can be accurately recognised without familiarity cues from dynamic displays of point-light sources placed on upper/lower-body joints, respectively. Further, they also pointed out how changes in the degree of arm-swing or in walking speed can interfere with this recognition. More recently, gender recognition has had an important impact in computer vision, where researchers have developed several approaches based on 2D-3D facial or full-body analysis (see [10] for a survey). However, relatively little is currently known about the effect of gender on the perception of emotion from body movement; the majority of studies within psychology and neurosciences have focused on perception of emotion from facial expressions, showing that females are better at perceiving emotion from facial expression than males (e.g. [11]), and that different brain regions are activated by females and males when viewing facial expressions that are expressing sadness and happiness [12]. Further, Bartneck et al. [13] studied the effect of both culture and gender on the emotion recognition from complex expressions of avatars.

Tracking movement is not a new domain of research and there are a number of approaches that have been used in the past. One of the most common techniques is motion capture using body sensors or markers. These systems are typically expensive and usually require the sensors or markers to be positioned at selected places on the user. Although researchers have developed wearable systems that can capture movement for mapping onto virtual characters [14], there are other alternatives including computer vision approaches. The advances of vision-based human motion capture have been well documented [15] and they are becoming more popular. For our experimental implementation we focused on the later approaches by utilising Microsoft Kinect as a low-cost alternative for capturing motion. The maximum distance Kinect can operate is 5 metres and random error accuracy ranges from a few millimetres at 0.5m to 4cm of error at 5m [16], providing reasonable accuracy for some categories of motion recording.

3   Data Collection from Actors

A corpus of emotional gestures was recorded from the performances of male and female actors using a Microsoft Kinect as follows.

Two amateur actors (1M:1F) were recruited to act six basic emotional states: anger, disgust, fear, happiness, sadness and surprise. The actors were instructed about the final goals of the emotional gesture mapping experiment and provided their written consent for using the recorded video and numerical data for research purposes.

The actors were instructed to stand facing the camera and were asked not to move beyond the boundaries of a square area marked on the center of the stage. This constraint has been imposed to minimize potential tracking problems, such as occlusion, which may occur due to the use of a single Kinect if the actors were free to walk around the stage.

Each performed gesture involved the actor starting from and returning to a *starting* pose (i.e., standing still with arms along the body). Each gesture lasted up to 6 seconds. Actors could decide the gesture starting time by clapping their hands, after which the 6 second interval was measured. At the end of the recording interval, a sound informed the actor that they should return to the starting pose.

For each of the 6 emotional states the actor had to perform 10 repetitions, with a break of approximately 15 seconds between consecutive repetitions. The emotional expressions were performed in the following order: anger, sadness, happiness, surprise, fear, disgust.

Before performing the 10 emotion repetitions, actors were prepared with a short predefined scenario in order to support them. For example, for sadness: "You are listening to your iPod, when it drops, you pick it up, but it won't work."

Kinect Studio (part of the Windows Developer Toolkit) was used to record the actors, saving the information required for the mapping of motions to the characters described in Section 5. After each gesture was performed by the actor, a Kinect data file was generated containing colour and depth information (Figures 3a and 3b). Thus the actors were recording at the same session and the virtual characters were mapped at a later stage.

4   Pre-experiment User Study

From the corpus of gestures recorded in the data collection phase (Section 3), three gestures per emotion per actor were selected to form a final set of gestures that were as diverse as possible for each emotion.

A categorisation task was performed in order to identify those gestures from the actors that were most recognisable for each emotion. Twenty participants took part in this pre-experiment user study, which utilised a six-alternative forced choice paradigm: participants were asked to watch the video stimuli of the real actors and in each case indicate which one of the six basic emotions they thought was being expressed. While a forced choice paradigm does not allow participants to deviate from the proposed alternatives, it forces them to select the single closest option matching their judgement, which was desirable for the purposes of this study.

Fig. 1. The interface of Kinect Studio

The face and hands of the actors in the videos were blurred so as not to interfere with the focus of the study, which is upper body movement. For each actor and for each emotion, the gesture with the highest recognition rate was selected (Table 1). A few gestures had the same recognition rate: in these cases, the gesture whose expressed emotion was the most highly rated/less misclassified across all emotions for that specific gesture was selected for the character mapping phase, described in the next Section.

Table 1. Recognition rates of the body movements performed by the actors

	Anger	Disgust	Fear	Happiness	Sadness	Surprise
Female actor	75%	35%	50%	85%	90%	55%
Male actor	85%	75%	65%	85%	90%	70%

5   Character Mapping

Starting from the collected actors' data (Section 3) and the corresponding recognition rates (Section 4), the character mapping stage involved two free pre-made 3D character embodiments, one male and one female, that were chosen from Mixamo[1].

---

[1] http://www.mixamo.com

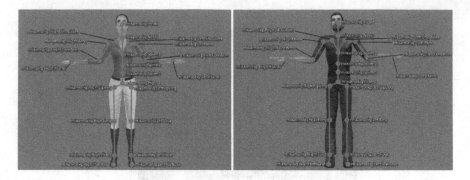

Fig. 2. The virtual character's skeleton data generated by the auto-rigging process

The mapping between the actors' motions and characters was conducted using a custom made real time skeleton motion tracking application developed in Visual Studio 2012 using the Microsoft for Windows SDK and Digital Rune Engine [2], which was used for rendering. This engine extends the XNA functionality making it easy to integrate the Kinect SDK in the engine.

As described in Section 3, movement tracking was conducted using the Kinect SDK that analyses the depth data from the camera and provides skeleton data (see Figure 2). This data consists of the movements of a set of joints. However, these joints differed from those in the characters (Figure 2). An auto-rigging service from Mixamo was used to create the same skeleton system for both characters, which was imported into our application.

Next, joints were mapped from the Kinect skeleton matching the actors' motions to the skeleton used in the virtual characters, i.e., the Hip_Center joint was mapped to the mixamorig:Hips0. This enabled the skeleton of the virtual character to copy the movements of the actors standing in front of the camera. Kinect Studio was used to connect the recording to our application for rendering, which was recorded using the Fraps [3] video recording utility. Female and Male Actors (FA and MA) were mapped onto both Female and Male Characters (FC and MC): a total of 24 videos were created during this phase (6 emotions x 2 actors x 2 characters).

There were a number of limitations to recording with a single Kinect: In particular, there is no finger tracking so the hands of the character are not mapped and remain in the same position in the generated videos. As in the case of the videos of the original performing actors, a blurring effect was placed on the head and hands of the virtual characters.

For each video, the process consisted of (1) a recording played in Kinect studio (Figure 3a and b), (2) a Fraps recording of the output of our application (Figure 3c) and (3) application of the blurring effect applied to the video (Figure 3d). The outputs of this process were the set of final mapped videos of virtual character movements to be used in the experiments, described in the next Section.

---

[2] http://www.digitalrune.com

[3] http://www.fraps.com

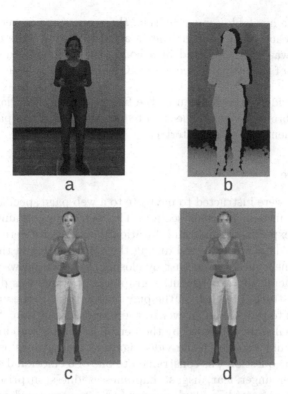

Fig. 3. RGB data output from the camera (a); depth data output from the camera (b); mapped avatar using the recorded data (c); blurred video using Sony Vegas (d)

6 Experiment

This section describes the experiment and methodology employed to assess the following hypothesis: *when the gender of a virtual character is congruent with the gender of an original actor, the recognition rate of the expressed emotion is higher.*

6.1 Participants

Twenty-four anonymous participants took part in the experiment. They were contacted by sending an invitation letter to a number of research mailing lists.

The order of the 24 videos the participants had to evaluate was randomised by using a 24 24 latin square. Each user was assigned to a different row of the square, consisting in a randomised sequence of 24 videos. This approach allowed for a balancing of practice effects across participants.

In order to ensure that participants were assigned all 24 sequences from the latin square, a PHP script[4] automatically assigned the first element of a pool

---

[4] The script is freely available for research purposes at the address:
   https://sourceforge.net/projects/phptestproject/.

containing all the available sequences (i.e., the sequences not yet evaluated by participants) to each participant as they started to perform the experiment. If the experiment was not completed in 3 hours, the assigned sequence was put back in the pool of the available sequences. Otherwise the sequence was marked as "completed".

To play back videos, the script uses the free version of JW Player [5]. Also, it performs a web browser version check to reduce the risk of compatibility issues with the experiment web-based interface.

6.2 Procedure

The participants were instructed to navigate to a web page specified in an email message as explained in previous section. The web page contained a brief description of the experiment goals and duration. Participants were also informed that no personal data was collected during the experiment and that they could leave the experiment at any time just by closing their web browser.

After commencing the experiment, a graphical interface was displayed. Participants were instructed to click on the play button to start the video playback. They were asked to provide an answer to the proposed question ("Do you think that the emotional state expressed by the person is:") after watching each video entirely. They could also watch the video again as many times as they wished. The answer to the question was constrained to one of 6 emotional states listed in alphabetical order: anger, fear, disgust, happiness, sadness, surprise. Participants were not allowed to provide a blank answer (e.g., "no emotion" or "other").

6.3 Results

In order to investigate the effects of gender mapping on the perception of emotion in the virtual stimuli, a statistical analysis was performed. Two Wilcoxon tests ($N = 24$) were performed for each emotion, one for each actor, for a total of twelve tests. As the data is not normally distributed, the Wilcoxon test was preferred to the t-test.

In each Wilcoxon test, the gender of the virtual character used to map the original actor's movement was considered as the independent variable (two levels), while the emotion rating (i.e., the accuracy performance) was considered as the dependent variable (one level). Each Wilcoxon test aimed to explore whether there is a significant difference in the rating of a specific emotion between stimuli in which the body movement expresses that same emotion when the virtual character's gender is congruent with that of the original actor and stimuli in which the virtual character's gender is not congruent with that of the original actor.

Results showed a significant effect of the virtual character's gender on the emotion rating in three cases. When anger is expressed by the female actor, the ratings of anger are significantly higher for the female virtual character

---

[5] http://www.longtailvideo.com/jw-player

$(z = -2.236, N = 5, p = 0.01)$. When fear is expressed by the male actor, the ratings of fear are significantly higher for the male virtual character ($z = -1.633, N = 6, p = 0.05$). When happiness is expressed by the female actor, the ratings of happiness are significantly higher for the female virtual character ($z = -2.121, N = 8, p = 0.017$).

While the ratings of anger are substantially high, the ratings of fear and happiness are not, although they are above chance level (see Table 2 for a summary of the means and standard deviations for the Wilcoxon test). This is in contrast to the results from the pre-experiment user study, which showed higher recognition accuracies for happiness and fear in the real stimuli. This discrepancy is possibly due to tracking and mapping issues related to the Kinect data, since some movements are not tracked with a high accuracy.

Table 2. Means and standard deviations for the Wilcoxon tests: significant differences between mean values are highlighted with a star (FA-to-FC = female actor to female character; FA-to-MC = female actor to male character; MA-to-MC = male actor to male character; MA-to-FC = male actor to female character)

	Female actor	Male actor
Accuracy	*FA-to-FC $\mu = 71\%, \sigma = 0.46$	MA-to-MC $\mu = 54\%, \sigma = 0.51$
anger	*FA-to-MC $\mu = 50\%, \sigma = 0.51$	MA-to-FC $\mu = 71\%, \sigma = 0.46$
Accuracy	FA-to-FC $\mu = 17\%, \sigma = 0.38$	MA-to-MC $\mu = 75\%, \sigma = 0.44$
disgust	FA-to-MC $\mu = 8\%, \sigma = 0.28$	MA-to-FC $\mu = 71\%, \sigma = 0.46$
Accuracy	FA-to-FC $\mu = 13\%, \sigma = 0.34$	*MA-to-MC $\mu = 29\%, \sigma = 0.46$
fear	FA-to-MC $\mu = 17\%, \sigma = 0.38$	*MA-to-FC $\mu = 13\%, \sigma = 0.34$
Accuracy	*FA-to-FC $\mu = 29\%, \sigma = 0.46$	MA-to-MC $\mu = 29\%, \sigma = 0.46$
happiness	*FA-to-MC $\mu = 4\%, \sigma = 0.20$	MA-to-FC $\mu = 38\%, \sigma = 0.50$
Accuracy	FA-to-FC $\mu = 87\%, \sigma = 0.34$	MA-to-MC $\mu = 92\%, \sigma = 0.28$
sadness	FA-to-MC $\mu = 79\%, \sigma = 0.42$	MA-to-FC $\mu = 87\%, \sigma = 0.34$
Accuracy	FA-to-FC $\mu = 25\%, \sigma = 0.44$	MA-to-MC $\mu = 46\%, \sigma = 0.51$
surprise	FA-to-MC $\mu = 29\%, \sigma = 0.46$	MA-to-FC $\mu = 42\%, \sigma = 0.50$

7   Conclusion

This paper presented an initial experiment studying the effects of gender mapping on the perception of emotion from virtual behaviour. We mapped emotional body movements generated by real actors onto virtual characters using data tracked with a Kinect. Movements generated by a female actor were mapped onto a female and a male character, and movements generated by a male actor were mapped onto a male and a female character.

Our hypothesis was that when the gender of the virtual character is congruent with the gender of the original actor the perception of emotion is higher. Results indeed showed that when the virtual character's gender is congruent with the gender of the original actor, perception of emotion is higher, but only for the emotions anger, fear and happiness, in three out of the twelve cases considered in our analysis.

Results need to be further validated by collecting a larger corpus of emotional gestures, also performed by actors from different cultures. However, despite the current limitations of Kinect, we believe that our approach should be further probed, as the possibility to use inexpensive equipment is desirable for developing, for example, more portable and wearable virtual and augmented reality systems.

References

1. McDonnell, R., Jörg, S., McHugh, J., Newell, F.N., O'Sullivan, C.: Investigating the role of body shape on the perception of emotion. ACM Transactions on Applied Perception (TAP) 6(3), 14 (2009)
2. Courgeon, M., Clavel, C., Tan, N., Martin, J.-C.: Front view vs. Side view of facial and postural expressions of emotions in a virtual character. In: Pan, Z., Cheok, A.D., Müller, W. (eds.) Transactions on Edutainment VI. LNCS, vol. 6758, pp. 132–143. Springer, Heidelberg (2011)
3. Castellano, G., Mancini, M., Peters, C., McOwan, P.W.: Expressive copying behavior for social agents: A perceptual analysis. IEEE Transactions on Systems, Man and Cybernetics, Part A: Systems and Humans 42(3), 776–783 (2012)
4. Shotton, J., Fitzgibbon, A., Cook, M., Sharp, T., Finocchio, M., Moore, R., Kipman, A., Blake, A.: Real-time human pose recognition in parts from single depth images. In: Proceedings of the 2011 IEEE Conference on Computer Vision and Pattern Recognition, CVPR 2011, pp. 1297–1304. IEEE Computer Society, Washington, DC (2011)
5. Zibrek, K., Hoyet, L., Ruhland, K., McDonnell, R.: Evaluating the effect of emotion on gender recognition in virtual humans. In: Proceedings of the ACM Symposium on Applied Perception, SAP 2013, pp. 45–49. ACM, New York (2013)
6. Ennis, C., Egges, A.: Perception of complex emotional body language of a virtual character. In: Kallmann, M., Bekris, K. (eds.) MIG 2012. LNCS, vol. 7660, pp. 112–121. Springer, Heidelberg (2012)
7. Mancini, M., Castellano, G., Peters, C., McOwan, P.W.: Evaluating the communication of emotion via expressive gesture copying behaviour in an embodied humanoid agent. In: D'Mello, S., Graesser, A., Schuller, B., Martin, J.-C. (eds.) ACII 2011, Part I. LNCS, vol. 6974, pp. 215–224. Springer, Heidelberg (2011)
8. Castellano, G., Mancini, M., Peters, C.: Emotion communication via copying behaviour: A case study with the greta embodied agent. In: Proceedings of the AFFINE Workshop, Hosted by the ACM ICMI 2011 Conference (2011)
9. Kozlowski, L.T., Cutting, J.E.: Recognizing the sex of a walker from a dynamic point-light display. Perception and Psychophysics 21(6), 575–580 (1977)
10. Ng, C., Tay, Y., Goi, B.-M.: Recognizing human gender in computer vision: A survey. In: Anthony, P., Ishizuka, M., Lukose, D. (eds.) PRICAI 2012. LNCS, vol. 7458, pp. 335–346. Springer, Heidelberg (2012)
11. Babchuk, W.A., Hames, R.B., Thompson, R.: Sex differences in the recognition of infant facial expressions of emotion: the primary caretaker hypothesis. Ethology and Sociobiology 6, 89–101 (1985)
12. Lee, T., Liu, H., Liao, W., Wu, C., Yuen, K., Chan, C., Fox, P., Gao, J.: Gender differences in neural correlates of recognition of happy and sad faces in humans assessed by functional magnetic resonance imaging. Neuroscience Letters 333(1) (2002)

13. Bartneck, C., Takahashi, T., Katagiri, Y.: Cross-cultural study of expressive avatars. In: Third International Workshop on Social Intelligence Design (2004)
14. New Scientist. Cheap sensors could capture your every move,
    http://www.newscientist.com/article/
    dn12963-cheap-sensors-could-capture-your-every-move.html
    (accessed at: April 8 2013)
15. Moeslund, T.B., Hilton, A., Krüger, V.: A survey of advances in vision-based human motion capture and analysis. Comput. Vis. Image Underst. 104(2), 90–126 (2006)
16. Khoshelham, K., Elberink, S.O.: Accuracy and resolution of kinect depth data for indoor mapping applications. Sensors 12(2), 1437–1454 (2012)

AR Navigation System
Using Interaction with a CG Avatar

Hirosuke Murata, Maiya Hori, Hiroki Yoshimura, and Yoshio Iwai

Graduate School of Engineering, Tottori University
101 Minami 4-chome, Koyama-cho, Tottori, 680-8550, Japan

Abstract. This paper describes a navigation system that is guided by a CG avatar using augmented reality (AR) technology. Some existing conventional AR navigation systems use arrows for route guidance. However, the positions to which the arrows point can be unclear because the actual scale of the arrow is unknown. In contrast, a navigation process conducted by a person indicates the routes clearly. In addition, this process offers a sense of safety with its expectation of arrival at the required destination, because the user can reach the destination as long as he/she follows the navigator. Moreover, the user can communicate easily with the navigator. In this research, we construct an AR navigation system using a CG avatar to perform interactively in place of a real person.

1 Introduction

Guidance systems based on display devices that are fixed in their environment, such as digital signage, can be found in public spaces. These systems require installation spaces and have high equipment costs. Guidance systems using mobile phones have been developed as one method to overcome these problems. As an example of the guidance systems that are offered by mobile devices, sophisticated applications using augmented reality (AR) technology are widely used, although they depend on the level of technological advancement of the device. AR is a technology that provides a digitally enhanced view of the real world. Conventional AR navigation systems[1][2] use arrows for guidance along a route. However, the positions to which the arrows are pointing can be unclear because the actual scale of the arrow is unknown. In contrast, when navigation is guided by a person, it is easy to understand the directions given intuitively. Furthermore, this navigation mode provides a sense of safety with the expectation of arrival at the desired destination, because the user can reach the destination as long as he/she follows the navigator. In addition, the user can communicate directly with the navigator.

In this research, we implement a CG avatar using AR technology to perform interactively with the user in place of a human navigator. It is easy for the user to understand the directions intuitively through interactions with the CG avatar. Additionally, the reliability can be improved by giving the CG avatar a favorable image.

R. Shumaker and S. Lackey (Eds.): VAMR 2014, Part I, LNCS 8525, pp. 274–281, 2014.
© Springer International Publishing Switzerland 2014

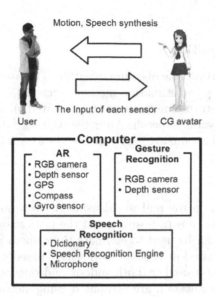

Fig. 1. The concept of the proposed method

2   AR Navigation System Based on Interaction with a CG Avatar

Figure 1 shows the concept of the proposed method. The user can communicate by speech and gestures with a CG avatar that has been superimposed on the real world. These communications are realized using speech recognition, gesture recognition and AR technologies. We use various sensors to monitor the user's behavior. Movements and speech are generated for the CG avatar that correspond to this behavior. The user, wearing a head-mounted display (HMD), is then guided by the CG avatar in real time. The CG avatar can perform several actions, including walking, waiting, pointing, gazing and greeting. It is also necessary to show that the CG avatar is standing on the ground for realism and we must consider the occlusions that are derived from real objects such as walls and buildings. These occlusions are realized by detecting the ground and measuring the depths of the objects using a depth sensor.

2.1   Speech Recognition

Speech recognition technology is required to conduct a conversation and provide explanations using the CG avatar. The user's speech can be recognized using a large vocabulary continuous speech recognition engine, such as Julius[3]. Various set speeches are generated in advance using a speech synthesis technique[4]. After the speech recognition process, the corresponding required speech is then spoken by the avatar.

2.2 Gesture Recognition

Gestures play an important role in communication. The user's gestures are recognized using a 3D hand pose estimation method, such as [5]. The avatar's various actions to be taken when guiding the user are generated in advance, similar to the method used for the avatar's speech. After the user's gesture is recognized, the corresponding required actions are performed by the avatar using AR techniques.

2.3 AR Technology

To overlay CG objects on the real world using AR technology, the application needs to know both the camera position and the camera orientation. There are several methods that can be used to estimate the camera position and orientation, including vision-based methods[6] and sensor-based methods. Because our system is intended to be used in both indoor and outdoor environments, the camera position and orientation are estimated using various sensors. A Global Positioning System (GPS) device, a gyroscope, and a compass are used for the estimation process in outdoor environments. In indoor environments, a vision-based method, a wireless LAN-based system and an Indoor MEssaging System (IMES)[7] are used for the estimation process. By switching between these methods, depending on the environment, the system can be operated over a wide area. The CG avatar can be superimposed on specific locations using the estimated camera position and its orientation.

To realize the interactions with the CG avatar, it is necessary to implement various avatar motions. The required motions are as follows. The movements that are necessary for the avatar itself are, "walking", "run", "go upstairs", "go downstairs", and "waiting". As motions that are required for the guidance process, "greeting", "hand gesture", "eye contact", and "representation of emotions" must all be implemented. Additionally, to make the user feel as if the CG avatar exists in the real world, we need further techniques such as detection of the ground and occlusion culling. These functions are achieved by using a depth sensor to obtain depth information for objects in the real world.

3 Experiment

In our experiments, we show the results of the construction of our navigation system using the CG avatar in both the indoor and outdoor environments. In the indoor environment, the CG avatar gave a poster presentation instead of a real person, as shown in Fig. 2. Occlusion culling is considered based on use of the available depth information, as shown in Fig. 3. The camera position and the posture are estimated using a magnetic sensor (3SPACE FASTRAK, Polhemus). The occlusion culling process is implemented using a depth sensor (Xtion Pro Live, ASUS).

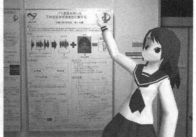

(a) Turning the avatar's gaze on the user

(b) Explaining the description of the poster

Fig. 2. Examples of a poster presentation

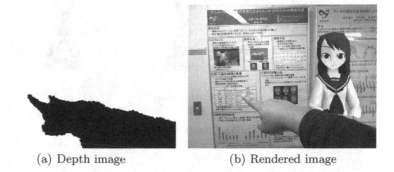

(a) Depth image

(b) Rendered image

Fig. 3. Example of the CG avatar when considering occlusions

The interactions of the CG avatar are conducted using the Wizard of Oz (WoZ) method[8]. The operator controls the CG avatar in response to the user's behavior and speech. The CG avatar contains 120 bones, and various avatar movements can be implemented as shown in Fig. 4. These movements are played along with the speeches that were generated previously, such as a greeting and an explanation of the presentation. The CG avatar can also cope with the user's questions by generating speech interactively via a keyboard input. In a demonstration, the CG avatar was able to give a presentation coupled with interactions with the users. From assessment of some of the users' opinions, we found that the users could feel like the CG avatar actually existed in front of them.

In the outdoor environment, the CG avatar acts as a guide. Figure 5 shows the user's appearance in the outdoor environment. The camera posture is acquired using a compass and a gyroscope. The CG avatar is superimposed in such a position that the avatar appears to be leading the user. In this experiment, the navigation processes are conducted by an operator using the WoZ method. The user looks at the walking avatar and decides on the direction of movement at some forks in the road. The navigation was carried out using five paths that were determined in advance, and these paths are unknown to the users. One path

(a) bow   (b) blink   (c) shake of avatar's
                                                head

(d) pointing   (e) thinking   (f) nodding

Fig. 4. Movements of the CG avatar

is selected in random order for each user. There are three forks in each path. Figure 6(a) shows an example of the ground truth that was predetermined by the operator. The trajectory of the user's movement acquired by GPS is shown in Fig. 6(b). From this figure, we see that the navigation has been conducted correctly. Examples of the user's view are shown in Fig. 7. The numbers of branches were three at points A and B, and two at points C and D. Users can arrive at the desired destination by simply following the CG avatar, as shown in Fig. 7.

To investigate the validity of the proposed method, subjective evaluations using questionnaires were conducted with 15 subjects. For comparisons, the following five methods were implemented.

- (a) Person
  A person guides the user, who is wearing the experimental apparatus.
- (b) CG avatar (the proposed method)
  A CG avatar guides the user, and the avatar exists at all times.
- (c) CG avatar only at forks
  A CG avatar appears only at forks in the road.
- (d) Arrows
  Arrows guide the user, and the arrows exist at all times.
- (e) Arrows only at forks
  Arrows appear only at forks in the road.

Fig. 5. User's appearance

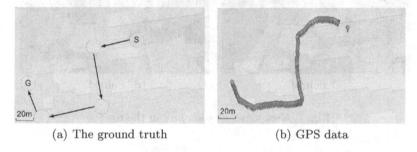

(a) The ground truth   (b) GPS data

Fig. 6. The trajectory of the user's movement

The questionnaires are used to rank the methods in terms of "Sense of safety", "Likability of the system", "Availability", "Reliability", "Visibility", "Responsiveness", and "Likability of the navigator". The evaluation was rated with scores from 1 (not felt at all) to 6 (felt extremely strongly).

The results of the questionnaires are shown in Fig. 8. From the results of the questionnaires, the proposed system exceeds the navigation by arrows method in terms of "Sense of safety", "Likability of the system", "Reliability", and "Likability of the navigator". With respect to "Likability of the system", the proposed system exceeds all other methods, including navigation by a person. The "Reliability" of the proposed method has a higher score than the methods where navigation guides appear only at forks in the road. In terms of "Visibility" and "Responsiveness", no significant differences can be observed between the methods.

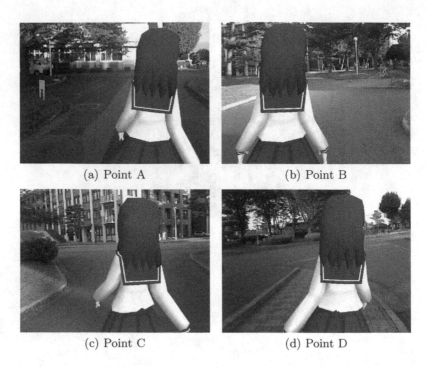

(a) Point A   (b) Point B

(c) Point C   (d) Point D

Fig. 7. User views at each fork in the road

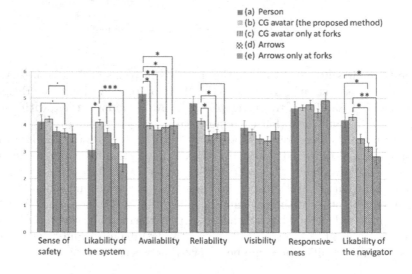

Fig. 8. Results of the questionnaires

4   Conclusion

This paper describes a navigation system where the user is guided by a CG avatar using AR technology. In the indoor environment, a poster presentation given by the CG avatar was demonstrated and the importance of user interactions has been shown. In the outdoor environment, the CG avatar acted as a guide and the navigation process was conducted correctly. From the results of subjective user evaluations, it was found that the proposed system has high likability and was preferred to the methods based on navigation by arrows in terms of their sense of safety and reliability. In our future work, we intend to automate the process that was carried out using the WoZ method in this work.

Acknowledgment. This work was supported by JSPS KAKENHI (Grant No. 24118705).

References

1. Kanbara, M., Nagamatsu, A., Yokoya, N.: Augmented reality guide system using mobile projectors in large indoor environment. In: Proc. Workshop on Personal Projection via Mobile and Wearable Pico Projection, pp. 16–19 (2010)
2. Yahoo!japan, http://maps.loco.yahoo.co.jp/promo/spn/map/
3. Julius, http://julius.sourceforge.jp/en_index.php?q=index-en.html
4. Open JTalk, http://open-jtalk.sourceforge.net/
5. Oikonomidis, I., Kyriazis, N., Argyros, A.: Efficient model-based 3D tracking of hand articulations using kinect. In: Proc. of the British Machine Vision Conference, pp. 101.1–101.11 (2011)
6. Klein, G., Murray, D.: Parallel tracking and mapping for small AR workspaces. In: Proc. International Symposium on Mixed and Augmented Reality (2007)
7. Manandhar, D., Kawaguchi, S., Torimoto, H.: Results of IMES (indoor messaging system) implementation for seamless indoor navigation and social infrastructure platform. In: Proc. of Int'l Technical Meeting of the Satellite Division of the Institute of Navigation, pp. 1184–1191 (2010)
8. Fraser, N.M., Gilbert, G.N.: Simulating speech systems. In: Computer Speech and Language, pp. 81–99 (1991)

Virtual Humans for Interpersonal and Communication Skills' Training in Crime Investigations

Konstantinos Mykoniatis[1,2], Anastasia Angelopoulou[1,2], Michael D. Proctor[2], and Waldemar Karwowski[2]

[1] Modeling & Simulation Graduate Program, University of Central Florida, Orlando, FL 32816, USA
{kmykoniatis,aangelopoulou}@knights.ucf.edu
[2] Institute for Advance System Engineering, Department of Industrial Engineering and Management Systems, University of Central Florida, Orlando, FL 32816, USA
{Michael.Proctor,wkar}@ucf.edu

Abstract. Virtual Humans (VHs) have been employed in multidisciplinary fields to advance interpersonal skills critical to many professional, including law enforcement agents, military personnel, managers, doctors, lawyers and other professionals. Law enforcement agencies in particular have faced a growing need to develop human to human interpersonal training to increase interviewing and interrogation skills. In this paper, we present a prototype VE that has been developed to provide law enforcement agents with effective interview and interrogation training and experiential learning. The virtual training environment will need to be tested and formally evaluated to verify the benefits compared to live exercises and traditional training techniques.

Keywords: Virtual Human, Training, Law enforcement agents, Interpersonal Skills, Virtual Environment.

1 Introduction

Virtual Humans (VHs) are the subjects of research in multidisciplinary fields, ranging from computer sciences (computer generated forces), healthcare and education industries to military and entertainment applications. Even though VH research has evolved rapidly over the last years (Gratch et al. 2002; Rickel et al. 2002; Swartout 2006, Swartout 2010), few studies have focused on how to employ VHs to advance interpersonal skills through training in interviewing, negotiating, leadership, cultural awareness, tactical questioning, or eliciting information (Hubal et al. 2001; Kenny et al. 2007). These interpersonal skills are critical to many professional, including law enforcement agents, military personnel, lawyers, doctors, managers, supervisors and other professionals.

Law enforcement agencies in particular have faced a growing need to develop human to human interpersonal training to increase interviewing and interrogation skills.

R. Shumaker and S. Lackey (Eds.): VAMR 2014, Part I, LNCS 8525, pp. 282–292, 2014.

This kind of training is traditionally conducted through live exercises, "talk and chalk" lectures, role playing, group discussions or non-experiential media learning. These techniques have led to a critical training gap since students are provided with limited practice time and limited variety of scenarios (Hubal et al. 2001). Regarding interrogation training, agencies typically use a variety of techniques and tools to train investigators in developing skills to identify deception indicators, ranging from verbal communication to non-verbal cues. This kind of training is time consuming as it is accomplished through practical interrogation with known suspects of committed crimes (Luciew et al. 2011). Although some existing Virtual Environments (VE) provide physical skills' training, team training, or even strategy and tactics, their overall limitation is that human user's interactions with the VHs are usually restricted to shooting activities (Kenny et al. 2007).

The purpose of this paper is to help fill the gap in the interpersonal skills training in the field of law enforcement. To this purpose, a prototype VE has been developed to provide law enforcement agents with effective interview and interrogation training and experiential learning. The prototype VE was built in Unity3D Pro, using, Maya 2013, 3DsMax, SonicAcid Pro and the VH toolkit which was provided by the University of Southern California (USC) Institute for Creative Technologies (ICT). The developed VE simulates a variety of aspects, from the physics of objects to realistic human behavior. The VHs have three attributes: they are believable, i.e. able to mimic human behavior and express realistic emotions in order to draw the human user into the scenario; they are responsive, meaning they are capable of interacting with trainees and other VHs via text or spoken dialogues; and they are interpretable, so that the user will be able to interpret the verbal and nonverbal cues in their responses.

2   Existing Virtual Environments for Training Interpersonal Skills

In this section, we review existing VEs in the field of crime investigation. If properly used, VEs can be useful training tools. VEs have been used for intercultural communication training (Kim et. al 2009), clinical interviewing (Kenny et al. 2008), and police officer training (Hubal et al. 2003), to name a few. Some examples of VEs developed for training interpersonal skills are briefly described below.

The JUST-TALK training system (Fig. 1) was developed to assist law enforcement agents in managing situations involving mentally ill people and responding appropriately. The overall objective of the JUST-TALK project was to improve law enforcement training using Natural Language Processing and Virtual Reality technology (Frank et al. 2002).

Another VE training example is the Tactical-Questioning system (Kenny et al., 2007), which allows trainees to interview a suspect of a bombing incident (Fig. 2).

Fig. 1. The JUST-TALK Virtual Environment (Source: Frank et al., 2002)

Fig. 2. Tactical Questioning System (Source: Kenny et al., 2007)

Finally, an immersive criminal investigator prototype developed for training investigations of child physical and sexual abuse is presented (Luciew et al. 2011). This system has two modes: the "interview training" mode, which enables investigators to experience a virtual interview with a victim of child abuse (Fig. 3); and the "interrogation training" mode, which allows investigators to virtually interrogate a suspect of sexual assault (Fig. 4).

Fig. 3. A virtual interview subject (Source: Luciew et al., 2011)

Fig. 4. A virtual interrogation subject (Source: Luciew et al., 2011)

3   Attributes of the VE Training System Prototype

Our goal is to build an interactive VE and VHs that will improve interpersonal skills training to benefit Law Enforcement Agents, i.e. advance their interviewing and inter-rogation techniques, critical skills for the success in the current working environment. We propose an interactive training tool to teach investigators how to conduct effective interviews. The proposed tool allows for natural and interactive dialog between the trainee and the VH.

The system has two modes: the "pre-interview mode" and the "training segment" mode. In the "pre-interview mode", the trainee is first introduced to a simulated scena-rio. The scenario is like a short video clip, which has the purpose of providing informa-tion and evidence to the trainee about the criminal case. The simulated scenario of the prototype follows below. The owner of a house has been murdered during a Halloween Party. Then, the trainee is presented with a list of possible suspects and applicable "police" profiles, a list of evidence from the scene and other relevant information and events occurred before and after the murder, as depicted in Fig.5 and Fig. 6.

After reviewing potential suspects and taking appropriate notes, the trainee is pre-sented with a target "training segment." In the "training segment", the trainee can interact with the VHs and interview one VH suspect at a time until a conclusion is made.

The *VE Training System Prototype* allows for the following interactions:

- The trainee can navigate within the VE to collect data, crime evidence and cues (Fig. 7).
- The trainee can interview VHs about the crime, i.e. the guests of the house, in or-der to determine their involvement. Each VH is capable of answering a number of questions that are relevant to the investigation case.
- The trainee can observe verbal and non-verbal behaviors, and deception cues by interacting within the VE and VHs. The ability to detect deception cues is a critical skill for law enforcement agents. The proposed training system is capable of aug-menting this type of skill.

POLICE PROFILE

NAME	John Morgan
DOB	January 13, 1972
HEIGHT	1 meter, 80 cm
WEIGHT	112 kg
HAIR	Grey
EYES	Brown
Writes	Left hand

Notes: John Morgan is Brad's three years older cousin. He was M&S Inc. employee since 2000. John is the Chief Human Resources Officer of M&S Inc. He hired Jenny Miller six months ago. In his prior report he claimed that Brad had problems with his wife, who was jealous of his new secretary.

POLICE PROFILE

NAME	Jenny Miller
DOB	July 20, 1986
HEIGHT	1 meter, 68 cm
WEIGHT	60 kg
HAIR	Brown
EYES	Green
Writes	Right Hand

Notes: Jenny Miller was born in Pennsylvania. Jenny had been Brad's private secretary for six months. She was hired to M&S Inc. by John Morgan, from Human Resources Department. In her prior report she said : "I can't believe my boss was murdered!"

POLICE PROFILE

NAME	Rachel Anderson Morgan
DOB	February 8, 1980
HEIGHT	1 meter, 65 cm
WEIGHT	67 kg
HAIR	Blond
EYES	green
Writes	right hand

Notes: Rachel Anderson had been married to Brad for 3 years. Rachel has inherited M&S Inc. from her father. Rachel found her husband dead and called 911 at 21:45. In her prior report she was grieving... " This can't be real! I can't believe my love is really dead! She did it, Jenny did it!"

POLICE PROFILE

NAME	Jack Morris
DOB	January 13, 1955
HEIGHT	1 meter, 85 cm
WEIGHT	112 kg
HAIR	Grey
EYES	Brown
Writes	Left hand

Notes: Jack Morris was a friend of Rachel's father, and the Chief Financial Officer (CFO) of M&S Inc. In his prior report he said: "I was enjoying the music on the living room, when the thunderbolt stroke and then...blackout! While I was searching for a lighter, I heard two gun shots, BANG! BANG! Oh my God! I can't believe it! Brad my boy! You can't be dead! Please officer, forgive me I am shocked..."

Fig. 5. "Police Profiles" (the VH suspects) in the Prototype

Fig. 6. Collected Evidence Screenshot in the Prototype

Fig. 7. Scenes taken from the VE Prototype

A stochastic model produces responses to the trainee's questions, which are selected from a pre-scripted list of possible questions. The VE enables the trainee to gain experience in asking proper questions and distinguishing between deceptive and truthful responses.

4   Prototype Focus on Deception Cues

In the developed prototype interviewing skills training is a major component. The opportunity for a realistic interaction with subjects capable of demonstrating cues related to truthfulness and deceit is a proven benefit. Research indicates that the virtual training environment can improve trainees' ability to detect deception by helping them identify the right cues (Lane et al. 2010). The trainee should ask the proper questions and identify common cues of truth-telling and deceit. Cues to deception are commonly divided into the three categories: verbal, nonverbal, and vocal. Verbal cues come from the content of the speaker's statement. Examples include declaration of lack of memory or self-references. Nonverbal cues include eye contact, posture, hand movement and can be observed individually by the suspect's behavior. Vocal cues can be a sound or the tone of the suspect's voice used to send a particular message and not an actual word. Vocal cues are significant, since they may help the trainee understand the message behind the words by either confirming or discrediting the message.

A person's body language is a form of mental and physical ability of human nonverbal communication, consisting of body posture, gestures, facial expressions, and eye movements, which can tell whether a suspect may lie (DePaulo, et al. 2003). In the prototype the VH characters can perform some of the natural human characteristics via the integrated SmartBody system within the VHToolkit. Deception indicators include self-fidgeting, posture shifts, response length, and verbal and vocal uncertainty. The simulated VHs may have a nervous habit, such as fidgeting their hair or wringing their hands, which can indicate when they might lie. Other VHs may exaggerate their emotions and then suddenly return to normal. A VH suspect who is lying is more likely to take a defensive posture, such as crossing his/her arms and remaining stiff. Fig.8 Illustrates a sample of different postures, gestures, facial expressions, and eye movements of a VH character.

Fig. 8. Examples of VH's nonverbal behavior in the VE Prototype

The first step in creating the VHs' profiles was to decide on incidents that would provide the environment for the interviews. The law enforcement scenario that was chosen for the simulation was a murder. Four VH characters were used as the main suspects. In this version of the system, the VHs use basic nonverbal behaviors in their speech, but they are not high fidelity modeled to deceit. For instance, the VHs do not have facial expressions or eye movement based on their emotional state.

The trainee can interact with the VHs by asking questions via either an integrated typed interface or an automated speech recognition system that provides animated and oral responses from the VHs. The training focus is primarily on helping the trainee to:

- Ask the appropriate questions (Socratic Method, Improve skill of investigative interviewing or interrogation of non-cooperative suspects).
- Identify deception cues (Verbal, Non Verbal, and Vocal).

5   Intelligent Tutoring Capability in Prototype System

The proposed system is capable of supporting an intelligent tutoring system. The *first phase* of the developed prototype focused on the construction of the VE, VHs, and interactive dialogues.

The *second phase* would focus on the effective implementation of intelligent tutor's elements, such as:

- Levels of interactions (novice, intermediate, expert). Different simulated scenarios would be provided for different level of training experience
- Feedback on the accomplished tasks
- Hints

- Applying Socratic instructional theory of learning to improve questioning skills
- Cumulative scoring and analysis of trainees' solutions to determine trainees' progress.

The training process would be based on the Socratic Learning Theory (Woolf, 2001). This learning theory is a teaching strategy derived from Socrates (Greece 469-399 B.C) and it is based on the belief that each person contains the essential ideas and answers to solve problems. By applying the Socratic Method trainees would improve their questioning skills and seek to discover the subject of matter, since their goal is to know what they do not know.

The intelligent tutor would assist the trainees in finding out and correcting their own misconceptions by asking the trainees instructive questions. The tutor would also track the trainee's performance and record, analyze and evaluate the questions, decisions and actions without interfering with the trainee's efforts. The tutor would be designed to motivate and provide an After Action Review (AAR) of the trainee's performance after the completion of the scenario to validate the skills the trainee has acquired. The tutor would also be able to provide oral feedback to the student after the interview is completed, by making suggestions to the trainee for future actions.

Finally, the *third phase* would include a pilot testing and evaluation of the effectiveness of the intelligent tutoring system. The evaluation findings will be judged by law enforcement key stakeholders and this information will be reused to improve the existing system.

6   Audio in the VE Prototype

As the visuals of the simulated scenario unfold, audio and sound effects can convey emotions such as excitement, and fear. According to Brown (1994), *"it is the combination of the visuals with music that makes the viewers feel those emotions and affects the users' subjective sense of presence or "being there"."* For the audio production of this project, we used the Sony ACID Pro, which is a professional digital audio workstation software program. Audio tracks were produced for:

- VE background music
- VHs realistic voices and vocal cues
- Natural Phenomena sound effects, such as raining and thunder strike sound effects
- Audio sounds visible within the VE, such as VHs' voices and vocal cues, footsteps, door-opening, gunshot, CD/radio music player.

"Music is used in two modes within films: diagetic and non-diagetic" (Robertson et al., 1998). Diegesis is a Greek term for "recounted story". In other words, the diegesis is the total world of the story action. Diegetic music can come from a sound source visible on the screen or a source implied to be occurred within the narrative of the virtual scenario. Examples of diegetic sounds in the developed VE are the VHs' voices, sounds made by VH's or other objects in the story, and music attributable to some source coming from instruments within the VE such as Hi-Fi CD/radio music player or jukebox.

Non-diegetic music comes from a sound source which is neither part of the narrative, nor attributable to a source in the virtual scenario. This type of music comes from outside the space of the simulated story events. Non-diegetic sounds can be sound effects, such as narrator's commentary, added to underline a dramatic effect. Non-diegetic music is usually used to affect the emotions of the audience. It can be used to cue the audiences to feel uncomfortable; to build up tension; to point out an approaching disaster or to indicate a love affair. Examples of non-diegetic sounds in the developed VE are the sound effects added to indicate an upcoming argument between VHs or to prepare the trainees for the crime to be committed.

7   Expected Benefits of the Proposed VE

The overall training system aims to help train law enforcement agents to conduct effective interviews and interrogations, to interpret the verbal and non-verbal communication of their subjects, to improve their abilities, such as cognitive, sensory, psychomotor skills (Fleishman et al, 1991) and to cultivate and improve analytic and decision making skills. The system will allow the simulation of a variety of VE scenarios, increasing the trainee's situational awareness, as situations can be repeated over and over with no further training costs.

Trainees will be provided with more practice time, increased access to training and consistent training experience, leading to improvements of their problem-solving abilities. Benefits will also include saving time and reducing training costs, individualized tutoring, realistic and engaging experience to provide valuable law enforcement training.

8   Discussion and Future Work

In this paper, we have discussed the need for training law enforcement agents to conduct effective interviews and interrogations. We reviewed existing VEs and proposed a virtual training environment that could fill the gap in this kind of training using VH suspects of criminal cases. This training system could be used to supplement real-world training, enhancing interviewing skills and reducing training cost, when compared to traditional interpersonal skills training. The weakness of using traditional methods, such as recorded videos or "chalk and talk" lectures when training interpersonal skills, is that traditional methods are not able to provide experiential learning and evaluate the trainee's ability to conduct investigative interviews, even though they can evaluate recognition skills.

Artwork of the VHs, the VE and any background music are important parts in a simulation because they contribute in sustaining the trainee's attention, interest, and motivation. However, these elements are usually underestimated (Kenny et al. 2007). An effort was made to implement a simulated scenario of animated VHs with realistic appearance, natural behavior, believable sound effects and atmospheric background music. Efforts were also made for the simulation of the effects of rain, water, candle fire and lighting.

Future work will focus on the advancement of the prototype system to an intelligent tutoring system. The trainee will be able to experience a variety of real-life training scenarios and will be provided with the time needed to develop the necessary skills, while receiving analytic feedback. The virtual training environment will need to be tested and formally evaluated to verify the benefits compared to live exercises and traditional training techniques.

References

1. Brown, R.S.: Overtones and Undertones. University of California Press, Berkeley and LosAngeles (1994)
2. DePaulo, B.M., Lindsay, J.J., Malone, B.E., Muhlenbruck, L., Charlton, K., Cooper, H.: Cues to deception. Psychological Bulletin 129(1), 74 (2003)
3. Fleishman, E.A., Mumford, M.D., Zaccaro, S.J., Levin, K.Y., Korotkin, A.L., Hein, M.B.: Taxonomic efforts in the description of leader behavior: A synthesis and functional interpretation. Leadership Quarterly 2(4), 245–287 (1991)
4. Frank, G., Guinn, C., Hubal, R.: JUST-TALK: An application of responsive virtual hu-man technology. In: The Interservice/Industry Training, Simulation & Education Confer-ence (I/ITSEC), vol. 1. National Training Systems Association (January 2002)
5. Gratch, J., Rickel, J., André, E., Badler, N., Cassell, J., Petajan, E.: Creating Interactive Virtual Humans: Some Assembly Required. IEEE Intelligent Systems 54–63 (July/August 2002)
6. Hubal, R.C., Frank, G.A.: Interactive training applications using responsive virtual human technology. Children 21, 25 (2001)
7. Hubal, R.C., Frank, G.A., Guinn, C.I.: Lessons learned in modeling schizophrenic and depressed responsive virtual humans for training. In: Proceedings of the 8th International Conference on Intelligent User Interfaces, pp. 85–92. ACM (January 2003)
8. Kenny, P., Hartholt, A., Gratch, J., Swartout, W., Traum, D., Marsella, S., Piepol, D.: Building interactive virtual humans for training environments. In: The Interser-vice/Industry Training, Simulation & Education Conference (I/ITSEC), vol. 2007(1). National Training Systems Association (January 2007)
9. Kenny, P., Parsons, T., Gratch, J., Rizzo, A.: Virtual humans for assisted health care. In: Proceedings of the 1st International Conference on PErvasive Technologies Related to Assistive Environments, vol. 6. ACM (July 2008)
10. Kim, J.M., Hill, J.R.W., Durlach, P.J., Lane, H.C., Forbell, E., Core, M., Hart, J.: BiLAT: A game-based environment for practicing negotiation in a cultural context. International Journal of Artificial Intelligence in Education 19(3), 289–308 (2009)
11. Lane, H.C., Schneider, M., Michael, S.W., Albrechtsen, J.S., Meissner, C.A.: Virtual humans with secrets: Learning to detect verbal cues to deception. In: Aleven, V., Kay, J., Mostow, J. (eds.) ITS 2010, Part II. LNCS, vol. 6095, pp. 144–154. Springer, Heidelberg (2010)
12. Luciew, D., Mulkern, J., Punako, R.: Finding the Truth: Interview and Interrogation Train-ing Simulations. In: The Interservice/Industry Training, Simulation & Education Con-ference (I/ITSEC), vol. 2011(1). National Training Systems Association (January 2011)
13. Rickel, J., Marsella, S., Gratch, J., Hill, R., Traum, D., Swartout, W.: Toward a new generation of virtual humans for interactive experiences. IEEE Intelligent Systems 32–38 (2002)

14. Robertson, J., de Quincey, A., Stapleford, T., Wiggins, G.: Real-time music generation for a virtual environment. In: Proceedings of ECAI 1998 Workshop on AI/Alife and Entertainment (August 1998)
15. Swartout, W.: Virtual Humans. In: Twenty-First National Conference on Artificial Intelligence (AAAI-06) (Senior Paper), Boston, MA (2006)
16. Swartout, W., Gratch, J., Hill, R., Hovy, E., Marsella, S., Rickel, J., Traum, D.: Toward Virtual Humans. AI Magazine 27(1) (2006)
17. Swartout, W.: Lessons Learned from Virtual Humans. AI Magazine 31(1) (2010)
18. Woolf, B.P.: Building intelligent interactive tutors: Student-centered strategies for revolutionizing e-learning. Morgan Kaufmann (2010)

The Avatar Written upon My Body: Embodied Interfaces and User Experience

Mark Palmer

UWE Bristol, Coldharbour Lane, Franchay, Bristol BS16 1QY
`Mark.Palmer@uwe.ac.uk`

Abstract. There is a growing consensus that the perception of our body is emergent and has a plasticity that can be affected through techniques such as the Rubber Hand Illusion (RHI). Alongside this we are seeing increased capabilities in technologies that track and represent our movements on screen. This paper will examine these issues through the RHI and conditions such as Complex Regional Pain Syndrome (CRPS) and consider the possibilities offered by these technologies for therapeutic use. It addition it will examine the issues raised for all users, asserting that we have reached a point where we can no longer afford assume that these are merely tools of representation.

Keywords: Avatar, Body Image, Complex Regional Pain Syndrome, Motion Sickness, Emergent.

1   Introduction

This paper will propose that advances in computational graphics and physical computing have reached a point where they are no longer merely tools of representation. Instead it will argue that because perception is increasingly understood as an emergent phenomenon, the representation and 'mapping' that computing now provides can affect bodily perception. This will draw upon work conducted to develop a tool to allow patients with Complex Regional Pain Syndrome (CRPS) to describe their perceptions of their body.

It will initially outline the nature of CRPS and the way the altered bodily perceptions problematizes the communication of the condition for patients. Having drawn attention to the fact that the body is not the given we often assume to be, the problem of motion sickness and virtual systems will be considered. This will focus on research asserting that motion sickness does not arise from sensory conflict but needs to be considered as ecological and emergent phenomena.

We will then consider the Rubber Hand Illusion (RHI) and the plasticity of bodily perception it highlights, looking at how the representation of the body might affect its perception. This will draw upon recent research concerning the RHI and patients with CRPS as well as work examining the affect that varying the representation of movement can have upon patients with Fibromyalgia. The paper will then return to examine these issues in relation to the discoveries made through the creation of a body

R. Shumaker and S. Lackey (Eds.): VAMR 2014, Part I, LNCS 8525, pp. 293–304, 2014.
© Springer International Publishing Switzerland 2014

image tool for use with patients with CRPS. The paper will then conclude by considering the opportunities and dangers that the combination of physical computing and representation present in therapeutic settings and normal use.

2　Complex Regional Pain Syndrome

Phantom Limb Syndrome (PLS) and Complex Regional Pain Syndrome (CRPS) were both identified by Dr Silas Weir Mitchell during the American civil war. Although now relatively well known, PLS had been thought to be an unusual phenomenon experienced by a limited number of amputees; often the condition was not reported as amputees feared they would not be believed or thought mentally affected. Now it's widely recognized as a common experience among amputees [1].

Similar circumstances appear to have affected our understanding of CRPS. CRPS is a chronic pain condition associated with the body's extremities affecting single or multiple limbs. The pain experienced often involves extreme and contradictory sensations of heat. There can also be the perception of the dramatic enlargement of parts of a limb, or that parts are missing or do not belong to their body [2, 3]. The affected region can possess heightened sensitivity and painful reactions to everyday sensations such as the touch of clothing, yet alongside this sensory discrimination in the affected region is reduced. The result is that patient's perception of their affected limb is different from its objective appearance and people with CRPS have reported they have found it hard to talk about their experiences of altered body perception. Indeed the frustration of trying to understand and convey their symptoms caused one of the patients we worked with to say that 'I really thought I was losing it.'

At present there are no objective tests for CRPS so diagnosis relies on signs and symptoms meeting a diagnostic checklist [4]. CRPS is defined as either CRPS-I or II dependent on the presence (II) or absence (I) of identifiable nerve damage. The condition is thought to be initially triggered by a peripheral insult but it rapidly evolves into a centrally driven condition for which there is currently no cure. Self-portrait sketches or drawings made by therapists are currently used to monitor changes in the condition, but this is limited by the individual's capacity to draw. As a result of this in 2010 a team at the UWE Bristol and the Royal National Hospital for Rheumatic Diseases in Bath instigated a project examining the use of tool utilizing a 3D avatar to monitor these changes. We will examine the results arising from testing the tool in a clinical setting; however prior to doing this we will challenge the assumptions that are often made concerning the perception of our own body.

3　Motion Sickness

Developers using the Oculus Rift have encountered significant problems with motion sickness. The source appears to be a problem present since the invention of immersive virtual reality (IVR) [5] deriving from the latency between the use of sensors to gain motion data and its use to update the users' view, resulting in motion that is felt but not immediately seen. Alongside this the use of virtual motion that does not possess a physical equivalent, results in 'movement' that is seen but not felt. It's thought that conflict between these perceptions of motion result in the body assuming it has absorbed a toxin, the sensation of nausea and the resulting 'desire' to evacuate it.

The supposition that motion sickness results from a conflict between visual and vestibular data has been unchallenged for over 100 years [6] even though blind people experience motion sickness [7]. Within the digital motion sickness is not limited to IVR and significant numbers experience it playing video games [8] and the cause has again been assumed to be a conflict between vision and the vestibular system. Whilst some are more prone than others, the recording of game play has allowed active and passive subjects to be exposed to the same visual and vestibular stimuli [9]. What was discovered was that the incidence of motion sickness was significantly increased in 'passive' subjects. If subjects significantly increase their chance of experiencing nausea simply due to the passive nature of the experience, discordance no longer appears to be a sufficient condition for motion sickness.

Work by Stroffregen [10] has shown suffers of motion sickness exhibit a postural instability prior to the onset of symptoms which is absent from those free of motion sickness. He has proposed that rather than arising from sensory incompatibility, motion sickness arises from an inability to maintain posture. The 'edge' players appear to have over those who passively experiencing virtual environments arises from their ability to anticipate and accommodate changes within the virtual environment, thereby lessening its impact upon their posture. The relationship between subject, environment and action is described by Stroffregen as the ecological approach to perception. Action is the fundamental 'unit of analysis' such that no one factor can be examined separately; the relationship between the body and its environment being central to maintaining stability. Focused as we are on tasks within an environment, environmental changes can impair our stability and affect our ability to act. We can use this instability to determine changes to the environment and adapt to them (such as when we gain 'sea legs'). As a result Stoffregen refers to sensory conflict as '*hypothetical; ...an interpretation of facts, rather than a fact itself*'. Rather than possessing senses that have individual frames of reference that compete suggesting incompatible states, '*Patterns of intermodal stimulation make available information about properties of the environment that influence the control of behavior*' [10]. The information that arises between senses differs from that which is derived from individual senses, as such he asserts this as an emergent property.

The question this begs is that if an ecological approach to perception and action is the fundamental 'unit of analysis' and knowledge of the environment is an emergent process, as a part of this might not the body need to be considered in the same way?

4   The Rubber Hand Illusion and Representation

Through what has become known as the rubber hand illusion (RHI) cognitive neuroscience has demonstrated that there is plasticity in the perception of the body. Discovered by Botvinick and Cohen [11] the RHI results in participants perceiving a rubber hand belongs to their body. This was achieved by placing a life size rubber in front of a participant, whilst placing their own hand close but hidden from view behind a standing screen. Participants were asked to look at the rubber hand whilst their and the rubber hand were brushed simultaneously. All ten of the participants taking part in their study reported that at some stage they felt the sensation where they saw the rubber hand and many stated they felt that the rubber hand was their own. Participants were also exposed to the illusion for periods of up to half an hour. After they were asked to move their free hand along a straight edge under the table until it aligned with the position they perceived their other hand. It was found that this caused a shift in participants' perception between the perceived and actual position of their hand (referred to in later studies as a proprioceptive drift) dependent on duration of the illusion. Botvinick and Cohen proposed this was the result of the 'spurious reconciliation of visual and tactile inputs' distorting participants' sense of position. Like motion sickness notions of sensory conflict underpin this, but here a reconciliation of those sensations has been assumed, but what might allow this? Is, as is often assume, my body a given onto which sensation is mapped effectively shaping perception or is the body built from its sensations?

Tsakiris and Haggard [12] sought to examine this. To test if there was a top down influence, they investigated whether congruent and incongruent positioning of real and rubber hands would influence susceptibility to the illusion. In additions tests to see if a neutral object might be incorporated into the body were used. Incongruent positioning involved turning the rubber hand -900 so its fingertips pointed towards the hidden hand in what would be an anatomically improbable position. Although the RHI occurred using congruent positioning, incongruent positioning and the neutral object both led to its absence. Their use of a neutral object also resulted in a proprioceptive drift away from the object which they described as a 'perceptual repulsion'. This was contrary to the earlier results of Armel & Ramachandran [13] who appeared to show a neutral object (which in their tests was a table top) could become incorporated into the body schema. Tsakiris and Haggard proposed this repulsion was the outcome if self-attribution did not to occur.

They examined whether the RHI involved a bottom up association of sensation by stimulating individual fingers and asking participants to indicate the perceived position of an adjacent digit. If the illusion involved a bottom up process the test might demonstrate significant differences in the perceived relative positions of digits following stimulation. The outcome was that although there was some drift, it was not significant and broadly relative to the fingers receiving the stimulation. Given that the RHI did not occur with incongruent positioning and adjacent fingers 'followed' stimulated ones, Tsakiris and Haggard asserted that the illusion resulted from the integration of visual input with a pre-existing representation of the body; a bottom up combination of visual and tactile data was a necessary, but not sufficient condition in the creation of the illusion. However this already appears to make the assumption that perception results from one or the other; what if this were considered similarly to Stroffregen's ecological approach to motion sickness? What if the perception of our body is an emergent phenomenon that possesses a plasticity, but one where intermodal sensation reaches its 'own' perceptual limits?

Ehrsson, Holmes and Passingham [14] felt it was ... *important to find out whether an illusory feeling of ownership can be induced in the absence of visual input...* Blindfolding participants, they moved the subjects own hand to touch the rubber hand whilst simultaneously touching the participants remaining hand in the 'same' place and discovered the RHI could be generated using synchronous touch *without* the involvement of vision. Contrary to Tsakiris and Haggard's assertion that visual and tactile data is a *necessary* condition for the RHI, the discovery that the RHI can be created without the active involvement of vision means this may not be the case.

Further research by Petkova, Zetterberg and Ehrsson [15] has shown that although the direct involvement of vision is not required in itself, vision appears to influence our capacity to experience the RHI. Referring to Ehrsson's earlier work as the "somatic" RHI they describe how it was used "to compare the multisensory representation of the body in blind and sighted individuals." This involved a comparison between participants who had been blind since birth and a group of aged matched sighted participants. Their outcomes were remarkably clear in that only 10% of blind compared to 67% of sighted participants experienced the illusion in any way. Additionally blind participants stated the illusion was "totally absurd" or that "they could not even imagine the illusion".

As possible explanation for the lack of the RHI in the blind group they noted behavioral studies showing those who have been blind since birth do not appear to map somatosensory sensation in external co-ordinates the way the sighted do [16, 17, 18, 19]. The lack of visual experience appears to effect the way other sensations work together, influencing the way the body is perceived. The phenomenologist Edmund Husserl stated that "The Body is in the first place the medium of all perception...the zero point of orientation... "[20]. Although the body is an object with parts that can be perceived "just like other things" [21] Husserl notes this only applies to visual appearances and that visual perception of our own body is not the same as tactile sensation, something touching which is touched [22]. In fact Husserl asserted that a "subject whose only sense was the sense of vision could not at all have an appearing body" [23]. What is interesting about Petkova's work is that that the sensation of the touching which is touched appears to only occur in those who have had sight, here there is a mapping of two sensations so they become one. The RHI appears to be the result of the hand touching and the one which is touched being 'pulled' into the same space.

But does any of this apply to virtual or augmented reality? Ehrsson et al [24] explored whether the illusion could be generated using a virtual limb. Computer graphics were used to provide users with a stereoscopic 3D view of a virtual arm extended in front of them. The outcome was that participants' sense of possession of the virtual arm was broadly similar to those demonstrated in the RHI. Yuan and Steed [25] took this further by testing whether this might be experienced within IVR and "an illusion very similar to the rubber hand illusion is "automatically" induced by active use of the virtual body in an IVR." Their use of a head mounted display provided a first person perspective that occluded participants' views of the physical environment and their body. Asserting a weakness of prior RHI studies to have been the passivity of participants, users were asked to undertake a series of tasks using their right hand to hold a wand to control virtual tasks such as placing 'balls' through 'holes' in a 'table'. Their left was immobile to enable the placement of galvanic skin response (GSR) sensors and avoid any movement that might introduce unwanted variability to the data. Since participants were seated at a table, this also enabled the use of the wand to judge the position of the user's arm using inverse kinematics and to appropriately 'map' the position of the avatar's arm to the user's. Using questions broadly similar to Botvinick and Cohen's their results showed participants experiencing a similar sense of ownership as seen in the RHI, as well as a rejection of the illusion when using a neutral 'object'. The GSR demonstrated that threat to the virtual body produced a positive response. As a result Yuan and Steed claimed they had 'shown that an "IVR arm ownership illusion" exists'. Given the work of Ehrsson and Steed we can see that the effect of the RHI can be extended from the physical into the virtual worlds.

Recent work by Reinersmann has examined the susepticablity of those with CRPS to the RHI [26]. The expectation was that patients with CRPS would not experience the illusion due to the disruption to cortical plasticity assumed to exist as a result of the condition [27]. Contrary to expectations those with CRPS experienced the RHI illusion to the same extent as healthy participants. However it was found that patients who felt strongly that their affected limb did not belong to them experienced a weaker form of the illusion. However understanding a 'normalized' perception of the body as intact and CRPS as something that breaks this representation may be problematic. If bodily perception is emergent, rather than being broken, what we may be seeing is a comples system that is being expressed differently. What is particulary interesting is the reduced level of the RHI in those who did not feel their own limb belonged to them. Given that the RHI occurs within CRPS, we should perhaps first consider whether factors that affect the creation of the RHI in other groups might be at work within CRPS. Given that CRPS patients experience their limb to be different to its visual appearance, the 'perceptual repulsion' a neutral object has been shown to generate in the work of Tsakiris and Haggard might be the underlying cause of this.

As Yuan and Steed noted many of the studies involving the RHI have not included activity. Here it is interesting to note a study involving Fibromyalgia (FMS). FMS is a condition similar to CRPS with symptoms including widespread pain, hypersensitivity to sensory stimuli, phantom swelling of limbs, reduced sensitivity to the position of limbs and motor abnormalities such as tremors or slowness in movement. Investigating whether these symptoms might be the result of a dysfunctional relationship between motor and sensory systems McCabe et al [28] conducted tests using a mirror/whiteboard to create varying degrees of sensory conflict through the representation of congruent/incongruent limb movements. The outcome was that 89.7% (26 out of 29) of patients with FMS reported changes in perception compared with 48% of a healthy control group. The sensations included "... disorientation, pain, perceived changes in temperature, limb weight or body image. Subjects described how these symptoms were similar to those they experienced in a "flare" of their FMS. This led us to conclude that some sensory disturbances in FMS may be perpetuated by a mismatch between motor output and sensory feedback." Whilst appearing to play a role within FMS, we should note that healthy participants also reported changes in perception. Rather than being a phenomena linked to the pathology of FMS, the results appear to indicate the underlying 'structure' of sensation is such that incongruent representation of movement can also affect body perception in healthy subjects. The impact of FMS appears to make those who suffer from the condition all the more vulnerable to new anomalies. Clearly results such as these ought to be of concern to anybody making use of systems that track and represent the movements of users.

5   Unseen Truths

The contradictory sensations experiences resulting from CRPS make it difficult for patients to talk about their condition. As one noted of their experiences prior to diagnosis "*...it's a very strange thing ... I really thought I was losing it.*" Following a diagnosis of CRPS, self-portrait sketches or drawings made by clinicians are used in its assessment. This can be revealing because patients often haven't fully engaged with these sensations, appearing to keep these contradictions at a distance rather than 'inhabit' the sensation. As one patient noted "*...it's quite new to me because I hadn't really thought about this until I came in here.*" In addition the differences between sensation and appearance was often commented upon *The right side of my whole body actually feels quite normal, there no problem with that I don't have any difference in perception to what I see with that...*

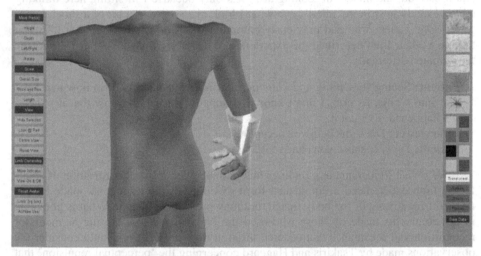

Fig. 1. Image Created of CRPS affected limb using the second version of the tool which added the ability to use particle effects to depict sensations

A specification for the tool was established using data from a previous study of body perception [29] and consultation with a person with CRPS. It was decided the tool should allow the manipulation of the scale, position and surface texture of body segments whilst allowing these to be removed if desired. Scaling would include the length and making parts thicker and thinner. The movement of parts was to allow their separation as well as their placement in anatomically impossible positions. Colors and textures were to aim to provide an opportunity to represent feelings of burning, cold, rough, smooth and lack of substance. Finally the tool should allow the camera to orbit the 'avatar'. A prototype was created that fulfilled these criteria and the research was approved by the Local NHS Research Ethics Committee and the tool was tested with consenting patients.

Ten participants used the first version of the application in a single consultation with the research nurse. Audio recordings were made of the participants using the application allowing immediate reactions to the tool to be captured. Immediately after using the tool participants were asked to complete a structured questionnaire with the research nurse with questions to ascertain their views and experience of using the tool. When asked 'Did you find using the body perception application an acceptable way to communicate how you view or feel about your limb or body parts?' all participants reported that it was a good method; for themselves and to help clinicians understand their perceptions of their body. They were also unanimous in the view that the tool was better than the standard interview undertaken earlier in their admission and was much more adaptable than a clinician's sketch and found it easy to use in consultation with the research nurse. Because discussing their condition can raise their levels of pain participants were also asked whether using the tool caused increased pain and distress. In most cases this was not an issue but in some instances increased pain was experienced, but what was surprising was that benefits were also expressed "It wasn't that I disliked using it, it's just... for me as I say to visualize that how I feel I felt a bit emotional, but the more I'm looking at it, it's only because I'm sitting here thinking that is exactly how in my mind's eye what I look like so it was a bit of a shock I suppose." One patient who had previously commented "I don't like looking at it" when talking of their limb described the experience of the Body Image Tool and the image they created differently...

> **Patient:** Seeing something and knowing that it's your hand is errm how can I put that into words, its erm, I don't know it I suppose accepting now that it's there, it's happened, I've got it..
> **Interviewer:** Does this help you accept it?
> **Patient:** *Yeah*, because you can see it...

If we revisit Reinersmann's findings that patients with a stronger rejection of an affected limb experienced a diminished form of the RHI, the comments made by patients during testing of the body image tool may provide an insight. What is noticable in the comments made by those who used the body image tool are the moments of recognition and acceptance that occured through its use. Here we should consider the observations made by Tsakiris and Haggard concerning the 'perceptual repulsion' that occurred if self-attribution of the rubber hand did not to occur. Patients often commented upon the difference they preceived between the sensation and appearance of their limb. Often these are not 'minor' contradictions, the disparity between experience and appearance is often marked "I know there are fingers there and I even move them, I can't see fingers when I try closing my eyes to see it, I don't see anything, I just see a big blob..." One patient commented that when they saw their physical limb "There is a sense now of repulsion, I think is the word, I don't like looking at it." Given this it seems that the lack of the RHI in those who felt that their limb didn't belong to them could plausablily result from the sense that the limb didn't belong to them.Nevertheless it is also important to note that overall the discovery was that those with CRPS experienced the RHI, as a result it may be that those who did not experience it had reached the kind of intersensory limit that prevented its formation. In relation to these instances it would be interesting to know if a more accurate depiction of the affected limb, perhaps using the combination of the body image tool and an augmented reality system such as that used by Ehrsson et al [24] would alter the veracity of the illusion.

The treatment of CRPS and PLS has also involved the use of Graded Motor Imagery (GMI). GMS is a development of a technique used by Ramachandran to treat PLS [30]. It uses a series of graded steps to treat the pain associated with a range of conditions related to the nervous system. Patients suffering from these conditions often exhibit a diminished ability to be able to discriminate between images of the part affected from the left and right hand side of the body. The first step of the treatment involves showing patients a series of images asking them to identify which side of the body they belong, with the exercises being aimed at increasing the ability to discriminate through changes achieved via perceptual plasticity. The next step is to ask patients to imagine moving their affected limb with the aim being that the activity exercises mirror neurons associated with the effected limb. Finally the use of mirror box is employed to see the affected limb moving (which in Ramachandran's work led to a reduction in the painful clenching felt within the phantom limb) and within conditions such as CRPS to gradually encourage actual movement of the affected limb alongside the one being mirrored. Moseley has achieved a noticeable reduction of the pain suffered by patients with CRPS and PLS [31] however this has so far not been something that has been reproduced in clinical settings [32]. Indeed was noted that

> "As GMI is now recommended practice, it is important to understand that treatment failure is not necessarily a patient's or a therapist's fault, but may reflect that we do not yet fully understand what the active ingredients of this complex intervention are, and how it interacts with other therapeutic strategies."

As we have seen if it is the case that patients with CRPS may not experience the RHI due to a 'repulsion' based on an incompatibility between the felt experience and appearance of a limb this might also affect the capacity of GMI as an intervention. In fact incongruent motions might have a negative effect. Once again a starting point might be the use of a virtual limb attuned to the perceived experience of the patient might achieve outcomes where they are able to identify with the image more immediately.

6   Conclusion

Stroffregen has noted that improvements in technology are leading to an increase in the reports of its side effects [32]. The effects go beyond those of motion sickness and include changes in users' movements after the use of these systems. He notes that

> "Enactive interface systems, such as Wii and Kinect, are associated with widespread anecdotal reports of motion sickness.
>   Ignoring this problem is not likely to make it go away. Similarly, the use of disclaimers (e.g., "use of this product may lead to motion sickness") is a legal rather than a practical solution."

Indeed he goes on to note that

> "Rather than relying on brute technological development, a meaningful solution to the problem of interface side effects will need to emerge from a better understanding of the perceptual-motor dynamics of human movement."

Given that work by McCabe [28] has demonstrated that the use of the incongruent representation of limb movements can create symptoms similar to FMS in healthy participants, the perceptual dynamics to which Stroffregen goes beyond the relationship that exists between the body and the environment. What we now have to address are the perceptual dynamics that inform the perception of the body itself. At present most tracking technologies are simply applied to avatars with idealized proportions. In some instances the disparity between the ideal and the real may be such that it will affect the user's perception of their body (beyond those pressures we usually associate with ideal physical forms).

Paradoxically we have also seen that the use of these technologies may provide more effective means to therapeutically track and address conditions such as CRPS. As a result of her findings Reinersmann notes that treatments should now include "interventions that address the distorted body image which appears to affect sensory functions in a top-down manner". In some ways this might first include the recognition and representation of the sensations experienced by those with CRPS. This might also be addressed in such a way that these are mapped onto an avatar which they move through motion tracking. Interestingly one possible (although not favored) reasons for the greater level of success achieved by Moseley's use of GMI was that "Reducing Pain related fear in CRPS may actually reduce pain and perhaps the clinicians in the RCTs better captured this effect" [32]. The spatial awareness of those with CRPS is affected by the condition and often limbs are held out of harm's way; it may be the case that representing the proportions of the limb as it is perceived might allow a greater confidence in moving the limb. Given that no references are made to the range of movement made using the affected limb by the participants in either the RDC or clinical use of GMI the 'active ingredients of' a 'complex intervention' might involve tracking the movements of both limbs involved. It is also the case that the use of tracking technology and the use a virtual mirror might also allow the appropriate differentiation in motion between limbs to be shown to participants as they enter the third stage of their treatment.

Stroffregen has noted that one solution to motion sickness might be to "design interfaces that are deliberately different form the relevant real-world situations." Anyone who has suffered motion sickness due to the head bob used in games such as Call-of-Duty will probably prefer a first person view that does not do this. What is interesting is that a simpler approach does not diminish an interface but makes it more effective. For a very long time the activity of artists has focused on stripping out unwanted sensation in order to drive at the heart of a matter. Although we might use the phrase 'less is more' when talking about such activity achieving less requires a greater insight into the matter at hand. Gaining an understanding of how representations of the body and its movements will allow us to achieve this in such a way it benefits users and will allow the development of new therapeutic techniques and systems.

References

1. Fraser, C.M., Halligan, P.W., Robertson, I.H., Kirker, S.G.B.: Characterising phantom limb phenomena in upper limb amputees. Prosthetics and Orthotics International 25, 235–242 (2001)
2. Moseley, L.: Distorted body image in complex regional pain syndrome. Neurology 65, 773 (2005)
3. Lewis, J.S., Kersten, P., McCabe, C.S., McPherson, K., Blake, D.: Body perception disturbance: A contribution to pain in Complex Regional Pain Syndrome. PAIN 133(1-3), 111–119 (2007)
4. Harden, R.N., Bruehl, S., Perez, R.S.: Validation of proposed diagnostic criteria (the "Budapest Criteria") for Complex Regional Pain Syndrome. Pain 150(2), 268–274 (2010)
5. Kolasinski, E.: US Army Research Institute. 19950630 166. United States Army Research (1995)
6. Irwin, J.: The pathology of seasickness. Lancet 2, 907–909 (1881)
7. Ashton, G.: Susceptibility To Acute Motion Sicknes. Blind Persons Aerospace Med. 41, 650 (1970)
8. Merhi, O., Faugloire, E., Flanagan, M., Stroffregen, T.: Motion Sickness, Console Video Games, and Head-Mounted Displays. Human Factors 49(5) (2007)
9. Chen, Y., Dong, X., Chen, F., Stroffregen, T.: Control of a Virtual Avatar Influences Postural Activity and Motion Sickness. Ecological Psychology (November 2012)
10. Riccio, G., Stroffregen, T.: An Ecological Theory of Motion Sickness and Postural Instability. Ecological Psychology, 195–240 (1991)
11. Botvinick, M., Cohen, J.: Rubber hands 'feel' touch that eyes see. Nature 391, 756 (1998)
12. Tsakiris, M., Haggard, P.: The Rubber Hand Illusion Revisited: Visuotactile Integration and Self-Attribution. Journal of Experimental Psychology: Human Perception and Performance 31(1), 80–91 (2005)
13. Armel, K.C., Ramachandran, V.S.: Projecting sensations to external objects: Evidence from skin conductance response. Proceedings of the Royal Society of London: Biological 270, 1499–1506 (2003)
14. Ehrsson, H., Holmes, N.P., Passingham, R.E.: Touching a Rubber Hand: Feeling of Body Ownership Is Associated with Activity in Multisensory Brain Areas. The Journal of Neuroscience 25(45), 10564–10573 (2005)
15. Petkova, V., Zetterberg, H., Ehrsson, H.: Rubber Hands Feel Touch, but Not in Blind Individuals. PLoS One 7(4) (2012)
16. Röder, B., Rösler, F., Spence, C.: Early vision impairs tactile perception in the blind. Curr. Biol. 14, 121–124 (2004)
17. Röder, B., Kusmierek, A., Spence, C., Schicke, T.: Developmental vision determines the reference frame for the multisensory control of action. Proc. Natl. Acad. Sci. U.S.A. 104, 4753–4758 (2007)
18. Azanon, E., Longo, M.R., Soto-Faraco, S., Haggard, P.: The posterior parietal cortex remaps touch into external space. Curr. Biol. 20, 1304–1309 (2010)
19. Yamamoto, S., Kitazawa, S.: Reversal of subjective temporal order due to arm crossing. Nat. Neuroscience 4, 759–765 (2001)
20. Husserl, E.: Ideas Pertaining to a Pure Phenomenology and to a Phenomenological Philosophy Book 2, p. 61. Kluwer (Original work published posthumously 1952), Dordrecht (1980); (Rojcewicz, R., Schuwer, A., trans.)

21. Ibid, p.152
22. Ibid, p.155
23. Ibid, p.158
24. Slater, M., Perez-Marcos, Ehrsson, H., Sanchez-Vives, M.V.: Towards a digital body: the virtual arm illusion. Frontiers in Human Neuroscience 2, Article 6 (2008)
25. Yuan, Y., Steed, A.: Is the Rubber Hand Illusion Induced by Immersive Virtual Reality? In: IEEE Virtual Reality 2010, pp. 95–102 (2010)
26. Reinersmann, A., Ocklenburg, S., Landwehrt, J., Krumova, E.K., Der Schmerz, M.C.: The rubber hand illusion in patients with complex regional pain syndrome. Successful illusion induction shows multisensory integration [Article in German] Der Schmerz 27(5), 513–516 (2013)
27. Swart, K., Stins, J., Beek, P.: Cortical Changes in complex regional pain syndrome (CRPS). European Journal of Pain (2008)
28. McCabe, C.S., Cohen, H., Hall, J., Lewis, J., Rodham, K., Harris, N.: Somatosensory Conflicts in Complex Regional Pain Syndrome Type 1 and Fibromyalgia Syndrome. Current Rheumatology Reports 11, 461–465 (2009)
29. Lewis, J.S., Kersten, P., McCabe, C.S., McPherson, K., Blake, D.: Body perception disturbance: A contribution to pain in Complex Regional Pain Syndrome. PAIN 133(1-3), 111–119 (2007)
30. Ramachandran, V.S., Rogers-Ramachandran, D.: Synaesthesia in Phantom Limbs Induced with Mirrors Proceedings of the Royal. Society of London 263(1369), 377–386 (1996)
31. Moseley, G.: Graded motor imagery for pathologic pain - A randomized controlled trial. Neurology 67, 2129–2134 (2006)
32. Johnson, S., Hall, J., Barnett, S., Draper, M., Derbyshire, G., Haynes, L., Rooney, C., Cameron, H., Moseley, G.L., de, C., Williams, A.C., McCabe, C., Goebel, A.: Using graded motor imagery for complex regional pain syndrome in clinical practice: Failure to improve pain. European Journal of Pain. Apr. 16(4), 550–561 (2012)
33. Stroffregen, T.: Interface solutions for interface side effects? In: BIO Web of Conferences, vol. 1 (2011)

How Does Varying Gaze Direction Affect Interaction between a Virtual Agent and Participant in an On-Line Communication Scenario?

Adam Qureshi[1], Christopher Peters[2], and Ian Apperly[3]

[1] Edge Hill University, Psychology Department Ormskirk, Lancashire, UK
[2] KTH Royal Institute of Technology, School of Computer Science and Communication, Valhallavagen 79, 100 44 Stockholm, Sweden
[3] University of Birmingham, School of Psychology Edgbaston, Birmingham, UK
qureshia@edgehill.ac.uk, chpeters@kth.se, i.a.apperly@bham.ac.uk

Abstract. Computer based perspective taking tasks in cognitive psychology often utilise static images and auditory instructions to assess online[1] communication. Results are then explained in terms of theory of mind (the ability to understand that other agents have different beliefs, desires and knowledge to oneself).The current study utilises a scenario in which participants were required to select objects in a grid after listening to instructions from an on-screen director. The director was positioned behind the grid from the participants' view. As objects in some slots were concealed from the view of the director, participants needed to take the perspective of the director into account in order to respond accurately. Results showed that participants reliably made errors, attributable to not using the information from the director's perspective efficiently, rather than not being able to take the director's perspective. However, the fact that the director was represented by a static sprite meant that even for a laboratory based experiment, the level of realism was low. This could have affected the level of participant engagement with the director and the task. This study, a collaboration between computer science and psychology, advances the static sprite model by incorporating head movement into a more realistic on-screen director with the aim of a.) Improving engagement and b.) investigating whether gaze direction affects accuracy and response times of object selection. Results suggest that gaze direction can influence the speed of accurate object selection, but only slightly and in certain situations; specifically those complex enough to warrant the participant paying additional attention to gaze direction and those that highlight perspective differences between themselves and the director. This in turn suggests that engagement with a virtual agent could be improved by taking these factors into account.

Keywords: Theory of mind, on-line communication, gaze direction, engagement.

1   Introduction

The aim of this study is to develop existing studies that have used static images in order to assess online communication [1] and have assessed gaze direction as a

---

[1] Online in this context means active interaction with an agent, not online as in internet-based communication.

R. Shumaker and S. Lackey (Eds.): VAMR 2014, Part I, LNCS 8525, pp. 305–316, 2014.
© Springer International Publishing Switzerland 2014

facilitatory factor [6], and relate the findings to engagement. This was achieved by manipulating the gaze direction of a director who instructed participants to select objects in an online communication scenario. This builds on [1] by incorporating head movement in order to change the gaze direction of the director and on [6] by including a condition that is predicted to inhibit correct object selection by the participant. As the rationale for the study and predictions derive from both theory of mind and communication literature, the introduction will cover each of these in turn, followed by a description of the prior studies methodologies.

1.1   Theory of Mind

Theory of mind is commonly defined as the ability to understand that others have different beliefs and mental states to you [11]. In addition, it also covers the ability to compute another person's perspective and to use the information from that perspective [12]. It also refers to being able to use that information to interpret behaviour or utterances.

The majority of psychological research on theory of mind has been developmental [12], and the classic test of theory of mind understanding is the false belief task [15]. Explicit understanding of false beliefs has been shown to develop by around 4-6 years old [15]. More recent studies have found that perspective-taking ability develops in infants [7] prior to the ability to pass false belief tasks.

The development of theory of mind has been associated with executive function and language ability [3] [5]. There is evidence that perspective-taking is cognitively efficient and automatic [12], but that more complex processes (such as false belief inferences) require executive processes [4]. Perhaps analogously, selecting perspectives is also thought to require executive processes [12]. This is supported by evidence from animal studies that show that chimpanzees exhibit low-level perspective taking abilities but are unable to understand false beliefs [2].

In summary, theory of mind may involve a cognitively efficient, perhaps innate, module that allows us to take perspectives. Dealing with different perspectives with respect to selecting which one to process and/or take information from may require executive processes – the latter develop over infancy, perhaps explaining why infants are able to pass simple (and implicit) tasks requiring perspective taking, but are unable to pass explicit false belief tasks until approximately ages 4- 6. An ability requiring executive resources is likely to be more flexible than one that does not, but due to this requirement it is also more error-prone and likely slower.

1.2   Communication

Theory of mind appears key to successful communication, as research on everyday communication [4] and conversational pragmatics [13] [14] suggest that to successfully communicate speakers and listeners must be able to take account of one another's knowledge, beliefs and intentions. However, this research assumes either implicitly or explicitly that such inference and use of information about mental states occurs quickly and efficiently. Psychological research on theory of mind suggests that inferring mental states may well occur quickly and efficiently (c.f. cognitively efficient perspective taking) but that using that information may not (c.f. executive resources needed for perspective selection).

During communication in real life, listeners can often see a speaker's eyes, and evidence suggests that information about eye gaze is used rapidly online to resolve ambiguous reference [6]. Results suggest that eye gaze has an automatic, reflexive orientating effect on attention. However, this effect may not always be reflexive or hard-wired. There is evidence that eye gaze is a flexible cue that can be rapidly re-mapped – it is a source of information whose use can be modified according to communicative context. Eye gaze may then help in using information from a perspective once that perspective is calculated.

1.3   Experimental Method

Experiments in cognitive psychology often use static imagery to assess communication. The task developed in [1], based on a study by [7] required participants to move objects in a 4 x 4 grid as instructed by a director with an different perspective to the participant (Fig.1).

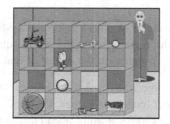

Fig. 1. Relational trial - instruction 'move the small ball one slot down'

The correct object was mutually visible to both the participant and director, whereas the competitor object was visible only to the participant. However, the competitor object was often a better referent to the instruction given.

Participants were shown the grid as it appeared from their own and from the director's perspective, so emphasizing the perspective-taking component of the task.

Critical instructions required the participant to make simple theory of mind inferences as they needed to calculate the perspective of the director and to use information from that perspective to interpret the instructions correctly.

Results showed participants made errors in object selection. The pattern of results suggested that they were able to calculate and take the director's perspective, but did not efficiently use the information gained. These errors suggest that participant fail to restrict the domain of potential reference to the 'common ground' of objects that were mutually visible / mutually known to themselves and the director.

Errors were attributed to egocentric bias: initial interpretation of an instruction (in this case) is based on information available to oneself, and "common ground" is optionally used to detect and correct errors from this initial interpretation [1] [7].

However, the director in the study was a static computer sprite wearing sunglasses. This experiment does not therefore include many cues which are normally part of conversation, such as eye gaze. As the eye gaze of a speaker is processed before the linguistic point of determination [6], this could suggest that participant's initial starting point is not egocentric: they attempt to use eye gaze to help resolve ambiguity before they hear any instructions. This means they do take information from other perspectives into account if a.) it is useful and b.) they are given the opportunity to do so. Processing of eye-gaze is low-level and relatively automatic (though can involve flexibility and remapping), but it is still a constraint whose influence can be weighted differently given the nature of the communicative context (c.f. other conversationally based sources of information).

This study [6] used instructions / referents that were ambiguous as to which object should be identified, but the eye gaze of the (human) director was always at the target object (facilitatory). The study that the current experiment is based on removed eye gaze as a factor by having the director wear sunglasses [1]. The current experiment builds on both studies by examining how participants deal with eye gaze as both a potentially facilitatory and inhibitory factor in object selection, and how this may be taken as a proxy for engagement with the director and their instructions.

2   Method

We used the design of [7] and [1] of a 4x4 grid, and systematically varied the gaze direction of the director in three conditions (the white square indicates the quadrant that the director is looking at, focusing on the center of that quadrant):

- Focus on mutually visible object (critical gaze, Figure 2 (R))
- Focus on an occluded object (competitor gaze, Figure 2 (L))
- No head movement (director looks straight ahead throughout the experiment)

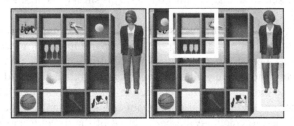

Fig. 2. Relational trial - instruction: 'move the small ball down one slot'. (L): Competitor gaze. (R): Critical gaze.

Participants were shown an example grid from their own perspective and also from the director's perspective, and were explicitly told that the director would have no knowledge of objects that were in slots that were covered from their side and that they could not see. Therefore participants were made aware that there was a difference in perspective between themselves and the director, and that it might be necessary to take the director's perspective into account in order to respond correctly.

The instructions took the form of critical, control and filler questions. Critical and control questions were either ambiguous (referring to one of two items with the same name) or relational (referring to one of three items differing in spatial location or size). Control and critical grids were identical apart from a filler item replacing the critical item in the former (Figure 2 (L) shows a critical relational grid with a golf ball as the best referent for the instruction, but the tennis ball as the correct response when taking the director's perspective into account; Figure 2 (R) shows a control relational grid with no object present in the top-right slot (in the actual experiment this slot was occupied by an airplane). The best referent for the control instruction (move the small ball down one slot), from both the participant and director's perspective, is the tennis ball).

We investigated how participants process eye gaze by using three gaze direction conditions: (1) Critical: when the gaze of the director focused on the center of the quadrant containing the correct object (mutually visible to both participant and director). (2) Competitor: when it is focused on the quadrant containing the competitor object (only visible to the participant, so possibly increasing interference between self perspective and information). (3) When it has no informational value to the participant (default condition, as in the original experiment).

Based on the pilot study of [1], which showed that static cartoon eyes (with no head movement) of the director was enough to give the impression that he was referring to specific objects in the array, we assume that gaze direction is an additional source of information available when computing another persons perspective. The default condition in this experiment has the director looking directly at the participant. There should be no information from that gaze direction that can be used by the participant with respect to object selection.

Previous work used a starting point of the director looking at the center of the grid. Anecdotal evidence suggested that some participants did not look at the director or take into account the head movement. In this study each trial with the director looking at the participant in order to capture attention and promote engagement. The control condition was also changed from prior studies, where the director's gaze was focused on the centre of the 4x4 grid, to one where the director looked directly at the participant for the duration of the trials. Again, this was due to anecdotal evidence that participants could not distinguish where the director's gaze was directed (between the competitor, critical and grid-center control conditions).

We assume that the computation of the director's perspective occurs in conjunction with processing of gaze direction: it is additional information contained within the information gained by computing another's perspective. This information could then facilitate use of this information (by focusing on the critical object quadrant – accentuating common ground), inhibit use of this information (by focusing on the competitor object quadrant, possibly enhancing privileged ground of participant), or neither (focus on the participant).

If eye gaze is a constraint that can be weighted differently given the nature of the communicative context, then it would be expected that when the information from gaze direction does not disambiguate the reference to an object (critical gaze) or interfere with the selection of the correct object (competitor gaze), then the participant would not need to use the information from gaze direction but only the information gained from computing the perspective of the director. Therefore errors should arise from not using the information from the perspective of the director as in the original study (default condition).

When gaze direction contains relevant information for the disambiguation of the reference to an object or interferes with the selection of the correct object, we assume that the participant will use this information in addition to the perspective of the director. As this information cues participants to the quadrant in which either the critical or competitor object is located, we predict that if the information gained from computing the director's perspective is used, the critical gaze condition will increase accuracy and decrease response times in selection of the correct critical object (accentuate common ground; prediction 1). We also predict that the competitor gaze condition will decrease accuracy and increase response times in selection of the correct critical object (accentuate privileged ground; prediction 2). And finally, the default condition, where the gaze direction is focused on the participant, is not predicted to affect accuracy or response times (prediction 3). We also predict that the level of engagement between the participant and director could be indicated by increased speed and accuracy in the facilitatory gaze direction condition, and decreased speed and accuracy in the competitor gaze direction condition; therefore:

Prediction 1) Focus on mutually visible object (critical condition) = ↑ accuracy, ↓RT
Prediction 2) Focus on occluded object (competitor condition) = ↓ accuracy, ↑ RT
Prediction 3) Focus on participant (default condition) = ~ accuracy, ~ RT

3   Results

3.1   Error Rates

A 3 x 2 x 2 mixed ANOVA was conducted, with gaze condition (competitor v critical v default) the between-subjects factor and trial condition (control v experimental) and trial type (ambiguous v relational) the within-subjects factors.

There was a main effect of trial condition (control < experimental; $F (1, 56) = 215.41$, $p \leq 0.01$, $\eta p2 = 0.79$), a main effect of trial type (ambiguous < relational; $F (1, 56) = 92.57$, $p \leq 0.01$, $\eta p2 = 0.62$). There was no main effect of gaze condition ($F (2, 56) = 1.88$, $p = 0.16$, $\eta p2 = 0.06$).

There was no interaction between trial condition and gaze condition ($F (2, 56) = 1.45$, $p = 0.24$, $\eta p2 = 0.05$) or between trial type and gaze condition ($F (2, 56) = 1.51$, $p = 0.23$, $\eta p2 = 0.05$). There was an interaction between trial condition and trial type ($F (1, 56) = 73.33$, $p \leq 0.01$, $\eta p2 = 0.57$) but not between gaze condition, trial condition and trial type ($F (2, 56) = 1.38$, $p = 0.26$, $\eta p2 = 0.05$).

The interaction between trial condition and trial type was investigated by collapsing the gaze condition factor. Analyses showed that there was a significant difference between the control and experimental trial conditions in the ambiguous trial type condition (control < experimental; $F (1, 58) = 133.46$, $p \leq 0.01$, $\eta p2 = 0.70$) and in the relational trial type condition ($F (1, 58) = 171.80$, $p \leq 0.01$, $\eta p2 = 0.75$).

There was a significant difference between ambiguous and relational trial types (ambiguous < relational) in the control trial condition ($F (1, 58) = 10.44$, $p \leq 0.01$, $\eta p2 = 0.15$) and in the experimental trial condition ($F (1, 58) = 83.34$, $p \leq 0.01$, $\eta p2 = 0.59$).

The pattern of the interaction replicates that found in [1]. The error rates are shown in Table 1.

Table 1. Error rates by gaze condition, trial condition and trial type

Condition (n)	Control (mean (sd))		Experimental (mean (sd))	
	Ambiguous	Relational	Ambiguous	Relational
Competitor (20)	0.10 (0.31)	0.25 (0.44)	1.75 (1.41)	4.15 (2.43)
Critical (21)	0.05 (0.22)	0.29 (0.46)	2.19 (1.44)	4.81 (2.82)
Default (18)	0.11 (0.32)	0.33 (0.59)	2.11 (0.90)	5.78 (2.44)

3.2 Response Times

A 3 x 2 x 2 mixed ANOVA was conducted, with gaze condition (competitor v critical v default) the between-subjects factor and trial condition (control v experimental) and trial type (ambiguous v relational) the within-subjects factors.

There was no main effect of trial condition (F (1, 58) = 3.44, p = 0.07, $\eta p2$ = 0.06), but there was a main effect of trial type (relational > ambiguous; F (1, 58) = 198.08, p $\leq$ 0.01, $\eta p2$ = 0.77). There was also no main effect of gaze condition (F (2, 58) = 1.70, p = 0.19, $\eta p2$ = 0.06).

There was no interaction between trial condition and gaze condition (F (2, 58) = 1.89, p = 0.16, $\eta p2$ = 0.06) or between trial type and gaze condition (F (2, 58) = 0.27, p = 0.76, $\eta p2$ = 0.01). There was an interaction between trial condition and trial type (F (1, 58) = 4.60, p = 0.04, $\eta p2$ = 0.07) and between gaze condition, trial condition and trial type (F (2, 58) = 3.35, p = 0.04, $\eta p2$ = 0.10).

The response times are shown in Table 2.

Table 2. Response time (ms) by gaze condition, trial condition and trial type

Condition (n)	Control (mean (sd))		Experimental (mean (sd))	
	Ambiguous (ms)	Relational (ms)	Ambiguous (ms)	Relational (ms)
Competitor (20)	2641.56 (451.77)	3422.32 (797.87)	2892.04 (685.24)	3198.75 (669.06)
Critical (21)	2545.97 (229.90)	3098.36 (288.70)	2800.05 (381.31)	3262.76 (515.25)
Default (20)	2566.35 (288.75)	3028.32 (326.88)	2582.67 (291.97)	3076.08 (405.73)

The interaction between trial condition and trial type was investigated by collapsing the gaze condition factor. Analyses showed that there was a significant difference between the control and experimental trial conditions in the ambiguous trial type condition (control < experimental; F (1, 60) = 15.70, p $\leq$ 0.01, $\eta p2$ = 0.21) but not in the relational trial type condition (F (1, 60) = 0.00, p = 0.99, $\eta p2$ = 0.00).

There was a significant difference between ambiguous and relational trial types (ambiguous < relational) in the control trial condition (F $_{(1, 60)}$ = 180.94, $p \leq 0.01$, η_p^2 = 0.75) and in the experimental trial condition (F $_{(1, 60)}$ = 41.62, $p \leq 0.01$, η_p^2 = 0.41).

This is shown in Figure 3:

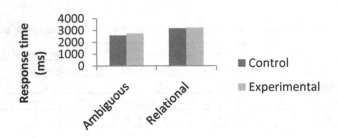

Fig. 3. Response time by trial condition and trial type (collapsed across gaze condition)

The interaction between gaze condition, trial condition and trial type was initially investigated by separate 2 x 2 within-subjects ANOVAs (trial condition x trial type).

Competitor Gaze Condition. There was no main effect of trial condition (F $_{(1, 19)}$ = 0.02, p = 0.90, η_p^2 = 0.00), but there was a main effect of trial type (ambiguous < relational; F $_{(1, 19)}$ = 57.37, $p \leq 0.01$, η_p^2 = 0.75) and an interaction between trial condition and trial type (F $_{(1, 60)}$ = 6.21, $p \leq 0.02$, η_p^2 = 0.25). There was a main effect of trial condition (control < experimental) in the ambiguous trials (F $_{(1, 19)}$ = 8.76, $p \leq$ 0.05, η_p^2 = 0.32) but not in the relational trials (F $_{(1, 19)}$ = 1.54, p = 0.23, η_p^2 = 0.01). There was a main effect of trial type (ambiguous < relational) in the control trials (F $_{(1, 19)}$ = 54.72, $p \leq 0.01$, η_p^2 = 0.74) and in the experimental trials (F $_{(1, 19)}$ = 5.45, $p \leq$ 0.05, η_p^2 = 0.22), though the latter effect was much smaller.

Critical gaze Condition. There was a main effect of trial condition (control < experimental; F $_{(1, 20)}$ = 7.34, $p \leq 0.05$, η_p^2 = 0.27), a main effect of trial type (ambiguous < relational) F $_{(1, 20)}$ = 57.87, $p \leq 0.01$, η_p^2 = 0.73) but no interaction between trial condition and trial type (F $_{(1, 20)}$ = 0.48, p = 0.50, η_p^2 = 0.02). There was a main effect of trial condition (control < experimental) in the ambiguous trials (F $_{(1, 19)}$ = 8.95, $p \leq$ 0.05, η_p^2 = 0.31) but not in the relational trials (F $_{(1, 19)}$ = 2.06, p = 0.17, η_p^2 = 0.09). There was a main effect of trial type (ambiguous < relational) in the control trials (F $_{(1, 19)}$ = 121.37, $p \leq 0.01$, η_p^2 = 0.86) and in the experimental trials (F $_{(1, 19)}$ = 14.46, $p \leq$ 0.01, η_p^2 = 0.42), though the latter effect was smaller.

Default Gaze Condition. There was no main effect of trial condition (F $_{(1, 19)}$ = 0.47, p = 0.50, η_p^2 = 0.02). There was a main effect of trial type (ambiguous < relational; F $_{(1, 19)}$ = 107.17, $p \leq 0.01$, η_p^2 = 0.85), but no interaction between trial condition and trial type (F $_{(1, 19)}$ = 0.11, p = 0.74, η_p^2 = 0.01). There was a main effect of trial type (ambiguous < relational) in the control trials (F $_{(1, 19)}$ = 95.04, $p \leq 0.01$, η_p^2 = 0.83) and in the experimental trials (F $_{(1, 19)}$ = 37.68, $p \leq 0.01$, η_p^2 = 0.67), though the latter effect was slightly smaller. There was no main effect of trial condition in the ambiguous trials (F $_{(1, 19)}$ = 0.16, p = 0.69, η_p^2 = 0.01) or in the relational trials (F $_{(1, 19)}$ = 0.32, p = 0.58, η_p^2 = 0.02).

A one-way ANOVA was conducted to investigate the differences between the gaze conditions for the different trial condition and trial type combinations. There was no main effect for control ambiguous trials (F (2, 58) = 0.46, p = 0.64, $\eta p2$ = 0.02), experimental ambiguous trials (F (2, 58) = 2.18, p = 0.12, $\eta p2$ = 0.07) or experimental relational trials (F (2, 58) = 0.63, p = 0.54, $\eta p2$ = 0.02). There was a marginally significant effect for control relational trials F (2, 58) = 3.26, p $\leq$ 0.05, $\eta p2$ = 0.10, though post-hoc tests revealed there were no significant differences (all p's > 0.05). The overall pattern of results is shown in Figure 4.

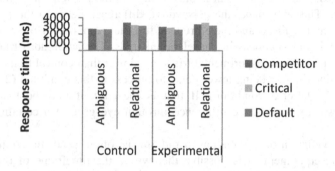

Fig. 4. Response time by gaze condition, trial condition and trial type

The error rates show no difference between the gaze conditions and replicate the findings of [1]. Although there are also no differences between gaze conditions in response times, there is an interaction between gaze condition, trial condition and trial type. Further analyses suggest that this interaction is caused by there being a significant difference between control and experimental conditions in the ambiguous trials for both the critical and competitor gaze conditions[2]. This is contrast to there being no difference between control and experimental conditions in the default gaze condition. The higher response times in experimental conditions would be expected due to the theory of mind inferences needed. However, this is not the case for relational trials in any gaze condition, though they do have a longer, but not significant, response time for both the critical and default gaze conditions. In the competitor gaze condition, the experimental relational trials are faster than the control relational trials, albeit not significantly so. This suggests that the director looking at the competitor object (in fact the wrong object that they have no knowledge of) helps the participant select the correct object, but only in the relational trial type (and in the experimental condition).

- Critical condition = no effect (no additional information after perspective calculation); experimental > control (amb
- Competitor condition = experimental relational is faster due to violation of expectation, ambiguous no difference
- Default condition = no effect (no information after perspective calculation).

---

[2] All gaze conditions show the same pattern of relational trials having a longer response time than ambiguous trials, both in the experimental and control trial conditions.

4   Discussion

The pattern of response times of the relational trials in the competitor gaze condition could be explained in terms of the violation-of-expectation paradigm that has been used with infants as an implicit measure: they will attend longer to situations that are unusual compared to those that they 'expect' or do not find unusual. Participants expect that if the director is going to look at an object that could be the referent of their instruction, it will be the one that they can see (critical gaze). If that is true, then the director looking at an object that is only visible to the participant would violate that expectation. This may make the perspective difference between the participant and the director more salient, and therefore lead to faster responses. However it is unclear as to why this only happens in the relational trials. The ambiguous trials follow the opposite pattern, where experimental trials are slower than control trials. It is possible that this is due to there being fewer items to process in this condition (2, as compared to 3 in the relational condition). If that is the case, it may be that participants only process any perspective difference through eye gaze at a certain threshold of complexity.

As the violation-of-expectation paradigm is often used in conjunction with eye-tracking equipment, it is possible that within the timeframe of the instruction, they may attend proportionally more to the gaze direction / head movement of the director in the competitor group than in the critical group. This would support the idea that they do not expect her to look at what is an occluded object from her perspective.

As it appears that participant only take eye gaze into account in certain situations, engagement may be promoted in online communication when a.) situations are sufficiently complex for participants to require the additional information it can provide, and b.) perspective differences between the participant and director are accentuated by the area or object the director is gazing at. However, it must be noted that these differences in response time are around 200ms and not significant, though the pattern is promising.

4.1   Future Work

Currently the director's gaze direction moves from looking at the participant to focus on the centre of the quadrant where the critical object is located (critical gaze), to focus on the centre of the quadrant where the competitor object is located (competitor gaze), or does not move and continues to be directed at the participant (default gaze). A further manipulation could involve the director focusing on any random quadrant that does not contain the critical object. Manipulation of eye gaze within head movements may also provide a more naturalistic representation of gaze direction, as static eyes within a moving head are not rated as realistic [9]. In order to assess whether participant are paying particular attention to head movement and gaze direction in the competitor gaze group (as suggested by a violation-of-expectation explanation) would require the use of eye-tracking equipment. This is currently ongoing work (a method without head movement has been created using Experiment Builder, the proprietary experimental design software for the EYELINK-1000 plus eye-tracking hardware.

The next step is to incorporate an agent with head movement into the experiment). A further plan is to replace the virtual agent with video capture of a human confederate who will act as the director (with head movement), and also to replace the virtual agent with an arrow that replicates the movement of the virtual agent with respect to prompting participants to attend to a particular location. The former will compare the level of engagement and attention participants have for a virtual versus a human agent, and the latter will compare the same between a virtual agent, human agent and a symbol that has inherent cuing properties. All of these will be done in conjunction with eye-tracking equipment.

5   Summary

Overall it appears that when gaze direction contains information that increases the saliency of any perspective difference, participants are faster in selecting the correct object. However, participants appear to either ignore or not use facilitatory information that could be gained from gaze direction, and this increase in engagement is shown only in the competitor gaze direction condition and in the relational trials. This could be explained by the violation-of-expectation paradigm, and a complexity threshold at which using information from eye gaze direction is triggered.

If processing of gaze direction and engagement was automatic, an effect of the facilitatory gaze condition on the speed and accuracy of object selection (either negative due to there being more information to process, or positive due to the information aiding the resolution of the instruction) would be expected. Therefore it is possible, with the current data, to suggest that processing gaze direction, and hence engaging further with the director, while fast and presumably then cognitively efficient, is a process that can be 'ignored' in certain situations. Specifically, it can be ignored where it provides no additional information to that gained by computing another's perspective or in situations where the level of complexity is not sufficient for participants to need the additional information it can provide. Aspects such as naturalistic blinking may increase engagement enough to 'override' any (conscious or unconscious) propensity to ignore gaze direction. This study is also of potential significance to human-machine interaction and engagement [16], for example, in collaborative situations between humans and artificial humanoid entities, where variations in their relative positioning with respect to each other and the environment, and accompanying perceived behavioural cues (real or artificial), may facilitate or hinder interaction performance.

References

1. Apperly, I.A., Carroll, D.J., Samson, D., Qureshi, A., Humphreys, G.W., Moffatt, G.: Why are there limits on theory of mind use? Evidence from adults' ability to follow instructions from an ignorant speaker. Quarterly Journal of Experimental Psychology 63(6), 1201–1217 (2010)
2. Call, J., Tomasello, M.: Does the chimpanzee have a theory of mind? 30 years later. Trends in Cognitive Science 12(5), 187–192 (2008)

3. Carlson, S.M., Moses, L.J., Claxton, L.J.: Individual differences in executive functioning and theory of mind: An investigation of inhibitory control and planning ability. Journal of Experimental Child Psychology 87, 299–319 (2004)
4. Clark, H.H., Marshall, C.R.: Definite reference and mutual knowledge. In: Joshi, A.K., Webber, B., Sag, I. (eds.) Elements of Discourse Understanding, pp. 10–63. Cambridge University Press, Cambridge (1981)
5. de Villiers, J.G., Pyers, J.E.: Complements to cognition: a longitudinal study of the relationship between complex syntax and false-belief- understanding. Cognitive Development 17, 1037–1060 (2002)
6. Hanna, J.E., Brennan, S.E.: Speakers' eye gaze disambiguates referring expressions early during face-to-face conversation. Journal of Memory and Language 57, 596–615 (2007)
7. Keysar, B., Lin, S., Barr, D.J.: Limits on theory of mind use in adults. Cognition 89, 25–41 (2003)
8. Onishi, K.H., Baillargeon, R.: Do 15-Month-Old Infants Understand False Beliefs? Science 308(5719), 255–258 (2005)
9. Peters, C., Qureshi, A.: A Head Movement Propensity Model for Animating Gaze Shifts and Blinks of Virtual Characters. Computers and Graphics, Special Issue on Graphics for Serious Games 34(6), 677–687 (2010)
10. Peters, C., Qureshi, A., Apperly, I.A.: Effects of gaze direction of a virtual agent in an online communication game. European Society of Philosophy and Psychology, Ruhr-Universität Bochum (August 2010)
11. Premack, D.G., Woodruff, G.: Does the chimpanzee have a theory of mind? Behavioral and Brain Sciences 1, 515–526 (1978)
12. Qureshi, A., Apperly, I.A., Samson, D.: Executive function is necessary for perspective-selection, not Level-1 visual perspective-calculation: Evidence from a dual-task study of adults. Cognition 117, 230–236 (2010)
13. Sperber, D., Wilson, D.: Relevance: Communication and Cognition, 2nd edn. Blackwell, Oxford (1986)
14. Sperber, D., Wilson, D.: Pragmatics, modularity and mindreading. Mind & Language. Special Issue on Pragmatics and Cognitive Science 17, 3–23 (2002)
15. Wellman, H.M., Cross, D., Watson, J.: Meta-analysis of theory-of-mind development: The truth about false belief. Child Development 72, 655–684 (2001)
16. Peters, C., Castellano, G., de Freitas, S.: An exploration of user engagement in HCI. In: Proceedings of the Affect-Aware Virtual Agents and Social Robots (AFFINE) Workshop, International Conference on Multimodal Interfaces and Workshop on Machine Learning for Multimodal Interaction (ICMI-MLMI 2009), Boston, MA, USA, November 6 (2009)

Developing Virtual and Augmented Environments

An Image Based Approach to Hand Occlusions in Mixed Reality Environments

Andrea F. Abate, Fabio Narducci, and Stefano Ricciardi

VRLab, University of Salerno
{abate,fnarducci,sricciardi}@unisa.it

Abstract. The illusion of the co-existence of virtual objects in the physical world, which is the essence of MR paradigm, is typically made possible by superimposing virtual contents onto the surrounding environment captured through a camera. This works well until the order of the planes to be composited is coherent to their distance from the observer. But, whenever an object of the real world is expected to occlude the virtual contents, the illusion vanishes. What should be seen behind a real object could be visualized over it instead, generating a "cognitive dissonance" that may compromise scene comprehension and, ultimately, the interaction capabilities during the MR experience. This paper describes an approach to handle hand occlusions in MR/AR interaction contexts by means of an optimized stereo matching technique based on the belief propagation algorithm.

Keywords: mixed reality, hand occlusion, disparity map.

1 Introduction

As the number of augmented and mixed reality applications available on a variety of platforms increases, so does the level of interaction required, possibly leading to the emergence of challenging visualization issues. To this regard, it is worth to note that the illusion of the co-existence of virtual objects in the physical world (the essence of MR paradigm) is typically made possible by so called video-based[1] see-through approach in which the rendering of virtual contents is superimposed onto the surrounding environment captured in real time by means of a proper transformation. This trick works well until the order of the planes to be composited is coherent to their distance from the observer (see Fig. 1_Left). But, whenever an object of the real world is expected to occlude the virtual contents, the illusion vanishes since the order of rendered planes does not lead to a correct visualization (see Fig. 1_Right). As a result, what should be seen behind a real object could be visualized over it instead, generating a "cognitive dissonance" due to the loss of spatial coherence along the axis normal to camera plane that may compromise scene comprehension and, ultimately, the interaction capabilities during the MR experience.

---

[1] Optical see-through is the other well known option for MR/AR, but besides being less diffused it is inherently less suited to support processing of environment visualization.

R. Shumaker and S. Lackey (Eds.): VAMR 2014, Part I, LNCS 8525, pp. 319–328, 2014.
© Springer International Publishing Switzerland 2014

Fig. 1. *Left:* A virtual model of a keyboard rendered onto a captured frame of real environment to augment it. The hand positioned along the right side of the keyboard does not ruins the Mixed Reality illusion. *Right:* The same MR scene, but as the hand is positioned over the keyboard, it is occluded by the virtual content.

This paper describes an image-based method aimed to address effectively hand occlusion in many MR/AR interaction contexts without any additional hardware, apart from video see-through goggles enabling stereo-vision. In brief, the proposed method composites the rendered virtual objects onto the incoming video see-through streams according to a disparity map encoding real-to-virtual visualization order at a pixel level as a gray-scale image by means of stereo matching. We optimize the performance of the algorithm by segmenting the input image between hand and not-hand regions via a skin-tone filtering in the HSV color space (less affected from lighting conditions than RGB space). The purpose of this segmentation is twofold. From the one hand it is possible to reduce the region of interest (that directly affects the computational cost of the disparity map) to a cropped region of the original frame, on the other hand the contour of the segmented hand region is used as a reference to improve the edge sharpness of the disparity map.

The rest of this paper is organized as follows. Section 2 presents previous works related to this research. Section 3 describes the overall system's architecture and each of its main components. Section 4 reports about first experiments to assess the advantages and the limitations in the proposed approach. Finally, Section 5 draws some conclusions introducing future directions of this study.

2   Related Works

Hand occlusion in augmented reality is a challenging topic and scientific literature presents diverse approaches to it. In particular, displaying occluded objects in a manner that a user intuitively understands is not always trivial. Furmanski et al. [1] in 2002 developed new concepts for developing effective visualizations of occluded information in MR/AR applications. They designed some practical approaches and guidelines aimed at evaluating user's perception and comprehension of the augmented scene and distances. Many researchers aimed at solving the incorrect occlusion problem by analyzing various tracking methods or by integrating vision-based methods with other sensors [2]. Lee and Park proposed to address this issue in AR environment introducing the usage of an Augmented Foam [3]. A blue foam mock-up is overlaid with a 3D virtual object, which is rendered with the same CAD model used for mock-up production. By hand occlusion correction, inferred by color-based detection of the foam, virtual products and user's hand are seamlessly synthesized. The advantage of the augmented foam is that it is cheap and easy to cut allowing to realize simple and complex shapes. On the other hand, it imposes that for all augmented objects has to be present in the scene the physical counterpart made of foam. A color-based similar approach is discussed by Walairacht et al [4]. They exploited the chroma-key technique to extract only the image of the hands from a blue-screen background merging the image of the real hands and the virtual objects with correct occlusion. Although chroma-key is particularly fast and efficient, it requires the use of a colored background that represents a not feasible solution in many environments. In addition, it does not provide any information about real objects in the scene and their spatial distances. Buchmann et al [5] also handled hand occlusions in augmented reality exploiting marker-based methods to determine the approximate position/orientation of user's hands and, indirectly, their contour to fix the visualization order. The disadvantages are the inconvenience to wear specific gloves featuring fiducials on each finger and the rough level of accuracy in the segmentation of the hand from the background. In the field of medicine, Fischer et al [6] exploited a Phantom tracker and anatomic volumetric models in order to support surgical interventions resolving occlusions of surgery tools. They presented a simple and fast preprocessing pipeline for medical volume datasets which extracts the visual hull volume. The resulting is used for real-time static occlusion handling in their specific AR system, which is based on off-the-shelf medical equipment. Depth/range cameras (e.g. the Kinect by Microsoft) have also been proposed [7][8][9] to provide a real-time updated depth-image of the surrounding world that can be conveniently used to evaluate whether a pixel from the captured environment is closer to the observer than the corresponding rendered pixel of virtual content, or not. This technique can lead to a more accurate result and also enables evaluating distances of real objects in the scene and their inter-occlusions with virtual objects. However, it requires additional hardware (usually an infrared pattern emitter and a dedicated infrared camera) and it should match the field-of-view of the see-through cameras, to works effectively. The generation of a disparity map by using stereo matching techniques [10][11] represent the most suited choice to correctly segment user's hands in AR environments. Results produced by this technique are comparable to the ones form depth cameras without requiring dedicated hardware, which is a central aspect of this study. In our proposal, the disparity map is generated by a belief propagation global algorithm [12] that exploits GPU's highly parallel architecture to speed up required calculations and to provide real-time performance. Some ad-hoc improvements aimed at further reducing the computational cost of the original algorithm are discussed in the following section.

3 System Description

The overall system architecture is shown in Fig. 2. The diagram highlights the main elements in the image-processing pipeline. The user wears a HMD with two embedded cameras enabling stereo vision. Two separated video streams, from left and right camera respectively, capture the real scene from a different perspective point. On each stream, a simple and fast skin detection technique detects the user's hands in the scene. The binary image is used to apply a vertical crop to the original frame that preserves the region, including the foreground and the background, where the hands appear. On that crop two disparity maps, the one for the real scene captured and the other for the rendered content, are generated by exploiting a stereo-matching with belief propagation technique. The disparity maps are used to estimate the position of the hands in the field of view with regards to the virtual scene. The occlusion correction is achieved by comparing them and combining the result with a skin-based segmentation of the hand. An edge blurring pass is applied to the segmentation in order to smooth the edges of the hand region. The combination of disparity map with blurred color-based segmentation of hands produces a cleaner approximation of the occlusions that can be applied as top-level layer of the augmented streams sent to the HMD displays.

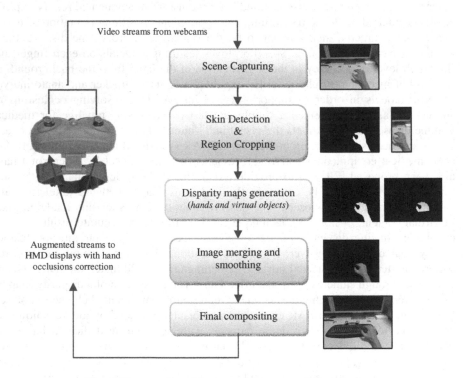

Fig. 2. The overall architecture of the approach proposed

More in detail, the first step consists in capturing the scene observed by the user through the webcams mounted on the HMD. Since the HMD is intended for a stereoscopic vision, the streams from left and right camera capture the scene from a slight different point of view. Each of the two streams is therefore separately augmented by rendered virtual contents throughout the pipeline. Even though this implies a greater computational cost of the augmenting algorithm, it preserves the binocular vision of human eyes leading to a more reliable augmentation of the scene and the occlusion correction. Fig. 3 shows one frame captured by one of the cameras mounted on the HMD while the user wears it.

Fig. 3. The scene captured by one of the cameras mounted on the HMD

To keep computational cost of the following steps slow, the frame is properly cropped so that the algorithm can focus the execution only on the relevant portion of the entire frame. The cropping is performed by a simple and fast skin color-based technique. It converts the video frame from the RGB to the HSV color space in order to have a simply way of filtering the color of naked hands by proper ranges of hue and saturation, thus leading to a gray-scale mask. Fast closure operators enable removing little irrelevant blobs in this mask and filling holes (if any) in main closed regions (the hands in our context). Every pixel inside the region boundaries (the hands' contour) is therefore set to full white (see Fig 4a). The intersection of this first mask with the rendered content's alpha channel (see Fig 4b) results in a new mask which limits the region on which the disparity maps of rendered content has to be computed (see Fig 4c). To this aim, stereo matching with belief propagation [12] is therefore performed on these cropped regions.

By processing only a limited region of the whole scene, we manage to reduce the computational costs of this step, which is the most time consuming in the processing pipeline. Firstly the matching costs for each pixel at each disparity level in a certain range (disparity range) are calculated. The matching costs determine the probability of a correct match. Afterwards, the matching costs for all disparity levels can be aggregated within a cross-shape neighborhood window. Basically the loopy belief propagation algorithm first gathers information from a pixel's neighbors and incorporate the information to update the smoothness term between the current pixel and its neighboring pixels, and to iteratively optimize the smoothness term thus resulting in global energy minimization. Each node is assigned to a disparity level and holds its matching costs. The belief (probability) that this disparity is the optimum arises from the matching costs and the belief values from the neighboring pixels. For each iteration, each node sends its belief value to all four connected nodes. The belief value is the sum of the matching costs and the received belief values. The new belief value is the sum of the actual and the received value and is saved for each direction separately. This is done for each disparity level. Finally, the best match is the one with the lowest belief values defined by a sum over all four directions [13] resulting in the final hand(s) disparity map. The main factor that affects every stereo-matching technique is the number of disparity ranges considered during the matching cost function. The more values are considered the more the disparity map is reliable but, the more the cost increases. Considering our main goal of performing a fast hands occlusion correction, we reduce the number of disparity ranges. We refine the both rough disparity maps obtained by composing it with the corresponding crop of the binary image from skin detection acting as alpha layer (one pass of edge blur allows to smooth the edges of the color-based segmentation).

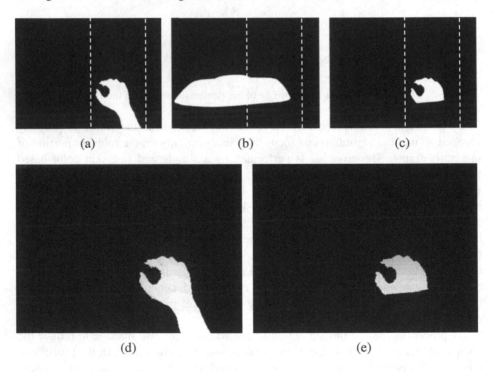

(a)   (b)   (c)

(d)   (e)

Fig. 4. Skin detection with closure functions refinement (a). Alpha channel of augmented objects rendered onto the video stream (b). Disparity map of user's hand segmented from the scene by the skin color-based detection (d). Disparity map of the crop of the region where augmented virtual contents overlap the hand (e).

Fig. 5. Compositing and final result. The original real background shown in Fig. 3 is composited according to the disparity map of the scene enabling a correct visualization and a meaningful interaction (note that hand's casted shadow is not currently handled by the proposed method).

The result is a smoother segmentation of user's hands (see Fig. 4d) that can be used for final compositing. For what concerns the rendered content, it would be simpler and faster to exploit the accurate depth info contained in the Z-buffer, but matching it coherently to the depth levels encoded in the hand(s) disparity map would be a not trivial task. The final composited frame is obtained by comparing pixel-wise the gray level of the two disparity maps. The pixel whose gray level is lower than its homologous is considered not-visible from the observer's point of view and is discarded. Fig. 5 shows an example of the final result in which the hand of a user interacting in a MR environment is properly composited onto the augmented content.

4   First Experiments

We performed a preliminary experimental trial of the proposed technique in a MR environment on a test-bed featuring an i7 Intel quad_core processor and an Nvidia GTX760 graphic board equipped with 1152 cores and 2 GB of VRAM. The user worn a Trivisio HMD that features stereo capturing by two embedded webcams (752x480 resolution, 6oFPS) and stereo vision by two 800x600 LCD displays.

Even though the technique proposed in this paper exploits time consuming algorithms, it meets the requirements of real-time application because it works only on a fraction of the whole captured scene. In addition, the improvement provided by utilizing graphics hardware acceleration makes possible to combine the time demands of stereo matching with typical marker-based tracking of the user on a stereo video stream.

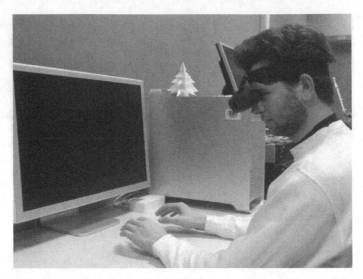

Fig. 6. A user wearing the Trivio HMD during the experimental trial

In Table 1 have been summarized the performance during the experimental session. In particular, the table shows the frame per second achieved by the solution proposed when the disparity maps are generated for 16 and 32 ranges of disparity values. During the experimental trial the user is free to move his/her hands thus implying a size of the crop of the scene that varies over time. We observed that, in normal condition of interaction, the number of pixels of user's hand covers about 1/8 to 1/6 of the whole scene for over 60% of the experimental session. When the distance between user's hand and the point of view results shorter, e.g., the user brings his/her hands closer to the cameras, the stereo matching works on a wide crop of the scene leading to a drop in performances to the limit of a smooth real-time rendering. Future improvement of our method will take into account such issue providing an adaptive amount of disparity levels to consider during the matching cost function.

Table 1. Frame per second recorded during the experimental trial at different size of the cropping region of the scene

Crop size *(fraction of the whole scene, which consists of 360960 pixels (752x480))*	# disparity levels	
	16	**32**
	FPS	**FPS**
< 1/8 (~ 45120 pixels)	56	48
< 1/6 (~ 60160 pixels)	42	33
< 1/4 (~ 90240 pixels)	31	22
< 1/2 (~ 180480pixels)	25	12

5   Conclusions

We presented a technique to address hand occlusion in real time when interacting in a Mixed Reality environment. The approach, designed around the stereo matching belief propagation algorithm and ad-hoc enhancements, meet the main design requirements of finer segmentation of user's hands, distance dependant occlusions, and natural interaction. Binocular scene capture and stereo rendering of virtual contents improve depth perception of real environment while stereo matching allows to estimate the distance from the observer and real/virtual objects in the scene.

The subjective system evaluation, performed by testers in an experimental environment, highlights the potential of the proposed approach, even though issues related to the hardware used (the reduced HMD's resolution/field-of-view, rough hands segmentation under rapid user's movements) have to be more carefully addressed to achieve a robust system behavior. In particular, the generation of the disparity maps for the hands when they occupy the most of the framed scene. Even though these enhancements are inherently effective only on naked hand region, even not-naked arms can be reasonably handled by the disparity info alone. As a further development of this technique, besides improving the quality of the disparity map, we are currently trying to address the incorrect visualization of the shadows casted by the hands when they should be projected onto a virtual object.

According to first users evaluations, the combination of augmentation and the detection of occlusions worked well, providing an intuitive interaction paradigm suited to a wide range of application contexts. For these reasons we expect to improve the solution proposed in this paper to resolve, by stereo-matching techniques, occlusion issues in wide environment where people are free to move around and occlude big one to one scale virtual augmenting objects.

References

1. Furmanski, C., Azuma, R., Daily, M.: Augmented-reality visualizations guided by cognition: Perceptual heuristics for combining visible and obscured information. In: Proceedings of the International Symposium on Mixed and Augmented Reality (ISMAR 2002), pp. 215–320. IEEE (2002)
2. Shah, M.M., Arshad, H., Sulaiman, R.: Occlusion in augmented reality. In: Proceedings of the 8th International Conference on Information Science and Digital Content Technology (ICIDT 2012), pp. 372–378. IEEE (2012)
3. Lee, W., Park, J.: Augmented foam: a tangible augmented reality for product design. In: Proceedings of the Fourth IEEE and ACM International Symposium on Mixed and Augmented Reality, pp. 106–109. IEEE (2005)
4. Walairacht, S., Yamada, K., Hasegawa, S., Koike, Y., Sato, M.: 4+ 4 fingers manipulating virtual objects in mixed-reality environment. Presence: Teleoperators and Virtual Environments. MIT Press Journal, 134–143 (2002)
5. Buchmann, V., Violich, S., Billinghurst, M., Cockburn, A.: FingARtips: Gesture Based Direct Manipulation in Augmented Reality. In: Proceedings of the 2nd International Conference on Computer Graphics and Interactive Techniques (GRAPHITE 2004), pp. 212–221. ACM (2004)

6. Fischer, J., Bartz, D., Straßer, W.: Occlusion handling for medical augmented reality using a volumetric phantom model. In: Proceedings of the ACM symposium on Virtual reality software and technology (2004), pp. 174–177. ACM (2004)
7. Corbett-Davies, S., Dunser, A., Green, R., Clark, A.: An Advanced Interaction Framework for Augmented Reality Based Exposure Treatment. In: IEEE Virtual Reality (VR 2013), pp. 19–22. IEEE (2013)
8. Gordon, G., Billinghurst, M., Bell, M., Woodfill, J., Kowalik, B., Erendi, A., Tilander, J.: The use of dense stereo range data in augmented reality. In: Proceedings of the 1st International Symposium on Mixed and Augmented Reality (2002), p. 14–23. IEEE Computer Society (2002)
9. Seo, D.W., Lee, J.Y.: Direct hand touchable interactions in augmented reality environments for natural and intuitive user experiences. Expert Systems with Applications 40(9), 3784–3793 (2013)
10. Kanade, T., Okutomi, M.: A stereo matching algorithm with an adaptive window: Theory and experiment. IEEE Transactions on Pattern Analysis and Machine Intelligence, 920–932 (1994)
11. Medioni, G., Nevatia, R.: Segment-based stereo matching. In: Computer Vision, Graphics, and Image Processing, pp. 2–18 (1985)
12. Yang, Q., Wang, L., Yang, R., Wang, S., Liao, M.: NisterD.: Real-time global stereo matching using hierarchical belief propagation, in: The British Machine Vision Conference, pp. 989–998 (2006)
13. Humenberger, M., Zinner, C., Weber, M., Kubinger, W., Vincze, M.: A fast stereo matching algorithm suitable for embedded real-time systems. Computer Vision and Image Understanding 114(11), 1180–1202 (2010)

Assembly of the Virtual Model with Real Hands Using Augmented Reality Technology

Poonpong Boonbrahm and Charlee Kaewrat

School of Informatics, Walailak University, Nakorn si Thammarat, Thailand 80161
{poonpong,charlee.qq}@gmail.com

Abstract. In the past few years, studying in the field of Augmented Reality (AR) has been expanded from technical aspect such as tracking system, authoring tools and etc. to applications ranging from the fields of education, entertainment, medicine to manufacturing. In manufacturing, which relies on assembly process, AR is used for assisting staffs in the field of maintenance and assembly. Usually, it has been used as a guidance system, for example using graphical instructions for advising the users with the steps in performing the maintenance or assembly operation. In assembly training, especially for small, expensive or harmful devices, interactive technique using real hands may be suitable than the guiding technique. Using tracking algorithm to track both hands in real time, interaction can occurs by the execution of grasp and release gestures. Bare hand tracking technique, which uses gesture recognition to enable interaction with augmented objects are also possible. In this paper, we attempted to use marker based AR technique to assemble 3D virtual objects using natural hand interaction. By applying the markers to fit on fingertip and assigned the corresponding virtual 3D finger that have physical properties such as surface, volume, density, friction and collision detection properties to them, interaction between fingers and objects could be executed. This setup was designed on a PC based system but could be ported to iOS or Android, so that it would work on tablet or mobile phones as well. Unity 3D game engine was used with Vuforia AR platform. In order to grab and move the virtual object by hand, the shape of the virtual finger (Vulforia's target) has been investigated. Appropriate friction coefficient were applied to both virtual fingers and the object and then at least two virtual fingers were force to press on the 3D virtual object in opposite directions so that frictional force is more than gravitational force. To test this method, virtual model of LEGO's mini-figures which composed of five pieces, was used and the assembly could be done in just a short time. Comparing with other popular technique such as "gestures recognition", we have found that our technique could provide more efficient result in term of cost and natural feeling.

Keywords: Augmented Reality, Manufacturing, Assembly Process, Virtual Object Assembly.

1 Introduction

The goals of Augmented Reality (AR) assisted assembly are to make assembly training more effective in terms of time used, cost and being able to interact naturally.

R. Shumaker and S. Lackey (Eds.): VAMR 2014, Part I, LNCS 8525, pp. 329–338, 2014.
© Springer International Publishing Switzerland 2014

In the manufacturing field, AR-based assembly system can be grouped into two categories i.e. AR-based guidance assembly and AR-based assembly training. In AR-based guidance assembly, the assembly is guided by texts or graphics to assemble parts, for example, placing texts, graphics or 3D models on top of real world machines and explaining or creating animations of how to work on the real machine step by step. Some automobile manufacturers are planning to use this technology as a means to assist service staffs in their technical work. Using AR in assisting assembly as a guiding system is proving to be very useful for assembling large and complex equipment. This technique has gained popular acceptance for real time assembly and real time maintenance processes for the last few years. For AR-based assembly training, AR is used to create an environment for assembly training. In this case, the emphasis is based on how to make the assembly process more realistic like performing them in real life. Researches on applying physical properties to the virtual objects to help assembly more naturally had been done and proved to be easy in training, but it still lacks of the "touch" feeling which may be necessary in some experiments. In order to make the training more natural, the users must learn from practicing with their own hands. Bare hand tracking technique, which uses gesture recognition to enable interactions with augmented objects was used by many researchers. By using tracking algorithm to track hands or fingers in real time, interaction may occur by the execution of grasp and release gestures. Even though, this technique seem to be suitable for assembling small devices which are usually assembled by hand but more work needs to be done in terms of easiness to use, precision and response time.

2   Related Work

Researches in the area of Augmented Reality assisting Assembly process have been done for quite some time. Pathomaree N. [1] used graphical instructions and virtual objects for advising the user with the assembly steps and the targeted positions in assembly task. This research also indicated whether the user performed actions correctly or not. Wang Y., et al. [2] had studied several key aspects in AR-based assembly system such as occlusion handling, collision detection and human-computer interaction. A prototype system was implemented to illustrate on how to apply these techniques. An example of AR assisted assembly had been developed by Woll, R., et al. [3], as a serious game for teaching an apprentice mechanic about the components of car's power generator and how these components were assembled. The application has been implemented on smart phone running the Android operation system. With AR technology, users could obtain interactive experiences in the spatial arrangement of components. Tang, A. et al. [4] had evaluated the effectiveness of spatially overlaid instructions using augmented reality (AR) in an assembly task comparing with other traditional media such as user manual and CAI. Results indicated that by overlaying 3D instructions on the workspace, reduction time could be reduced by 10-15% with the error rate of 82%, particularly in cumulative errors. All of these researches gear towards assisted assembly by using AR as guidance in improving speed and quality of assembly processing. For improving skill in assembly, users must be able to perform the assembly process in real environment or at least feel like performing in real one and AR can fit in this situation. Using AR, users can obtain experiences in performing assembly tasks in both real and virtual space. Besides that, users can practice at any time and any place with a minimum cost of performance. Therefore, many users can gain more experiences in assembly process at one time. To make AR assisted assembly more realistic, researchers have used many techniques. Boonbrahm, P. et al. [5] had applied physical properties to the virtual objects to help assembly more natural. This technique had been done and proved to be easy to train users in performing assembly processes, but it still lacks of the "touch" feeling which may be necessary in some experiments.

In order to interact with virtual objects with real hand, either bare hand or with some special equipment, many techniques were introduced by other researchers and our research is related or based on those earlier works. Lee, M., et al. [6] had developed a 3D vision-based natural hand interaction method based on hand direction calculation and collision detection between the user's hand and augmented objects. Results showed that users would have a seamless interaction in AR environments with the tracking accuracy of the hand interaction varied from 3mm to 20 mm depending on the distance between the user's hand and the stereo camera. The drawbacks were that, by using a single finger for interaction, there were some error from calculation and the application was limited. Bare hand tracking technique, which uses gesture recognition to enable interaction with augmented objects are also possible. Wang, Z.B., et al. [7] developed an effective hand segmentation method based on a Restricted Coulomb Energy (RCE) neural network for bare hands interaction in the AR assembly environment. An experiment using two fingertips to control virtual objects to simulate assembly in a 2D space was conducted. The results demonstrated that the proposed bare-hand interaction method was robust and effective. But since the fingertips tracking algorithms were executed in a 2D space, there was no depth information. Li, Y. and Shen, X. [8] studied on how users interacted with virtual objects by hands using the real-time collision detection between virtual and real objects based on 3D tracking of hand. Using a pair of common web cameras to collect images and track the points on hands which were marked by color blocks, then the stereo vision calibration algorithm was achieved. Finally, the accurate collision detection was achieved by calculating the relative positions between real hand and virtual objects real-time. Choi, J [9] proposed an augmented reality interface that provided natural hand-based interaction with virtual objects on mobile phones. The proposed method consisted of three steps: hand detection, palm pose estimation, and finger gesture recognition. A virtual object was rendered on his/her palm and reacted to hand and finger movements. The most popular technique for real hand interaction in AR, is tracking hands in real time. The interaction between hands and virtual objects occurs by the execution of "grasp and release" gestures. Figueiredo, L., et al. [10] proposed and evaluated a solution for direct interaction with augmented objects on tabletop applications through hand tracking and gesture recognition. Kinect device was used for hand tracking and the interaction was performed by a grasp and release gesture recognized by the distance between thumb and forefinger. If there was an augmented object within the region between these fingers points and the evaluated distance was short enough, the object was grabbed. But if the distance increased the object was released.

Even though, these techniques seem to be suitable for the assembly of small devices that are usually assembled by hand but some setup still need special equipment or special setup which is too complicate to be done easily. In order to make virtual assembly training more efficient for users, it is still needed more work done in term of easiness of use, precision and response time.

3   System Development

In this paper, we attempted to use marker based AR technique to assemble 3D virtual objects using natural hand interaction. By applying the markers to fit on fingertip and assigned the corresponding virtual 3D finger which had physical properties such as surface, friction, volume, mass and collision detection properties, interaction between fingers and virtual objects could be executed. This technique was similar to "grasp and release" gestures. But instead of using image recognition concept, interaction between objects that had physical properties was used. In this setup, Unity 3D game engine was used on Vuforia platform. Unity is a fully integrated development engine for creating games and other interactive 3D content. Qualcomm's Vuforia platform made it possible to write a single native application that run on almost all smartphones and tablets. In order to grab the virtual object by hand, friction were applied to the surface of both virtual fingers and of the object and then at least two virtual fingers (thumb and index finger) were forced to press on the 3D virtual object in opposite direction. Since there were forces applied to the virtual object and with some appropriate friction between the surfaces of virtual object and virtual fingers, lifting the object could be done easily. Moving the object around was possible by moving the hand to the destination point. Details of the setup could be divided into 3 steps as follows.

3.1   Step 1: Create a Virtual Fingers

In Vulforia, targets that were representatives of real-world objects, which could be detected and tracked, occurred in many types such as image, cylinder, text or user-defined. In this case, we used cylinder target since it would fit in our fingers nicely. Besides that, the look and feelings were more realistic, which made them more natural in action. Rectangular shapes were suitable for grabbing rectangular virtual object since the surface contact between the two objects was large (see Fig.1(a)). Problems with this shape occurred when the surface of virtual object and the surface of the rectangular finger were not in paralleled or the contact surface were not large enough, like when grabbing the cylindrical virtual objects as shown in Fig. 1(b).

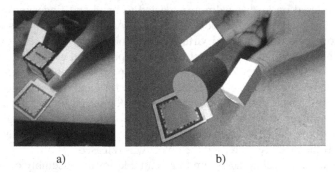

a)   b)

Fig. 1. Grabbing virtual object with rectangular virtual fingers a) Rectangular shape object b) Cylindrical virtual objects

Using octagon shape of virtual fingers created another problem. Octagon shape had many edges. If one of the edges touched the virtual object, it would push the object away, making it hard to grab as shown in Fig. 2.

Fig. 2. Grabbing virtual object with octagon virtual fingers

Since the shape of the target make big impact on the grabbing situation, trying to make less edges and make the surface in parallel with the object surface as possible, seem to be the good decision. By making the target as a small flat surface attached to the markers, we have found out that it did not improve much in term of grabbing ability. The reason for this is due to the fact that the contact surface is too small to make it possible for grabbing and lifting as shown in fig. 3.

Fig. 3. Grabbing virtual object with cylindrical virtual fingers

For cylindrical shape target (called capsules), the shape look like the real finger, so it should be the perfect solution in term of realistic movement. Since the contact surface didn't improve much in this case, improving the cylindrical virtual finger which have the properties of rigid body, by adding another layer of low mass model on top of cylindrical shape virtual finger, make it easy to grab the virtual objects. This low mass layer performed as an elastic layer just like the real finger, make grabbing more realistic as seen in Fig. 4.

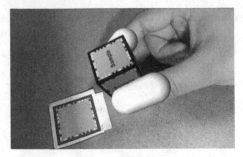

Fig. 4. Grabbing virtual object with 2 layers of cylindrical shape virtual fingers

3.2   Step 2: Apply Physical Properties to the Virtual Objects

Since the setup should give real experience in performing the assembly function such as lifting, dropping, moving the virtual objects, then both fingers and the assembly part should have physical properties. Adding the physical properties to the virtual object could be done on unity 3D platform, but precise calculation of a given values have to be done. For virtual object, in order to perform as a real object, mass, gravity force, frictional coefficient and rigid body properties such as collision detection have to be applied to the virtual object. For virtual fingers to be able to grab the virtual object, some physical properties for rigid body such as mass and collision detection have to be applied also. To make them more realistic, the virtual finger should have rigid body properties inside and elastic skin outside. With this setup, the virtual finger will have collision detection function to detect the object in contact and also have better grab due to the properties of the surface. To understand the situation, the forces applied to the objects are illustrated in Fig. 5.

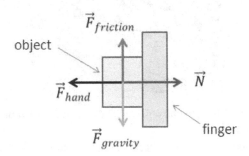

Fig. 5. The forces applied to the objects from finger grabbing

Since the virtual object, that will be grabbed, have weight (mass x gravity), it tends to drop due to the gravitational force. To grab the object and be able to lift it up without dropping it, the frictional force must be equal or higher than the force due to gravity.

$$F_{friction} \geq F_{gravity}$$

with

$$F_{friction} \leq \mu_s N$$

Since N is the force that the object react to the force applied by the virtual finger in opposite direction with equal amount and μ_s is the frictional coefficient that was assigned to the surface of the object, then we can control and make them equal or more than gravitational force. With the value of frictional force more than gravitational force, lifting or assembling the virtual objects by using two fingers can be done easily.

3.3   Step 3: Testing the Concept

Preliminary test of this method on different shape objects was done using "shape sorter" toy concept, in which we had to grab 3D virtual objects in the shape of cube, hexagon and cylinder, and placed them in the right "opening" spots. By placing different shape objects, one by one, in to the base, using two virtual fingers grabbing, we found that this could be done easily with the "touch" feeling.

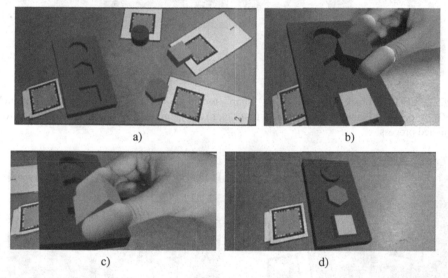

Fig. 6. Testing the concept with "shape sorter" toy (a) "Shape sorter" base with 3 virtual objects (b) Placing hexagon into the base using 2 finger grabbing (c) Placing hexagon into the base (d) Finished process

To assemble a model with many parts, calculations on the direction, distance and matching procedure were made so that the matching parts could be "snapped" together. To test this assembly method, we simply used four virtual LEGO's blocks to form a rectangular block and the result was more than satisfied. These LEGO blocks were used because they had exact positions that can be snapped together when attached at the right position. Details of the assembly is shown in Fig. 7.

Attempting to try more sophisticated assemblies, virtual model of LEGO's minifigures which composed of five pieces of virtual parts, were used. The parts are base unit, leg unit, body unit, head and hat (as seen in Fig. 8 (a)). With two virtual fingers grabbing and "snap" technique, the assembly could be done in just a short time with the feeling just like assembling by real hand.

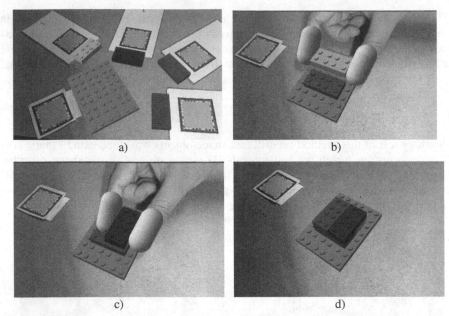

Fig. 7. LEGO's block assemble using "snap" technique (a) LEGO's base with 4 virtual LEGO blocks (b) Placing LEGO block's first layer (c) Placing LEGO block's second layer (d) Finished process

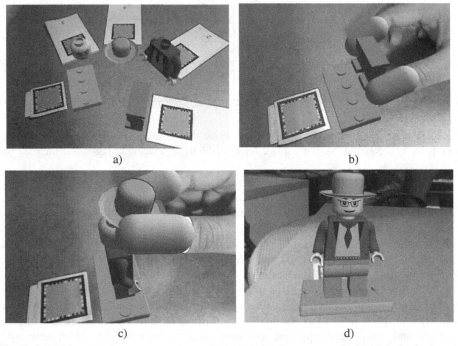

Fig. 8. LEGO's mini figure assemble (a) LEGO's mini figure parts (b) Placing the leg's part into the base (c) Placing the hat on (d) Finished process

4   Result and Discussion

Comparing the techniques used in this setup and other techniques used by other researchers, we have found that our techniques is more efficient in term of cost, effectiveness and easy to use. For example, in our setup, there is no need for extra equipment except webcam. In term of effectiveness and easy to use, since the virtual fingers is covered on the real fingers, making it felt like user's own fingers, so grabbing virtual object even a small one could be done naturally. In other popular technique such as "gestures recognition", we have found that our technique provided more natural feeling. This may be due to the fact that "grasp and release gestures" are executed in 2D space, so the information used for interaction with 3D virtual object has no depth. But in our experiment, both virtual fingers and virtual object are in 3D world so the interaction could occur in many dimensions. Besides that, there is no precision setup for special equipment such as kinect device or special cameras, setup time can also be reduced. And since this experiment is built on Unity 3D, porting them to other platform like iOS or Androids for running on tablets could be done easily.

5   Conclusion

This virtual fingers technique proved to be useful for assisting hand assembly of small devices because it provides the feeling of real manual assembly without using sophisticated devices, so training can be done many times until the technician understands and gains confidence in assembling real devices. The same concept can be applied for games that need the "natural touch" feeling like chess or other board games. In conclusion, with this technique, human-computer interaction in performing the assembly operation in the AR environment can be improved especially in "touch and feel".

References

1. Pathomaree, N., Charoenseang, S.: Augmented Reality for Skill Transfer in Assembly Task. In: The 14th IEEE International Workshop on Robot and Human Interactive Communication (RO-MAN), Nashville, Tennessee, USA, August 13-15 (2005)
2. Wang, Z.B., Shen, Y., Ong, S.K., Nee, A.Y.C.: Assembly Design and Evaluation based on Bare-Hand Interaction in an Augmented Reality Environment. In: International Conference on Cyber Worlds, pp. 21–28 (2009)
3. Woll, R., Damerau, T., Wrasse, K., Stark, R.: Augmented reality in a serious game for manual assembly processes. In: 2011 IEEE International Symposium on Mixed and Augmented Reality - Arts, Media, and Humanities (ISMAR-AMH), pp. 37–39 (2011)
4. Tang, A., Owen, C., Biocca, F., Mou, W.: Experimental Evaluation of Augmented Reality in Object Assembly Task. In: Proceedings of the International Symposium on Mixed and Augmented Reality, ISMAR 2002 (2002)
5. Imbert, N., Vignat, F., Kaewrat, C., Boonbrahm, P.: Adding Physical Properties to 3D Models in Augmented Reality for Realistic Interactions Experiments. Procedia Computer Science 25, 364–369 (2013)

6. Lee, M., Green, R., Billinghurst, M.: 3D natural hand interaction for AR applications. In: 23rd International Conference on Image and Vision Computing (IVCNZ 2008), New Zealand, vol. 1(6), pp. 26–28 (November 2008)
7. Wang, Z., Shen, Y., Ong, S.K., Nee, A.Y.-C.: Assembly Design and Evaluation Based on Bare-Hand Interaction in an Augmented Reality Environment. In: International Conference on CyberWorlds (CW 2009), vol. 21(28), pp. 7–11 (2009)
8. Li, Y., Shen, X.: A Real-time Collision Detection between Virtual and Real Objects Based on Three-dimensional Tracking of Hand. In: 2010 International Conference on Audio Language and Image Processing, ICALIP 2010, pp. 1346–1351 (2010)
9. Choi, J., Park, H., Park, J., Park, J.-I.: Bare-Hand-Based Augmented Reality Interface on Mobile Phone. In: IEEE International Symposium on Mixed and Augmented Reality 2011, Science and Technology Proceedings, Basel, Switzerland, October 26-29, pp. 275–276 (2011)

Future Media Internet Technologies for Digital Domes

Dimitrios Christopoulos[1,*], Efstathia Hatzi[2], Anargyros Chatzitofis[3],
Nicholas Vretos[3], and Petros Daras[3]

[1] Virtual Reality & 3D Department, Foundation of The Hellenic World,
Poulopoulou 38, 11851 Athens, Greece
[2] Project Coordination Department, Foundation of The Hellenic World,
Poulopoulou 38, 11851 Athens, Greece
{christop,echatzi}@fhw.gr
[3] Information Technologies Institute, Center for Research & Technology,
Thessaloniki, Greece
{tofis,vretos,daras}@iti.gr

Abstract. The paper outlines the primary challenges and principles for museums and venues that wish to accommodate social and Future Media Internet (FMI) technologies, incorporating the experiences gathered through the EXPERIMEDIA project experiments.

Keywords: Future Museums, New Media, Infrastructure, Smart Devices, EXPERIMEDIA Project.

1 Introduction

"The next generation of museums and venues was envisioned as a composite of three metaphors: an information seeking space, a social gathering space and a new artefact, embodying social processes and projects" [1]. Certainly new internet technologies have many engaging uses within a museum context. But which of these technologies, museums choose to sustain with their limited resources should be guided by larger questions of accessibility and inclusiveness. It's easy to equate participatory culture with social media but it is also important to distinguish between them. Henry Jenkins of MIT [2], clearly states the case for focusing on the growing culture of participation rather than exclusively on the interactive technologies that support it. Jenkins defines this culture of participation as one:

- With relatively low barriers to artistic expression and civic engagement.
- With strong support for creating and sharing one's creations with others.
- With some type of informal mentorship whereby what is known by the most experienced is passed along to novices.
- Where members believe that their contributions matter.
- Where members feel some degree of social connection with one another.

---

* Corresponding author.

R. Shumaker and S. Lackey (Eds.): VAMR 2014, Part I, LNCS 8525, pp. 339–350, 2014.

Many museum professionals argue that there are some visitors for whom participatory experiences might be entirely off-putting. This is true, but the converse is also true. There are many people who engage heavily with social media and are incredibly comfortable using participatory platforms to connect with friends, activity partners, and potential dates.

Building on the experience of the Foundation of the Hellenic World (FHW) with social media and other adaptive technologies, particularly during the EXPERIMEDIA project [3], we discuss the primary challenges associated with the use of participatory elements in traditional digital dome shows. The use of such elements may draw in audiences for whom creative activities and social connection are preconditions for cultural engagement.

The initial section of this publication presents what has been done so far regarding large audience dome interactions and our proposed enhancements. The next section describes the technological FMI components used to implement the enhancements and how the experiment was conducted in order to validate these. Further sections analyze the experiment results and establish various impact factors. The concluding section presents future extensions.

2   Dome Audience Interactivity

The Foundation for the Hellenic World (FHW) is a world leading institution known for its use of 3D facilities and production in culture and heritage [4]. As many high tech museums it deploys advanced 3D virtual reality (VR) installations for virtual tours through reconstructions of heritage sites. Its real-time dome theater 'Tholos' projects imagery on a tilted hemispherical reflective surface of 13m in diameter.

Museums strive constantly to incorporate interactivity to exhibits or virtual reality shows because research has shown that it fosters learning and provides a unique visitor experience [5]. Unfortunately digital dome shows usually host large audiences where the common interactivity techniques and mechanics don't work. Therefore ongoing research is performed on methods incorporating audience interaction and gaming environments in the immersive space of a dome theater [6]. Traditional modes of interaction include button/joystick devices on visitor chairs and wherever possible the usage of dedicated museum educators which adapt the show and can conduct interactive question-answer sessions [7]. Another approach is to use camera based techniques in order to capture the crowd movement for controlling in-game objects or initiating actions [8].

Although research is actively conducted in order to use FMI for learning [9], sports [10][11] or museum visits[12], its potential usage for large audience participation and for enhancing visitor experience in digital dome shows has been largely ignored.

The standard mode of operation of the Tholos may be graphically modeled as in Figure 1. It is easy to see that this is a mainly one-way communication system, as the museum educator controls the system, thus specifying what the Tholos system will project to the visitors, while at the same time commenting on it.

Our proposed mode of operation to enhance the Dome visitor experience provides three additional activities:

1. Before entering the show, the participants are able to use a dedicated AR smart-phone application to deepen their knowledge on specific artifacts which will be shown later in the VR show.
2. Live video streaming allowed the contents of the VR show to be broadcast to the internet to be viewed by academic experts and to cast a video feed of the remote experts onto the dome screen.
3. A Facebook based mobile application was developed that allows visitors and experts to connect to a dedicated event page and post messages during the VR walk-through.

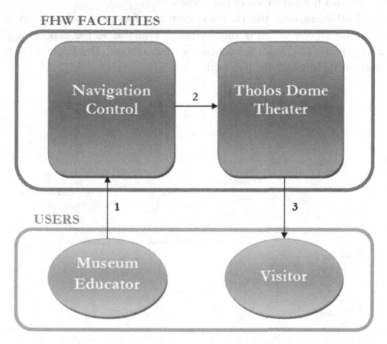

Fig. 1. Standard mode of operation of the Tholos

3 FMI Technologies in the Dome

The actual experiment, which was performed to evaluate the FMI extensions, was conducted as part of the EXPERIMEDIA framework over 2 days with a total of 18 participants. The proposed FMI mode of operation essentially consists of two operational parts and aims to enhance the education experience in at least three ways: by allowing multiple perspectives, situated learning and transfer of knowledge. The first part takes place before the show, and uses augmented reality technologies. The second part takes place during the show and includes live streaming and social media usage.

3.1   Live Streaming

Since the Experts are on a remote location, the main motivation is to allow real-time interaction between the Experts and the Visitors. To this end, the experts must see and hear of what is shown in the dome and of any questions coming from the audience. Additionally the audience must hear and see the experts.

The actual connectivity and communication between the components is shown in Figure 2. In the bottom part we can see that the museum educator holds the navigation control, which specifies the content that should be displayed to the visitors. This is the typical scenario for the utilization of the Tholos.

With the FMI extensions, the Tholos system also forwards the rendered stream to the video stream server, which in turn makes it available to the experts' application along with the audio feed from the educators' microphone. The Experts use a simple web browser portal to watch the live feed.

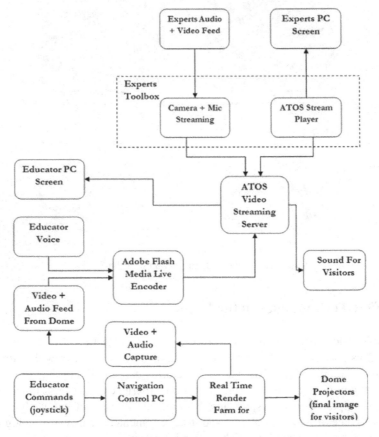

Fig. 2. Flow of information and component diagram for the experiment

3.2   Augmented Reality

The potential power of Augmented Reality (AR) as a Learning tool is its ability to leverage smartphone capabilities to create immersive learning experience [13]. Before entering the show, the participants are able to use a dedicated AR smartphone application to deepen their knowledge on specific artifacts, which will be shown in the VR show.

A dedicated space just before entering the show was created using markers on exhibition tables. These markers can be recognized by an application which superimposes virtual objects on top of the real ones, by tracking the position and orientation of the markers. With the help of FHW historians four points (Figure 3) were identified that are related to Miletus (i.e., the topic of the Tholos projection that was used in the experiment to test the new enhancements). Specifically:

- Point 1 is a 3D reconstruction of a bed that could be found in the city.
- Point 2 is a 3D reconstruction of a building that could be found in the city.
- Point 3 is a physical reconstruction of an ancient ship.
- Point 4 is coupled with the reconstruction of an amphora.

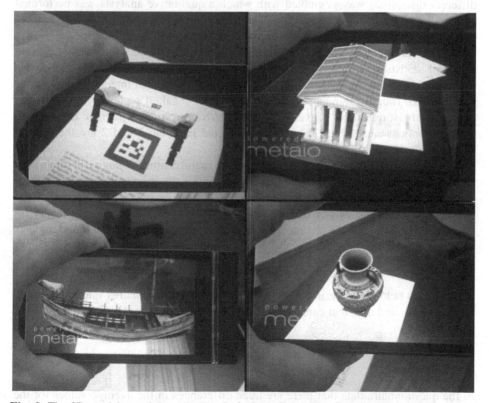

Fig. 3. The 3D models used for AR. Top-Left: Bed, Top-Right: Temple, Bottom-Left: Ship, Bottom-Right: Amphora

3.3   Social Networks

In order to leverage the power of social media, a Facebook based mobile application has been developed that allows visitors to connect using their personal credentials to a dedicated event page. Using their mobile device the visitors can communicate with each other and with the experts by posting messages during the VR walkthrough. The experts used a specialized web application to connect to the Facebook event page for chatting with the participants and also embedded a simple flash player for watching the Tholos video stream remotely form their office.

4   The Experiment

For evaluation purposes the participants were asked to fill out structured questionnaires. In a duration of two days there were two runs of the experiment inside the Tholos with a total of 18 participants. Each run took 1 hour to complete, with the participants spending 10 min. in the AR event, 35-40 min. inside the show and 10-15 for live Q&A with the remote expert. On the last day a focus group with 4 people of different disciplines was assembled with which a qualitative analysis was performed using simple conversation techniques. The focus group was consisting of an archaelogist/museologist, a curator, a 3D expert and a museum pedagogy expert.

Despite the medium number of samples, the number of questions allows a wide range of statistical values, correlations and graphical charts to be produced. We present below some statistics that we find most informative and interesting. Questions are translated roughly and abbreviated. A standard 1-5 Likert scale (1=Low, 5=High) is used for most questions. The exception is Yes/No questions which are treated with 2 values only (1=no, 2=yes). The values depicted in Table 1 and 2 are the median values of all the answers.

The friends and volunteers of the museum are mainly either young professionals or students studying on relevant to the museum activities disciplines (museology, digital archaeology, education, 3D programming and design etc), or professionals of the same disciplines. This of course meant that the testers were a group specifically invited to participate and not just random visitors of the venue, the main demographics of the tester group were:

- Mainly women (78%), high academic background, between 26-40 years of age

In the tables below we are including the data of the questionnaires interrelated with the comments and data that came out during the focus group for the relevant group of questions.

4.1   Pre Show

In the questionnaire data that there are huge differences in the average values for the different points. It is clear that points such as the ship and the amphorae have made a bigger impression than for example the bed and we discussed it in this focus group. The participants indicated two different patterns:

- The images of the bed and less of the building were considered less detailed than those of the ship and the amphorae (probably because of the rendering angle)
- The bed was considered to be quite out of context presented on its own without other objects of daily use of the same category.

Also people would be willing to pay money for such an application. This is probably the safest way to conclude that the augmented reality component did enhance their experience considerably. Although we tried to correlate the quality of the images to the quality of the experience (e.g. in the case of the bed) it looks like the overall experience is not dampened by a not so top quality image.

Table 1. Questionnaire analysis for the AR event. All results except where it is designated show the values with 1=Low, 5=High.

Question	Value
Q1: Was the device difficult to have on you? (1=no, 2=yes)	1,22
Q2: General clarity of images in the applications.	4,22
Q3: Clarity of the bed image	4,39
Q4: Clarity of the building image	4,83
Q5: Clarity of the ship image	4,94
Q6: Clarity of the amphorae image	4,78
Q7: General interest factor of the content	4,61
Q8: interest factor of the bed	4,00
Q9: interest factor of the building	4,50
Q10: interest factor of the ship	4,94
Q11: interest factor of the amphorae	4,72
Q12 : General Educational added value of the application	5,00
Q13 : Educational added value connected to the bed	4,50
Q14 : Educational added value connected to the building	4,72
Q15 : Educational added value connected to the ship	4,78
Q16 : Educational added value connected to the amphorae	4,74
Q17 : Was it fun to use the application?	4,83
Q18: Was it fun to watch the bed?	3,22
Q19: Was it fun to watch the building?	4,80
Q20: Was it fun to watch the ship?	4,89
Q21: Was it fun to watch the amphorae?	4,85
Q22: Would you pay 1 euro for this service? (1=no, 2=yes)	1,83
Q23: Would you pay 1 euro for this service if there were more interest points included? (1=no, 2=yes)	1,89
Q24: Would you pay 1 euro for this service if there were more interest points included like the bed? (1=no, 2=yes)	1,89

4.2   During the Walkthrough

The Facebook application and the ability of concurrent written communication of the visitors with the expert, as well as between themselves resulted in more questions being asked and answered. The whole walkthrough got instantly more social and exciting allowing the visitors to acclimatize very quickly to the tour and become much more focused. Even the occasional whispers amongst friends diminished since they were using messages to communicate.

The focus group discussion confirmed the questionnaire findings that in many occasions it was quite distracting trying to use the smart device during the Tholos show. The remote expert added value to the information that was given by the local guide but according to questionnaires and focus group results this service is something that people would pay for but not so willingly as for the Augmented Reality service.

Table 2. Questionnaire analysis for inside the show. All results except where it is designated show the values with 1=Low, 5=High.

Question	Value
Q25: was it clear why the specific images were used? (Tholos application) (1=no, 2=yes)	1,78
Q26: was there added educational value to the replies of the expert? (1=no, 2=yes)	1,89
Q27: Was it fun to use the application inside the Tholos?	4,61
Q28: Was the quality of the image and of the sound acceptable during the interaction with the expert?	4,67
Q29: Was it easy to use the Q&A application and its software?	4,44
Q30: The interaction with the remote expert added value to the experience?	4,67
Q31: How much distracting was the use of the smart phone during the show?	3,33
Q32 : Would you like to have permanently in each show a remote expert appearing except the museum guide?	3,44
Q33: How much would you like to have a permanent service with smart phones in the Tholos?	3,89
Q34: The quality of the image of the expert was good (yes/no)	4,11
Q35: The quality of the sound of the expert was good (yes/no)	4,11
Q36: Was there delay in the reception of the expert's voice. Were you annoyed by the time lapse between the question of the audience and the reply of the expert? (1=no, 2=yes)	1,56
Q37 : Which service you liked more in the Tholos (1=Q&A, 2=Expert discussion)	1,44
Q38 : Would you play 1 euro for the Tholos service? (1=no, 2=yes)	1,69
Q39 : Would you pay 1 euro for this service if there have been more interactive services? (1=no, 2=yes)	1,72

5   Impact of FMI

The experiment had three major impacts.

Visitor socializing: visitors could communicate with each other and to the expert providing a fertile ground for social activities. The AR event allowed them to explore and interact as a group, the streaming and social network components to communicate during the show without disturbing the main presentation.

Learning: The AR preshow event besides being very interactive disseminated historical information. It created a link and high anticipation about the VR show because the artefacts seen in the AR app are actually seen later in the show. The usage of a dedicated social application and live video streaming during the show allowed visitors to ask freely without hesitation and interruption. The museum educators witnessed an increase in the amount of questions asked especially during the live video session conversations with the remote expert.

Economic: User evaluation showed that the additions can also have a financial impact since most of the visitors were willing to pay additionally for experiences. Also the publicity through the live video feed and chat resulted in higher visitor number on the website and Facebook profile of the museum.

5.1   Parameters that affected impact

We established certain critical factors which could affect the success of using these tools for Dome shows and museums.

Ratio of Devices/Visitor: To experience these technologies the museum relies on the visitor to bring his own equipment, meaning his mobile phone or tablet. If the ratio of devices per visitor is very low the social aspects and the enhanced learning is tremendously impacted. The visitors without mobile phones cannot participate in the AR and social activities making oral questions.

Quality of Wi-Fi Signal: Without a reliable and working internet connection these technologies are rendered useless. We specifically had to increase and install Wi-Fi spots so as to ensure the whole venue's coverage. The exception lies with the AR event which is autonomous in that respect.

Duration and Order of AR Event: Initially we tried to use the AR points after the show scattered around the museum in order to motivate visitor exploration. This proved not functional since many visitors could not find the interest points or had the time and energy after a VR walkthrough of 40 minutes. The AR event should be easily accessible and for a short period of time when combined with a traditional show.

Number of Visitors: We run the last experiment with a number of 18 visitors and had 1 expert. The focus group discussion and through observation it resulted that the expert had difficulty in answering all these questions on time and could easily overlook questions or comments. Often the visitors had to wait before getting a response. As the Tholos is a VR system of 130 seats it is evident that a scale in visitors need a analogous scale in experts to have any real value.

Social app and Web App UI: The user interface of the social app which is used by the visitors and web app of the expert are of utmost importance. The UI should be self explanatory, easy to use and should not force the visitor to look at it all the time. During all experiment runs we witnessed a lot of failures and problems in that regard. The UI of the mobile app was desktop oriented and required constant button presses and usage of menus. The answers were not refreshed automatically and the visitor for forced to press the 'Refresh" button repeatedly.

This resulted in visitors missing large parts of the show, since they were forced to monitor it constantly. The UI has to try keep people in a heads-up mode to make sure that they are also looking at the historical and art information presented. Therefore a simple design is needed which enables the visitor to quickly find the interest point he wants. It should also feature some form of feedback in the form vibration or a visual indication when an answer to a question arrived.

Latency versus Quality: During video streaming major latency issues were experienced which could range to up to 7 seconds. During the show and interaction with the expert a temporal loss of quality both in picture and in some for also in audio could be accepted but the latency issue made it difficult to conduct a live asks and answer section

6   Avatar Embodiment

Although not incorporated into the experiment described here the next milestone for usage of new FMI technologies in digital domes is avatar embodiment. Avatar embodiment allows the experts to puppeteer a virtual character created by an external authoring application. The process requires that the character mesh is attached to an articulated structure of control elements called bones. Bones can be viewed as oriented 3D line segments that connect transformable joints (such as knees or shoulders). Avatar embodiment within the FHW use case is achieved by allowing users to create avatars, rigged with a pre-defined 17-joints hierarchy (similar to the OpenNI joint tracking structure), as in [14].

The Microsoft Kinect was a breakthrough device for the easy capturing of 3D information. This fact led to the enormous penetration of the FMI ideas to a very wide audience, yet many inefficiencies remain unsolved. EXPERIMEDIA developed sophisticated algorithms to cope with these inefficiencies. The algorithms provide information correction from inaccurate depth estimation, constrain the Kinect's calculated human skeleton data to physical poses to enhance reliability, as well as many more enhancement that are suitable for avatar motion. Therefore, EXPERIMEDIA clearly offers a unique combination of algorithms that pave the way for more novel application domains.

The goal of using the avatar motion within the FHW context is to provide the means to put the expert on the scene. By doing so, visitors will have the change to meet in "person" with the expert's avatar, which can respond in real-time. It is a step beyond the common practice until now with either voice interaction and/or text messages. The sensation of a guided tour within a museum guided from the expert's avatar will provide a higher immersion sensation to the visitors of the Tholos. Quality of Experience (QoE) measures will be defined to finally assess the overall feedback of the visitor's experience.

7   Conclusion

Museums are increasingly using technology to reach an audience outside their walls. As technology and all its tools change, so do the challenges facing museums. In this paper we have reported on the experience of incorporating such new or emerging technologies in the operations of the FHW museum. It seems that whilst the technology itself is mature enough and it certainly brings added value to what is offered to the visitor, there are some fine lines to tend to as the developers' perspective is not necessarily in line with the museological perspective of things.

There is also significant frustration among curators that museums are leaping ahead with new technologies without proper evaluation. Therefore this experiment despite having a rather limited number of participants provides an very informative pilot study into the possibilities that exist in using future internet technologies for domes. it not only established a proposed method of implementation but also ratified the impact it had on the visitor experience and the several factors that could limit the results.

The three areas where the suggested enhancements had the most impact are of primary importance to any museum venue and vital to its survival and educational goal.

Acknowledgement. The research leading to these results is partly funded by the EU Community's FP7 ICT under the "EXPERiments in live social and networked MEDIA experiences" project (Grant Agreement 287966).

And also by the EU Community's FP7 ICT NO under the "Virtual Museum Transnational Network " project (Grant Agreement 270404)

References

1. Bearman, D.: Representing Museum Knowledge. In: Marty, P.F., Jones, K.B. (eds.) Museum Informatics, Routledge, New York (2008)
2. Jenkins, H. (P. I.), Purushotma, R., Weigel, M., Clinton, K., Robison, A.J.: Confronting the Challenges of Participatory Culture Media Education for the 21st Century. The MIT Press, Cambridge (2009)
3. Boniface, M., Phillips, S., Voulodimos, A., Osborne, D., Murg, S.: Technology Enablers for a Future Media Internet Testing Facility. NEM Summit (2013) (accepted)
4. Christopoulos, D., Gaitatzes, A., Papaioannou, G., Zyba, G.: Designing a Real-time Playback System for a Dome Theater. In: Proceedings of Eurographics 7th International Symposium on Virtual Reality, Archaeology and Intelligent Cultural Heritage, VAST (2006)
5. Falk, J.H., Dierking, L.D.: Learning from museums: visitor experiences and the making of meaning. AltaMira Press, Walnut Creek (2000)
6. Apostolellis, P., Daradoumis, T.: Audience Interactivity as Leverage for Effective Learning in Gaming Environments for Dome Theaters. In: Wolpers, M., Kirschner, P.A., Scheffel, M., Lindstaedt, S., Dimitrova, V. (eds.) EC-TEL 2010. LNCS, vol. 6383, pp. 451–456. Springer, Heidelberg (2010)

7. Christopoulos, D., Apostolellis, P., Onasiadis, A.: Educational Virtual Environments for Digital Dome Display Systems with Audience Participation. In: Workshop on Informatics in Education (WIE 2009), Corfy, Greece, September 12 (2009)
8. Maynes-Aminzade, D., Pausch, R., Seitz, S.: Techniques for interactive audience participation. In: Proceedings of the Fourth IEEE International Conference on Multimodal Interfaces, Pittsburgh, PA, USA (2002)
9. Gil-Solla, A., et al.: REENACT: Future Media Internet Technologies for Immersive Learning about Historical Battles and Wars. In: eChallenges Conference (2013)
10. Eriksson, M.: Elite Sports Training as Model for Future Internet Practices. In: European Sociological Association Conferences, ESA 2013 (2013)
11. Daras, P., Zarpalas, D., Posio, E., Vatjus-Anttila, J.: Sharing the jogging experience between remote runners. In: 3D-Live Demo at the 15th IEEE International Workshop on Multimedia Signal Processing (MMSP), Pula, Italy, September 30-October 2 (2013)
12. Antoniou, A., Lepouras, G., Lykourentzou, I., Naudet, Y.: Connecting physical space, human personalities, and social networks: The Experimedia Blue project. In: Charitos, D., Theona, I., Gragona, D., Rizopoulos, H., Meimaris, M. (eds.) Proceedings of the International Biennial Conference Hybrid City, Subtle Revolutions, May 23-25, pp. 197–200. University Research Institute of Applied Communication, Athens (2013)
13. Dunleavy, M., Dede, C.: Augmented Reality Teaching and Learning. In: Handbook of Research on Educational Communications and Technology, pp. 735–745. Springer, New York (2013)
14. Sanna, A., Lamberti, F., Paravati, G., Rocha, F.D.: A kinect-based interface to animate virtual characters. Journal on Multimodal User Interfaces, 1–11 (2012)

Fast and Accurate 3D Reproduction
of a Remote Collaboration Environment

ABM Tariqul Islam[1], Christian Scheel[1], Ali Shariq Imran[2], and Oliver Staadt[1]

[1] Visual Computing Lab, Dept. of Comp. Science, University of Rostock, Germany
[2] Gjøvik University College, Norway
{tariqul.islam,christian.scheel,oliver.staadt}@uni-rostock.de,
ali.imran@hig.no

Abstract. We present an approach for high quality rendering of the 3D representation of a remote collaboration scene, along with real-time rendering speed, by expanding the unstructured lumigraph rendering (ULR) method. ULR uses a 3D proxy which is in the simplest case a 2D plane. We develop *dynamic proxy* for ULR, to get a better and more detailed 3D proxy in real-time; which leads to the rendering of high-quality and accurate 3D scenes with motion parallax support. The novel contribution of this work is the development of a *dynamic proxy* in real-time. The *dynamic proxy* is generated based on depth images instead of color images as in the Lumigraph approach.

Keywords: 3D reproduction, remote collaboration, telepresence, unstructured lumigraph rendering, motion parallax.

1 Introduction

Recent advancements in display technology have made a tremendous influence on the research related to displaying realistic and interactive representation of a scene. Moreover, because of availability of low-cost color and depth cameras, systems capable of displaying such 3D representations have become cost effective, and many applications, such as elearning and remote collaboration, are including large camera arrays to support 3D visualization of a scene [1][2]. Nowadays, we see camera arrays consisting of different camera types, on either side of a remote collaboration setup, for capturing the whole scene [1]. In order to provide an immersive meeting experience, a remote collaboration system should provide the users with a real-time reproduction of the collaborating environment and also a way to interact properly with the distant participants [3].

A number of research projects have been carried out to provide such an interactive 3D representation; our focus is on remote collaboration or telepresence system, as depicted in Fig. 1. We can see in Fig. 1 that image acquisition is taking place on the local site of the telepresence system and then transmitted to the remote site where 3D scene is visualized on the display. Although, the area of 3D representation of a scene has been explored during the last few years [4][5][6], high-quality reconstruction and immersive interaction method is still an

R. Shumaker and S. Lackey (Eds.): VAMR 2014, Part I, LNCS 8525, pp. 351–362, 2014.

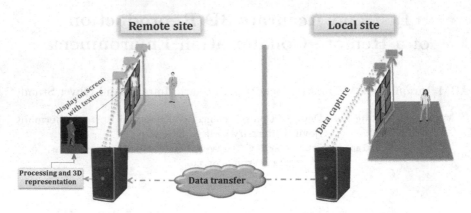

Fig. 1. Illustration of a telepresence system with 3D representation of the scene

open problem. Most of the existing approaches either suffer from slower reconstruction speed or from visible artifacts on the represented scene. Moreover, the huge dynamic data, generated from camera arrays, adds additional problem of data transmission [7].

We present here an approach for high-quality 3D rendering of a remote collaboration scene, with real-time rendering speed, by means of expanding the Unstructured Lumigraph Rendering (ULR) method [8]. In the ULR approach, the authors use a 3D proxy, which is in the simplest case a 2D plane. A more complex proxy would be, for example, an arbitrary triangle mesh. In our work, we develop a *dynamic proxy* for getting a better and more detailed 3D proxy in real-time; which leads to a high-quality 3D scene representation. The proxy in ULR doesn't get updated when the scene is changed in real-time; our novel idea of generating dynamic proxies help to remove this obstacle and get updated in real-time. Like any other proxy, which supports motion parallax, our developed system with *dynamic proxy* also supports motion parallax; thus, proper interaction for the represented scene is obtained. Dynamic proxies also help to avoid generating huge dynamic data by reducing the number of required cameras. GPU implementation of our idea leads to achieving real-time rendering of the represented scene. We map the texture from color images on top of the depth images which are obtained from a set of Microsoft kinects. We also adapt a recently developed depth camera calibration method [9] for our system. The rest of the paper is organized as follows: in section 2, we present some related work for 3D scene representation; in section 3, we present a brief description of ULR method; section 4 describes details of our system; in section 5, we describe our system setup and implementation details; in section 6, we present our results and some existing limitations and finally, in section 7, we conclude our paper.

2 Related Work

Maimone and Fuchs, in [10], present a telepresence system in which the users can view a 3D representation of the scene captured by a set of kinects placed on the remote site. On the basis of per pixel quality assessment, they merge overlapping depth contributions. Although, the system generates dynamic scene from arbitrary position, it suffers from lower rendering speed issues when more enhancement parameters, for removing interference issues, are activated [10]. Researchers also generated such 3D representations by combining textures from 2D video stream on top of the depth information obtained from depth cameras [1][4]. They obtain 3D representation by projecting the foreground silhouettes backwards onto 3D plane and refine it by view-dependent depth estimation [5]. Beck et al. presents an immersive telepresence system [11] where a set of kinects is used to capture the scene. They apply similar 3D reconstruction method as in [10]. Although, they provide an immersive interaction experience through a complex setup, the visual appearance is not quite satisfactory. Hansung et al. present a dynamic 3D scene representation approach [5] for outdoor environments.

For producing a 3D representation of a scene, researchers very often use image-based rendering (IBR) approach rather than traditional three-dimensional graphics [8]. Gortler et al. present an IBR method, named as *Lumigraph* [12], which is capable of reconstructing an accurate ray from a limited number of acquisition cameras. Shum et al. propose an alternate approach [13], which use low precission depth correction for lower dimensional Lumigraph method. Buehler et al., in [8], have presented an IBR method, called ULR. We discus briefly about ULR in the next section.

3   Unstructured Lumigraph Rendering

The ULR algorithm [8] generalizes two IBR approaches – *Lumigraph* [12] and *View-Dependent Texture Mapping* [14]. ULR has three input parameters – a polygon mesh that represents the scene geometry, an unstructured image set and camera pose information for each image. The authors refer the polygon mesh as *geometric proxy* which is in principle similar to the *proxy* stated in [15].

In the ULR, a *camera blending* field determines how each input camera is weighted to reconstruct a pixel. Each pixel of the reconstructed image is calculated from the weighted average of the corresponding pixels of the input images [8]. The blending weight function w_{ang} and normalization of blending weights $\widetilde{w}_{ang}(i)$ are calculated as in Eq. 1 and Eq. 2.

$$w_{ang}(i) = 1 - \frac{penalty_{ang}(i)}{thres_{ang}} \tag{1}$$

$$\widetilde{w}_{ang}(i) = \frac{w_{ang}(i)}{\sum_{j=1}^{k} w_{ang}(j)} \tag{2}$$

In Eq. 1, $penalty_{ang}(i)$ is the angular difference between a ray from a virtual camera (the new viewpoint) and the ray of i-th input camera to the point where the ray from the virtual camera intersects the proxy. The $thres_{ang}$ angle is the largest $penalty_{ang}$ of the k-nearest cameras.

4   System Description

Most of the existing telepresence systems, such as the *extended window metaphor* (EWM) [7] and [11], suffer from generating huge dynamic data because of using large number of cameras. We develop a *dynamic proxy* which combines the depth images from the depth cameras in addition to the basic idea of the ULR approach. Since, scene geometry information is used, ULR can reproduce a new view using few number of input camera images.

However, ULR has its own limitation as well; the *proxy* in ULR doesn't update when the scene is changed in real-time. To resolve this, we develop *dynamic proxy* for representing the scene in 3D from a new view-point; thus, it supports depth images for creating a new depth image out of existing depth images which can be used as a proxy. *Dynamic proxies* also help to reduce the processing time significantly, because they generate arbitrary view-points only for the part of the scene which is visible from a particular view rather than for the whole scene.

4.1   Dynamic Proxy Generation

The data of the depth cameras should be merged to generate the *dynamic proxy*; the *dynamic proxy* is then used to render the scene from a new point of view. To generate a *dynamic proxy*, depth information is first obtained with the Microsoft kinects; then, the depth values are passed through a median filter for noise reduction. We choose the median filter in order to preserve the edges of the objects inside a scene. Then the filtered points of each kinects are transferred to a common coordinate system. The camera extrinsics, via calibration, must be known for transferring the 3D points to a common coordinate system.

For each camera, a triangle mesh is generated from the 3D points of that camera that are transferred to a common coordinate system. For the creation of the triangles, the neighbor relationships of the 3D points are used for each camera. For each 3D point, a check is performed whether the immediate-right, lower-right and bottom neighbors are still present in each case after filtering. If a 3D point does not have at least two neighbors, no triangle is created. When there are two neighbors, one triangle is created and when there are three neighbors, two triangles of the 3D point are generated. To remove unwanted triangles between object edges and object background or foreground object, triangles are removed, in which the distance between two points is above a threshold.

For each pixel, a ray R_i is cast from the position of the virtual camera V into the scene. For each ray, the intersection points S_{ik} with the triangle meshes T_k are calculated, see Fig. 2(a). When a ray has multiple intersections with the triangle mesh of a camera, only the closest one to the virtual camera is taken. When a ray has intersection points with the triangle meshes of several cameras, the depth values of this intersection points are blended through a weighting. Instead as in the *Lumigraph* [12], where best color information is searched, here we look for the best depth information.

The weighting is performed by comparing the angle between the rays of the cameras to their 3D points and the rays from the virtual camera to these points.

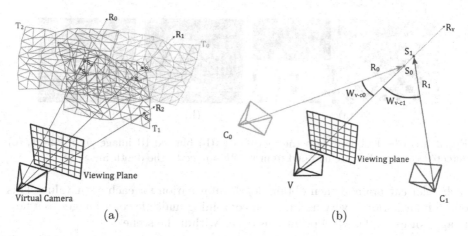

Fig. 2. (a) Rays R_i cast from the virtual camera V; S_{ik} intersection points, T_k triangle meshes. (b) Weighting the angles W_{V-C_i} between the rays; C_i kinects.

Smaller angle between the ray of a camera and the ray of the virtual camera indicates a higher weighting for the point from the camera.

The weighting also takes into account that a intersection point of a ray, from the virtual camera, that lies far behind other intersection points from the ray, is not used. Because, it is assumed that this point then belongs to another object or to another side of the same object. The total weight ω is defined as follows:

$$\omega = \rho \cdot \theta \tag{3}$$

$$\rho = v_\tau \cdot d_\tau \tag{4}$$

In Eq. 3 and Eq. 4, θ, ρ, v_τ and d_τ refer to the angle, penalty, position threshold and distance threshold respectively. $v_\tau = 0$, if a point lies outside a given scene, otherwise 1 and $d_\tau = 0$, when an intersection point from the view of the virtual camera is more than a threshold value behind a different intersection from the same ray. If one of these two variables is 0, the total weight ω is set to 0. θ is a weight for the angle between a ray of the virtual camera and a ray of a kinect to a point in the scene (see Fig. 2(b)). θ is calculated and normalized (see, *blending shader* in section 5.1) like in Eq. 5. Acceleration techniques must be applied to calculate the intersection of a ray with a triangle mesh, since it is computationally very expensive to test the ray with each triangle.

To accelerate the *dynamic proxy* generation, we use GPU acceleration technique (see section 5.1). The generated *dynamic proxy* can then be used for the ULR. The important point for using the *dynamic proxy* with the ULR is to interlace the processing of the color cameras in the processing of the depth cameras; this is required especially for a GPU implementation to get real-time performance. Moreover, it is also necessary to calibrate the color cameras with respect to the depth cameras, or to calibrate all cameras to a specific world coordinate system. It is also possible to generate a *dynamic proxy* from the perspective of

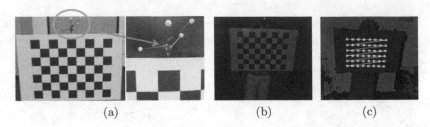

(a)   (b)   (c)

Fig. 3. (a) Checkerboard with the rigid body, (b) blurred IR image [9] of kinect, (c) detected corners that are mapped from the IR image to the depth image [9]

each color camera and then obtain depth information for each color value. This depth information is very useful when combining multiple color images to a new image, for example, when occlusions occur within the scene.

4.2   Camera Calibration

There exist a number of works for depth camera calibration; for our proposed 3D scene rendering system, we adapt the work [9], by Avetisyan et al. It uses a 3-D lookup table to support per-pixel and per-distance mapping at every pixel in the depth image. For finding the *intrinsic* and *extrinsic* parameters [9], we use the standard checkerboard based approach. The calibration method uses a rigid body attached to the standard planar checkerboard as shown in Fig. 3(a). During the calibration, the rigid body is being traced by well calibrated 12 DOF (degrees of freedom) OptiTrack [16] system.

After obtaining the mapping between infrared (IR) and depth images of the kinects, we transfer the corner coordinates from the IR image into the depth image [9]. Illustration of the resulting depth images with the detected corners is shown in Fig. 3(b) and 3(c). This approach doesn't need any hard mechanical setup or distance measuring tools. The ground truth values are recorded by the real-time tracking system and are used for calculating real distances of the points that are extracted from the checkerboard pattern. Moreover, this approach supports simultaneous depth correction for multiple kinects.

5   System Setup and Implementation

We use two kinects as depicted in Fig. 4 for capturing the scene. For displaying the rendered 3D scene, we use a display wall which consists of 24 DELL 2709W displays; the color cameras are integrated on the bezels of the displays. The display wall has a combined resolution of 55 Mio pixels. For tracking purpose, we use the 12 DOF OptiTrack [16] system. We develop the system with C++ and use libfreenect from OpenKinect as camera driver libraries. For this work, we use a single Macbook Pro, with 2.3 GHz intel i7 processor and NVIDIA GeForce GT 650M 1024 MB graphics card.

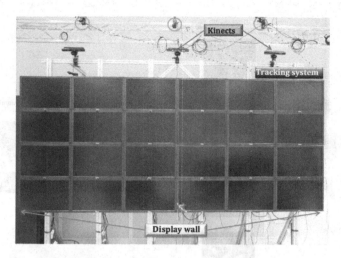

Fig. 4. Lab setup with kinects, tracking system and display wall

5.1   GPU Implementation

To accelerate the generation of the *dynamic proxy*, we approach for a GPU implementation of our method. The implementation is sub-divided into three shader programs in OpenGL – a filter shader, a rendering shader and a blending shader. OpenGL version 2.1 and GLSL version 1.2 is used for the implementation. The illustration of the workflow is depicted in Fig. 5. We can see in Fig. 5 that, after the scene is captured by the camera set, each camera data goes, at first, to filter shader, then to render shader and then, they are blended at the blender shader and finally, the *dynamic proxy* for the scene is generated. A brief description of the functionalities of the shaders is given below.

Filter Shader. The filter shader is used for noise reduction in the depth values. It filters the depth values of the kinects by a 5x5 median filter.

Render Shader. In the render shader, the real point values from the depth values of the kinects are calculated and transferred to a common coordinate system. Also the weighting of each point is performed here. The weight ω and penalty ρ are calculated as in Eq. 3 and Eq. 4; to calculate the angle θ in Eq. 3, we use the following formula:

$$\theta = \cos^{-1}\left(\frac{R_k \cdot R_v}{|R_k| \cdot |R_v|}\right) \cdot \frac{\theta_\tau}{\frac{\pi}{2}} \tag{5}$$

In Eq. 5, θ_τ is the threshold value for angle θ; R_k and R_v are the rays from the kinects and the virtual camera V respectively. θ_τ is 0 if θ is bigger than $\frac{\pi}{2}$, otherwise 1.

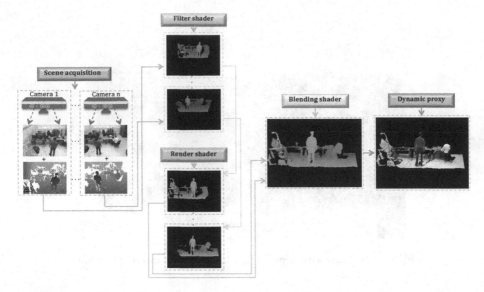

Fig. 5. Illustration of workflow for GPU implementation

Blending Shader. In the blending shader, the depth values in the textures from each camera are blended together based on their weights. For each pixel the weight ω_i, calculated like in Eq. 7, for camera i of n cameras is multiplied with a normalization factor f; f is calculated as in Eq. 6. The depth values Z_i of the n kinects are blended on the basis of the weights ω_i to get final depth Z, as in Eq. 8. The blended depth values are stored in a final resulting texture which represents the *dynamic proxy*.

$$f = \frac{1}{\sum_{i=0}^{n-1} \omega_i} \tag{6}$$

$$\omega_i = \omega_i \cdot f \tag{7}$$

$$Z = \sum_{i=0}^{n-1} Z_i \omega_i \tag{8}$$

6   Results

We are able to achieve real-time rendering speed (29.88 fps) by implementing our idea with the GPU implementation. Table 1 shows the time required for different sectors of the processing pipeline. From table 1, we can see that, each image takes 33 ms to process, in which the rendering takes only 4 ms and most of the time is consumed to transfer camera data from the camera to the system for processing. Fig. 6 shows the 3D rendering of an object (a bag on a chair) from various view-points inside the test scene. Fig. 7 shows the 3D rendering, via *dynamic proxy*, of a scene with a person and objects in the test environment. Fig. 8 shows the 3D rendering of the test environment; on the top row, it shows a person in different positions, on bottom row, it shows different view-points of a person sitting behind a desk.

Table 1. Time measurement for 1100 images (1024 × 768 res)

Image per sec.	29.88
Time per image	33 ms
Get camera data to computer	28 ms
Filtering	1 ms
Rendering	4 ms

As a limitation of our system, we observe presence of holes on the represented 3D scene at the intersection of two kinects; this is caused due to the interference problem of multiple kinect projectors. We plan to solve this issue by capturing the image stream for kinects on different time domains; by switching the stream from one kinect to the another very fast. We can also solve this by software based solutions as described in [10]. Since our focus in this paper is on a faster and accurate 3D representation of a scene, we overlook the interference issue and keep it as a future work.

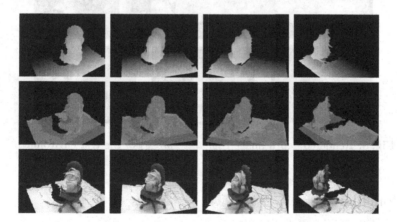

Fig. 6. Top row: depth image (*dynamic proxy*), middle row: camera weighting (for 2 kinects), bottom row: final output with texture

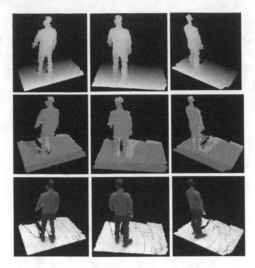

Fig. 7. Top row: *dynamic proxy* (depth image), middle row: camera weighting (for 2 kinects), bottom row: *dynamic proxy* with texture

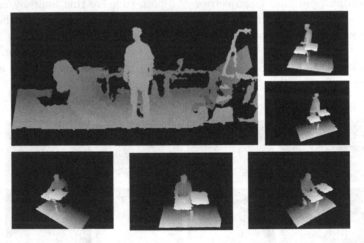

Fig. 8. Rendered depth image (*dynamic proxy*) of the test environment

7   Conclusion

Modern display technology along with availability of cheaper cameras have influenced remote collaboration systems to incorporate large camera array to capture and transmit the recorded data, to be represented as 3D scene on display, to other side of the collaborating environment. Until today, a method providing both real-time reproduction speed and high visual quality is far from achieving. We present an approach for high quality rendering of the 3D representation of a remote collaboration scene along with real-time rendering speed by expanding the ULR method. We develop a *dynamic proxy* for ULR, to get a better and more detailed 3D proxy in real-time; which leads to a better quality rendering of the 3D scene. Our system also supports motion parallax for the represented 3D scene. Although, we observe some holes at the interference point of two kinects, it can be solved with existing solutions. As a future work, we plan to extend our method for a networked camera system for generating arbitrary view-points for multiple users.

Acknowledgments. This work was supported by the EU FP7 Marie Curie ITN "DIVA" under REA Grant Agreement No. 290227 and by the German Research Foundation (DFG) within the research training group GRK 1424 MuSAMA. We thank Razmik Avetisyan for his valuable suggestions in camera calibration. We would also like to thank the anonymous reviewers for their valuable comments and suggestions.

References

1. Maimone, A., Bidwell, J., Peng, K., Fuchs, H.: Enhanced personal autostereoscopic telepresence system using commodity depth cameras. Computers & Graphics 36(7), 791–807 (2012)
2. Marcus, R., Alan, R.: Developing Interaction 3D models for e-learning applications online, http://shura.shu.ac.uk/5306/1/developing_3d_models_for_e-learning_applications.pdf (last accessed October 30, 2013)
3. Edwards, J.: Telepresence: Virtual Reality in the Real World [Special Reports]. IEEE Signal Processing Magazine 28(6), 9–142 (2011)
4. Petit, B., Lesage, J.-D., Menier, C., Allard, J., Franco, J.-S., Raffin, B., Boyer, E., Faure, F.: Multicamera real-time 3d modeling for telepresence and remote collaboration. International Journal of Digital Multimedia Broadcasting 2010, 247108, 12 pages (2009)
5. Kim, H., Guillemaut, J.-Y., Takai, T., Sarim, M., Hilton, A.: Outdoor Dynamic 3-D Scene Reconstruction. IEEE Transactions on Circuits and Systems for Video Technology 22(11), 1611–1622 (2012)
6. Maimone, A., Fuchs, H.: A first look at a telepresence system with room-sized real-time 3d capture and life-sized tracked display wall. In: ICAT (November 2011)
7. Willert, M., Ohl, S., Staadt, O.G.: Reducing bandwidth consumption in parallel networked telepresence environments. In: VRCAI, pp. 247–254 (2012)
8. Buehler, C., Bosse, M., Mcmillan, L., Gortler, S., Cohen, M.: Unstructured lumigraph rendering. In: Proceedings of the 28th annual Conference on Computer Graphics and Interactive Techniques ACM, S. 425–432 (2001)
9. Avetisyan, R.: Calibration of depth camera arrays (Master thesis). Dept. of computer science, University of Rostock, Germany (2013)
10. Maimone, A., Fuchs, H.: Encumbrance-free telepresence system with real-time 3D capture and display using commodity depth cameras. In: 2011 10th IEEE International Symposium on Mixed and Augmented Reality (ISMAR), 137–146 (2011)
11. Beck, S., Kunert, A., Kulik, A., Froehlich, B.: Immersive Group-to-Group Telepresence. IEEE Transactions on Visualization and Computer Graphics 19(4), 616–625 (2013)

12. Gortler, S.J., Grzeszczuk, R., Szeliski, R., Cohen, M.F.: The lumigraph. In: SIGGRAPH, pp. 43–54 (1996)
13. Shum, H.-Y., He, L.-W.: Rendering with concentric mosaics. In: SIGGRAPH, pp. 299–306 (1999)
14. Debevec, P., Taylor, C., Malik, J.: Modeling and rendering architecture from photographs. In: SIGGRAPH, pp. 11–20 (1996)
15. Eisemann, M., De Decker, B., Magnor, M., Bekaert, P., De Aguiar, E., Ahmed, N., Theobalt, C., Sellent, A.: Floating textures. In: Computer Graphics Forum Bd, vol. 27, S. 409–418. Wiley Online Library (2008)
16. OptiTrack, http://www.naturalpoint.com/optitrack/ (last accessed January 25, 2014)

From Image Inpainting to Diminished Reality

Norihiko Kawai, Tomokazu Sato, and Naokazu Yokoya

Graduate School of Information Science, Nara Institute of Science and Technology
8916-5 Takayama, Ikoma, Nara 630-0192, Japan
{norihi-k,tomoka-s,yokoya}@is.naist.jp

Abstract. Image inpainting, which removes undesired objects in a static image and fills in the missing regions with plausible textures, has been developed in the research fields of image processing. On the other hand, Diminished Reality (DR), which visually removes real objects from video images by filling in the missing regions with background textures in real time, is one of the growing topics in Virtual/Mixed Reality, and considered as the opposite of Augmented Reality. In this paper, we introduce the state-of-the-art of image inpainting methods and how to apply the image inpainting to diminished reality.

Keywords: image inpainting, diminished reality, augmented reality.

1 Introduction

Image inpainting, which removes undesired objects in a static image and fills in the missing regions with plausible textures, has been developed in the research fields of image processing. On the other hand, Diminished Reality (DR), which visually removes real objects from video images by filling in the missing regions with background textures in real time, is one of the growing topics in Virtual/Mixed Reality, and considered as the opposite of Augmented Reality. Diminished reality can be used for various applications. For example, some pieces of furniture may be removed to simulate different arrangements (Fig. 1(a)), signboards can be removed for landscape simulations (Fig. 1(b)), and augmented reality (AR) markers can be hidden to achieve seamless fusion between virtual objects and the real world [1–3]. Diminished reality methods can be classified into two categories: One uses actual background images by capturing them in advance or with multiple cameras, and the other generates a plausible background by applying an image inpainting technique. For scenes in which the actual background of a target object cannot be observed, or for cases where it is burdensome for users to capture the background, we can employ the latter method. In this paper, we focus on the image inpainting-based diminished reality approach, and introduce the state-of-the-art of image inpainting methods and how to apply the image inpainting to diminished reality. In addition, we briefly introduce our recent diminished reality method and its results [4].

R. Shumaker and S. Lackey (Eds.): VAMR 2014, Part I, LNCS 8525, pp. 363–374, 2014.
© Springer International Publishing Switzerland 2014

(a) Furniture removal   (b) Signboard removal

Fig. 1. Example applications of diminished reality. Images on the left are inputs, and those on the right are our results.

2   Image Inpainting for Removing Objects

In this section, we introduce the state-of-the-art image inpainting methods. We then introduce searching methods for speeding up image inpainting.

2.1   Image Inpainting Methods

Image inpainting (also referred to as image completion) methods can be largely classified into two categories: One uses information only around the target region, and the other uses the similarity of textures. The former approach fills in the missing regions by calculating pixel values considering the continuity of pixel intensity from the boundary of the missing region assuming thet neighbor pixels have similar pixel values. As the representative method, Bertalmio et al. [5] propagate colors along edges by using partial differential equations. This type of method is effective for small image gaps like scratches in a photograph. However, the resultant images easily become unclear when the missing regions are large because the methods cannot generate complex textures in principle. Therefore, the latter approach has been intensively developed these days.

This approach uses textures in an image as exemplars based on the assumption that textures appropriate for missing regions are similar to those in the remainder of the image. The methods in this approach can be classified into two categories. One is based on successive texture copy and the other on global optimization. In the former approach, the application of texture synthesis technique to image completion was originated by Efros et al. [6]. In this method, texture is successively copied to the boundary of the missing regions. Although this method can generate complex textures in the missing regions, the quality of synthesized texture largely depends on the order of copy. For this problem, in order to maker more plausible textures, the order of texture copy has been determined with some criteria (e.g., the number of fixed pixels in a patch and strength of an edge in [7]). Nevertheless, these methods still have the problem that a discontinuous texture tends to be generated by the greedy fill-in order.

In order to settle this, global optimization-based methods have been proposed. As the representative method in this approach, Wexler et al. [8] generate optimal textures in missing regions by minimizing an objective function based

Fig. 2. Results of our image inpainting method [10]

on pattern similarity between the missing region and the reminder of the image. Specifically, the objective function is minimized by iterating two processes: searching for a similar pattern in the reminder of the image, and updating pixel values in the missing regions. Although this method can generate complex and good textures for many images, unnatural textures are still generated due to the paucity of available samples in the image. To increase available samples, there have already been some attempts in terms of photometric and geometric expansion of patterns. For example, our previous methods in [9, 10] allow brightness transformation of texture patterns to utilize patterns with the same geometry but different brightness, and use symmetric patterns. Fig. 2 shows example results of our method. Darabi et al. [11] use screened poisson to adjust color and symmetric, rotating, scaling patterns. However, it is difficult to automatically and appropriately estimate parameters of geometric transformation because various changes in texture patterns exist in ordinary photographs. Therefore, some methods are proposed for dealing with various changes in geometric patterns with manual interactions [12, 13].

2.2 Searching Method for Speeding Up Image Inpainting

In the exemplar-based method mentioned above, it takes much time to exhaustively search for similar patterns. For this problem, an approximate nearest neighbor search algorithm "PatchMatch" has been proposed [14]. This method propagates pixel positions of similar patterns when we make correspondences between pixels in the missing region and the reminder of the image pixel by pixel by raster scan. In addition, it also gives a good correspondence seed with random search. This method was improved for dealing with geometric changes in texture patterns as "Generalized PatchMatch" [15]. By using these search methods, the computational time of image inpainting is drastically improved from several tens of minutes to a few seconds.

3 Image Inpainting-Based Diminished Reality

In this section, we introduce six methods [1–4, 16, 17] in the field of image inpainting-based diminished reality. These methods basically assume that target objects are fixed in the 3D environment. A target object in research [1–3] is an AR marker, and the others target general objects. We review these methods in terms of four factors: (1) real-time processing, (2) the temporal coherence of textures, (3) the quality of image inpainting, and (4) the determination of mask regions in which foreground textures are to be replaced with background ones.

3.1   Real-Time Processing

As mentioned in Section 2, it still takes at least a few seconds for inpainting methods to fill in missing regions. Therefore, just applying an image inpainting method to each frame cannot remove objects in real time. To overcome the problem, three approaches have been proposed. One uses a very simple approach, and one alters a conventional image inpainting method to reduce the computational cost, and the other employs a semi-dynamic approach.

As regards a simple approach, Siltanen [1] mixed several specific pixel values around the target region. Although this method can rapidly generate textures, it is difficult to generate natural and complex textures using such a simple approach. As the second approach, Herling et al. [16] basically applied the the combination of methods in [18] and [14] with use of grayscale and reduction of resolution. Although the method achieved the real-time performance, the quality of inpainting decreased compared with the original inpainting method. Herling et al. [17] have also proposed a different diminished reality method by improving the energy function used in [16] using spatial cost to quicken the energy convergence. They also employed a parallel processing for searching process. By these, the quality is quite improved compared with their previous method. As the third approach, Korkalo et al. [2] and we [3, 4] proposed a semi-dynamic approach, which conducts two processes concurrently: image inpainting for a key frame, and the overlay of the inpainted texture with geometric and photometric adjustment for every frame. In this approach, though target objects are hidden with incomplete textures until the image inpainting finishes, advanced image inpainting methods can be applied. For example, in our paper [4], image inpainting method [10], which considers photometric and geometric pattern changes, was applied to diminished reality.

3.2   Temporal Coherence of Textures

For the temporal coherence of textures, the methods in [1, 16] basically generate textures for every frame. Therefore, they tend to cause unnatural changes in geometry between frames. Although Herling et al. [16] attempt to reduce texture flickering between frames by propagating patch correspondences in image inpainting from frame to frame, it is insufficient to achieve geometric consistency between frames taken with large camera motion. To overcome this problem, Herling et al. [17] improved their original method [16] by employing a homography, and thus determined the search areas in the next frame by assuming the background around the target object to be almost planar. Our previous method [3] also used a homography to synthesize an inpainted result when hiding an AR marker. These methods successfully preserve the temporal coherence of planar scenes. In addition, in our most recent paper [4], we approximated the background of the target objects by combining the local planes. For this, the scene around the target object is divided into multiple planes, whose number is automatically determined, and inpainted textures are successfully overlaid on the target object using multiple homographies by considering the estimated planes and camera-pose given by visual-SLAM (Simultaneous Localization and Mapping).

3.3 Quality of Image Inpainting

As mentioned above, Siltanen [1] mixed several specific pixel values for filling in missing regions. Therefore, the quality is insufficient if the textures in surrounding background are complex. To synthesize more natural textures for diminished reality, Herling et al. [16] applied an example-based image inpainting method [18], and they have also improved their energy function by considering spatial costs [17]. In their methods, the whole input image is searched for texture patterns that are similar to that around the target region, and pixel values in the target region are determined using similar patterns. Generally, although example-based inpainting methods yield good results, they produce unnatural results when an image's regular patterns have a distorted perspective.

To solve this problem, using the idea of perspective correction in image inpainting [12, 13], our previous method [3] corrected the perspective distortion using an AR marker, meaning that the size of regular texture patterns could be unified. Unlike the methods [12, 13] that requires manual interactions, we calculated a homography based on the assumption that an AR marker exists on a plane. In our most recent method [4], we have extended this idea for 3D scenes using 3D geometry to deal with perspective correction in 3D scenes. Specifically, we have generated multiple rectified images, one for each of the estimated planes. In addition to this, we have added a constraint to automatically limit the search region using structures around a target object, thus increasing the quality of inpainted textures.

3.4 Determination of Mask Region

Mask regions (those that include target objects) have to be found in every frame to ensure that the objects are removed from the image. Objects such as AR markers [1–3] can easily be tracked using software libraries (e.g., ARToolkit [19]), allowing the mask regions to be determined in real time. In other cases, various approaches are used to track the target objects and find the mask regions. For example, an active contour algorithm has been applied to detect and track objects [16], but this method is not robust for textured backgrounds. For this problem, several feature points that store the appearance of the image are set around the target objects, and the image is segmented into the mask and other regions in every frame by tracking the feature points [17]. Although this method

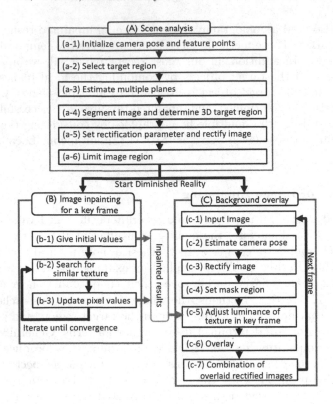

Fig. 3. Pipeline of our diminished reality technique

works well for scenes with textured backgrounds, it has the limitation that the entire object must always be in the video frame. In our method [4], we robustly determine the mask regions in all frames by tracking the 3D volume that includes target objects in 3D space using camera pose, rather than by tracking the object in 2D space. In this approach, the target objects do not always have to be in the video frame.

4   Diminished Reality Considering Background Structures

In this section, we briefly introduce our method [4], which achieve real-time diminished reality for 3D scenes by approximating the background by multiple local planes, and show experimental results of the method.

4.1   Pipeline of Our Diminished Reality Technique

Figure 3 shows the pipeline of our diminished reality technique. Our method first analyzes the target scene (A). Diminished reality is then achieved by a semi-dynamic approach that conducts two processes concurrently: example-based image inpainting for a key frame (B), and the overlay of the inpainted texture

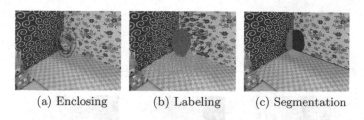

(a) Enclosing   (b) Labeling   (c) Segmentation

Fig. 4. Scene analysis

for every frame (C). Although process (B) is not performed in real-time, users can start applications immediately by performing processes (B) and (C) concurrently. Within several seconds of starting process (B), we can experience diminished reality with a completely inpainted result. In the following, we describe processes (A), (B), and (C) in detail.

4.2 Scene Analysis

As pre-processing for diminished reality, the target scene is analyzed and the image is divided into multiple images to improve the quality of image inpainting. Specifically, the camera pose and 3D coordinates of feature points are first estimated by initializing visual-SLAM (a-1). A user then manually selects a region that includes target objects by enclosing the region, as shown in Fig. 4(a) (a-2). The frame when the user finishes enclosing the region is set as a key frame and is used for image inpainting in process (B). Next, feature points around the target region are picked up, and normal vectors of the feature points are calculated using the 3D coordinates of feature points. Each feature point is then classified into multiple groups based on mean-shift clustering using the normal vectors as shown in Fig. 4(b), and a plane is fitted to the feature points of each group using LMedS (Least Median of Squares) (a-3). All the fitted planes are projected onto the image plane, and each pixel is assigned to the plane that is nearest to the camera. According to this assignment, the whole image, including the missing region, is segmented as shown in Fig. 4(c). In addition, the 3D target region is generated from the 2D selected region using the fitted planes and feature points on the target object, so the 3D region must include the target object (a-4). Next, as shown in Fig. 5, the perspective distortion of the key frame is corrected by calculating a homography matrix for each plane as if each plane was captured by a camera in front of it, and the information for rectifying subsequent frames is stored (a-5). Finally, we limit the search region in which textures can be used as exemplars for inpainting in process (B) based on the segmented image (a-6).

4.3 Image Inpainting for Multiple Rectified Images

We apply an example-based image inpainting method to each rectified and limited image of the key frame. Our framework can adopt arbitrary example-based

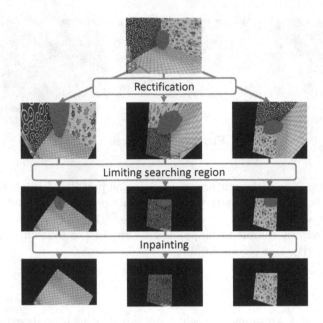

Fig. 5. Rectification and region limitation for inpainting

methods that use global optimization. After initializing parameters of the missing regions, e.g., the average value of boundary pixels, the inpainting method iterates two processes in order to minimize an energy function based on the similarity between missing regions and the remainder of the image. The first process searches for similar patterns (b-2), and the second updates pixel values in the missing regions (b-3). In each iteration, process (B) stores the tentative inpainted result in the memory shared with process (C). After the energy converges, the completely inpainted result is stored and used in process (C).

4.4   Real-Time Overlay of Inpainted Textures

In process (C), after capturing an image (c-1) and calculating a camera pose using visual-SLAM (c-2), a rectified image is generated for every plane using the current camera pose and information for rectification (c-3). On each rectified image, a mask region is then determined by projecting the 3D target region from the optical center of the current frame's camera onto each plane (c-4). Next, the mask regions are filled in using the texture in the rectified images of the key frame in which the object regions are inpainted. Because there is usually some difference in the luminance of the key frame and the current frame, we adjust the luminance of the key frame's texture (c-5). Here, we estimate luminance changes in the mask region from the changes in the surrounding region using rectified images between the key frame and the current frame. Finally, the texture of each rectified image of the key frame is overlaid on the mask region of each rectified image of the current frame. The rectified images are transformed to the original

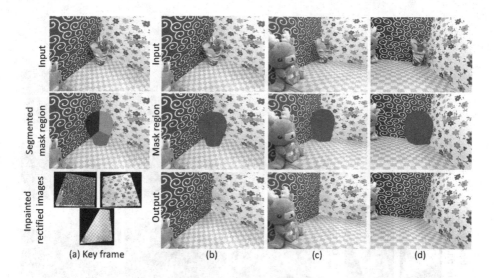

Fig. 6. Experiment for the scene with three textured planes: (a) key frame, (b)–(e) subsequent frames

appearance of the current frame using homographies (c-6), and these are then combined to produce the final output (c-7).

4.5   Experimental Results

We show experimental results in three environments. In the experiment, we used a PC with Windows 7, Core i7-3820QM 2.7 GHz CPU, 8 GB of memory, and a GeForce GT 650M GPU for input images of resolution 640 × 480 captured by a USB camera (Logicool Qcam Pro 9000). The GPU was used for image rectification in process (C). We used PTAM [20] for the visual-SLAM and inpainting methods [10]. In Figs. 6 to 8, Fig. (a) shows the key frame, with the top row showing the input image, the middle row showing the segmented mask region, and the bottom row showing the inpainted results of rectified images. Figs. (b) to (d) show subsequent frames captured from various viewpoints; the top row shows input images, the middle row shows the mask regions, and the bottom row shows output images.

First, we show the results of the indoor scene in Figs. 6. In this scene, textures are successfully generated in the target region, and the temporal coherence is preserved. Second, we show the results for the outdoor scene in Fig. 7, in which the optical parameter of the camera automatically changes with camera motion because of the large difference in luminance between sunny and shady areas and the low dynamic range of the camera. In this scene, the mask region of the key frame is inpainted when the camera's optical parameter adjusts to a shady area, as shown in Fig. (a). The optical parameter is adjusted according to this shady area in Figs. (b) and (d), and to sunny areas in Fig. (c).

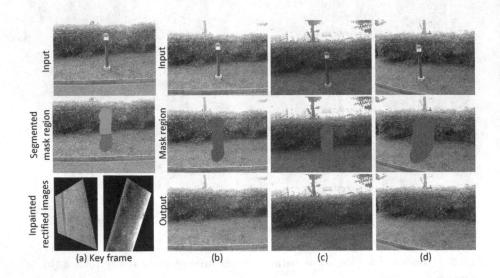

Fig. 7. Experiment for a scene with the camera's optical parameter changed: (a) key frame, (b) to (e) subsequent frames

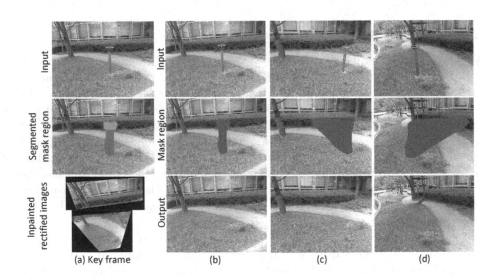

Fig. 8. Experiment for a scene in which the target object is distant from the background objects: (a) key frame, (b) to (e) subsequent frames

Finally, we show the results for the outdoor scene in Fig. 8, in which the target object is distant from the background objects. In this scene, the mask region is larger, as the camera position is farther from the key frame position, as shown in the middle images of Fig. (c). Nevertheless, plausible textures are overlaid on the mask region, as shown in the bottom images of Fig. (c). However, when the target object overlaps the background tree, as in Fig. (d), the tree texture is distorted in the mask region. This is because our method assumes that objects in each rectified image, such as the bottom image of Fig. (a), exist on each plane, and the textures of the current frame are generated by transforming the texture in each rectified image of the key frame using the relevant homography.

The computational time for scene analysis is less than 100 milliseconds, and the frame rate of diminished reality is about 20 to 30 fps. The frame rate decreases as more planes are estimated.

5 Conclusion

This paper introduced image inpainting methods and their application to diminished reality. In addition, we introduced our image inpainting-based diminished reality method, which conducts image inpainting and overlay processes concurrently, and showed experimental results for various environments.

Currently, in the field of image inpainting-based diminished reality, there are still only a few methods, and the applicable situation is limited to some extent. In future, we should deal with various situations. For example, target objects are moving, the structure and texture of background are complex, illumination variously changes. To achieve this, diminished reality techniques will be developed with techniques of Computer Vision, Augmented Reality, and Computer Graphics.

Acknowledgements. This work was partially supported by Grants-in-Aid for Scientific Research Nos. 23240024 and 24700118 from the Ministry of Education, Culture, Sports, Science and Technology.

References

1. Siltanen, S.: Texture generation over the marker area. In: Proc. Int. Symp. on Mixed and Augmented Reality, pp. 253–254 (2006)
2. Korkalo, O., Aittala, M., Siltanen, S.: Light-weight marker hiding for augmented reality. In: Proc. Int. Symp. on Mixed and Augmented Reality, pp. 247–248 (2010)
3. Kawai, N., Yamasaki, M., Sato, T., Yokoya, N.: Diminished reality for AR marker hiding based on image inpainting with reflection of luminance changes. ITE Trans. on Media Technology and Applications 1(4), 343–353 (2013)
4. Kawai, N., Sato, T., Yokoya, N.: Diminished reality considering background structures. In: Proc. Int. Symp. on Mixed and Augmented Reality, pp. 259–260 (2013)
5. Bertalmio, M., Sapiro, G., Caselles, V., Ballester, C.: Image inpainting. In: Proc. SIGGRAPH, pp. 417–424 (2000)

6. Efros, A.A., Leung, T.K.: Texture synthesis by non-parametric sampling. In: Proc. Int. Conf. on Computer Vision, pp. 1033–1038 (1999)
7. Criminisi, A., Pérez, P., Toyama, K.: Region filling and object removal by exemplar-based image inpainting. IEEE Trans. on Image Processing 13(9), 1200–1212 (2004)
8. Wexler, Y., Shechtman, E., Irani, M.: Space-time completion of video. IEEE Trans. on Pattern Analysis and Machine Intelligence 29(3), 463–476 (2007)
9. Kawai, N., Sato, T., Yokoya, N.: Image inpainting considering brightness change and spatial locality of textures and its evaluation. In: Proc. Pacific-Rim Symposium on Image and Video Technology, pp. 271–282 (2009)
10. Kawai, N., Yokoya, N.: Image inpainting considering symmetric patterns. In: Proc. Int. Conf. on Pattern Recognition, pp. 2744–2747 (2012)
11. Darabi, S., Shechtman, E., Barnes, C., Goldman, D.B., Sen, P.: Image melding: Combining inconsistent images using patch-based synthesis. ACM Trans. on Graphics 31(4), 82:1–82:10 (2012)
12. Pavić, D., Schönefeld, V., Kobbelt, L.: Interactive image completion with perspective correction. The Visual Computer 22(9), 671–681 (2006)
13. Huang, J.B., Kopf, J., Ahuja, N., Kang, S.B.: Transformation guided image completion. In: Proc. Int. Conf. on Computational Photography, pp. 1–9 (2013)
14. Barnes, C., Shechtman, E., Finkelstein, A., Goldman, D.B.: PatchMatch: A randomized correspondence algorithm for structural image editing. ACM Trans. on Graphics 28(3), 1–11 (2009)
15. Barnes, C., Shechtman, E., Goldman, D.B., Finkelstein, A.: The Generalized Patch-Match Correspondence Algorithm. In: Daniilidis, K., Maragos, P., Paragios, N. (eds.) ECCV 2010, Part III. LNCS, vol. 6313, pp. 29–43. Springer, Heidelberg (2010)
16. Herling, J., Broll, W.: Advanced self-contained object removal for realizing real-time diminished reality in unconstrained environments. In: Proc. Int. Symp. on Mixed and Augmented Reality, pp. 207–212 (2010)
17. Herling, J., Broll, W.: Pixmix: A real-time approach to high-quality diminished reality. In: Proc. Int. Symp. on Mixed and Augmented Reality, pp. 141–150 (2012)
18. Simakov, D., Caspi, Y., Shechtman, E., Irani, M.: Summarizing visual data using bidirectional similarity. In: Proc. IEEE Conf. on Computer Vision and Pattern Recognition, pp. 1–8 (2008)
19. Kato, H., Billinghurst, M.: Marker tracking and hmd calibration for a video-based augmented reality conferencing system. In: Proc. Int. Workshop on Augmented Reality, pp. 85–94 (1999)
20. Klein, G., Murray, D.: Parallel tracking and mapping for small AR workspaces. In: Proc. Int. Symp. on Mixed and Augmented Reality, pp. 225–234 (2007)

A Semantically Enriched Augmented Reality Browser

Tamás Matuszka[1,2], Sándor Kámán[1], and Attila Kiss[1]

[1] Eötvös Loránd University, Budapest, Hungary
{tomintt,kasraai,kiss}@inf.elte.hu
[2] Inter-University Centre for Telecommunications and Informatics,
Debrecen, Hungary

Abstract. Owing to the remarkable advancement of smartphones, Augmented Reality applications have become part of everyday life. Augmented Reality browsers are the most commonly used among these applications. The users can search and display interesting places from the physical environment surrounding them by means of these browsers. Some of the most popular AR browsers use only one data source and the openly available datasets are not used. In contrast, the main objective of Linked Open Data community project is to link knowledge from different data sources. This pursuit makes it easier to retrieval information, among others. In this paper, an Augmented Reality browser was presented. Information derived from Linked Open Data was used by the browser as data source. Due to this, the system is able to handle more data sources.

Keywords: Augmented Reality, Semantic Web, Location-based Services, Linked Data.

1 Introduction

Augmented Reality applications, which combine the real and virtual worlds in real-time, are more and more widespread nowadays. The history of Augmented Reality dating back to the last few decades, when the hardware possessed by researchers was typically weaker than nowadays. As a result, the use of different, expensive as well as uncomfortable wearable devices (for instance, computer in backpack, head-mounted display) was necessary. Due to the advancement of hardware, computer graphics and mobile information technology, Augmented Reality has been widespread in the everyday use as well. Instead of expensive, inconvenient devices; the small, affordable and convenient smartphones can be used as a platform for Augmented Reality.

In the past few years, several Augmented Reality applications have been published in the field of medical applications, education, tourism, etc. [15], [7], [3]. Among these, perhaps the most widely used application is the Augmented Reality browser that combines the traditional Augmented Reality application with the Internet browsing. This kind of Augmented Reality takes advantage of the

R. Shumaker and S. Lackey (Eds.): VAMR 2014, Part I, LNCS 8525, pp. 375–384, 2014.

user's current geographical location and location-based information can be superimposed into the real life view. A typical example is when the user looks around with the mobile phone and could see the icons which represent restaurants located near in the real-life view. The most important criterion of a browser is the amount and variety of accessible data [12]. The current augmented reality browsers (e.g. Junaio[1], Layar[2], Mixare[3]) use only one data source and the openly available datasets are not used. Wikitude built on Augmented Reality Markup Language (ARML)[4], Mixare and Layar use hidden and proprietary data structures [24]. In contrast, the main objective of Linked Open Data (LOD) [5] community project is to link knowledge from different data sources. Several publicly available data source can be found on the Internet in semantically represented format. A wider knowledge base can be obtained by means of interlinked data sources. The Linked Open Data can be used for data source of Augmented Reality browser as well, as opposed to one data source, which is used by the recently browsers.

In this paper, a Linked Data-driven Mobile Augmented Reality browser will be discussed. The Semantic Web was used for data integration and data retrieval purposes. The Semantic Web is able to manage the data available on the Internet [2]. A lot of publicly available datasets have been published in semantically form currently. The Semantic Web stores the information in RDF (Resource Description Framework) statements about resources in the form of subject-predicate-object expressions. These expressions are known as triples in RDF terminology [13]. Information can be obtained from these data sources with SPARQL [20] query language that is able to retrieve and manipulate data stored in RDF format. With the help of this application, a user can navigate and collect local-aware information. A sensor-based tracking approach was combined with RDF processing of related geographical data. The used data come from semantically represented data source from the Linked Open Data. A map-based navigation is also provided by the system. We have implemented our browser on Android operation system which allows for a widespread of usability. One of the main challenges was correctly positioned the displayable virtual elements on the screen of mobile phone. For this purpose, a mathematical model [24] was used.

The organization of the rest of this paper is as follows. After the introductory Section 1, we outline the preliminary definitions in Section 2. Section 3 deals with the related work. Then, the details of our system is described in Section 4. Finally, the conclusion and our future plans are described in Section 5.

2   Preliminaries

In this section, the concepts that are necessary for understanding are defined. We provide insight into the basic concepts of Semantic Web and Augmented Reality.

---

[1] http://www.junaio.com/

[2] https://www.layar.com

[3] http://www.mixare.org

[4] http://openarml.org

A possible way to manage the data available on the Internet is to use the Semantic Web [2]. The Semantic Web aims for creating a "web of data": a large distributed knowledge base, which contains the information of the World Wide Web in a format which is directly interpretable by computers. *Ontology* is recognized as one of the key technologies of the Semantic Web. An *ontology* is a structure $\mathcal{O} := (C, \leq_C, P, \sigma)$, where C and P are two disjoint sets. The elements of C and P are called *classes* and *properties*, respectively. A partial order $\leq_C$ on C is called class hierarchy and a function $\sigma: P \to C \times C$ is a signature of a property [23]. The Semantic Web stores the knowledge base as *RDF triples*. Let I, B, and L (IRIs, Blank Nodes, Literals) be pairwise disjoint sets. An *RDF triple* is a $(v_1, v_2, v_3 \in (I \cup B) \times I \times (I \cup B \cup L))$, where v_1 is the subject, v_2 is the predicate and v_3 is the object [19].

Augmented Reality applications are more and more widespread nowadays. With its help the real physical environment can be extended by computer generated virtual elements creating the illusion that the two worlds coexist. Augmented Reality has two different types. The first one is the marker-based Augmented Reality and the second one is the position based Augmented Reality. The marker-based one uses a so-called marker. This marker allows the registration of the virtual object in the physical space. The position based Augmented Reality depends on the user's physical position which is determined by GPS coordinates [16].

According to Azuma's definition, an Augmented Reality system combines real and virtual reality; is interactive in real-time and is registered in 3D [1]. Another, formal definition for the same concept was given by us [18]. A quintet $\langle M, VE, T, \varphi, \xi \rangle$ is called as Augmented Reality system, where M is the set of markers, VE is the set of virtual elements, T is the set of transformations, φ is the mapping function and ξ is the transformation function. Let IB, PB (image-based markers and position-based markers) be two disjoint sets. Then, M can be written as follows: $M = IB \cup PB$. Let I, V, S and K (images, videos, sounds, knowledge base) be pairwise disjoint sets. In this case, $VE = I \cup V \cup S \cup K$. The T set contains geometric transformations, namely translation (τ), rotation (ρ) and scale (σ). In addition, let L be the set of 3D vectors. Every $v \in VE$ virtual element has an $l \in L$ vector. This l vector stores the position of v virtual element. The function $\varphi: M \to VE \times L$ maps a virtual element and its relative initial position to a marker. The last part of the quintet is the transformation function ξ. The function $\xi: M \times VE \times L \times T \to VE \times L$ transforms a virtual element corresponding to the given marker with a given transformation in real-time. The current Augmented Reality systems can be modeled by the above definition.

In this paper, we present an $\langle M|_{PB}, VE|_{KB}, T, \varphi, \xi \rangle$ Augmented Reality system, where the set of markers is restricted to position-based markers (i.e. the markers are limited to position-based type) and the set of virtual elements is restricted to knowledge base (i.e. the virtual elements are solely location-aware information). This knowledge base is stored in RDF triples and it derived from DBpedia [4] that is included in Linked Open Data. The function φ assigns relevant information based on the latitude and longitude coordinates of the places represented by markers.

3   Related Work

Augmented Reality has been thoroughly researched over the last few years. Several early projects have been started which aims to create augmented reality browser. The [9] presents a location-, and spatial-aware system which enables the integration of existing information systems with virtual objects in easily way. Feiner et al. describe a wearable Augmented Reality prototype and a campus information system case study in [6]. A backpack, head-worn display and hand-held display were required by the user of prototype to the navigation. Rekimoto, Ayatsuka and Hayashi in [22] show a system that is able to assign virtual content (e.g. audio, video) to physical location. The user of system can see these virtual contents as an Augmented Reality post-it. A head-mounted display (HMD) has to be worn by the user also in this case. Kooper and MacIntre present in [11] a general Augmented Reality system, which connects physical locations with World Wide Web. Head-mounted display is also required in this case.

The usage of inconvenient backpack and HMD has become unnecessary due to the improvement of hardware of mobile phones and the spread of smartphones. The smartphones can be used for browsing purpose instead of uncomfortable wearable devices. Kähäry and Murphy in [10] show a hand-held, video-see through Augmented Reality system, which can interact with the surrounding environment through a simple interface. Luna et al. describe a navigation system in [14] that has an Augmented Reality view as well. They claim that their system is friendlier than the similar applications which enable the users to navigate along streets. They argue that the navigation along known places (e.g. shops, monuments) is friendlier than the original solution. Traditional navigation system cannot deal with the user's preferences, the environment and omitted important information: the user context. A system based on the POIs which provides different paths depending on the user preferences was proposed by the authors, so that path leads to a specific target through the well-known places. An open architecture and corresponding prototype is presented by Hill et al. in [8]. Hill's system allows quickly mobile Augmented Reality application development. HTML authoring tool, client-side JavaScript and database connection with AJAX were used for this purpose. The main advantage of the system is the easy content creation according to the authors.

Today, there have been some attempts to combine Semantic Web and Augmented Reality. In a previous paper [17] we have tried to combine the advantages of Augmented Reality and Semantic Web to provide indoor navigation. In this work, we describe an indoor navigation system which uses Augmented Reality for visualization of navigation. The storage of data which are necessary to the navigation was based on ontology. In addition, the possible paths are generated by rule-based inferences. In another previous work [16] we present the conception of a general, Semantic Web-based Augmented Reality system. Due to this framework, the user would navigate through arbitrary areas and get context-aware information. Martín-Serrano, Hervás and Bravo show a touristic Android application in [15] that uses Web 3.0 technology tools to data extraction from various data sources with help of publicly available services on the Internet.

Ontology was used for determining the user's context. In addition, the application provides a recommendation system that based on rule-based inferences. Schubotz and Harth describe a case study in which Linked Open Data [5] is combined with spatial and encyclopedic data sources. The resulting data was transformed to Web3D renderable format. The most LOD browser supports only navigation and exploratory discovery and the query visualization happened in table and list view. Instead, they present a system that uses Web3D for visualization the result of a LOD query [21].

4   Details of the Prototype

In this section, we overview the motivation and the basic functions of our system. Afterwards, we describe the architecture of the prototype. Finally, we present the mathematical model which was used to position the displayable virtual elements on the screen of mobile phone.

4.1   Motivation

Imagine, that you are in a foreign city or you just have a few free hours and you do not know what interesting places are in the near. Maybe you are hungry too. It would be great, when you could somehow find out, what kind of places are in the near, which you are interested in. Of course you can ask somebody, but he or she may not know every place in the city. It would be great, if you could reach a database, from which you could get a lot of information about your environment.

In these or similar situations our application can help for you. You have to nothing else to do, just grab your smartphone with Android operating system and start the application. The browser connects to the DBpedia database and downloads the information about your near environment. You can see where are the sights and attractions. With the help of Google Maps, the program can easily plan a direction for you, so you will not be lost. You can also get information from the selected point, which is also downloaded from DBpedia.

4.2   The Basic Functions of the Browser

The main objective of our Linked Data-drive Mobile Augmented Reality browser is to help navigate the users through the environment and to gather local-aware information. These information come from the most well-known semantic dataset, namely DBpedia, which contains the knowledge of Wikipedia in semantic form. DBpedia contains the latitude and longitude coordinates of numerous places, therefore it can be used as geographical data source. A sensor-based tracking approach was combined with RDF processing of DBpedia. The GPS (Global Positioning System) is used for get the objects position on the whole surface of Earth. It is supported by the satellites around the planet. In order to set our position, the GPS receiver has to communicate with 4 satellites in the case of 2D positioning, and 5 satellites in case of 3D positioning. In our application, we only use 2D positioning. There are weaker and cheaper GPS receivers in the cellphones, which are perform better with network access. The phone downloads the orbital position of the satellites and that way the weaker receiver can find them faster.

Fig. 1. The Augmented Reality view of the browser

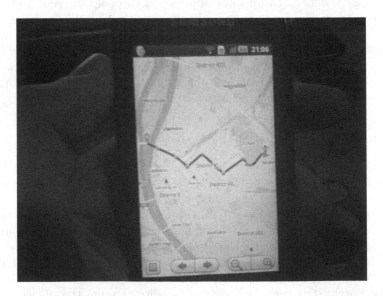

Fig. 2. Map view, the direction is provided by Google Maps

When the user starts the application, he or she can see the POI-s on the real-world view via camera's display. The data of POI-s are originally stored in DBpedia and were converted to POI by a transformation step. The main activity includes a special POI, which has a differential icon, depicted in Figure 1. This POI is the active one, the user can read informations about them in the bottom of the screen which contains the name of active POI as well as the distance from the current position of the user. Further information can be obtained from the active POI based on the DBpedia on the Info activity. This view contains the corresponding photos and a short description about the POI. A map-based navigation is also provided by this view, the user can get the direction with the help of Google Maps from the Info activity which can be viewed on Figure 2.

4.3   The Architecture of the System

The system is separated into two parts: the database and the client. The database is the DBpedia itself, while the client was implemented on Android operation system which allows for a widespread of usability. The schematic diagram of the architecture can be seen on the Figure 3.

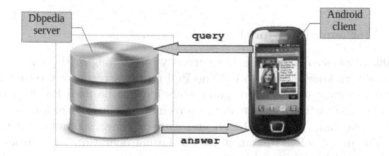

Fig. 3. The system architecture

The database contains RDF triples. The DBpedia is built on the Virtuoso database handler system which is the first cross-platform server, which implements web, file and database server functionalities. The DBpedia-based data is queried from the client with using AndroJena API which is a porting of Jena semantic web framework to the Android platform. Jena is a free and open source Java framework for building Semantic Web and applications. The client connects to DBpedia and sends a SPARQL query to it, which will run on the DBpedia server. Figure 4 depicts an example SPARQL query. The given result was processed by the client. The client makes POI objects from these data. To take account of the low computing capacity of the cell phones, we limited the size of the queries in 100 rows.

```
PREFIX  geo:  <http://www.w3.org/2003/01/geo/wgs84_pos#>
PREFIX  rdfs:  <http://www.w3.org/2000/01/rdf-schema#>
PREFIX  dbpedia-owl:  <http://dbpedia.org/ontology/>
SELECT  ?label ?lat ?long ?abstract ?pic WHERE {
        _:a geo:lat ?lat .
        _:a geo:long ?long .
        _:a rdfs:label ?label .
        _:a dbpedia-owl:abstract ?abstract .
        _:a dbpedia-owl:thumbnail ?pic .
        FILTER(?lat - 35.341846 <= 0.05 &&
               35.341846 - ?lat <= 0.05 &&
               ?long - 25.148254 <= 0.05 &&
               25.148254 - ?long <= 0.05 &&
               lang(?label) = "en" &&
               lang(?abstract) = "en"
               )
} LIMIT 100
```

Fig. 4. SPARQL query which collects data of POI-s

4.4   The Mathematical Model

Several difficulties occur during on the correctly positioning of the virtual elements. In order to know, where to put the POI on the screen, we used a lot of mathematical calculations. A lot of parameters have to be used for determine the position of the virtual element on the screen of mobile device, for instance the longitude, latitude, altitude of POI and camera; range, azimuth and pitch of device. The details of the parameters, the formal definitions as well as the mathematical model can be read in [24].

5   Conclusion

In this paper a mobile Augmented Reality browser was presented, which extracts the information from Linked Open Data, in contrast to the similar current browser. In that case, only one data source is used by the recently applications. Semantic Web was used for information retrieval as well as a sensor-based tracking approach was combined with RDF processing. Due to the Augmented Reality browser, the user is able to display the surrounding related geographical data from DBpedia, extract information about them, and navigate to the selected place as well. The browser was implemented on Android operation system which allows for a widespread of usability.

In the future, we are planning to integrate another data sources by using Semantic Web technologies. In order to validate the work we have carried out, a more in-depth investigation into data integration is needed. We are intending to use not only semantic data sources, but also arbitrary geographical data sources (e.g. Foursquare, Google Places API, Facebook API) as well. We also want to implement a touristic, sightseeing application with recommendation system. The user can set certain conditions (for instance the available time, maximal distance, interested sights) and the system proposes some sightseeing trips which contain the maximal number of given attractions. We would like to formalize this task and give a mathematical solution for it as well.

Acknowledgments. This work was partially supported by the European Union and the European Social Fund through project FuturICT.hu (grant no.: TAMOP-4.2.2.C-11/1/KONV-2012-0013) and TAMOP-4.2.2.C-11/1/KONV-2012-0001 supported by the European Union, co-financed by the European Social Fund.

References

1. Azuma, R.T.: A survey of augmented reality. Presence 6(4), 355–385 (1997)
2. Berners-Lee, T., Hendler, J., Lassila, O.: The semantic web. Scientific American 284(5), 28–37 (2001)
3. Billinghurst, M., Dünser, A.: Augmented reality in the classroom. Computer 45(7), 56–63 (2012)
4. Bizer, C., Lehmann, J., Kobilarov, G., Auer, S., Becker, C., Cyganiak, R., Hellmann, S.: DBpedia-A crystallization point for the Web of Data. Web Semantics: Science, Services and Agents on the World Wide Web 7(3), 154–165 (2009)
5. Bizer, C., Jentzsch, A., Cyganiak, R.: State of the LOD Cloud, http://wifo5-03.informatik.uni-mannheim.de/lodcloud/state/
6. Feiner, S., MacIntyre, B., Höllerer, T., Webster, A.: A touring machine: Prototyping 3D mobile augmented reality systems for exploring the urban environment. Personal Technologies 1(4), 208–217 (1997)
7. Hansen, C., Wieferich, J., Ritter, F., Rieder, C., Peitgen, H.O.: Illustrative visualization of 3D planning models for augmented reality in liver surgery. International Journal of Computer Assisted Radiology and Surgery 5(2), 133–141 (2010)
8. Hill, A., MacIntyre, B., Gandy, M., Davidson, B., Rouzati, H.: Kharma: An open kml/html architecture for mobile augmented reality applications. In: 2010 9th IEEE International Symposium on Mixed and Augmented Reality (ISMAR), pp. 233–234. IEEE (2010)
9. Hohl, F., Kubach, U., Leonhardi, A., Rothermel, K., Schwehm, M.: Next century challenges: Nexus an open global infrastructure for spatial-aware applications. In: Proceedings of the 5th Annual ACM/IEEE International Conference on Mobile Computing and Networking, pp. 249–255. ACM (1999)
10. Kähäri, M., Murphy, D.J.: Mara: Sensor based augmented reality system for mobile imaging device. In: 5th IEEE and ACM International Symposium on Mixed and Augmented Reality (2006)
11. Kooper, R., MacIntyre, B.: Browsing the real-world wide web: Maintaining awareness of virtual information in an AR information space. International Journal of Human-Computer Interaction 16(3), 425–446 (2003)
12. Langlotz, T., Grubert, J., Grasset, R.: Augmented reality browsers: essential products or only gadgets? Communications of the ACM 56(11), 34–36 (2013)

13. Lassila, O., Swick, R.R.: Resource Description Framework (RDF) Schema Specification,
    http://www.w3.org/TR/rdf-schemahttp://www.w3.org/TR/rdf-schema
14. Ma Luna, J., Hervás, R., Fontecha, J., Bravo, J.: A friendly navigation-system based on points of interest, augmented reality and context-awareness. In: Bravo, J., López-de-Ipiña, D., Moya, F. (eds.) UCAmI 2012. LNCS, vol. 7656, pp. 137–144. Springer, Heidelberg (2012)
15. Martín-Serrano, D., Hervás, R., Bravo, J.: Telemaco: Context-aware System for Tourism Guiding based on Web 3.0 Technology. In: 1st Workshop on Contextual Computing and Ambient Intelligence in Tourism, Riviera Maya, Mexico (2011)
16. Matuszka, T.: Augmented Reality Supported by Semantic Web Technologies. In: Cimiano, P., Corcho, O., Presutti, V., Hollink, L., Rudolph, S. (eds.) ESWC 2013. LNCS, vol. 7882, pp. 682–686. Springer, Heidelberg (2013)
17. Matuszka, T., Gombos, G., Kiss, A.: A New Approach for Indoor Navigation Using Semantic Webtechnologies and Augmented Reality. In: Shumaker, R. (ed.) VAMR 2013, Part I. LNCS, vol. 8021, pp. 202–210. Springer, Heidelberg (2013)
18. Matuszka, T., Kiss, A.: Alive Cemeteries with Augmented Reality and Semantic Web Technologies. In: Proceedings on ICHCI 2014 (accepted, 2014)
19. Pérez, J., Arenas, M., Gutierrez, C.: Semantics and Complexity of SPARQL. In: Cruz, I., Decker, S., Allemang, D., Preist, C., Schwabe, D., Mika, P., Uschold, M., Aroyo, L.M. (eds.) ISWC 2006. LNCS, vol. 4273, pp. 30–43. Springer, Heidelberg (2006)
20. Prud'hommeaux, E., Seaborne, A.: SPARQL Query Language for RDF, http://www.w3.org/TR/rdf-sparql-query/
21. Schubotz, R., Harth, A.: Towards Networked Linked Data-Driven Web3D Applications. In: Dec3D (2012)
22. Rekimoto, J., Ayatsuka, Y., Hayashi, K.: Augment-able reality: Situated communication through physical and digital spaces. In: Second International Symposium on Wearable Computers, Digest of Papers, pp. 68-75. IEEE (1998)
23. Volz, R., Kleb, J., Mueller, W.: Towards Ontology-based Disambiguation of Geographical Identifiers. In: I3 (2007)
24. Zander, S., Chiu, C., Sageder, G.: A computational model for the integration of linked data in mobile augmented reality applications. In: Proceedings of the 8th International Conference on Semantic Systems, pp. 133–140. ACM (2012)

Mobile Augmentation
Based on Switching Multiple Tracking Method

Ayaka Miyagi, Daiki Yoshihara, Kei Kusui, Asako Kimura, and Fumihisa Shibata

Graduate School of Information Science and Engineering, Ritsumeikan University
1-1-1 Noji-Higashi, Kusatsu, Shiga, 525-8577, Japan
miyagi@rm.is.ritsumei.ac.jp

Abstract. This paper presents a localization mechanism for mobile augmented reality systems in various places. Recently, variety of image-based tracking methods have been proposed: artificial marker based methods, and natural feature based methods. However, localization done with only one tracking methods is difficult in all situation. Therefore, we propose a system, which enables users to continually track in various situation by dynamically switching the multiple localization methods. Our proposed mechanism consists of clients, a switcher, and servers. The server estimates the camera pose of the client, and the switcher selects the outstanding localization method. Furthermore, we employed real-time mapping to continually estimate the position and orientation even if the camera is apart from the prior knowledge of the environment. After localization, the newly updated mapping result is stored in the server. Thus, we could continually track even if the environment has changed.

Keywords: mixed reality, localization, tracking.

1   Introduction

Recently, Mixed Reality (MR) has become increasingly important. In particular, mobile MR systems that could be used in wide area are attracting attentions. One of the most important issues for mobile MR systems is to estimate the device's position and orientation accurately in real-time. Therefore, a variety of tracking methods have been proposed: artificial marker based methods, natural feature based methods. However, it is next to impossible to use the only single method to cope with all the conceivable environments. To successfully accomplish localization in diverse environments, we propose a mechanism which dynamically switches multiple localization methods depending on the usage environment.

In this paper we describe a localization mechanism that switches multiple tracking methods to track in wide area environment using client-server model. The mobile device communicates with the switcher, which selects a suitable tracking method. The selected method changes dynamically according to the surroundings of the device. Additionally, we have applied real-time mapping to continue each tracking method without any prior knowledge.

R. Shumaker and S. Lackey (Eds.): VAMR 2014, Part I, LNCS 8525, pp. 385–395, 2014.

2   Related Work

The simple way to estimate camera pose is a marker based method that place an artificial marker in the environment. For example, Wagner *et al*. has applied ARToolKit [1] by Kato *et al*. for PDA [2]. This method obtains camera position and orientation by detecting the four corners of the marker. In general marker based method has small computational cost. However, these kinds of methods need to always detect a marker from a captured image. Also, placing these markers in an environment is visually obtrusive because the markers usually have an obvious colors and shapes to improve their detection rate. We have proposed a less noticeable marker based method using a poster [3-4], but could not solve the former problem. On the other hand, hence performance of the mobile device has improved significantly in recent years, a variety of feature based methods have been proposed. The methods that apply planar constraint using features are [5, 6]. This method could achieve a robust localization using a plane, such as a poster. However, compared to the marker based method, it is believed that this method is suited for occlusion, but in general the processing speed is slow.

Meanwhile, Arth *et al*. has proposed a mobile based localization method that construct a 3D map of the feature points [7]. Thereafter, Arth *et al*. has also proposed a localization method using panoramic image [8]. This method could be done in wide field of view in outdoor scene by using a panoramic image generated from the images acquired from mobile device. However, the proposed method presupposes the rotation of the camera, although translation is not mentioned. As method capable of performing a translation are method created by Oe *et al*[9] and Ventura *et al*[10] that build a 3D map using image obtained from omnidirectional camera, and localize using 3D point and key frames. However these feature based methods could not be done in an environment where there are less features detected. Also, it is difficult to localize in environments where there are similar patterns due to the error when matching the feature points.

For other feature based localization method contains PTAM [11, 12] which construct the 3D map and estimate the position and orientation of the camera in parallel threads. This method construct the 3D map in real-time, so it could localize without the need to determine the 3D position of the feature points in advance. However, this method could not measure the absolute coordinate of the camera in the environment. As a result, it could not be applied directly to application such as navigation that uses the information depended on the absolute position. Furthermore, as the 3D map expands, the optimization of the detected feature points would become heavy for the mobile phone, and the accuracy of the position and orientation of the camera may lack due to the error contained in feature points as the feature points increases.

Another method created by Castle *et al*. is PTAMM [13]. This method creates multiple maps simultaneously to widen the area of localization. However, since each map is independent, it could not create MR applications that extend over multiple maps.

These proposed methods limit its place to be used. Therefore, wide range localization could not be done with single method.

3   System Architecture

3.1   Overview

Figure 1 shows the conceptual image of our switching mechanism. The proposed mechanism switches each method to realize both wide and various locations in tracking.

The system is composed of client-server model. The Server estimates the initial position and orientation with high processing loads. Subsequently, to ensure estimation in real-time, the light processing camera tracking is been done on the client side. Additionally, in order to ensure the extensibility and load balance executed in the server for the newly proposed localization, we provide each localization method with each server. By analyzing the calculated result of each server in the switcher, the overall throughput does not depend on the number of localization method employed. To improve the stability of the overall system, we also applied sensor based localization and real-time mapping. For the sensor based method, we used geomagnetic sensor, acceleration sensor, and a GPS built in the mobile device. The real-time mapping could perform the localization to continue even after when each localization method fail in tracking.

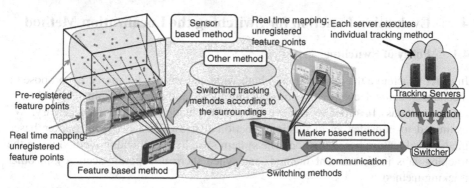

Fig. 1. The concept of our proposed mechanism. The system switches the tracking method according to the surroundings of the device and executes real-time mapping to continue the pose estimation.

3.2   Flow of the System

The proposed method contains three components: client, server, and switcher. The server manages each localization method to estimate the client's position. The switcher selects the superior tracking method to be used by the client. The client achieves the real time localization by camera tracking.

1. Requests to choose a tracking method (Client)
   The client gets a captured image and GPS information, and sends them to the server.
2. Request to estimate position and orientation (Switcher)
   The switcher sends the captured camera image and GPS information to each server.
3. Estimate position and orientation of the camera (Server)

Each server receives the captured camera image and GPS information and estimates the position and orientation.

4. Sends back the position and orientation to the switcher (Server)
   Each server sends back the estimated position and orientation to the switcher.
5. Selects the superior tracking method (Switcher)
   From the estimated position and orientation provided by the each server, the switcher selects the highly accurate tracking method.
6. Notify the tracking method to the client (Switcher)
   The switcher notifies the tracking method and sends the estimated initial position and orientation to the client.
7. Real-time tracking (Client)

From the received information, the client estimates its position and orientation in real-time. In this moment, the client periodically sends a captured camera image, position and orientation of the camera, and GPS information to the server. The system continually repeat (1) thorough (6) and switch into the superior tracking method for client.

4   Evaluation Function for Switching the Localization Method

4.1   Policy of Switching

In order to achieve the localization in both wide and various locations, we proposed a mechanism that selects the most outstanding localization method from several localization methods. In order to achieve this, an evaluation function is necessary. We examined to consider an evaluation function that switches between marker based method and feature based method. The system switches the tracking method when the tracking fails in the current method, and when there is superior accuracy in other tracking method.

We have decided to set the evaluation formula for evaluating the adaptability of the localization method. The localization that has the highest value from the formula will be considered as the worthiest localization method to be used.

4.2   Evaluation Function

To switch into the superior localization method, various elements could be considered such as re-projection error and positional relationship of the marker.

Thus, we have parameterized individual element of each localization method. We have gradually added the parameters and select the highest score. Currently, the localization method is switched using the following formula (1).

$$S_i = M_i + (-E_i) \tag{1}$$

The number of localization method is i, evaluation value for each localization method is S_i. M_i is a parameter for each method. E_i is the average re-projection error. For M_i, it is possible to select the method with priority by setting the values to appropriate natural number.

4.3   Fail-Safe

Evaluation formula described in the previous section selects localization method when estimation of the position and orientation succeeds. When all the initial localization fails in all methods or when the tracking could not achieve stable estimation, we roughly estimate the localization using GPS and direction sensor. In particular, the position of the camera is determined by the value of the GPS. The yaw is determined by magnetic sensor. Also, the estimation of roll and pitch is determined by gyro sensor. However, even when we use the sensor based localization, the switcher continuously receive localization methods from the server. When switcher select a localization other than sensor based method, we process the newly selected localization method to start.

5   Real-Time Mapping

5.1   Overview of Real-Time Mapping

In the following, we describe the real-time mapping process which has been employed in the proposed mechanism.

While it is possible to dynamically switch into localization method according to the location used for tracking, the camera path and the movement will be limited with the conventional method. Therefore, we estimate the 3D position of the feature points from camera image in real-time parallel with the tracking. However, real-time mapping process could not estimate the camera position in world coordinate. For this reason, we have employed real-time mapping process, which we designed to suit each localization method.

5.2   Real-Time Mapping for Marker Based Method

Processing Flow of Real-time Mapping for Marker Based Method. With the localization method with the marker-based method, we estimate the 3D position of the feature point around the marker and continually track, even when the camera is distant from the marker.

We used PTAM proposed by Klein et al. [11] for mapping process. Mapping the feature points of a large amount in high speed, PTAM has achieves stable process by asynchronously updating the environment model in parallel threads. When performing the marker based method, we use both the conventional localization method and PTAM in parallel thread to estimate the 3D position of the feature points.

Since PTAM could not define the coordinate, we have converted the scale from the amount of movement from the camera and with the transformation matrix; we convert 3D positional points that were mapped with PTAM to absolute coordinate.

Initial Map. In the following, we include the process of building the initial map.

1. Select the first frame that succeeded in position and orientation with the marker-based method.
2. Select the second frame that moved parallel to the direction of optical axis.
3. We estimate the 3D position using the correspondence of selected keytrames.

In order to realize the process (2), it is necessary to determine if the localization method has moved parallel other than optical axis. To determine the movement of the mobile phone, we use gyroscope that is built into a device.

Switching Mechanism. The accuracy of camera tracking in PTAM depends on the number of feature points detected from the camera image. Therefore, when the marker is captured within the camera image, the marker is superiorly selected. The tracking is switched into PTAM when the camera is distant from the marker. In addition, since two approaches could not run simultaneously due to the low computational power in mobile device, marker based method and PTAM run in separate thread to reduce the processing speed.

5.3   Real-Time Mapping for Feature Based Method

Flow of Real-Time Mapping for Feature Based Method. In the proposed mechanism, we assume the feature points to be extracted and stored from prior knowledge. We will describe a method for introducing the mapping process. We will describe in detail with Landmark Database (LMDB) as example.

In LMDB method, the feature point is registered in prior. With the 3D-2D matching correspondence, the LMDB are constructed. Therefore, it is difficult to estimate the camera position and orientation when the camera is distant from the constructed area. Unlike the marker based method, the feature points will gradually decrease as the camera moves apart from the constructed environment. Without using the previously stated marker based real-time mapping method, we proposed a method to add and update a new feature points as landmark in real-time. By using the position and orientation estimated by the priory registered landmarks and added landmarks, we realized to continually track even when camera is apart from the constructed LMDB. We also update the database, so the newly added landmarks could be used next time.

Adding the Landmark in Real-Time. To add the landmark in real-time, it is essential to estimate the 3D position of the feature in real-time. In PTAM, they use a triangulation from two frames to estimate the camera position. This method has a simple calculation, so the 3D position of the features could be estimated immediately, but depending on the selected frame, the camera position and orientation would include a major error. PTAM uses large quantities of feature and repeatedly optimize the mapping to decrease this error. However feature based methods like LMDB, would fail in tracking when 3D reconstructed features and new detected features are simultaneously tracked.

To achieve highly accuracy in estimation, we used the flow listed below.

1. Determine whether the 3D position is estimated in current frame
   Without using the 3D position estimated by all the frames, we use frames that include a great quantity of feature with small re-projection error. We also observe certain parallax compared to the previous frame. The tracking thread verifies if the position and orientation estimation is satisfied in each frame.

2. Correspondence using additional keyframe

We add the keyframe that meets these listed conditions in the mapping thread. At this time, we use Lucas-Kanade [15] to correspond each feature from the previous keyframe.

3. Estimate 3D position of the feature

When there are parallax compared to the previous frame, and when keyframe are obtained and stored, we estimate the 3D position of the feature using the multiple keyframes. This newly detected landmark will be stored. We also remove the feature that contains major errors. Specifically, we re-project 3D position for all frames, and calculate the average value of the re-projection error for each frame. We delete these feature that has re-projection error in certain threshold.

Update the LMDB Obtained from Real-Time Mapping. Using the real-time mapping, we update the registered information of Landmark in database. With the real-time mapping, we could perform camera tracking in location outside the constructed landmark. However, the initial position and orientation could not be estimated to the place where landmark does not exist. Therefore, we store the information of the feature points which was detected in real-time mapping in the server, and register it in the database as a new landmark to update the database. Due to the changes in environment, we exclude landmarks from database that could not correspond to the feature detected while tracking. With this approach, even when there are changes in the environment, we could easily update the database.

This approach is done with online process and offline process. The online process stores the 3D position of the feature detected in real-time mapping, image information of each keyframes, and position and orientation of the camera. Furthermore, in order to prevent decrease in accuracy and capacity in data-base, we register feature with high utilization rate. We calculate the utilization rate by the following equation (4). U_i is the utilization rate, I_i is the number of times that are considered as inlier when using RANSAC. F_i is the total number of frames that contain the added landmarks. The utilization rate is stored in the server and used in the offline process.

$$U_i = \frac{I_i}{F_i} \qquad (4)$$

The offline process builds additional landmarks and eliminates other landmark that has low utilization rates. The landmarks with low utilization rate are deleted and others are registered into the database.

6   Experiment

We have qualitatively evaluated our switching system in both outdoor and indoor environment. For the server we have employed ARToolKit[1], SFINCS-PM[3-4], and LMDB[9]. The equipment used for client, switcher and server is listed in Table 1. The resolution is 640 x 480.

Table 1. Specification of the client, switcher and server

	Client	Switcher & Server
Device	4th iPad	Notebook PC
OS	iOS 6	Windows7 x64
CPU	Apple A6X 1.4GHz	Intel Core i7 2.8GHz
RAM	1GB	8.0GB

6.1   Camera Tracking

In this experiment, we check whether our proposed mechanism selects the superior tracking method by comparing the true value. The true value is measured with robotic arm. Fig.4 shows the environment of the experiments. The coordinate system is set to x-axis to be parallel to the camera path, and y-axis to be opposite direction of gravity, and z-axis in the front direction.

Fig. 2 shows the camera position of each method. From the estimated camera position, the LMDB is switched into ARToolKit from 185 frames; ARToolkit is changed into LMDB from 305 frames. Lastly LMDB is switched into SFINCS-PM method from 441frame. We could see that the estimation in camera position changes according to the motion of the robotic arm. Fig. 3 shows the localization done inside the room.

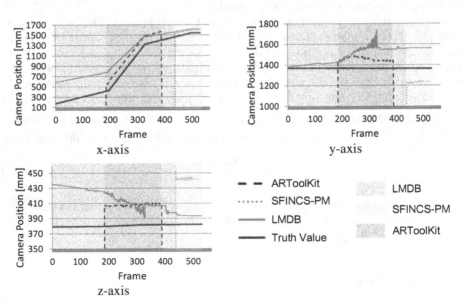

Fig. 2. Comparison of localization result

| LMDB | ARToolKit | ARToolKit | SFINCS-PM |

Fig. 3. Result of tracking inside the room

6.2   Tracking Using Real-Time Mapping

We checked the operation of the updated LMDB using real-time mapping described in Ch.5.3.3 with feature based LMDB method. The experiment is done in indoor scene. The LMDB is constructed in scene listed in Left Top of Fig 4. The black and white ARToolKit plus markers are used for setting the world coordinate. We perform the localization using real-time mapping in each database after changing the position of the object after constructing LMDB (Fig 4). After updating the LMDB, we execute the camera tracking using LMDB and compare with the camera position with pre-updated LMDB (Fig. 5). Further, in order to compare the initial camera position, we compare the number of times the initial camera position is estimated (Fig. 6).

With the pre-updated LMDB, the camera tracking failed from 180 frames. However with the updated LMDB, we could continually track even when the object is moved after the constructed LMDB.

Fig. 6 shows the result of estimating the initial camera position started form 10 location. In the pre-updated LMDB, we could only estimate five locations. With the updated LMDB, it has become possible to estimate 9 locations.

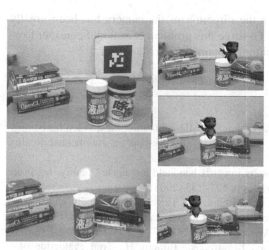

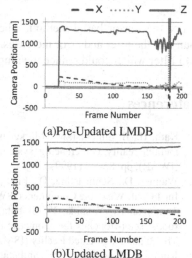

(a)Pre-Updated LMDB

(b)Updated LMDB

Fig. 4. Indoor Scene. Left Top: Constructed LMDB. Left Bottom: Object is moved after constructed. Right: Tracking using updated LMDB.

Fig. 5. Tracking result using the conventional database and updated database using real-time mapping

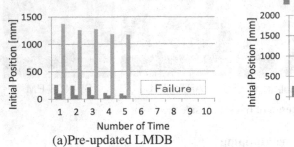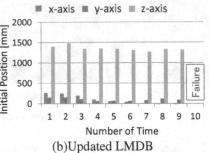

(a)Pre-updated LMDB   (b)Updated LMDB

Fig. 6. Initial position

7   Conclusion

In this paper, we have proposed a mechanism to achieve mobile augmentation in various places by dynamically switching the multiple localization techniques. The proposed mechanism is executed on the server. The localization is achieved in various environments by selecting the superior method. Furthermore, when the tracking fails, the tracking is switched to real-time mapping. With the feature based method, the mapping result obtained from real-time mapping is updated in the database. Therefore, we could continually track in environments that have changed.

For future works, our evaluation formula for switching uses the weight defined by user and re-projection error. However, we should also consider the processing time and positional relationship of the camera and the marker. For future works, we will investigate the events that occur while tracking and make an advanced evaluation formula.

For the sensor based method, when the direction of the camera has been greatly changed, the jitter and error increases. To solve this problem, we should consider low-path filter which could reduce the amplitude obtained from the sensor.

References

1. Kato, H., Billinghurst, M.: Marker tracking and HMD calibration for a video-based augmented reality conferencing system. In: Proc. Int'l Workshop on Augmented Reality (IWAR), pp. 85–94 (1999)
2. Wagner, D., Schmalsting, D.: First steps towards handheld augmented reality. In: Proc. Int'l Conf. Wearable Computers (ISWC), pp. 127–135 (2003)
3. Tenmoku, R., Yoshida, Y., Shibata, F., Kimura, A., Tamura, H.: Visually elegant and robust semi-fiducials for geometric registration in mixed reality. In: Proc. Int'l Symp. on Mixed and Augmented Reality (ISMAR), pp. 261–262 (2007)
4. Kubo, Y., Komurasaki, S., Shibata, F., Kimura, A., Tamura, H.: Trial evaluation of a marker-based geometric registration method using a TrakMark data set. In: Proc. Int'l Workshop on Benchmark Test Scheme for AR/MR Geometric Registration and Tracking Method (TrakMark), pp. 6–9 (2012)

5. Pirchheim, C., Reitmayr, G.: Homography-based planar mapping and tracking for mobile phones. In: Mixed and Augmented Reality (ISMAR), pp. 27–36 (2011)
6. Kurz, D., Olszamowski, T., Benhimane, S.: Representative feature descriptor sets for robust handheld camera localization. In: Proc. Mixed and Augmented Reality (ISMAR), pp. 65–70 (2012)
7. Arth, C., Wagner, D., Klopschitz, M., Irschara, A., Schmalstieg, D.: Wide area localization on mobile phones. In: Proc. Int'l Symp. on Mixed and Augmented Reality (ISMAR), pp. 73–92 (2009)
8. Arth, C., Klopschitz, M.: Real-time self-localization from panoramic images on mobile devices. In: Proc. Int'l Symp. on Mixed and Augmented Reality (ISMAR), pp. 37–46 (2011)
9. Oe, M., Sato, T., Yokoya, N.: Estimating camera position and posture by using feature landmark database. In: Kalviainen, H., Parkkinen, J., Kaarna, A. (eds.) SCIA 2005. LNCS, vol. 3540, pp. 171–181. Springer, Heidelberg (2005)
10. Ventura, J., Höllerer, T.: Wide-area scene mapping for mobile visual tracking. In: Proc. Int'l Symp. on Mixed and Augmented Reality (ISMAR), pp. 3–12 (2012)
11. Klein, G., Murray, D.: Parallel tracking and mapping for small AR workspaces. In: Proc. Int'l Symp. on Mixed and Augmented Reality (ISMAR), pp. 1–10 (2007)
12. Klein, G., Murray, D.: Parallel tracking and mapping on a camera phone. In: Proc. Int'l Symp. on Mixed and Augmented Reality (ISMAR), pp. 83–86 (2009)
13. Castle, R., Klein, G., Murray, D.W.: Video-rate localization in multiple maps for wearable augmented reality. In: Proc. Int'l Symp. on Wearable Computers (ISWC), pp. 15–22 (2008)
14. Chum, O., Matas, J.: Matching with PROSAC - progressive sample consensus. In: Proc. Conf. on Computer Vision and Pattern Recognition (CVPR), vol. 1, pp. 220–226 (2005)
15. Lucas, B.D., Kanade, T.: An interactive image registration technique with an application to stereo vision. In: Proc. Image Understanding Workshop, pp. 121–130 (1981)

Hand Tracking with a Near-Range Depth Camera for Virtual Object Manipulation in an Wearable Augmented Reality

Gabyong Park, Taejin Ha, and Woontack Woo

KAIST UVR Lab., S. Korea
{gypark,taejinha,wwoo}@kaist.ac.kr

Abstract. This paper proposes methods for tracking a bare hand with a near-range depth camera attached to a video see-through Head-mounted Display (HMD) for virtual object manipulation in an Augmented Reality (AR) environment. The particular focus herein is upon using hand gestures that are frequently used in daily life. First, we use a near-range depth camera attached to HMD to segment the hand object easily, considering both skin color and depth information within arms' reaches. Then, fingertip and base positions are extracted through primitive models of the finger and palm. According to these positions, the rotation parameters of finger joints are estimated through an inverse-kinematics algorithm. Finally, the user's hands are localized from physical space by camera-tracking and then used for 3D virtual object manipulation. Our method is applicable to various AR interaction scenarios such as digital information access/control, creative CG modeling, virtual-hand-guiding, or game UIs.

Keywords: Hand Tracking, HMD, Augmented Reality.

1 Introduction

Today, as cameras and HMDs are smaller and lighter, wearable computing technology is garnering significant attention. There are many interface systems for obtaining digital information about the object, space, or situation in which a user is interested. Of the various user interfaces, the hand is naturally anticipated as a major focus for wearable computing technology.

In wearable computing, considerable research has advanced the development of natural user interfaces with a hand. [1–5] proposed a hand-tracking and pose estimation technology, through pattern recognition or tracking a hand after initializing, which is appropriate in a fixed camera environment. On the other hand, [7-8] proposed a system that is suitable for moving-camera-view situations. The algorithm for bare hand-based user interface in fixed environment of a camera is not appropriate to HMD wearable interfaces like our system. The algorithm has difficulties with background learning, because of the camera's movement; thus, it cannot estimate hand pose well. In moving-camera-view scenarios with HMD, as far as we are aware, researchers have used mainly color information. But this has limits in 3D motion recognition.

R. Shumaker and S. Lackey (Eds.): VAMR 2014, Part I, LNCS 8525, pp. 396–405, 2014.
© Springer International Publishing Switzerland 2014

For the interactions with virtual objects registered in real world, using a hand, the system has to coordinate successfully between the real object and the hand.

We propose methods for a user wearing HMD to manipulate the virtual object with their own hand in a wearable AR environment, without a desktop-based interface with a mouse and keyboard. Concretely, from skin color and depth information, it extracts positions of the tips and bases of fingers based on its models of the finger and palm. Then, to estimate the rotation parameters of a finger's articulations, an inverse kinematics algorithm is used, which considers the damping ratio using the position of a fingertip and the base of the finger. Finally, for AR applications, gesture-based interaction is processed with coordinates between hand and real object.

We focus on the accuracy and stability of gesture estimation. For this, we model a finger and palm through a convex body. The features of a palm and a finger are extracted stably. This enables the detection module to be robust in nearly real time. In addition, through the hand gestures, virtual objects are manipulated. Figure 1 shows our application scenario. A user who wants to go on a trop can select virtual objects (e.g., area) augmented on the virtual globe object. The user can adjust the virtual object's position, orientation, or size for detailed observation.

This paper is composed of the following components: Section 2 introduces related works about hand tracking, and Section 3 describes our systems with hand-tracking. Next, Section 4 shows the experiment for accuracy and stability of our hand-tracking module. Finally, we introduce the conclusions regarding our system and options for future work in this area.

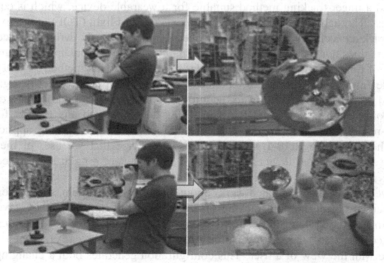

Fig. 1. Bare hand user interaction on video see-through HMD with a RGB-D camera

2   Related Works

There is extensive extant research on hand tracking. To track the motion of a hand, various methods have been developed. A hand has 26 Degrees of Freedom (DOF) [10].

Using this fact, model-based approaches were developed by [1-2]. This proposed 3D tracking of hand articulations by using RGB-D camera like Kinect. This hypothesizes the hand motion with Particle Swarm Optimization (PSO), and estimates tracking accuracy through pixel estimations of the color and depth map. [2] has expanded upon this version, applying the algorithm to two hands. This shows robust tracking results for each hand and its fingers. [1-2] performed detection procedures through initializing. By a model-based approach, this shows very robust tracking of the fingers' self-occlusion.

A feature-based approach was developed by [3-4]. This proposed a method for estimating the gestures of the hand by recognizing patterns from off-line learning. This system sets up the RGB-D camera in a position in which it is looking down, and requires a user to wear a special glove with a particular, identifiable pattern [3]. By this method of pattern recognition, up to two hands are tracked. The user can interact with virtual objects registered to the real world. In the present, furthered version, a method is proposed that does not require special gloves [4]. These methods take advantage of shape features; but this method, in certain situations, has difficulty recognizing certain motions.

Another approach, based on artificial neural networks, is proposed by [5]. This develops the system to track the torso and hands with a Self-Organizing Map (SOM). This does not require off-line learning, and it enables the algorithm to operate in an ARM-based platform. Thus, this offers a simple and speedy algorithm to track hand motion.

Using detection of fingertips and a palm, methods were developed by [6–9]. [6] proposed a finger-tracking method suitable for a wearable device, which is equipped on a wrist. Through depth information based on Time of Flight (TOF), it has excellent finger-tracking accuracy. Because the device is equipped on the wrist, self-occlusion of fingers does not incur. [7] recognized a hand's pose with polar coordinates. The number of fingers is counted by these polar coordinates. This method is suitable for wearable environments because it operates well only if the hand object is segmented well. [8] proposed the algorithm for acquiring coordinates of a hand from a camera, using points of the fingers and the palm. This does not need any marker for augmented-reality interaction and is, thus, useful for wearable computing applications. [9] is the near-range RGB-D camera, the same device that we use. In the hand-tracking module of that device, the fingertip and center of a palm are tracked. This operates in real time and robustly.

As we described in the related works about hand-tracking system, some researchers have focused on full-motion tracking of a hand. For this approach, they gave some constraints to the system, like a fixed camera and special glove [1–6]. Unless they have exceptional accuracy, for wearable AR environments, the camera's view should coincide with the view of a user. This configuration generates both a changing environment as well as difficulties of initializing for detection.

Although not tracking full DOF motion, some researched methods [7–9] are suitable for wearable AR applications, using the hand. [7-8] do not take enough advantage, however, of a hand's depth information, and so they cannot track a hand's 3D motion very well. In the module included in [9], especially when tracking bending fingers, the tracking accuracy is also problematic, with limited hand pose.

We focus on the hand-motion-tracking for wearable AR environments. Tracking is conducted robustly, using the featured information of fingertip, base, and palm, which are extracted easily in spite of the moving-camera view. In other words, through RGB and depth information, regardless of the changing environmental scene, a hand's features are extracted stably. Specifically, this makes it possible to estimate gestures used frequently in our daily life, such as pointing, pinching, grasping, translation, and rotation. Finally, for interaction with virtual objects adjusted to the real world, relative coordinates between a hand and the real object are calculated. On this basis, a user can manipulate virtual objects in a wearable AR environment.

Our contributions are as follows:

- Hand-tracking is conducted robustly regardless of the changing scene, considering the range a user can reach with an arm. It is also a suitable configuration for wearable augmented reality interaction, because the camera view coincides with that of the user.
- The fingertips, base of a finger, and a palm are detected robustly, regardless of the changing environment. This feature is used to track a hand and estimate gesture of it, used frequently in our life.

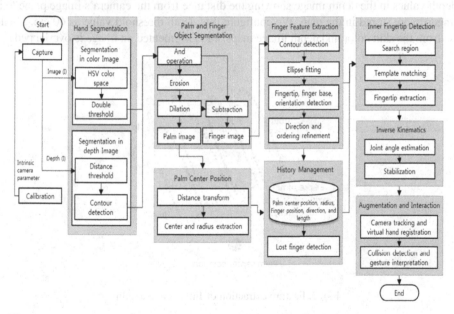

Fig. 2. Proposed hand tracking algorithm for manipulating virtual objects in wearable AR

3   System

Figure 2 shows a block diagram of our system. This is the algorithm that tracks a hand for 3D user hand interaction with a RGB-D camera in wearable AR environments. First, from RGB image and depth image through the camera, hand–object segmentation is conducted according to HSV color space and fingers' objects; the palm's is segmented through morphological operation. When modeling the fingers and a palm, featured information includes the center/radius/direction of a palm, the position of a fingers' tip and base, and ordering. In addition to that, using a depth template of fingertips and motion information of the fingers and a palm, in the case of bending fingers inward, 3D position of fingertips can be extracted. After that, from the extracted 3D position of fingertips and their bases, rotation parameters are estimated using an Inverse Kinematics (IK) algorithm. Finally, virtual objects are registered to a real object, and coordinates between a virtual object and the real hand are derived. In this system, a user can interact with virtual objects with their own hand.

3.1 Palm and Finger Object Segmentation

From the RGB and depth image, the objects composing a hand are segmented [11]. First, for robust segmentation according to light condition, the RGB color space is converted to HSV color space. The skin color space is attained through a double threshold about S and V components. Additionally, depth segmentation by the region that a user can reach with the hand makes it possible to segment hands and objects robustly and easily. To this end, depth values in the depth image showing the distance from the camera's image plane to a fingertip are stored in the map. We configure this depth threshold value as 60 cm. Finally, from the skin color and depth image maps, each segmented an image is overlapped.

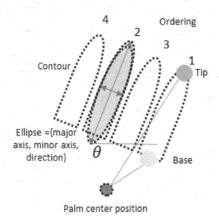

Fig. 3. Feature extraction of fingers and a palm

From this segmented hand image, the image is further segmented into one for the fingers and one for the palm to estimate a hand's subspecialized poses. For this step, a hand image is segmented through simple morphological operations such as erosion, expansion, and subtraction [9].

A palm's center position and radius are calculated by a distance transform [13]. Later, for estimating the poses of fingers by the IK algorithm, the positions of the fingers' tips and bases are needed. Finger objects are modeled by ellipse-fitting. As shown in Figure 3, the finger's base point of is calculated by minimizing of the distance from a point in a palm's circle model to a point in a finger's ellipse model.

This method is advantageous, allowing as it does the stable extraction of the fingers' base, even when the fingers are bending.

Through the above procedure, when fingers are bent inward to the palm, the position of the fingertip is not detected, although one of the bases is found. This is because the points of ellipse models do not include the fingertip in the image plane. Given this problem, we cannot recognize many gestures on the basis of fingers' motions. Thus, we should extract the fingertips' positions by another approach, such as the use of depth information.

To detect the position of the fingertips, we take care of their motion information. When one bends a finger inward toward the palm in the present frame, the convex body modeled is not detected. So, through the trace of a fingertip stored in some previous frames is known the fact that this fingertip is in the region of the palm. The image's region is set according to the direction in which the fingertip moved, and the Zero-mean Normalized Cross Correlation (ZNCC) [14] is calculated, using the depth template stored in the off-line procedure. As figure 4 shows, one point having a high score is extracted, which estimates the position of the fingertip detected. This point and the base point detected from model-fitting are used in experiment as input parameters for an inverse-kinematics algorithm.

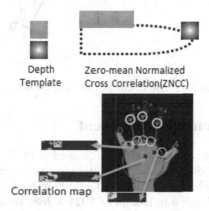

Depth Template   Zero-mean Normalized Cross Correlation(ZNCC)

Correlation map

Fig. 4. Fingertip detection using depth template

3.2   3D Hand Model Reconstruction Using Damped Least Squares Based Inverse Kinematics

To estimate the rotation poses of fingers, we use an IK algorithm. We apply it to our system, which is a damped least-square-based inverse-kinematics algorithm that [12] has proposed. This method, unlike other algorithms, can estimate rotation parameters stably by controlling the damping ratio. To take advantage of this algorithm, the position of end-effector and reference like fingertips and finger's base is detected. From [section 3.1] we proposed, the positions are considered as input, and rotation parameters are estimated. Like figure 5, we model virtual hand controlled from camera image for estimation.

We denote $\vec{s}$ as position vector from base point and $\vec{t}$ as target position vector detected from camera image, θ as a joint's rotation parameter, λ as damping ratio parameter, and set L1, L2, L3 as the joint's length. Thus, the IK algorithm solves optimizing problems as follows:

$$\Delta\theta^* = argmin(\ \|J\Delta\theta - \vec{e}\|^2 + \lambda^2\|\Delta\theta\|^2) \tag{1}$$

$J(\theta)$ can be considered as a $3 \times n$ matrix (n represents the number of DOF for one finger). The Jacobian $J(\theta) = \partial S/\partial\theta$ is also computed. $\Delta\theta^*$ is added repeatedly to present θ up to that threshold distance to reach the value we have set. This distance is denoted as $\vec{e}$, the distance between a finger's tip and base. By control of λ, stability is regulated. We set the threshold distance as 0.1 and the damping ratio as 1000.

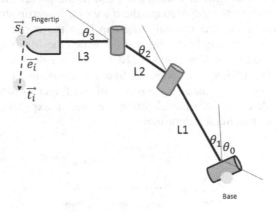

Fig. 5. Inverse kinematics for pose estimation

4   Implementation and Experiment

The proposed method runs on a computer equipped with i7 Core, 8GB RAM, Ge-Force GT 520M. The RGB-D camera is an Intel creative-gesture camera with a resolution of 640 × 480 for color images, and 320 × 240 for depth images. The HMD used is VUZIX 920AR, which has a resolution of 1024 × 768. To track the extrinsic parameter of a hand object, Sixense magnetic [15] is attached to the hand.

The base of the magnetic tracker is arranged on the reference coordinate of AR space, which quadrates the coordinate system. For the vision module, we use the openCV library, experiment with the IK module with the openGL library, and implement a demo with Unity 3D [16].

To enable a user to interact on a 3D virtual object with his own hand in AR space, a camera's extrinsic parameter is calculated and the local-reference coordinate is set in real space. According to this coordinate, the virtual object is registered in real space. This distinguishes the interface module for AR interaction from simply overlaying virtual objects in an image. Also a hand's extrinsic parameter is calculated, according to coordinates in real space. Figure 6 shows how coordinates interact with virtual objects. In other words, through the algorithm proposed in sections 3.1 and 3.2, this system estimates a hand's motion and enables a user to interact with virtual objects registered in real space.

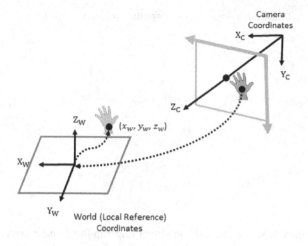

Fig. 6. Relative coordinate between a hand and real object

Two experiments compare our performance in detecting fingertips with Softkinet-ic's hand tracking module. Figure 7 show the performance, numbering finger detection in both the outside and inside of the palm. We configure our experiments, which involve bending and stretching fingers, in the regular sequence. Accurate detection of the number of fingers implies accurate detection of the fingertips' positions. The existing method showed some detection error outside of the palm and the method could not detect the finger inside of the palm properly. The method we propose, on the other hand, could detect fingertips robustly and stably. Figure 8 represents the quantitative experimental results of the inverse-kinematics algorithm applied to our system. It shows one fingertip's position in a virtual hand and the corresponding position of a fingertip of a real hand. The error boundary is 15mm (±5mm), including 15mm for camera error.

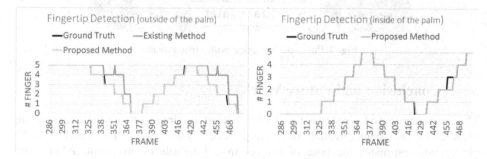

Fig. 7. Fingertip detection (Outside and inside of the palm)

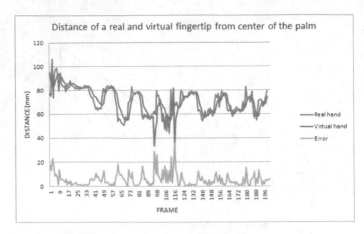

Fig. 8. Distance of a real and virtual fingertip from a palm center

Fig. 9. Piano performance with virtual avatar

5   Conclusion and Future Work

This paper proposed a system for tracking hand motion with a near-range depth camera for augmented-reality interaction. Our system does not need special gloves, and estimates the pose of fingers in a wearable environment. After that, it helps a user wearing an HMD to interact with one's hand on virtual objects augmented from a real object of his interest. According to the miniaturization and weight-lightening of such devices as cameras and HMDs, this system will be used heavily in the wearable-computing environment for AR application.

This system does not consider the self-occlusion of the fingers that occurs when the camera view changes. In future works, we will make the hand-tracking system robust to the self-occlusion of the fingers. It will estimate more poses of the fingers and have a greater number of interaction applications. Figure 9 shows our future scenario. A user can perform a virtual piano, registered on a physical table. The user can play the piano together with augmented virtual avatar. To realize this kind of application scenario, we will enable finger pose estimation under self-occlusion of the fingers.

Acknowledgment. This work was supported by the Global Frontier R&D Program on <Human-centered Interaction for Coexistence> funded by the National Research Foundation of Korea grant funded by the Korean Government (MSIP) (NRF-2010-0029751).

References

1. Oikonomidis, I., Kyriazis, N., Argyros, A.A.: Efficient model-based 3D tracking of hand articulations using Kinect. In: Proceedings of the 22nd British Machine Vision Conference, BMVC 2011, University of Dundee, UK, August 29-September 1 (2011)
2. Oikonomidis, I., Kyriazis, N., Argyros, A.A.: Tracking the articulated motion of two strongly interacting hands. In: Proceedings of the IEEE Conference on Computer Vision and Pattern Recognition, CVPR 2012, Rhode Island, USA, June 18-20 (2012)
3. Wang, R.Y., Popovic, J.: Real-Time Hand-Tracking with a Color Glove. ACM Transaction on Graphics (SIGGRAPH 2009) 28(3) (August 2009)
4. Wang, R.Y., Paris, S., Popovic, J.: 6D Hands: Markerless Hand Tracking for Computer Aided Design. ACM User Interface Software and Technology, UIST (2011)
5. Coleca, F., Klement, S., Martinetz, T., Barth, E.: Real-time skeleton tracking for embedded systems. In: Proceedings SPIE, Mobile Computational Photography, vol. 8667D (2013)
6. LEAP MOTION, https://www.leapmotion.com (access date: February 5, 2014)
7. Wachs, J., Kölsch, M., Stern, H., Edan, Y.: Vision-Based Hand-Gesture Applications, Challenges and Innovations. Communications of the ACM (February 2011)
8. Lee, T., Höllerer, T.: Handy AR:Markerless Inspection of Augmented Reality Objects Using Fingertip Tracking. In: Proceedings of the IEEE International Symposium on Werarable Computer(ISWC), Boston, MA (October 2007)
9. SOFT KINETIC, http://www.softkinetic.com (access date: February 5, 2014)
10. Albrecht, I., Haber, J., Seidel, H.-P.: Construction and Animation of Anatomically Based Human Hand Models. In: Eurographics Symposium on Computer Animation, p. 109. Eurographics Association (2003)
11. Ram Rajesh, J., Nagarjunan, D., Arunachalam, M., Aarthi, R.R.: Distance Transform Based Hand Gestures Recognition for Powerpoint Presentation Navigation. Advanced Computing 3(3), 41 (2012)
12. Wampler, C.W., Leifer, L.J.: Applications of damped least-squares methods to resolved-rate and resolved-acceleration control of manipulators. Journal of Dynamic Systems, Measurement, and Control 110, 31–38 (1988)
13. Ha, T., Woo, W.: Bare hand interface for interaction in the video see-through HMD based wearable AR environment. In: Harper, R., Rauterberg, M., Combetto, M. (eds.) ICEC 2006. LNCS, vol. 4161, pp. 354–357. Springer, Heidelberg (2006)
14. Brunelli, R.: Template Matching Techniques in Computer Vision: Theory and Practice. Wiley
15. SIXENSE, http://sixense.com/ (access date: February 5, 2014)
16. Unity3D, http://unity3d.com (access date: February 5, 2014)

Matching Levels of Task Difficulty for Different Modes of Presentation in a VR Table Tennis Simulation by Using Assistance Functions and Regression Analysis

Daniel Pietschmann[1] and Stephan Rusdorf[2]

[1] Chemnitz University of Technology, Institute for Media Research, Chemnitz, Germany
[2] Chemnitz University of Technology, Department of Computer Science, Chemnitz, Germany
daniel.pietschmann@phil.tu-chemnitz.de,
stephan.rusdorf@informatik.tu-chemnitz.de

Abstract. UX is often compared between different systems or iterations of the same system. Especially when investigating human perception processes in virtual tasks and associated effects, experimental manipulation allows for better control of confounders. When manipulating modes of presentation, such as stereoscopy or visual perspective, the quality and quantity of available sensory cues is manipulated as well, resulting not only in different user experiences, but also in modified task difficulty. Increased difficulty and lower user task performance may lead to negative attributions that spill over to the evaluation of the system as a whole (halo effect). To avoid this, the task difficulty should remain unaltered. In highly dynamic virtual environments, the modification of difficulty with Fitts' law may prove problematic, so an alternative is presented using curve fitting regression analyses of empirical data from a within-subjects experiment in a virtual table tennis simulation to calculate equal difficulty levels.

Keywords: Virtual Reality, Performance, User Experience, Spatial Presence, Table Tennis Simulation.

1 Introduction

The user experience (UX) of a given technology is a central research question in HCI. For example, social and behavioral sciences are interested in cognitive and physiological short-term and long-term effects on the user and the role that the perception has in the user experience (UX) as a whole.

UX is often compared between systems or within different iterations of the same system. The experimental manipulation of investigated variables within the same system allows for better control of confounders [1] than when comparing different systems. Still, a general drawback is an unintentional difference in task difficulty in different experimental conditions. The more difficult the task and the less successful the user, the more negative his subjective UX with the system is: Negative attributions from failing the task spill over to the evaluation of the system as a whole (halo effect). A possible solution is to create equally difficult tasks in all experimental conditions.

R. Shumaker and S. Lackey (Eds.): VAMR 2014, Part I, LNCS 8525, pp. 406–417, 2014.

In this paper, we present a method to match difficulty using interval-scaled task assistance functions and regression curve fitting. A case study (within-subjects design with five participants) is presented, using an immersive table tennis simulation (3x4 m high resolution Powerwall with active stereoscopy and a table tennis racket as input device). Goal of the experiment is to use assistance functions of the simulation to achieve a subjectively equal difficulty of the user task within all presentation conditions of the simulation.

2   User Experience and Spatial Presence

UX is often defined as an umbrella term for all qualitative experiences a user has while interacting with a given product, and it reaches beyond the more task-oriented term usability (for an overview, see [2] or [3]). The ISO definition of UX focuses on a "user's perception and responses resulting from the use or anticipated use of a product, system, service or game" (ISO FDIS 9241-210:2010). Several other concepts are closely related to UX, such as immersion [4], flow [5], cognitive absorption [6] or (tele-) presence [7-9].

Presence is often referred to as a "sense of being there", and occurs, "when part or all of a person's perception fails to accurately acknowledge the role of technology that makes it appear that she/he is in a physical location and environment different from her/his actual location and environment in the physical world" [10]. Presence can therefore be understood as a part of the larger user experience framework. The sensation of being physically situated within an immersive and virtual spatial environment (self-location) and the perceived possibilities to act within such an environment are part of the spatial presence construct [9, 11]. The focus lies on the mediated spatial environment, which – instead of reality – is perceived as primary interaction space.

In the two step process model of spatial presence formation from Wirth and colleagues [9], the first step is the construction of a spatial situation model (SSM). This spatial situation model is a mental model [12] of the spatial environment that the user unconsciously constructs, based on different available spatial cues and relevant personal spatial memories and cognitions [13]. Spatial sensory cues are part of a theory of selective visual attention in cognitive psychology [14], linked mostly to the visual modality. Static monocular cues like relative size, height in the visual field, texture effects of objects, occlusion or accommodation are the most important cues to act as building blocks of a mental model of a spatial environment [15, 16]. Dynamic monocular cues like motion parallax or binocular cues like stereopsis and convergence also provide information for depth perception. Furthermore, spatial audio, haptic and vestibular cues can are incorporated into the SSM [11]. The quality of the SSM is determined by the quantity and consistency of spatial cues available [9]. Media factors, attention allocation processes as well as user factors (situational motivation, domain-specific interest, and spatial visual imagery) also influence the process of constructing a SSM.

The second step of the model relies on a rich SSM to construct spatial presence. Based on the theory of perceptual hypotheses [17], users constantly check their environment for inconsistencies in perceived representation and their sensory feedback. A rich SSM results in perceiving the mediated environment as the primary reference frame of action, and spatial presence is constructed as a consequence.

When referring to UX in this paper, we distinguish between UX as a general concept in terms of ISO 9241-210 and spatial presence as specific part of the overall UX. Several measures, especially questionnaires, have been developed to assess the UX of a given system. The AttrakDiff [18] and the User Experience Questionnaire [19] are both valid post test tools for quickly assessing hedonic or pragmatic qualities. For spatial presence, the MEC Spatial Presence Questionnaire [20] offers a suitable tool, which has been validated in a series of studies with different media environments.

3   Goals of the Simulation

In a series of studies, we investigate the effects of quality and quantity of spatial cues in Virtual Reality simulations on spatial presence formation, using an immersive table tennis simulation. Given the important role that visual perception of distance plays in a user's experience within a virtual environment, depth perception in particular was among the first topics investigated by VR researchers [21-23]. In order to support training and performance in virtual environments, it is essential to provide necessary sensory cues that are required for the task, e.g. hitting the ball in our scenario. These cues can be presented in a multitude of different modalities, including different viewing perspectives and stereoscopic presentation. Our research focus lies on the influence of perspectives and stereoscopy of game-related scenarios and different aspects of UX, such as presence or enjoyment.

Studies on the current trend to use stereoscopic presentation or natural user interfaces in the video game industry (Nintendo Wii; Microsoft Kinect; Sony Move) found mixed results on their effectiveness to enhance the UX [24-27]. But often, commercially available game systems lack the sensory quality of real immersive virtual environments such as VR, whereas most VR simulations lack the entertainment quality of video games. Tamborini and colleagues [28] as well as Persky and Blascovich [29] investigated presence and aggressive feelings in a video game and a comparable VR application. They found no relevant differences in perceived presence in VR or standard video games. VR applications however have the advantage, that they can be modified in much more detail to accommodate certain modalities. Also, in experimental research, the manipulation of investigated variables (like perspective) within the same system allows for better control of confounders [1, 30].

3.1   Difficulty, Challenge and User Experience

In VR, perspective and stereoscopic presentation are believed to significantly contribute to task performance [31]. Our research focuses on influences of spatial cues on perception and resulting effects (e.g. presence, enjoyment) and individual user factors (e.g. motivation, visual spatial imagery) instead of just performance. The task's difficulty is a confounder is this design: When the quantity and quality of spatial cues is reduced, there is less information available for the construction of a rich spatial situation model, which is one of the research questions of the experiment. But simultaneously, the difficulty of the task increases, because of less accurate information available to base user decisions on (e.g. where to position the racket, where to move, etc.) If the difficulty of the task is too high for the skill level of the user, it may result in failure and frustration [5]. The more difficult the task and the less successful the individual user is, the more negative is his subjective user experience with the system. Negative attributions from losing the game spill over to the evaluation of the system as a whole (halo effect). In order to investigate the user's perception of stimuli within the simulation in different presentation modalities, each modality should have the same subjective task difficulty.

A number of studies investigated performance and user experience in different media contexts. A review from Chen and Thropp [32] on frame rate effects of virtual performance and user experience identified critical thresholds for various tasks (e.g. tracking, placement, target recognition). Fu and colleagues [33] compared physical and virtual task performances of a 3D Fitts' point-to-point reaching task in different visualization conditions and between collocated and non-colocated workspaces. They found no difference in the task performance, as their task primarily relied on a single user's performance. Zhang and colleagues [34] found that appropriate auditory or visual feedback cues of a virtual assembly simulation improved task performance and improved user experience, confirming the importance of multimodal sensory cues for task difficulty.

3.2   Fitt's Law

Fitt's law [35] serves as a model predicting the time required to move an object into a target area with a rapid, aimed motion. It greatly contributed to user interface design and evaluation, including different input devices (e.g. [36]) and immersive 3D VR [37].

$$MT = a + b \log2 \left(\frac{A}{W} + K \right) \tag{1}$$

Fitt's law allows to calculate the average movement time MT, with a given start/stop time of the device a, the inherent 1/speed of the device b, the amplitude A of the motion (distance to reach target), and the width W of the target area along the axis of the motion. Both a and b have to be determined empirically by fitting a straight line to measured data.

The equation poses a speed-accuracy tradeoff: Targets that are further away or smaller require more time to acquire. The "law of crossing" [38] is based on Fitt's law and relates to the time to move an object across two goals on a trajectory. Furthermore, the "law of steering" [39] also includes drawing curves, or movement paths in VR environments.

Altogether, Fitt's law provides a good rationale for adjusting the task's difficulty in the current user study. The approach employed in this paper is similar: To account for the difference in task difficulty, we implemented the ability to adjust the hit box size of the table tennis racket (racket radius) and optimize the ballistic trajectory of the ball (help level). A bigger hit box of the racket made the simulation more tolerant in positioning the swings. A higher help level results in the system adjusting the ballistic trajectory of the ball, so that it hits the opponent's side of the table with a higher probability.

The table tennis simulation is highly dynamic with different target positions and starting positions of the users (i.e. different distance to target in three-dimensional space) as well as dynamic movement time. Our approach therefore focused on average performance values, such as ball hit ratios. If racket radius and help level can be modified to achieve a similar average hit ratio, users would subjectively experience the same difficulty level, judging from their actual performance in the game. In this case, it is sufficient to focus on subjective difficulty instead of objective task difficulty for controlling frustration effects from poor subjective performance. Users may still perform differently because of different skill levels, but the confounder is controlled for in all experimental conditions. To achieve this, we used regression analyses on case study data to calculate appropriate levels the assistance functions of the simulation.

4   User Study

The simulation was developed to include different presentation techniques. It is possible to manipulate the perspective of the user: Beside a subjective ("first-person") perspective, an objective ("third-person") perspective can be employed, where the camera is detached from the tracked perspective of the user and can be positioned anywhere in the scene. This allows to construct a scene that resembles the standard presentation mode for most video games, such as Wii or Xbox Kinect games. Additionally, the stereoscopic effects can be modified freely.

The setup allows the investigation of several research problems concerning display modalities. Altogether, this allows not only to compare research results on video game systems with our setup, but allows for a systematic manipulation of different aspects of the table tennis experience, which is not possible with existing video games.

When playing table tennis without stereoscopic presentation, the spatial cues are reduced and it's more difficult to hit the ball in the game than with binocular depth cues present. A subjective camera allows the user to view the scene perspectively correct from any viewing angle while moving his head. A static camera limits the depth perception, as the user can only see a predetermined viewing angle, further reducing spatial cues – the game should get even more difficult. As it includes more spatial cues, the influence of perspective should be greater on the difficulty than the type of presentation

In order to investigate only the user's perception of stimuli within the simulation in different presentation modalities, each modality should have the same difficulty. We employed a 2×2 within-subjects design (presentation × perspective) where spatial information is partially reduced: A1B1 (monoscopic presentation/static camera), A1B2 (mono/dynamic camera), A2B1 (stereoscopic presentation/static) and A2B2 (stereo/dynamic). Reduced spatial information results in lower performance and a presumably lower UX and spatial presence.

4.1   Apparatus and Task

The immersive table tennis simulation consists of a rear projection system, a tracking system and an application host and is housed in a university VR lab. The system is a state of the art enhancement of the first iterations [40, 41]. The projection screen (4 x 3m) is divided into four screen tiles, each worked by an Epson EHTW 8100 projector. Together the four projectors show high-resolution stereoscopic images necessary for the application. The Rendering is done using parallel rendering on several graphic cards on four PCs. The application runs on a separate PC and requires two tracked objects: Stereoscopic shutter glasses and the table tennis racket each contain several tracking targets (Figure 1).

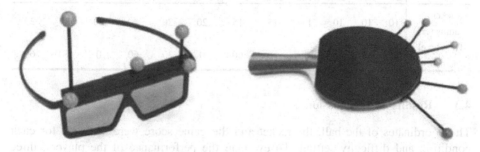

Fig. 1. Two objects with tracking targets used for the simulation

The tracking of the glasses (standard 5 targets) is needed to compute the correct visual perspective in the scene, the racket (6 targets) is used as the main input device. The tracking is achieved using four ARTtrack1 cameras, running on a separate computer. The simulation uses four cameras to reduce marker occlusion due to the fast, wide range movements of the table tennis scenario. The software application is based on the scene graph library V3D [42] and is employing spatial audio, realistic game physics, a virtual opponent AI and animation. Overall, the simulation was received well in the past (e.g. on IEEE VR2005, CeBit 2006) and could be used by users with no prior VR experience.

The users were tasked to play a 10 minute match of table tennis against an AI opponent for each of the four presentation modality conditions. The game difficulty decreased over time in each condition.

4.2   Procedure

We recruited five participants, who were pre-selected on the basis of their respective table tennis experience. They stated their experience on a 5-point scale between 1 and 5 with "1" having no experience at all and "5" playing table tennis professionally. One participant plays professional table tennis (5), another plays semi-professionally (4), two have minor expertise (2; 3) and one participant has no prior game experience at all (1). All participants had no prior VR experience. The difficulty was manipulated using an increasing racket radius size (10cm; 15cm; 20cm; 30cm) and help level

(0%; 30%; 60%). Each participant completed all four conditions in a different sequence (due to learning effects) with starting values for racket radius size of 10cm
and help level of 0%. Every 30 seconds, the values were increased, resulting in decreasing game difficulty (Table 1). During the experiment, all simulation variables
(coordinates for the position of the ball, player head, racket, game score, etc.) were
chronologically recorded in a log file.

After the game session, all participants filled out the AttrakDiff [18] and the User
Experience Questionnaires [19] for an overall UX evaluation of the simulation.

Table 1. Experimental sequence for each condition

Time	0s	30s	60s	120s	180s	240s	300s	330s	390s	450s	510s	570s
Racket radius (cm)	10	10	10	15	15	15	20	20	20	20	20	20
Help level (percent)	0	30	60	0	30	60	0	30	60	0	30	60

4.3   Results and Discussion

The coordinates of the ball, the racket and the game score were analyzed for each
condition and difficulty setting. To evaluate the performance of the players, three
measures were computed from the raw data: the play-back-ratio (ratio of successfully
returned serves) the points scored and the average distance of the center of the ball to
the center of the racket, when the player hit the ball. Since our goal is a smooth gameplay experience with several rallies, we did not include simple hit-ratios in the
analyses, but focused on play-back-ratios as indicator for the difficulty.

As hypothesized, the mode of presentation significantly impacted play-back-ratios,
$F (3, 43) = 3.004$, $p < .05$. In general, our assumption holds: The more spatial cues are
available, the better the performance. After analyzing assistance variables, help level
was dropped since only racket radius significantly affected performance, $F (3, 6) =
10.967$, $p < .01$, $\eta^2 = .85$).

To achieve an equal difficulty level, we set the target play-back-ratio to 75%, so
that an average player can play the simulation rather easily and to encourage positive
emotions during gameplay due to high self-efficacy [43]. To calculate the difficulty
level at $y = 0.75$, we fitted the data on the logarithmic regression function to calculate
required racket radii ($R^2_{mono/static} = .97$; $R^2_{mono/dynamic} = .92$; $R^2_{stereo/static} = .80$;
$R^2_{stereo/dynamic} = .74$; Figure 2).

The values for $x = f (y)$ were calculated: Mono/static (racket size = 25.1cm),
mono/dynamic (racket size = 20.4cm); stereo/static (racket size = 17.9cm); ste-
reo/dynamic (racket size = 20.7cm). The estimated values for racket radius should
allow average users to achieve similar game performance metrics, based on play-
back-ratio for a smooth gameplay. Of course individual skill will still be determining
the performance of a single participant, whereas on average, we expect an equal difficulty distribution over all modalities.

The calculated values for racket size in the various conditions were used in a later study (N = 130) with a between-subjects design investigating the specific role of presentation mode and perspective on spatial presence, instead of UX of the system as a whole. The resulting mean values of play-back-ratio lay within a standard deviation of 0.75: Empirical values were M = 0.78 (0.17) for mono/static, M = 0.74 (0.14) for mono/dynamic, M = 0.73 (0.13) for stereo/static and M = 0.79 (0.13) for stereo/dynamic. These results suggest, that the calculated values worked well. Average users experienced similar subjective task difficulty, thus eliminating frustration/challenge of the task as influence of subjective user experience or spatial presence.

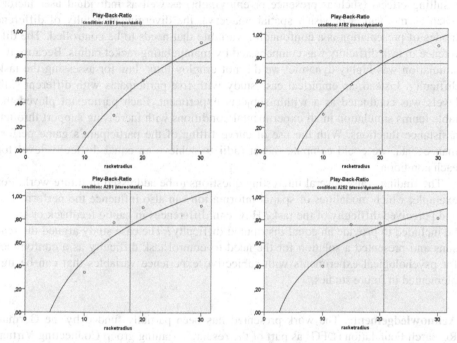

Fig. 2. Play-back-ratio with fitted logarithmic function

Results for the AttrakDiff and User Experience Questionnaires were computed using the AttrakDiff Online Resource (www.attrakdiff.de) and SPSS. With values ranging from -3 to 3, the means for hedonic (identification with the system, HQ-I; and stimulation through the system, HQ-S) and pragmatic quality (PQ) for AttrakDiff suggest a neutral assessment of the overall system (M_{PQ} = -0.1; M_{HQ-I} = 0.2; M_{HQ-S} = 1.0). System attractivity was also evaluated little above average (M_{ATT} = 0.8). This evaluation can also be supported by the UEQ data. On a range from 0 to 1, the factors attractiveness (M_{att} = 0.61), dependability (M_{dep} = 0.45), efficiency (M_{eff} = 0.53), and perspicuity (M_{per} = 0.48) indicate a neutral assessment. Novelty (M_{nov} = 0.66) was evaluated above average by all users, due to the fact, that they have never used a VR system before.

5   Discussion, Conclusion, and Application

In this paper we investigated difficulty levels of different modes of presentation of a virtual table tennis simulation game. Stereoscopic presentation and dynamic camera perspective were manipulated to reduce the quantity and quality of available spatial cues within the simulation. As expected, more spatial cues lead to a better overall performance and a reduced perceived game difficulty for the users. In conditions with reduced spatial cues, users performed worse than in the other conditions. For experiments investigating the effects of reduced spatial cues on the user's perception and resulting effects (such as presence or enjoyment) as well as individual user factors (such as motivation or visual spatial imagery), the diverging difficulty of different modes of presentation is a confounding variable that needs to be controlled. The difference in task difficulty was compensated by manipulating racket radius. Because the simulation was highly dynamic, we did not employ Fitts' law for assessing the task difficulty. Instead, an empirical case study with five participants with different skill levels was conducted as a within-subjects experiment. Each participant played the table tennis simulation in all experimental conditions with increasing support through assistance functions. With the use of curve fitting of the participant's game performance data, we could compute racket radii to achieve an equal difficulty level for each condition.

The findings raise several interesting questions to be addressed in future work. For example, which modalities of spatial information can also influence the performance and perceived difficulty of the task? How can differences in haptic feedback or sound be included to provide an equal distributed difficulty? The case study argued the reasons and presented a solution for the need to control task difficulty as a confounder for psychological experiments with subjective experience variables that can be implemented in future studies.

Acknowledgements. The work presented has been partially funded by the German Research Foundation (DFG) as part of the research training group Connecting Virtual and Real Social Worlds (grant 1780).

References

1. McMahan, R.P., Ragan, E.D., Leal, A., Beaton, R.J., Bowman, D.A.: Considerations for the use of commercial video games in controlled experiments. Entertainment Computing 2, 3–9 (2011)
2. Bernhaupt, R. (ed.): Evaluating user experience in games. Concepts and Methods. Springer, London (2010)
3. Krahn, B.: User Experience: Konstrukt definition und Entwicklung eines Erhebungs instruments. [User Experience: Definition of the construct and development of measurements]. GUX | Gesellschaft für User Experience mbH, Bonn (2012)
4. Murray, J.: Hamlet on the holodeck: The future of narrative in cyberspace. MIT Press, Cambridge (1997)

5. Csikszentmihalyi, M.: Beyond Boredom and Anxiety: Experiencing Flow in Work and Play. Jossey-Bass, San Francisco (1975)
6. Agarwal, R., Karahanna, E.: Time flies when you're having fun. Cognitive Absorption and beliefs about information technology use. MIS Quarterly 24, 665–994 (2000)
7. Lombard, M., Ditton, T.: At the heart of it all: The concept of presence. Journal of Computer-Mediated Communication 3 (1997)
8. Minsky, M.: Telepresence. Omni 45–51 (June 1980)
9. Wirth, W., Hartmann, T., Böcking, S., Vorderer, P., Klimmt, C., Schramm, H., Saari, T., Laarni, J., Ravaja, N., Gouveia, F.R., Biocca, F., Sacau, A., Jäncke, L., Baumgartner, T., Jäncke, P.: A process model of the formation of spatial presence experiences. Media Psychology 9, 493–525 (2007)
10. ISPR, http://ispr.info/about-presence-2/about-presence/
11. Vorderer, P., Wirth, W., Saari, T., Gouveia, F.R., Biocca, F., Jäncke, F., Böcking, S., Hartmann, T., Klimmt, C., Schramm, H., Laarni, J., Ravaja, N., Gouveia, L.B., Rebeiro, N., Sacau, A., Baumgartner, T., Jäncke, P.: Constructing presence: Towards a two-level model of the formation of spatial presence. Unpublished report to the European Community, Project Presence: MEC (IST-2001-37661). Hannover, Munich, Helsinki, Porto, Zurich (2003)
12. Johnson-Laird, P.N.: Mental models: Towards a cognitive science of language, inference, and consciousness. Cambridge University Press, Combridge (1983)
13. McNamara, T.P.: Mental representations of spatial relations. Cognitive Psychology 18, 87–121 (1986)
14. Posner, M.I., Snyder, C.R., Davidson, B.J.: Attention and the Detection of Signals. Journal of Experimental Psychology: General 109 (1980)
15. Gibson, J.J.: The ecological approach to visual perception. Houghton Mifflin, Boston (1979)
16. Surdick, R.T., Davis, E.T., King, R.A., Hodges, L.F.: The Perception of Distance in Simulated Visual Displays: A Comparison of the Effectiveness and Accuracy of Multiple Depth Cues Across Viewing Distances. Presence 513–531 (1997)
17. Bruner, J.S., Postman, L.: On the perception of incongruity: a paradigm. Journal of Personality 18, 206–223 (1949)
18. Hassenzahl, M., Burmester, M., Koller, F.: AttrakDiff: A questionnaire for measuring perceived hedonistic and pragmatic quality. [AttrakDiff: Ein Fragebogen zur Messung wahrgenommener hedonischer und pragmatischer Qualität]. In: Mensch & Computer 2003. Interaktion in Bewegung, pp. 187-196. B.G. Teubner (2003)
19. Laugwitz, B., Held, T., Schrepp, M.: Construction and evaluation of a user experience questionnaire. In: Holzinger, A. (ed.) USAB 2008. LNCS, vol. 5298, pp. 63–76. Springer, Heidelberg (2008)
20. Vorderer, P., Wirth, W., Gouveia, F.R., Biocca, F., Saari, T., Jäncke, F., Böcking, S., Schramm, H., Gysbers, A., Hartmann, T., Klimmt, C., Laarni, J., Ravaja, N., Sacau, A., Baumgartner, T., Jäncke, P.: MEC spatial presence questionnaire (MEC-SPQ): Short documentation and instructions for application, Report to the European Community, Project Presence: MEC, IST-2001-37661 (2004)
21. Barfield, W., Rosenberg, C.: Judgments of azimuth and elevation as a function of monoscopic and binocular depth cues using a perspective display. Human Factors 37, 173–181 (1995)
22. Kline, P.B., Witmer, B.G.: Distance perception in virtual environments: Effects of field of view and surface texture at near distances. In: 40th Annual Meeting on Human Factors and Ergonomics Society, pp. 112–116. Human Factors and Ergonomics Society (1996)

23. Loomis, J.M., Knapp, J.M.: Visual perception of egocentric distance in real and virtual environments. In: Hettinger, L.J., Haas, M.W. (eds.) Virtual and Adaptive Environments, pp. 21–46. Erlbaum, Mahwah (2003)

24. Rajae-Joordens, R.J.E., Langendijk, E., Wilinski, P., Heynderickx, I.: Added value of a multi-view auto-stereoscopic 3D display in gaming applications. In: 12th International Display Workshops in conjunction with Asia Display, Takamatsu, Japan (December 2005)

25. Skalski, P., Tamborini, R., Shelton, A., Buncher, M., Lindmark, P.: Mapping the road to fun: Natural video game controllers, presence, and game enjoyment. New Media & Society 13, 224–242 (2010)

26. Takatalo, J., Kawai, T., Kaistinen, J., Nyman, G., Hakkinen, J.: User Experience in 3D Stereoscopic Games. Media Psychology 14 (2011)

27. Elson, M., van Looy, J., Vermeulen, L., Van den Bosch, F.: In: the mind's: No Evidence for an effect of stereoscopic 3D on user experience of digital games. In: ECREA ECC 2012, preconference Experiencing Digital Games: Use, Effects & Culture of Gaming, Istanbul, Turkey (September 2012)

28. Tamborini, R., Eastin, M.S., Skalski, P., Lachlan, K., Fediuk, T.A., Brady, R.: Violent Virtual Video Games and Hostile Thoughts. Journal of Broadcasting & Electronic Media 48, 335–357 (2004)

29. Persky, S., Blascovich, J.: Immersive Virtual Environments versus traditional platforms: Effects of violent and nonviolent video game play. Media Psychology 10, 135–156 (2007)

30. Hartig, J., Frey, A., Ketzel, A.: Modifikation des Computerspiels Quake III Arena zur Durchführung psychologischer Experimente in einer virtuellen 3D-Umgebung. [Modification of the video game Quake III Arean for psychological experiments in a virtual 3D environment]. Zeitschrift für Medienpsychologie 9, 493–525 (2003)

31. Barfield, W., Hendrix, C., Bystrom, K.-E.: Effects of Stereopsis and Head Tracking on Performance Using Desktop Virtual Environment Displays. Presence: Teleoperators and Virtual Environments 8, 237–240 (1999)

32. Chen, J.Y.C., Thropp, J.E.: Review of Low Frame Rate Effects on Human Performance. IEEE Transactions on Systems, Man, and Cybernetics - Part A: Systems and Humans 37, 1063–1076 (2007)

33. Fu, M.J., Hershberger, A.D., Sano, K., Cavusoglu, M.C.: Effect of Visuomotor Colocation on 3D Fitts' Task Performance in Physical and Virtual Environments. Presence-Teleop Virt. 21, 305–320 (2012)

34. Zhang, Y., Fernando, T., Xiao, H.N., Travis, A.R.L.: Evaluation of auditory and visual feedback on task performance in a virtual assembly environment. Presence-Teleop Virt. 15, 613–626 (2006)

35. Fitts, P.M.: The information capacity of the human motor system in controlling the amplitude of movement. Journal of Experimental Psychology 47, 381–391 (1954)

36. MacKenzie, I.S., Zhang, S.X.: The design and evaluation of a high-performance soft keyboard. In: ACM Conference on Human Factors in Computing Systems - CHI 1999, pp. 25–31. ACM (1999)

37. Watson, B.A., Walker, N., Woytiuk, P., Ribarsky, W.R.: Maintaining usability during 3D placement despite delay. In: IEEE Virtual Reality Conference 2003. IEEE Computer Society (2003)

38. Accot, J., Zhai, S.: Beyond Fitts' Law: Models for trajectory-based HCI tasks. In: ACM SIGCHI Conference on Human Factors in Computing Systems, CHI 1997, pp. 295–302. ACM (1997)

39. Zhai, S., Accot, J., Woltjer, R.: Human Action Laws in Electronic Virtual Worlds: An Empirical Study of Path Steering Performance in VR. Presence 13, 113–127 (2004)

40. Rusdorf, S., Brunnett, G.: Real Time Tracking of High Movements in the Context of a Table Tennis Application. In: ACM Symposium on Virtual Reality Software and Technology 2005. ACM (2005)
41. Rusdorf, S., Brunnett, G., Lorenz, M., Winkler, T.: Real Time Interaction with a Humanoid Avatar in an Immersive Table Tennis Simulation. IEEE Transactions on Visualization and Computer Graphics 13, 15–25 (2007)
42. Lorenz, M., Rusdorf, S., Woelk, S., Brunnett, G.: Virtualiti3D (V3D): A system independent, real time-animated, three dimensional graphical user interface. In: IASTED Int. Conf. on Visualization, Imaging, and Image Processing, VIIP 2003, pp. 955–960. ACTA Press (2003)
43. Klimmt, C., Hartmann, T.: Effectance, self-efficacy, and the motivation to play video games. In: Vorderer, P., Bryant, J. (eds.) Playing Video Games: Motives, Responses, and Consequences, pp. 132–145. Lawrence Erlbaum, Mahwah (2006)

A Pen Based Tool for Annotating Planar Objects

Satoshi Yonemoto

Graduate School of Information Science, Kyushu Sangyo University, Japan
yonemoto@is.kyusan-u.ac.jp

Abstract. In recent augmented reality (AR) application, marker-less tracking approaches are often used. Most marker-less tracking approaches force user to capture the front view of a target object during the initial setup. We have recently proposed two image rectification methods for non-frontal view of a planar object. These methods can be applied to reference image generation in marker-less AR. This paper describes a pen based tool for annotating planar objects. Our tool builds upon several interactive image rectification methods, and supports registration of AR Annotations, marker-less tracking and annotation overlay.

Keywords: image rectification, marker-less tracking, AR annotation.

1 Introduction

In recent augmented reality (AR) application, robust tracking algorithm is used, which does not use any artificial markers. It is known as marker-less tracking [1]. In general, most planar objects in natural scenes are observed in non-frontal view. Most marker-less tracking approaches force user to capture the front view of a target object during the initial setup. In online use, user cannot always capture a front view image (e.g., large sign-board and building surface). We have recently proposed two image rectification methods for non-frontal view of a planar object [9] [10]. These methods can be applied to reference image generation in marker-less AR. Now, we have developed a pen based tool for annotating planar objects. This tool enables on-line registration of AR annotations, marker-less tracking and annotation overlay. The following functions are realized: live image view, image rectification (reference image generation) and registration of AR annotations. In live image view mode, registered objects are tracked and then the corresponding AR annotations are overlaid.

Image rectification method is often used in text detection in natural scene [2] [3]. In most text detection methods, two approaches are taken. The first is vanishing point estimation [4] [5]. The second is quadrangle estimation [6]. A quadrangle is warped into a rectified text area (i.e., a rectangle), correcting any perspective distortion. In document images used in OCR, text lines are regularly aligned in paragraph, so rich horizontal lines are stably extracted. Two text lines and the vertical stroke boundaries are often used as a quadrangle clue [4]. Our method is one of quadrangle estimation methods extended to general planar objects.

Image rectification methods should be used in dependence on appearance of each target object. Therefore, our tool is equipped with several interactive methods.

R. Shumaker and S. Lackey (Eds.): VAMR 2014, Part I, LNCS 8525, pp. 418–427, 2014.

2   Overview

2.1   Image Rectification Algorithm

In the proposed method, it is assumed that target image has rich horizontal and vertical lines. If a target object has a rectangular shape such as book and poster, then their corner points are clearly observed. In this case, the reference image is easily acquired from their points (Fig. 3). The proposed method can also be applied to non-rectangular objects such as circular objects. This idea is realized by using horizontal (or vertical) lines with target object, that is, these lines always become horizontal, correcting any perspective distortion. We assume that at least two horizontal lines and two vertical lines would be observed. Our method is one of quadrangle estimation methods [9]. A quadrangle with a target object is constructed by picking up 4 points or 4 lines in an image. The projection of a rectangle is a quadrangle. Our approach to find such quadrangle is summarized as follows (see Fig. 1): First, specify the region of interest in an interactive way. Next, extract horizontal and vertical line segments in the target image by using probabilistic Hough transform [11]. Then, make a quadrangle hypothesis from their line segments. Finally, warp the quadrangle into a rectangle and then, evaluate whether re-projected line segments will be horizontal (vertical) or not. The goodness function is defined by total error with the warped horizontal and vertical lines. The important point is whether extracted lines will be transformed horizontal (vertical) or not. As a result, the underlying problem is equal to a search problem for a combination of 4 line segments. Fig. 2 shows an example of several quadrangle hypotheses generated from the extracted line segments. The line segments are extracted only in the region of interest. The quadrangle hypotheses q1, q2 and q3 are shown (each goodness is also described in parentheses). Quadrangle hypothesis indicates a combination of different 4 line segments that are selected from among the extracted line segments. In Fig. 2, q3 is the best quadrangle with the max goodness 327. 4 line segments that are part of the quadrangle q3 are also shown.

Image Rectification Algorithm	
Step 1	Extract horizontal / vertical line segments (check the proper baseline if box based)
Step 2	Select 4 line segments & generate a quadrangle hypothesis q_i
Step 3	Warp q_i into a rectangle & evaluate the goodness
Step 4	Find the best quadrangle with max goodness

Fig. 1. Our image rectification algorithm

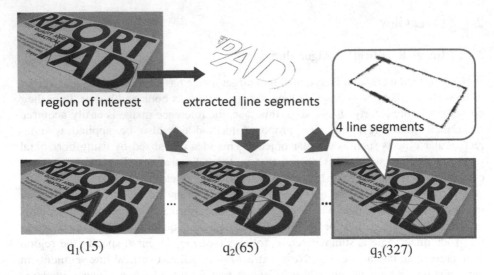

region of interest   extracted line segments

4 line segments

$q_1(15)$ $q_2(65)$ $q_3(327)$

Fig. 2. Quadrangle hypotheses

2.2   Interactive Methods for Image Rectification

To acquire a fronto-parallel image, we can use any one of 4 interactive methods: (A) 4 corner points based, (B) line selection based, (C) user-stroke based and (D) box based. That is, user can select a region of interest in different way. Fig. 3 shows our interactive methods. Method A is used for only rectangular objects. From 4 corner points (which are manually selected by user), the rectified image is generated by warping. Method B is used when user can observe at least two horizontal lines and two vertical lines in the region of interest. User draws their lines on the screen. Note that our method can also use invisible lines existing virtually in the image. In method C, user can directly paint a stroke(s) on a region of interest. Pen size can be selected in advance. Multiple strokes are also supported. In this method, it is assumed that user stroke direction is parallel to a horizontal baseline. In method D, user can specify a bounding box (or freehand area selection) as a region of interest. In this case, user does not clearly define the baseline. To find valid baseline, we take a hypothesis and test approach. Thus, method B, C and D are semi-automatically controlled. After selecting a region of interest, our image rectification algorithm is executed. Image cropping is performed by user (auto-cropping is also supported). The cropped image is registered as a reference image.

Fig. 4 shows two examples of method A (4 corner points based). Fig. 5 shows the results of method B (line selection based). Two horizontal lines (invisible lines) and two vertical lines are picked up by user. The best quadrangle is overlaid in the figure. The rectified image is shown as a fronto-parallel image. Fig. 6 shows the results of method C (user-stroke based). User-strokes are represented by red circles. The baseline is parallel to the bounding box of the strokes. Fig. 7 shows the results of method D (box-based). Valid baseline is automatically determined.

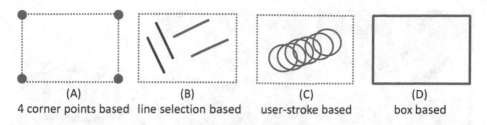

(A)	(B)	(C)	(D)
4 corner points based	line selection based	user-stroke based	box based

Fig. 3. 4 Interactive methods for image rectification

book   poster

Fig. 4. 4 corner points selection based method. (left) book (right) poster.

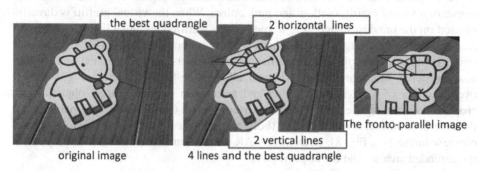

the best quadrangle   2 horizontal lines

The fronto-parallel image

2 vertical lines

original image   4 lines and the best quadrangle

Fig. 5. Line selection based method

original image and user stroke   the best quadrangle   the fronto-parallel image

Fig. 6. User-stroke based method

original image and the box   the best quadrangle   the fronto-parallel image

Fig. 7. Box based method

2.3   Registration of AR Annotations

After image rectification, AR annotations are registered for the cropped reference image. Our tool supports the following AR annotations: image texture (virtual graffiti), text, url and transparent marker. Virtual graffiti annotation can be created online, directly painting on the target image (i.e., the preview image) or the reference image. It can be painted on the extended area around the target region. Fig. 8 shows an example of a virtual graffiti (yellow and pink color). When the virtual graffiti is directly painted on the preview image, it is warped into a rectified texture. Given 4 point correspondences with a target region, a homography is computed [12] [13]. The computation is proceeded by the same rectification process as method A. Text and url are also registered. Transparent marker is realized by a see-through overlay. Fig. 9 shows two examples of marker-less tracking and annotation overlay. Target objects were cropped and then registered in advance. Virtual graffiti (top) is created by painting on the reference image. Virtual graffiti (bottom) is created by directly painting on the preview image (see Fig. 8). In this case, AR annotation is overlaid and displayed on the extended area around the target region.

2.4   Marker-Less Tracking

We have implemented marker-less tracking algorithm based on keypoint based descriptors and the trackers (SURF) [7]. It is one of the state of the art trackers, and it is often used at the base of many visual tracking problems. In our marker-less tracking algorithm, the tracker can use any kind of planar object as long as sufficient texture information is available. 4 corner points can be estimated as the tracking result. Thus, AR annotation (i.e., virtual graffiti) can be overlaid and displayed on the area corresponding to the target object on the screen. In Fig. 9, the tracking results are shown. Using 4 corner points of a planar object, real-virtual camera pose parameters can be estimated [2] [12]. Although our tool is capable of displaying any 3D annotations such as 3D text and CAD model, our tool supports only 2D annotations to provide a way that is convenient for a user.

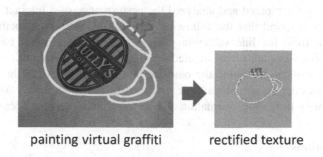

painting virtual graffiti   rectified texture

Fig. 8. Virtual graffiti creation

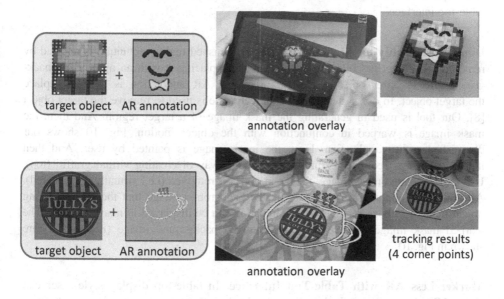

target object   AR annotation

annotation overlay

target object   AR annotation

annotation overlay

tracking results
(4 corner points)

Fig. 9. Marker-less tracking and annotation overlay

3 Experiments

3.1 Implementation

We have implemented our tool on a tablet PC with digitizer pen (OS: windows 8, CPU: Intel Core i7, memory: 8GB and screen: 11.6-inch). Real images are captured using a rear facing camera device. Marker-less tracking is implemented with OpenCV library. Virtual graffiti creation is implemented with OpenGL library.

3.2   Experimental Evaluation

In experiments, we compared and analyzed the performance of 3 interaction methods (B, C and D). We found that the following conclusions. Although method B takes relatively much time for line selection process, the desired results can be easily acquired. Invisible lines are often selected for figures have a symmetric structure. In method C, user strokes determine the baseline that is used to extract horizontal and vertical line segments, so use of multiple strokes affects the accuracy. Although method D takes only a little time, estimation of false baseline affects the accuracy.

3.3   Applications

At present, our tool is used in our practical AR applications. We have implemented prototype versions of "diminished reality for marker-less AR", "marker-less AR with table-top interface".

Diminished Reality for Marker-Less AR. Diminished reality technique is realized by removing an object or collection of objects and replacing it with an appropriate background image. After object detection, projecting AR annotation is built to replace the target object. In our system, inpainting technique is used to remove the target object [8]. Our tool is used in generating the mask image of a target region. And then, the mask image is warped in conjunction with the object motion. Fig. 10 shows our diminished reality application. First, the mask image is painted by user. And then it is registered as rectified texture by the similar way of creating virtual graffiti (top). Using the extended mask image, the target object is removed (i.e., virtually disappeared). And then, AR annotation is overlaid on the background image that the corresponding object region has been removed. AR annotation can be displayed in marker hiding. The warped mask image (middle) and the removed background image (bottom-left) are shown in Fig. 10.

Marker-Less AR with Table-Top Interface. In table-top display style, user can share AR annotations with the other people. Using marker-less tracking technique, AR annotations can be displayed on table-top display that puts a target object. That is, they are displayed below (around) the moving object. Fig. 11 shows our table-top display application. Target object is a teddy. Both table-top display and the target object are constantly captured by a web camera (left). According to the object location, AR annotation should be projected on the display screen. Using both the tracking results and the display position (4 corner points) in the web camera view, AR annotation is projected and then displayed on the screen (right). If user has an AR glasses (i.e., wearable display), the prototype system can provide the mix world. That is, AR annotations are displayed in both the front and back of the target object [15].

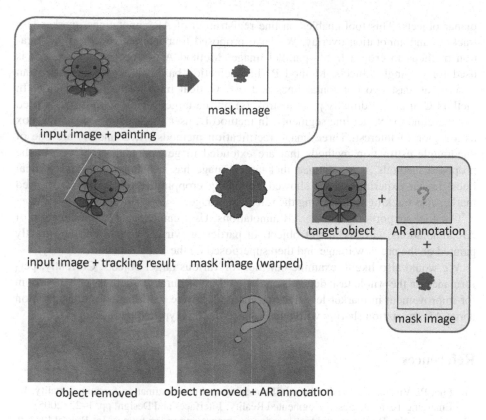

Fig. 10. Diminished reality application

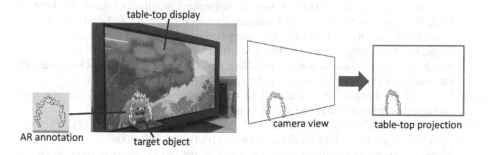

Fig. 11. Table-top display application. (left) table-top display and the target object. (right) conversion from camera view to table-top view.

4   Conclusion

We proposed a pen based tool based on image rectification method for non-frontal view of a planar object. This tool is designed to support online task of annotating planar objects. This tool enables on-line registration of AR annotations, marker-less tracking and annotation overlay. We have proposed four interactive image rectification methods to crop a fronto-parallel image. Method A (4 corner points based) is used for rectangle objects. Method B (line selection based) is used when user can observe at least two horizontal lines and two vertical lines in the target region. In method C, user can directly paint a stroke(s) on the target region. The stroke is used as a baseline to extract line segments. In method D, user can specify a bounding box as a region of interest. Three image rectification methods (B, C and D) are one of quadrangle estimation methods that are extended to general planar objects. In the proposed methods, it is assumed that target image has rich horizontal and vertical lines. In our experiments, we showed promising cropping results. And we showed marker-less tracking results using the reference image.

Our tool supports registering AR annotations. User can execute online creation of AR annotations with the target object. In particular, virtual graffiti can be directly painted on the preview image and then superposed on the live image immediately.

We would also like to examine our tool for various target objects. Currently, performance on the whole task depends on the tracking accuracy. There is probably room for improvement in marker-less tracking method. Future work includes consideration about AR annotation sharing with other users, which is typified by Stiktu [14].

References

1. Fue, P., Vincent, L.: Vision based 3D tracking and pose estimation for mixed reality. In: Emerging Technologies of Augmented Reality: Interfaces and Design, pp. 1–22 (2005)
2. Jain, A., Yu, B.: Automatic text location in images and video frames. In: Proc. 14th Intl. Conf. on Pattern Recognition, vol. 2, pp. 1497–1499 (1998)
3. Fragoso, V., et al.: TranslatAR: A Mobile Augmented Reality Translator. In: Proc. of IEEE Workshop on Applications of Computer Vision (WACV), pp. 497–502 (2011)
4. Clark, P., Mirmehdi, M.: Estimating the orientation and recovery of text planes in a single image. In: Proceedings of the 12th British Machine Vision Conference (2001)
5. Yin, X.-C., et al.: Robust Vanishing Point Detection for MobileCam-Based Documents. In: International Conference on Document Analysis and Recognition. IEEE (2011)
6. Lu, S., et al.: Perspective rectification of document images using fuzzy set and morphological operations. Image and Vision Computing 23(5), 541–553 (2005)
7. Bay, H., Ess, A., Tuytelaars, T., Gool, L.V.: Speeded-Up Robust Features (SURF). Computer Vision and Image Understanding Archive 110(3), 346–359 (2008)
8. Telea, A.: An image inpainting technique based on the fast marching method. Journal of Graphics Tools 9(1), 23–34 (2004)
9. Yonemoto, S.: An interactive image rectification method using quadrangle hypothesis. In: Proc. of International Conference on Image Analysis and Processing (ICIAP 2013), pp. 51–60 (2013)
10. Yonemoto, S.: A Reference Image Generation Method for Marker-less AR. In: Proc. of 17th Conference Information Visualisation, pp. 410–415 (2013)
11. Matas, J., Galambos, C., Kittler, J.V.: Robust Detection of Lines Using the Progressive Probabilistic Hough Transform. CVIU 78(1), 119–137 (2000)

12. Hartley, R., Zisserman, A.: Multiple view geometry in computer vision. Cambridge University Press, New York (2001)
13. Zhang, Z., He, L.-W.: Note-taking with a camera: whiteboard scanning and image enhancement. In: Proceedings of International Conference on Acoustics, Speech, and Signal Processing (ICASSP 2004), vol. 3 (2004)
14. Stiktu, http://stiktu.com/
15. Yonemoto, S.: Seamless Annotation Display for Augmented Reality. In: Proc. of International Conference on Cyberworlds, p. 37 (2013)

Author Index